P9-CQD-648

MILITANT MINORITY

British Columbia Workers and the Rise of a New Left, 1948–1972

Militant Minority tells the compelling story of British Columbia workers who sustained a left tradition during the bleakest days of the Cold War. Through their continuing activism on issues from the politics of timber licences to global questions of war and peace, these workers bridged the transition from an Old to a New Left.

In the late 1950s, half of BC's workers belonged to unions, but the promise of postwar collective bargaining quickly turned into disillusionment as inflation rose and automation steadily displaced workers. A new and increasingly rebellious working class emerged, made more diverse by the growing participation of woman and urban workers from the burgeoning public sector. This New Left, influenced by traditional forms of labour militancy, took part in strikes, occupations, and picketing, visibly challenging the socio-economic status quo and contributing to a change in government, the election of the newly formed New Democratic Party in 1972.

Grounded in archival research and oral history, *Militant Minority* provides a valuable case study of one of the most organized and independent working classes in North America during a period of ideological tension and unprecedented material advance.

BENJAMIN ISITT is an assistant professor of history at the University of British Columbia, specializing in social movements in twentieth-century Canada and the world.

Militant Minority

British Columbia Workers and the Rise of a New Left, 1948–1972

BENJAMIN ISITT

UNIVERSITY OF TORONTO PRESS
Toronto Buffalo London

Toronto Buffalo London
www.utppublishing.com
Printed in Canada

ISBN 978-1-4426-4194-5 (cloth)
ISBN 978-1-4426-1105-4 (paper)

Printed on acid-free, 100% post-consumer recycled paper with vegetable-based inks

---

Library and Archives Canada Cataloguing in Publication

Isitt, Benjamin, 1978–
Militant minority : British Columbia workers and the rise of a New Left, 1948–1972 / Benjamin Isitt.

Includes bibliographical references and index.
ISBN 978-1-4426-4194-5 (bound) ISBN 978-1-4426-1105-4 (pbk.)

1. Working class – British Columbia – History – 20th century. 2. Working class – Political activity – British Columbia – History – 20th century. 3. New Left – British Columbia. I. Title.

HD8106.5.I85 2011 305.5′620971109045 C2011-901979-5

University of Toronto Press acknowledges the financial assistance to its publishing program of the Canada Council for the Arts and the Ontario Arts Council.

University of Toronto Press acknowledges the financial support of the Government of Canada through the Canada Book Fund for its publishing activities.

This book has been published with the help of a grant from the Canadian Federation for the Humanities and Social Sciences, through the Aid to Scholarly Publications Program, using funds provided by the Social Sciences and Humanities Research Council of Canada.

To Melissa, Aviva, and troublemakers everywhere

Contents

List of Tables and Illustrations

Tables

Appendices

Illustrations (section follows page 80)

Acknowledgments

In this work I am indebted to many people. Greg Kealey supervised the original dissertation with a blend of intellectual stimulation, friendship, and critical insight, and provided a research fellowship that started it off. The University of New Brunswick history department, particularly David Frank, Linda Kealey, Margaret Conrad, Gary Waite, Marc Milner, Carole Hines, and Elizabeth Adshade, created a collegial atmosphere that made my apprenticeship as a historian engaging and fun. The University of Victoria and University of British Columbia history departments provided supportive postdoctoral homes during the transition from thesis to book. I also wish to thank the team at University of Toronto Press, particularly Len Husband, Frances Mundy, Judy Williams, and anonymous readers, whose engaging and constructive feedback contributed to a sharper analysis and smoother narrative flow. The Social Sciences and Humanities Research Council of Canada provided generous financial support. Archivists were friendly and helpful in the face of last-minute requests for materials and photocopying at the Library and Archives Canada, University of British Columbia Special Collections, British Columbia Archives, University of Victoria Archives and Special Collections, Greater Victoria Public Library, Thomas Fisher Rare Books Library, and McMaster Archives and Research Collections. The office of the Information Commissioner, Ottawa, helped speed the release of RCMP Security Service files on BC labour unions.

This study is strengthened immensely by the unique perspectives of workers who made history in postwar BC. I wish to thank these 'troublemakers' for welcoming me into their homes and breathing life into a story otherwise confined to dusty newspapers and old records: Grace Tickson, Ben Swankey, Grace Stevens, Betty Griffin, Maurice Rush,

Dave Barrett, Eileen Dailly, Norm Levi, Hilda Thomas, Bill Doherty, John Fryer, Paul Phillips, and Kevin Neish. Peers and mentors helped develop my interpretive framework, pointed me toward fresh sources, and improved earlier drafts, including Craig Heron, Thom Workman, Eric Sager, Foster Griezic, Patricia Roy, Allen Seager, Elaine Bernard, Joan Sangster, Bryan Palmer, Alvin Finkel, Jeff Taylor, Matthew Lamb, Patrick Webber, Kirk Niergarth, and Janis Thiessen. Finally, I thank family and friends – particularly Melissa Moroz, my daughter Aviva, and my parents Linda and Julian – who provided support and respite from rigorous intellectual work.

Benjamin Isitt,
Victoria, British Columbia

Abbreviations

AFL	American Federation of Labor
AUCE	Association of University and College Employees
BCFL	BC Federation of Labour
BCFU	BC Federation of the Unemployed
BCGEA	BC Government Employees' Association
BCGEU	BC Government Employees' Union
BCPC	BC Peace Council
CAIMAW	Canadian Association of Industrial Mechanical and Allied Workers
CASAW	Canadian Association of Smelter and Allied Workers
CAUT	Canadian Association of University Teachers
CCL	Canadian Congress of Labour
CCF	Co-operative Commonwealth Federation
CCFA	Canada-China Friendship Association
CCU	Council of Canadian Unions
CCW	Congress of Canadian Women
CCYM	Co-operative Commonwealth Youth Movement
CEW	Committee for the Equality of Women
CEWU	Canadian Electrical Workers Union
CIO	Congress of Industrial Organizations
CIV	Citizens for the Improvement of Vancouver
CIW	Canadian Iron Workers
CLC	Canadian Labour Congress
COPE	Committee of Progressive Electors
CPC	Communist Party of Canada
CPCML	Communist Party of Canada – Marxist-Leninist

CPL	Canadian Party of Labour
CSU	Canadian Seamen's Union
CUCND	Combined Universities Campaign for Nuclear Disarmament
CUPE	Canadian Union of Public Employees
CUPW	Canadian Union of Postal Workers
CYC	Company of Young Canadians
FPCC	Fair Play for Cuba Committee
IAM	International Association of Machinists
IBEW	International Brotherhood of Electrical Workers
ICA Act	Industrial Conciliation and Arbitration Act
ILWU	International Longshoremen and Warehousemen's Union
IUMMSW	International Union of Mine, Mill and Smelterworkers (Mine-Mill)
IWA	International Woodworkers of America
JCCA	Japanese Canadian Citizens Association
LPP	Labor-Progressive Party
LSA	League for Socialist Action
MISC	Movement for an Independent Socialist Canada
NAC	National Action Committee on the Status of Women
NBBC	Native Brotherhood of British Columbia
NDP	New Democratic Party
NDY	New Democratic Youth
NLC	New Left Committee
NPA	Non-Partisan Association
NUPE	National Union of Public Employees
PPWC	Pulp, Paper and Mill Workers of Canada
Pulp & Sulphite	International Brotherhood of Pulp, Sulphite and Paper Mill Workers
PW	Progressive Workers Movement
RCMP	Royal Canadian Mounted Police
RWP	Revolutionary Workers Party
SEL	Socialist Educational League
SF	Socialist Fellowship
SIC	Socialist Information Centre
SORWUC	Service Office and Retail Workers' Union of Canada
SPC	Socialist Party of Canada

SUPA	Student Union for Peace Action
SWP	Socialist Workers Party
TEAM	The Electors' Action Movement
TLC	Trades and Labor Congress of Canada
TUEL	Trade Union Education League
TURB	Trade Union Research Bureau
UFAWU	United Fishermen and Allied Workers' Union
USWA	United Steelworkers of America
VDLC	Vancouver and District Labour Council (CLC)
VLC	Vancouver Labour Council (CCL)
VOW	Voice of Women
VTLC	Vancouver Trades and Labour Council (TLC)
WCSU	West Coast Seamen's Union
WILPF	Women's International League for Peace and Freedom
WIUC	Woodworkers Industrial Union of Canada
YS	Young Socialists/Ligue des Jeunes Socialistes

MILITANT MINORITY

British Columbia Workers and the Rise of a New Left, 1948–1972

Introduction

'Any book which incites the downtrodden working man to revolt should be removed,' declared Doris Lougheed, a member of the Victoria Library Board, during the city's 'book burning' incident of 1954.[1] I hope this book is worthy of that description. Happily, the Victoria library's controversial collection was spared, in the face of public protest that saw college students burn the mayor in effigy, but at least one 'red' librarian was not so fortunate (fired for left-wing associations). The proposal to burn *The Communist Manifesto* and other subversive books arose at a tense time, and from circumstances of a regional and international character. Across British Columbia, a tug-of-war raged between workers and employers, a conflict over resource wealth, the rules of labour relations, and the scope of the welfare state. Internationally, a Cold War raged, a global struggle between capitalism and communism that enlisted partisans on both sides, provoked crises in political parties of the 'Old Left,' and exposed a stubborn group of workers who did not fit easily into either side and thus laid the groundwork for a 'New Left': the militant minority.

This book examines the militant minority, the layer of working-class women and men who challenged the premises and practices of politics and labour relations in postwar BC, sustaining the tug-of-war while kindling an independent working-class flame. Labour historian David Montgomery helped revive the term 'militant minority,' workers who 'endeavored to weld their workmates and neighbors into a self-aware and purposeful working class.'[2] They belonged to the broader working class but they also stood apart, adhering to a world view and to a way of life that conflicted with the Cold War drive for conformity prevailing in 1950s and 1960s North America. These workers' aspirations did not end with the comforts of colour television, chromed Chevrolet sedans, modern suburban homes, and the 'recreational democracy' of hunting, fishing, and camping in the hinterland (pursuits facilitated by the distinct political economy of the postwar years).[3] Though no strangers to such comforts, the militant minority lived and breathed politics and they spearheaded movements for economic justice and political change. They belonged to the Co-operative Commonwealth Federation (CCF), the Labor-Progressive Party (as the Communist Party was called between 1943 and 1959), and more marginal currents such as Trotskyism, and sometimes they belonged to several parties at the same time. These militants had their eye on both domestic and international affairs, from the politics of timber licences and electricity to global questions of war and peace from Korea to Cuba to Vietnam. This militant minority occupied a tangible economic space – leading unions and parties – and also a more ephemeral ideological one, providing the bridge between the 'Old Left' and 'New Left' in Cold War BC.

While the militant minority ascribed to a world view that was more radical and more independent than the working class generally, these workers shared the common experience of the benefits and dangers of the expanding postwar economy. The theory of Fordism helps us to understand postwar economic relationships. As Gordon Hak recently observed, 'Unions, by maintaining high wages and a disciplined workforce, contributed to this stability and governments, too, took on a major role.'[4] The politics of postwar BC, particularly the politics of labour, reflected Fordist relations. The 'long boom' of North American capitalism that ran roughly from 1948 to 1972 provided a degree of economic prosperity for BC's working people, who leveraged through their labour collective agreements and through the 'social wage' of an expanding welfare state a level of affluence without historical precedent. It was in this brief window that a majority of BC workers escaped poverty for the first time, with steadily rising incomes, holidays with pay, and social protections against illness, workplace injury, unemployment, and old age. During this long boom, many BC workers approached the 'good life,' to use a popular Social Credit slogan of the day. But the militant minority demanded more.

The long boom's veneer of affluence concealed looming structural problems, which undermined workers' economic security and served as catalysts for militant action. Inflation led to spiralling costs for food, energy, and other necessities of life, eroding workers' wage gains at the bargaining table and amplifying the distance between labour and management. Automation eroded job security, as employers embraced new technologies that allowed them to replace workers with machines, prompting major disputes such as the 1965 Burrard Inlet oil refinery workers' strike that nearly escalated into a provice-wide general strike (a dispute that grew from an illegal sitdown strike by a handful of workers in a single refinery). Workplace safety, an old concern, assumed urgency in the face of the dangers confronting workers in BC's fast-paced postwar economy, graphically demonstrated in 1958 when the half-built Second Narrows Bridge collapsed, claiming the lives of nineteen ironworkers. Structural unemployment, unheard of during the war and rare in the early postwar years, became entrenched as blue-collar resource-extraction jobs gave way to more tenuous tertiary-service jobs; union density declined from a historic peak of 54 per cent of wage workers in 1958, as employment fell in absolute and relative terms in the traditional bastions of union strength: sawmills, logging camps, coal mines, and shipyards.[5] While the public sector grew substantially, enlisting many woman workers who joined the paid labour force in record numbers, these workers were often denied the fruits of union protection and were vulnerable as state revenues tightened, emerging as a new locus of militancy. The convergence of these factors, the underbelly of Fordism and the long boom, was not easily resolved within the postwar rules of labour relations, and therefore strained established Old Left labour unions and parties while fuelling illegal 'wildcat' strikes and 'breakaway unions' in pulp and paper, smelting, hard-rock mining, and other sectors (led, as always, by the militant minority).[6]

By the early 1970s, the gaps in the 'good life' and this underbelly of Fordism were becoming apparent – not just to the militant minority but to a broader layer of BC workers. Insecurity wrought by inflation, automation, unemployment, and dangerous working conditions hinted that the long boom was fading, at the same time that anger grew against more local grievances, such as the indiscriminate use of court injunctions against workers in labour disputes and a proliferation of anti-labour laws. The result was the most intense labour unrest in a generation, a wave of strikes and lockouts that peaked in the summer of 1972. That year, one out of every three BC union members walked picket lines, paralysing the forestry and construction sectors and prompting police raids on a dozen union offices on orders of the attorney general.[7] In this context, the ruling political coalition fractured, the Social Credit party led by W.A.C. Bennett that had enjoyed an unbroken twenty years in office through an alliance of the regional petty bourgeosie and large resource corporations. On 30 August 1972, British Columbians voted to change their government. The New Democratic Party (NDP) was elected to power, the first social-democratic government in BC's history and a successor to the Old Left CCF. The independent working-class flame kindled by the militant minority had borne fruit.

New Left

This work examines the transition from one left formation to another, grouped around the 'matrix-event' of the Cold War, to employ Ian McKay's terminology (itself borrowed from the *Annales* school), 'a moment that reshapes hegemony at both its profoundest structural levels and its conscious levels.'[8] The pages that follow provide a 'horizontal history,' surveying connections within and between BC's postwar working-class formations, which, however divided, belonged to a common tradition pursuing 'a path out of the labyrinth of a persisting liberal order.'[9] A continuum linked these left formations, as Maurice Isserman demonstrated in his important study of the American left, *If I Had a Hammer: The Death of the Old Left and the Birth of the New Left* (1987).[10] Like Isserman, I challenge the emphasis on rupture that is common to the North American historiography of the New Left, an approach that frequently begins with Ann Arbor in 1960 and Port Huron in 1962. The New Left's history is one of continuity rather than rupture, continuity provided in BC by the activism of the militant minority in the labour, peace, and women's movements. This book builds on works by Myrna Kostash, Cyril Levitt, and others to offer a regionally focused case study, a Canadian equivalent to Isserman that engages the emerging literature on the 1960s. As Bryan Palmer recently noted, 'however much the 1960s were about new developments and abrupt change, these were also times that existed in the shadows of what had gone before.'[11] Like Isserman and Palmer, my historical lens is focused on questions of class and power, linking the stories of the Old and New Left through the agency of BC's militant minority.

The growth of the New Left signified a rejection of the postwar settlement of legalized collective bargaining and incremental gains through welfare-state social security measures. Rather than a compromise, as the prevailing historiography suggested, BC's postwar labour relations climate more closely resembled a tug-of-war, a pitched conflict between workers and employers over the rules of collective bargaining, the distribution of the resource wealth, and the scope of worker entitlements provided by the welfare state.[12] In Nelson Lichtenstein's words, the postwar settlement was 'a limited and unstable truce,' an uneasy arrangement where labour won the right to bargain but management maintained a wide prerogative over the work process and the allocation of profits.[13] Palmer described it as 'an unevenly applied and reluctantly implemented accord.'[14] In a recent study of BC's forest industry, Gordon Hak argued that 'confrontations over wages, though hardly revolutionary, challenged the rights and powers of capital.'[15] Evidence from BC during the long boom demonstrates the persistence of the tug-of-war, which took the form of protracted strikes in logging, fishing, construction, manufacturing, public services and motley sectors, and coalesced into strong labour opposition to specific labour laws, such as Bills 33, 39, 42, 43, 87, and 128. The labour relations system itself was a major arena of contestation, with workers and employers jockeying over the laws of union certification, bargaining, and picketing, and rulings of the Labour Relations Board and Workmen's Compensation Board; in 1956, Bea Zucco led a one-woman sitdown strike on the steps of the provincial legislature demanding worker compensation benefits. Confrontation rather than compromise was the norm.

The growth of the New Left also reflected changes in the structure of BC's working class, as women and ethnic minorities demanded equality within the labour force and within the institutions of labour and the left. The proportion of women wage earners as a percentage of all BC wage earners rose from 16 to 34 per cent between 1941 and 1971, but wages in all sectors lagged far behind those of men.[16] Postwar collective bargaining had structured the BC workforce in gendered and racialized ways. As Gillian Creese argues, straight seniority provisions disadvantaged women workers, workers of colour, and younger workers, because these groups lacked opportunities for continuous employment available to white men, and therefore acquired less seniority. For working women, 'work interruptions linked to family responsibilities' and a lack of access to male-dominated jobs relegated them to an inferior position in this gendered and racialized workforce.[17] Even white-collar unions with many women members, such as Office and Professional Employees Local 378 at the BC Electric Company (after 1961, BC Hydro), failed to institute equality in their ranks; men dominated leadership positions in a union where half the membership was female.[18] As Sylvia Bashevkin and others have demonstrated, women were often relegated to a 'pink-collar ghetto' of clerical work and auxiliary social functions in unions and left-wing parties, while men enjoyed the prestige and influence of the podium and press.[19] As an activist in the CCF Women's Council observed in 1949:

> In spite of our profession of progressive thinking, too many men and women are still conditioned to the belief that women's place is in the home. If this is not the case why is it that when a choice has to be made as to who shall attend a club meeting and who shall put junior to bed, Dad goes to the club and Mom stays home?[20]

Inequality on the left fuelled explicitly feminist forms of political and labour activism, energizing the women's liberation movement as a new source of militancy.[21]

Changes in Canadian immigration policy also altered the demographic and cultural composition of BC's postwar working class and gave shape to the New Left. In 1949, war-time regulations banning Canadians of Japanese origin from the coast were lifted and immigration from China, virtually eliminated from the 1920s to the 1940s, revived as the trade-union movement finally abandoned its historic demand for 'Asiatic exclusion.'[22] In 1948, both the CCF and the LPP assailed a Coalition government edict to lumber operators to dismiss eight hundred Japanese-Canadian loggers, a move the *CCF News* suggested was reminiscent of 'Hitler's brutality against racial minorities' and contrary 'to all the decent principles for which the war was fought.'[23] The social-democratic party accused the Coalition of 'raising the issue of race in the hope that people may again be diverted from their own economic problems.'[24] Communist leader Nigel Morgan suggested it was hypocritical to extend employment rights to Asian-Canadian workers during the wartime labour shortage and then revert to 'cruel and arbitrary discrimination.'[25] In the legislative assembly, CCF MLA Rupert Haggen described Japanese Canadians as 'good citizens,' demanding an end to 'racial discrimination.'[26] Communists and social democrats also sank roots in the South Asian community, among Indo-Canadian woodworkers in Port Alberni and other districts, a trail blazed by Darshan Singh Sangha, an active LPPer who later served as a Communist legislator in India's Punjab state.[27] In urban Vancouver, the militant minority joined Black and Jewish activists in the Vancouver Joint Labor Committee to Combat Racial Discrimination, an early expression of the postwar human rights movement.[28]

Moves toward unity were uneven, demonstrating stubborn prejudices and the gulf between indigenous workers and BC's non-indigenous working class. Living conditions on Indian reservations and the racist residential school system (which persisted in BC until 1983) kept many indigenous people a world apart from the non-indigenous working class. As Andrew Parnaby noted in his study of longshore workers, 'Squamish men … faced the additional burden of being Indian. In a racially segmented labour market that meant working a more dangerous and less lucrative commodity, and in a racist society that meant contending with the significant pressures of the colonial state.'[29] The CCF and communists attempted to bridge this divide, with CCF MLA Frank Calder winning election as BC's first indigenous legislator in 1949, the first provincial election in which indigenous people could vote.[30] Among unions, the communist-led United Fishermen and Allied Workers' Union (UFAWU) stood out in its efforts to forge unity with indigenous fishers in the Native Brotherhood of BC (NBBC).[31] UFAWU secretary Homer Stevens, whose grandmother belonged to the Cowichan and Songhees First Nations, attended the NBBC's 1950 convention in Bella Bella, which he described as an example of 'brotherhood in action.'[32] Two years later, Calder told delegates at the UFAWU annual convention that the 'Native Brotherhood should actually be part of the Union,' that 'there should only be one body of fishermen, one union in the province of BC as far as the fishing industry is concerned.'[33] Such sentiments undermined efforts by BC Packers and the Canadian Fishing Company (Canfisco) to foment divisions along ethnic lines. As Calder told the 1952 UFAWU convention: 'The companies try to keep us apart.'[34] At remote Namu, indigenous women fish-plant workers took direct action, removing segregated toilet signs labelled 'Indian' and 'White.'[35]

By the 1960s, the indigenous political tradition was changing, influenced by the militant Red Power movement and the American Indian Movement (AIM), which would attract considerable interest in BC when Leonard Peltier faced extradition proceedings before a Vancouver judge.[36] For a generation, open political organizing had been effectively banned, by police harassment of activists and Indian Act measures that made it illegal to obtain funds or legal counsel in pursuit of land claims. The NBBC had waged a covert campaign through its organ *Native Voice* and Squamish activist Andrew Paull formed the North American Indian Brotherhood during the war.[37] An RCMP report on Red Power noted that 'early in 1953 our attention was drawn to the formation of a new provincial political party in British Columbia … the Indian Independence Party.'[38] Organizational efforts intensified in the 1960s, buoyed by

Nisga'a legal advances and broader political radicalization; coastal and interior Salish nations formed the Confederation of Native Indians of British Columbia at a meeting in Musqueam in 1966, while the Union of British Columbia Indian Chiefs emerged in 1969 in opposition to the federal White Paper.[39] By the late 1960s, the Native Alliance for Red Power (NARP) had formed its own 'patrol' force, consisting of indigenous youth on the watch for police brutality – borrowing the tactics of the Black Panthers in the United States.[40] Trotskyists in the Vancouver Young Socialists held public forums on Red Power, 'establishing contact with the Indian community,' while Capilano band member James Beynon contested a 1968 North Vancouver provincial by-election as a Communist candidate, declaring: 'For over a hundred years the old line parties of Capitalism have subjected the Canadian Indian to poverty, humiliation, and discrimination.'[41] On the eve of the NDP's 1972 victory, an RCMP agent reported on efforts to 'form an Indian faction of the NDP at Williams Lake.'[42]

Political change was tied to these developments and to the emergence of a 'new working class,' as employment shifted from rural areas into cities and from the extractive resource industries to technical and professional occupations, with corresponding demands for union recognition.[43] The historic locus of working-class militancy – the blue collar, male-dominated resource-extraction sectors and the Old Left parties – gave way to more diffuse forms of organization and activism. Left politics expanded beyond the Cold War-hardened militant minority to include mobilized youth in the labour, peace, women's, student, and counterculture movements.

Mirroring trends across North America and Europe, the break from established institutions, both social democratic and communist, was embedded in the internal history of those institutions. The tension between democracy and organization, Roberto Michels's famous 'Iron Law of Oligarchy,' became acute as working-class parties responded to the Cold War. Michels helps us understand the history of BC's left, as workers were compelled to organize in their struggle for economic and political justice, but butted against the conservative tendencies inherent in all human organizations. In Michels's words: 'Who says organization says oligarchy.'[44] The operation of bureaucracy, examined in an earlier period of BC labour history in Mark Leier's *Red Flags and Red Tape*, is pursued in this book into the postwar years with particular reference to the political institutions of workers.[45] The ambiguous record of labour and socialist governments in Britain, New Zealand, Australia, and

Saskatchewan, and the Cold War shift within the CCF from avowedly socialist to reformed liberal policies, produced disillusionment among the militant minority, creating an openness to new political vehicles.[46] Among BC communists, top-down practices fuelled internal crises which were aggravated by state-supported anti-communism and its virulent Cold War variant, McCarthyism, leading to atrophy as opportunities for the renewal of members and views were lost.[47] The Khrushchev revelations and Soviet invasions of Hungary and Czechoslovakia discredited the alternative system that was being established in the Soviet bloc.[48] Trotskyist and allied radical groups that had operated on the margins provided a pole of attraction to leftists and labour militants, as did Maoist formations and issue-based movements against the nuclear bomb, for environmental protection, and in support of liberation movements both at home and abroad.

In 1972, a political vehicle that represented a compromise between the Old Left and New Left – and drew strength from the province's deep socialist tradition, its class-based party system, its militant labour movement, and decades of electioneering expertise – succeeded in harnessing the sentiments of the new working class and diverse social protest movements, capturing the reins of legislative power from a politically fragmented provincial bourgeoisie. The Dave Barrett NDP government (1972–5) represented a new chapter in the political history of BC's working class.[49]

Origins and Agency

Though hardly exceptional, the pattern of colonization in British Columbia spawned the militant labour tradition. On the 'corporate industrial frontier' immigrant workers from the British Isles confronted undisguised exploitation, while Asian workers faced low wages, virulent racism, and demands for 'Asiatic exclusion.' Conditions of life and work in BC's mines, logging camps, and railroad camps reinforced a Marxian critique of capitalism and spawned militant industrial unions such as the Industrial Workers of the World and radical political formations such as the Socialist Party of Canada.[50] As Paul Phillips observed a generation ago in the only existing survey of BC labour history, 'there was an articulate, able and often charismatic socialist leadership to take control of the BC labour movement during its formative period.'[51] This tradition of militancy and radicalism – the origins of the militant minority – shaped industrial relations and partisan politics for the duration of the twentieth century.[52] The militants sunk roots in various industries and forged strong unions before the era of 'industrial legality.'[53] Scholarly treatment of BC's political economy by Phillips, Martin Robin, Philip Resnick, Paul Knox, and others has focused largely on the period prior to the 1930s, and the study at hand therefore extends this approach – grounded in the intersection of social class, economics, and political power – beyond the Second World War.[54]

The collective agency of this militant minority and British Columbia's broader working class produced two distinct outcomes in the postwar years: 1) a level of union density unsurpassed on the North American continent (54 per cent of wage earners belonged to unions in 1958); and 2) a class-polarized party system that more closely resembled European patterns of partisan alignment than North American 'brokerage' politics.[55] While BC workers never broke away from the free enterprise mould that distinguished North American economics and politics in the Cold War era, at the initiative of the militant minority they challenged employers' industrial and political power and they altered the institutions of capitalism. The experience of BC's militant minority therefore has much to say to workers outside the province. It signifies the limits of working-class agency in North America: both the capacity of organized workers to alter the conditions of life and work and the barriers imposed by a political and economic system that privileged employers' interests.

The historic conflict between labour and capital over the distribution of power and wealth was influenced in postwar BC by a complex of state institutions that favoured employers. From the actions of police on picket lines, to Royal Canadian Mounted Police (RCMP) Security Service surveillance of labour organizations, to injunctions issued by provincial court judges, to the rulings of the quasi-judicial Labour Relations Board and Workmen's Compensation Board, to statutes and regulations emanating out of the provincial legislature, to the amended Elections Act of 1951, state power was exercised to the benefit of employers more often than workers. Laws and programs that benefited workers (such as social security provisions, state medicine, and collective bargaining apparatus) were largely concessions from employer-oriented governments dependent on working-class votes. The Hospital Insurance Act of 1948 was implemented by BC's Coalition government prior to an election, but its confused funding formula contributed to the Coalition's demise. The labour relations system, while allowing for incremental improvements in living standards and job security, entrenched management rights and employer dominance in the provincial economy.

Opposition by employers and the state was only the most overt barrier to workers' agency, as an array of cultural institutions perpetuated a world view detrimental to labour's goals, broadcasting employer-oriented messages for working-class consumption.[56] Alternative media such as the *CCF News, Pacific Tribune*, and *The Fisherman* sought to challenge this bias, but they lacked the frequency and circulation of employer-controlled media. In August 1950, Vancouver radio station CKMO cancelled a taped broadcast by UFAWU secretary Homer Stevens quoting facts on the effects of the atomic bomb, in the midst of a 'Ban-the-Bomb' peace campaign and the fifth anniversary of the Hiroshima bombing.[57] Vancouver dailies similarly refused to publish advertisements from the Canadian Peace Congress urging readers to sign the Ban-the-Bomb petition.[58] In 1954, the Canadian Broadcasting Corporation's Prince Rupert affiliate, CFPR, refused air-time to the Prince Rupert Trades and Labour Council's Union Label Committee because the script was deemed 'controversial.'[59] Strongly influenced by the Cold War, these cultural institutions bolstered support for individual rather than collective responses to social problems, undermined the militant minority's position within the broader working class, and discredited the potential of working-class agency as a force for social change.

This point, however, must not be overstated. Agency is exhibited by working people in diverse ways, not just on militant picket lines or raucous protest demonstrations. Those workers who shunned labour unions and leftist political parties, and embraced Liberal, Conservative, and Social Credit politics – or no politics at all – exercised agency. During periods of apparent industrial quiescence, workers exercised agency through shirking, absenteeism, insubordination, and subtle or overt sabotage. Workers exercised agency through their creativity in the work process.[60] They also exercised agency outside the workplace: in patterns of migration, in the act of human reproduction, in leisure activities and art, in lifestyle choices, and in social institutions such as churches, service clubs, and athletic associations. As historian Paul Thompson has suggested, the cumulative choices of individuals have probably had a greater impact as an agent of social change than 'the acts of politicians which are the usual stuff of history.'[61] Mark Leier calls for an appreciation of working-class agency on its own terms, defining class as 'a daily, lived experience, as accessible and as plain as race and gender, even if workers do not articulate it with the precision of a sociologist or translate it into a vote for a socialist candidate.'[62]

Having waged a successful war against fascism in Europe and Japan, Canadian workers were determined to win an extension of democracy at home. The outcome was by no means predetermined, but in historic strikes – by Windsor autoworkers in 1945 and Hamilton steelworkers and British Columbia loggers in 1946 – Canadian employers, along with the federal and provincial governments, were compelled to confer a degree of permanence on concessions granted during the war. Most significant was a set of bargaining rights, enacted by federal Order-in-Council and then embodied in provincial legislation, requiring employers to recognize, and negotiate with, unions freely chosen by workers. This historic advance in labour rights paved the way for incremental improvements in wages, benefits, and working conditions. Buttressed by an expanding social wage, which provided insurance for unemployment, workplace injury, sickness, and old age, BC workers approached the 'good life.' Even so, these working-class gains did not translate into labour peace. Rising prices eroded wage gains, and the Cold War intruded on the freedom of workers to choose unions and leaders to defend their interests. The ambiguous postwar victory of BC's working class laid the foundation for the rank-and-file revolt of the 1960s.

As in other frontier societies, BC's population was influenced by a low birth rate and a preponderance of men, many of whom worked in the resource-extraction sectors. In 1931, there were 124 men for every 100 women in the province. During the postwar decades this imbalance levelled off, as the total population more than doubled from 1.1 million people in 1948 to 2.3 million in 1972. However, men continued to outnumber women in hinterland areas. While the province-wide ratio in 1951 was 105 men for every 100 women, this figure soared to 123 among the non-farming rural population.[63] The geographic distribution of men and women helps explain the low birth rate: young men were over-represented in rural areas, while young women were over-represented in urban areas.[64] BC's postwar demography, and its political culture, were also influenced by inter-provincial migration, which fluctuated widely from year to year, reflecting volatile employment conditions in the export-dependent economy. In 1961, with unemployment exceeding 10 per cent, net inter-provincial migration hovered around zero; by 1965, this number soared to 25,000 as unemployment dropped to 4.5 per cent.[65] More than half of British Columbia residents in the years 1948 to 1972 were born outside the province.[66] As political scientist Edwin R. Black observed in 1967, 'A steady influx of new people ... tends to inhibit the growth of incipient local custom' and weaken ties to traditional political and social institutions.[67]

Political change in postwar BC reflected volatility in the labour relations system, which promised gains but ultimately spawned rank-and-file discontent.[68] 'Contentious issues of workplace control or class solidarity were ... shunted aside in the rush to consumerism,' historian Peter McInnis noted.[69] Consumerism displaced socialism as the goal of many trade-union leaders, as Canadian Congress of Labour secretary-treasurer Pat Conroy confirmed in a 1947 speech to the Canadian Club in Ottawa: 'If labour can secure what it wants under free enterprise it will stay with the system.'[70] The social wage provided by an expanding welfare state, combined with incremental material gains in wages and benefits secured through the formalized bargaining relationship, represented the limit of labour's postwar victory. In contrast to the economic privation of the pre-Second World War era, and the arbitrary authority of capital, the postwar settlement represented an unprecedented improvement in the condition of BC's working class. However, in contrast with the historic objective of a socialist society that would transcend capitalism, the postwar settlement fell short.

Between these two objectives a tension emerged, one that widened into an open breach in the 1960s; dissident unions, led by communists, such as the United Fishermen and Allied Workers' Union (UFAWU), Vancouver Civic Outside Workers, and Mine, Mill and Smelter Workers (Mine-Mill), retained a radical philosophy throughout the Cold War and were excluded from the central bodies of organized labour. By the 1960s, they were joined by secessionist unions such as the Canadian Iron Workers (CIW), Pulp and Paper Workers of Canada (PPWC), and Canadian Association of Smelter and Allied Workers (CASAW). The rise of these dissident or 'alternative' labour organizations underscored the role of the militant minority in postwar labour relations.[71] American domination of BC's industrial unions contributed to the breakaway sentiment, as did the perceived benefits of a confrontational approach. Moderate labour leaders' efforts to achieve material gains through negotiation and political lobbying were often blocked by intransigent employers and an aggressive, employer-friendly provincial government. BC was distinct in postwar Canada for the enduring, albeit minority, strength of the Communist Party and for the relatively high rate of striker-days, a reflection of BC's militant tradition and volatile economic climate.

Working-class politics changed in postwar British Columbia, reflecting Cold War crises in established Old Left parties and structural changes in BC's economy and working class. The basic antagonism of interests between labour and capital continued to motivate expressions of collective action, but the fabric and practice of working-class life changed. Tightly knit working-class communities were diffused by the automobile and suburban housing; leisure became more compartmentalized with the advent of the television age; the causes of socialism and trade unionism appeared less important in a period of rising incomes and social security.[72] The CCF retreated from its explicitly socialist doctrine in favour of reform liberal policies, while the Communist Party's influence in BC's powerful industrial unions declined. The Communists were rarely a competitive electoral force; only in the provincial and federal elections of 1945 did the several thousand votes mustered by Communist candidates influence the outcome in BC. Meanwhile, structural changes were transforming BC's working class. Infrastructure expansion and public-sector growth created new loci of militancy, while women's increased participation in the paid labour force altered dynamics within and between unions. A new working class emerged that was more diverse, educated, white-collar, and urbanized than the old resource-extraction workforce.

Against this backdrop, the militant minority – CCF and communist dissidents, and Trotskyists in the Revolutionary Workers' Party (RWP) – nurtured an oppositional political culture in the labour, peace, and women's movements that enjoyed a resurgence in the 1960s. Rank-and-file workers and students gravitated behind a New Left, which assumed the name of a British movement and rallied around issues of nuclear arms, environmental protection, and liberation movements at home and abroad. This New Left developed distinct cultural styles, myriad organizational forms, and emerged as the most visible force challenging the socio-economic status quo in North America and beyond.[73] While this New Left lacked the institutional cohesion of the older left formations, it coincided with the upturn in rank-and-file labour militancy, embodied in 'illegal' wildcat strikes, workplace occupations, and breakaway unions. Tactically, BC's New Left was influenced by traditional forms of labour militancy – strikes, occupations, picketing – and the philosophy of 'non-violence' popularized by Mahatma Gandhi and the American civil rights and anti-war movements. In 1972, this ferment within BC's working class contributed to a wave of strikes and a change in government, which brought labour closer to power.

This book has three principal objectives: (1) to restore political economy, and an emphasis on labour institutions, as valid subjects of working-class and social history; (2) to provide a regional Canadian equivalent to Isserman's study of the transition from the Old Left to the New Left, a 'horizontal history' grounded in the major political traditions of the Canadian working class and broader economic and political currents; and (3) to expand our understanding of BC's political culture, class-polarized party system, and volatile labour-relations climate in a way that is relevant to a wider, interdisciplinary Canadian and international literature.[74] Chapter 1 explores the economic and political context within which the postwar working class engaged politically. Chapter 2 assesses the fortunes of BC's Communist Party during the Cold War, examining external and internal crises that provided an opening for new expressions of political radicalism. Chapter 3 considers changes in the social democratic CCF, which moved away from socialism and contributed to the appeal of the New Left. Chapter 4 explores radical currents outside the mainstream working-class parties, such as Trotskyism and Maoism, and examines the New Left ferment in the postwar peace movement. Chapter 5 traces the 'unhinging' of workers from established industrial institutions, culminating in the breakaway unions and rank-and-file revolt of the 1960s. Chapter 6, finally, explores how these political and industrial changes culminated in the NDP's 1972 victory.

Informed by rich archival sources, by labour and left-wing newspapers including the *Pacific Tribune*, *CCF News*, and the *Fisherman*, by government records, and by the personal stories of working-class people who made history in postwar BC, this work draws from a wide body of source material. It provides a wealth of detail that may appear daunting to nonspecialist readers. However, the narrative conveys the complexity and fluidity of the province's left-wing tradition. In compiling oral history, I sought out leaders and rank-and-file workers from the CCF-NDP, Communist Party, and New Left traditions, and from labour unions and women's auxiliaries. These informants were selected because of their proximity to the themes and events examined in this work. As Paul Thompson has argued, oral history forces historians 'to come out of the closet and talk to ordinary people,' restoring to them 'the oldest skill of their own craft.' Moreover, oral history facilitates the writing of a history 'which leads to action: not to confirm, but to change the world.'[75]

This work tackles an ideologically charged subject, one which holds appeal for historians of kindred ideological commitments. However, as James Naylor suggests, labour and working-class historians must strive toward an understanding of 'the sources of conflict within the labour movement' while avoiding 'fighting old battles' tied to their particular ideological commitments.[76] They must avoid imposing what Craig Heron calls 'the search for simon-pure class consciousness' on the past, 'since it sets a standard of perfection in class behaviour that has never been met anywhere outside theoretical texts.'[77] The tenor of debate – between warring communist factions after 1956, between 'socialists' and 'social democrats' in the CCF-NDP, between supporters of 'International' and breakaway unions – often assumed an extra-wordly character, at times clouding the larger struggle against private control of the provincial economy. It is with these cautionary words in mind that I embark on the minefield that was working-class politics in postwar BC. Informed by the insights of the new social history, the interpretive narrative that follows sheds fresh light on the process of political change within BC's working class – institutionalization and deinstitutionalization in the face of Cold War crises, and then reformation as the remnants of the Old Left were transformed by the militant minority and an ascendant new working class. It examines the political development of one of the most militant, unionized, and politically independent working classes on the North American continent, during a period of historic material advance.

CHAPTER ONE

The Political Economy of British Columbia

> We are concerned with the control of the forests and the mineral wealth, the natural gas and the hydro power of the province. If these resources belong to the people, then the CCF says the people should control them through the legislature.
>
> Robert Strachan, BC CCF Leader, 1956[1]

In postwar British Columbia, the essential fact of economic life was that the province's natural resource wealth belonged to the Crown, even as *de facto* control remained in private and increasingly American hands. Resource exploitation drove the provincial economy, spawning robust working-class challenges and the political coalition that took shape as Social Credit. Throughout this period, working-class militants challenged the prerogrative of private resource firms and offered a sustained critique of the 'give-away' of the 'people's resources' by first the Coalition that governed from 1941 to 1952 and then by the Social Credit coalition that succeeded it until 1972. While the landscape of British Columbia politics changed after the 1952 election – as populism of the right and left displaced Liberal and Convervative loyalties – the basic political economy demonstrated continuity rather than change. Its primary features were the tug-of-war between labour and capital over resource wealth, corporate consolidation and rising opposition to American resource firms, and the challenge that confronted rival sections of the capitalist class in responding to the political agency of the working class.[2]

Tug-of-War: Postwar Industrial Relations

Rather than a compromise, as some scholars have suggested, the industrial relations climate in postwar BC is better described as a tug-of-war between labour and capital, a pitched conflict over the balance of power in the provincial economy, the limits of labour's social wage, and control of resource wealth. In 1947, the federal government's wartime jurisdiction over labour relations lapsed; BC's Industrial Conciliation and Arbitration Act (ICA Act), passed in 1937, was substantially amended to incorporate the changes in federal Privy Council Order (PC) 1003 during the war. BC's Coalition-controlled legislature approved Bill 39, which like PC 1003 banned mid-contract strikes and mandated government-supervised strike votes and grievance-arbitration language.[3] 'Its machinery was geared to the demands of big business,' alleged the *Pacific Tribune*, newspaper of the Labor-Progressive Party (LPP), as the Communist Party was called between 1943 and 1959: 'When the policies of big business provoked strike action, the machinery broke down.'[4] LPP leader Nigel Morgan, a woodworker, concurred: 'Bill 39 was specifically designed by its Coalition sponsors to obstruct the trade union movement of BC in use of its bargaining power to secure just wage demands, shorter hours, greater safety and better conditions on the job.'[5]

In January 1948, the average industrial wage in BC was $40.49 per week, far below the $72.98 the LPP-aligned Workers' Educational Association estimated was necessary to provide adequate living standards for a family of four.[6] Federal and provincial 'decontrol' policies contributed to a sharp increase in consumer prices, from milk, butter, bacon, and other foodstuffs to petroleum and rental housing, while the Coalition introduced a 3 per cent sales tax in March 1948 that cut into workers' earnings.[7] As a working-class woman wrote, 'we have to stretch household finances and what our husbands earn is the root of our problem.'[8] The wages and working conditions of male workers were, therefore, of immediate concern to working-class women:

> Whatever action most women take, it all springs from one desire – to maintain some security for their families and help to preserve peace. That's why thousands of women have been out with roll-back prices petitions in an effort to bring down living costs. That's why women are taking jobs to ease the family burden and inevitably are being drawn into union activity to increase their wages and protect their jobs.[9]

The Vancouver chapter of the LPP-aligned Congress of Canadian Women (CCW) lobbied Vancouver City Council to pressure the federal government for action against rising prices. 'It is becoming impossible for working mothers to stretch their dollars any further,' local president Marie Godfrey said.[10]

In early 1948, the 30,000 members of the International Woodworkers of America (IWA) BC district, confident in the wake of their successful thirty-seven-day strike in 1946 and led by LPPer Harold Pritchett and other communists, were preparing for bargaining, as were coal miners, civic workers, fishers, and packinghouse workers at twenty-eight fruit and vegetable plants in the Interior.[11] Printers at Vancouver's *Daily Province* newspaper, members of the International Typographical Union, had been on strike for eighteen months; West Coast merchant-marine officers, backed by the Canadian Seamen's Union, tied up shipping on Burrard Inlet in a dispute with the Shipping Federation.[12] 'With the cost of living rising daily, the workers are preparing a drive for higher wages,' the *CCF News* reported in January 1948.[13]

Divisions among the province's labour organizations – between CIO and AFL unions, affiliated respectively with the rival Canadian Congress of Labour (CCL) and Trades and Labor Congress of Canada (TLC), and between a CCF-aligned 'White Bloc' and communists for control over the powerful CIO unions – provided opportunities for an employer-driven campaign to rewrite the ICA Act to their benefit. In the legislative session of spring 1948, the Coalition introduced amendments to the ICA Act making it possible to decertify unions that engaged in unauthorized strikes, requiring a government-supervised vote on an employer's final offer, and removing a clause protecting unions against spurious lawsuits.[14] Bill 87, tabled in April 1948, ignored extensive lobbying efforts of CCL and TLC unions: 'This bill is dictated by the Canadian Manufacturers' Association and the BC Bar Association,' provincial CCF leader Harold Winch charged. 'It is not concerned with the interests of the trade unions.'[15] His father, Ernest Winch, MLA for Burnaby, said the anti-communist tone of debate reminded him of the anti-socialist attacks he suffered as a labour organizer in the 1920s: 'You'd blacklist me in this House if you could.'[16] All twenty-seven amendments proposed by the CCF were voted down by Coalition MLAs. However, the labour-appointed representatives on the new Labour Relations Board (LRB) – compensated to the tune of $5,000 per year – supported Bill 87.[17] According to the *Fisherman*,

> The ICA Act of 1947 was worse than PC 1003 and the pre-war ICA Act, and the 1948 amendments further weakened the position of trade unions on the crucial issues of their status as legal entities and the right to strike. The only effective amendment to the present Act would be its repeal and its substitution with an entirely new Act.[18]

This question, of amending the existing act or replacing it with new legislation, revealed the Red-White split and divided the Victoria Trades and Labour Council, which narrowly voted 32 to 31 to place itself on record 'as being against the ICA Act in its entirety.'[19]

The new LRB was a peculiar institution, ostensibly neutral but slanted in favour of employers. George Wilkinson of Victoria, the TLC representative, belonged to the local Chamber of Commerce and had participated in a 1947 employer lobby on Bill 39.[20] Other members of the board – Harry Strange for the CCL, and former Saanich MLA MacGregor McIntosh and F.W. Smelt representing employers – were appointed nearly ten months after Bill 39 created the LRB; at the time of their appointments, the five-member board still lacked a permanent chairman. This was interpreted by the *CCF News* as proof that the Coalition was 'not particularly concerned about the efficient functioning of the Labor Relations Board.'[21] Even with the LRB stacked in employers' favour, however, labour scored some victories. In spring 1948, the Vancouver Boilermakers successfully contested the certification of a company union at the Dominion Rustproofing Co. plant in Burnaby. 'We have now set a precedent,' union president Bill White told the Vancouver Labour Council (CCL).[22]

However, other precedents detrimental to labour were emerging out of the courts and the nascent LRB. A Court of Appeal ruling against the Nanaimo Laundry Workers' Union established 'the right of the government to prosecute a trade union.'[23] A second ruling by the appeal court, pertaining to a dispute between the Steelworkers and the Vancouver Machinery Department, 'extended the principle so that it is now possible for employers to bring civil suit for damages against trade unions.'[24] IWA Local 1-71 and the IWA BC District Council were brought before the BC Supreme Court for a sit-down strike against an arbitrary increase in camp board from $1.50 to $2.00 per day. The company, Smith and Osberg Ltd., alleged an 'illegal strike,' while organized labour maintained such strikes 'could not exist.'[25] Citing earlier action against the Steelworkers and the *Daily Province* printers, the *Pacific Trib-*

une warned that 'an attempt is being made to make a criminal out of the whole labour movement.'[26]

Labour negotiations in 1948 took place within the sixfold context of (1) legalized, though circumscribed, bargaining rights for workers; (2) escalating prices for foodstuffs and other necessities of life, following the lifting of wartime price controls and the introduction of the provincial sales tax; (3) the emergence of a White Bloc within labour's ranks that was attempting to wrest control of powerful industrial unions from Communist leadership; (4) the advent of the Cold War between the capitalist West and Communist East with a corresponding ideological assault on militancy and radical political alternatives; (5) structural changes in BC's resource sectors; and (6) the resurgence of centrifugal rifts between rival sections of the provincial bourgeoisie.

Organized Capital and Political Power

From the earliest days of colonial government in British Columbia, political power was based on economic power – Crown ownership of land, timber, fish stocks, rivers, and subsurface energy and mineral rights invested government with a determining role in BC's economy, a role that could not be ignored by any group or individual concerned about its economic interests. From the vast landholdings of the Hudson's Bay Company and Governor James Douglas, through the coal interests and 1.9-million-acre land grant of the Dunsmuir clan, through the timber licences granted to H.R. MacMillan, the oligarchs of BC industry understood the importance of controlling the reins of government.[27] State subsidies were integral to resource extraction, which emerged as the pillar of economic activity. Raw materials – initially sea-otter furs and later coal, fish, and timber – were exported for manufacture and consumption elsewhere; forays into processing and value-added manufacturing were spasmodic and ephemeral.[28] In 1903, after Nanaimo coal miners elected a socialist to the legislature, the non-partisan electoral system was replaced with a party system mirroring old-world Conservative/Liberal alignments.[29] Predictably, the Conservative administration that governed BC for the next thirteen years favoured the interests of employers more often than workers.[30] In 1913, it deployed the militia against striking Vancouver Island miners; 179 workers were arrested and imprisoned.[31] While BC's party system had its desired effect, ensuring the orderly alternation of Conservative and Liberal majorities for four decades, independent working-class politics remained a permanent, if minority, presence in the BC Legislature.[32]

The pattern of colonization and industrial development helps explain BC's tradition of instability in industrial relations, and also the strength of working-class political parties. However, as Theresa Kerin demonstrated, the idea that economic power is more open in frontier societies is contradicted by evidence; control has remained in the hands of 'a cohesive, homogenous, closed group of men' in the Vancouver metropolis.[33] Robber barons of the Dunsmuir variety may have faded as capitalism became more complex, but the manipulation of public office for private gain remained a mainstay of political life, as Martin Robin and Thomas Sanford demonstrated in their interpretations of the 'company province.'[34] The Pacific Great Eastern Railway – forerunner to the BC Railway – was a major source of controversy and patronage.[35] Similarly, in the postwar era, the young Social Credit administration was seriously battered in its second term when Lands and Forests Minister Robert Sommers was convicted and jailed for accepting bribes in the granting of timber licences.[36] Bruce Hutchinson, Liberal editor of Victoria's *Daily Times*, commented on this kind of graft in 1950: 'Vancouver is ruled by the most garish tycoons produced to date in Canada … In the shelter of this mushroom aristocracy, and usually with the aid of its campaign funds, Vancouver has produced some of the worst politics in Canada.'[37]

A tension existed throughout the twentieth century between the political ambitions of rival sections of BC's capitalist class and the need for unity in the face of the working-class challenge. At the polls, this tension was demonstrated in the elections of 1941, 1952, 1972, and 1991, when the dissolution of ruling-class coalitions provided the opportunity for victory by the working-class coalition that marshalled behind the CCF-NDP banner. In 1941, vote-splitting between Liberals and Conservatives allowed the CCF to capture a plurality of the vote, forcing a wartime Coalition government that held power until 1952; when divisions again became apparent, the Liberal-led Coalition introduced Bill 108, changes to the Elections Act that replaced the first-past-the-post, simple-majority electoral system with a transferable or 'alternate voting' system.[38] Future Liberal leader Pat McGeer described the new voting system as W.A.C. Bennett's 'ladder to power.'[39] Ronald Worley, Bennett's executive assistant, acknowledged this fact: '(CCF leader) Harold Winch was quick to make it clear he did not favour the bill, because he claimed that it was being instituted solely to keep his socialists out of office. How right he was! It did!'[40]

The Coalition that governed until 1952 was an unstable amalgam of partisan jealousies and conflicting regional and industrial interests, the product of a shotgun wedding necessitated by the CCF's electoral threat. Liberal premier Thomas Dufferin Pattullo (1933–41) had laid the groundwork for an interventionist provincial state, advancing a program of 'socialized capitalism' in a package of policies Margaret Ormsby described as the 'Little New Deal.'[41] Under the slogan 'Work and Wages,' the Pattullo government responded to the 1930s depression with a proto-Keynesian program of public works; public boards were established with jurisdiction over industrial relations, agricultural marketing, public utilities, and the price of coal and petroleum. In 1941, however, Pattullo failed to win a majority, and refused co-operation with the Conservatives, believing that a 'broader and bigger liberalism' was actually 'a patched up Toryism.'[42] Pattullo was unceremoniously dumped by his party and replaced by his finance minister John Hart, who formed a Coalition government with R.L. Maitland's Conservatives.[43] In 1945, Coalition leaders negotiated an electoral saw-off of constituencies to avoid direct competition between Liberal and Conservative candidates. The result was the successful containment of the CCF threat, which had risen to power in Saskatchewan on a wave of wartime support for economic planning and social security.[44]

While Bennett described the Hart Coalition government as 'the best government BC ever had,' he described the second Coalition government, led by Byron 'Boss' Johnson, as the province's worst.[45] The ascendancy of Johnson as Coalition premier in 1947 coincided with the 'orderly decontrol' program of federal and provincial governments and a shift toward free-enterprise policies: prices of basic foodstuffs were deregulated, a sales tax was implemented, the Industrial Conciliation and Arbitration Act was amended despite labour's intense lobbying efforts, and the 'Aluminum Bill' and Forest Act provided huge concessions to private industry.[46] In 1948, LPP provincial leader Nigel Morgan accused the Coalition of being 'completely under the domination of the big monopolists in the lumber, mining, hydro-electric, and petroleum industries.'[47]

Under pressure from the CCF opposition in the legislature and extra-parliamentary opposition from the LPP and other groups, the Coalition was cognizant of the need to retain working-class votes. BC citizens had voted 59 per cent in favour of public hospital insurance in a 1937 plebiscite, and Pattullo had passed (but never proclaimed) an act establishing such a scheme, but the issue languished. In 1948, the vote-conscious Coalition implemented a compulsory, contributory provincial hospital-insurance program, based on a maximum annual premium of $33 per family, with remaining costs to be covered by a $2-million provincial stabilization fund and a municipal payment of 70 cents per patient per day. It quickly became apparent, however, that this financial arrangement was inadequate, producing escalating deficits for the BC Hospital Insurance Service (BCHIS) that sapped political capital from the Coalition. In its first fifteen months of operation, the BCHIS incurred cost overruns of $4.5 million.[48] The Coalition preferred to raise premiums rather than allot funds from general revenue, despite a petition bearing 250,000 signatures favouring such a move. Finance Minister Herbert Anscomb, the Conservative leader, told the legislature he was not prepared to raise taxes 'to finance ventures in socialism.'[49] Health costs were only one area of rising government expenditures. Social service costs more than doubled between 1947 and 1948, from $9 million to $19 million, prompting the Coalition to establish the 3 per cent 'Social Service and Municipal Aid' retail sales tax; total provincial expenditures grew from $77 million in 1948 to $164 million in 1951.[50] The weakness of the Liberal-Conservative Coalition was exposed in October 1951, when its candidate, Victoria mayor Percy George, finished third in an Esquimalt by-election that was won by the CCF.[51] The final break occurred in January 1952, when Anscomb publicly released the terms of a federal-provincial tax agreement before informing the premier or cabinet.[52]

Hospital Insurance was a major issue in the 1952 election, which also featured plebiscites on the extension of daylight saving time and relaxation of the province's archaic liquor laws. The Conservatives campaigned for a return to a voluntary hospital-insurance system, while the Liberals and CCF defended the public system, as did the upstart Social Credit party of W.A.C. Bennett.[53] The Kelowna hardware merchant had first been elected as a Conservative in South Okanagan in 1941 and mounted two unsuccessful bids for the party leadership, along with a failed 1948 federal by-election campaign (losing to CCFer Owen Jones, mayor of Kelowna and a hardware merchant himself). Bennett frequently found himself on the opposite side of issues within his party and the Coalition caucus, defecting to sit as an independent during the Coalition's dying days.[54] He linked up with the ruling Social Credit ad-

Table 1.1 Popular support for Social Credit in BC, 1937–53

Election Year	% of popular vote	# of votes	# of candidates	# elected
1937	1.15	4,812	18	0
1941[a]	–	–	0	0
1945	1.42	6,627	16	0
1949[b]	1.65	11,536	16	0
1952[c]	27.20	209,049	47	19
1953[c]	37.75	274,771	48	28

Source: British Columbia, *Statement of Votes*, 1937–1953

[a] Mired in divisions, Social Credit did not field a single candidate in 1941. Horsfield, 'The Social Credit Movement in British Columbia,' 58–62.

[b] The 1949 figures reflect the combined totals for the rival BC Social Credit League and Social Credit Party. British Columbia, Statement of Votes, 1949

[c] These elections were contested under the Alternative Vote or 'transferable ballot' system. Elkins, 'Politics Makes Strange Bedfellows,' 3–26.

ministration in Alberta and the party's fringe following in BC, the remnant of several splits and sects that had received a meagre 1.7 per cent of the vote in 1949 (see table 1.1).[55] Bennett invested $10,000 of his own funds and toured the province by car to prop up the skeletal campaigns of forty-six Social Credit candidates, none of whom had served in the legislature with the exception of another erstwhile Tory, Tilly Rolston of Point Grey. According to political scientist Martin Robin, Bennett 'disengaged the elite, in order to engage the masses.'[56] In August 1952, after the labyrinthine counting procedures of the new Alternative Voting system had unfolded, Bennett was proclaimed premier of a minority Social Credit government (in an election that would likely have been won by the CCF under the old voting system). In the spring of 1953, he engineered his own defeat in the legislature, won a majority mandate in the subsequent election, and repealed the Elections Act changes, returning BC to the first-past-the-post system.

Bennett had staved off the socialist threat and retained control of government for the province's employing class.[57] As CCF MLA Frank Calder, the first indigenous person elected to the BC Legislature, observed prior to the election, Social Credit represented 'a new form of Coalition.'[58] To be sure, sections of the elite were wary of Social Credit. Residual loyalty to the Liberal and Conservative parties remained, and neither party would die in the decades that followed. The Social Credit victory of 1952, however, *was* significant. Bennett came to symbolize the

Table 1.2 Occupational background of cabinet ministers (1947–74)

	Coalition (%)	Social Credit (%)	NDP (%)
Executives/Managers	30	4	0
Small business	40	19	15
Lawyers	20	13	15
Teachers	0	21	8
Other professionals	10	21	23
White collar	0	4	23
Skilled trades	0	0	8
Semi-skilled	0	13	8
Farmers	0	8	0

Source: Addie, Czepil and Rumsey, 'The Power Elite in BC,' 30.

defence of free enterprise from the socialist hordes, but he also represented a change in the face of private enterprise. His party occupied a distinct location in BC's class structure, representing the regional petty bourgeoisie, 'small to medium-sized businessmen, ranchers, orchardists, retail merchants, and struggling private enterprisers of all types,' who resented the economic influence of the Lower Mainland.[59] Gordon Hak described Social Credit's 1952 breakthrough as a populist response to structural changes in BC's economy, particularly the rapid postwar expansion of large resource firms, which fuelled political alienation of the petty bourgeoisie in the hinterland.[60] Social Credit harnessed resentment against the established order, 'resentment of the educated by the uneducated, of metropolitan interests and attitudes by rural and semi-frontier areas, of the denominations by the sects, of the private and public bureaucracies by the small entrepreneur.'[61] This class basis is apparent in table 1.2, comparing the occupational backgrounds of Coalition, Social Credit, and NDP cabinet ministers.

Social Credit's economic strategy reflected its class basis: distanced from the economic elite of the Vancouver-Victoria metropolis, Social Credit pursued a strategy of 'province building' – 'opening up' the vast resource-rich hinterland Interior through government spending on transportation and energy infrastructure to ensure the easy flow of exportable commodities.[62] 'The opening up and development of new resources in the central and northern Interior, essential to the further expansion of the economy, require costly transportation facilities,' the government argued in a 1953 proposal for federal-provincial cost sharing.[63] Transportation expansion focused on highways, roads, and bridges; completion of the government-owned Pacific Great Eastern railway, a pariah for previous governments that Bennett extended to the Peace Country and restored to profitability under the aegis of the British Columbia Railway; and coastal passenger and freight movement by sea, under the publicly owned British Columbia Ferry Authority, created in 1958 during a protracted labour dispute.[64] Highways, bridges, and the BC Railway improved access to mountainous and remote areas, while hydroelectric developments on the Peace and Columbia rivers supplied employment and cheap power for Interior industries. To meet the needs of the expanding Interior resource sectors, new or 'instant' service and processing towns emerged, such as Kitimat and Mackenzie.[65] Established towns on major transportation arteries, such as Kamloops and Prince George, saw considerable postwar growth. In the Peace Country, extending from the eastern slopes of the Rocky Mountains to the Alberta and Yukon border, oil and gas extraction and dam construction provided major engines of growth. From an extreme metropolis-hinterland dichotomy at war's end, BC diversified demographically to an extent, with growing medium-sized urban centres in the regions.[66]

For twenty years, W.A.C. Bennett enjoyed an unbroken term as premier of BC. Long an advocate of preferential voting during the Coalition, Bennett made peace with first-past-the-post when he found himself at the helm of a majority party. In two by-elections conducted under first-past-the-post in the mid-1950s, Social Credit candidates won easily, defeating Liberal leader Gordon Gibson Sr. in Lillooet and Conservative candidate Douglas Jung in Vancouver Centre (the first Chinese Canadian to contest a legislative seat).[67] In 1956, Social Credit capitalized on economic boom conditions to win re-election with a stronger majority, capturing 39 of 52 seats and nearly 46 per cent of the vote (see appendix C). While CCF MLA Tony Gargrave described Social Credit as 'a rebuilt Conservative party' with 'a flamboyant premier who carries a mediocre cabinet,' and the *Pacific Tribune* claimed that party's grassroots base was 'drying up,' voters remained loyal to the government.[68] Before the election, LPP leader Nigel Morgan had offered an assessment of the political climate, warning that Bennett intended to take advantage of other parties' weakness to 'wipe out his opposition in the Legislature':

> Premier Bennett sees this moment as most favourable for his government and its big business backers. The Sommers case is all nicely tied up in the courts. The Liberals have lost considerable ground and are busy trying to mend political fences in preparation for a fall or early spring federal elec-

> tion. The CCF organization is weakened by a bitter inner fight over the Winnipeg decision to amend the Regina Manifesto which has demobilized many of its best workers.[69]

The *Pacific Tribune* described Social Credit in terms once reserved for the Coalition, as 'a right-wing, reactionary government intent on stripping this province of its future independent industrial development for the sake of a few quick millions in the treasury.'[70]

'54-40 without a Fight'

During the Second World War, the Coalition had appointed Supreme Court Chief Justice Gordon Sloan to head a Royal Commission on BC's forest resources, responding to public concern over rapid deforestation and industry's concern for stability in timber supply.[71] The 1945 Sloan Report advocated a system of 'sustained yield management,' whereby large tracts of Crown timberland would be leased to private firms in perpetuity, providing the incentive for private enterprise to replant logged areas and invest capital in processing and transportation infrastructure. The CCF, which had earlier advocated nationalization, contented itself with demanding increased taxation of logging firms, wooed by the promise of guaranteed employment.[72] CCF forestry critic Colin Cameron, noted for his left-wing views, told the Sloan Commission his party could accept a continuing role for private enterprise. The new arrangement embodied 'the best features of public and private ownership,' according to BC's chief forester.[73]

Sloan's recommendations, which formed the basis of the 1947 Forest Act, had far-reaching implications for small and medium-sized operators and the overall pattern of land tenure and forestry in BC. Pulp-and-paper production displaced sawmilling as the locus of the industry, while secondary processing moved from metropolitan Vancouver and Victoria to emerging hinterland centres closer to the source of wood fibre – single-industry towns such as Port Alberni, Mackenzie, Quesnel, and Castlegar. The trend toward merger intensified, on the heels of BC Forest Products, formed after the war out of dozens of regional logging and milling firms, with an infusion of eastern-Canadian, American, and British capital. Ontario industrialist E.P. Taylor, who had served with logging baron H.R. MacMillan as a 'dollar-a-year man' in the wartime production efforts of C.D. Howe, oversaw the formation of BC Forest Products.[74] In 1951, MacMillan merged his company with a major competitor, Bloedel, Stewart and Welch, to form MacMillan-Bloedel; the merged company soon amalgamated with the Powell River Company to become BC's largest forestry firm.[75] Provincial forester D.M. Carey told the 1956 BC Natural Resources Conference that access to Crown timberlands by small operators had declined markedly between 1945 and 1955: small operators controlled only 8.5 per cent of the land base, compared to 20 per cent for the H.R. MacMillan Export Company.[76]

The Forest Management Licence (FML) system recommended by Sloan and implemented by the Coalition was vulnerable to abuse, placing control of immense resource wealth at the disposal of partisan government officials (as would soon be proven during the Sommers Scandal). Small regional operations gave way to vertically integrated oligopolies. The Truck Loggers' Association, representing small operators, lambasted the anti-competitive practices of large firms and corruption in the granting of licences. Before the scandal broke, a second Sloan Commission was appointed to review the new forest policy. The vulnerable Bennett government concurred with Sloan's recommendations; FMLs were renamed Tree Farm Licences, and the term 'in perpetuity' was replaced with a twenty-one-year lease, but the trend toward consolidation and vertical integration continued. Edwin R. Black observed in 1967 that 'small loggers without ready access to prime stands of timber are rapidly going out of business.'[77]

In the Cold War climate of the 1950s, the LPP was one of the few voices advocating a qualitatively different forest policy, as the CCF all but abandoned socialization at its 1956 Winnipeg convention and, under pressure from the IWA, refused to attack private control of the forests.[78] In their brief to the second Sloan Commission, the communists argued that FMLs

> have been largely responsible for a sharp growth of monopoly with the Big Five companies seizing major control of BC's forest industry, and driving hundreds of little operators to the wall in areas like the Alberni Valley, the Kootenays, up-Coast and on Vancouver Island.[79]

The communists described the FML system as 'a betrayal of the people's trust,' and urged a 'public forest management plan.' Citing figures showing MacMillan-Bloedel's net profit in 1954 exceeded the total forest revenue accruing to the BC government, the LPP demanded the restoration to public ownership of lands alienated to private monopolies, and the formation of regional 'public working circles' under the administration of a BC Forest Resources Commission.[80]

A growing feature of this working-class critique was opposition to American control of BC's resource wealth. A continuum can be traced from Communist opposition in the 1940s, through the CCF's economic nationalism in the 1950s, to the more generalized outcry against American penetration associated with the New Left in the 1960s and the left-nationalist current in organized labour. BC's dependence on foreign capital and markets had historical antecedents, but this process intensified after the United States surpassed Britain as Canada's major trading partner in the 1920s. The war fuelled greater cooperation, such as the Alaska Highway project, and American penetration was cemented in the postwar years. As federal finance minister Douglas Abbott told Parliament in December 1947: 'We are making every effort to achieve the needed integration.'[81] The IWA's communist president, Harold Pritchett, suggested federal policies were facilitating 'the exporting of logs to the United States in a greater volume than ever before, which means the BC sawmill workers will have less work.' In fishing, the American Can Company had closed its Vancouver operations and indefinitely laid off the plant's workers 'because Canadian fish is no longer being canned in BC, but is being sent across to the United States in a raw state to be processed,' Pritchett claimed.[82]

This sentiment was echoed by Homer Stevens, communist secretary of the fishermen's union, who urged 'greater protection of resources ... which are presently being picked up by American vessels and taken directly to the market.' Extending Canada's territorial waters would ensure 'greater utilization by Canadian fishermen and greater processing here in Canada' – a proposal opposed by British Columbia Packers Ltd., the Canadian Fishing Company (Canfisco), and other industry groups.[83] While fishing paled in comparison to forestry in terms of employment and production value, it remained a major economic activity along the coast. Five thousand workers were employed as fishers in the mid-1950s, with another 13,000 employed as shoreworkers; profitability, however, remained concentrated in the canning, processing, and marketing of fish, activities dominated by BC Packers and American-controlled Canfisco.[84] Reflecting the concentration of economic power, logging baron H.R. MacMillan served as president of BC Packers from 1933 to 1946, and retained control of the company into the 1950s.[85] Salmon accounted for 70 per cent of the total value of the catch in the 1950s, while the remainder consisted of halibut, cod, other bottom-fish, and shellfish.[86] In order to challenge the power of the fishing combines, fishers and shoreworkers merged their several unions into the United Fishermen and Allied Workers' Union (UFAWU) in 1945 and formed producer co-operatives in communities up and down the coast: at Prince Rupert, Masset, Sointula, Tofino, Ucluelet, Steveston, and Ladner.[87]

BC's pulp and paper industry exemplified postwar economic relationships: pulp mills were built with American capital, tooled with American machinery, reliant on American replacement parts, their semi-processed products destined for American markets, with value to be added by American workers. 'The whole economy of this province will be increasingly subjected to "boom and bust" policies of Wall Street,' the *Pacific Tribune* warned: 'Pulp is the convenient form in which the forest wealth of our province is smuggled across the line as a raw material for US finishing industries. Consequently, thousands of Canadians are being deprived of jobs that these secondary industries would provide.'[88] '54-40 without a Fight' was how the *Pacific Tribune* described the granting of the Forest Management Licence No. 1 under the terms of the 1947 Forest Act. The Celanese Corporation of America, based in New York, received timber rights to 800,000 acres of Crown land in northwestern BC in exchange for constructing a new pulp mill near Prince Rupert; the pulp was then exported to Ohio for the manufacture of rayon.[89] 'The American concern is receiving the huge pulp stands free, gratis and for nothing,' the Communists lamented.[90] In the 1950s, LPP provincial leader Nigel Morgan described a proposed pulp pipeline from BC to Washington State as 'blind stupidity,' estimating it would cost 1,000 worker-days of employment for every 100,000 board feet of exported pulp.[91] BC workers would be relegated to the position of 'raw producers for US manufacturing.'[92]

In 1951, only 23 per cent of BC's workforce was employed in manufacturing, considerably below the figure for Ontario and Quebec.[93] Manufacturing that did exist, particularly for export, was primarily in the extractive resource sectors. Half of manufacturing in 1951 was in wood products, a trend that intensified with the transition to pulp and paper production; fully half of BC woodpulp was exported for manufacture in eastern Canada, Europe and the United States, while 80 per cent of BC newsprint was exported to the United States.[94] 'The Coalition, subservient to the demands of home-grown monopolists who are the partners of Wall Street, is bartering away the heritage of the people to American interests,' the *Pacific Tribune* opined in 1948.[95]

Table 1.3 Commodity exports as a percentage of total production, 1955

Lumber	55
Wood pulp (sold as such)	87
Newsprint	89
Metals: Aluminum	100
Copper	100
Lead	65
Silver	75
Zinc	65
Asbestos	60
Fish and fish products	55
Tree-fruits	60

Source: British Columbia, Documentary Submission to the Royal Commission on Canada's Economic Prospects (Victoria: Government of British Columbia, 1956), 48.

The Coalition's defeat in 1952 failed to produce any significant change in economic policy, or any diminution of American penetration. While Social Credit claimed in its submission to the Gordon Commission on Canada's Economic Prospects that it sought to 'impart the highest utility to our natural products before selling them on the world's markets,' BC remained an exporter of raw or semi-processed commodities throughout Bennett's twenty-year rule (see table 1.3). Investment was similarly derived from outside the province. Domestic capital underpinned public utilities and tertiary services, but 'development in the natural-resource-based industries ... has been largely dependent on foreign capital,' Social Credit conceded in 1956.[96] Bennett visited New York bondholders in the summer of 1956, prompting LPP provincial leader Nigel Morgan to infer that the premier 'no doubt was advised on how to handle the Columbia, the Panhandle and Forest Management Licenses, etc., for the Yankee trusts.'[97] In its own brief to the Gordon Commission, the LPP suggested that 'Canadian monopoly capital has no independent national existence but is a junior partner of US capital and is under its domination' – a sentiment echoed at the 1956 convention of the BC District of the LPP-aligned Mine, Mill and Smelter Workers, reflecting the broader Communist line on American imperialism.[98]

Private ownership and American investment extended into mineral and oil and gas development, provoking a similar working-class critique. A traditional locus of militancy, mining was undergoing substantial change, from coal to the base metals of lead, zinc, and copper, and to a lesser degree gold and silver, and the opening of the Peace River Country's petroleum resources and the Aluminum Company of Canada (Alcan) smelter at Kitimat. New technology and depletion of the most accessible and highest grades of coal weakened the power of miners. When 11,000 coal miners from Vancouver Island to Alberta's Crow's Nest Pass went on strike in 1948 against contract work and demanding a straight pay scale of $14 per day, a miner from Cumberland warned: 'To us old timers it seems what they are trying to do is get a separate agreement for Vancouver Island, thereby causing a split in our organization.'[99] CCF MLA Sam Guthrie of Nanaimo appeared on the same platform as communist Harold Pritchett, in a rare display of unity. Miners earned on average less than $30 per week, while the *Pacific Tribune* estimated profits of $536 per miner per year based on the increased price of coal.[100]

During this period, oil and gas came to play an increasingly prominent role in BC's economy, triggering the same debates over private and foreign ownership. Foreign-owned Shell Oil and Imperial Oil waged a 'capital strike' in February 1948, cutting the supply of gasoline to local gas stations to apply pressure on the provincial government and the Coal and Petroleum Control Board, which regulated the price of fuel.[101] 'The oil dictators feel perfectly safe now in staging their sit-down strike which is working hardship not only on the public generally, but on the gas-station operators,' the *CCF News* declared.[102] The companies won an increase of three-and-a-half cents per gallon (originally demanding five cents), while the executive council of the BC Federation of Labour (CCL) demanded the province 'take over the oil companies and operate them in the interests of the general public.'[103] This demand intensified as oil and gas development proceeded in northeastern BC. Completion of the Alaska Highway and discovery of oil at Leduc, Alberta, heightened attention to the region's petroleum potential, among the largest untapped reserves in North America, estimated at two trillion cubic feet by Texas geologist Ralph Smith in a study for the US Federal Power Commission. In 1947, the Coalition abandoned a Depression-era policy establishing a public monopoly on oil and gas exploration in the Peace River Country and gas was tapped at Fort St John Well No. 1 in 1951. By mid-decade, a dozen wells were in operation with construction underway on the Westcoast Transmission pipeline to Vancouver and the US; an industry representative lamented that 'as a poor cousin of Alberta's healthy, wealthy industry, its potentialities are still overlooked by many of our citizens and some of our industrialists.'[104] In 1956, Social Credit granted a monopoly on residential gas distribution to the BC Electric Company (BCE), prompting CCF accusations that the government had 'sold its soul' for campaign funds; energy critic Arthur Turner favoured extending the utility under the publicly owned BC Power Commission (BCPC), a demand echoed by the LPP's Maple Ridge club.[105] During the federal 'Pipeline Debate,' the TLC and CCL jointly opposed the deal with Trans-Canada Pipelines Ltd. as 'a gigantic giveaway of a priceless and irreplaceable resource.'[106] Oil and gas was emerging as a new locus of labour militancy: a 1965 oil refinery workers' strike on Burrard Inlet nearly escalated into a province-wide general strike, while breakaway unions took hold among smelterworkers at Kimitat and Trail and hard-rock miners in the interior.[107]

Hydroelectric development on BC's mighty waterways also served as a flashpoint for working-class opponents of private enterprise and American influence. For decades, labour had demanded nationalization of the BCE, dubbed 'BC Collectric' by the communists, a pillar of private enterprise that operated municipal electricity systems, generating dams, and the public transit systems of Vancouver and Victoria.[108] Demands for nationalization grew during the war, endorsed by the mayors of Vancouver and Victoria, as the BCE responded with 'free months' of residential electricity in the winters of 1944 and 1945, and the Coalition passed the Electric Power Act (1945), establishing the BCPC with the narrow mandate of rural electrification and a limited budget of $10-million.[109] Private firms, such as the Consolidated Mining and Smelting Company at Trail and Aluminum Company of Canada (Alcan) at Kitimat, were permitted to generate hydroelectric power for industrial purposes.[110] In 1947, BCPC launched its first major foray into public power generation, the Elk Falls dam near Campbell River, which the LPP viewed as a subsidy to private pulp interests – Bloedel's mill at Port Alberni, Western Timber's mill at Duncan Bay near Campbell River, and MacMillan's Harmac mill south of Nanaimo.[111] In the 1950s, the business-oriented mayor of Nanaimo joined the chorus of voices demanding an expansion of BCPC operations, but Bennett's Social Credit government anticipated that private investment in hydroelectric development would 'continue substantially unaltered.'[112]

This manoeuvring coincided with international negotiations over the future of the Columbia River, BC's second-largest waterway, which had caused major flooding downstream in Washington and Oregon states. The Americans drove the negotiations after the war, hoping to curb the river's 'flashy flow' and expand its potential for hydro power, already tapped by the Grand Coulee Dam (the world's largest when it was completed as a New Deal project in 1942). However, in the late 1950s talks slowed, reflecting rivalry between the governments of BC and Canada, and specifically between Bennett and Diefenbaker's senior BC minister, Justice Minister E. Davie Fulton of Kamloops. Bennett struck a separate deal with American industrialist Henry Kaiser for a dam at Mica Creek – estimated at $18-million worth of power for a meagre $2-million, triggering vigorous opposition from the CCF and LPP. 'When you export power you export jobs,' CCF MLA Bob Strachan told the legislature. 'You are chasing out the young men of this province, forcing them across the border to get jobs.' The premier responded to Strachan's statements by storming out of the legislative chamber but ultimately abandoned the Kaiser deal.[113]

In 1960, the CCF made hydro nationalization the centrepiece of its election campaign and cut heavily into Social Credit support; the ruling party dropped to 39 per cent of the vote and 32 seats, compared with 33 per cent and 16 seats for the CCF, alongside four Liberals.[114] Bennett had warned that the CCF plan would ruin 'the climate of investment' in BC.[115] However, within a year, the premier borrowed a page from the CCF platform and nationalized the BCE, forming the British Columbia Hydro and Power Authority. Behind this decision was the festering fight with Fulton and Bennett's 'Two-Rivers Policy,' based on the simultaneous development of the Columbia and the Peace River in the northeast. Bennett had secured a deal with Swedish millionaire Axel Wenner-Gren for construction of a massive Peace River dam, but the BCE refused to purchase Peace River power, believing transmission costs were too high. The premier responded by seizing the assets of the BCE. In August 1961 – the day before the New Party convention in Ottawa transformed the CCF into the New Democratic Party (NDP) – Bennett convened a special session of the BC legislature to pass legislation nationalizing the BCE and Peace River Development Company. 'The purpose of this Bill is plain,' Bennett told the legislature:

> It converts the BC Electric into an agency of the Crown, and entrusts it with the development under public power of the Peace River project which will be the largest single power project in the world. When this project is under way – and make no mistake, it will be under way rapidly and vigorously – it will provide not just hundreds of jobs, but directly and indirectly tens of thousands of jobs for the people of this province.[116]

Tenders were issued and construction began on the Peace River Dam, named after the premier upon completion in 1967. Meanwhile, the US agreed to purchase surplus BC power and the Columbia River Treaty became law in 1964. Construction on the Duncan, High Arrow, and Mica projects – the three retention dams stipulated in the treaty – proceeded apace, under public ownership but with American funds.[117] A 'No Strike, No Lockout' agreement was signed with the building-trades council representing fourteen unions employed on the Peace and Columbia projects, providing a measure of labour peace for this rapidly expanding sector.[118]

Sections of BC's left remained critical of the Columbia River Treaty, which had been signed by American and Canadian negotiators in 1961 but stalled in the House of Commons over fears that the Americans received a disproportionate benefit.[119] In 1962, a communist-led car calvalcade wound its way through the Interior to the banks of the Columbia, highlighting the harmful impact on BC's future industrial development.[120] There were also concerns over displacement, notably the dislocation of 2,000 indigenous and rural residents in the flooded areas, particularly along the shores of the Arrow Lakes between Revelstoke and Castlegar.[121] Proto-environmentalists, meanwhile, questioned the flooding of healthy stands of timber in the Peace and Columbia valleys and the impact on fish stocks.[122] Such views were largely sidelined, however, in the modernist drive for economic 'growth,' a philosophy widely shared by labour, industry, and the state. Bennett's vision of hydroelectric development aimed to provide low-cost energy for the expanding resource-processing sectors while serving as an engine of general economic activity and employment in BC's Interior, the locus of Social Credit support. When these domestic considerations came in conflict with the international debate over the flow of the Columbia, and the profit considerations of the BCE, Bennett took action atypical of a free-enterprise politician: public ownership (emulating earlier moves to hydro nationalization by free-enteprise governments such as the Ontario Conservatives).[123] Bennett cast himself as the defender of BC interests against the 'sell-off' represented by the Columbia Treaty, but a different interpretion can be drawn. As the assistant general manager of the BC Power Commission told industry leaders in 1956,

> Our energy planning must transcend considerations of boundaries – municipal, utility or international, and considerations of ownership. The whole of the Pacific Northwest must be viewed as one field, in which all

> forms of energy must be fully developed, fully interconnected and fully integrated, without regard for politics either of business or of government.[124]

Creation of Crown-owned BC Hydro provided a stable, expanding supply of cheap power for the province's resource-processing sectors – which were dominated by foreign firms. Fully 75 per cent of hydroelectricity generated in BC in 1967 was for industrial purposes.[125]

In one area, however, hydroelectric development was curbed in the face of competing industrial interests and the political constituency they represented. The untapped energy potential of the Fraser, BC's largest river, was never harnessed for electricity generation. The damming of the Fraser, proposed with the Moran Dam project north of Lillooet in 1951, and favoured by Bennett as 'the cheapest and most pollution free source of power for British Columbians,' would have damaged the river's salmon stocks, affecting thousands of jobs directly and indirectly.[126] As UFAWU secretary Homer Stevens stated in a 1956 Vancouver radio address, 'Why should one resource be destroyed in order to develop another when it is fully possible to develop our power and still protect our salmon?'[127] In the face of these political considerations, Social Credit left the Fraser untouched.[128]

In the 1960s, opposition to American control of BC resources was generalized more broadly across the working class, driven in part by growing opposition to the US war in Vietnam, and also opposition to American domination of BC labour unions. The presence of US military bases in the BC hinterland – the 'Pinetree Line' radar bases at Baldy Hughes (near Prince George), Mount Lolo (near Kamloops), and Puntzi Lake (near Williams Lake) – fuelled fears that BC was a target for nuclear attack.[129] In the terminology of the New Left, BC represented a peripheral satellite or client in the continentalist North American economy, providing raw materials for US centres of manufacturing.[130] New Left student leader Jim Harding debunked as a 'myth' the view that American capital was essential to develop BC's natural resources. 'Most so-called foreign investment actually develops from profit gained within Canada,' Harding argued, suggesting that surplus value from BC resources financed the capital investments of American firms.[131] Discussing the 'lesson' of the Columbia River Treaty, Harding concluded: 'When a satellite tries to co-operate with an imperial power it always gets screwed.'[132]

Tied to American control of BC resources was tariff policy and free trade, which remained a point of divergence between provincial and federal politicians, reflecting a regional cleavage in Canada's economic elite. The east-west trading relationship imposed inflated costs on BC's export industries and bolstered support for free trade. BC industrialists looked askance at the tariff-protected manufacturing sector of eastern Canada and discriminatory freight rates, which drove up the cost of capital inputs for BC industry and reduced the competitiveness of BC commodities in international markets. As Addie, Czepil, and Rumsey argued, BC's economic elite realized it was better off dealing 'directly with the American metropolis instead of through central Canada,' ending its subordinate position in the Canadian metropolis-hinterland structure.[133] In its 1956 submission to the Gordon Commission, the Social Credit government called for a 'critical examination' of national tariff policies, in the belief that 'by and large, removal of international trade restrictions should be encouraged.' Only in the area of agriculture did the government concede that 'some protection may be necessary' – reflecting the centrality of food production in Bennett's Okanagan and Fraser Valley base.[134]

The Role of the State?

While the extraction and processing of natural resources dominated economic life, changes were afoot in the postwar years, transforming BC's economy and its working class. As appendix E demonstrates, between 1941 and 1971, employment in logging, fishing, and mining fell from 11.8 per cent of total employment to 4.9 per cent, as technology enabled employers to replace workers with machines. In the same period, tertiary services grew from 18 per cent of the labour force to 31 per cent.[135] Tourism emerged second only to forestry by the 1970s.[136] 'Service, trade, and manufacturing...are the industries of expansion as British Columbians change from being drawers of water and hewers of wood to a society demanding increasingly more goods and services in an increasingly complex society,' the provincial department of labour noted in 1970.[137] Coinciding with trends in other jurisdictions, the greatest postwar growth was in healthcare, education, and government services, which expanded from 7.6 to 18.5 per cent of BC's labour force. These were industries dominated by women, who held one out of every two service jobs in BC in 1971, and accounted for 46 per cent of union members in the sector.[138]

While the Bennett government, like the Coalition before it, privileged infrastructure over social spending, the scope of government services expanded dramatically in the postwar era, as it did across North America and the western world. Under pressure from a buoyant continental labour movement, and faced with the spectre of an expanding communist bloc globally, BC employers were prepared to make concessions to the working class that augmented incomes with a social wage of government benefits. This postwar welfare state was gendered, as Nancy Christie and others have argued, and never as extensive as European models.[139] However, growth of BC's provincial state swelled the public sector and intensified the decades-long struggle for collective bargaining rights. Direct government employment grew from 10,641 to 54,855 workers between 1941 and 1971, a fivefold increase as government's share of the labour force expanded from 3.10 to 6.48 per cent; indirect government employment in healthcare and education further augmented BC's public sector (see appendix E).[140]

The spending priorities of Social Credit were laid bare in a 1955 brief to the Gordon Commission on Canada's Economic Prospects: large-scale public investment in energy and transportation infrastructure, as a stimulus to private investment in the profitable resource-extraction and processing sectors. The government's brief provided a twenty-year (1955–75) forecast of provincial and municipal capital expenditures, including $1.2-billion (in 1955 dollars) on highways, roads, and rail infrastructure, and $524 million on hydroelectric development (which excluded the American funds for the three Columbia Treaty dams). In contrast, $260 million was allotted for schools and universities, and $210 million for hospital construction.[141] In 1959, CCF Alberni MLA John Squire proposed diverting 'one or two millions from highways to education' to contain spiralling university tuition fees.[142] As Liberal leader Patrick McGeer later suggested, 'any hope that the province would make a strong commitment to the human resource went down the two rivers along with the $1.5-billion that was poured into them during the peak construction years of 1963–1970.'[143]

In 1960, Social Credit appointed a Royal Commission to study BC's education system, headed by UBC's Dean of Arts and Sciences Sperrin Chant. The Chant Commission, like similar bodies in other provinces, was 'set up in response to a general feeling that education in North America was "soft" and not equal to the challenge posed by the scientific advances made by Russia in the "Sputnik" era,' an educator with the Vancouver school board noted.[144] Chant recommended a return to the 'puritan ethic' in education, the view that youth be educated to serve a useful function in society, in contrast to the permissive approach based on free choice in the selection of studies to develop the individual's talents to the fullest. High levels of unemployment in 1958–60 fuelled this view, which was articulated in stark economic terms by Bennett's deputy minister of education, G. Neil Perry:

> A certain *minimum investment* MUST be made in each individual to bring him up to the lowest acceptable common denominator in a developed society, that is, to become a viable person able to survive in a competitive economic environment, capable of earning an income sufficient to care for the basic needs of a family.[145] (emphasis original)

The Chant Commission recommended a major expansion in vocational training for youth, to prepare them for the workforce. In 1962, UBC president John Macdonald released another report, *Higher Education in British Columbia and a Plan for the Future*, advocating the expansion and diversification of BC's post-secondary system.[146] Social Credit adopted many of Macdonald's recommendations and by the end of the 1960s, six vocational schools were operating in BC, alongside four junior colleges, with three more under construction.[147] In the university sector, the University of British Columbia (established as a stand-alone institution in 1915) was joined by the University of Victoria and Simon Fraser University (SFU) in the 1960s; postsecondary enrolment grew from 6,300 students in 1955 to over 30,000 by 1970.[148] Employment at BC colleges and universities mushroomed from 2,407 in 1961 to 8,895 a decade later.[149]

This massive expansion of post-secondary education was viewed with a critical eye by a growing body of students, who identified with the radical politics of the New Left and joined the militant minority. According to SFU student Jim Harding, the postwar era gave rise to the 'education plant,' which he described as 'branch-plants tied to the interests of neo-capitalism.' Citing the UBC Forestry Department, which 'trains people for the lumber industry,' and business administration at SFU, 'which trains people to help manage labour and profits,' Harding identified this postwar 'education plant' as the locus of the new radicalism of the 1960s. This conformed with the view of philosopher Herbert Marcuse, an intellectual leader of the New Left, who theorized that students had displaced workers as the revolutionary class in industrialized societies.[150] Reflecting worldwide trends, BC's postsecondary students formed a distinct subculture, rejecting the functionalist view of education and embracing direct action, most notably in 1968 when students occupied the SFU administration building, culminating in 114 arrests.[151]

The growth of education signalled larger structural changes in BC's working class. As Harding observed, the 'old working class' rooted in the extractive industries was augmented by a new working class based in technical and professional occupations.[152] Employment in logging, fishing, mining, and hunting declined in absolute terms in the years 1941–71, while education experienced a sevenfold increase in employment, from 2 to 6 per cent of BC's labour force.[153] This new working class was at the centre of the New Left ferment, and provided a core constituency for the NDP's 1972 victory.

Social Credit was not immune from the militants' critique of its resource and social policies, nor was it immune from centrifugal tensions emanating from the divergent interests of rival sections of the capitalist class. The resource sectors tended toward merger and integration, as the costs of extraction, processing, and marketing concentrated profitability in the largest firms. Bennett grappled with the challenge of serving the interests of regional middle-class entrepreneurs in a resource-dependent economy that tended toward oligopoly and metropolitan control. Cognizant of the need to maintain working-class support, Bennett appeased resource corporations that were integral to his strategy of employment, government revenue, and economic growth. He navigated a fine line between the classical liberal view where government ensured a free market for profit-making – which in BC meant unhindered access to resources by large corporations – and a more interventionist approach better suited to the interests of small private enterprise. Social Credit, 'the party *of* small businessmen,' served as 'the party *for* big business.'[154] This tension was evident in the Columbia River controversy, between the promise of quick cash and jobs the Kaiser and Wenner-Gren deals would have entailed, and the more orderly pattern of development favoured by the federal government.

Throughout his twenty-year reign, W.A.C. Bennett marshalled an unwieldy coalition of free-enterprise forces against the political threat of labour, and its primary political vehicle, the CCF-NDP. While the Liberals retained nearly 20 per cent of the vote throughout Bennett's tenure, Social Credit remained the principal means of containing the socialist threat. In 1972, the contradictions inherent in Social Credit's governing coalition bubbled over, giving rise to a resurgence in Conservative support and paving the road to NDP victory. The business monopoly on political power was broken.

CHAPTER TWO

Moscow on the Fraser

In January 1948, Homer Stevens, organizer of the United Fishermen and Allied Workers' Union (UFAWU), was prevented from entering the United States for a meeting of the International Fisheries Commission. Stevens belonged to the Labor-Progressive Party (LPP), as the Communist Party was then called. 'It appears that the United States now has the power to interfere in the affairs of Canadian unions to the extent of seeking to dictate which members may represent fishermen at such international gatherings,' Stevens wrote in the *Fisherman*.[1] In the postwar years, Stevens and other BC labour militants navigated a turbulent path of confrontation with employers and the state – and confrontation within their own organizations. In the 1960s Stevens served a year in prison for defying a court injunction that he order striking Prince Rupert trawlers back to work. Upon his release, Stevens found himself in a bitter conflict within the BC Communist Party. Livid over what he called the 'Warsaw Pact invasion of Czechoslovakia,' Stevens stormed out of the party's 1968 convention and publicly resigned his membership.[2]

The experience of Homer Stevens in BC's Communist Party and broader working-class movement provides a revealing window into the militant tradition at the height of the Cold War – complementing a literature on Canadian communism that has focused either on its national contours or the pre-Second World War period.[3] In organized labour, the peace movement, and provincial and local government politics, communists such as Stevens sustained a radical political current that challenged the assumptions and structures of postwar capitalism – cutting against the grain of Fordist accommodation and the expanding postwar economy. BC communists were far from perfect; they often failed to extend their analyses of militarism and exploitation to the Soviet Union and grappled with the process of institutionalization prevalent in all organizations. In the Communist Party, the Cold War had a particularly devastating effect, curbing opportunities for renewal of members and views, which led to atrophy and fuelled inner-party strife. However, like Stevens, communists contributed to, and were influenced by, the ideological ferment of the 1950s and 1960s – the searching for fresh responses to domestic and international crises.

Red Wars

The UFAWU was just one organization with communist leadership in the postwar years. As Irving Abella writes, BC's labour movement was, until 1948, 'almost a personal fiefdom of the Communist party.'[4] It was communist organizers whose inspired efforts during the Depression era laid the foundation for BC's powerful industrial unions. Among loggers, fishers, miners, longshore workers, shipyard workers, and the unemployed, communists extolled the benefits of collective action in the face of blacklisting, intimidation, and violence by employers and the state. Responding to a wartime ban, the party rebranded itself the Labor-Progressive Party (LPP), retaining the name until 1959. However, the structures and culture of postwar capitalism undermined the party, which was already weakened by the expulsion of provincial LPP leader Fergus McKean in 1945 as the national leadership flirted with Mackenzie King's Liberals.[5] An Iron Curtain divided BC's working class and eroded communist strength. Tim Buck, national LPP leader, wrote in 1948: 'The monopolists will fight. They will strive to weaken Labor at home – by union smashing, by red-baiting, by bribing corrupt weaklings, by the use of capitalist governments and courts. They will strive to counteract the growing dynamic inspiration of Socialism abroad, by threats of war.'[6]

Developments on Vancouver Island signalled the arrival of the Cold War in BC, as business interests invoked the 'red bogey' to contain militant expressions of working-class agency. During a 1948 coal miners' strike and a dispute with civic workers, the Nanaimo Board of Trade considered a proposal from businessman Stan Dakin to investigate 'Communist infiltration and activity in Nanaimo.'[7] Wartime political alignments divided the local population, as labour gravitated toward communism and business flirted with fascism. Marko Vitkovich, a Nanaimo coal miner and war veteran, was charged with defamatory libel when he circulated a letter describing Dr Mladen Giunio Zorkin, who had moved to Vancouver Island in 1947, as 'a Ustachi hangman.' Appealing to the local Yugoslav community, Vitkovich accused Zorkin of seeking to organize chapters of Yugoslav fascists in Nanaimo, Chemainus, Cumberland, Courtenay, and Port Alberni.[8] The Vitkovich-Zorkin case illustrated class divisions in the area, described by Ross Johnson as 'the cradle of socialism in Canada.'[9] Nanaimo Mayor George Muir organized a rally for Zorkin, attended by Conservative MP George Pearkes, calling for a vast Island-wide 'anti-subversive' organization. Labour, meanwhile, mobilized in Vitkovich's defence, holding a 700-strong rally and forming the Defend Nanaimo Labor Committee. The president of the United Mine Workers' Nanaimo local, Ed Webb, considered the charges against Vitkovich 'a direct attack on Nanaimo labor.'[10] Growing anti-Communism in the working-class communities of Vancouver Island revealed larger processes underway in BC and beyond.

Revelations of a Soviet spy ring by Ottawa cypher clerk Igor Gouzenko in 1945 had ended the brief entente between East and West, the wartime coalition that had united Soviet Communism with the capitalist democracies in the fight against fascism. As several scholars have argued, the Gouzenko Affair inaugurated the Cold War in Canada. The lone Communist in the House of Commons, Fred Rose of Cartier, was expelled from parliament and served four years in prison for violating the Official Secrets Act; dozens of alleged spies were arrested and detained without access to legal counsel, lives were destroyed, and a Royal Commission on Espionage investigated the leaking of state secrets within the Canadian civil service.[11] As future Prime Minister Louis St Laurent predicted in 1947: 'In my lifetime we shall engage in the greatest and most destructive war ever waged in the history of mankind; to preserve our Christian civilization from the spread of atheistic bolshevism.'[12] This war was both domestic and international; Prime Minister William Lyon Mackenzie King told the Liberal National Advisory Council in January 1948 that military preparations were necessary against those countries that rejected the capitalist system. His under-secretary of state for external affairs, Lester Pearson, called for a military alliance against communism, an idea embodied in the North Atlantic Treaty.[13] The sentiments of Canadian leaders reflected growing unease in all capitalist countries over Soviet expansion in Eastern and Central Europe, and the strength of Communist parties from China, Korea, and Vietnam to France and Italy.[14]

According to Whitaker and Marcuse, Canadian unions 'became part of the culture of the Cold War, and an effective means of disseminating it.' Purges of communists 'were damaging to the very fabric of working-class organization,' since they divided trade unionists and drove 'some of the most dedicated and effective organizers and militants out of the movement, or to its margins.'[15] This process unfolded in BC, where the communist stronghold established during the Depression and war – in powerful industrial unions such as the woodworkers and in the Vancouver Labour Council (CCL) and BC Federation of Labour (CCL) – was eroded in 1948 by an ascendant CCF-aligned 'White Bloc.' Those red unions that retained their communist leadership – the United Fishermen and Allied Workers' Union (UFAWU), BC district of the International Union of Mine, Mill and Smelter Workers (Mine-Mill), Vancouver Marine Workers and Boilermakers, and Vancouver Civic Employees' Union (Outside Workers) – were subjected to raids, discriminatory legislation, and employer blacklisting. They were consigned to the margins of BC's working-class movement, excluded from the central bodies of organized labour.[16]

The Red Wars of '48, as this period is remembered, reflected developments distinct to BC, but also a North America-wide assault on communist unionism. The American Taft-Hartley Act (1947) substantially amended the National Labor Relations Act or Wagner Act of 1935, part of Roosevelt's 'New Deal' concessions to American labour. Taft-Hartley was the legislative embodiment of postwar anti-communism, requiring union officers from the local to international levels to take anti-communist oaths. But Taft-Hartley went much further. Under the guise of fighting communism, the legislation altered the balance of industrial relations to the benefit of employers, prohibiting the 'closed shop' and secondary boycotts, and extending the powers of the National Labor Relations Board to prevent strikes.[17]

The prevalence of American-controlled 'International' unions in Canada meant that Taft-Hartley had a direct impact on domestic labour relations, delineating who could or could not run for senior positions in International unions. Moreover, the spirit of Taft-Hartley pervaded various US agencies. Six BC officials of the IWA, including International president Harold Pritchett, were denied entry into the United States by decision of a special board of inquiry, because the LPP had distributed 5,000 copies of the *Communist Manifesto*. While this decision was later reversed, the bias against communist unionists was evident. Jack Scott, delegate from Trail to Mine-Mill's 1948 international convention, was similarly turned away at the US border. This was seized upon by the *Trail Times* – 'notorious mouthpiece of the views of Consolidated

Mining and Smelting Co.' – to 'sow dissension in the ranks of Trail local 480.'[18] In February 1948, Charlie Millard, the Steelworkers' Canadian director, endorsed statements of US Senator Robert A. Taft to the effect that communists were 'infiltrating' Canada to escape prosecution under Taft-Hartley.[19] When deportation proceedings were initiated against Reid Robinson, Mine-Mill's International vice-president, the BC district sent a strongly worded resolution to Mackenzie King, warning that any attempt to prevent International officers from entering Canada would be interpreted as 'discriminatory against Labor, since similar action is not taken against any representative of business management.'[20] Robinson was deported despite labour opposition.

The Canadian Manufacturers' Association (CMA) and other industry groups lobbied for the inclusion of Taft-Hartley type language in BC's Industrial Conciliation and Arbitration (ICA) Act. During debate on the Bill 87 amendments in spring 1948, a fourteen-member CMA delegation visited Victoria and submitted a brief stating: 'Collective bargaining agents should comprise men and organizations which stand for the upholding of the law of the land and the maintenance of present governmental institutions.' Communists accused the CMA of proposing 'Hitlerite clauses,' which they said already existed in the labour laws of Alberta, Quebec, and Prince Edward Island, 'whittling away the last vestiges of free trade unionism, and paving the way for corporate state technique in labor relations.' At least one Coalition MLA, Don Brown of Vancouver-Burrard, advocated the inclusion of a Taft-Hartley clause in the ICA Act, but the strength of the labour lobby appears to have prevented such a move.[21] In January 1948, the Mining Association of BC refused to provide input on the Metalliferous Mines Act at any meeting where representatives of the LPP-controlled Mine-Mill union were present.[22]

Labour's Cold War traced its origins to internal antagonisms extending back to the 1920s, when distinct communist and anti-communist blocs emerged in BC unions, divisions which ossified during the 'Third Period' as the Comintern condemned social democrats as class traitors and 'social fascists.'[23] Periodic attempts at unity were rebuffed by a CCF leadership distrustful of Communist 'tactics.'[24] Pro-unity sentiments resurfaced during the war, with the LPP applying for affiliation to the CCF in 1943, but these moves were stymied by CCF leaders and culminated in the expulsion of Bert Herridge, CCF MLA for Rossland-Trail; Herridge contested the 1945 federal election as a 'People's CCF' candidate and won.[25] While CCFers such as Herridge moved closer to the LPP, CCF leaders moved in the opposite direction and attempted to wrest control of organized labour from communists. In 1943, the CCL endorsed the CCF as 'the political arm of labour.' Backed by the powerful United Steelworkers, the CCF and CCL laid siege to the bastions of communist strength in BC.[26] In 1948, this campaign finally bore fruit.

In January 1948, CCFer George Home of the United Packinghouse Workers scored what the *CCF News* described as a 'complete victory' over the LPP in executive elections to the Vancouver Labour Council (CCL). Home won the presidency over LPPer Ed Leary of the Fur and Leather Workers, 79 votes to 65, and members of his slate captured other executive positions. The LPP, however, attributed its defeat to the 'unbalanced representation' on the council. Three large LPP-controlled unions – IWA 1-71, IWA 1-217, and the Marine Workers and Boilermakers – paid one half of all per capita dues to the council, yet their 11,000 members were represented by only 21 delegates, far fewer than delegates from smaller unions. The new executive wasted no time consolidating its narrow victory. At the next meeting, Home marshalled a resolution through the divided council endorsing an executive recommendation 'to help elect CCF candidates to civic offices.'[27]

The tide was turning against the LPP. At the party's 1948 provincial convention, held in Vancouver in March, 128 delegates representing 71 clubs re-elected Nigel Morgan provincial leader by acclamation. Tim Buck addressed a capacity crowd of 3,000 party loyalists, unveiling the new slogan 'unity to elect a CCF government.' This implicitly acknowledged the LPP's weakness as an electoral force, and also the abandonment of the strategy of supporting Liberals, which had cost the CCF seats in 1945 (and reflected the Soviet Union's short-lived *rapprochement* with liberal capitalism during the war).[28] At the University of British Columbia, Buck was assailed by a group of 'hoodlums,' who prevented a planned speaking engagement.[29] In Port Alberni, police tore down posters for the film *Journey for Peace*, by Denny Arsenault, delegate to the 1947 World Youth Festival in Prague. The film played to a packed house nonetheless. Later in 1948, the town council refused to grant the LPP a permit for a 'prices parade' against the rising cost of beef. When the LPP and Housewives' Consumer League marched in defiance, a motion of censure for 'flouting the law' was rejected by a vote of 3–2; the council instead passed a resolution calling on Ottawa to re-impose controls on beef prices.[30]

Government officials, employers, and national and international labour leaders overtly supported the white challenge in BC's red unions.

When BCFL president and CCL regional director Danny O'Brien – an LPP 'fellow-traveller' – was arraigned on a trumped-up 'morals' charge during the 1947 debate on the Bill 39 amendments to the ICA Act, national CCL leaders including Aaron Mosher and Pat Conroy refused to support the BC union leader. O'Brien was subsequently acquitted, but not before the CCL executive had transferred his responsibilities to avowed whites Bill Mahoney and Dan Radford.[31] The Red Wars extended through BC and Canada, including the Canadian Seamen's Union and the robust Vancouver Marine Workers' and Boilermakers' union.[32] In May 1948, the TLC-affiliated labour councils of Victoria and Vancouver endorsed anti-communist resolutions, a stance 'almost identical' to the Canadian Chamber of Commerce and the CMA, communists alleged. Jack Phillips, communist secretary of the Vancouver Civic Outside Workers, insisted that: 'This [TLC] council is big enough to support men like [Birt] Showler and [Tom] Alsbury and Communists like me.'[33] LPP provincial organizer Maurice Rush said his party was 'proud of the fact that thousands of workers in democratic elections return well known communists to office year after year,' calling on BC workers to reject red-baiting, to avoid a situation where 'the boss gains and the worker loses.'[34] Another communist, Bill White of the Vancouver Boilermakers, criticized the strategy of the CCF-aligned White Bloc: 'The CCF wasn't near as effective at organizing and wasn't too interested in it. Their approach was to move in on already established unions and take them over at the top.'[35]

In March 1948, the LPP scored an important victory when its slate retained control of the IWA's BC District executive by a margin of 3–1, despite the efforts of logging operators, International officers, and the *Vancouver Sun* newspaper to support the White Bloc. Ernie Dalskog, elected district president, warned that red-baiting attacks in the press were aimed not only at the LPP but 'at the destruction of the trade union movement and we should make no mistake about it.'[36]

A disastrous April 1948 speech by LPPer Harvey Murphy, Mine-Mill's western director, during the BCFL Labour Lobby in Victoria, provided fodder for the LPP's opponents. Under the influence of alcohol, Murphy reportedly said that Bill Mahoney, chief organizer of BC's White Bloc, 'knew what to do when the boss lowered his pants.'[37] Murphy was subsequently charged by the CCL and suspended for two years from Congress activities, including participation in the BCFL where he served as vice-president. Comments in the *Mineworker* critical of CCL president Mosher's stand during a railworkers' dispute triggered the suspension of the entire Mine-Mill union. In the words of Al King, a Mine-Mill leader at Trail, a majority of CCL unions 'were out to destroy the most progressive ones, the ones they called "red."'[38]

The White Bloc was aided by a vitriolic press campaign designed to discredit the LPP leadership, led by *Vancouver Sun* columnist Jack Webster. 'I consider myself a reasonably fair reporter except the way I treated the Communists in the early days,' Webster admitted in his memoirs, conceding that he 'led the witchhunt in print.'[39] LPP leaders believed the entire 'Murphy Incident' had been engineered by Mahoney, Webster, and their anti-communist backers to neutralize Mine-Mill's influence in BC's central labour bodies, and specifically 'to enable the CCL disruptionists, on the eve of the BC Federation of Labor convention either to rule or wreck that valuable tribune of British Columbia labor.'[40]

When the BCFL's 1948 convention met in Vancouver in September, 22 Mine-Mill delegates were refused seating because of the suspension. Their absence was decisive in executive elections, with Home defeating Pritchett 66–65 for secretary-treasurer and CCFer Stewart Alsbury defeating LPPer Alex McKenzie by the same margin for second vice-president. Overall, the new nine-member executive counted five whites to three reds, while Mahoney believed Danny O'Brien, who was re-elected president, would 'always gravitate toward power.' Midway through voting, Mahoney and Home suspected a certain delegate from the Retail Wholesale union 'had voted for the Commie candidate,' O'Brien for president and Bill Stewart for first vice-president. Home sat beside the delegate to 'help him mark his ballot,' and ensured whites won all subsequent positions.[41] *Pacific Tribune* editor Tom McEwen called the Mine-Mill suspension 'a move to enable a "white" bloc of assorted social democrats and careerists to win the power of leadership they could not hope to win otherwise.'[42] Despite Mahoney's prediction, O'Brien resigned from the presidency two months later, citing 'complete disagreement with the so-called majority' on the executive after a 6–5 vote favouring the IWA's white bloc.[43] As if to rub salt in the wounds, Steel launched a raid on Mine-Mill's certification at the Vancouver Engineering Works.[44] The only solace for the LPP came at the TLC's 1948 convention, held in Victoria in October, when the national leadership adopted a tolerant stance toward communism. TLC president Percy Bengough told delegates that their 'executive has consistently opposed the introduction into Canada of any of the features of the Taft Hartley law as in operation in the United States.'[45] Bengough, mindful of the voting strength of communist delegates and engaged in a conflict with Frank Hall, vice-president of the Brotherhood of Railway and Steamship Clerks, could not afford to disassociate himself from the left. However, a deal was struck whereby Alex Gordon, UFAWU business agent, agreed not to stand for re-election as TLC vice-president for BC.[46]

The last major battleground in the 1948 Red Wars was the IWA, the province's largest union and a bastion of LPP strength, which was 'recognized as setting the wage pace in BC.'[47] Contract negotiations between 30,000 IWA members and logging operators in 1948 were undermined by conflict between supporters of International president Jim Fadling and the BC district's communist leadership. The defeat of Fadling's slate earlier that year failed to stem the White challenge. Building from an anti-communist beachhead in New Westminster local 1–357, the White Bloc extended its influence among BC woodworkers, aided by weekly 'Voice of the IWA' radio broadcasts sponsored by the International Board and Webster's columns in the *Sun*. To the communists, Webster was 'a fingerman for the lumber bosses and their "white bloc" allies.'[48] In July, Fadling ordered an investigation into the finances of the BC district and invited Mahoney to Portland, Oregon to discuss strategy. Three BC locals and the District Council responded by demanding Fadling's resignation, while the *Tribune* accused the International president of 'throwing mud, whether red-baiting or the equally time-worn method of financial charges.'[49] In August, the IWA negotiating committee applied for conciliation and announced it was holding a strike vote in abeyance. This prompted the industry-backed *British Columbia Labor Letter* to speculate that the communists were afraid to strike: 'The union leaders have a healthy respect for the teeth in the amended ICA Act ... and ... do not want to place themselves in a position where the union might be decertified by the labor board and a new and non-communist crowd might gain the bargaining representation.'[50]

BC's industrial relations apparatus was putting the brakes on worker militancy and isolating militant leaders. In the language of the LPP, 'concealed Taft-Hartley decertification clauses' hindered the bargaining power of the IWA.[51] When the IWA's appointee on the conciliation board, Harvey Murphy, agreed to a 13 per cent wage increase in September, the White Bloc intensified its attack. The *CCF News* predicted the wage award 'will be very disappointing to the workers.'[52] Fadling, meanwhile, claimed the district leadership would have achieved the same result in direct negotiations with employers, and that conciliation was merely an opportunity for LPP grandstanding. As the IWA's

International convention in Portland approached, pro-LPP delegations were elected in Victoria local 1–118, Mission local 1-367, Vancouver local 1-217, and Port Alberni local 1–185. All delegates pledged to remain in Canada if a single delegate was denied entry into the United States. As a demonstration of strength, the District leadership laid charges with the CCL against Mahoney for participating 'in a factional meeting of the members of IWA Local 1-217 (Vancouver) which was without authority and was organized to foment disruption of the local and the district…in violation of the constitution.'[53]

On 3 October 1948, the conflict between whites and reds peaked. The IWA's BC District Council voted to sever connections with the International and form the independent Woodworkers Industrial Union of Canada (WIUC). The decision was made after US Immigration denied entry to forty left-wing IWA delegates, amid rumours that the International Board intended to place the District under trusteeship.[54] The decision to secede derived, however, from the LPP's BC Provincial Committee, where party heavyweights including Pritchett, Murphy, and Morgan debated the issue into the night of 2 October before a majority finally voted to split.[55]

While LPP leaders claimed to respect the autonomy of the unions they represented, major decisions in LPP-controlled unions rested with the party. 'It was the party running things at that time,' concedes Betty Griffin, an LPP member whose husband Hal served on the Provincial Committee during the split.[56] Fadling, who was denied the floor during the decisive District Council meeting, declared the LPP had lost control of the BC locals and was 'trying to destroy them.' He suggested that Pritchett's radio address the night of the split, taped before the District Council had made its decision, demonstrated the LPP leader's 'contempt for the rank and file'; so too did the leadership's refusal to put the WIUC idea to a referendum vote. Foreshadowing future developments, Fadling said the BC District had not been abolished 'by the action of a few Communist-led disruptionists.' His BC lieutenant, Stewart Alsbury, president of the 5,000-strong New Westminster local 1-357, said the 'recently signed wage contracts with the operators are the property of the IWA.'[57]

A skirmish ensued over the assets and certifications of BC's largest union, with the courts, LRB, and logging operators favouring the IWA over the nascent WIUC. Fadling was granted an injunction by Supreme Court Justice J.M. Coady declaring the proceedings of the 3 October district council meeting *ultra vires* (outside the powers of the District), and impounding all assets and accounts. Within a week, BC Forest Products announced that its contracts with the IWA remained in force and that it would deal only with IWA representatives, who were granted privileged access to camps and mills. When a strike erupted at MacMillan's Iron River camp on Vancouver Island over the dismissal of two WIUC workers, the Fadling forces collaborated with the company and provincial police to escort strike-breakers through WIUC picket lines; Alsbury was severely beaten and hospitalized. By the time the Iron River strike was called off in April 1949, the WIUC challenge had been contained. Only nine of thirty-four applications for certification had been granted by the LRB. WIUC vice-president Ernie Dalskog spent a month in jail for defying a court order to hand over $130,000 in strike funds to the IWA. Hjalmar Bergren, the WIUC's business agent and a veteran of the Cowichan Valley organizing drives of the 1930s, was sued and lost his Vancouver home and savings. The forty-two district council members who had voted to split were barred from holding IWA cards. By the summer of 1949, in the midst of contract negotiations, the breakaway union conceded its inferior position, urging a 'shoulder to shoulder fight' with the rival IWA; in August 1950, the WIUC was finally abandoned by party leaders, with the exception of a lone local in distant Cranbrook.[58]

Lembcke and Tattam conclude that 'disaffiliation from an International union was easy to declare, but difficult to consolidate.' Indeed, the 'October Revolution' of the IWA's communist leadership strengthened the hand of anti-communists.[59] In a perceptive doctoral thesis, Stephen Gray emphasizes the distance between the union's rank-and-file and its communist leaders, who viewed themselves as 'the "spearhead" of the Canadian labour movement.'[60] LPPers such as Erni Knott were effectively blacklisted from the industry, because of lifetime bans on IWA membership and 'closed shop' agreements they had helped negotiate. 'Officially I was expelled from the union because of my support, in the quarterly district council meeting, for the resolution to break away from the international,' Knott recalls. 'The real reason was because I was a well-known active communist.'[61] Retrospectively, communists admitted there were flaws in the secessionist strategy. 'The party made a big mistake,' concluded Grace Tickson, an LPP member whose husband Walter left logging to become a fisherman. 'They didn't really go to the membership, and ask them whether they would approve ... So that was wrong. They should have made a campaign, or found out how many people were for it. But they didn't. They just did it.'[62] Betty Griffin agrees:

> For the first time in my life I nearly made a long distance phone call to Tim Buck to get him to stop them, because to me, right away it was the wrong thing to do. It was a split decision on the executive that they would form a union – the WIUC. Well, you just don't do that.[63]

Success distorted the perspective of Pritchett and other IWA leaders, Griffin suggests:

> They didn't realize they were beginning to lose touch with the membership. It is easy when you have a full time job and suddenly you're getting a really good paycheque … It had gone to [Pritchett's] head a little bit … Going through years, tough years, and the depression and the war years, suddenly, you were ... wow! You're powerful … Well, it split the workers of course.[64]

Bill White, communist president of the Vancouver Marine Workers and Boilermakers who left the party in 1949 amid charges of 'adventurism,' suggests the LPP's domineering ways undermined its influence in BC labour – foreshadowing a critique that was prominent in the splits of the 1950s and 1960s. 'Officially Tom [McEwen] and Nigel [Morgan] had no connection with our union at all, but there they were sending in orders just as obvious as hell – and this went on all the time.' The LPP's meddling in internal union affairs diluted its claim to represent a superior social system: 'Hiring instead of being a tool of the bosses became a tool of the Party … This was that old Communist thinking that they were on a holier plane … They're supposed to eliminate privilege, not just take in from one group and give it to another.'[65]

Red Unionism

The Red Wars of '48 curbed communist power in BC unions, but failed to eradicate it entirely. As the *Financial Post* newspaper observed in a 1953 exposé:

> Strategically placed as Canada's Gateway to the Pacific and as an ever-growing source of much strategic material for the Canadian and allied

> defense effort, British Columbia today is one of Canadian Communism's most fertile spawning grounds, a bastion in the over-all Canadian Communist disruptive strategy.[66]

In the UFAWU, Mine-Mill, Vancouver Civic Outside Workers, Vancouver Marine Workers and Boilermakers, International Brotherhood of Electrical Workers (IBEW), West Coast Seamen's Union, Canadian Communications Association, and International Longshoremen and Warehousemen's Union (ILWU), communists held leadership positions throughout the Cold War.[67] CCFer Tom Alsbury alleged in the *Vancouver Sun* in 1956 that 'one third' of BC's organized workers – 68,000 of 187,000 – belonged to communist-led or -influenced unions.[68] The RCMP Security Service noted in 1962 that 16,000 communists were employed in 'various industries in Canada' and that 'a small minority of Communist delegates' controlled the BCFL convention: 'The Communist Party of Canada influence cannot be measured by numerical strength. They are able, highly trained and experienced trade unionists who by skilful infiltration and manouvering [*sic*], are able to successfully dominate a vastly larger group.' Another RCMP agent suggested that communists affiliated with the Trade Union Research Bureau (TURB), which represented BC unions in dealings with employers and government boards, 'could do a lot of harm to the economic structure of this province.'[69]

Communist influence extended into the International Brotherhood of Pulp and Sulphite and Paper Mill Workers (Pulp & Sulphite), the Brotherhood of Painters, Decorators and Paper Hangers, the United Brotherhood of Carpenters and Joiners, the International Jewelry Workers, the Plumbers' Union, the Fruit and Vegetable Workers, and the IWA, despite an anti-communist by-law adopted after the WIUC split. Later, public-sector unions including the Hospital Employees' Union (HEU), Canadian Union of Public Employees (CUPE), BC Government Employees' Association (BCGEA), and BC Teachers' Federation (BCTF) developed communist leaderships at the local level, following the legacy of Jack Phillips and the Vancouver Civic Outside Workers.[70] In 1965, communists and fellow-travellers in the Oil, Chemical and Atomic Workers' International Union nearly triggered a province-wide general strike. In November 1972, Bill Stewart of the Marine Workers and Boilermakers was elected BCFL vice-president, a move that would have been unfathomable a decade earlier.[71] The enduring, albeit minority, communist presence in BC unions sustained a current of militancy throughout the 1950s, inhibiting conciliation between the classes and the pattern of compromise that developed in other Canadian provinces. Facing internal and external competition from communists, non-communist leaders in BC were more inclined to embrace militant action and a confrontational stance with employers.

The UFAWU, formed out of several occupational groups in 1945, was the locus of communist strength in Cold War BC. Sidelined in the postwar drive for 'industrial legality,' fishers were denied certification under BC's labour laws, considered 'co-adventurers' rather than workers entitled to union protection, creating greater space for militant leadership.[72] Indeed, the Vancouver *Province* suggested the UFAWU had 'the tightest Communist control of any union on the North American continent. It has life and death power over BC's second largest industry through a leadership hierarchy that is solid Communist from top to bottom.'[73] Homer Stevens, who served as organizer (1946–8), secretary (1948–70), and president (1970–8), embodied the union's commitment to militancy and class confrontation with employers and governments. He belonged to the Communist Party from 1944 (when he left the CCF) until 1968, travelling with the 'Beaver Brigade' to the World Youth Festival in Prague in 1947 and helping build a 'youth railroad' in Tito's Yugoslavia.[74] BC fishers had affirmed at their 1947 convention that 'we as a union will refuse to be intimidated or in any way forced to deviate in the slightest degree from our officially declared and democratically determined union objectives by red-baiting attacks upon any of our members or our officers.'[75]

The UFAWU, which merged with the Canadian Auto Workers in 1996, was a militant and socially progressive labour organization. Stevens was elected first vice-president of the BC Peace Committee at its founding in 1950, and UFAWU business agent Alex Gordon attended the second World Peace Congress in Sheffield, England in November 1950. In December 1950, the UFAWU executive wired Prime Minister St Laurent urging an end to the Korean War through negotiation. Elgin 'Scotty' Neish, president of the Victoria UFAWU local, attended the Asian and Pacific Rim peace conference in Beijing in 1952, where he told delegates that 'as long as the cold war policies and the building up of armaments are being pursued, the living standards of the working people will continue to get worse.'[76] Back in Canada, a flotilla of fishing boats descended on Victoria's Inner Harbour in 1952 to pressure politicians in the legislature for the extension of workers' compensation benefits to fishers.[77] The UFAWU and its women's auxiliaries waged a determined campaign for a Canadian coast guard – a step taken by the Diefenbaker government in 1962 – stressing the importance of 'saving lives and rescuing vessels in distress.'[78] In 1961, the UFAWU sent a fraternal delegation to a Trade Union Congress in Communist Cuba. Betty Griffin suggests that a strong democratic culture in the UFAWU sustained the relationship between LPP leaders and the rank and file: 'in the fisherman's union, they would never pay their staff people more than the fisherman's wage or the cannery worker's wage, ... the [wage of the] highest paid worker.'[79]

The UFAWU paid a price for its intransigence. The parent TLC declared at its 1949 convention that 'no known Communist can hold office in the Congress or its provincial and central bodies.' UFAWU delegate Tom Parkin was subsequently prevented from running for chairman of the VTLC's organizing committee. The Victoria Trades and Labor Council also debated the issue, and in a vote boycotted by left-wing delegates, incorporated the 'no known Communist' clause into its constitution by a 40–8 vote.[80] In September 1950, the TLC adopted a foreign policy statement supporting the Korean War and declaring the Stockholm 'Ban the Bomb' Appeal subversive; a Congress official summed up the policy on left-wingers: 'We'll liquidate them.'[81] In November 1950, Stevens and Neish were barred from a BC conference of TLC unions, an action Neish described as an 'unprincipled attempt to introduce thought control and fascist suppression into the trade union movement.' Street Railwaymen's delegate Chuck Stewart warned: 'If this keeps up we'll be eliminated one by one, piecemeal fashion, until this meeting will be attended by mechanical robots.' Neish was stripped of his Victoria TLC credential a week later, on grounds of his association with the Victoria Peace Council and the 'Ban the Bomb' campaign. UFAWU delegates boycotted the council in protest, as a similar scenario unfolded in Prince Rupert. The *Fisherman* called the treatment of Neish 'ignorance and stupidity at its worst.'[82] In the mid-1950s, Neish, a navy veteran, was expelled from the Royal Canadian Legion because of his 'subversive' peace activities and criticism of the Korean War.[83]

In 1953, the TLC suspended the UFAWU and barred its delegates from all central labour bodies until the union took 'all reasonable and necessary measures to rid itself of communist leadership and leanings.'[84] The suspension coincided with a failed raid by the Seafarers' International Union (SIU) and notorious racketeer Hal Banks, aided by the BC Gillnetters' Association, which briefly won control of the UFAWU Campbell River local.[85] In May 1956, 3,000 documents were seized from the union's Vancouver headquarters as part of an investigation under the Combines Investigation Act, centring on the UFAWU's legal status as a trade union.[86]

In mining, where the 8,000-strong western district of Mine-Mill was the second largest union in BC, red-baiting was also prevalent. The communist leadership of Mine-Mill Local 480 at Trail had established certification at the Consolidated Mining and Smelting Company (CM&S, after 1966 Cominco), a notorious bastion of company unionism; Local 480 led a successful strike in 1946 that secured among the highest wages in North America. However, in 1950, the United Steelworkers of America (Steel) launched a raid at Trail, paying the CCL $50,000 for jurisdiction in the sector, Mine-Mill leaders alleged.[87] With the active participation of CCL organizers Mahoney and Herbert Gargrave (a former CCF MLA), Steel courted Mine-Mill members and engineered the defection of the entire Local 480 executive, 'traitorous officers who walked out on the rank and file,' as regional director Harvey Murphy described them.[88] Al King, who was elected Local 480 president at an emergency meeting following the defections, said one positive result of the Steel raid was 'the elimination of the company union elements,' workers who had been admitted into Local 480 as a compromise measure.[89]

Both sides sent heavyweights to Trail, Charlie Millard for the CCL-Steel and International president John Clark for Mine-Mill. Steel collected union cards from a majority of CM&S workers – 2,200 of 4,000 workers – but failed to collect initiation dues at the time the cards were signed, or administer membership oaths, two requirements under the ICA Act. A mass meeting in Vancouver's Pender Auditorium deplored Steel's tactics and urged the LRB to reject Steel's application for certification. In May 1950, the LRB denied certification, signalling what the *Fisherman* described as 'a victory for all workers who strive for unity in the labour movement.'[90] The *Vancouver Sun*, however, described the LRB's decision as 'disturbing to the public at large.'[91] Ross Dowson of the Trotskyist Revolutionary Workers Party (RWP) suggested that 'Mine Mill has been saved by the Labor Board but in the long run it seems likely ... that Steel will take over.'[92] Mine-Mill's position was strengthened, however, when it achieved joint certification (or 'industrial certification') of Trail smelterworkers with miners at the Sullivan Mine in Kimberley, the world's largest lead-zinc mine, preventing a situation where the employer could 'use the mine against the smelter' – and putting 'an almost insurmountable barrier in Steel's way.'[93]

Mirroring jurisdictional conflict in Sudbury and northern Ontario mining centres, conflict between Mine-Mill and Steel exposed Cold War divisions in labour's ranks. At its 1950 convention, the CCL empowered its executive to expel any union that was considered 'Communist-dominated.'[94] Pierre Berton published an exposé in *Maclean's Magazine* in 1951, warning that Mine-Mill's influence over a heavy-water facility at Trail imperilled national security; CM&S's secret 'Project 9' plant, the first Canadian site to produce heavy water and supply the US atomic and hydrogen bomb projects, was heavily guarded by RCMP officers under Federal Bureau of Investigation (FBI) surveillance. LPP official Maurice Rush, however, dismissed these allegations as 'absurd,' playing into the public's A-bomb fears.[95] The *Financial Post* echoed Berton's warning, describing BC as 'an ever-growing source of much strategic material for the Canadian and allied defense effort' and 'one of Canadian Communism's most fertile spawning grounds.'[96] In May 1952, when the LRB finally put the CM&S certification to a vote, Mine-Mill defeated Steel with 1,949 to 1,669 votes, with 48 workers favouring 'no union.'[97] Steel spent $500,000 to unseat Mine-Mill influence in Canada, and with the exception of northern Ontario gold mining, met with little immediate success. Despite the LPP victory, Murphy warned that low unemployment in BC's mining industry 'is not based upon peace-time markets, it is based on war booms,' with BC's base metals sector 'one of the prize war babies.' Labour's weakness was the result of employers' success in 'spreading a vicious, violent propaganda' and 'splitting labour.'[98]

Vancouver was also a hotbed of red unionism, even after the 1948 rout of the IWA. The Vancouver Civic Employees' Federal Union Local 28 (Outside Workers), a directly chartered local of the TLC, had elected communist officers in 1947 and was a bastion of LPP strength; its entire delegation to the 1949 TLC convention voted against expelling the LPP-led Canadian Seamen's Union.[99] In 1950, the union's two delegates to the TLC's Montreal convention, union secretary Jack Phillips and business agent Donald Guise, were refused credentials because they 'were, or were suspected of being, communists.'[100] Phillips and Guise didn't deny this claim, but argued that in three years under their leadership, membership in the local had increased from 600 to 1,600 and Vancouver civic workers had won improvements in wages and working conditions that placed them at the top of all civic workers in Canada: 'As a result of such accomplishments, reactionary interests in British Columbia became increasingly hostile to our union because of the influence which our gains had on the labor movement.'[101] The TLC action was condemned by Vancouver and Victoria Gas Workers Federal Union 225, and the UFAWU executive and several locals. When the TLC ordered the resignation of the Outside Workers' executive, returned with a solid majority only months earlier, the membership stood by their officers. A mass meeting attended by 900 civic workers declared 'we could not agree to this demand.'[102] TLC regional vice-president Carl Berg responded by suspending seventeen members and organizing a dual union, but this attempt failed in the face of rank-and-file support for the local leadership.[103]

A 'communist-scare' in the IWA produced a sharp reaction in the mid-1950s by district and International officers determined to keep control of the previously red union. Indications of mounting communist strength in Vancouver Local 1-217, the largest BC local, resulted in the January 1955 expulsion of millworker Gordon Elder, an LPP candidate in the 1953 federal election. Elder and other Local 1-217 members had mobilized one-third of the vote in executive elections. Elder was charged with violating a by-law adopted after the WIUC split, prohibiting membership in communist, fascist, or Nazi parties. His trial, attended by International president Al Hartung of Portland, recommended expulsion, a move approved at a membership meeting. Following the controversy, the BC District leadership moved to amend the International constitution to permit disciplinary action 'against those members suspected of working in the Communist cause,' removing the burden of proving party membership.[104] A similar case arose in 1960, after Local 1-217 member George Lakusta ran as the Communist candidate in Delta. Lakusta appealed to the trial board 'to reject witch-hunting; to refuse to become a party to importation of McCarthyism into the Canadian labor movement ... to reject the bosses' trick of divide and rule.'[105]

Police interference helped weaken LPP influence in red unions. The RCMP cooperated with the anti-communist SIU to root out communists on west coast ships, and isolate the West Coast Seaman's Union, the remnant of the once-powerful CSU. The Canadian Labour Relations Board assisted this effort by revoking the seamen's certification with Branch Lines Ltd.[106] In Vancouver Local 213 of the International Brotherhood of Electrical Workers (IBEW), suspected communists were harassed by RCMP agents. John McCuish, a former IWA officer who had been blacklisted after the WIUC split, accused police of a 'crude form of intimidation' after they visited his home and inquired into his political associations and beliefs. 'In case of war, we have got to know who are loyal Canadians,' the officers told McCuish, according to an affidavit.[107] IBEW Local 213 had established a closed shop on electricians' work in Vancouver, meaning that expulsion from the union – on whatever grounds – prevented workers from practising their trade. McCuish accused employers, the RCMP, and the International union of conspiring to oust communists and other left-wingers from the local. At a union trial in February 1956, dismissed by communists as a 'kangaroo court,' McCuish was found guilty of violating the IBEW constitution, but permitted to retain employment provided he pay union dues and refrain from criticizing the leadership. He was suspended from union activities and offices for fifteen years, without voice or vote in local union affairs. For the second time in a decade, McCuish was persecuted for his politics and barred from trade-union activity. As the *Pacific Tribune* observed: 'RCMP techniques in the cold war years has [*sic*] taken on new characteristics, among them that of "visits" to workers' homes and places of employment to intimidate, threaten and cajole. The cajolery is generally used upon young workers the RCMP hope to enlist as stools in unions and political organizations.'[108]

A year earlier, IBEW 213 had been placed under trusteeship, as two International envoys arrived in Vancouver and 'almost overnight, managed to transform a democratic and progressive union, by silencing progressive voices with threats of expulsion from the union, job and industry; by dividing the local into small industrial sections; banning all union meetings and elections and imposing the arbitrary power of an "appointed" executive on the union membership.'[109] Local 213 business agent George Gee was expelled because of his close association with the LPP, on grounds that included attendance at a Paul Robeson Peace Arch concert; attendance at the 1950 funeral of William 'Ol Bill' Bennett; his description of CCFer and VTLC president Tom Alsbury as 'Fearless Fosdick'; and the renting of office space in Local 213's Vancouver building to Mine-Mill director Harvey Murphy.[110] The campaign against IBEW 213's left leadership extended beyond Vancouver. At the new Alcan smelter in Kitimat, the company and the International collaborated to ensure certification of apolitical IBEW Local 344, in the midst of a strong organizing drive by Local 213. The Kitimat project 'had been given defense priority by the federal government,' the *Pacific Tribune* noted.[111]

The anti-communist drive extended through various industries and unions, both large and small. William George Skinner, a veteran of the Spanish Civil War, was expelled from the Wood, Wire and Metal Lathers Union in 1956 after demanding an audit of the International and other democratic measures. The union's western organizer described Skinner, vice-president of Vancouver Local 207, as 'a disruptive element' and cited his involvement in the Mackenzie-Papineau Battalion as grounds for expulsion. Despite being re-elected by the local membership, Skinner remained expelled, and he was terminated by Dominion Sound Equipment Ltd. because he did not hold a union card. Local 207 was placed under trusteeship.[112]

Red-baiting in the house of labour crystallized around the case of Myron Kuzych, a Vancouver boilermaker who challenged the 'closed shop' certification of the LPP-led Marine Workers and Boilermakers. Kuzych's protracted legal battle was financed by leading industrialists in BC and eastern Canada, and made its way to the Privy Council in London. In 1950, the *Fisherman* had warned that a Court of Appeal ruling favourable to Kuzych would, if unchallenged, 'force unions to accept into membership scabs and employer-paid union-busters of every stripe.'[113] A confidential fundraising letter circulated to leading businesses by Dr H.T. James, managing director of Pioneer Gold Mines, named donors representing such firms as Crown Zellerbach, Standard Oil, Macmillan Export Company, and BC Electric; the Canadian Bankers Association Pacific section discussed the Kuzych case at a 1956 meeting.[114] The *Pacific Tribune* sought to knit together this complex web of what it called anti-communist union-busting:

> The Canadian Bankers Association, the powerful monopolies and corporations, the RCMP and the trade union bureaucrats, are joined in an unholy alliance to wreck unions – under the pretext of 'saving them from Communism.' The bankers plan the campaign and together with the monopolists supply the finances, the RCMP compile the 'dossiers' and the trade union bureaucrats swing the axe.[115]

As the AFL-CIO merged in the United States and the 1956 'unity' convention of Canadian labour approached, BC workers debated whether red unions should be eligible for affiliation to the new Canadian Labour Congress (CLC). Vancouver Local 506 of the Shipwrights', Boatbuilders' and Caulkers' union called for the purging of communist officers before any 'Red officered' unions be permitted to join.[116] CCFer Tom Alsbury, VTLC president, addressed the Civil Liberties Union at the University of British Columbia, alleging that one-third of BC's organized workers remained under communist leadership or influence. The

Province newspaper reported prominently on Alsbury's remarks, while the *Sun* ran a series of columns by the anti-communist labour leader. 'We should get on with the job of sweeping out this whole subversive mess,' Alsbury advised.[117] In the Vancouver Labour Council (CCL), a motion of censure against the TLC president was ruled out of order, a ruling that delegates sustained with a 44–12 vote. 'From a factual standpoint they can be compared only to the writings of professional stool-pigeons, red-baiters and renegades who write for a price,' Tom McEwen commented bitterly in the *Tribune*.[118] Jack Phillips, secretary of the Vancouver Civic Outside Workers, accused Alsbury of 'chasing red shadows' and warned: 'Once we open our doors to McCarthyism, the basic liberties of the nation are seriously endangered. The experience of the trade union movement in the US should prove this point to any unbiased person.'[119] Within the VTLC, a delegate from the Vancouver Street Railwaymen's Union described the *Sun* articles as 'a comfort to employers who could use the publicity to weaken the effectiveness of trade unions.'[120]

At the national level, LPP labour secretary William Kashtan warned that undemocratic practices were creeping into the new CLC even before it was formed. Kashtan cited a provision for biannual, rather than annual, conventions, a departure from accepted practice in the TLC and CCL. 'The trade union bureaucracy has been clamoring for years to end annual conventions,' Kashtan warned. 'The rank and file have greater guarantees of impressing their views on Congress policy' with annual conventions, he claimed, and 'the trade union movements everywhere, apart from the United States, meet annually.'[121] However, at the CLC's founding convention delegates agreed to meet every second year and approved a constitutional provision barring 'any organization controlled or dominated by communists, fascists or other totalitarians.'[122] Exposing the façade of labour 'unity,' BC's red unions remained outside Canada's new house of labour.

Peace Activism and McCarthyism

Persecution of communists was fuelled by domestic class relations, and also by mounting international tension between the Soviet Bloc and the alliance of capitalist democracies that coalesced behind the United States in the North Atlantic Treaty Organization (NATO). Opposing the Truman Doctrine of 'Soviet containment,' communists in Canada and other NATO countries were viewed as fifth columns of subversion, appendages of Soviet foreign policy whose demands for peace and disarmament blunted the military capacity of the non-communist West. The formation of the Communist Information Bureau (Cominform) in 1947 had restored the organizational link between Canadian communists and the Soviet Union, a relationship that had been suspended with Stalin's dissolution of the Third International during the war. Throughout the Cold War, BC communists campaigned for a ban on nuclear weapons and for universal disarmament, and against military subjugation of colonial peoples.[123]

BC communists led picketing against the *SS Colima* in late 1947, to prevent the shipment of Canadian warplanes to Kuomintang China. They hosted a 1948 lecture by Dr James Endicott, former missionary to China and an outspoken peace activist, on corruption in the Chiang Kai-Shek regime. Later that year, they led opposition to the signing of the North Atlantic Treaty, which they argued undermined the United Nations, and they opposed the Marshall Plan as a tool of economic imperialism. In 1950, communists mobilized support for the 'Ban the Bomb' petition and opposed the Korean War, which party organizer Maurice Rush described as 'strictly contrary to world law as embodied in the UN charter.'[124] A solidarity network was built in BC during the Rosenberg-Sobell spy trials in the United States, which resulted in the 1953 executions of Ethel and Julius Rosenberg. Through their efforts in the BC Peace Council and Congress of Canadian Women (CCW), communists extended peace activism beyond local LPP clubs and red unions. Signalling the origins of the largest peace campaign of the postwar era, the *Pacific Tribune* reported on developments in Vietnam in 1948, where 'the aims of American imperialism clash with national aspirations of the people.'[125]

To be sure, the communist-led peace campaigns conveniently jelled with the strategic imperatives of the Soviet Union. Calls for disarmament and a ban on the atomic bomb acknowledged the USSR's military vulnerability in comparison with NATO armies; support for third-world liberation movements weakened NATO influence globally while strengthening the reach of the Soviet bloc. As the BC council of the Young Communist League argued in 1962, 'Canada should be the nation that shows the lead in establishing friendship with the socialist countries. This requires an independent foreign policy for Canada, a policy of trade and exchange.'[126] Communists and fellow-travellers may have been motivated by a legitimate desire to prevent nuclear annihilation and another world war, but their peace activism was undermined by a failure to extend the critique of militarism and imperialism to the Soviet Union. While Dan Cardoni, a fisherman from Quathiaski Cove on Quadra Island, wrote rhetorically in 1950: 'Are you willing to use the same yardstick for measuring our own actions as we use to measure the Russians?,' this same logic was never applied to the Soviet heartland.[127] This incongruity laid the foundation for ideological and organizational crises, when the USSR deployed military force to preserve its authority in Hungary and Czechoslovakia. It also laid the basis for a peace movement that operated more independently of the Communist Party.

In the 1950s, however, the Communist Party and its front organizations were the major locus of peace activism in BC. Communists organized the first BC Peace Conference in May 1950, which endorsed the Stockholm Appeal for 'the unconditional prohibition of the atomic weapon,' and formed the BC Peace Committee, precursor to the BC Peace Council and an affiliate of the Canadian Peace Congress. In dozens of BC communities, communists organized local Peace Councils to wage the 'Ban the Bomb' campaign on the ground, with BC aiming for 75,000 signatures toward a 500,000 Canadian quota.[128] Civic worker Aubrey Burton of Trail provided a keen description of the LPP's peace strategy in a 1950 letter to Ross Dowson, national secretary of the Trotskyist RWP:

> Their current line on this question seems to be this: Their program is not pacifist but rather is a realistic evaluation of the political development of the masses. Their aim is the mobilization of all classes and ideologies that desire peace, to unite with them in a struggle against imperialistic capitalism's war drive. The issue, they further maintain, cannot at this time be one of Socialism, because it would be impossible to rally the people behind such a purely political issue. Nor could any other tactic be pursued such as the class basis approach because the working-class is not sufficiently conscious of the issues at stake, and because the issue is peace, an issue which all classes are interested in. As the struggle for peace continues it will more and more assume a political basis as the issue grows in intensity, and though the weaker and vacillating elements will probably succumb to capitalist pressures, the majority will realize through experiences and educational efforts that until capitalism is abolished that war will be inevitable. Thus the peace movement will assume a more permanent form and instead of being an anti-war alliance it will become a Peoples Front in the struggle to establish Socialism.[129]

LPP members and fellow-travellers in the Peace Councils went door-to-door collecting signatures on the Stockholm 'Ban the Bomb' petition, while LPP-led unions including the Vancouver Civic Outside Workers, UFAWU, and Mine-Mill Local 480 at Trail endorsed the Stockholm Appeal; as an RCMP agent reported, the WIUC's Cranbrook office was adorned with a large placard entitled 'Stockholm Appeal,' described by the press as 'a mischievous and evil thing' that only 'idealists, idiots and traitors' would support.[130] In August 1950, Jack Phillips, Vancouver Civic Outside Workers secretary, and four others, were arrested by Vancouver police for 'Ban the Bomb' canvassing on a downtown street corner. 'I believe the "right to petition" is a farce unless one can stand on a street and ask people to sign petitions,' Phillips said.[131]

When US and Canadian troops moved against North Korea in mid-1950, LPP official Maurice Rush issued a pointed letter to Vancouver *Sun* columnist Elmore Philpott, his opponent in a 1949 New Westminster federal by-election:

> You justify US intervention in the internal affairs of Asiatic countries by dragging out the anti-communist bogey. You take the stand that every protest movement, every attempt by colonial peoples to throw off the horrible burden of imperialist domination, is willy-nilly a Russian communist plot. You have been bitten by the anti-communist bug and seem to be running a temperature, and in your delirium you have publicly declared yourself as favoring [*sic*] large-scale military action involving the lives of Canadian boys to prevent the colonial peoples from breaking their chains and settling their own affairs.[132]

Vancouver communists organized public meetings with Rev. Hewlitt Johnson, the 'Red Dean' of Canterbury, and Dr Endicott, national spokesperson of the Canadian Peace Congress, who accused the Allies of using germ warfare against North Korea. The Canadian government considered indicting Endicott, according to lawyer Harry Rankin, 'but backed off when they realized how much evidence he held to support his claims.'[133] The BC Peace Council hosted a performance by American musician Earl Robinson, to mobilize opposition to the Korean War.[134]

An episode that symbolizes the defiance of BC communists during the Cold War centres on an unlikely series of musical concerts at the Peace Arch border crossing at Blaine, Washington. Between 1952 and 1955, the LPP and BC District of Mine-Mill defied immigration restrictions by hosting annual performances by American actor and musician

Paul Robeson. Robeson suffered two-pronged discrimination, as a communist at the height of the Cold War and an outspoken Black man as the civil rights movement gathered strength in the American South. The first concert, held 18 May 1952, was prompted after US border officials prevented Robeson from *leaving* the United States to perform at a Vancouver concert organized by Mine-Mill. Robeson performed the labour ballad 'Joe Hill,' via telephone, but Mine-Mill sought greater publicity and organized the first Peace Arch concert, attended by 40,000 trade unionists and supporters from BC and Washington State. According to Mark Kristmanson, 'a globalized filtration system conditioned the movements of persons according to their perceived allegiances,' and the 'cultural civil war' of the Cold War years 'left no obvious trace' of Robeson's culturally charged performances at Blaine – though a sound recording survives.[135] In 1956, US border officials finally permitted Robeson to enter Canada; he performed at a Mine-Mill concert in Sudbury and for a capacity crowd, 2,800-strong, at Toronto's Massey Hall. However, later that year, immigration minister Jack Pickersgill banned Robeson from entering Canada, prompting the Vancouver branch of the League for Democratic Rights to condemn attempts 'to erect an iron curtain around Canada.'[136]

Support for national liberation movements in developing countries was a consistent theme of communist peace activism, alongside demands for an A-bomb ban. Cheddi Jagan of Guyana visited Vancouver communists in 1954, after his elected government was overthrown by British forces and he served jail time for defying an order to remain in Georgetown; in 1957, Jagan was again elected prime minister of Guyana. Solidarity was also forged with leftist dissidents who visited BC from Francoist Spain and Greece under the Junta regime. *Pacific Tribune* editor Tom McEwen joined a Canadian delegation to China in September 1956 to attend the eighth congress of the Chinese Communist Party. After the 1959 Cuban Revolution, BC communists formed the Canada-Cuba Friendship Society and lobbied for diplomatic recognition of the Castro government, the first anti-capitalist regime in the western hemisphere.[137]

Throughout the Cold War, BC communists retained close relations with the Soviet Union, and travelled to the socialist heartland on numerous occasions. In 1956, LPP leader Tim Buck addressed the historic Twentieth Congress of the Communist Party of the Soviet Union, where Khrushchev made his famous Stalin revelations. 'Through you I extend fraternal greetings from the peace-loving people of Canada to the great heroic people of the USSR,' said Buck.[138] BC leader Nigel Morgan also attended the fateful Twentieth Congress.[139] All the major figures in the BC party made pilgrimages to the Soviet Union, receiving first-class treatment that likely shaped their perception of the country and its communist leadership. Grace Tickson and her husband Walter spent a year and a half in Russia in the early 1960s, attending classes at Moscow University and enjoying the cultural amenities of the capital, including the Bolshoi Theatre and the Tchaikovsky Hall. Betty Griffin travelled to the Soviet Union three times; Ben Swankey went four times. Al King, communist president of Mine-Mill Local 480 at Trail, travelled to Moscow in the mid-1950s and visited the Red Square tomb of Industrial Workers of the World (IWW) leader William 'Big Bill' Haywood; King was strip-searched and had his personal journal and address book confiscated upon his return to Canada.[140]

BC communists and 'fellow-travellers' suffered discrimination at the hands of police agencies and employers. The RCMP Security Service kept a watchful eye on the LPP and groups considered 'front' organizations, infiltrating union meetings and collecting publications including *Civil Liberties Digest*, published by the Vancouver branch of the League for Democratic Rights, and the Hungarian-language newspaper *Magyar Hirado*. The RCMP contemplated a major crackdown against the BC LPP in 1951, but decided against the plan 'because it would have exposed the force's sources' in the party.[141] That year, the St Laurent Liberals introduced amendments to the Criminal Code that would have made criticism of the government's foreign policy punishable by death, even during peacetime, imposed penalties of five years' imprisonment for criticism of the RCMP, and defined forms of labour protest as 'sabotage,' punishable by ten years in prison. A National Council of Democratic Rights formed in response to the legislation, and in concert with labour and the CCF forced the government's retreat.[142] The *Vancouver Sun*, however, claimed in an editorial that 'only plain suckers would give money or in any way aid a campaign of deception aimed at hamstringing the government in writing any type of effective treason law for this dangerous atomic age.'[143] Responding to this kind of thinking, communists such as Jack Phillips renewed calls for a Canadian Bill of Rights.[144] In 1955, the RCMP staked out the LPP's Vancouver city convention, examining every delegate who entered the convention hall, prompting city secretary Maurice Rush to file a complaint with Attorney General Robert Bonner against 'police state practices.'[145]

Betty Griffin, a Burnaby schoolteacher and lifelong Communist Party member, describes the repressive climate in Cold War BC:

> They turfed out every red union – electrical workers, the fishermen ... It was a very turbulent time and it was tough because the RCMP was harassing people at the local level. When Harry Rankin was a labour lawyer and running for city council, they would [visit his wife] Jonnie Rankin and threaten her. 'She wouldn't be getting family allowance,' etc. Well, we had made arrangements with an older couple in White Rock to take the kids because we figured we're going to be declared illegal again.[146]

Griffin's views were shaped by an earlier experience of anti-communist repression, the wartime ban, when police interned party leaders and suppressed the *Advocate*, a newspaper edited by her husband Harold. According to Griffin:

> The witch-hunting that went on in Canada was incredible too, just like the United States. The first Ban the Bomb petition – the Stockholm Petition – trying to get signatures on that was hell. People took practically their lives in their hands, going house to house. They'd practically throw you down the stairs, talk about peace or 'Ban the Bomb', you were flaming bloody reds, you dirty commie so-and-sos. Ha![147]

Grace Tickson, who contested the 1953 provincial election as the LPP candidate for Nanaimo, described the period as 'the heights of the Cold War.' As an activist in the UFAWU auxiliary and the Nanaimo chapter of the CCW, Tickson grew accustomed to opposition for her 'unladylike' activities, singling out the anti-communist efforts of businessman Mladen Zorkin. Nonetheless, Tickson believes McCarthyism was more muted in Canada. She tells of an encounter with an American couple outside the Communist Party offices on Commercial Street in downtown Nanaimo in the late 1950s. 'They were really astounded that we could come out in the open like that, and have it on the street ... Nobody shot at us. In some countries, Christ, they'd shoot me, you know, if they knew you were a communist. But we didn't have to put up with that.'[148]

BC communists may have avoided the murderous violence that prevailed in other countries, but persecution persisted. Discrimination in employment altered the lives of individual workers, shunting them out of their chosen trade or profession and unleashing years of financial insecurity. John M. Marshall, a Victoria librarian, lost his job in 1954 because of his past association with 'Red-tinged organizations,' including the Canadian Peace Congress and the *Westerner*, a left-wing newspaper published out of Winnipeg.[149] Victoria's chief librarian, Thressa Pollock, tendered her resignation in the midst of the Marshall affair as a protest against interference by the Library Board. Elgin 'Scotty' Neish, an LPPer and president of the Victoria UFAWU local, purchased radio time where he accused the Library Board of imposing 'a McCarthyite system of political screening for those they want to hire.'[150] Even the anti-communist Victoria Trades and Labour Council (TLC) and CCF constituency association supported Marshall's appeal for re-instatement, as did an array of religious and civic leaders. Despite these efforts, John Marshall never again worked as a librarian in Victoria. In the midst of the Marshall affair, Victoria Mayor Claude Harrison incited a storm of controversy when he proposed the burning of 'subversive' books, which Alderman Robert MacMillan described as a 'threat to democracy.'[151] Doris Lougheed, a member of the Library Board, said 'Any book which incites the downtrodden working man to revolt should be removed.'[152]

Anti-communism extended into the professions. In 1948, the Benchers of the Law Society of British Columbia obstructed efforts by LPP members and fellow-travellers to gain admission to the Bar. Changes to the Legal Professions Act, like similar changes to the ICA Act, empowered the Benchers to reject lawyers and law students on grounds of an ill-defined 'moral character' and 'apparent fitness.'[153] Norman Littlewood, a war veteran, was refused entry to UBC's law school because of his association with the LPP, but won admission on appeal. Gordon Martin, however, was prohibited from practising law because he had contested the 1945 election as an LPP candidate and retained membership in the party; Martin later opened a TV repair shop in Nanaimo. The *Pacific Tribune* interpreted these developments as 'the opening wedge of a drive by narrow big business political interests to restrict entry into the professions' for LPPers, CCFers, and 'other democratically minded people,' 'stultifying the professions and introducing two categories of citizenship.'[154] Harry Rankin, a Vancouver lawyer who narrowly passed the anti-communist screen in 1948, and again in 1972, described the Benchers' actions as 'political intimidation ... letting a whole generation of law students know that it was unacceptable to do any real thinking about change.'[155]

Despite persecution, BC communists sustained an alternative working-class culture throughout the Cold War. Party leader Nigel Morgan toured the province by car, maintaining contact with clubs and individual communists in BC's remote communities. During the controversy over the Columbia River Treaty, communists organized a car cavalcade that wound its way through the Interior to the banks of the Columbia.[156] The party organized regular social functions through clubs and ethnic associations including the Finnish Organization of Canada, United Jewish People's Order, and Association of United Ukrainian Canadians. Youth activity was maintained in the National Federation of Labour Youth (NFLY) and Young Communist League (YCL). Kevin Neish, son of Elgin 'Scotty' Neish, recalls growing up in this milieu: 'I got my politics by osmosis ... It wasn't indoctrination. But it couldn't be helped. I was walking picket lines. I was on my mother's knee while she was knitting shawls for Vietnamese children.' Neish visited Communist Cuba in 1966, at age ten, with his mother, Gladys, on a tour organized by the Canada-Cuba Friendship Society. He has fond memories of the annual Labour Day picnics held on Parksville Beach, where communists from across Vancouver Island gathered for an authentic salmon barbecue:

> We'd have a huge gathering, hundreds of people. Huge amounts of food ... Potato salad and pop and ice cream and watermelon by the ton. And lots of politics and speeches and music. We'd play on the beach. They had a softball game and tug-of-war and they'd set up a volleyball net ...We went every year for years ... A friendly, safe place to be.

While Neish was never active in the YCL, he remembers attending an event one summer where young people were addressed by party leaders and a folk singer told the children, 'I'm here just to let you know that Communists really don't have forked tails.'[157]

Neish's recollections aren't entirely positive, however. In 1961, his father received a letter from a US Immigration official stating: 'You are hereby placed on notice that hereafter it will be unlawful for you to enter the United States for any purpose. If you enter the United States, you will be subject to arrest and deportation, and possible criminal prosecution.'[158] Neish recalls attending a peace vigil in the early 1960s, in front of the Hudson's Bay Company store in Victoria, with his mother, Gladys. 'I remember people berating us and spitting at us. That's what I remember as a little kid. One of my first memories. Somebody spitting at my mom, spitting at her feet for being against the Vietnam War.' Neish remembers his mother

> knitting blankets for the Vietnamese children and families. She would be always knitting, and she would be knitting dark camouflage colours. It had an impact on me as a kid. She'd explain why it had to be greens and browns and dark colours. It couldn't be the usual bright colours that she knit because they were being shipped over to North Vietnam for the families to use in the streets. When they were trying to hide, you had to have these camouflage-coloured knitted shawls and blankets. Strange stuff for a kid to understand.

When his father, Elgin, was away from home on his fishing boat, Neish recalls his mother wrapping a pillow around the family telephone, which rang incessantly through the night. 'When dad wasn't home, the anti-communist or anti-union people in town, especially when they got out of the bars, they'd phone up to threaten mom and harass us. So she wrapped it with a pillow, just to let it ring at night and ignore it. I didn't realize that was unusual until I got a little older.'[159]

Relations with the CCF-NDP were always shaky, particularly in the wake of the 1948 Red Wars. Grace and Walter Tickson, like other communists on Vancouver Island, attended CCF and NDP picnics, and worked in coalitions with members of the social-democratic party. Grace Tickson suggests, however, that she got along with 'some of them. Not all of them, mind you.' Dave Stupich, a left-winger who narrowly lost the Nanaimo seat to Social Credit in 1953, 'wasn't that good, as far as the party was concerned.'[160] While Communists were philosophically committed to a transformation away from capitalist property relations, in the electoral realm they focused on more earthly pursuits. Doris Blakey, LPP candidate in a 1953 Victoria by-election, ran on a platform of trade, jobs, pensions, tax relief, and civil rights, accusing Social Credit of 'allowing the same cold war policy of the Liberals and Tories to take precedence over the needs of the people,' while the CCF opposition was 'afraid to speak out.'[161] Despite this criticism, the LPP usually refrained from challenging incumbent CCF MLAs, pursuing the policy laid down in 1948 of 'Unity to Elect a CCF government.' Only in those ridings where CCF victory was highly unlikely, or in the multiple-member Vancouver ridings, did the LPP consistently run candidates. However, formal cooperation was not on the table. Tickson recalls a telephone conversation between her husband and provincial leader Bob Strachan: 'We wanted to sit down with the CCF and figure out if we should run people.... And he wouldn't. He said no. Wouldn't have anything to do with us.'[162]

The Crisis of '56 and Splits

Conflict in BC's labour and peace movements combined with ugly internal splits. Soviet premier Nikita Khrushchev astounded delegates at his party's Twentieth Congress, delivering a secret speech on 25 February 1956 that reverberated through the international communist movement. It was described by the Toronto *Globe and Mail* as 'Russia's Tragedy,' but the *Pacific Tribune* put on a brave face, calling the gathering 'a historic, optimistic, inspiring Congress,' Russia's 'hour of triumph.'[163] Nigel Morgan had attended the Congress, but along with other international delegates was excluded from the secret session.[164] Khrushchev described 'glaring violations of revolutionary legality' under Stalin, but warned delegates that 'we cannot let this matter get out of the party, especially not to the press ... We should not give ammunition to the enemy; we should not wash our dirty linen before their eyes.'[165] But the contents of Khrushchev's speech made their way into the press, via a Polish journalist, Israel's Shin Bet security agency, and the CIA, appearing in a *New York Times* exposé in June. When Soviet tanks rolled into Budapest in November – after reformist premier Imre Nagy announced that Hungary was breaking from the Warsaw Pact – disillusionment in the LPP and other communist parties erupted.[166]

In July 1956, Albert Pacey of Woodfibre, BC had responded to the Khrushchev revelations in a letter to the *Pacific Tribune*:

> Canadian Communists failed to respond to warning signs and thus made their own contribution to the Stalinist distortion. When sincere and proven party members raised doubts as to the justice meted out to some individuals in the purges (e.g. imprisonment of Arvid Lahti) no real check was made and if the doubtful one persisted, Trotskyite was a convenient tag ... 'The great discussion' should not only deal with the shortcomings of the Communist Party of the Soviet Union ... It should deal, too with the shortcomings of Canadian socialists and communists.[167]

At the national level, communist leaders split on whether the LPP had gone far enough in distancing itself from Stalin and the Soviet Union. In particular, Jewish members including former Ontario MPP (1943–55) Joe Salsberg cited systemic anti-Semitism in the USSR.[168] In typically pedantic prose, the party's official history concedes that:

> From 1956 to the end of the decade was a most difficult period for Cana-

> dian Communists … Imperialism seized upon the so-called Stalin revelations and the attempted counter-revolution in Hungary as an opportunity to be fully exploited in a massive ideological offensive. This was a period of intense ideological crisis inside the LPP. Essentially, the party was engaged in a struggle between Leninism and revisionism.[169]

In a series of National Committee meetings in 1956, controversy raged, spawning the resignation of six Quebec LPP officials, demands for Tim Buck's resignation, and consolidation of power by the old party leadership.[170]

According to Jack Scott, who was a LPP member in BC at the time, 'Out here, it didn't hit that hard.' The BC party held general membership meetings where 'a lot of bitter words were thrown around,' but the major crisis raged in the national leadership.[171] Grace Tickson suggests the crisis of 1956 provided an excuse for those already unhappy with the party's fortunes: 'Some of them wanted to leave and they had an excuse. They were wanting to go anyhow 'cause things weren't going right. We weren't getting the influence we had before.'[172] Ben Swankey, then Alberta LPP leader (1945–57), who would soon relocate to BC, attended the National Committee meetings and concedes that Salsberg and the revisionists' criticism of Soviet anti-Semitism was justified:

> They were right, and most of us who disputed that spoke from ignorance and wouldn't accept what was actually happening. Because the Soviet Union could do no wrong. You got suspicious of everything that was anti-Soviet. It made it hard to understand that some of it was true … I think I went along with the general line of the leadership of the party, which was wrong.

According to Swankey, 'we lost a lot members … After '56, you never had the same faith in the party … [There was] no real democracy. It was lip democracy. The central bodies would formulate things, and then you go down to the branches and you study them and talk about them, and then you go back to the central office and they would decide … The Canadian party was taking its leadership from the Comintern.'[173]

In the midst of the Hungarian crisis, the LPP's National Committee held a special plenum in Toronto, meeting for thirteen days 'in an atmosphere of unprecedented disorder and hostility.'[174] The two camps were divided roughly equally, but the gathering closed on 9 November with adoption of a motion from BC leader Nigel Morgan withdrawing earlier criticism of the CPSU.[175] Morgan's stance reflected orthodoxy in the BC leadership; in June 1956, the BC Provincial Committee had burned a *Canadian Tribune* supplement containing the text of Khrushchev's speech. Like Tom McEwen and other BC heavyweights, Morgan was consistently aligned with Buck. According to Jack Scott, 'Morgan always wants to live with the big guy.'[176] Carried in an 18–11 vote, with one abstention, Morgan's resolution revealed the minority position of the 'revisionists' and the supremacy of the orthodox 'Leninist' line. The Leninists captured a clear majority on the NEC. At a second National Committee plenum in December 1956, a proposal from Salsberg and others advocating 'a Canadian path to socialism' was rejected 21–7. In January 1957, the NEC attributed the Hungarian crisis to the counter-revolutionary activities of 'internal and external reactionary and fascist elements.'[177]

The revisionists' defeat was confirmed at the LPP's sixth national convention in Toronto in April 1957, where Buck was re-elected party secretary by a standing vote of 116–28. Penner, however, suggests this was 'the beginning of Buck's decline as leader.'[178] Resolutions from BC clubs reveal the depth of dissent. The Rossland-Trail Club noted that 'party membership has fallen off considerably … and our press sales have dropped badly,' proposing the rotation of national conventions between Toronto, Winnipeg, and Vancouver among other measures. The Aldergrove Club viewed 'the party's drift to the right with anxiety. Instead of being a leader in the class struggle we are developing into a debating society.' Andy Hogarth of Courtenay expressed concern over the cult of the individual, and proposed abolishing the position of party leader. The Campbell River Club went further, proposing amendments that 'the present existing Canadian democracy be utilized as the point of departure to a socialist and communist democracy.' The Cowichan Club, meanwhile, urged a discontinuation of fraternal travel by party officers, since 'the answer to our problems are [*sic*] here in Canada and not in other lands.'[179]

The *Advocate*, a dissident newspaper released at the 1957 convention, urged that 'only an alerted rank and file, determined to stay and fight, can settle accounts with LPP misleadership and contribute to the restoration in Canada of a genuine revolutionary movement.'[180] The Trotskyist Socialist Educational League (SEL) saw in these developments a 'big opportunity for us to build our movement, put some flesh on our bones.' SEL accused the LPP leadership of opportunism 'because it does not serve the interests of socialism in Canada but the interests of the bureaucracy in Russia.'[181] As Steve Hewitt has observed, the RCMP Security Service fanned the flames of discord during the crisis of '56. 'K' Branch forwarded a forged letter to LPP members, purportedly from a member disenchanted over the Khrushchev revelations. Buck demanded a public inquiry into RCMP activities, insisting they violated basic civil rights.[182]

The crisis of '56 inaugurated a protracted period of doubt and dissension in the BC LPP. Disputes resurfaced between BC leaders and dissidents, such as Jack Scott, who captured a third of the vote in one election for the BC Provincial Committee, and sparred periodically over the affairs of People's Co-op Bookstore. Scott recalls serving with Harry Rankin on the bookstore board and preventing the banning of *Doctor Zhivago*.[183] In 1959, the national LPP convention restored the name Communist Party of Canada (CPC). To some BC party members this was a mistake. 'I know I opposed it,' recalls Swankey. 'I thought it would not do us any good. We had made a certain reputation as the LPP, and I thought it was a step backward. It would make us more sectarian than ever.'[184] Harold Griffin, a member of the BC Provincial Committee and associate editor of the *Fisherman*, felt the same way. 'Hal always thought we should have just kept it the Labor Progressive Party,' says Betty Griffin. 'Communist Party just raises a barrier.'[185]

Discord raged in the BC Communist Party in the 1960s, creating a political vacuum that contributed to the appeal of the New Left. Disunity in the BC CPC reflected internal power struggles and also debates in the international communist movement. In 1962, Nigel Morgan intervened to bring the BC section of the YCL in line with the national YCL leadership, after a dispute arose over distribution of the newspaper *Advance*.[186] However, the major crisis in the early 1960s centred on a dispute between party leaders and alleged Maoists associated with Vancouver's 'Special Club,' a unique amalgam of left currents that counted former party organizer Jack Scott among its members. 'It is often thought that our differences with the Party were over the question of China versus the Soviet Union,' Scott recounts. 'That's not so. We were sympathetic to China in the arguments that were taking place, but our differences with the Party were based on differences of policy for Canada.'[187]

The Special Club had originated in 1961 among left-wing CCFers, 'all working class,' Scott suggests, activists in unions including the Oil and Chemical Workers, Plumbers, Teamsters, Printing Trades, Carpenters, and Electricians. The club included oil workers' president Jerry Lebourdais and (according to Scott) Bert Herridge, CCF-NDP MP for Kootenay West (1945–68). As a party report stated, 'because of anti-Communist restrictions in their organizations they asked that their membership be kept "confidential."'[188] The BC Provincial Committee approved the club's formation and assigned Charlie Caron to organize and lead the group, which consisted of about thirty members and developed links in the early 1960s with the NDP Socialist Caucus. The club wreaked havoc in the Communist Party, waging 'sort of a guerilla warfare' on issues ranging from an unauthorized delegation to Cuba to the Norris investigation into the gangster-ridden SIU. The club sent anonymous letters to party units, publicizing positions that deviated from the provincial leadership, but its members were determined to remain inside the CPC until they were expelled.[189]

It was in this context that the simmering dispute between the Chinese and Soviet communist parties broke into the open. Yugoslavia's break with the USSR in 1948 had foreshadowed tensions that widened in the 1950s and 1960s, with the BC party remaining firmly in the Russian camp. When Khrushchev reneged, under US pressure, on a Stalin-era agreement to assist the Chinese in developing nuclear weapons, the Chinese leadership responded with bitter invective against the Soviet premier. After the 1962 Cuban missile crisis, the Chinese argued that the USSR should have pursued a policy of no compromise with US imperialism, but CPC leaders defended the Soviet position on grounds that any other action would have led to nuclear war. Leslie Morris and Bill Kashtan travelled to Beijing in 1962, via Moscow, on behalf of the CPC, but lacked the influence to bring about a resolution – which struck at the root of the Soviet policy of 'peaceful co-existence.' While the Indonesian and Albanian communist parties fell squarely under the Chinese orbit, CPC leaders were loyal to Moscow, exacerbating tension with the rank and file. Jack Scott and a dozen other Vancouver communists in the Special Club formed a Canada-China Friendship Association in October 1963, openly declaring their sympathy with the Chinese line. 'We used the China-Soviet issue quite deliberately as an opportunity to come out into the open and embarrass the bloody Party leadership as far as we could,' Scott recalls.[190]

Scott had first raised the Sino-Soviet dispute in the mid-1950s, when a series of articles from the *Peking Review* were circulated in pamphlet form, but BC leaders downplayed any divisions. However, in the 1960s, the conflict erupted, in tandem with growing disagreement over domestic policy. Party organizer Charlie Caron described the Canada-China

Friendship Association as 'an alternative central committee,' and tense debate at the 1963 national convention failed to resolve the rift between the Special Club and party leaders. Scott described a domestic policy pledging to 'Put Monopoly Under Control' as 'goddamn ridiculous,' evidence of the leadership's lack of commitment 'to keep the idea of socialism alive.' After the convention, Bill Kashtan, future party leader, flew to Vancouver to impress the national line on the renegade club, but met with little success.[191]

The final break occurred in spring 1964. Scott and other Special Club members organized a public meeting on the Sino-India border dispute, which saw the USSR providing military aid to India. The BC Provincial Committee ordered Scott not to speak, but he defied the order and addressed a capacity crowd in Vancouver's Teamsters Hall on 21 March 1964 – 'the biggest left-wing meeting in the city for years.'[192] Two months later, Caron attended the weekly Special Club meeting, on behalf of the provincial executive, and announced that the club was dissolved and that any member wishing to remain in the party should raise the matter with him on an individual basis.[193] Scott was singled out for his role in the March meeting, charged with refusal to carry out a direct Party order, and following a trial in August 1964 received a letter from Nigel Morgan informing him of his expulsion from the CPC.[194]

The charges against Scott and the Special Club's dissolution reverberated through the BC party and beyond. Scott sent an appeal to the National Committee, circulating mimeographed copies to party members as far away as the Essex County Club, consisting of dissident autoworkers in Windsor, Ontario. Scott argued that 'if there is no safeguard to protect one club against such arbitrary action, then there is obviously no protection for any club – except perhaps the wrath of an aroused membership.'[195] Scott and two colleagues travelled across Canada to drum up support for a new 'Labor-Progressive Movement,' later called the Progressive Worker Movement. Though dismissed by the BC Provincial Committee as 'factional ... anti-Party elements,' Scott and his group received support from sections of the BC membership.[196] Respected communists including Elgin 'Scotty' Neish took issue with the methods used to expel Scott and apparent violations of the party constitution. As Neish's son Kevin recounts:

> There was a dispute in the party, and Dad defended the Maoist side. He was well versed in Communist positions. I believe he might have been rousted out because of that. A lot of people got kicked out at that time, for

> 'Maoist tendencies.' But he was either invited back or went back. It didn't stop him. He just carried on working. He was a Marxist. It didn't matter whether he was a member of any party. He was still a Marxist.[197]

The Communist Party's official history plays down the impact of Maoism in Canada: 'As in other countries where they were unable to effect a split, the Chinese Maoists sponsored the formation of ultra-left violence-prone splinter groupings based on petty-bourgeois fringe elements mainly in the universities.'[198]

The ousting of Scott and the Special Club failed to stem internal conflict. Caron, the former party stalwart, became embroiled in a dispute with Nigel Morgan and the Provincial Committee, centring on the party's Vancouver City Committee. According to Maurice Rush, then *Tribune* associate editor, Caron 'entertained many leftist ideas' and sought to move the City Committee 'toward adopting left-sectarian positions,' such as equating the struggle for peace with the struggle against capitalism, a stance circulated in a leaflet at a Vancouver peace march. Caron and the City Committee, like earlier dissidents, corresponded with clubs around the province. This prompted the Provincial Committee to hold a series of 'very stormy meetings' to 'undo the harm that the City Committee had done.' Harold Pritchett and Donald 'Dusty' Greenwell were the only City Committee members to vote against the left-sectarian positions, Rush claims.[199] The provincial committee's views are reflected in a 1966 report on 'Party Organization and Style of Work,' offering a thinly veiled criticism of the City Committee leadership:

> Our perspective on civic politics will require the closest relations between the clubs and the City Committee. Forms of organization will have to be worked out to establish these ties. It will also require the selection of a City Committee which will display a great deal of wisdom and concreteness in its leadership in the period ahead. The committee must be capable of sound political judgement and they should have mass connections with the various areas of public activities.

Party work had assumed 'the character of a ritual, rather than the character of Marxist leadership,' the report claimed, and club activities were divorced from 'the struggles of the people,' suggesting it might be 'necessary to re-organize some clubs.'[200]

In November 1967, the dispute spilled over into the party's UBC Campus Club. Joe and Ann Irving resigned, citing disagreement with

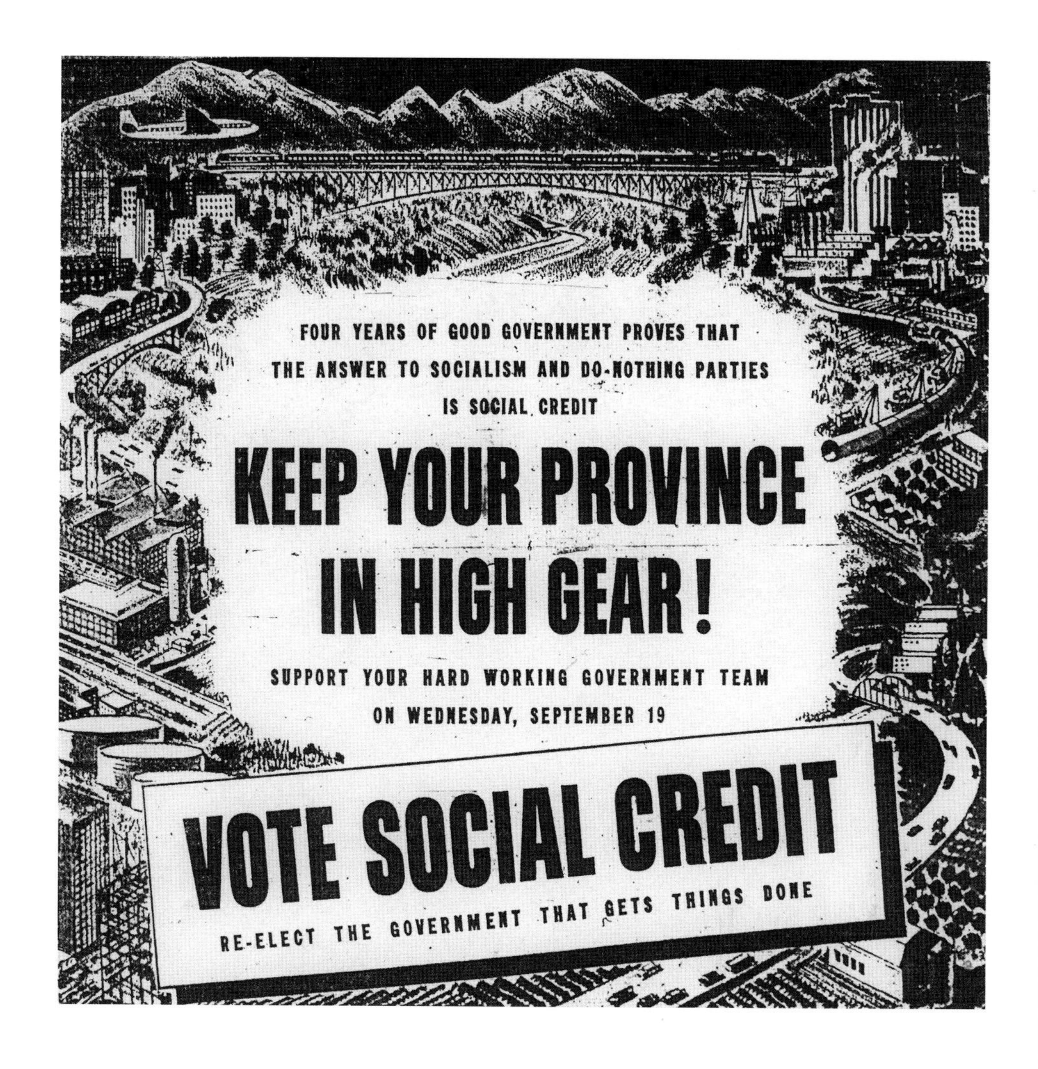

Social Credit election poster, 1956. The modernist imagery conveys the optimism that animated W.A.C. Bennett's 'province-building' agenda, reflecting buoyant conditions in BC's expanding postwar economy. Many working-class voters responded to these populist appeals for the 'good life,' returning Social Credit to power in seven consecutive elections.

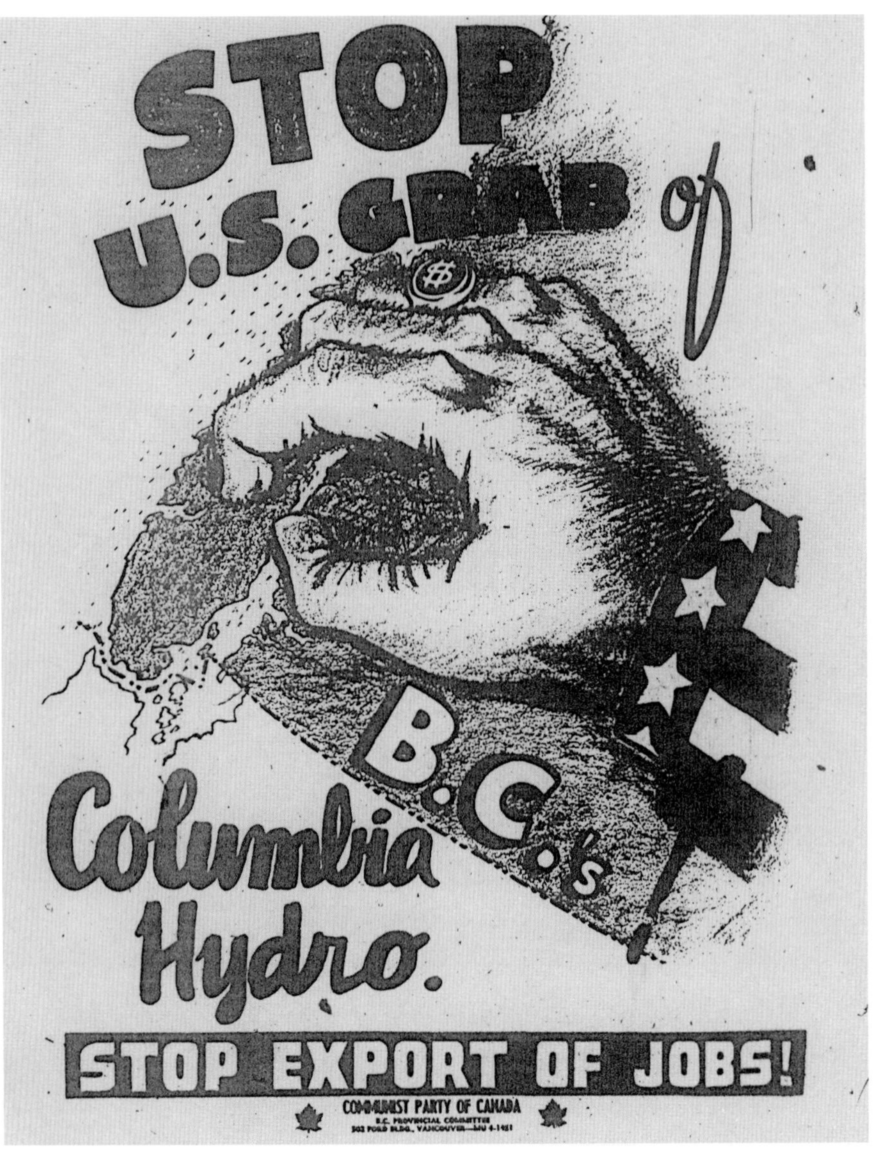

Communist Party leaflet opposing the Columbia River Treaty, c. 1962. The agreement between Canada and the United States was viewed by the militant minority as a 'sell-out' of the people's interests and a hindrance to the province's industrial potential.

Ready to Go . . . "Compensation For All Fishermen"

Flotilla of fishing boats at the BC legislature, 1952. Organized by the United Fishermen and Allied Workers Union (UFAWU), the protest demanded unemployment benefits for fishers, whom the state and employers deemed 'co-adventurers' rather than workers entitled to the benefits of union certification and the social wage.

The Fisherman

Representing The Organized Fishermen And Shoreworkers of British Columbia

VOL. XII. No. 31 (509) VANCOUVER, B.C., OCTOBER 3, 1950  Price Fiv

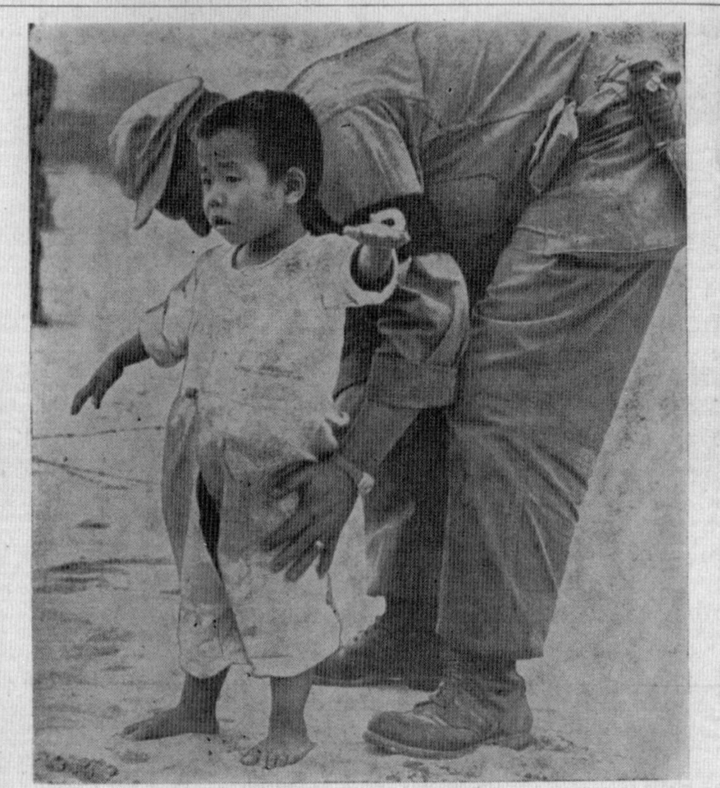

No Comment Required It is hardly necessary to express any comment on the picture above: it speaks for itself. The soldier frisking the Korean tot is an American GI — a pitiful scene in a tortured land.

New P
For Fa

New prices for f
waters Monday, Octob
ermen and Allied Work

The new prices are
four cents over mi
established in agreeme
isting between the U
and Operators.

Prices established are
lows:

CHUMS

- Johnstone Strait
per pound.
- Mainland, East C
Vancouver Island and
River. 12 cents per pour
- Below Estevan
West Coast, 10 cen
pound.
- Above Estevan
West Coast and abov
Caution. 9 cents per po

COHO

- Below Cape Caut
below Estevan. 20 ce
pound.
- Above Cape Caut
Estevan. 18 cents per

In granting the in
operators stipulated th
are based on the A
market and if the marl
tuates downward, they
the right to lower thes

Korean boy and an American GI, 1950. Published in the early stages of the Korean War, the caption 'No Comment Required' conveys the communist-led UFAWU's wholesale rejection of American and NATO foreign policy. The UFAWU occupied a leadership position in BC's postwar peace movement.

Trade with China march, BC Legislature, 1950s. Aligning themselves with the 'enemy' in the Cold War, BC communists agitated for the lifting of the western blockade against China, imposed in the wake of the Communist victory over the Kuomintang in 1949.

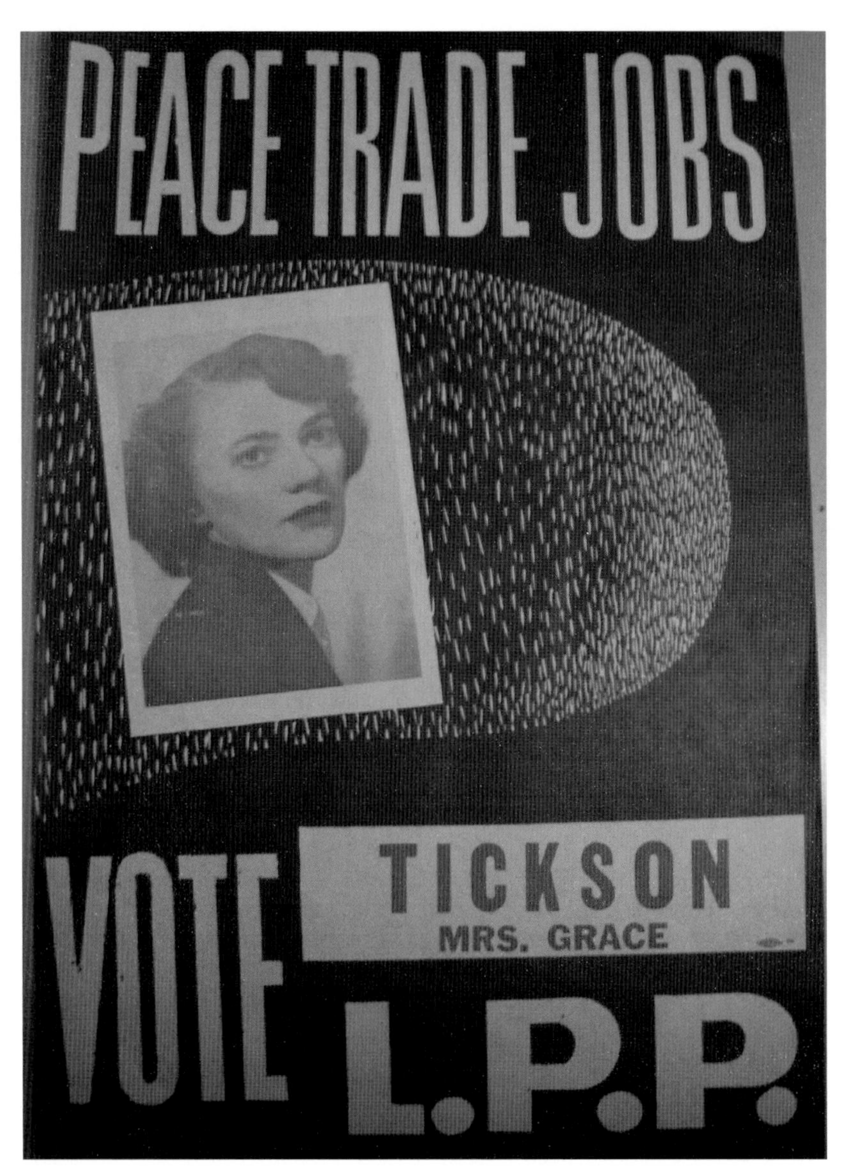

Grace Tickson election poster, Nanaimo, 1953. Tickson, a court stenographer and activist in the Congress of Canadian Women, contested the Nanaimo constituency in the 1953 election as a candidate of the Labor-Progressive Party (LPP), as the Communist Party was then called.

Cuba meeting sponsored by the Young Communist League, Vancouver, c. 1961. BC's militant minority formed strong relations with the rebel island after the Batista regime was defeated by Castro's July 26th Movement.

Elgin 'Scotty' Neish, Fidel Castro, and Gladys Neish, Havana, 1961. Scotty Neish, president of the UFAWU's Victoria local and a card-carrying Communist, had been expelled from the Victoria Trades and Labour Council and the Royal Canadian Legion in the 1950s for left-wing associations. Gladys Neish, a 'feminist Marxist' according to her son, never joined the Communist Party but was a lifelong peace worker: 'In that era the party was very patriarchal.'

Delegates at the annual convention of the Women's Auxiliary of the UFAWU, Vancouver, 22 March 1962. This layer of working-class women occupied a distinct location in BC's postwar political economy, bridging a 'militant mothering' tradition and the more explicitly feminist politics of the Women's Liberation Movement.

Camp Woodsworth, Gabriola Island, BC, 1950s. The Co-operative Commonwealth Federation, like other left formations, extended its work into the cultural realm, seeking to provide its activists with a sense of belonging and a social home in a chaotic geopolitical and ideological space. Members addressed one another with the greeting 'Comrade,' reflecting traditions the CCF inherited from the old Socialist Party.

Woman's sitdown dramatizes plight of silicosis victims

By BERT WHYTE

Mrs. Bea Zucco of New Westminster, mother of four children who staged sitdown strikes with three of them at the Workmen's Compensation building here and in front of the Legislative Buildings in Victoria, forced authorities to act this week on her husband's claim to compensation for silicosis. Labor Minister Lyle Wicks said that Jack Zucco, a patient in George Pearson TB Hospital here, has been found to have "minimum qualifications" for compensation.

Mrs. Zucco's dramatic action turned the spotlight of publicity on the plight of scores of miners in B.C. who have become unfit for work because of silicosis and other lung conditions arising from silicosis.

Silicosis is not a disease, but a condition arising from inhalation of the dust of rock, sand or flint. Miners are its chief victims.

For many years International Union of Mine, Mill and Smelter Workers has fought the battle for compensation on behalf of miners suffering from silicosis. It has been a long, hard struggle.

The 13th Mine-Mill district convention held here recently pressed for a change in that part of the Workmen's Compensation Act dealing with silicosis, which requires a man to demonstrate loss of earning capacity, even though the X-rays may reveal a substantial change in the chest condition.

Labor Minister Lyle Wicks, addressing the Mine-Mill parley, told delegates he had acted on the union's 1954 submission with respect to a reciprocal arrangement for miners who travel from one province to another, and who later learn that they have developed silicosis.

Union position is that miners who contract silicosis in one province and then move to a job in another province should be eligible for compensation.

But this is still not law.

Leo Nimsick (CCF Cranbrook) raised the question in the House last month, and also delivered a radio address on the subject. He said:

"One of the grim jokes of our present legislation is the definition of silicosis: 'Silicosis shall mean a fibrotic condition of the lungs caused by dust containing silica and evidenced by specific X-ray appearances, accompanied by a substantially lessened capacity for work.'

"This means that no matter how much silicosis is shown on the X-rays there is no hope of a man getting compensation as long as he continues to work.

"That is why we find many men with families, who cannot afford to lay off work, continuing to deteriorate until the silicosis is complicated with some other disease, which finally disables them altogether; then it is not silicosis which disables them, but the new disease and this may be heart disease, asthma, bronchitis, or what have you, and then they are denied compensation on those grounds.

"If a person is receiving a silicosis pension for years, and he dies from carcinoma of the lungs, asthma, or any other cause except what he is compensated for, his widow is not entitled to the widow's pension."

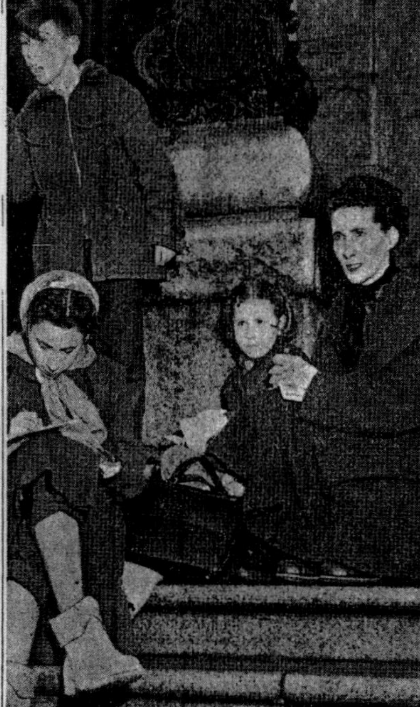

Mrs. Zucco, wife of a New Westminster silicosis victim, is shown here as she staged her sitdown on the steps of the Legislative Buildings in Victoria. With her are three of her four children, Margaret, 13; Johnny, 11, and Sylvia, 6.

Mrs. Zucco staged her sitdown strikes in protest against the government's refusal to grant a silicosis pension to her husband, Jack, 44, a miner for 20 years and a tuberculosis patient for six years.

She made it clear that she was not battling for her family alone.

"I want the regulations changed so that if a man works in a mine as my husband did and then gets TB it should be accepted that TB was brought on by silicosis," she told reporters.

Mrs. Zucco and her three older children turned up at the Workmen's Compensation Board office here February 23 carrying "on strike" placards, a big box of sandwiches and a red blanket.

On February 27 she and her family shifted their sitdown to the wet granite steps of the Legislative Buildings in Victoria, and soon got some action from vote-conscious politicians.

Labor Minister Lyle Wicks interviewed her and later told the House he was considering her husband's case. He said that Dr. A. R. Riddell of Toronto, a silicosis expert, had reported finding "nothing in this case to support a case of silicosis" and that Zucco's case was one of pulmonary tuberculosis.

Mrs. Zucco sat tight and public indignation mounted.

This week Wicks said that the Workmen's Compensation Board would reopen the case for final decision, and admitted that Zucco has "minimum qualifications" for compensation benefits.

The fight for victims of the "great killer," silicosis, goes on. It is still far from won, but Mrs. Zucco's stand, which dramatised the battle waged by Mine-Mill over the years, has helped create public pressure which should hasten changes in legislation.

Last weekend a resolution passed unanimously by delegates attending a Greater Vancouver convention of the Labor-Progressive party demanded that "the Lieutenant-Governor-in-Council remove those members of the Compensation Board who are making no attempt to fulfil the intent of the Workmen's Compensation Act."

The Zucco case may open the door and force a re-examination of many more cases which have been repeatedly brought before the authorities by Mine-Mill officials.

Bea Zucco's sit-down strike at the BC legislature, 1956. The mother of three staged this 'one-woman protest' in a bid for workman's compensation benefits for herself and her children, arising from her husband's affliction with silicosis from work in the mines. Zucco ultimately won her battle, but not before she was evicted from her home and was obliged to place her children in foster care.

RIGHT HON. JOHN. G. DIEFENBAKER,
PRIME MINISTER OF CANADA,
OTTAWA, CANADA.

Dear Sir:

I believe that Canada's participation in NATO & NORAD are contrary to the interests of Canadians.

Canada's acceptance of nuclear weapons would identify us as a member of the camp of war instead of peace. I believe that Canada's position should be one of withdrawing from NATO and NORAD, and refusing to accept nuclear weapons on Canadian soil. We should adopt a policy of positive neutrality to work for peace.

In order to safeguard the future of our families, we urge that your government should take every measure possible to achieve that end.

(Signed) ....

This leaflet is published by the Women's Committee, Vancouver Island Region, Communist Party of Canada.

Your comments are welcome, and should be addressed to:

Mrs. Myrtle Bergren,
Box 260,
Lake Cowichan, B.C.

MOTHER'S DAY 1961!

WHICH CHILD FOR CANADA?

Communist Party of Canada Women's Committee peace leaflet, Lake Cowichan, 1961. The committee invoked strong imagery to warn of the dangers of nuclear war.

THE ARMS RACE? OR

THE HUMAN RACE?

No Nuclear Arms For Canada

HEAR

PROFESSOR J. GORDIN KAPLAN

JOHN B. WITCHELL

Thursday, February 9, 8:30 p.m.

QUEEN ELIZABETH AUDITORIUM

SPONSORED BY THE B.C. COMMITTEES ON RADIATION HAZARDS

Radiation Hazards poster, Vancouver, February 1961. The anti-nuclear movement, both in BC and internationally, provided an important continuum between the activism of the Old Left and New Left.

2★★★★ THE PROVINCE, Monday, March 28, 1966

STOP the WAR in Vietnam

Viet Nam protest marchers held up traffic along Broadway on trek to the courthouse.

Babes-in-arms join city peace parade

More than [illegible] students, move on before trouble started friends they are losing around not a police uniform in sight

Vancouver peace march, 26 March 1966. By the late 1960s, the peace movement had expanded beyond the Cold War–hardened militant minority to include growing numbers of students, youth, and upwardly mobile members of the urban middle class. The headline conveys the changed demographic of BC's left and the rising movement against the Vietnam War.

—William E. John

Panthers Stride at UVic

In uniforms of black leather jackets and berets and sporting semi-automatic rifle, members of the militant Black Panther Party from Seattle's ghetto stride toward Student Union Building at University of Victoria. However, objective of, left to-right, Bruce Hayes, Bobby White, and Bobby Harding Sunday night was to talk, not destroy. See story Page 18.

Black Panthers, armed, visit the University of Victoria campus, August 1968. Demonstrating linkages with the American left, these activists from Seattle were invited to speak to students in BC's capital city. Reflecting the rebellious mood of the era, the activist on the left is holding a rifle.

MAY DAY EDITION

Pacific TRIBUNE

Vol. 7, NO. 18 Vancouver, B.C., Friday, April 30, 1948 Five Cents

Coalition provoking unrest

'UNIONS WON'T STAND FOR DESTRUCTION BY LAW'

WINCH---TURNER

PEACE

SOLIDARITY

Unity for world peace

CCF battles against anti-labor Bill 87

VICTORIA, B.C. — "The trade unions of this province are determined that their unions shall not be destroyed—law or no law. They won't just sit down and let their unions be put out of business."

This is how Arthur Turner, (CCF, Vancouver East) summed up the attitude of the labor movement to Bill 87 as the CCF opposition and Tom Uphill (Labor, Fernie) battled point by point in the legislature Tuesday to defeat the Coalition government's vicious amendments to the ICA Act—the notorious Bill 39 of last year.

"This bill is dictated by the Canadian Manufacturers Association and the B.C. Bar Association. It is not concerned with the interests of the trade unions," Harold Winch, CCF leader, charged.

Winch's charge was effectively substantiated in committee by Herbert Gargrave (CCF, Mackenzie) when he read CMA representations to the government and showed that they were little different from the amendments proposed by the government in Bill 87.

With Labor Minister Gordon S. Wismer still clinging to the fiction that Bill 87 would protect labor's interests and Coalitionists Alan MacDonell (Vancouver Centre) and A. R. MacDougall (Point Grey) furnishing the red-baiting lie to his claims, the government rammed the bill through the House. Other Coalitionists displayed their concern for labor's interests by disruptive heckling and voting down all the 27 amendments proposed by the CCF.

E. E. Winch (CCF, Burnaby) answered MacDougall's assertion that the amendments would "protect the unions against self-avowed communists" by stating:

"This talk about avowed communists reminds me of my younger days when I was very undesirable to employers who broke our unions and blacklisted me and others who were avowed socialists.

"You'd blacklist me and others in this House if you could," he declared.

"You can't bring the red bogey in here and get away with it," Arthur Turner told red-baiting Coalitionists.

Continued on page 4
See BILL 87

'Abbott threw prices brief back at me'

By MARK FRANK

OTTAWA.—Are you one of the 709,573 people who signed the Housewives' Consumer Association brief calling on the King government to restore price controls at 1946 levels?

If you are, you're probably pretty indignant at the government's arrogant refusal to receive the petition—it was finally delivered to Prime Minister King's Laurier House residence — and you want to know why.

This account of the interview forced on Finance Minister Douglas Abbott by Mrs. Rae Lucock, president of the new Housewives and Consumers Federation of Canada, as related by her to a meeting of consumer delegates in Lisgar Collegiate here, reveals the government's desperate efforts to evade general public protest against high prices by using the red smear technique.

Somebody had tipped Mrs. Lucock off on the whereabouts of the finance minister. He was in the cafeteria sipping coffee.

"I found him in the lunch room," Mrs. Lucock told delegates.

"Taking my courage into my hands, I walked up to his table, bowed a little stiffly, and said: 'How do you do? I'm Mrs. Lucock of the Housewives Consumer Association.'

"I held out my hand and he shook it. Then he said he would be glad to speak to me personally, but not as a member of the delegation. Well, that was all right.

"'Rightly or wrongly you're being used as a communist front,' the minister told me. Well, I showed him our constitution. He said he was quite sure I was a sincere woman. I told him the group was not formed for political purposes but to take care of prices. It had been formed 11 years ago.

"What could I do with the petitions, I asked. Where could I take them? 'Nothing to offer,' said the minister. 'Suggest you write a letter to A. D. P. Heeney, secretary of the cabinet and ask him to receive them.'

"'But I will not even examine them or look at them,' he said.

"Then some time during the interview, I showed him our brief. 'I won't accept a brief,' said the minister, 'send it to me by mail.'

"I asked him not to be so rude to us. The minister relented, took hold of the brief, then suddenly threw it back on the desk at me. 'No, I won't receive it either,' he declared.

"He didn't give it back to me, he threw it back at me."

Labour's response to Bill 87, amendments to the Industrial Conciliation and Arbitration Act, April 1948. The shape of BC's postwar industrial relations system was hotly contested, as labour and management sought to tip the balance of power to their benefit.

Strike Vote at Rivers Inlet, March 1959. This UFAWU meeting on the wharf at Duncanby Landing reflected militancy among BC fishers and shoreworkers, who staged the first industry-wide general strike that year, tying up ships from the mouth of the Fraser in the south to Prince Rupert on the north coast.

UFAWU activists celebrate George North's release from Oakalla prison, 1959. North, as editor of the *Fisherman* newspaper, had been jailed by BC Supreme Court Justice Norman Whitaker for publishing the editorial 'Injunctions Won't Catch Fish Nor Build Bridges.' North is sitting on the shoulder of UFAWU secretary Homer Stevens (in centre of photo below banner).

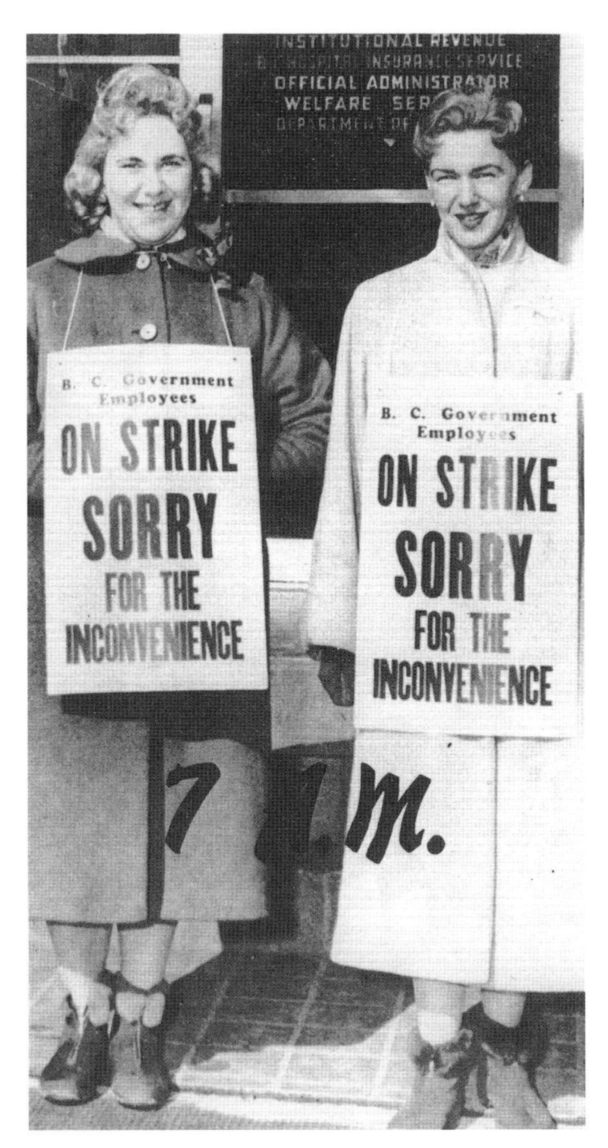

BC Government Employees' Association (BCGEA) picketers during the 'Four-Hour Strike' of 13 March 1959. A high point of civil servants' decades-long struggle for collective bargaining rights, the walkout prompted the Social Credit government of the day to hastily amend BC's Constitution Act, making it illegal to 'picket, watch, or beset' any government building.

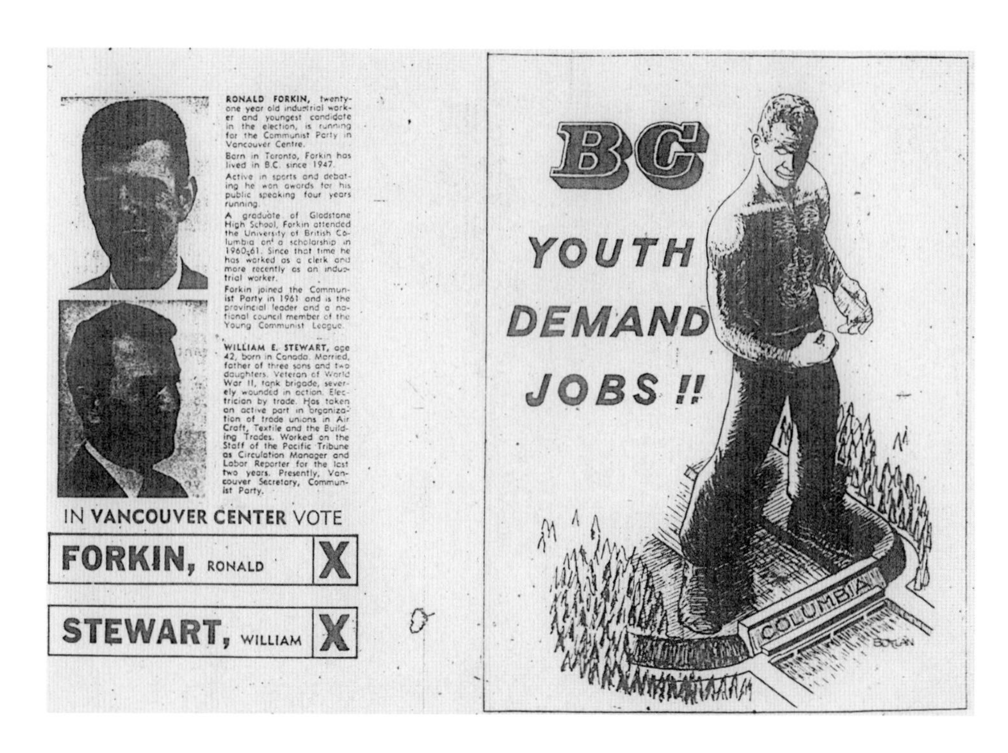

RONALD FORKIN, twenty-one year old industrial worker and youngest candidate in the election, is running for the Communist Party in Vancouver Centre.

Born in Toronto, Forkin has lived in B.C. since 1947.

Active in sports and debating he won awards for his public speaking four years running.

A graduate of Gladstone High School, Forkin attended the University of British Columbia on a scholarship in 1960-61. Since that time he has worked as a clerk and more recently as an industrial worker.

Forkin joined the Communist Party in 1961 and is the provincial leader and a national council member of the Young Communist League.

WILLIAM E. STEWART, age 42, born in Canada. Married, father of three sons and two daughters. Veteran of World War II, tank brigade, severely wounded in action. Electrician by trade. Has taken an active part in organization of trade unions in Air Craft, Textile and the Building Trades. Worked on the Staff of the Pacific Tribune as Circulation Manager and Labor Reporter for the last two years. Presently, Vancouver Secretary, Communist Party.

IN **VANCOUVER CENTER** VOTE

FORKIN, RONALD **X**

STEWART, WILLIAM **X**

BC

YOUTH DEMAND JOBS !!

Communist provincial election leaflet, Vancouver Center, 1963. By the 1960s, growing numbers of young workers challenged the premises and practices of BC's postwar labour relations regime. The 'rank-and-file' revolt reflected anger generated by inflation, automation, and structural unemployment, grievances not adequately addressed through arbitration procedures and collective bargaining apparatus. The Communist Party sought to remain relevant by connecting with these rebellious young workers.

The Sun

'NO A-BOMB FC
SAYS INDIA'S SI

Rhodesia Se
Negro Chan

Former Prime Minist
As Wilson Makes Fi

It followed the detention of a former prime minister known to favor majority rule and an 11th-hour plea by Britain against a unilateral declaration of independence by Rhodesia.

Only a few hours after Prime Minister Ian Smith rejected a British proposal for a Commonwealth premiers mission to visit Salisbury to discuss the independence issue, Prime Minister Wilson sent a cable pleading with the Rhodesian leader not to declare unilateral independence and to continue negotiations.

Wilson discussed the crisis by telephone with Canadian Prime Minister Lester Pearson in Ottawa today.

Government sources said Wilson also was in touch with Australian Prime Minister Sir Robert Menzies and other Commonwealth leaders.

Today, Smith announced that he would meet formally with his cabinet Wednesday and observers expected a decision on independence made then.

Shortly after Wilson's cable was received in Salisbury, the Rhodesian government imposed a 12-month restriction order on former prime minister Garfield Todd as he was about to leave for Britain to take part in a teach-in on Rhodesia at Edinburgh University.

The order restricted Todd to his farm at Shabani, 250 miles south of Salisbury.

Speaking only 24 hours after he had been served with the order, Todd said:

"This restriction came as quite a surprise to me. Of course, as they have banned African nationalist leaders who oppose them it was logical that I should also be considered, but I never

Please Turn to Page Two
See: "Crisis"

HEFTY SHOVE by RCMP officer sends picket reeling back after picket refused officer's order to move from in front of British American Oil Co. truck attempting to leave strikebound Burnaby plant.

—George Diack Photo

Mounties, Pickets Scuffle In Oil-Strike Encounter

By WAYNE MacDONALD

Scuffling broke out between RCMP officers and pickets at the British American Oil Company's Burnaby marketing plant today shortly after a BA tanker docked with five million gallons of refined products.

The incident came when some 30 pickets blocked two BA trucks trying to leave the dock area of the plant. Eight RCMP officers shoved and pushed the pickets from in front of the trucks.

Two pickets were knocked to the ground, but were not injured.

Police were assailed by shouts of "scab herders," "Yankee lovers" and "Finks."

No arrests were made.

Earlier, a scuffle broke out between a union picket and an unidentified man whom the picket termed "a Communist." The picket kicked a camera out of the man's hand, smashing it.

This incident occurred when the camera-toting man took a picture of the picket, and the picket, who refused to give his name, shouted he did not want his photograph taken by Communists.

WATCHED DOCKING

The pickets, some of them carrying placards of the Oil, Chemical and Atomic Workers Union which is striking against BA, had been watching the tanker dock prior to the fight with police.

Tempers were running high because the men said the tanker, the BA Canada, which is normally based in Montreal, was bringing in enough gasoline and other products to keep BA's British Columbia stations supplied for two months.

(A company spokesman said the tanker had taken on its cargo in the Caribbean.)

After the tanker had safely docked, the pickets noticed the two BA trucks coming up the hill and ran over to block them.

ORDER GIVEN

Police, who had been cruising past the area all morning, arrived a few minutes later and ordered the pickets to let the trucks through.

Police said the men were standing on private property.

'EYES DOWN'

Cameramen Shun Queen

LONDON (Reuters) — Photographers staged a down-cameras strike when the Queen arrived here from Scotland today because they were kept 70 yards away.

About two dozen photographers waited to take press pictures when the Queen and Prince Philip returned from their Scottish holiday at Balmoral Castle.

Police kept the photographers well away from the point where the Queen left the train.

In protest, the photographers placed their cameras on the ground.

$100,000 Oat Fire

MOOSE JAW (CP) — Fire of undetermined origin Monday caused damage estimated at $100,000 to the oat mill of the Robin Hood Flour Co. plant in downtown Moose Jaw.

3 CANADIANS ABOARD MISSING UN PLANE

VIENTIANE, Laos (Reuters) — An aircraft

RCMP officers and strikers clash at a British American Oil Co. refinery on Burrard Inlet in Burnaby during the oil workers' strike, November 1965. Triggered by an illegal sit-down strike by a handful of workers in a single refinery, the dispute centred on automation and nearly erupted into a province-wide general strike. W.A.C. Bennett intervened at the eleventh hour to broker a settlement.

UFAWU march at the BC legislature, opposing court injunctions and the jailing of union secretary Homer Stevens and president Steve Stavenes, c. 1967. The labour leaders were jailed for nearly a year for defying a court injunction that they order striking Prince Rupert trawlers back to work.

Communist poster opposing Bill 33, the Mediation Commission Act, 1969. The BC Federation of Labour initially called for a boycott of the Mediation Commission, which was entrusted with far-reaching powers to intervene in labour disputes, and threatened a general strike to force the repeal of the legislation. However, divisions in labour's ranks – centring on tensions between established labour leaders and a more militant rank and file – prevented a unified working-class response.

BC Government Employees' Union (BCGEU) banner flown over the provincial legislature in Victoria, 15 December 1969. The banner refers to W.D. Black, provincial secretery under Bennett and therefore employer of all government workers. Two months earlier, the civil servants had transformed their association into a union, as they ramped up their campaign demanding 'Collective Bargaining Right Now!' This was granted in 1973, after the NDP had assumed the reins of government.

The British Columbia New Democratic Party legislative caucus, 1967. From left to right: (bottom row) Randolph Harding, Bob Strachan, Eileen Dailly, Bill Hartley, Leo Nimsick; (top row) Frank Calder, Fred Vulliamy, Dave Stupich, Tom Berger, Dr Ray Parkinson, Dave Barrett, Bob Williams, Ernest Hall, Alex MacDonald, Rae Eddie.

'peaceful coexistence' and the party's organizational functioning. Correspondence between the UBC Club and the City Committee cites Joe Irving's 'agreement with Fergus McKean's criticism of inter-class alliances put forward in "Communism versus Opportunism"' – the issue at the heart of the BC LPP leader's 1945 expulsion.[201] Like many disenchanted communists in the 1960s, Joe Irving joined the Trotskyist League for Socialist Action (LSA), which observed that the CPC was 'rapidly losing its last bases of support in the labor movement' and remained 'the servile instrument of the Soviet bureaucracy, wedded to the strategy of peaceful coexistence which marks off Canada, in the foreseeable future, as part of the capitalist realm.'[202] BC party units lamented waning member participation. 'There seems to be a lack of party participation in peace work,' the Delta-New Westminster regional committee noted, 'even though this is the number one question on the world agenda.'[203]

Ben Swankey, who served on the Provincial Committee, was appointed chair of a special 'Ideological Committee' that toured the BC clubs, hearing the views of the rank and file. Swankey recalls the anger of members at being excluded from decision-making. He developed his own criticisms of the party's internal functioning and the principle of democratic centralism. 'I fought hard for the elimination of democratic centralism, which I didn't think was very democratic,' Swankey recalls. At a National Convention in the late 1960s he found himself in the minority. 'The top leadership, they didn't like the idea at all.' Swankey retained his party membership, however, amid a growing awareness that 'decisions should be made in Canada, and not elsewhere.'[204]

The year 1968 produced a new wave of defections and expulsions, as the USSR again deployed force in Eastern Europe. Many BC members were appalled when Soviet tanks quashed moves to establish 'socialism with a human face' in Czechoslovakia. UFAWU secretary Homer Stevens circulated a letter from prison criticizing developments in Czechoslovakia and expressing confidence in the Alexander Dubcek government. 'It sounded to me that the Soviet Union was trying to dictate everything that was going on in Eastern Europe despite promising they weren't going to do that any more,' Stevens recalled. Shortly after his release, Stevens attended the 1968 BC convention where the tone of discussion prompted him to publicly resign from the party and walk out of the meeting, 'not because of events in Czechoslovakia but because of the actions of the party here.'[205] At this time, Stevens had already fallen out of favour with the provincial leadership, allowing his name to stand for nomination for provincial secretary, which implied replacing Morgan, who was ill. Stevens provided a seventeen-page explanation to the Provincial Committee outlining his disagreement with the CPSU and objections to the application of democratic centralism in the Canadian party. The committee dismissed Stevens's criticisms in predictable language, implicating him with the 'anti-Party group,' the City Committee dissidents who resigned *en masse* prior to a special convention in early 1969.[206] According to Ben Swankey:

> Homer was called an individualist. I think that's partly due to the fact that he didn't agree with the party sometimes. Which made him an individual and us right. Sometimes we accuse people in the trade-union movement of being 'individualists.' They may be quite right ... [Homer] had a very strong sense of democracy.[207]

Stevens was only the most high-profile member to leave the party during the Czechoslovakian crisis, though he returned two years later after concluding that the CPC was 'a human organization after all.'[208] Another BC dissident, Charlie Boylan, a UBC alumnus and editor of the YCL organ *Scan*, also left; accused of stealing funds, Boylan took the *Scan* subscription list and migrated toward Maoism and Hardial Bains's Communist Party of Canada (Marxist-Leninist).[209] Many BC members abandoned radical politics entirely. Jerry Lebourdais, a militant oil worker who was expelled with Jack Scott, 'became a hippy,' Swankey recalls. 'He found the struggle too hard.'[210]

Rush describes these 'major inner-party upheavals' of the 1960s as 'part of the consequences of the pressures on the Party arising from the Cold War' – a view echoed in the party's official history: 'the Cold War had cost the party an entire generation.'[211] Bill White, who left the LPP in 1949 amid charges of 'adventurism,' was more criticial, describing the party as a 'closed shop': 'The leadership has barely changed for thirty years and there's very little youth coming in. It's an old men's club where most of the members are life members. It's at a dead end.'[212] This lack of renewal in party ranks is apparent from an RCMP report on the 1963 Vancouver City Convention: delegates were on average forty-three years old and had belonged to the party for fifteen years – since 1948.[213]

The loss of the Communist Party's depression-era and wartime leaders – Fergus McKean, Malcolm Bruce, Bill White, Jack Scott, Scotty Neish, Homer Stevens – signalled its sharp decline in the Cold War years. According to White, 'there were hundreds like that. It's harder to think of guys who stayed in than it is guys who got out.'[214] In 1948, Tim Buck had written that the Communist Party 'has no interests whatsoever apart from the interests of the working people.'[215] However, evidence from BC suggests that Buck was wrong. The Communist Party, like all institutions – political or otherwise, left or right – had an institutional interest of self-preservation, which prevented a forthright assessment of the state of socialism in Russia and Eastern Europe, and encouraged authoritarian tendencies in the Canadian party. As Michels argued in his classic study of German social democracy, this institutional interest tended toward conservatism and a separation of leaders from the rank and file.[216] In the Communist Party, the Cold War combined with institutional pressures in a particularly devastating way. Persecution in the labour and peace movements placed the party on the defensive, which produced atrophy as opportunities for renewal of views and members were destroyed. Jack Phillips, communist secretary of the Vancouver Civic Outside Workers (now CUPE 15), reflected on this tension in BC's communist movement: 'We knew it wasn't perfect, but we were willing to overlook its imperfections because we felt it had a dynamism, it had a logic, and above all it had a soul. That was the soul of the people.'[217] The Communist Party, warts and all, helped sustain an oppositional working-class culture in Cold War BC.

CHAPTER THREE

Socialism Postponed

> There must be no doubt in the mind of any CCF member that the first task of a CCF administration will be the swift and ruthless removal of the major sources of wealth production from private hands to those of the community. It must be made clear that all our program of social services and economic expansion rests on that first bold revolutionary action.[1]
>
> Colin Cameron,
> President's report to 1947 BC CCF convention

While communists looked to the Soviet Union for inspiration, the Co-operative Commonwealth Federation (CCF) pursued the gradualist parliamentary path of the Tommy Douglas government in Saskatchewan and the Labour governments that rose to power in the United Kingdom, Australia, and New Zealand at the end of the Second World War. During the 1930s and 1940s – years of economic depression and war – socialism was embraced by a wide of layer of British Columbians as a realistic – indeed, a necessary – alternative to the capitalist system. Voters rallied behind the BC CCF, which formed the official opposition in the BC legislature in 1933 and captured a plurality of the popular vote in 1941, prompting the Coalition of Liberals and Conservatives. Conditions at home and abroad suggested that capitalism had broken down, a critique the pre-CCF Socialist Party of Canada (SPC) had promoted since the turn of the century. While they disagreed with communists on the necessity of force to transcend capitalism, CCFers embraced an ideology and an aggressive political program for a new social order. However, after 1945, as capitalist forces consolidated power and made concessions that adapted, and preserved, the capitalist system, while declaring *de facto* war on the USSR, the prospect of socialist victory appeared increasingly distant. 'Make no mistake about this,' warned Dorothy Gretchen Steeves, a former North Vancouver MLA (1934–45) and prominent leftist, in 1947: 'The present anti-Communist drive will become a drive against any organization and individual which threatens their vested interests and that means the CCF.'[2]

Within the BC CCF, some leaders and members adapted their ideology and strategy to this changed political climate. Others in the militant minority, however, refused. To these party militants, winning elections was not acceptable if it meant a sacrifice of principles. The old debate between 'catching votes' and 'making socialists,' which traced its lineage to the old Socialist Party, continued to demarcate ideological factions in the party.[3] Electoral defeat in 1949 was interpreted differently by the factions; the left pointed to 'opportunism,' while the right emphasized 'irresponsible statements' by the left.[4] Anti-communism in the postwar era 'induced a retreat from socialism,' Martin Robin concludes, bolstering centrists at the expense of the left.[5] Socialist and labour governments in Saskatchewan and other jurisdictions were confronted with the realities of governing in a capitalist world, at the height of the Cold War. Limited nationalizations were followed by more modest social-welfare policies.[6] These policies, which provided security against illness, unemployment, and old age, considerably improved the living and working conditions of the working class, but they fell short of the expectations of many CCF activists, who remained committed to large-scale socialization as part of the transition away from capitalism. Public pronouncements by national CCF leaders such as M.J. Coldwell – 'the consummate Cold War social democrat'[7] – inflamed leftists, who controlled the party organization in BC. In 1950, conflict between the left and right erupted at the National CCF Convention in Vancouver, spawning the Socialist Fellowship, a left-wing 'party within a party' that derived its name from a kindred British faction.

Mired in conflict, the BC CCF failed to capitalize on the collapse of the Liberal-Conservative Coalition. The upstart Social Credit party took advantage of the 1951 Elections Act amendments and a political vacuum to win the 1952 and 1953 elections. In 1954, this period of intense inner-party conflict culminated in the resignation of Rodney Young, one-time CCF MP and an outspoken leftist.[8] The BC CCF reached a nadir of electoral strength in 1956 – 28.3 per cent of the vote and 10 seats in the 52-seat legislature.[9] That year, the national CCF replaced the Regina Manifesto, with its pledge to not 'rest content until it has eradicated capitalism,' with the more modest Winnipeg Declaration of principles. 'Economic prosperity and cold-war hysteria generated a sense of social and political conservatism in the late forties and most of the fifties,' party stalwart David Lewis wrote in his memoirs.[10] The CCF retreated from socialism as it moved closer to organized labour, responding to electoral weakness with the New Party movement and the New Democratic Party in 1961.

Roots

Left-wing electoral strength was extended and consolidated in BC's regions as the twentieth century unfolded, sinking roots in industrial strongholds in urban and rural areas where the extraction and processing of the raw commodities of wood, fish, and minerals dominated economic life. From the lead-zinc smelter at Trail to the coal mines of Nanaimo to the sawmills of urban Vancouver, working-class people demonstrated a sustained refusal to accept the political leadership of their bosses. Leo Nimsick, Cranbrook MLA from 1949 and mines minister in the Barrett government, and Cedric Cox, who succeeded Ernest Winch as Burnaby MLA in 1957, were charter members of Mine-Mill Local 480 at Trail; Nimsick was on the bargaining committee that negotiated Local 480's first collective agreement in 1944.[11] In one corner of the province, the southeast, the coal economy gave rise to persistent class loyalties and BC's lone Labour MLA: Tom Uphill of Fernie, who served forty unbroken years in the legislature.[12]

Benefiting from enduring frontier characteristics and from an influx of class-conscious British immigrants, BC's working class developed a political culture that was independent from the old-line parties and collectivist in orientation. This politics found organizational expression in the Socialist Party, based in Vancouver, which elected several MLAs to the provincial legislature and imbued the CCF with a class-conscious, Marxist strain.[13] Throughout the 1940s and 1950s, the party was officially known as the BC-Yukon section of the CCF, indicating the late arrival of partisan politics in the northern frontier. In autumn 1948, party leader Harold Winch toured the Yukon and Northwest Territories, suggesting in a report to the national leadership that 'the people of the North feel rather neglected as citizens of Canada.'[14]

In the 1940s, the levers of power in the BC CCF were squarely in the hands of the Marxian left wing, embodied in the father-son team of Ernest and Harold Winch. These militants viewed themselves as standing to the left of the Communist Party, owing to the class collaborationism of communists beginning with the Popular Front era.[15] The defection of dissidents into the short-lived BC Constructive party in late 1930s had strengthened the control of the Winches, a bricklayer and an electrician respectively, who deftly positioned themselves as the guardians of BC Marxism.[16] Those who strayed too far to the left, however, such as Port Alberni socialist A.M. Stephen, who advocated a united front with communists, were expelled.[17] According to Walter Young,

> The chief figures in the movement in British Columbia were, without any doubt, committed socialists, but their commitment was no less self-seeking than that of any politician, however much they would lard their disagreements with pious statements of socialist dogma.[18]

Elaine Bernard argues, however, that it is wrong to assume that 'ideology is "invariably" a cover for personal conflict or personal ambition.'[19] As party dissident Doug Cameron recalled years later, the Winches used George Weaver – the foremost Marxist theoretician in the CCF – 'to gun down the intellectual left in the party.'[20] The chair of the party's Women's Committee described 'the presence of an aristocracy of old Socialists,' who created a hostile climate for those uneducated in the tenets of Marxism.[21]

The dominance of the left distinguished the BC CCF from the national party and other provincial sections. Members addressed one another in party meetings with the greeting 'Comrade,' reflecting traditions the CCF inherited from the old Socialist Party, which provoked scorn during the Cold War period.[22] Angus MacInnis, Vancouver South MP (1930–57), and Grace MacInnis, Vancouver-Burrard MLA (1941–5), MP (1965–74), and daughter of J.S. Woodsworth, frequently found themselves at odds with the BC section. In 1940, Angus had resigned from the CCF National Council, citing a lack of support from CCF leaders in BC.[23] A year later, he wrote to national secretary David Lewis, expressing concern with the otherworldly character of the BC party:

> I believe the CCF has at this time the greatest opportunity we have ever had if we know how to take advantage of it. The country is ripe for a lead that it will not get from either of the old parties ... We must, however, go out for a program that will have a close relation to reality, that will accept

> conditions as they are with all the imperfections and, if you like, contradictions which meet us on every hand. Out of this mess we must point the way which will take us step by step to the new social order.[24]

CCF MLA Laura Jamieson echoed this view, urging a departure from the party's Marxian roots: 'That early influence has persisted apparently to a great extent ... I think, however, the CCF in BC can and should take a more constructive action.'[25] The gap between the party and the world, identified by Zakuta, took longer to narrow in BC than in other provinces.[26]

Throughout its history, foreign policy and cooperation with the Communist Party were persistent sources of conflict in the BC CCF. Pitting elements in the provincial party against the national leadership and other provincial sections, a socialist perspective on foreign affairs surfaced on a range of issues: Canadian participation in the Second World War; the independence of India from Britain; cooperation with the Soviet Union; support for the United Nations; Canadian participation in NATO; the banning of atomic weapons; the Korean War; recognition of Red China; and Canadian and German rearmament.[27] Factions were drawn along the lines of 'left' and 'right,' but there was overlap and inconsistency in the stances of members and leaders. Predictably, the party newspapers – the *Federationist* and, after 1943, *CCF News* – were major battlegrounds, as were executive elections and policy debates at provincial and national conventions. By the end of the decade, the moderate faction was increasingly successful at curbing the power of the left, aided by the national leadership and the Cold War.

The Cold War and the CCF

The ideological shift in the CCF, nationally and provincially, was an uneven and protracted process. In January 1948, a *CCF News* correspondent objected to a provincial executive directive against picketing the *SS Colima*, 'which is being prepared to carry arms to the reactionary forces of Kuomintang China.'[28] The Victoria-Oak Bay CCF constituency association deplored 'the action of the federal government in sending arms to either side in the civil war in China.'[29] In May 1948, the BC CCF provincial convention went on record opposing the North Atlantic Treaty and elected Dorothy Steeves as provincial president.[30] A week later, alleged Trotskyist Rodney Young was elected CCF MP for Vancouver Centre, a development that inflamed moderates.[31] In August, delegates at the National CCF convention defeated, on a 56–94 vote, a resolution from the National Council opposing nationalization of the banks.[32] The same convention, however, overwhelmingly endorsed the European Recovery Plan (Marshall Plan), despite a Manitoba CCF resolution opposing the plan on grounds that it provided 'military aid to reactionary regimes to use against attempts to establish socialism in Europe.'[33] Rod Young was among those delegates attempting to bring federal policy in line with the Manitoba resolution. Also in 1948, the BC CCF readmitted Bert Herridge, Kootenay West MP, who had been expelled in 1945 for advocating cooperation with communists; the death of the sitting Coalition MLA, and an impending by-election in the working-class district, fuelled the party's rapprochement with Herridge and his 'People's CCF' organization.[34]

The growing distance between the BC CCF and national CCF leaders was evident when Steeves, BC CCF president and a former North Vancouver MLA, was prevented from providing a full report to the national convention. Widely acknowledged as the foreign policy expert in the CCF, Steeves authored the weekly *CCF News* column 'A Socialist View of World Affairs,' which declared in July 1948: 'A few years ago, it was easy for socialists to call for the liberation of colonial peoples. Today, in a two-bloc world, the problem is not so simple. The elimination of one imperialism may open the way for the introduction of a new brand of the same kind.'[35] Despite this ostensibly balanced stance, Angus MacInnis complained in a confidential letter to David Lewis that Steeves's columns were 'getting worse ... putting equal blame on the Western Powers and the Soviet Union,' indeed, 'the chief blame on the United States.' MacInnis asked that Lewis raise the matter with Coldwell and party chairman Frank Scott, as the world situation was 'too critical' for the CCF 'to be confused or frustrated or to be suspicious of the leaders in the movement.'[36] Lewis responded, lamenting the 'anti-Americanism' in Steeves's column and her opposition to rearmament and NATO, but his tone was more conciliatory. He proposed entering into a private correspondence with Steeves 'to bring the national point of view a little more clearly before her.'[37]

Ideological conflict in the CCF was influenced by the party's relations with the Communist Party.[38] According to Angus MacInnis, 'the hangover from our old pacifism and our hope of the Russian Revolution as a forerunner of socialism are muddling our thinking in the present international situation,' creating a following for leftists such as Steeves and Colin Cameron.[39] 'Unity to Elect a CCF Government,' the slogan unveiled by the LPP in 1948, elicited a mixed response in the CCF. John Price, an old labour militant from the Kootenay mining town of Silverton, traced a continuum between Marx and Engels's *Communist Manifesto*, the Soviet Constitution, and the CCF's Regina Manifesto: 'The CCF has done good work in exposing the pretences of the old line parties, its prospects for the future depend on unity with Communist and non-Communist workers against a common enemy ... It cannot do the job alone.'[40]

Such views were anathema to CCF leaders desperate to distance themselves from Soviet Communism. Outspoken leftist Colin Cameron – BC CCF past-president, former Comox MLA (1941–5), and future Nanaimo MP (1953–8, 1962–8) – wrote that it was 'the authoritarian structure of the communist parties which constitutes the gulf between socialists and communists today.'[41] Cameron's views were influenced by defeat in a 1948 Saanich by-election, where the Coalition effectively invoked the red bogey:

> The most brilliant stroke of business performed by the Coalition was the arrangement whereby the LPP candidate was withdrawn and the communists launched a high-powered campaign supposedly in support of the CCF ... [which] was no doubt responsible for turning away the few hundreds which were required for a CCF victory.[42]

George Weaver, the CCF's Marxist theoretician, provided a scathing attack on the Soviet brand of communism, which 'appropriated to itself the name Communist' and thus 'deluded the workers of all countries, and has, moreover, put into the hands of the bourgeoisie a whip.'[43] Some CCFers, however, objected to Weaver's attack. 'Maybe Weaver's wrong ideas and self-centred egotism had something to do with the CCF debacle in Saanich and Cariboo,' Mrs J.H. Hodges of New Westminster wrote in the *CCF News*. 'You know common people don't like to be talked down to, as though they were not intelligent. We like the CCF paper and will vote CCF, but we think Weaver and his ilk are a detriment instead of a help.'[44] Anticipating the phenomenon that would later be called McCarthyism, the *CCF News* issued a warning:

> The fact that we condemn communism should not divert us from the realization that the democratic liberties which constitute the only worthwhile heritage of nineteenth century capitalism are now in danger of being destroyed in order to perpetuate the power of a ruling class.[45]

Even avowed anti-communist Angus MacInnis recognized the danger inherent in the Cold War's ideological assault; in April 1948, he spoke out in the House of Commons against proposed amendments to the Criminal Code that would have outlawed the Communist Party 'not because they have committed illegal acts, but because they have ideas which we do not like.'[46]

In organized labour, the White Bloc challenge of 1948 strengthened the position of CCF trade unionists, but failed to eliminate communist leadership in several powerful unions, including the UFAWU and Mine-Mill. MacInnis described the 1948 TLC convention, held in Victoria, as 'a great disappointment,' and confided to Lewis that the 'CCF following in the AF of L is not strong enough to make any impression.' In contrast, 'the influence of the Communists is very strong, and the amazing thing is to find the Liberal and Conservative members of the Executive and of the unions working with them.'[47] A year later, however, CCFer Tom Alsbury, a school principal and future Vancouver mayor, won the chairmanship of the AFL-affiliated Vancouver Trades and Labour Council's (VLTC) Press Committee, making him editor of the *Labor Statesman* newspaper. 'It was thought that the old time trade unionists and the CCF could defeat the LPP candidates,' Alsbury informed Grace MacInnis. He described his new role as a 'key position,' since the editor had 'plenty of influence in writing editorials and selecting material to go into the paper.'[48] The next year, Alsbury was elected VTLC vice-president.[49] When communist delegates from the UFAWU were denied the right to contest council offices, a delegate named Rigby questioned whether the statement 'To each the political party of his Choice' should continue to adorn the *Labor Statesman*'s masthead.[50]

Alsbury, the MacInnises, and their allies in the 'moderate' faction were no less committed to improving the conditions of BC's working class, but they objected to the strident statements and radical resolutions of the left wing, which they considered harmful to the CCF's electoral objectives. Between 1945 and 1949, the BC CCF won only one of six provincial by-elections.[51] Two federal by-election victories, including the defeat of W.A.C. Bennett in Yale, failed to stem the perception that a change in policy was needed.[52] The drop in CCF support in the provincial and federal elections of June 1949, and the loss of seats, appeared to confirm that BC voters were not ready for socialism. In the 15 June 1949 provincial election the CCF's share of the popular vote dipped from 37 to 35 per cent, and its representation fell from 11 seats to 7. The total number of CCF voters, however, increased by nearly 70,000.[53]

While the LPP contested only two seats, preventing a split in the left-wing vote, the emergence of Social Credit candidates in several ridings introduced a new dynamic that would emerge as a major obstacle to CCF success.[54] After the election, Saskatchewan premier Tommy Douglas wrote Grace MacInnis, lamenting 'the reduction in numbers and the loss of some former members.'[55] Two weeks later, voters returned to the polls for a federal election. CCF support increased from 29.4 per cent in 1945 to 31.5 per cent, but the party was reduced from 6 BC seats to 3, as the Coalition strategy of running either a Liberal or Conservative candidate was extended to several federal ridings. Nationally, the CCF fell from 32 seats to 13.[56]

In a post mortem, Lorne Ingle, national research secretary, could not 'escape the feeling that some events in British Columbia contributed more to our losses than any other thing we did.' He cited opposition to NATO and 'the disruptive work of the Communists in Trade Unions that should have been overwhelmingly on our side.' Ingle was losing tolerance 'for views divergent to the majority opinion in our party.'[57] Eugene Forsey, CCL research director, expressed similar views in a letter to Grace MacInnis, regretting her defeat in Vancouver South: 'It must be sickening to have a seat where you really have reason to hope, and then to miss out, partly because of some of the peculiar "problems" of the BC CCF.'[58] Angus MacInnis conceded this point: 'The CCF did not build itself up in the minds of the people as an alternative – opposition, even. I regret to say that responsibility for that must in large measure be assumed by the movement in British Columbia … We did everything we possibly could to lose both elections.'[59]

War on the Left

> I think the next couple of years are crucial for the CCF. It is no accident, in my opinion, that our membership is falling. People are not going to follow a party that doesn't know where it is going itself. There cannot be two different sets of leaders, each going in a different direction.[60]
>
> Angus MacInnis, April 1950

In the aftermath of the 1949 defeats, the campaign began in earnest to unseat left-wing influence in the BC CCF. Applying tactics that had effectively eroded LPP strength in organized labour, powerful forces in the national CCF and BC section turned against dissidents in their own ranks.[61] This effort was imbued with a sense of urgency, as the party's biennial National Convention was scheduled to take place in Vancouver in July 1950. At a National Council meeting in Winnipeg in January 1950, BC delegates were ridiculed for proposing changes to the national constitution that played into the hands of the leftists, who were anxious 'to drive a wedge between British Columbia and the rest of Canada.'[62] At a provincial council meeting the next month, the left maintained the upper hand, accusing the MacInnises of being 'secretly engaged in a strong rightist sabotage thrust at the CCF's vitals.'[63] Gladys Webster, a moderate, commented: 'I can only learn how to meet these tactical moves in the hard school of experience':

> Colin, Rod, and cohorts watch carefully and make their moves skillfully. Things happened for them at the beginning and end when the attendance was scanty. Then, far too many able debaters were missing – MacInnises, A. Webster, F. McKenzie, L. Jamieson. I had phoned Laura and had coaxed Arnold to come – but they didn't.[64]

In the Burrard constituency, the right was more successful, easily outnumbering leftists in proposing of a slate of officers for the upcoming provincial convention at Penticton.

These preparations paid off. Bruce Woodsworth described the proceedings in a letter to his sister and brother-in-law: 'In a nutshell the convention from our standpoint was a great success because *we* won – the Cameron pseudo-revolutionaries were routed.'[65] Controversy over the Steelworkers' raid on Mine-Mill Local 480 at Trail, which had threatened to erupt at the convention, was averted when two Trail CCF Club delegates were prevented from speaking.[66] Woodsworth attributed 'the moderates' success largely to the spadework which [the MacInnises] did during the past year, plus the carrying out of carefully laid plans by a large number of clubs both at the Coast and in the Interior.'[67] The right took all but two executive positions (Rod Young as second vice-president and Dorothy Steeves as National Council rep); however, late in the evening, following a debate on NATO and disarmament, the left succeeded in passing a resolution that placed the BC CCF on record 'opposing any further expenditures on arms and urges the CCF members of the House of Commons to voice this opposition to arms expenditures.' Delegates voted to forward this resolution to the upcoming National Convention 'for favourable consideration by that body.'[68] Upon learning of the resolution, Angus MacInnis regretted not having attended the Penticton convention, and felt that 'Our delegates are to be criticized for not attending the evening session in larger numbers. They should know by this time that the disrupters in the movement will take advantage of occasions such as this to get resolutions through that they could not get through if there were a full attendance of delegates.' He stressed the importance of electing sympathetic delegates to the National Convention, to prevent a reversal of the progress that had been made 'in eliminating obstructors.'[69]

As the National Convention approached, Grace wrote to David Lewis, informing him that 'the Steeves-Young axis' had been working hard, and had 'more than 50% of the BC delegates on their side.'[70] Nonetheless, they were 'losing fast and they know it.' Grace advised caution among national party leaders, suggesting an outburst from Coldwell or other officers 'would be absolutely fatal to our hopes of making the split come where it should – in the BC delegation.' In light of the disarmament resolution, conflict was inevitable. 'National Office pressure would be the worst thing,' she warned.[71] The left, for its part, was confident: 'I think we can keep Gracie in order, even if we have to raise the ashes of her father to do it,' Steeves confided to Cameron, as ally Ernie Winch prepared a special convention-edition *CCF News* article on J.S. Woodsworth's 'proletarian apprenticeship' on the docks of Vancouver, entitled 'Birth of a Socialist.'[72] In the midst of this manoeuvring, the Langford CCF Club laid charges against the Sooke Club, which had adopted a resolution urging CCF affiliation to the Trotskyist Fourth International.[73]

The 1950 National CCF Convention opened in Vancouver at the end of July. The Korean War had broken out a month earlier, and the national executive, meeting prior to the convention, endorsed the UN action, a stance Coldwell confirmed in a press conference on the eve of the convention.[74] This pre-emptive strike by the national leadership inflamed the left. But BC delegates and other dissidents were in the minority. A resolution was passed rejecting the Stockholm 'Ban-the-Bomb' petition, which demanded 'the unconditional banning by all countries of the atomic weapons.' BC MLAs Ernie Winch, Leo Nimsick, and Arthur Turner had signed the petition, which was circulated by the Canadian Peace Congress, but the moderates viewed the Congress as an LPP front and would have nothing to do with it.[75] Another major issue decided in favour of the 'moderates' was a resolution to draft a revised statement of principles, signalling a move away from the overtly anti-capitalist language of the Regina Manifesto, which committed the CCF to eradicate capitalism.[76] Finally, the convention approved constitutional amendments 'that will allow the N.E. [National Executive] to assume the powers of discipline of the Provincial sections in the event that the P.E. [Provincial Executive] does not take such action. In plain words it means now that the N.E. can compel the P.E. to take any action that the Coldwell gang wishes.'[77] The most graphic display of ideological polarization in the party surrounded the appearance of a pamphlet titled *Is the Labour Party the Way to Socialism?*, which led to a confrontation between BC leftist Eve Smith and national secretary David Lewis, and Smith's dismissal as chair of the BC section's Political Education Committee.[78] After the convention, Lorne Ingle, who had been elected to succeed Lewis as national secretary, wrote to Grace MacInnis, thanking her 'for the excellent help and advice you gave before the convention started.'[79]

The BC left wing was inflamed by the convention proceedings, particularly the treatment of Eve Smith. Eighty delegates and observers held their own meeting across the street in the ballroom of the Georgia Hotel, and the next month, at a Left Wing Conference in Vancouver, they formed a Socialist Caucus of the CCF. Rod Young moved a motion to 'disaffiliate from the CCF,' arguing that it was 'impossible to put forward Marxian ideas within the Movement,' but a large majority favoured remaining in the CCF.[80] Smith acted as secretary of the group, which soon adopted the name Socialist Fellowship, after a kindred faction in the British Labour Party. Prominent CCFers took an interest in the Fellowship, including Steeves, Cameron, Wallis Lefeaux, future provincial leader Bob Strachan, future MLAs Bill Hartley and David Stupich, and railroader Lefty Morgan.[81] The Fellowship met regularly through 1950 and early 1951, establishing strongholds in the Stanley Park and Hillcrest CCF Clubs and local units in Victoria, Nanaimo, Kamloops, Hedley, and Trail; agitation extended into the Co-operative Commonwealth Youth Movement (CCYM), which was abolished by the BC CCF executive the next February.[82] Resolutions were sent to clubs and constituency associations throughout BC and Canada, and efforts were made to establish a dues base. The journal *Material for Thought*, published by Lefeaux, was endorsed as the Fellowship's official organ.[83]

Cameron, however, expressed concern with the group's direction, seeing its purpose as socialist 'education within the mass of the movement, not the organisation of a separatist movement.'[84] Cameron's position was likely influenced by a threat from Alsbury, who sat on the provincial executive, to have him expelled.[85] According to Cameron, the Fellowship's activities were creating 'a furtive and conspiratorial atmosphere.' If the left acted strategically, it could emerge out of the

January provincial council meeting 'in control of the BC section's policies,' Cameron believed, but the present direction, such as a resolution critical of the UN, would allow the reactionaries 'to come out stronger than ever.'[86] Cameron's fears were confirmed. Following the January meeting, provincial secretary Jessie Mendels provided a detailed report outlining the Fellowship's activities and plan of organization, exposing the left to charges of being 'a disruptive inner caucus.' The right had been in a position where it could have been 'completely routed,' Cameron felt, but the Fellowship had put the left in a false position and on the defensive.[87]

The moderates – Grant MacNeil, Jessie Mendels, Gladys Webster, Arnold Webster, Alex MacDonald, Frank McKenzie, Laura Jamieson, Tom Alsbury, and others – focused their efforts on 'building the anti-wrecking machine' in Burrard, where the Fellowship was recruiting new members and pushing for a motion of censure against Mendels.[88] They met discreetly on Saturday nights to formulate strategy.[89] MacNeil, provincial president, confided to Grace MacInnis that 'our fight at the moment is to prevent the Fellowship gaining complete control of the next Provincial Convention.'[90] In March, he succeeded in having a resolution approved by the provincial executive, declaring that membership in 'the Socialist Fellowship is an offence against the Constitution of the CCF, punishable by expulsion'; this move won unanimous approval of the National Council but was rejected by the BC provincial council.[91] MacNeil alleged that the Trotskyist RWP was attempting to infiltrate the CCF through the Fellowship.[92] Laura Jamieson advocated a hard line, wishing to 'name specific people and have them expelled,' including the entire Stanley Park Club. If the convention got out of hand, she proposed having a national officer 'step in and more or less take charge ... They are going to blame us and claim we are dictatorial whatever we do ... We might as well be hung for a sheep as a lamb, especially if being hung (or hanged) is the price of saving the CCF in BC.'[93] Jamieson's hard-line stance was favoured by Grace MacInnis.[94] However, Harold Winch, BC CCF leader, sought to reconcile the warring factions, advising provincial council delegates in April to 'forget everything and start out fresh,' which moderates believed contributed to 'the defeat of the executive' recommendation against the Fellowship. MacNeil, Alsbury, and Alex Macdonald visited Victoria to rake Winch over the coals; at a meeting in Winch's apartment, attended by the entire CCF caucus (excluding Leo Nimsick and Frank Calder), MLAs promised to go out to the constituencies to ensure 'good delegates are sent to the Convention.'[95]

The Fellowship controversy was related to ongoing struggles against BC's red unions, which created tension in the CCF legislative caucus. In Trail, the epicentre of Steel's 1950 raid on Mine-Mill, Trotskyist Aubrey Burton observed that 'the CCF has been virtually split in this working class city by the union raiding tactics of their CCL leadership and the repercussions may well cost the CCF their remaining influence throughout the whole of the Kootenays.'[96] Nimsick, CCF MLA for Cranbrook and a charter member of Local 480, threatened to vote against the caucus to prevent CCF interference in the Steel-Mine-Mill fight. While the Labor Relations Board had disallowed Steel's application for certification, CCF MLAs were 'preparing their case against the Labor Relations Board,' MacNeil informed Grace MacInnis. Nimsick demanded a halt to this interference, a position 'supported by Gretchen [Steeves] and evidently by the Fellowship,' which alleged 'that the trade union struggle against Communist domination is undemocratic.'[97] Fellowship supporters threatened to raise the matter at the 1951 provincial convention, believing that the CCF's 'further cooperation with CCL-PAC [Canadian Congress of Labour-Political Action Committee] will "water down our Socialism."'[98]

In the Fellowship, already strained relationships were amplified by threatened disciplinary action. 'The Fellowship, due to diverse elements, is on the verge of falling apart anyway, and this might be the fatal blow,' MacNeil predicted.[99] Some leftists, such as Steeves, Cameron, and Hartley, began distancing themselves from the Fellowship and returned to the CCF fold.[100] Others, such as Eve and John Smith, and Doug Cameron, left the party.[101] One dissident CCFer in New Westminster, Georges LaFrance, threw away his membership card, suggesting his belief 'in revolutionary political action' was 'completely incompatible with the reform political action of the CCF'; LaFrance planned to join either the Socialist Party of Canada or the LPP.[102] By the time the provincial convention opened in May 1951, the Fellowship had officially disbanded.[103] MacNeil was re-elected president, cementing the power of the right, though Jamieson lost her position on the executive and Steeves retained her seat.[104] Writing at the time, Eve Smith succinctly described the ideological conflict in the CCF:

> This movement must decide whether or not it is going to be a socialist movement, or merely a social democratic party. Those terms now represent two schools of thought that I know we all understand quite well. I am not going to waste our time giving definitions of Marxian Socialism and

democratic socialism, except to say that Marxian Socialism is essentially democratic.[105]

By November 1951, the right had finally succeeded in wresting control of *CCF News* from Steeves. 'Gretchen says we haven't heard the last of it,' Laura Jamieson wrote to Grace. 'They fight every inch, naturally. *CCF News* was about their last citadel.'[106]

The 1952 Election and Realignment of the Party System

The left and right wings of the BC CCF polarized on the eve of a generational upheaval in partisan alignments. The Liberal-Conservative Coalition, born a decade earlier to contain the CCF's electoral threat, imploded. In the spring session of 1951, Attorney General Gordon Wismer, a Liberal, introduced amendments to the Elections Act implementing the controversial single transferable ballot.[107] According to future Liberal leader Pat McGeer, the device was intended 'to keep the socialists out of office.'[108] An October 1951 Esquimalt by-election, the final count before the new system came into force, illustrated the consequences of divisions among free-enterprise forces: CCFer Frank Mitchell took 38 per cent of the vote, defeating Liberal, Conservative, and Social Credit candidates to capture a seat never before held by the CCF.[109] Harold Winch lambasted the Elections Act amendments, which were designed to prevent such an outcome: 'It is without doubt the most ridiculous Elections Act in the democratic world.'[110]

The Coalition's collapse coincided with renewed interest in labour political action. The CCL's 1951 convention, held in Vancouver, had reaffirmed support for the CCF, and also urged unification with the rival TLC.[111] However, no formal mechanism existed for labour affiliation. Trade unionists such as MacNeil, Alsbury, and George Home held leading party positions, and MLAs including the Winches, Nimsick, and Arthur Turner retained close union connections, but the BC CCF operated at arm's length from BC unions. Moderates sought to strengthen labour ties while the left viewed such moves with suspicion. 'Your prediction that Grant would turn the CCF into a union machine is now coming true,' Steeves told Cameron in June 1951. That month, the provincial executive bypassed the CCF Trade Union Committee and formed a special committee to 'study' trade union relations, particularly for candidate nominations. Steeves viewed this as an attempt 'to eliminate people with whom Tom Alsbury "can't work,"' and prevent leftists including Cameron and Stupich from winning Vancouver Island nominations. Moderates, however, claimed the committee was necessary to curb a Liberal plan, developed in concert with the IWA, to run 'independent Labour' candidates against the CCF.[112]

Tensions in the labour movement contributed to the CCF's 1952 defeat. That spring, Labour MLA Tom Uphill of Fernie invited every BC union local to a Vancouver conference to consider a 'united program' for the election of labour candidates, under the aegis of a Labour Representation Committee. CCFers saw an attempt to forge a new Labour Party, but UFAWU business agent Alex Gordon insisted the conference was merely intended 'to draft a program' 'without creating further divisions in the general political situation in the Province.' Fishermen's secretary Homer Stevens, a communist, cautioned that union locals should require 'overwhelming support' before endorsing a candidate or party, to avert a situation that would 'split any local down the middle.'[113] In the June 1952 election, the CCF won a plurality of votes, but under the single-transferrable ballot Social Credit edged out the CCF, 19 seats to 18. Importantly, W.A.C. Bennett claimed he was in possession of a signed letter from Uphill, indicating that the Labour MLA, eyeing the Mines portfolio, would prop up a Social Credit government.[114]

The expanded CCF caucus of eighteen grew increasingly restless with the leadership of Harold Winch, who had held the post continuously since Rev. Robert Connell's defection in 1936.[115] 'There has been a feeling that we were close to power and that any ineptitude in meeting events might set us back ten or twenty years,' Frank McKenzie observed. 'I am sure that Harold has felt this very keenly.'[116] Tension was apparent even before the legislature reconvened. Winch favoured delaying formulation of the CCF house strategy until Social Credit's strategy had been unveiled, but the caucus and provincial executive disagreed. Earlier in 1952, Winch had suffered a personal rebuke when the CCF provincial convention called for a rollback of hospital insurance premiums despite his advice to the contrary. On a more personal level was Winch's ongoing battle with alcoholism and other medical problems. During the 1952 campaign, he developed inflammation of the tendons in his arm, a condition that required sedatives. In January 1953, he embarrassed CCF MLAs and officers when he attended a meeting with British Labour MP (and future prime minister) Harold Wilson in an intoxicated state. Leading CCF members were 'convinced that the CCF is not strong enough under Harold's leadership to win an election,' Arnold Webster confided to Angus MacInnis.[117] However, in March 1953, MacNeil observed that there 'is a good atmosphere in the caucus. Harold is showing up well, and is this year taking time to work with the new members.'[118] 'As a parliamentarian he is without a peer in the house,' Frank McKenzie wrote, and 'no one has ever stumped this province as thoroughly as Harold did.'[119]

In late March 1953 Winch resigned in a sea of controversy.[120] Bennett had engineered his own defeat in the house, and Winch visited Lieutenant Governor Clarence Wallace, a shipyard owner, offering to assume the premiership with Uphill's backing. Wallace, however, declined Winch's offer and dissolved the legislature. Neither the CCF caucus nor the provincial executive had approved Winch's action and CCF whip Arthur Turner publicly chastised the provincial leader. The executive did not ask Winch to reconsider his resignation, and instead nominated Vancouver parks board trustee and school principal Arnold Webster for the leadership, a move unanimously approved at the CCF convention two weeks later, in April 1953.[121] The CCF was in poor shape to fight another election.

Social Credit was re-elected with a legislative majority in June 1953 – with 28 seats to 14 CCF, 4 Liberal, 1 Conservative, and the indomitable Uphill as a Labour MLA – and promptly repealed the Elections Act changes, cementing the realignment of BC's party system.[122] The CCF remained a competitive electoral force, but the failure to win power after the demise of the Coalition, and the loss of votes and seats to Social Credit, unleashed a prolonged period of recrimination and self-doubt. The party's improved showing in the August 1953 federal election – from three BC MPs to seven, including Colin Cameron in Comox and Harold Winch in Vancouver East – was marred by Rod Young's candidacy in Vancouver Centre, which the provincial executive had disallowed but the provincial convention endorsed.[123] 'I am sure that we have not heard the last of the Rod Young matter,' McKenzie confided to Grace MacInnis.[124] Indeed, they hadn't. At the 1954 provincial convention in Vancouver, Young declared defiantly that he was 'proud to have people tell me I'm a Communist' and knew 'at least fifty former Communists in the CCF.'[125] Young's remarks were reported in the press, and in an attack led by Alsbury, an emergency resolution was debated requesting Young's resignation from the CCF; while the motion was defeated 52–55, the provincial executive subsequently suspended Young on the eve of the National CCF convention, prompting his resignation.[126] According to Elaine Bernard, Young personified the ideological struggle in the party, and his resignation signified the demise of the BC CCF's Marxian tradition:

> The charges of irresponsibility and vanity leveled against Young were designed, or at least served, to disguise very real political differences under a covering of personal abuse. It further contributed to the right wing's ability to make the left the scapegoat for the party's failures. Rod Young became the stick with which the right successfully beat the left.[127]

David Lewis, however, maintains that Rod Young 'did a lot of harm during his years of activity.'[128] The CCF left had become a casualty of circumstance and the Cold War.

Debate raged in the CCF as the left descended into a subordinate role in the party. At the 1955 BC convention – the largest since 1940 – where two leftists (Steeves and Ernest Winch) won election to the six-member provincial executive and the trial of twenty-three North Vancouver members stirred controversy, the left and right wings offered conflicting interpretations of the crisis facing the party.[129] David Stupich, a former Fellowship member who was defeated for the presidency, lambasted the moderates' 'Program of Action' as an attempt 'to reassure capitalism that it has nothing to fear from the election of a CCF government.'[130] Meeting *in camera*, delegates debated Trotskyist infiltration, highlighted by the circulation of the mimeographed sheet *Box 16*, named after a Vancouver post office box.[131] The ruling group attributed the party's electoral decline to the loss of members in 1950 and 1951, which it blamed on the Socialist Fellowship:

> In 1952 the opportunity arose for the CCF to bring to government in this province the strength, knowledge and skill we had been preparing for 19 years. Outwardly it appeared that the CCF was the only party capable of picking up the reins dropped by the senile Coalition. The truth was that our party has been bled by the Socialist Fellowship ... A few more votes for the two CCF candidates in a single riding, Vancouver-Burrard, would have resulted in the formation of a CCF government and could have changed the course of British Columbia history. Those extra votes would have been won, had Vancouver-Burrard not been weakened by the long Fellowship struggle in the constituency. There were other ridings, too, which could have been won, but were lost by narrow margins because of the havoc wrought in 1950 and 1951.[132]

Left-wing CCFers, associated with the *Box 16* group, advanced a starkly different analysis, grounded in a long-range view of CCF history:

> The greatest danger to our movement has never been from forces outside it, but rather from a tendency toward disintegration and decay from within ... The Co-operative Commonwealth Federation was just that. A *federation* of many groups and sub-groups *united by their intention* of achieving social ownership and control of the means of wealth production but *divided* sharply by their knowledge or ignorance of the class nature of society, the nature of capitalism and the nature of the historical process by which man advanced.[133] [emphasis in original]

The left pointed to the impact of the Cold War in the BC CCF:

> the instruments through which the base of the Movement expresses itself have been sadly weakened by the inroads of war hysteria; the trend towards conservative attitudes as a result of the long sustained false prosperity of a 'war economy' and its twin brother 'cold war economy' has further enabled careerists to entrench themselves in office. Yet despite appearances, they feel insecure.[134]

Though highly coloured with the bias of an aggrieved faction and the sting of defeat, this criticism was valid. The 'war hysteria' and relative prosperity of the postwar period *did* change the CCF. In provincial and federal politics, as Walter Young argued, the CCF changed from a depression-era protest movement to a professionalized political party.[135] As Zakuta pointed out, this process of institutionalization altered the relationship between members and leaders, and moderated the party's political program.[136]

In the midst of the Fellowship controversy and as the Korean War strained his own relations with the national party, Angus MacInnis fell ill, possibly with intestinal cancer.[137] He reflected on the state of the CCF in a letter to Coldwell:

> If the party is not to fade out, as all third parties in Canada have done, we must get down to sound thinking and hard work ... First we must find why the aspirations of the people do not seem to go beyond the status quo, that is, the policies of the Liberal party. We must try to find why the prestige of the CCF has fallen since 1948 ... There is a sort of deadly apathy

that has to be overcome. In the early days of our movement there were two things that spurred our people to action. There was, first, the deplorable condition caused by the depression and second, the idealism of the new society. The first of these has disappeared with the prosperity of the war which has continued into the present, despite high prices. But the new society seems so far away. They are discouraged and are not prepared to do the hard work which is necessary to build a socialist society.[138]

Nadir

In the mid-1950s, the BC CCF reached its organizational and electoral nadir. Consumed by a Cold War struggle against its Marxian left wing, the CCF failed to take advantage of the collapse of the Liberal-Conservative Coalition. Realignment of BC's party system left the CCF no closer to power. In March 1956, Arnold Webster resigned as BC CCF leader.[139] The Vancouver school principal and parks board trustee had struggled from the outset. After his inaugural speech as Vancouver East MLA, Webster confided to Angus MacInnis that 'the whole atmosphere of the Legislature leaves me unimpressed and unhappy.'[140] In 1955, Dorothy Steeves wrote that 'Arnold is discouraged, he knows he isn't fitting the bill ... he would be better off to go back to teaching, but who would come in his place?'[141] When the BC CCF executive withdrew a forestry brief calling for socialization, under IWA pressure against any radical moves,[142] Steeves expressed a loss of faith in the party to which she had devoted her life since the early 1930s:

I feel utterly down. The CCF has become nothing, a ghost. If we got beaten through standing for something, it wouldn't be so awful, but it is because we have no principles any more. Well, this is my last election, I shall have to reorganize my life in some way. Let the rightists have it, I'm not going to stand for executive positions any more, let them go to hell in their own way. This forestry business is the last straw.[143]

The *Pacific Tribune* adopted a similar view in February 1956:

CCF members, from Arnold Webster down, have made the fatal political error of battling the Socreds on their chosen grounds. They have been content, in the main, to challenge isolated statements and items in the Throne and budget speeches, instead of boldly attacking the government on its whole program of giving away the province's natural resources.[144]

A month later, Webster resigned and the CCF was in the throes of a leadership race. Bob Strachan, a British-born carpenter and Cowichan-Newcastle MLA since 1952, won the caucus's endorsement after Randolph Harding, Kaslo-Slocan MLA, declined to run. Strachan easily won the leadership at an April 1956 convention.[145] 'The CCF seems to have trouble deciding whether it is still socialist or not,' the *Vancouver Sun* observed, describing as 'a compromise' the selection of Strachan, a self-described 'militant socialist' who advocated policies that 'were not particular to militant socialism.'[146] While the Trotskyist *Workers Vanguard* challenged the BC CCF to 'become a party of the working class or a withered arm of outworn middle class liberalism,' other forces were pushing the CCF in moderate directions.[147] Moves were afoot at the national level to make CCF policy amenable to the merged Canadian Labour Congress (CLC).

The Regina Manifesto was a 'millstone' around M.J. Coldwell's neck, an Achilles heel in an era when political discourse was constrained by Cold War biases. Anti-communism cast an indiscriminate brush over all sectors of progressive thought, smearing the CCF's democratic program with allegations of totalitarianism more properly attributed to apologists of Stalinist Russia. National CCF leaders and their BC allies, like labour and socialist politicians in Europe and other liberal democracies, were prepared to abandon the scope of socialization envisioned in 1933, accepting a mixed economy that allowed room for private enterprise. To the Marxian remnants in the BC CCF, however, this willingness to compromise with capitalism was viewed as treason, an opportunistic attempt to 'catch votes' and abandon that long-held strategy of 'making socialists,' the development of socialist consciousness among a majority of BC voters. Social democracy groped for a short-cut to socialism that didn't exist, Marxists claimed, replacing socialist aims with reformed liberal ones. Aubrey Burton of Trail, a civic worker and member of the Trotskyist RWP, wrote to the *CCF News* in 1949 objecting to 'the tendency to water down our socialism':

> There is a danger to the CCF as it grows larger, and since it is a mass party, to absorb discontented ex-Liberals and mere social reformers at best and some outright political opportunists. These sort constitute a danger to our party, a very real danger, by their tactics of spreading their compromise-with-capitalism attitude, and it can only be resisted by a thorough educational program based on the aims and principles laid down in the Regina Manifesto.[148]

The debate over the Regina Manifesto struck at the root of CCFers' vision of the future society and represented a major turning point in the party's history.

In 1943, BC CCF leader Harold Winch had attracted national media attention when he declared in a Calgary speech that a CCF government would respond with the full force of the law to those who opposed its policies. Lending credence to allegations of the CCF's dictatorial designs, Winch reportedly warned, 'If capitalism says "No", then we know the answer – so did Russia.'[149] Socialization was hotly debated at the 1944 CCF convention in Montreal, where BC delegates led by Winch and Cameron helped defeat an attempt at conciliation with private enterprise.[150] However, at the 1950 Vancouver convention, delegates approved a resolution instructing the National Council to prepare an appendix to the Regina Manifesto, 'a statement of democratic socialist principles as applied to Canada and the world today.'[151] Coldwell told delegates that the concept of the class struggle was outdated and praised a similar policy review at the International Socialist Conference in Copenhagen in June 1950, which resulted in the Frankfurt Declaration.[152] Ernest Winch, however, declared that 'as long as the Regina Manifesto stands as an expression of the principles of the CCF we are safe.'[153] Cameron went further, accusing national leaders of doing 'irreparable damage to the socialist movement in BC,' and asserting that 'the class war is here and it won't be over until exploitation of the human race is over.'[154] Aubrey Burton wrote after the convention that:

> In return for lavish praise from the capitalist press they attempt to eradicate not the last vestiges of capitalism but rather the last remaining vestiges of socialist thought and principles within the CCF and reduce this once proud creation of the militant working-class under the defiant leadership of J.S. Woodsworth, to a petty imitation of the Liberal party.[155]

Despite the Vancouver decision to prepare a new statement of principles, disagreement among leaders and rank-and-file members, particularly in Saskatchewan and BC, prevented the issue from resurfacing at the 1952 and 1954 National conventions. Coldwell raised the matter at a January 1955 National Council meeting, but little progress was made.[156]

In January 1956, the National Council again debated the crisis facing the party. Tommy Douglas, the only provincial leader to win an election, identified a world reaction 'against the things in which we believe,' suggesting the 'tide was running with us' a decade earlier but had turned against the CCF. Capitalists had learned a great deal, applying Keynesian techniques 'to prevent violent fluctuation.' When the tide was running out, the 'movement must be deepened and broadened,' Douglas argued, making socialists who could win mass support in the trade unions, farm organizations, and cooperatives. He noted that beneath the veneer of prosperity and conservatism problems were mounting, such as fabulous wealth and automation. The time was nearing when the tide would turn again, and the CCF would have to bring other organizations – farmer, cooperative, labour – 'into a new alignment.'[157] Others, such as Angus MacInnis, insisted that socialism was 'not a state but a process' and that the CCF couldn't run the industries it said it would socialize. The CCF had to base its program 'on today,' on what people wanted today. William Irvine, veteran MP for the Cariboo in northern BC, who had sat beside Woodsworth in the 1921 Parliament, said it was 'not practicable to establish [a] socialist movement without a broad, mass industrial base.' His colleagues laid too much emphasis on electoral success, and instead should emphasize the 'kind of society we want.' Labour lawyer David Lewis closed the debate, arguing that capitalism, 'though still detestable, is not static.' The Regina Manifesto's assumptions were no longer valid, and people were frightened of the party's 'ultimate socialization objectives.'[158]

The outcome of this debate was, of course, the abandonment of the Regina Manifesto. The National Council appointed a committee to produce a final draft declaration of principles for the upcoming convention in Winnipeg. At the August 1956 convention, delegates overwhelmingly approved the revised statement, with the *Winnipeg Free Press* reporting that opponents of private enterprise could be 'counted on the fingers of one hand'; only fifteen dissidents supported a motion by twenty-eight-year-old Toronto activist Robert Kenzie to 'reaffirm those decisions on public ownership made at previous conventions.'[159] The *Vancouver Sun* commented approvingly, urging the CCF to 'move into the Liberal party.'[160] Delegates also rejected an appeal from fourteen Ontario CCF members expelled for belonging to the Trotskyist Socialist Educational League (SEL).[161] What could not be accomplished in 1950 was finally achieved in 1956. However, contrary to the hopes of its proponents, the adoption of the Winnipeg Declaration and dilution of CCF socialism did not halt the party's electoral decline. Indeed, many CCF leaders had already concluded that the party's fortunes were beyond repair; they sought a policy amenable to the new Canadian Labour Congress

(CLC), which had formed out of the Trades and Labor Congress and Canadian Congress of Labor, in anticipation of a political marriage. Sections of labour, however, resisted this drift, such as Oakville autoworkers who sent a telegram to the convention opposing the 'backwards step' of minimizing 'the wide chasm between the owners of the means of production and the workers of this county.'[162] Rarely mentioned in discussions of the 1956 convention is a second motion, presented by the Vancouver East delegation, endorsing the CLC's political action program, a move resisted by farmer delegates from Saskatchewan but approved with amendment.[163]

Delegates returned from Winnipeg as the BC CCF faced a provincial election, with a new leader and enduring inner-party strife. Bennett called the election in August 1956 hoping to take advantage of other parties' weakness and 'wipe out his opposition in the Legislature,' according to LPP leader Nigel Morgan, who described the situation facing the CCF and labour as 'a very serious one.'[164] The CCF fell from 14 to 10 seats as its share of the vote declined from 31 to 28 per cent. Social Credit consolidated itself as a majority party with 46 per cent of the vote and a commanding 39 of 52 seats. George Home, secretary of the unified BC Federation of Labour (BCFL), however, told the *Vancouver Sun* that union members had remained loyal to the CCF, and accounted for much of the party's popular vote.[165] He pointed to CCF victories in the industrial ridings of Alberni, Mackenzie, and New Westminster. Strachan, however, commented bitterly that the public was only interested in 'half a mile of black top,' referring to Bennett's much-touted road-building program.[166] Grace MacInnis, defeated in Point Grey, attributed Social Credit success to 'unlimited funds' in the party's war chest.[167] But Tommy Douglas conceded that 'The election caught the CCF organization in British Columbia in a transitional stage and they were not prepared to face an election.'[168]

Other voices attributed the CCF's decline to developments at Winnipeg. Morgan declared in a circular to LPP units that: 'The CCF organization is weakened by a bitter inner fight over the Winnipeg decision to amend the Regina Manifesto which has demobilized many of its best workers.'[169] In December 1956, a month prior to his death, Burnaby MLA Ernest Winch wrote to CCF national secretary Lorne Ingle protesting the deletion of the final sentence of the Regina Manifesto:

> I feel the action was put over by pre-arrangement by persons in prominent positions more concerned with immediate vote-catching than with long-

> range objectives based upon sound socialist principles ... In my opinion, the CCF has now surrendered the stand which distinguished it from all other political parties and sounded its death knell as a vital and revolutionary force in the political life of Canada.[170]

According to Dorothy Steeves, Rev. Robert Connell, the CCF leader who resigned in the 1930s because of its radicalism, 'would have felt perfectly at home in the CCF of 1956 which had changed its goal away from socialism to a mixed economy.'[171] A slew of CCFers left the party, such as railroad engineer Richard E. 'Lefty' Morgan, who helped form the short-lived Labour Party of Canada in autumn 1956. The Trotskyist SEL wavered from its 'entryist' stance and considered running candidates against the CCF. As a memo to SEL's national committee noted: 'Many workers who, in the past, voted CCF are not voting at all, or, as in BC, are voting Social Credit.'[172] Even in the victorious moderate camp, problems were apparent. VTLC vice-president Tom Alsbury, a future Vancouver mayor, told the 1957 BCFL convention: 'I am not a member of any party.'[173] Within a decade, Alsbury would run unsuccessfully as the Social Credit candidate in Vancouver-Burrard.[174] The BC CCF had reached its electoral and organizational nadir.

CHAPTER FOUR

Other Lefts

There was no clear rupture between an Old Left and a New Left in post-war BC. While a Student Union for Peace Action (SUPA) brief claimed in January 1967 that the New Left traced its origins to 'the death of the political parties and the old left,' a continuum linked these left formations.[1] Confirming Maurice Isserman's conclusions on the American left, the links between the working-class politics of the early Cold War years and the labour and youth radicalism of the 1960s were vibrant and real.[2] In the peace movement and organized labour, the militant minority of Old Leftists sustained an oppositional political culture that saw a resurgence in the 1960s, buoyed by the new working class and burgeoning student population. The Trotskyist movement straddled ideological and generational divides, providing a unique window into this continuous process of contestation, occupying a distinct location in a political space crowded by the Communist Party and the CCF. The seeds of the New Left can be traced to Cold War crises in these established Old Left parties and structural changes in BC's working class. As growing numbers of BC workers became disenchanted with both the Soviet and the social-democratic roads to socialism, and with the North American strategy of Fordist accommodation, independent political tendencies that had operated on the margins enjoyed a wider appeal. Trotskyist and Maoist groups, which had divorced themselves from the Soviet Union, wreaked havoc on the Old Left's depleted ranks and sunk roots in unions, youth organizations, and emerging 'new social movements.' The New Left retained the older emphasis on peace and labour issues, while pursuing an array of causes – the liberation struggles of women, aboriginals, workers of colour, students, and gays and lesbians, and environmentalism, which demanded protection of ecosystems and (like the Old Left) an end to nuclear testing. BC's left of the 1970s demonstrated continuity and change; it bore the imprint of the militant minority's earlier struggles but its form and substance had changed.

Trotskyism in Cold War BC

The origins of the New Left were grounded in the Old Left, in ideological and factional currents extending back before the Second World War. Where Isserman identifies Max Shachtman as a key figure in this historical continuum in the United States, Canada had Ross Dowson.[3] From the 1940s until the 1970s, Dowson was at the centre of the Canadian Trotskyist movement and its myriad organizational forms: the Revolutionary Workers Party (RWP) of the 1940s, the Socialist Educational League (SEL) and Socialist Workers Party (SWP) of the 1950s, the League for Socialist Action (LSA) and Young Socialists/Ligue des Jeunes socialistes (YS) of the 1960s. Though based in Toronto, Dowson retained a band of followers on the west coast and in the BC Interior, who pressured the CCF-NDP from the left, leading to periodic expulsions in the 1950s and 1960s. Vancouver was a bastion of Trotskyist strength in Canada. As Dowson confided in 1948, the maintenance of *Labor Challenge* and the national office 'depends almost entirely on the Vancouver branch.' Dowson ultimately found himself on the wrong side of a split in 1973, leaving the organization he had nurtured; however, in the postwar era he led the effort to forge a brand of revolutionary socialism distinct from the Stalinism of the LPP-CPC and reformism of the CCF-NDP – 'a revolutionary tendency untainted by the crimes of Stalinism.'[4]

The contours of Canadian Trotskyism are blurred by a historiographic emphasis on the mainstream, rather than the margins, of working-class politics. Studies by Bryan Palmer, Ian McKay, and Ian Angus illuminate this strain of Canadian socialism, while Elaine Bernard and Heather McLeod provide a unique window into Trotskyism in postwar BC.[5] As early as 1928, the *Labor Statesman*, newspaper of the Vancouver Trades and Labor Council, commented contemptuously that 'the Trotskyites have no friends outside of Russia and their friends inside are getting less and less.'[6] During the early 1940s, BC Trotskyists focused their efforts on labour and anti-war work, striking a position distinct from the CCF (which had critically endorsed Canada's war effort in 1939) and the Communist Party (which moved from opposition to a whole-hearted embrace after Hitler invaded Russia); three apparent Trotskyists were arrested and jailed in affluent Oak Bay in 1941 for possessing anti-war pamphlets.[7]

Trotskyists challenged LPP influence in powerful industrial unions including the Marine Workers and Boilermakers and the IWA. The 'no-strike' pledges signed by communist union leaders and their support for speed-ups and piece-work to boost the Allied war effort provided an opening for more militant shop-floor leadership.[8] Boilermakers' president Bill White was charged with 'consorting with anti-party elements' and accused of Trotskyism after he was spotted conversing with shipyard militant Gordie McQuillan, whom he described as 'one hell of a fine trade unionist.'[9] In February 1948, the LPP's Vancouver City Committee charged four members – George Black, Margaret Black, Pat Driscoll, and Renee Nelissen – with engaging 'in disruptive activities harmful to the working class,' for publishing the dissident sheet *Communist Voice*, which followed 'the typically Trotskyist policy of raising divisive and disruptive issues.'[10] In IWA locals 1–217 and 1–357, Trotskyists such as Lloyd Whelan, Reg Bullock, and Tom Bradley led a Rank and File Caucus that was instrumental in curbing LPP strength; Bullock had allegedly been 'pulled out of the shipyards in 1946–47' to 'defeat the Stalinist stranglehold on the IWA.'[11] These Trotskyist trade unionists navigated a delicate line between opposing the LPP and playing into the hands of anti-labour employers: 'They wanted to expose the mismanagement by the Stalinist union leaders, but not open the door to a generalized anti-socialist attack.'[12]

Trotskyist activism in BC's working class was most evident, however, in the strategy of 'entryism' in social democracy, which wreaked havoc in the BC CCF-NDP. 'The French turn as it is called in our movement is a tactical maneuver designed to overcome the general isolation that the revolutionary vanguard finds itself in today,' Dowson explained.[13] Dorothy Gretchen Steeves, CCF MLA for North Vancouver (1934–45), suggested the most vocal opponents of a United Front with communists in the 1930s had belonged to 'an extreme leftist group and were accused of being "Trotskyites"'; Rod Young was suspended from the CCF for associating with this group.[14] Trotskyists adopted a long-range view of relations with the CCF, as Dowson explained to a worker in Trail, BC:

> In 1937 the Canadian Trotskyists made an entry into the CCF, which appeared to offer great opportunities of work inside its ranks. We would have preferred to affiliate to it but this was denied us and so we entered

> to form a fraction around which we hoped to gather the militants. During the war we remained in the CCF advancing our ideas as best we could. In 1945 we concluded that there were greater opportunities to spread our ideas outside the CCF free from the censurous pressure of the bureaucracy and organized the independent party in 1946.[15]

This new party, the Revolutionary Workers' Party (RWP), formed after a failed attempt by Lloyd Whelan, chairperson of the BC CCF Trade Union Committee, to bring a revolutionary program to the floor of the 1946 CCF National convention.[16] Whelan, Bullock, Bradley (a former CCF organizer), Ruth Bullock (a CCF provincial council member), and Elaine MacDonald defected to form the Labor Challenge Club. In October 1946, the RWP was founded at a Toronto convention and affiliated to the Fourth International. The new party opened a Vancouver headquarters on Cordova Street and attracted militants from the CCF, such as William White of the Britannia Beach Mine-Mill local and William and Lillian Whitney of New Westminster. In December 1946, three members of the LPP's Ginger Goodwin Youth Club defected to the RWP.[17]

The RWP brought Dowson into contact with Trail civic worker Aubrey Burton. Letters between Dowson and Burton provide a unique window into class relations and working-class politics in the early Cold War years. In 1949, Dowson outlined the RWP's strategy, which opposed the LPP 'peace fronts' because 'they poison the workers with pacifist illusions which disorient the anti-war fight and so objectively pave the way for war.' The party's attitude toward the USSR was linked to the struggle against labour bureaucracy in Canada:

> We stand rigorously opposed to the capitalist war plans against the USSR. Wall Street is not interested in destroying the Kremlin oligarchy but the property relations that were achieved by the revolution and which have not yet been cancelled out by the Kremlin. The defense of the USSR – what is left of the October conquests requires however the destruction of the Kremlin bureaucracy just as the defense of the unions requires the destruction of the Greens, Bengoughs and Moshers and their replacement with a revolutionary leadership.[18]

Forging a revolutionary leadership in Trail, in the CCF and smelterworkers' union, was the object of Dowson's correspondence with

Burton. The RWP sought 'a clarification' in a political environmental crowded by the 'Stalinist' LPP and 'right-wing' CCF:

> Yes it is unfortunate that there is not greater unity in the left. But the responsibility for its present state of disintegration lies in large part at the door of the Kremlin oligarchy and their stooges across the globe whose criminal policies have brought defeat after defeat and disoriented a whole generation of revolutionaries. A new upsurge will see a clarification and a unification of all worthwhile elements – the hopelessly sectarian and muddleheads will be left by the wayside.[19]

Burton began distributing copies of *Labor Challenge* and building an oppositional presence in the Trail CCF Club and LPP-controlled Mine-Mill Local 480. In September 1949, Dowson commended Burton for a *Pacific Tribune* letter attacking 'the Stalinist Labor Progressive Party from a Marxist point of view. In this day of the cold war and the witch hunt this is a breath of fresh air.'[20]

In February 1950, Burton observed first-hand the Steelworkers' raid on Mine-Mill Local 480, as the left and right wings of the CCF clashed. 'On Feb 11 the Mosher-Millard bureaucracy launched their union-raiding campaign against the Stalinist dominated IUMM &SW,' Burton reported.[21] He attended the April 1950 BC CCF convention in Penticton, aided by travel funds from Local 480, despite 'behind-the-scenes attempts to prevent my getting there on the parts of Bert Gargrave, J. Quinn, the former MLA for this Riding.'[22] Burton and a CCYM delegate were the only RWP members in attendance. Burton described political polarization in the Trail CCF:

> There exists today within the local CCF movement here two distinct wings neither of which will have the least bit to do with the other. In short there exists in Trail now that for which we are working to bring about provincially, a clear clarification between the right and left within the CCF. The catch being that the 'left' here is gravitating rapidly towards the Stalinists.

Burton responded by organizing a public meeting in May 1950 'to establish a fighting socialist club by fighting Union men and women,' a CCF club free from LPP and 'moderate' influence.[23] He was elected president of Civic Workers Local 343 in Trail.[24] At Reg Bullock and Dowson's suggestion, Burton adopted the pseudonym Steve Rosslund to protect his work in the CCF, as controversy arose over the circulation of *Labor Challenge* to a CCF mailing list.[25]

Burton attended the stormy 1950 CCF National convention in Vancouver, distributing mimeographed materials from *Socialist Outlook*, bulletin of the British Labour Party's left wing, and organized a pre-convention caucus with BC 'left oppositionists' including Rod Young, Dorothy Steeves, Colin Cameron, Eve Smith, and Cranbrook MLA Leo Nimsick. However, a resolution Burton proposed opposing 'American armed forces in the Korean civil war' was rejected by Young and Steeves, who feared it would alienate the left. 'Colin Cameron and Eve Smith were the only two leading oppositionists that supported me at all,' Burton reported.[26] He met with other RWP comrades in Vancouver and Seattle, gaining 'an awareness of the Party as a force, not just as semi-isolated individuals.'[27] After the convention, Burton wrote to Young supporting 'a strong left-wing faction organized within the CCF' and suggested launching a newspaper akin to *Socialist Outlook*.[28] However, Burton confided to Dowson that he 'would prefer a clean break with the CCF now in favor of complete concentration on the trade union aspect such as the Stalinists are carrying through, whether openly as a Trotskyist or just as a trade union militant.'[29] 'Coldwell has finished his party in this area now,' Burton believed, but Dowson was more optimistic:

> The elements that have reacted so violently to Coldwell's open attacks on elementary class struggle principles are not the workers of Canada who have come into and are moving towards the CCF but the left overs from the past of the CCF – the SPers, the old fundamentalists. The workers as a whole in Canada know little of what did take place in the CCF convention and are not yet too concerned. They are not going to turn away from the CCF because of this convention ... This left that is developing now doesn't reflect the level of class understanding of the Canadian working-class or their class experience.[30]

Dowson's correspondence with Burton sheds light on conflicting leadership currents within BC's working class, and the nature of the new politics that was emerging in response to the Cold War:

> Within the lower ranks of the trade union bureaucracy there are shades of differences. Many of the lower ranks of the union leadership are only a few years removed from the shop, a few are leaders who were thrown

> up in the struggle, who were once militants and have got soft. Today in the unions they play much the same role as the Youngs, Eve Smiths etc play in the CCF. To a certain extent they are used as a left cover by the bureaucracy. To a certain extent they play an independent and critical role. At certain stages they act as a point of gravitation for militants like Young in the CCF in BC today. We have to handle them different. L C [*Labor Challenge*] has given Young and co a form of critical support – yet what is Rodney Young himself – a pretty treacherous cowardly, opportunist element. But compared to Coldwell he represents in a distorted way a progressive force and all critical elements tend to gravitate toward him. I have my own ideas of what will probably happen to Young but we want to contact these critical elements.[31]

While the RWP denounced Stalinism and top-down bureaucratic methods, it was not immune from internal strife. Whalen and Bradley were suspended, and a factional fight surfaced in the *RWP Bulletin* in spring 1950, prompting Burton to lament that if this was the level of debate in the party, 'we have small hope of ever persuading the rank and file workers to accept us as their vanguard.' Ironic in light of his own factional activities in the BC CCF, Burton warned that 'if we are not to degenerate into a mere sectarian group I think we had better tighten up our party discipline' and suggested seeking remedy through 'the International itself' if 'the rank and file fail to check it.'[32]

In the early 1950s, the line between RWP entryism and broader left criticism in the CCF became blurred: moderates attacked the Socialist Fellowship as a Trotskyist front, and the RWP's presence in the Fellowship lent credence to allegations of a 'party within the party.'[33] As Dowson admitted in April 1950: 'Our first loyalty is of course to our ideas and our party, but we have an orientation to the CCF so our second loyalty is to the CCF.'[34] He discussed the implications of 'total entry': 'What would happen to *Labor Challenge*? Well if we made a total entry it would fold up but we would within the shortest time possible publish some kind of legal CCF fraction organ to take its place.... I am inclined to believe that the Vancouver branch should carry out some fraction work in the BC section before attempting to carry out an entry.'[35] Following the 1950 Vancouver convention, Dowson observed that the 'Coldwell gang's' efforts to 'rip up the Regina Manifesto and create a lynch atmosphere against the BC section' were galvanizing left opposition in Eastern Canada. He anticipated the formation of 'something along the line of *our* Socialist Fellowship in the BLP,' highlighting the role of Trotskyists in the British left.[36] Dowson welcomed the Left-Wing Conference that met in Vancouver in August 1950, noting that the RWP's Vancouver branch had struck off 'three or four comrades to get into the CCYM.'[37] In October, Burton – by then executive secretary of the Trail CCF Club – spearheaded the organization of a Socialist Fellowship in Trail, consisting of militants from his own Civic Workers Local 343 and left-wing CCFers in Mine-Mill Local 480.[38]

The RWP maintained a separate party organization, but 'entryism' was the main strategy as the CCF Socialist Fellowship formed and then dissolved in 1950–1. Trotskyists debated whether the CCF represented the main agency for 'political action by labor' or whether it had degenerated into a 'rotten section of the resurrected corpse of the Second International.'[39] When Burton produced a report titled *Whether the CCF?*, questioning the logic of entryism, Dowson advised against breaking from the party: 'With the CCF label on us and with the protection that the Socialist Fellowship gives we can in essence be Trotskyists politically, we can say everything we want openly but "Join the RWP! Join the Fourth International!"'[40] Behind the scenes, Dowson grew weary of Burton's anti-entryist stance. In November 1950, he suggested Burton move to Vancouver for his 'final polishing off ... as a revolutionist.'[41] A year later, as two Ontario RWP activists travelled west, Dowson described Burton as 'a most erratic and confused comrade' with a 'complete orientation to the Stalinist LPP' who 'never did and still doesn't know the score. He doesn't understand what our orientation is about.'[42]

The RWP formally dissolved in spring 1952, suspending publication of *Labor Challenge* as Trotskyists made a 'total entry' into the CCF. Dowson's brother Murray envisioned 'a long stay in the CCF stretching over several years,' suggesting that 'the comrades in BC will have to restrain themselves from leaping ahead of the rest of the country due to the left-tradition of the West.'[43] There was 'not a public face to the Trotskyist organization' between April 1952 and December 1955, historian Elaine Bernard noted.[44] BC Trotskyists submerged their activity into the Vancouver faction Box 16 and Stanley Park CCF Club Forum. A protégé of Dowson's named Barry, who had moved to Vancouver from Toronto, ensconced himself in the Vancouver Centre CCF and Stanley Park Club, serving on the 1952 campaign committee that elected Laura Jamieson and Jim Bury to the legislature. Another Trotskyist, Angus MacPhee, a pulp worker and president of the Prince Rupert Trades and Labour Council, was also active in the 1952 Vancouver Centre campaign.[45] Trotskyists' effectiveness was blunted, however, by splits in the Fourth

International, which divided the Canadian membership.[46] At the 1955 BC CCF convention, party leaders attributed their woes to Trotskyist infiltration; the Ontario CCF had expelled fourteen members, prompting demands for similar action in BC.[47]

The expulsions contributed to the December 1955 decision to re-establish a public face, with the launching of *Workers Vanguard* newspaper and the Toronto-based Socialist Educational League (SEL), 'a product of the crisis that confronts the CCF.' SEL was committed to 'fight for a socialist CCF' and 'win affiliation to the CCF as the socialist education wing of the movement.'[48] After the CCF abandoned the Regina Manifesto at its 1956 Winnipeg convention, SEL contemplated fielding candidates in the next federal election, but maintained that the CCF was still 'an elementary and progressive break from capitalist politics.'[49] In BC, Trotskyists remained active in the Stanley Park CCF Club Forum, and helped form the Vancouver Socialist Forum and Socialist Information Centre (SIC) in the late 1950s, 'an arena where conflicting, competing and parallel views could meet.'[50] Led by Ruth Bullock and Malcolm Bruce, a veteran communist who had left the LPP in the 1940s, SIC opened a Vancouver meeting hall. Canadian Trotskyists maintained formal organizational ties through the Socialist Workers Party (SWP), an affiliate of the American organization that had formed in Canada 'following the shake-up of stalinism in 1956.'[51] At a 1960 convention, held in Vancouver, SWP militants endorsed 'the formal constitution of a national public socialist wing of the New Party.'[52]

Trotskyist entryism in the New Party, like earlier CCF activism, was undermined by in-fighting, which Dowson attributed to 'an atmosphere ... inimical to the full participation of newer comrades'; 'old timers,' because of their years of experience, tended 'to make decisions outside of the branch.'[53] Clashes erupted over the nomination of CCF candidates in Vancouver Centre, the appropriate structure for the New Party, and strategy in the Fair Play for Cuba Committee.[54] Ruth Bullock and Bill Whitney called for a separate BC newspaper, while Vancouver Branch 1 demanded Bruce's suspension as west coast editor of *Workers Vanguard*, citing his handling of copy and allegiance to the rival faction. The split divided the two Vancouver branches; Branch 1 favoured a 'deep entry liquidationist' policy while Branch 2 favoured 'a more open policy' – the majority viewpoint at the 1960 convention. A City Executive was formed to 'unite our public activities in preparation for the emergence of our projected more open national organization.'[55] Jerry and Ruth Houle, deployed to Vancouver to reconcile the warring factions, only aggravated the situation. Vancouver comrades inundated the Toronto headquarters with complaints, and Dowson recalled the Houles to Toronto in March 1961.[56] On the eve of the New Party convention, Vancouver-based SIC merged with Toronto-based SEL to form the League for Socialist Action (LSA). 'Past differences, sectarian pride, or vanity – all the barriers which have kept the socialists divided – must be broken down,' the *Vanguard* urged.[57] The birth of the LSA, more stable organizationally than earlier Trotskyist groups and focused on the NDP, signalled a new era in the history of the Fourth International in BC.

Other Lefts

Parallel to these efforts, CCF dissidents were moving in diverse directions. In August 1956, a group of Vancouver CCF members and fellow-travellers including Rod Young, Jim McKenzie, and Richard 'Lefty' Morgan responded to the Winnipeg Declaration by laying the groundwork for a new party. This Socialist Committee for the Organization of a Labour Party of Canada met regularly throughout 1956–7, drafting a provisional constitution and launching the monthly mimeographed sheet *Press*, which was attacked by *Workers Vanguard* because of its association with Young.[58] In March 1957, the committee endorsed Cedric Cox's CCF candidacy in a Burnaby by-election, because, though they were 'critical of his platform … he spoke as a working class candidate should.'[59] The group's Provisional Constitution was designed 'to retain power in the hands of the rank and file.'[60] Its Interim Manifesto declared that 'reform is not in the forefront and social ownership relegated to some distant future' (see appendix F). While articulating an 'Immediate Program,' the Manifesto concluded that 'we pledge ourselves never to rest content until we have eradicated capitalism from the earth.' Taking aim at the LPP, the Manifesto declared that 'the Labour Party will oppose any other party which seeks to place the socialists of one country under the direction of the socialists of another country,' and pledged to 'support all movements of colonial emancipation regardless of the short term disadvantages which may result.'[61]

The promised Labour Party never took shape. In early 1957, CCFer Dorothy Steeves observed that Young was 'completely at outs with the Trotskyites' and that *Press* was 'not much of an improvement over *Box 16*,' the earlier leftist CCF organ. 'Poor Rod, he has to be leading something, even a party with no members.'[62] Young, McKenzie, and Morgan continued meeting, as a discussion group that made contact with communist Jack Scott and his wife, Hilda: 'She belonged to the group. I never did. I couldn't get along with the lawyer [Young]. Him and I used to argue something terrible,' Scott recalls.[63] Around 1959–60, the group met in the Scott home and morphed into a CCF Socialist Caucus, which included communists, Trotskyists, and fellow-travellers and continued to publish *Press*, and later, the *Socialist Caucus Bulletin*. In June 1960, SIC organizer Jerry Houle noted that 'the *Press* group is still very much alive and appears to be stepping up its activities'; Young addressed the Stanley Park CCF Forum on the topic of 'Pre-Marxian Socialism,' his first public CCF appearance since leaving the party in 1954.[64] Young 'speaks clearly and very simply,' Houle reported, enjoying 'considerable influence, more than some of our comrades would admit,' especially with 'the youthful serious element.'[65] A month later, Houle lamented that 'the Young group exists because of our failure in BC,' with 'petty personal squabbles and unprincipled politics' driving away new members, a view confirmed by Jack Scott.[66]

Unlike many Trotskyists, veteran socialist Malcolm Bruce was non-sectarian, playing a lead role in Vancouver's Socialist Forum and submitting articles to *Press*, which Dowson described as 'scandalous,' insisting that 'our comrades should not be identified with that sectarian rag of Young's.'[67] Bruce defended his actions in a letter to SIC's Vancouver City Executive Committee: 'We must launch out on the great sea of the actual class struggle and not paddle our sectarian canoe in the placid backwaters of mere inner-party discussion which leads to impotence and stagnation.'[68] In February 1961, Bruce chaired a Socialist Forum meeting on the topic 'The Union Dues Check-Off: What Is It About,' with speakers from the Marine Workers and Boilermakers, Canadian Iron Workers, and International Longshoremen and Warehousemen's Union (ILWU).[69] Later in 1961, the Socialist Caucus organized a delegation to Cuba, independent of the CPC, CCF-NDP, and LSA leadership, and were 'the heart and soul' of the Columbia River for Canada Committee.[70] Some militants in this milieu joined the Communist Party's 'Special Club' while remaining NDP members.[71]

Lefty Morgan had rejoined the CCF in 1960 and was active in the Fair Play for Cuba Committee, discussing Cuba at the Stanley Park CCF Open Forum in May 1961. Morgan attended the 1961 NDP convention in Ottawa, and on that trip visited Detroit, where he met Raya Dunayevskaya, leader of a Trotskyist sect that had broken from the mainstream of American Trotskyism in the mid-1950s. Morgan became a subscriber and contributor to *News and Letters*, the publication of Dunayevskaya's Marxist-Humanist tendency. Dunayevskaya visited Vancouver in 1965 and delivered a talk at UBC. While Morgan retained NDP membership, he remained critical of the party's rightward drift and by the mid-1960s was no longer active.[72]

Jack Scott and other 'Special Club' dissidents responded to their 1964 expulsion from the Communist Party by touring the Prairie provinces, Ontario, and Montreal, laying the groundwork for a new Canadian socialist movement. A founding conference was held in Toronto's King Edward Hotel, but strategic disagreement with Toronto socialist Stephen Endicott (over the role of the revolutionary party) denied the Vancouver group a base in central Canada.[73] Scott and his comrades persisted, founding the *Progressive Worker* newspaper, pledged to 'renew the fight to revitalize the Revolutionary Working Class movement in Canada.'[74] The Progressive Worker Movement (PWM) developed branches in Vancouver, New Westminster, Nanaimo, and Victoria, and contacts among dissident communist autoworkers in Windsor, Ontario.[75] Scott's close ally Jerry Lebourdais was elected president of the Oil, Chemical and Atomic Workers local at the Shellburn refinery, reflecting *PW*'s concentrated base in organized labour: 'If you want to talk about a proletarian movement we were it.'[76] Lebourdais travelled to China in 1964 and in 1965 ran as the PWM candidate against NDP MP Harold Winch in Vancouver East.[77] Scott visited China several times and met personally with Chairman Mao.[78] During its six-year existence, *Progressive Worker* developed a subscription list with 1,500 names and a monthly circulation of 3,000, exceeding the actual sales of the communist *Pacific Tribune*, which 'were going in a bloody furnace.'[79] In June 1964, Canadian Communist leader Leslie Morris (who succeeded Tim Buck) bitterly described the new tendency as 'perhaps the most dangerous phenomenon ever to have overtaken the cause of Marxism in Canada'; *Tribune* editor Tom McEwen dismissed the PWM as 'this ultra-"Leftist" brand of Trotskyite provocation.'[80] However, the Trotskyist LSA was equally disdainful. The PWM was tainted by 'the insidious heritage of Stalinist theory and practice,' its work in the anti-war movement was marked by 'sectarianism and adventurism,' and its dismissal of 'international unions as pawns of US imperialism ... cut [the group] off from the living process of the labor movement.'[81]

Jack Scott viewed the mid-1960s as the PWM's heyday. 'For a few years we were able to play a small role within the class struggle in the Lower Mainland.' However, as the decade unfolded, 'the student movement began to dominate the scene' and 'we just petered out, stopped functioning really.'[82] A faction emerged around Vancouver activist Martin Amiable, accusing Scott and Lebourdais of dictatorial practices before breaking away. *Progressive Worker* ceased publication in June 1970, urging that 'the major activity of socialists at this point in Canadian history ought to be assisting the building of a truly broadly-based movement fighting for the independence of Canada from foreign domination.'[83] 'It was what we never wanted to be,' Scott suggests. 'A British Columbia group that was trying to move the whole bloody country.' According to Scott, workers were moving away from established organizations:

> A lot of people were sort of floating off and sort of doing their own things. Organizing little groups here and there and for some reason or another didn't want to become affiliated with anything in particular. This is the period of do your own thing sort of business. Sort of a revolt against organization.[84]

Among Trotskyists, the New Left presented opportunities for unprecedented growth but also exposed old contradictions. Malcolm Bruce left the LSA, which he had helped found, and joined the PWM.[85] The LSA and its youth wing, the Young Socialists (YS), worked with others on the left, even the Communist Party in the anti-Vietnam War movement, but tension was palpable.[86] Khrushchev's qualified reprieve of the errant Trotskyist tendency in 1956 failed to blunt Communist hostility.[87] As Ivan Avakumovic points out, communists 'knew that Trotskyist strength lay in the very age groups where the CPC had been notoriously weak since the beginning of the Cold War.'[88] The Young Communist League (YCL) dismissed the New Democratic Youth's 1961 platform as 'Trotskyite,' and when Jean Rands ran for Vancouver mayor in 1966, the Communist Party's City Committee 'warned any worker against voting for Rands ... because of her Trotskyite sponsorship which fosters disunity of the working class.'[89] The YS had declared confidently in 1965 that through its work in the NDY and the organ *Young Socialist Forum*, the Trotskyist youth movement had established 'the skeleton of a youth movement of national scope.'[90] By 1967, paid circulation of the newspaper surpassed 2,000 copies per issue, establishing YS as '*the* socialists' [emphasis in original].[91]

However, in 1968 conflict erupted between the LSA's Vancouver Branch and the national organization, prompted by disagreement over *Workers Vanguard* editorial policy and BC labour's response to Bill 33, the anti-labour Mediation Commission Act.[92] The split was aggravated by the old 'entryist' debate on maintaining parallel open and secret organizations. Vancouver Trotskyists, according to an internal bulletin, identified with San Francisco, rather than Toronto, and opposed entryism in the NDP.[93] A survey of new recruits in the Vancouver YS reflected a range of New Left interests: 'NDY-2 [members], Red Power-2, Anti-War-3, high school-1.' This was interpreted as having 'completely justified the decision for an open organization and maintaining a separate organization.'[94] However, at the LSA's 1968 convention, leading members including Rands and Allen Engler, *Workers Vanguard* west coast editor, were in the minority and publicly resigned from the LSA. A faction emerged in support of Rands and Engler's position, urging the 'direct propagation of Trotskyist ideas.'[95]

Other leftist splinter groups appeared around this time, reflecting the broader process of deinstitutionalization as the New Left rose in strength. The Canadian Party of Labour (CPL), a Maoist offshoot of the US Progressive Labor Party, which bore no connection to the earlier CCF-oriented formation, developed a core of BC militants.[96] The Workers' Communist Party, also Maoist, formed in Montreal after the 1970 FLQ crisis and developed a presence in BC.[97] Other groups included the Left Caucus and Internationalists (forerunner to the CPCML), and Simon Fraser University's Red Collective, which Scott dismissed as 'a ridiculous outfit.'[98]

The terrain of BC's revolutionary left was becoming crowded, influenced by ideological and organizational currents that rejected or at least criticized the Soviet Union as the central reference point for a revolutionary politics in Canada. The tide was moving away from the Communist Party at the same time that a growing layer of young people turned toward radical politics. In 1962, the YCL had claimed eight BC clubs and 'many contacts,' observing that:

> In a dozen ways Canadian young people are beginning to question government war policies, to ask why there are no jobs, to wonder at the lack of educational opportunities, and finally to question the reason for the continued existence of capitalism itself. We must become a part of this great ideological debate in a new way.[99]

However, by the end of the 1960s, the YCL was defunct, and McGill instructor Chuck McFadden, elected to the Central Executive Committee, was charged with the task of reorganizing the youth section.[100] Former party stalwarts such as Charlie Caron and Jack Scott had defected to the Maoists, while UBC student leader Charlie Boylan joined the renegade Communist Party of Canada (Marxist-Leninist) led by Hardial Bains.[101]

In 1970, Tommy Douglas, the federal NDP leader and Nanaimo-Cowichan-The Islands MP, rejected the tactical orientation of the Maoists: 'We do not accept the doctrine of the Maoists that "all power proceeds out of the mouth of a gun," because if we accept that concept what we are saying is that society will be dominated by those who have the most guns and the ruthless will to use them.'[102] Douglas made these remarks in the House of Commons, during debate on the War Measures Act and the October 1970 FLQ crisis. During what was described as Douglas's 'finest hour,' the veteran socialist remained firm in his commitment to the parliamentary road. However, a layer of young people was migrating toward the violent tactics of the Weather Underground and Red Army Faction. Hardial Bains's Vancouver followers in the CPCML gained notoriety for violently clashing with rival leftists, while this current would resurface in BC a decade later in the group Direct Action! and the 'Squamish Five' bombings.[103]

Anti-War

Opposition to militarism was the unifying thread for the diverse strains of BC's left. The dashed hopes of the immediate postwar years were conveyed in a 1948 *Pacific Tribune* column by Harold Griffin, titled the 'Crusade against Progress':

> Labor's concept of victory over fascism and their own had nothing in common. Labor saw, over the stacks of victory bonds, over the ships taking form on the ways, over the planes taking to the air, the beginning of a new way of life distinguished by its broader freedom and greater economic justice ... Now, the banks are reclaiming the victory bonds. The shipyards are closed down, the aircraft plants dismantled. Now a new promise is fashioned from the shattered pieces of the old. Now they have taken their enemy's weapons for their own, the ally in the fight for freedom and the partner in victory has become the new tyranny, the new enemy, and the way to peace is through the atom bomb and a new world war.[104]

Opposition to nuclear arms and colonial wars linked the Old Left activism of the 1940s and 1950s with the New Left ferment of the 1960s, even as the locus of activism shifted from labour-based parties to the student movement.

In December 1947, members of the Canadian Seamen's Union (CSU) launched a picket at Vancouver's Ballantyne Pier against the ship SS *Colima*, which was being loaded with warplanes and arms for Kuomintang China. Trade unionists, students, churchgoers, CCFers, and communists joined the CSU picket, while the Vancouver Trades and Labor Council (TLC) endorsed a resolution from the Women's International League for Peace and Freedom (WILPF) condemning the munitions shipment. The Chinese Workers' Protective Association commended this stand, with secretary H.C. Low accusing the Canadian government of 'prolonging the civil war in China.'[105] When the *Colima* was moved to Burrard Dry Dock for repairs, the LPP-led Marine Workers and Boilermakers refused to touch the ship. The protests were weakened, however, by the Red Wars in labour ranks. ILWU Local 501 pledged to load the ship and CCL president Aaron Mosher ordered an end to picketing, a directive echoed by the BC CCF executive. This prompted Robert Loosmore, of Ganges on Saltspring Island, to write in the *CCF News* that union contracts and CCF electoral considerations were less important than the aspirations 'of Chinese peasants who have for years been fighting for economic improvement.'[106] After a three-week delay, the *Colima* left Vancouver loaded with planes, small arms, and ammunition for the Kuomintang. By November 1948, as Chiang Kai-shek's toehold on the Chinese mainland neared its end amid labour strikes in Shanghai, Nanking, and along the Yangtze, the *Fisherman* commented: 'Chiang Kai-shek is tottering – all the American arms and explosives, all the dollars and credits have availed him nothing. The people are against him and his corrupt regime and they are too many for him and his allies.'[107] The SS *Islandside* loaded 5,000 tons of explosives and thirty Mosquito bombers at Ballantyne Pier, and communists and fellow-travellers were again on hand brandishing picket signs. 'Ottawa is rushing the death cargo to bolster the tottering Kuomintang regime,' the *Pacific Tribune* remarked.[108]

This campaign demonstrated divisions within BC's working class – but also the determination of the militant minority that challenged Cold War assumptions. In July 1948, Vancouver Labour Council (CCL) delegates had rejected an executive recommendation and supported the WILPF by building a peace float for the Pacific National Exhibition.[109] CCF women including Vancouver alderwoman Helena Gutteridge and former MLAs Dorothy Steeves and Laura Jamieson were active in the WILPF Vancouver branch. Local CCF Women's Committees, which extended to Port Alberni on Vancouver Island, opposed military recruiting in schools.[110] In 1950, B.P. Johnson, secretary of the Sooke CCF Club, demanded a CCF membership referendum on the Korean War, insisting: 'We must give all possible support to the fight of the colonial people for independence.'[111] As Trotskyist Aubrey Burton noted: 'Growing opposition to the Coldwell-Lewis leadership springs from the rank and file's opposition to war.'[112] The 1954 BC CCF convention placed itself on record opposing military involvement in Indo-China and declared that 'Canada should substantially decrease her own armed forces.'[113] Two years later, the BC Boys' Parliament rejected military conscription.[114] Even in the darkest days of McCarthyite witchhunts, resistance to militarism was palpable in BC.

The BC Peace Council (BCPC) was at the centre of peace activism in the 1950s. When the Royal Canadian Legion expelled LPPer and UFAWU leader Elgin 'Scotty' Neish in 1955, BCPC secretary Ray Gardner argued that 'the real issue facing all veterans today is the plan to rearm West Germany, to build a new Nazi army, and not whether you are or are not the chairman of a peace council.'[115] In January 1956, the peace council sent a delegation to the BC Legislature urging a ban on H-bomb tests; legislators later approved, by unanimous vote, a resolution urging the Canadian government 'to intensify its efforts to achieve world disarmament by international agreement through the United Nations Organization.'[116] The Vancouver Labour Council (CCL) backed the disarmament campaign, while the Non-Partisan Association (NPA)-dominated Vancouver City Council refused.[117] When the Congress of Canadian Women's BC council learned of a new round of US nuclear tests in the Pacific, the organization wired an appeal to Prime Minister St Laurent and MPs urging disarmament and federal action against H-bomb tests. As the *Pacific Tribune* reported, radiation from atomic and H-bombs that had already exploded in the atmosphere would result in the death, or prevent the birth, of 1.5 million human beings.[118] The Burnaby LPP endorsed the 1957 by-election campaign of CCFer Cedric Cox, declaring:

> Overshadowing all these issues is that of the H-tests. This may seem far removed from provincial politics. But as long as tests of nuclear weapons continue, the threat to peace remains and people everywhere are menaced by the incalculable consequences of radiation.[119]

Mirroring developments in the United Kingdom, where the Campaign for Nuclear Disarmament (CND) was born, the issue of nuclear testing was a motive force behind the emergence of an emboldened peace movement and a New Left. The Canadian Committee for the Control of Radiation Hazards, formed in 1959, developed a strong presence in Vancouver and collected more than 142,000 signatures on a petition against nuclear testing.[120] Camille Mather, CCF-NDP MLA for Delta (1960–3), and party dissident Eve Smith were active in the campaign, as was the Trotskyist LSA and Socialist Forum.[121] In 1960, the Vancouver Radiation Hazards committee hosted a talk by Dr Linus Pauling, the campaign's founder and Nobel Prize-winning chemist who had refused to participate in the Manhattan Project. The Socialist Forum issued a leaflet welcoming Dr Pauling to Vancouver, advocating a policy of 'unilateral disarmament' and a Canadian referendum on nuclear arms.[122] Later that year, an LSA activist described the composition of the emerging anti-nuclear movement, based on a Radiation Hazards meeting at UBC attended by 300 people: 'The vast majority of the audience were under forty, perhaps under thirty. Few people over fifty there. Relatively few workers with dirty hands and faces were in the audience.'[123] The LSA organized a protest picket at the Vancouver fallout shelter, while the Communist Party warned that US military bases in BC's hinterland – the 'Pinetree Line' radar bases at Baldy Hughes (near Prince George), Mount Lolo (near Kamloops), and Puntzi Lake (near Williams Lake) – made BC a target for nuclear attack.[124]

Peace activism was extending to new social groups and influencing Old Left parties. The Voice of Women (VOW), formed in 1960, pulled middle-class women into the campaign for peace and rapidly developed a national following.[125] At the 1960 CCF National convention, the last before the CCF gave way to the NDP, delegates went on record demanding Canada's withdrawal from NATO. While this position was reversed at the NDP's founding convention, as party leaders sought to present a moderate face, peace activism grew in the new party. NDP leader Tommy Douglas told the 1962 BCFL convention that the Cuban Missile Crisis demonstrated the validity of the NDP's position that Canada should not 'increase the membership of the nuclear club.'[126] The same BCFL convention went on record 'opposing nuclear weapons on Canadian soil.'[127] The Vancouver and District Labour Council had earlier condemned nuclear tests, 'despite an attempt at red-baiting by a member of the plumbers' union.'[128] In 1962 several anti-nuclear groups such as Citizens for Survival, Focus Society, and Gibsons Committee for Nuclear Disarmament federated to form the League for Total Disarmament, which staged two protests in 1963 at the Comox airbase, one of two acknowledged Canadian sites for nuclear-equipped US Air Force planes.[129]

The nuclear disarmament movement flourished on university campuses. The UBC Nuclear Disarmament Club was affiliated with the Combined Universities Campaign for Nuclear Disarmament (CUCND), which had formed in 1959 and issued the Montreal-based quarterly publication *Our Generation against Nuclear War*.[130] In October 1961, the UBC club sent a telegram to Nikita Khrushchev condemning 'the Soviet resumption of atmospheric testing' and commended the UBC student council for circulating a petition against atmospheric nuclear weapons tests. Club president Dorothy Thompson declared that 'the Disarmament Club does not endorse or affiliate with any political, religious, or ethnic organization or institution, its primary interest is human survival.'[131] When the CUCND organized a picket on Parliament Hill in Ottawa in October 1961, as a protest against the government's refusal to adopt a non-nuclear stand, the UBC club abstained because of travel costs, but club president Mike Audain said, 'We support the Ottawa campaign wholeheartedly.'[132] By 1963, the UBC club counted 130 members and forged links with the Student Christian Movement and off-campus disarmament groups; attempts were made to organize a CUCND club in Victoria.[133]

BC's peace movement and Old Left sympathized with anti-colonial struggles in Indo-China, Guyana, Algeria, and, after 1959, Cuba. The victory of Fidel Castro and his July 26th Movement, defeating the US-aligned Batista regime, was celebrated as an anti-imperialist victory at the doorstep of American imperialism. When Washington imposed an embargo on the Caribbean island, Vancouver Trotskyists launched the Fair Play for Cuba Committee (FPCC), picketing the US Consulate in November 1960.[134] Trotskyists worried about 'the Stalinists moving in and trying to take over,' with Dowson advising Vancouver comrades to assure moderate FPCC supporters, such as UBC professors, that 'it is not a CP *or a Trotskyist front*' (emphasis in original).[135] In labour's ranks, pulp worker Angus MacPhee won approval at the 1960 BCFL convention for a motion investigating the hiring of a former Batista henchman as a special consultant to AFL-CIO president George Meany; the convention also approved a recommendation to send a fact-finding mission to the island.[136] In 1961, around the time of the failed US invasion at the Bay of Pigs, communists and fellow-travellers formed the Canada-Cuba Friendship Society.[137] During the October 1962 Cuban Missile Crisis – triggered by Soviet attempts to deploy missiles to Cuba – a

BC Peace Council march wound its way through Vancouver, and NDP leader Tommy Douglas told the BC NDP convention, then in session, that: 'Some people talk of starting a war as if they were talking about going on a picnic – and this is a world where, if war comes, there will be no hiding place for any man, woman or child.'[138]

In the wake of the crisis, the *Ubyssey* student newspaper exposed a broad RCMP Security Service anti-subversion campaign on university campuses.[139] Tom Berger, NDP MP for Vancouver-Burrard, queried federal Justice Minister E. Davie Fulton on police surveillance during question period in the House of Commons.[140] While an agreement was later struck between the federal government, RCMP, Canadian Association of University Teachers (CAUT), and Canadian Union of Students, the RCMP ignored its provisions and maintained investigations at UBC, the new University of Victoria, and universities across Canada.[141] The target of state surveillance was expanding in the 1960s, as radicalism moved from labour-based parties to student groups.

The Diefenbaker Conservatives, Canada's only non-Liberal government between 1935 and 1979, deviated from the United States on a number of key foreign-policy issues. Diefenbaker continued diplomatic relations with Communist Cuba and exported wheat to Communist China. His government refused to bring Canada into the Organization of American States, which was considered a mechanism of US domination in Latin America.[142] Most significant, the Diefenbaker Conservatives refused to install nuclear warheads on Canada's Bomarc missiles, a decision that prompted the prime minister's defeat in the House and triggered the 1963 election. Nuclear-disarmament activists had campaigned against the Bomarc since 1959, and celebrated the Nuclear Test Ban Treaty of August 1963, the first concrete step toward *détente* between East and West. However, Lester Pearson's minority Liberal government was elected on the pledge to accept the warheads and on 31 December 1963 'kept its promise to US imperialism,' as communists described it.[143] Nuclear warheads arrived in Canada.

The campaign against the Bomarcs intensified. Larry Ryan, a Victoria postal worker, steered a resolution through the Victoria Labour Council demanding that the federal government 'declare a non-nuclear role for Canada.'[144] The Student Union for Peace Action (SUPA), which had evolved out of CUCND, organized its Kootenay Project and Comox Project, which launched 'an integrated three-pronged attack on the RCAF base,' combining research and community education with nonviolent direct action. 'This would be one of the first times that the three aspects of the peace movement's work have all been actively undertaken and integrated within the same community,' SUPA field secretary Peter Boothroyd claimed.[145] Demonstrating links between Canadian and American activists, a scuffle erupted at the Blaine border crossing when fifteen US activists were detained en route to Victoria for a fourteen-day march to Comox.[146]

The anti-nuclear campaign was tied to the escalating conflict in Vietnam. Canada never maintained combat troops in Vietnam, but mounting evidence of what was called 'Canadian complicity' helped consolidate a domestic anti-war movement. 'It was all linked,' recalls Kevin Neish, who grew up in the peace activism of the 1960s.[147] US secretary of state Henry Kissinger threatened to use nuclear weapons against Vietnam, echoing Truman's threat against China during the Korean War. As the YS noted in 1968:

> Vietnam is the biggest political issue today among Canadian youth, and the most immediate factor in their radicalization. The escalation of the war, the increasingly frequent and devastating revelations of the true nature of the war, and the growth of the anti-war movement across this continent, makes Canadian support for the war more and more untenable in the eyes of young people.[148]

In 1954, Canada had been appointed to the three-member International Control Commission (ICC), charged with monitoring the Geneva Accords that ended the first Indo-China war; but like Poland (which represented the communist bloc on the ICC), Canada was not neutral. The Communist Party insisted during the 1963 BC election that the Legislature 'demand an end to Ottawa's support of the US genocide actions in Vietnam and adherence to the 1954 Geneva Accord.'[149]

The movement against the Vietnam War attracted all elements of the BC left, both old and new. NDP activist Hilda Thomas, a UBC English instructor, was politicized by the Vietnam War and served as chair of Vancouver's Vietnam Action Committee. 'I was the token non-Trotskyist chair of that committee,' Thomas recalls.[150] Protests against the war intensified as American armed force increased, particularly after the manufactured Gulf of Tonkin incident of 1965. In August that year, thirty-nine youths were arrested for blocking Prime Minister Lester Pearson's motorcade in the Pacific National Exhibition parade in Vancouver.[151] Though dismissed as pawns of the Communist Party, the young people demonstrated the growing appeal of direct action. On 26

March 1966, a large peace march, 3,000 strong, wound its way through Vancouver, uniting 'youth, students, labour, clergy and progressives.'[152] The march was organized by SUPA, and NDP MLA Alex MacDonald told the crowd that 'the Vietnamese people have earned the right to be left alone.'[153] That spring, a strong anti-war caucus emerged in the BC Teachers' Federation, while the UFAWU Women's Auxiliary endorsed a Voice of Women (VOW) delegation to Ottawa, demanding Canada 'use its influence with the Johnson administration' to end the Vietnam War.[154] However, Canada's secretary of state for foreign affairs, Paul Martin Sr, echoed the 'Domino Theory' at the core of American policy in southeast Asia: 'if the North Vietnamese aggression with Chinese connivance succeeds, it will only be a matter of time before the next victim is selected.'[155] Highlighting Canadian complicity, NDP leader Tommy Douglas exposed Canada's annual sales of $300 million in war materials to the United States, for use 'in an undeclared war' in Vietnam, which he described as 'a bloody and barbaric incident that has no equal in our time ... The time for quiet diplomacy is over and the time for speaking out is here.'[156]

By the late 1960s, BC's anti-war movement included both Old Left trade unionists and a new layer of activists (see appendix G). Vancouver Labour Council secretary Paddy Neale sat on the city's Vietnam Coordinating Committee, 'the only leader of a labor council formally on a Vietnam coordinating committee'; on 27 April 1968 the committee organized a large demonstration in Vancouver.[157] Tom Clarke, the militant president of Vancouver IWA Local 1-217, served as master of ceremonies at a benefit concert for the National Liberation Front.[158] A shift in leadership was discernible. The YS focused its efforts in UBC's Committee to End the War in Vietnam and the high school-based Students against War in Vietnam.[159] A group of University of Victoria activists led a walkout of 4,000 Victoria high school students in November 1971, protesting US nuclear tests at Amchitka Island and the war in Vietnam. 'I remember as a kid walking out of school, marching downtown,' Kevin Neish recalls. 'UVic students were the ones leading it.'[160]

BC's burgeoning anti-war movement was underpinned by a tangible manifestation of resistance to American militarism: the thousands of American draft-resisters and their families who settled in the Kootenays and across BC.[161] On the domestic front, BC's New Left mobilized in support of the national liberation movement in Quebec. During the October 1970 Front de Liberation du Québec (FLQ) crisis, seven members of the activist group Vancouver Liberation Front were arrested under the War Measures Act; Dawson Creek schoolteacher Arthur Olson was fired for expressing sympathy with the FLQ, under a special provincial order-in-council.[162] Vancouver City Council attempted to thwart protests by entertaining a motion prohibiting public demonstrations deemed 'subversive.' Committee of Progressive Electors (COPE) alderman Harry Rankin defeated the motion, as Vietnam Action Committee chairperson Hilda Thomas, an NDP member, said: 'Never before has this committee been so harassed and intimidated.'[163] A rally against the War Measures Act took place at the Vancouver Court House, followed by an anti-Vietnam War march. On the first anniversary of the declaration of the War Measures Act, a group calling itself the October 16 Committee organized a march through downtown Vancouver to a federal building at Granville and Hastings.[164]

Student Power and the Youth Revolt

Long before the youth revolt of the sixties, BC students cast a critical eye on the political and economic landscape. In groups such as the Student Christian Movement (SCM), Young Communist League (YCL), Co-operative Commonwealth Youth Movement (CCYM), and Young Liberals, students debated social questions and challenged the logic of the Cold War.[165] When Victoria Mayor Claude Harrison called for the burning of 'subversive' library books in 1954, the Victoria College SCM, backed by the Liberal Club and International Relations Club, organized a protest where they burned an effigy of the mayor.[166]

Growth in post-secondary education underpinned the new radicalism. The Department of National Defence noted in 1963 that attendance at UBC 'continues to grow at a phenomenal pace ... from approximately 10,000 in 1958–59 to 14,000 in 1962–63.'[167] A more visible student movement emerged, one that operated at a distance from BC's working class. The Canadian Union of Students (CUS) highlighted the class bias in post-secondary education in a 1966 survey, which found that only 35 per cent of Canadian university students were from 'blue-collar' working-class families. While this marked an improvement from previous decades, the report noted that Canadian university students were 'by and large not representative of the Canadian class structure but rather bear the characteristics of the middle and upper classes of Canadian society.'[168] In 1959, CCF Cranbrook MLA Leo Nimsick had warned that a $100 tuition increase at UBC would make 'university more privileged.'[169]

Despite their distance from the working class, this new layer of students gravitated to issues long championed by working-class parties, such as nuclear disarmament and the liberation struggles of colonial peoples. In December-January 1964–5, the CUCND took a radical turn at a Regina conference and reinvented itself as SUPA.[170] At UBC, student radical Charlie Boylan, a Communist Party member, was elected first vice-president of the Alma Mater Society.[171] At SFU, Trotskyists were 'recognized activists' in Students for a Democratic University (SDU), and an RCMP agent warned that the LSA 'could become a very strong radical influence on youth organizations, both in the NDP and in the educational process.'[172] Activist Don Roebuck urged a shift in priorities from Vietnam to campus work, citing 'the superior organizing potential of a student syndicalist movement.'[173] Sections of the New Left, however, were disdainful of the student movement, which they dismissed as hopelessly middle class. 'The CP and Maoists have ignored the student power movement,' a YS internal bulletin suggested.[174] While SUPA retained 'a small group of experienced leaders, considerable financial resources and connections in the university establishments,' the LSA observed that the organization, 'after a meteoric rise, disintegrated due to its programmatic inadequacy.'[175] SUPA split at its 1967 general membership conference in Goderich, Ontario, spawning the short-lived New Left Committee (NLC), which urged a return to class-based, workplace-centred organizing.[176] However, the NLC had little presence in the western provinces and within months executive members declared that 'The NLC, as a political organization, has no useful role to play at present' and its 'active existence ... shall not and ought not to be pursued.'[177] A section of the NLC remained active, particularly in the Canadian Union of Students (CUS), but trouble loomed as students at several universities voted to leave CUS.[178]

In BC, the student movement peaked in 1968 at Simon Fraser University, where 114 students were arrested for occupying the administration building, demanding that universities 'be open and accessible to all who wish to use them.'[179] Following the occupation, the SFU administration clamped down on the restive Political Science, Sociology, and Anthropology (PSA) Department, appointing a committee of trustees to oversee the department's affairs and curb its radical experiments in participatory democracy. Professor Mordecai Briemberg, who had been elected department chair a week earlier despite the protests of the university president and dean of arts, issued a statement opposing this heavy-handed measure: 'We are attacked because we want to contribute our energy to assisting the people in the community who don't control the power and wealth of BC.'[180] A *Ubyssey* editorial echoed this sentiment, in the midst of a labour dispute between the UBC administration and non-academic staff: 'We'd better realize where our allegiance should lie. And it ain't with the administrators, the polluting pulp millers, the forest barons and the Socreds.'[181] Students at three working-class Vancouver high schools refused to cross a janitors' picket line in 1968.[182] From Carihi in Campbell River, to the innovative 'Knowplace' school in Vancouver's West End, to a proposed 'Free University' in Victoria, teachers and students were experimenting with egalitarian and participatory models of education.[183]

The SFU occupation coincided with a wave of student and youth unrest that enveloped Canada and other countries. From Paris to Chicago to Montreal's Sir George Williams (now Concordia) University, students were at the centre of major clashes with authority.[184] Unrest in Czechoslovakia, where reformist premier Dubcek sought to establish 'socialism with a human face,' confirmed that neither the American nor the Soviet model jelled with the aspirations of rebellious young people. Addressing a group of McMaster University students in 1969, federal NDP leader and Nanaimo MP Tommy Douglas expressed this discontent with the Cold War superpowers: 'in the interests of so-called peace the United States had systematically bombed the people of Vietnam and in the name of so-called security the Soviet Union sent its tanks rumbling into Czechoslovakia.' Douglas described the youth revolt as a

> protest movement against a society that has failed to meet man's deepest needs and which impedes the realization of man's finest aspiration ... It is the realization that the power structure is beyond their control and unresponsive to the public will that has generated the spirit of revolt in modern youth ... In this contest I am on the side of youth.[185]

Efforts to bridge the divide between the Old Left and emerging New Left could be discerned. In 1967, Old Leftist Colin Cameron, who preceded Douglas as Nanaimo MP and kindled the flame of Marxism in the CCF-NDP, had addressed Selkirk College students in Castlegar on the 'gulf between the generations':

> The sort of future it will be is being decided now. Slowly, painfully, day by day we are fashioning the future in which you will live. The ideas you and your generation are developing to-day can determine the sort of world in

> which your children will struggle to maturity. But to do so they must be translated into political terms ...[186]

However, many New Leftists, such as SFU student and former SUPA chairman Jim Harding, rejected the NDP's gradualism as 'welfare-state-capitalist,' reflecting party leaders' interests in 'stabilizing the present system' despite a program 'cloaked in socialist rhetoric.' NDP leaders, such as Tom Berger, were 'the upward mobile members of the status quo, deeply socialized in liberalism, accepting the tenets and techniques of repressive tolerance,' and therefore not surprisingly favoured taxation over the expropriation of monopolies. The NDP's grievance was not with capitalism *per se*, Harding argued, but with how the old middle class represented by Social Credit was managing the capitalist system:

> If the NDP were elected in BC it would amount to a replacement of the old middle class representation (from an earlier development of capitalism) by a new middle class of neo-capitalism. It would reflect not a defeat but a change in the management of capitalism.[187]

This rejection of reformism found a home in the left-nationalist Waffle faction, which railed against US imperialism from Canada to Vietnam, and mounted a vigorous challenge in the late 1960s and early 1970s. Outside the NDP, such views were echoed by Old Leftist Harry Rankin, the fellow-travelling radical lawyer and Vancouver alderman: 'I adamantly reject one type of compromise – that of joining a party whose sole business is to maintain the present capitalistic system with improvements.' Rankin, however, was critical of sections of the New Left, particularly those 'young radicals' who regularly attacked him 'for entering the political structure as it now stands ... It makes a hell of a lot more sense to be inside where the action is, dealing with the issues, accelerating change than to be outside just making noise!'[188]

The 1960s ended as young people gravitated to hands-on community projects in the government-sponsored Company of Young Canadians (CYC) and the in-your-face organizing style of the Yippie movement in the United States.[189] When Yippie leader Jerry Rubin delivered a speech at UBC in 1968, a crowd of 2,000 students marched on the university faculty club, raiding the liquor supply, climbing on furniture, smoking marijuana, burning dollar bills, and bathing nude in the ornamental pond.[190] According to Jim Harding, there was a sharp politicization in the youth culture in the late 1960s, 'from a primitive sub-culture, naively believing at first that "love", "flowers" and mere dropping-out were sufficient ... to viewing the state as their enemy.' BC youth responded to 'continuous' police harassment – exemplified in the 1971 Gastown 'riot' – by forming urban co-ops and communes, seaside and island communities, that provided 'a base and security for the counter culture.'[191] According to Michael Walzer, New Left radicalism 'was the radicalism of a generation for whom neither security nor money had ever been a problem.' The children of a generation that had struggled through the Depression and achieved a measure of security in the post-war years, New Leftists inherited, 'in addition to their comforts, only the vaguest idealism, corroded by a new and very strong feeling for the possible pleasures of private life.' They forged a new radicalism in juxtaposition to 'the various radicalisms' of their parents' youth.[192]

The relationship between BC's Old Left and New Left was apparent in the environmental movement that took shape in the 1970s. Resource exploitation on the province's rugged frontier had nurtured a strong conservationist ethos, which manifested itself in opposition to clear-cut logging during the war and the first Sloan Commission. After the war, the UFAWU advocated licence limitation and the enforcement of a twelve-mile boundary to protect Canadian fishing grounds; Dan Assu, Native Brotherhood vice-president and a herring skipper from Cape Mudge on Quadra Island, wrote: 'We are partners with other groups in the conservation of salmon. We are even missionaries in this respect.'[193] Suburban development and industrial pollution in the 1950s spurred an emerging environmental consciousness. Activists, including veteran CCF MLA Ernie Winch, campaigned for the humane treatment of animals and a ban on leg-hold traps.[194] In 1961, the Burnaby Citizens Association (BCA) contested the municipal election on the pledge to 'STOP pollution in Burnaby now,' and proposed pollution control standards to regulate the activities of oil refineries, sawmills, and other businesses within the municipality. The BCA demanded a noise pollution by-law, a ban on heavy trucks in residential areas at night, the development of Burnaby Lake into a 'recreation and wildlife preserve,' and the preservation of the Marine Drive area for farming.[195] Pollution also raised the ire of local residents in BC's hinterland. Communist-endorsed aldermanic candidate George McKnight, a pulp mill worker in Vancouver Island's Alberni Valley, demanded air control legislation to curb the high incidence of respiratory disease. He circulated a petition demanding 'provincial laws to prevent industrial contamination of our air, river and coastal waters; and ensure clean water on our lakes, rivers and beaches ... It will cost money, but these profitable industries can afford it.'[196]

Continuity between the Old Left conservationists and New Left environmentalists crystallized on the issue of atomic testing, which spawned the Radiation Hazards committees in 1959 and Greenpeace in 1971. 'Before Greenpeace, it was the socialist and peace movement that was fighting the open-air nuclear tests that the Americans were doing,' recalls Kevin Neish, whose communist fisherman father campaigned against nuclear tests on Amchitka in the Aleutian Islands.[197] By the late 1960s, diverse environmental concerns were coalescing into a discernible movement, exerting pressure on labour unions and established left parties. Communist millworker Erni Knott spearheaded grassroots efforts to protect the rainforests of Vancouver Island, while the BC NDP led legislative efforts to protect North Vancouver's Cypress Bowl and curb hydroelectric expansion in the Skagit Valley.[198] The party's 1970 convention, which elected Dave Barrett as leader, endorsed the nationalization of all industries 'that refuse to stop polluting the environment.'[199] The Victoria Labour Council took stances on industrial waste, domestic sewage, garbage, and pesticide use, and in February 1971 opposed the passage of Alaskan oil tankers along 'the vulnerable BC coast.'[200] Reflecting its historic commitment to environmental conservation, the UFAWU staged a 'sail-in' at Vancouver's English Bay on 11 June 1972 to protest the proposed transport of Alaskan oil. Later that year, a second 'sail-in' was staged in the north arm of the Fraser River, demanding advanced sewage treatment at the Annacis Island plant.[201] In this milieu, a group of Vancouver activists in the 'Don't Make a Wave Committee' chartered the fishing seiner *Phyllis Cormack* and sailed to Amchitka, pledged to make a 'green peace.'[202]

The rise of BC's New Left challenged and changed established working-class parties. In the myriad 'other lefts' of this chaotic era, the militant minority nurtured an independent political flame, experimenting with forms of social-movement politics that provided a bridge between the Old and New Left. Social-movement activism energized the depleted ranks of the Communist Party, which organized demonstrations in the early 1970s against the War Measures Act, a proposed increase in BC Hydro rates, and California grapes.[203] Within the NDP, the New Left chipped away at narrow Cold War policies and rigid institutional practices – sustaining an oppositional current that Trotskyists had pursued since the Second World War. The Waffle, like kindred groups, mobilized in opposition to US economic imperialism in Canada and US militarism in Vietnam. NDP members such as Hilda Thomas, a feminist, Waffler, and chairperson of Vancouver's Vietnam Action Committee, belonged to this emerging social-movement activism. The 'third force' in BC's Old Left – the Trotskyist movement in its several organizational forms – navigated between these shifting political currents and was transformed. Uniquely situated as the historic critic of both Stalinism and social democracy, Trotskyism influenced student and labour militants but grappled with internal strife.[204] By the early 1970s, BC's working-class movements had changed. More diverse in orientation and composition than the militant minority of the 1940s and 1950s, this New Left was returning to the explicitly anti-capitalist politics that the Cold War had sought to wipe out.

CHAPTER FIVE

New Militancy

> A very large part in the trend to the left has been the economic struggles of the workers. Increasingly over the last two years these struggles have risen in intensity. Militant forms of struggle such as 'wild-cat' strikes and mass picketing have developed. Because of the anti-labour laws and the use of ex-parte injunctions in labour disputes there has grown a greater awareness of the political relationships existing in our country. More and more the workers' demands have included political demands. Witness the threat of a general strike in BC ...[1]
>
> 'A New Wind from the East Side,' CPC City Committee report, c. 1966

The Communist Party attributed Harry Rankin's 1966 election to Vancouver City Council to 'the new turn to the left across the country and especially here in BC,' tied to growing working-class militancy. As discussed earlier, labour relations in postwar BC more closely resembled a tug-of-war than a compromise between labour and capital. Union certification procedures, the legality of strikes and picketing, the composition of the Labour Relations Board, the operation of the Workmen's Compensation Board, and the bargaining rights of public-sector workers were all hotly contested by unions and employers. Both organized groups sought to tip the balance of forces to their benefit. The supremacy of employers was entrenched in 'management rights' clauses that pervaded postwar agreements. Labour, however, often directed the agenda through the extent of union organization and the militant agency of its rank and file.

By the 1960s, structural changes in BC's working class and increased participation by women and public-sector workers changed the nature of working-class militancy and contributed to a rank-and-file revolt.[2] The temper of industrial relations was also influenced by rising living costs, by insecurity wrought by automation and unemployment, by rapid construction of transportation and energy infrastructure in hinterland areas, by volatility in commodity prices, by the intransigence of employers and governments to bargain in good faith, and by a growing frustration among rank-and-file workers with cumbersome collective bargaining procedures and the apparent complacency of established unions operating within this *status quo*. This frustration was tied to an emerging Canadian nationalist current, manifested in moves across the sectors to sever ties with American unions and forge new organizations. Tracing a continuum to earlier secessionist movements – the Industrial Workers of the World (IWW), One Big Union (OBU), All-Canadian Congress of Labour (ACCL), Committee for Industrial Organization (CIO), and communist-led Woodworkers Industrial Union of Canada (WIUC), which split from the IWA in 1948 – the breakaway movement of the 1960s and 1970s extended from 'blue-collar' resource workers at Castlegar, Crofton, Nanaimo, Kitimat, Prince Rupert, and Trail to the growing pool of white-collar workers in the cities. By 1972, this working-class unrest gave rise to levels of strike activity and striker-days unseen since the Second World War (see appendix A).

The Origins of Breakaway Unions

The origins of the breakaway unions can be traced much earlier than the 1960s – to the postwar industrial relations apparatus that created a distance between leaders and the rank and file; to the climate of recrimination and hostility that was the legacy of the 1948 Red Wars; and to the conservatism of International unions, which had spawned the IWW, OBU, and CIO. In BC's Kootenay region, the breakaway WIUC provided a tangible alternative to the Internationals with a militant presence in the forestry sector of the 1950s.[3] Legislative restraints on the right to picket and strike, a hallmark of labour relations in postwar BC, encouraged a tradition of law-breaking and contempt for governments, law enforcement, and the courts. Between 1946 and 1955, the BC Supreme Court received 69 applications for injunctions relating to labour disputes and granted all but two; from 1956 to 1965, this trend intensified, with the courts granting 224 of 226 applications for *ex parte* injunctions, where the union was denied notice or hearing. As Tom Berger, BCFL legal counsel, wrote in 1966: injunctions 'place the judiciary, as far as the labourer is concerned, in the ranks of the employers.'[4] The openly partisan rulings of provincial and federal politicians, Labour Relations Board and Workmen's Compensation Board appointees, and provincial court judges provoked the ire of organized workers.

In 1950, a joint meeting of the rival Vancouver Trades and Labor Council (TLC) and Vancouver Labour Council (CCL) demanded 'the immediate repeal' of emergency federal legislation ordering striking railroaders back to work. 'This bill is going to be the rocks on which the careers of many politicians are going to founder at the next elections,' Jack O'Brien, publicity chairperson of the fifteen unions involved in the dispute, told the crowd.[5] However, the 1950 Maintenance of Railway Operation Act stood, setting a pattern of government intervention that became the rule by the close of the twentieth century.[6] BC trade unionists railed against the decision of CCL leaders Frank Hall and Aaron Mosher to end the strike, before the legislation even came into force, but labour's weakness was apparent, a consequence of the Red Wars and labour laws designed to curb sympathetic job action.[7]

In the postwar era, organized labour focused primarily on winning union security and improving wages and benefits through negotiation and industrial action, but also applied political pressure on governments to regulate prices. The lifting of wartime price controls by the federal and provincial governments contributed to a sharp increase in consumer prices, for foodstuffs such as bread, milk, and meat, to petroleum, consumer durables, and housing.[8] Workers' wage gains were often stripped away by employers' price hikes. 'We shall be told that the rise is caused by the demands of organized labor for increased wages,' the *CCF News* quipped in August 1948. However, the real cause of inflation was the 'insatiable greed of industrialists' and the 'supine' attitude of the federal government.[9] In 1950 federal finance minister Abbott told Parliament:

> People do not like controls, and we have to recognize the fact that except in times of great crisis, they will resist them, evade and circumvent them ... [T]he government's policy is to counter the inflationary pressures that may be generated by our expanded defense program primarily by fiscal measures ... [10]

Such measures did little to alleviate the inflationary pressure on workers' wages, fuelling demands for wage increases in every round of bargaining. BCFL secretary-treasurer Pat O'Neil told UBC's CCF club in

1959 that 'instead of protecting the public from corporations, corporations are protected at the expense of the public.' [11] Later, this sentiment inspired campaigns against 'price-fixing' by food processing and distribution combines, and encouraged the formation of consumer co-operatives.[12]

BC labour's position was weakened in the 1950s by the lack of cooperation between TLC and CCL unions, animosity toward red unions, and growing institutional pressures. As Harvey Murphy told the 1952 UFAWU convention, the 'most violent propaganda' had brought about 'the practice of having individual unions go by themselves' to the provincial government, replacing the former joint 'Labour Lobbies' of TLC and CCL unions:

> Big shots have come up in the labor movement, high salaried officials who look, not to the rank and file any more, but who look for plaudits from the press of big business, and who are glorified by the Governmental Agencies, and who look for their promotion, not from the ranks of labor, but you see them stepping into Government office after they want to leave a Trade Union position, and who are not responsive today to the voice and control of the rank and file. This is what is happening today.[13]

The labour bureaucracy remained an obstacle to militancy in the postwar years, as the institutions of collective bargaining created distance between leaders and rank-and-file workers and lent credence to employers' anti-union attacks. [14] Murphy pointed to the unity of employers as an example for labour to emulate: 'I have never seen yet one employers association attacking another employers association insofar as labour legislation or its relationship with workers. The CMA in British Columbia unites them all. Why is it not possible among the workers to have that same unity?' The Seamen's Union had been

> smashed and obliterated ... because some government body refused to grant it license to operate. [But] whoever heard of the time when labor had to apply to a Government to have its Trade Union license. And yet, in actuality, that is the situation today. Greater powers bestowed on boards.[15]

Murphy identified a tension in postwar BC: the efforts of employer-oriented governments and the courts to curb working-class agency, and the predilection of workers to use their collective power to improve working and living conditions.

Even non-communist trade unionists retained a commitment to militant industrial action: in 1952, the IWA led a forty-five-day strike that accounted for more striker-days than disputes in all other industries combined in the years 1949 to 1956.[16] After the IWA strike, Local 1-80 president Tony Poje was sentenced to three months in Oakalla prison and fined $3,000 for defying a court injunction against picketing in Nanaimo.[17] In construction, building-trades unions 'led by conservative "business" unionists' accounted for 24 per cent of all strikes in BC in the 1950s, while Murphy's Mine-Mill was, according to Stuart Jamieson, 'relatively free of strikes of any consequence.' As Jamieson concludes: 'There is little or no reliable evidence to indicate that unions under radical leadership have engaged in larger, longer, or more frequent strikes than those under conservative leadership in British Columbia.'[18]

Where radical and moderate union leaders diverged was on their respective political strategies. Moderates, often linked to the CCF, placed greater emphasis on striking at the ballot box. In 1952, IWA secretary-treasurer George Mitchell called for 'a day of reckoning with those politicians who so flagrantly disregard the expressed views and needs of the Trade Union movement' and demanded the Industrial Conciliation and Arbitration (ICA) Act be amended:

> to safeguard and not handicap the procedures of genuine collective bargaining. The Labor Relations Board must be held to its responsibilities under an amended Act, to act not with bias against labor, but with even-handed justice toward labor's struggles to raise living standards.

Mitchell said the IWA was exploring 'ways and means for exercising a more direct influence on political decisions.'[19] In the 1952 general election, BC voters threw out the authors of the ICA Act, replacing the Liberal-Conservative Coalition with the untested Social Credit League. Emboldened by a legislative majority in 1953, W.A.C. Bennett replaced the hated ICA Act with Bill 22, the Labour Relations Act (1954), which was specifically designed 'to reduce the frequency and impact of industrial disputes,' but as Jamieson suggests, failed to have the desired effect: 'In the unstable economic, social, and political context in which industrial relations are carried on in British Columbia, even the best designed and most far-sighted labour disputes legislation (or the most severe and punitive for that matter!) would have little or no effect upon the recurrent cycle of industrial conflict in that province.'[20] At its 1954 convention, the BC CCF demanded the repeal of the new act, proposing a labour code 'designed to halt and avoid the trend of labor-management problems being referred to and decided by the courts, and to restore the traditional freedom of collective bargaining.'[21] George Home, BCFL president and a BC CCF executive member, described the act 'as one of the most vicious pieces of legislation in North America.'[22] Thwarted by the courts when they attempted to improve employment conditions by means of the strike, delegates at the BCFL's 1956 merger convention urged that 'all future appointments to the judiciary should be on the basis of merit, divorced from political considerations.'[23]

Militancy was a regular feature of BC industrial relations in the 1950s, setting the province apart from trends in the rest of Canada. Of seventy-one strikes in forestry in the years 1949–59, forty-seven were 'wildcat' or 'illegal' strikes that took place outside formalized bargaining procedures; in construction, forty-five of seventy-eight strikes were 'wildcat.'[24] The prevalence of wildcat strikes often demonstrated tension between rank-and-file workers in the hinterland and unions and corporations headquartered in Vancouver. A 1953 sawmill strike in the Kootenays erupted a day after IWA officials assured operators that workers would remain on the job.[25] In forestry and industrial construction, multi-employer collective agreements were negotiated between unions and corporations, reducing the number of 'interest' strikes during bargaining but creating a distance from the rank and file that triggered mid-contract disputes. 'Common grievances on the job tend then to develop into unauthorized or wildcat strikes,' Jamieson argues.[26] The wildcat phenomenon of the 1950s reflected volatility in BC's economy, particularly the boom-bust nature of its resource-extraction industries and cyclical construction sector. In the recession years of 1953 and 1958, construction declined by 14.5 per cent and 25 per cent respectively, in comparison with declines of 6 per cent and 2.3 per cent in Canada as a whole. In the boom years of 1955–7, construction expanded by 73 per cent in BC compared with a 36 per cent rise elsewhere, creating fierce competition for labour in the building trades and driving up wages and benefits to levels that cut deeply into profits once the boom subsided. The expectations of construction workers did not subside, however, triggering prolonged strikes by workers determined to win 'boom' wages from intransigent employers.[27]

Some labour leaders, however, were more conciliatory in their relations with employers and governments. In March 1956, on the eve of the TLC-CCL merger, VTLC secretary-treasurer Roly K. Gervin became a spokesperson for Construction Industrial Relations, an employer lobby group. 'Many years of union experience was thus suddenly placed at the disposal of the employers,' labour lawyer John Stanton observes.[28] A former RCMP officer, Gervin served as a Vancouver alderman with the business-aligned Non-Partisan Association. The *Pacific Tribune* attributed Gervin's defection to opposition from Bill Black, of the Hospital Employees' Union, and Everett King, of the Office Employees, to Gervin's attempts to stifle debate on the new CLC constitution.[29] Gervin's new employer was soon embroiled in a major controversy over the collapse of the Second Narrows Bridge on Burrard Inlet. The earlier case of George Wilkinson, Victoria TLC secretary and Chamber of Commerce member who participated in an employer lobby to the BC legislature (discussed in chapter 1), also highlighted this phenomenon of class collaborationism in BC labour's ranks.

Despite militant strikes to boost wages, few BC workers questioned the logic of postwar growth. A correspondent to the *CCF News*, W. Mackey of Ganges on Saltspring Island, deviated from the norm in challenging the materialism underlying labour's postwar bargaining strategy. Mackey took issue with the 'selfishness' of labour's postwar aims, an abandonment of the old socialist objective of 'the raising of the down trodden, the equalization of all who wanted to work, or were unable to do so.' Mackey articulated an internationalist critique of the growing disparity between workers in poor and rich countries: 'Can we continue boosting wages and profits for export goods, depending on loaned money to buy our goods? Should we do most of the world's production of goods and other nations do a very minor part of it?'[30] This view was echoed at the 1956 BCFL merger convention, when packinghouse worker Jim Bury reminded delegates: 'If we get a wage increase here it means driving a 1955 Pontiac instead of a 1952 Chev. To the Africans it means at least one proper solid meal a day.'[31] Tied to the rising current of anti-colonial liberation struggles, British Columbia's militant minority was cognizant of imbalances in the world economy. During his 1952 journey across the 'Bamboo Curtain' to Beijing, China for the Asia-Pacific Rim Peace Conference, communist fisherman Elgin 'Scotty' Neish anticipated future trading relationships: 'China would welcome trade from Canada. But that doesn't mean that they want Coca-Cola or nylon stockings. They are willing to trade on the basis of material and equal advantage ... I would say it's time our businessmen realized they are not dealing with infants and that you cannot blockade half the world.'[32]

This internationalist critique reflected a growing trend among BC unions to abandon xenophobic attitudes, which had divided workers for decades and impeded labour's bargaining strength. A Vancouver Joint Labor Committee to Combat Racial Discrimination was formed in 1950, 'one of the first cooperative projects between local TLC and CCL groups.'[33] The committee called for a Bill of Rights and a Fair Employment Practices Act, which would 'guarantee that all workers would be given the opportunity for a job and for promotion merely on the basis of their ability and not because they belong to a certain church or their ancestors happened to come from a certain country or that they don't happen to speak with an accent.'[34] Committee spokesperson Knute Buttedahl cited similar legislation on the books in Saskatchewan and Ontario, and stressed that passage of legislation was not sufficient, that a permanent commission had to be established 'to carry out the terms of such legislation.'[35] When Social Credit acceded to pressure with Bill 33, the Fair Employment Practices Act (1956) – outlawing discrimination in employment or trade-union membership on the basis of race, colour, or religious belief – the Vancouver branch of the LPP-aligned League for Democratic Rights described the move as 'a step in the right direction, but it doesn't go far enough.' Penalties against employers were insufficient and the complaints procedure 'too cumbersome,' the League claimed. Moreover, Bill 33 dealt only with employment discrimination, failing to address inequality in housing and accommodation: 'Many hotels will not accommodate a person whose skin is not white. A number of beer parlors in Vancouver will not serve mixed parties of negro and White people.'[36] Communists were at the forefront of moves toward racial equality, enlisting Chinese, Japanense, and Indo-Canadian organizers to work among fishers, loggers, and millworkers. In the 1963 provincial election, the LPP distributed 2,000 Mandarin leaflets in Vancouver's Chinese community.[37]

Other labour leaders, however, adhered to a more narrow Cold War politics. The year 1956 has been described as 'the year of mergers.' In 1955, the American labour movement had ended the twenty-year-old AFL-CIO split, paving the way for similar moves in Canada that gave rise to the CLC and unified BCFL.[38] However, the jurisdictional gymnastics associated with merging affiliates of the two central bodies unleashed an upturn in breakaway sentiment. There was also a nationalistic component, as Abella suggests: 'the Canadian labour movement was no longer effectively Canadian.'[39] While the CLC weakened the Internationals' hegemony by providing a cohesive union central, it also signalled the end of the more home-grown CCL. In BC, the desire of international officers to ensure the orderly development of unified affiliates produced tension with local leadership and rank-and-file workers, tension exacerbated by enduring anti-communism. In the summer of 1956, six BC union locals were under trusteeship, most of them communist-led.[40]

That year, Mine-Mill staved off a raid attempt at the new Alcan smelter at Kitimat, while its Nelson local waged a strike against Yale Lead and Zinc Mines Ltd. to win parity with other miners in the district. Seeking to escape the discriminatory provisions of Taft-Hartley, delegates to the 1956 BC District convention unanimously approved the formation of an autonomous Canadian Mine-Mill union, not because of 'a rift in the international union' but in order to conduct union affairs independently of US law.[41] Canadian members approved the creation of the 30,000-strong Union of Mine, Mill and Smelter Workers by referendum, with the consent of the International. As Al King, president of Trail Local 480 recounts, 'This wasn't a breakaway.'[42]

In other BC unions, however, alienation from US-controlled International leadership was fuelling breakaway sentiments and demands for autonomy and outright independence. As the *Woodpecker*, organ of the WIUC Cranbrook local, declared in 1955: 'In the "Mergers" that are taking place today in the International Unions, there is a dangerous trend to become an even more servile tool of US Imperialist policy and an accomplice to monopoly in Canada.'[43] Pulp and paper workers in the Western Council of the International Brotherhood of Pulp, Sulphite and Paper Mill Workers (Pulp & Sulphite) grew increasingly disenchanted, with Vancouver Local 433 business agent Orville Braaten founding the *Western Pulp and Paper Worker* in January 1956. The dissidents opposed merger talks with the IWA and clashed with International officers at Pulp & Sulphite's May 1956 Milwaukee convention, claiming jurisdiction over new mills in Alberta and Saskatchewan. Local 433 was the largest union of paper box and bag workers in Canada, but in 1957 the International relinquished jurisdiction to rival CLC unions. A Rank and File Committee for Democratic Action emerged, foreshadowing the 1963 split that gave rise to the Pulp and Paper Workers of Canada (PPWC, which changed its name to Pulp, Paper and Woodworkers of Canada in 1971).[44]

Other breakaway currents emerged at this time. In May 1956, fifty tunnel and rock workers on the West coast natural gas pipeline at Harrison Hot Springs staged a wildcat strike to protest a wage ceiling of $1.20 an hour – 40 cents below the prevailing BC rate – agreed to by the International Hod Carriers union (AFL), their parent union. The

International expelled the officers of Tunnel and Rock Workers Local 168, but a trustee was physically prevented from seizing the local's Vancouver headquarters. At a mass meeting in Pender Auditorium, declared 'unconstitutional and illegal' by the International, 1,000 workers pledged support to the expelled officers. 'We are within BC labor laws and we will fight for BC wages on the job,' expelled secretary Art Andres declared.[45] The trustee opened a separate office, attempting to establish a rival local, but the workers remained solid and forced the contractor, Sparling Davis Ltd., to accept a wage scale at the prevailing BC rates. While Local 168's delegates were unseated by the VTLC at the behest of the International, the Supreme Court of BC offered a rare ruling favourable to the rank and file, preventing interference with the local's bank account, mail delivery, 'contractual obligations,' agreements, and certifications.[46] When workers in Merritt, BC wildcatted for the higher rate, Local 168 won an increase of 30 cents despite the trustee's promise to get 'a boatload of Italian immigrants to man the job.' This victory was offset, however, by the granting of jurisdiction on all pipeline work to the International Labourers' Union (CIO) Local 602, under the trusteeship of CLC envoy Carl Berg. 'Seldom has the argument for Canadian trade union autonomy and inner-union democracy been so clearly illustrated,' the *Pacific Tribune* declared.[47]

To labour dissidents, the new CLC and BCFL were compliant tools of the Internationals, central bodies that hindered rather than advanced the emancipation of BC's working class. Provisions in the CLC constitution, such as biannual rather than annual conventions, despite pressure from communists and other left-wingers, were interpreted as proof that CLC leaders sought to contain militant working-class agency.[48] In November 1956, the merger was formalized at the BCFL convention. Despite talk of unity, delegates were not prepared to abandon the Cold War exclusion of LPP-led unions. Paper Makers Local 360 called on the BCFL to protest the CLC's exclusion of the Tunnel and Rock Workers and UFAWU, but the resolutions committee moved non-concurrence and delegates agreed. CCFer Tom Alsbury led the debate against the UFAWU, invoking the misdeeds of the USSR: 'We have seen in Hungary just how far they can go in forcing their views on people.' He reminded delegates that Homer Stevens had been granted an hour-long hearing at the TLC convention where the UFAWU was suspended, and that the UFAWU (along with Mine-Mill and the Vancouver Civic Outside Workers) was welcome to return to the mainstream of labour 'at any time they are prepared to accept democratic procedures and abide by the policies and constitution of our Congress.'[49] William Stewart of the Vancouver Marine Workers and Boilermakers suggested, however, that claims that 'the door is open' were hollow, and that divisions would impede the work of organizing the unorganized. He noted that the highest incomes in Canada were in Trail and Sudbury, cities covered by Mine-Mill agreements. 'We cannot say Mr. Chairman that we have a fully united labour movement here in Canada if we consistently tell a number of unions you are not coming in because we don't like your officers.'[50] Ray Haynes, narrowly elected to the BCFL executive council, called the question and a majority of BCFL delegates voted to keep the UFAWU outside their ranks. A motion on Trade Union Unity, submitted by Stewart's Marine Workers and Boilermakers, was rejected without debate, as was a resolution from Pulp & Sulphite Local 312 to 'enable the affiliation of all bona fide Trades Unions regardless of the personal beliefs of their officers or members.'[51] For the next decade and a half, pressure mounted for the UFAWU's admission.[52]

Despite these divisions, BC labour continued to win organizational and compensation gains. In July 1957, an industry-wide strike by coastal loggers was narrowly averted by the direct intervention of W.A.C. Bennett, who arranged an all-night bargaining session that awarded the IWA a 7.5 per cent pay increase and extensive fringe benefits.[53] As Labour Minister Lyle Wicks reported to the 1957 BCFL convention, 'we in BC have the highest hourly average wage in all of Canada.'[54] The next year, union density in BC reached its historic peak, with 53.9 per cent of workers organized into unions.[55] When workers on the Canadian Pacific Steamship Service paralysed transport between the mainland and Vancouver Island, an emergency sitting of Parliament passed the BC Coast Steamship Service Act (1958), the second instance of federal back-to-work legislation, which ended the strike. The CCF National Council issued a statement supporting the action, but condemned the Diefenbaker government for compulsory-arbitration provisions, which were 'unnecessary to a resumption of services' and violated 'the legitimate rights of the organized labour movement.'[56]

The 1959 Strike Wave

The collapse of the Trans-Canada Highway bridge, then under construction, at the Second Narrows of Burrard Inlet on 18 June 1958 highlighted the dangers facing workers in BC's fast-paced economy, and contributed to a fresh wave of strikes and injunctions. Nineteen workers were killed, most of them members of Local 97 of the International Association of Bridge, Structural and Ornamental Ironworkers. The contractor, Dominion Bridge, won a new contract to rebuild the bridge, but when the company's engineers expressed concern over the safety of the new structure, Ironworkers Local 97 went on strike. The strike was legal under the union's collective agreement, but Dominion Bridge was granted an *ex parte* injunction from Justice A.M. Manson directing Local 97 to order the strikers back to work, based on the anti-strike provisions of Bill 43, the new Trade-Unions Act (1959). Local 97's officers complied with the letter of the judge's ruling, but made it clear they did so under compulsion and that Manson's injunction was subject to appeal. The workers, predictably, remained on strike. Manson responded with a hastily convened hearing where he fined the union and its officers $19,000, or a year in prison.[57]

Legal action extended to other unions. George North, editor of the *Fisherman*, published the editorial 'Injunctions Won't Catch Fish nor Build Bridges' (appendix H) and was jailed by Supreme Court Justice Norman Whitaker – a former Liberal speaker of the BC legislature – and the Fisherman Publishing Society was fined $3,000. North had noted 'the closeness of companies and the courts' and lauded the 'sensible leadership' the striking Ironworkers provided to BC workers. He suggested Bill 43 could be 'made ineffective and wiped off the books' by 'trade union solidarity,' urging all BC unions to follow the Vancouver Building Trades Council and support the Ironworkers. Anticipating 'big strikes...in the lumber and fishing industries ... within the next few weeks,' North stated that 'United action by all labour can win these strikes despite the opposition of employers, government, and courts.' North spent a month in BC's Oakalla prison for his editorial.[58]

The 1959 Ironworkers' dispute was only one battle in a year of turbulent industrial relations. Bill 43, which supplemented the Labour Relations Act (1954), restricted picketing and strikes and gave the LRB and government the power to issue injunctions.[59] According to labour lawyer Harry Rankin, the legislation 'allowed companies to obtain injunctions practically at will against striking unions.'[60] The right to freely disseminate information during labour disputes, established in Supreme Court Justice Ivan Rand's famous 1946 ruling, was set aside. Bill 43 also weakened workers' bargaining power by prohibiting secondary picketing and confirmed unions' status as legal entities that could be sued for damages.[61] A second piece of legislation, Bill 128, outlawed civil-service strikes, amending BC's Constitution Act to ensure 'the continuation without interference or interruption of public services.'[62] These measures inflamed labour, while a pace-setting pension clause won by Mine-Mill Local 480 at Trail increased pressure on employers in other sectors.[63]

A strike by the National Association of Marine Engineers against the Northland Navigation Co. served as a test case for Bill 43's anti-picketing language, but the marine engineers won a favourable settlement after Vancouver unions devised the innovative tactic of posting columns of 'observers' in front of the plant – 'the Northland Formula.'[64] In July 1959, 27,000 IWA members struck 134 companies, paralysing BC's coastal forestry sector in a protracted strike. 'There can be no retreat by the workers in the face of government and boss-inspired injunctions,' the LPP's Woodworkers Club warned.[65] The woodworkers remained out for sixty-six days before settling with a 25 cent hourly pay increase over two years.[66] In late July 1959, the UFAWU also struck, from the mouth of the Fraser to Prince Rupert, the first industry-wide strike in fishing; the UFAWU had earlier won the dues check-off for shoreworkers, and in 1959 demanded higher wages, settling after twelve days.[67] A strike of shorter duration but great significance was the March 1959 walkout of 12,000 provincial civil servants, who struck for four hours demanding higher wages and bargaining rights.[68] This militancy, like a threatened strike of Vancouver Postal Workers during Christmas 1959, demonstrated the emerging phenomenon of public-sector unionism.[69]

The Fight for Public-Sector Unionism

Resource extraction and processing were the most important locus of BC's postwar economy, but the public sector expanded as never before, in tandem with growth of the Keynesian welfare state. BC's Hospital Insurance Act (1948) inaugurated a central role for the province in the provision of health services. The Hospital Employees' Union (HEU), founded in 1944 when male and female workers at Vancouver General Hospital merged their separate organizations, intensified its struggle for recognition and fair compensation. HEU expanded to nineteen locals in its first decade and began negotiating regional contracts in 1961 (rather than separate contracts with each hospital); in 1968 HEU achieved its first master agreement, bargaining with an employers' association representing sixty-six BC hospitals. That year, the federal Medical Care Act paved the way for public health insurance in every

Canadian province, a universal single-tier comprehensive system that labour had demanded for decades.[70]

Growth in public services and public employment was mirrored in education, where teachers had long struggled for adequate compensation and union recognition. The BC Teachers' Federation (BCTF), founded in 1917, had an ambivalent relationship with the broader labour movement. Like other white-collar workers, many teachers viewed themselves as 'professionals,' set apart from the industrial working class. BC labour's gains during the Second World War demonstrated the benefits of formal bargaining relationships and labour affiliation: wages soared among militant resource and manufacturing workers, while the salaries of teachers – employed by 400 school boards in BC's far-flung communities – fell behind. In December 1943, the BCTF affiliated with the TLC, and in 1947 won 'closed shop' recognition – all BC teachers were required by legislation to belong to the BCTF.[71] However, as the *Pacific Tribune* observed, 'few BCTF locals carried through the affiliation by sending delegates to local labour councils.'[72] The province improved conditions in the schools, as recommended by the Cameron Commission on education, and collective bargaining drove up teachers' salaries.[73] When Richmond janitors went on strike in 1953, teachers took no action.[74] In 1956, on the eve of the TLC-CCL merger, BC teachers again debated affiliation. Some teachers favoured severing ties in the view that union affiliation was 'incompatible with professional status.' But communists warned of the folly of this course, at a time when the BC School Trustees Association was pressing for 'merit-based' pay that threatened the teachers' hard-won salary gains.[75] However, in May 1956, BCTF delegates voted to withdraw from the TLC and remain outside the merged BCFL and CLC.[76]

From the outset, the BC Federation of Labour was oriented toward public-sector unionism. The HEU's William Black was elected founding president, and the 1956 merger convention adopted a resolution from the BC Government Employees' Association (BCGEA) calling for 'a properly regulated bargaining procedure ... with provisions for impartial arbitration of disputes,' a right that already extended to police, firefighters, teachers, and municipal workers.[77] As the *CCF News* had observed in 1948: 'With the exception of the provincial public servants in Saskatchewan, civil servants in Canada today enjoy far fewer rights than their opposite number in the leading democracies of the world.'[78] The BCGEA (formed as a province-wide organization in 1944 out of the earlier Provincial Civil Service Association) affiliated with the TLC in 1945.[79] Like teachers, provincial government workers were ambivalent about their relationship with the organized working class. However, conditions in the 1950s and 1960s underscored the need for stronger labour ties. The BCGEA stayed inside the BCFL and CLC, and in 1957 conducted a strike vote that won pay increases, the promise of a forty-hour week, and a public inquiry into bargaining rights.[80] UBC law professor A.W.R. Carrothers reviewed the 1948 Civil Service Act and recommended that collective bargaining be extended to civil servants, but 'kept separate from the Labour Relations Act,' rejecting the system then in operation in Saskatchewan. Carrothers opposed 'closed shop' recognition for the BCGEA and proposed binding arbitration as the final recourse for settling disputes, insisting that 'there was no statutory restriction on freedom to strike ... it is not in the collective nature of civil servants to strike.'[81] Sixteen BCGEA delegates were seated at the Victoria Labour Council in January 1958.[82]

In 1959, provincial government workers' grievances bubbled over, tied to the broader current of militancy. On 13 March 1959, 12,000 BCGEA members went on strike at 7 a.m., picketing government buildings across the province; by 10:30 a.m., Supreme Court Justice McInnes had issued an injunction against 'watching, besetting, and picketing,' and the BCGEA ended the strike, citing weak support in Victoria. Another judge, J.A. Ratten, declared that picketing government buildings amounted to 'a virtual blockade,' while the union said the issue was whether 'the law of the land is to apply equally to government employees.'[83] The legislature approved amendments to BC's Constitution Act a week later making it illegal to 'picket, watch, or beset any [government] building.'[84] Animosity between the BCGEA and Social Credit intensified. In October 1960 the government cut off payroll deduction of dues, citing affiliation to the BCFL, which was engaged in New Party talks with the CCF opposition. The timing of this move betrayed Bennett's fears of politically active public-sector workers. However, the BCGEA was not prepared to lose the dues check-off and immediately suspended affiliation, a move approved in a December referendum by 4,793–1,827 votes; delegates withdrew from labour councils across BC.[85] Despite this olive branch to Social Credit, the check-off was not restored until 1967. Membership and finances slumped by 40 per cent in the first year, as a team of several hundred volunteer shop stewards scrambled to collect dues. 'It almost destroyed them,' future general secretary John Fryer has suggested.[86] By the end of the decade, provincial government employees in all Canadian provinces with the exception of BC had won formal recognition and collective bargaining rights.[87]

BC's public-sector unions were less tainted by earlier Red Wars and spurred a new kind of unionism. Ben Swankey, former Alberta LPP leader who moved to Burnaby in 1958 and worked for the CPC's Trade Union Research Bureau, suggests there was a gender dimension. Cold War divisions weakened as

> all the women came into the labour movement from the public service. They didn't bring any anti-communism with them. They just brought a desire to organize. I think they were the decisive factor in making it a Canadian labour movement ... Women were mostly in the public service. And they were the least influenced by anti-communism ... They sure as hell didn't want any American control over Canada.[88]

Women accounted for a third of the 80,000 workers in the Canadian Union of Public Employees (CUPE), which formed in 1963 when the National Union of Public Employees (NUPE) merged with the smaller National Union of Public Service Employees (NUPSE) to create the CLC's second largest affiliate. The RCMP Security Service 'closely watched' these developments, claiming that Grace Hartman, a NUPE member and future CUPE secretary-treasurer, reported to 'the CP of C's Metro Toronto Labour Committee.'[89] While NUPSE unanimously favoured the merger, a majority of BC delegates at NUPE's final convention were opposed, believing it undermined local autonomy and the role of local staff representatives. They were defeated on a 232–71 vote. 'Several BC locals did not affiliate immediately with the new union,' CUPE BC's official history records.[90] The Vancouver Civic Outside Workers, barred from the house of labour for communist leadership, remained outside CUPE, striking successfully in 1964 and 1966 for higher wages and increased vacation time.[91] However, the aspiration of CUPE leaders to create 'the biggest national union in the country,' and a dispute with the CLC, created an opening for the red union: '[we] saw an opportunity of our local with this progressive policy getting into the national union and working in the labour movement from the inside,' secretary Jack Phillips recalls.[92] In 1967, CUPE threatened to withhold per capita dues and the CLC grudgingly accepted the affiliation of the Vancouver outside workers.[93]

Bargaining rights in the federal civil service came to the fore in a 1965 wildcat strike of Vancouver postal workers, who along with their

Montreal counterparts initiated a national strike, to win parity with other public-sector workers; as the *Vancouver Sun* noted, postal workers earned $3,000 less per year than police officers and firefighters and $2,000 less than labourers employed by the City of Vancouver.[94] Despite a court injunction prohibiting picketing and opposition from union leaders, Vancouver postal workers pulled off a 100 per cent shutdown of mail service in the Pacific metropolis.[95] Following the strike, leaders of the Canadian Postal Employees Association (CPEA) and Federated Union of Letter Carriers (FULC) were voted out of office, as CPEA reinvented itself as the Canadian Union of Postal Workers (CUPW).[96]

Wildcat Strikes

The pattern of government intervention, employer intransigence, and working-class militancy intensified in the 1960s, influenced by inflationary pressures, structural unemployment, and conflict over automation. The Communist Party took aim at 'a chronic unemployment situation that has been getting steadily worse ever since the end of the war, in good times and bad. Our vaunted free enterprise economy simply has not been able to provide jobs for the people.'[97] Communists proposed a thirty-hour work week to combat unemployment, which exceeded 63,000 in spring 1960.[98] The Trotskyist SWP helped organize the unemployed, supporting an effort by Courtenay militant David McGarvie to make 'the BC Federation realize they can't sit on their hands any longer.'[99] In response, the BCFL drafted a plan of organization for a British Columbia Federation of the Unemployed (BCFU), headed by the secretary-treasurers of the BCFL, local labour and building trades councils, a CLC representative, and five 'representatives of the Unemployed in British Columbia.'[100] The Victoria Labour Council, meanwhile, spearheaded an unemployed workers' union that rallied at the opening of the legislature in 1961.[101]

Fears of unemployment were heightened by automation in production, as employers undertook substantial capital investments to contain labour costs. Forestry exemplifies this trend: in the 1950s, output and profit increased substantially 'without any appreciable increase in the size of the labour force.'[102] Protracted strikes reflected the weakened bargaining position of forestry workers, who sought parity with workers in the overheated construction sector. Working-class grievances against automation mounted as workers in all sectors saw jobs replaced by machines. The Kensington LPP Club noted in 1957 that 'automation must be recognized as a revolutionary development in our life, bringing into focus the sharpest contradictions of capitalism.'[103] In the 1966 provincial election, the Communist Party demanded that labour be given 'full voice in planning and determining the benefits of automation.'[104]

Despite mounting working-class grievances, overt conflict was less pronounced in the early 1960s than it had been in the previous decade. Only two of thirty-four 'large' strikes in Canada from 1960 to 1966 occurred in BC – a 1964 strike of 4,700 office workers and lumber workers, and a 1966 strike of 13,000 logging and lumber workers.[105] However, this data conceals ambiguities in working-class unrest, and persistent sources of conflict between BC workers and employers. In August 1962, a dispute over seniority promotion of one millworker escalated into a ten-day wildcat strike that halted production at the MacMillan, Bloedel and Powell River Company's Somass plant in Port Alberni; the LRB granted the company permission to sue IWA Local 1-85 president Walter Allen and forty-eight workers for damages, while the BCFL demanded the prosecution be dropped.[106] Another 1962 strike, at Allied Engineering in Vancouver, led to mass pickets and a police attack in which Tom Clarke, militant president of the Marine Workers and Boilermakers, was bitten by a police dog.[107] A 1963 wildcat strike at the South Seas Mines in Ashcroft, a non-union shop, signified the mood on BC's resource frontier, where workers embraced job action in the absence of union protection.[108] Rank-and-file tradespeople challenged company officials and several Internationals during construction of the Northwood pulp and paper mill in Prince George, precipitating wildcat strikes.[109] In Squamish, construction of the $12-million FMC Chemical plant was halted when over 200 electricians, pipefitters, ironworkers, boilermakers, and machinists refused to cross 'mystery pickets,' as the Vancouver *Sun* described the unauthorized lines, during a 1965 dispute over room and board allowance.[110]

Social Credit pursued the familiar strategy of hindering workers' agency through restrictive legislation. Communists called for the repeal of Bills 43 and 128, and proposed a Bill of Rights that would 'guarantee the right to organize, to bargain collectively, to strike and picket' to all workers.[111] High wages and good working conditions 'were won through struggle by a powerful trade union movement,' communists claimed, rather than through the benevolence of employers and Social Credit.[112] The NDP took aim at Bill 42, amendments to the Labour Relations Act that outlawed the check-off of union dues for political purposes, while placing no equivalent restrictions on Social Credit's corporate backers.[113] In 1962, Social Credit considered further Labour Relations Act amendments, proposed by the Canadian Manufacturers' Association BC division, outlawing strikes by workers who belonged to unions representing a minority of workers in a multi-union plant.[114] The new militancy prompted proposals ranging from a Labour Court to binding arbitration for resolving disputes short of strikes. Also considered were joint Labour-Management committees to resolve conflicts during the 'no strike' period between rounds of bargaining.[115] Wildcat strikes intensified, J.T. Montague argues, 'as the scope of the issues that might go to bargaining widened.'[116]

In autumn 1965, a strike of oil refinery workers on Burrard Inlet nearly escalated into a province-wide general strike.[117] Initially confined to British American Oil, the strike spread in November to Imperial Oil and Shell refineries. The underlying issue was the Oil, Chemical and Atomic Workers' demand for job protection in the face of automation, and notification of the companies' intent to install new technologies. At the Shellburn refinery in Burnaby, where Jerry Lebourdais of the Progressive Worker Movement served as local president, the workers staged a sit-down strike. 'There was a lot of militant feeling throughout the industry in BC and a lot of workers were prepared to go, but they were looking to the leadership of the union and the leadership of the union didn't want to strike,' Jack Scott claims.[118] The oilworkers' Canadian director, J.R. Duncan, set a deadline for an agreement, threatening a shutdown of all BC refineries, while Social Credit labour minister Leslie Peterson warned: 'we cannot tolerate that type of action.'[119] Company representatives claimed to maintain 80 per cent production, as oil workers turned to secondary picketing and boycotts of suppliers and customers.[120]

On the Columbia River dam project, 350 construction workers respected an oil workers' picket line, temporarily halting work and prompting a court injunction. Another injunction limited picketing against Imperial Oil to the Ioco plant.[121] The Vancouver Labour Council, led by secretary-treasurer Paddy Neale, threatened a general strike if the BCFL did not act first, prompting the BCFL to canvass affiliates on a forty-eight-hour walkout. Officers of the IWA, PPWC, Building Trades, Marine, Transport, and Teamsters pledged support, establishing a Strike Coordinating Committee.[122] Social Credit claimed the strike was politically motivated, allegations NDP leader Bob Strachan described as 'complete and utter falsehood.'[123] Attorney General Robert Bonner threatened lawsuits against unions that violated the province's labour laws, while the Canadian Manufacturers' Association advised 'serious consequences' against any worker who joined a general strike.[124] CLC and International officers scrambled to avert a general strike, with the International Association of Machinists and the Teamsters announcing they would not participate in any illegal work stoppage.[125] In late November, Bennett brokered an agreement providing oil workers with a 35 cent hourly wage increase, input into automation, job-protection, and retraining.[126] BC labour stepped back from the brink of a general strike.

The next spring, Communist leader Nigel Morgan commented on the mounting unrest and the response by BC's economic and political elite:

> Big business fears the rising challenge to the so called 'residual rights of management' resulting from the technological revolution. They know that rising prices, rising taxes and today's phenomenally high profits are creating widespread social unrest, setting the stage for substantial gains by a united labor movement. They are preparing to provoke another major confrontation with labor, and Premier Bennett's plans for an election half way through the usual term of office, threatening to make the general strike of last fall a major issue, is part of that plot.[127]

Wildcats erupted as workers sought wage increases commensurate with the rising cost of living; large wage increases won through illegal strikes by Hamilton steelworkers and Sudbury Inco workers spurred militancy across the country.[128] In August 1966, these pressures erupted in the second nation-wide rail strike in Canadian history, when 110,000 workers in seventeen unions struck against the CPR and Canadian National Railway. An emergency sitting of Parliament legislated an end to the strike, awarding an 18 per cent wage increase, but several hundred BC railworkers remained off the job for four days until they received an assurance that there would be no reprisals.[129]

Breakaway Unions and Militant Leadership

The rising militancy intensified conflict between BC workers and International unions. In the wake of the Second Narrows bridge collapse and the 'unauthorized' 1959 strike, Vancouver ironworkers responded to attempted trusteeship by forming the breakaway Canadian Iron Workers (CIW) Local 1 in June 1960.[130] Also that year, the West Coast Seamen's

Union (WCSU), the Vancouver remnant of the once-powerful CSU, ended a four-year affiliation with rival SIU after seamen were ordered to cross a longshoremen's picket line.[131] The Trotskyist SWP discussed 'Canadian trade union autonomy and separatism' at its 1960 Vancouver convention.[132] The Communist Party, however, opposed the breakaway trend, issuing a leaflet urging 'Canadian autonomy for Ironworkers' and claiming 'the answer to US control and domination ... cannot be found in the secession of individual locals or in splinter movements.'[133] CIW challenged the International for certification in rural and urban centres, and led a 1962 strike that paralysed a half-dozen Vancouver construction sites when rank-and-file workers in other unions respected CIW picket lines. In the mid-1960s, CIW members picketed the BC legislature, demanding a public inquiry into the LRB's apparent bias and exposing a $150 initiation fee, collected by the Internationals, from workers on the Columbia and Peace dam projects.[134]

In Pulp & Sulphite, a jurisdictional dispute at the new Castlegar pulp mill and the harassment of BC dissidents Orville Braaten and Angus MacPhee by US border officials at Detroit contributed to the formation of PPWC in 1963.[135] The breakaway quickly captured certifications at Castlegar, Crofton, Woodfibre, and Prince Rupert, but PPWC Local 5, the 'converter local' vying for sixteen certifications at paper products plants in the Lower Mainland, had more difficulty. Pulp & Sulphite was led in BC by Pat O'Neil (not to be confused with Paddy Neale), secretary-treasurer of the BCFL, and collusion between the International, employers, and police stalled PPWC's growth at around 2,000 members.[136] In 1966, the LRB declared that PPWC was not a 'union under the meaning of the Act' and delayed certification votes at four mills that promised to double PPWC's membership. Harmac and Prince George (and later Skookumchuk) joined PPWC, but Port Mellon and Elk Falls stayed with the International.[137] In the midst of these certification drives, O'Neil and the RCMP were exposed for wiretapping PPWC's 1966 Vancouver convention.[138]

Working-class women were instrumental in PPWC's expansion into resource-processing towns on the coast and in the interior, and they played a leading role in the broader breakaway movement. Anne Royle, a research librarian and wife of a Harmac worker, organized a cavalcade of 200 cars and 800 workers from remote Gold River on northwestern Vancouver Island to the steps of the provincial legislature, demanding a secret ballot vote of the affected workers. A short while later, Royle set up a protest camp on the steps of the Labour Relations Board to press this demand.[139] In Prince George, the PPWC women's auxiliary collected 5,000 names on a petition that was presented to Labour Minister Leslie Peterson. Women were also active inside the PPWC. Local 11 member Karen Cooling from Gold River was elected secretary-treasurer of the Confederation of Canadian Unions (CCU), the breakaway labour centre.[140]

A key dispute in the breakaway movement was the April 1966 wildcat strike at the Lenkurt Electric plant in Burnaby. The IBEW had struck a deal with the company authorizing increased overtime during contract negotiations, but the Lenkurt workers walked out and 257 were fired. Relations with the International had been acrimonious since the 1950s, when a trustee was appointed to purge Local 213 of its communist officers.[141] The Lenkurt strike escalated when the IWA and other unions mobilized behind the fired workers, who continued to picket the plant; a court injunction against picketing led to a clash between police and picketers and thirty arrests. Four prominent BC labour leaders – Vancouver Labour Council secretary Paddy Neale, IWA Local 1-217 vice-president Tom Clarke (formerly of the Boilermakers), Marine Workers and Boilermakers president Jeff Power, and IBEW Local 213 business agent Art O'Keefe – received prison sentences ranging from three to six months, along with twenty-six other union activists who were fined a total of $3,100. 'We would act in the same manner if it became necessary,' said Neale, who was jailed for four and a half months.[142]

Lenkurt served as a lightning rod for BC opponents of American unions.[143] One of the wildcat's leaders, Jess Succamore, a thirty-four-year-old immigrant from Lancashire, England received a twenty-five-year suspension from IBEW membership and went on to serve as national secretary-treasurer of the breakaway Canadian Association of Industrial Mechanical and Allied Workers (CAIMAW) and president of the Council of Canadian Unions (CCU, renamed Confederation of Canadian Unions in 1973).[144] After the strike, Succamore and George Brown, assisted by the Progressive Worker Movement, founded the Canadian Electrical Workers' Union (CEWU), to hold together the 200 strikers who were never reinstated. In 1969, CEWU merged with Winnipeg-based CAIMAW, which took a militant turn in 1971, electing Succamore secretary-treasurer and moving its headquarters to Vancouver.[145] 'That's what came out of the Lenkurt strike,' Jack Scott suggests, 'the beginning of the independent Canadian labour movement in BC.'[146]

Lenkurt intensified BC labour's opposition to the anti-labour stance of Social Credit and the courts. 'Lenkurt sparked an all-out campaign by the labour movement against the use of injunctions, the jailing of labour leaders, and restrictive labour legislation imposed by the Social Credit government,' writes historian Elaine Bernard.[147] The BCFL organized an October 1966 conference on injunctions, financially supported the families of the jailed labour leaders, and distributed 100,000 pamphlets titled *Guilty Until Proven Innocent*; the BCFL's legal counsel, Tom Berger, produced a report on injunctions, as the BC NDP caucus and provincial council demanded that *ex parte* injunctions 'must be completely eliminated.'[148] The Communist Party's Delta-New Westminster regional committee discussed Lenkurt and the broader upturn in militancy:

> Labour has made many economic and political gains in BC in the last few years with 1966 putting a stop to a lot of apathy ... The workers at Lenkurt went on strike because of overtime and were sold out by their International and Local Presidents, but they were not discouraged and the province will long remember the co-operation that other unions gave to that struggle and the arrest of 30 trade unionists, with fines and jail sentences. Our labour leaders are willing to go to jail to defend their principles. On the other side the Socred government is pressing charges against the strikers and issuing injunctions to the monopolies.[149]

This message was reinforced in 1967, when a strike of Prince Rupert trawlers ended with the jailing of UFAWU secretary Homer Stevens and president Steve Stavenes and $25,000 in fines.[150] Four days into the strike the BC Supreme Court granted an *ex parte* injunction ordering shoreworkers to handle 'hot' fish, to prevent it from spoiling. Vessel owners won a second injunction directing the union to send a telegram informing 'all members concerned in the ... processing of ground-fish' to handle the cargo. Rather than comply, the UFAWU put the question to a membership vote, receiving an 89 per cent mandate against acting on the order. Justice Thomas A. Dohm, who would soon leave the bench to serve as president of the Vancouver Stock Exchange,[151] sentenced Stevens, Stavenes, and UFAWU business agent Jack Nichol to a year in Oakalla prison for contempt of court. While Nichol's conviction was overturned on appeal, Stevens and Stavenes served their full terms, after the federal solicitor general denied a request for clemency. They were released in July 1968 to a heroes' welcome.[152]

During the Prince Rupert strike, a trawl membership meeting in Vancouver organized a mass picket at Vancouver Shipyards, encouraging 'anyone who wishes to go on the picket line, no matter which union they belong to – men or women, to help us win this strike.'[153] But as Stevens recalls, CLC officers and staff 'used every means to discourage their affiliates from supporting us in any way.'[154] Morale waned as the strike dragged on, with Prince Rupert members joining the Deep Sea Fisherman's Union and, at the Prince Rupert Co-op, defecting to a breakaway union. In August, the strikers voted to return to work.[155] The strike was further weakened by a group calling itself the 'Marching Mothers,' which the central council of UFAWU Women's Auxiliaries dismissed in a radio broadcast as 'wives of the vessel owners' who 'speak for a tiny privileged minority.'[156] For one Marching Mother, Prince Rupert alderwoman Iona Campagnola, the trawlers' strike provided a springboard to political power: Campagnola was elected Liberal MP for Skeena in 1974, serving in the Trudeau cabinet and, later, as Liberal Party of Canada president and BC's lieutenant-governor.[157]

Isolated from the CLC and mainstream of Canadian labour, the UFAWU considered forming a rival union centre, influenced by PPWC's growth. Stevens recalls:

> We had fairly close relations with the PPWC, although some of their officers held that we were being contrary to our own principles because we were still trying to get reinstated in the CLC. They attempted to persuade us that the best route to go was to form a separate all-Canadian federation of labour. We chewed that over on various occasions but decided that it would be a mistake. It wasn't going to help in the long haul to simply have one more labour federation. So we decided against it.[158]

PPWC became an influential union, representing a majority of BC pulp and paper workers and honouring IWA picket lines during a 1967 strike. The IWA considered granting strike pay to PPWC members, which inflamed Pulp & Sulphite and exposed divisions in the BCFL, between a craft union faction grouped around Pat O'Neil and militants around IWA Local 1-217 leader Sid Thompson.[159] Allen Engler, west coast editor of the LSA's *Workers Vanguard*, observed:

> The craft unions are ... very hostile to the IWA [and] have made it clear that they want the IWA expelled if it does not toe the line ... We consider the Thompson caucus the basis for an alternative to the present leadership ... Since there has been considerable decline in the amount of employment in the sawmills in the last fifteen years there are militant activists in such key

> unions as Letter carriers, plumbers, and carpenters who were associated with the caucus at one time or others and still take leadership from it.[160]

The New Left situated its critique of organized labour in the context of postwar capitalism. Union leaders had embraced 'co-management,' SFU student leader Jim Harding claimed, accepting 'most, if not all, of the assumptions of capitalism and imperialism and, in their briefs to the elites, ask[ing] only for a larger slice of the pie.' However, issues of 'control' and the upturn in militancy 'were beginning to challenge established union bureaucracies ... Most old leftists have either accepted the capitalists' definition of the postwar "boom", or have so abstracted the class struggle that they can't understand the new tactics being used to contain labour.'[161] Radicals, including communists, had 'failed in many labour needs,' the LSA claimed, such as organizing 'women and youth.'[162] While organized labour was 'the most powerful instrument yet created by working people ... to defend and advance their interests,' its 'effective power' had been 'crippled' by state intervention. To the LSA, the 'new militancy' was an 'outgrowth of the mass of young workers entering the labor force in recent years, who do not bear the demoralizing burden of past failures and have no patience with the injustice of existing living standards and working conditions.'[163]

The new militancy extended across the industries, affecting white-collar workers who were traditionally ambivalent toward the organized working class. In 1965, the Federation of Telephone Workers, representing workers at the BC Telephone Company, affiliated with the BCFL and four years later waged their first strike in fifty years, winning a 20 per cent pay increase; in 1971, the telephone workers broke away from their International to join the new Canadian Federation of Communications Workers.[164] Other white-collar workers were similarly affected. Office and Professional Employees Local 378 grew in the 1960s from a base among clerical staff at the BC Hydro and Power Authority to include many private-sector firms. Local 378 members at International Power and Engineering Consultants Ltd., a former BC Electric Co. subsidiary, staged two wildcat strikes in 1968, while strikes were waged for union recognition at Federal Pacific Electric, Dominion Glass, and the Hertz and Avis car rental agencies.[165] In late 1969, after a strike at Simon Fraser University, the RCMP reported on efforts by professors and trade unionists 'to establish a working relationship.'[166]

Despite the increasingly restive rank and file, one bastion of BC's militant working-class tradition surrendered to a Cold War rival. In

1967, Mine-Mill merged with Steel. In northwestern BC, twenty-eight Mine-Mill members had died in a 1965 avalanche at the Granduc mine, and the union then lost certification to the 'Three Way Pact' – the International Building Labourers, Teamsters, and Operating Engineers Local 1005 – which negotiated a 'pre-contract agreement' before a new workforce was hired.[167] In 1966, the 15,000-strong Sudbury Inco local went over to Steel, as did Mine-Mill's American counterpart. 'A lot of rank and file members were tired of the endless raiding and wanted both unions to start fighting for their members instead of fighting each other,' recalls Al King, Local 480 president (1950–60) and Western District secretary (1960–7).[168] At a June 1967 convention, delegates voted 95–31 to join Steel, a decision Mine-Mill members affirmed by a 3–1 margin. In a bitter irony for partisans of independent unionism, the merger came into force on 1 July 1967, the centennial of Canada's confederation.[169] Interpretations vary widely. Labour lawyer John Stanton, who served as Mine-Mill counsel, described the merger as 'the tale of a political party and several of its leading members who sold out their own declared principles and manipulated an independent Canadian union, which they had done much to create, into a US-affiliated, business union.' Stanton accused western director Harvey Murphy of 'internal treachery' and 'unhealthy collaboration.'[170] Al King, however, denies such an allegation: '"Boss collaborator" is the last thing Harvey Murphy could ever be.'[171] This view is echoed by Allen Seager, who described Murphy as 'a responsible and honest trade unionist … a credit to his class.'[172] Critics cite key staff positions awarded to Mine-Mill president Ken Smith, secretary-treasurer William Longridge, and Murphy.[173] 'That's one thing I'll never be able to forgive about Harvey Murphy,' Bill White insists. 'He let the bastards get to him … I figured then and I still figure today that Steel is as phoney as a three-dollar bill.'[174] Murphy died in Toronto in 1977. However, in a 1972 letter to the *Trail Times*, as the breakaway CCU courted Cominco workers, he insisted that the 'merger was made under the direction of the Canadian membership.'[175]

Steel won control of the 3,000-member Trail local but two BC Mine-Mill locals broke away, the BC Diamond Drillers and the Domtar plant in New Westminster, following the lead of Falconbridge in northern Ontario.[176] Tension was brewing in other quarters. Discontent at the Alcan smelter in Kitimat, near Prince Rupert, gave rise to the breakaway Canadian Association of Smelter and Allied Workers (CASAW), which worked closely with CAIMAW and affiliated with the CCU.[177]

Steel had represented Alcan workers since 1956, when it signed a 'pre-contract' agreement during construction. In 1970, a bitter three-month strike ended with a 59 per cent ratification vote; rank-and-file dissidents invited PPWC to raid the smelter, but the LRB rejected certification on grounds that some union cards had been forged. The rank and file responded by forming CASAW, which won certification in a 1,172–385 vote in 1972.[178] Ray Haeussler, an Alcan worker and future CASAW national secretary-treasurer, discussed the role of nationalism: 'Let's be honest: we made the national issue an issue in order to get away from the Steelworkers. This thing started as dissatisfaction with the United Steelworkers of America, mainly with the strike.'[179]

Opposition to Internationals was rooted in shop-floor discontent, the desire for local control, and what the breakaways saw as a drain of workers' dues to the United States; a 1968 Revenue Canada report claimed that $68-million stayed in the US above and beyond expenditures.[180] Kitimat Alcan workers paid $200,000 per year prior to the breakaway, $120,000 of which went 'across the line.'[181] Breakaway sentiment was also influenced by the militarist policies of many Internationals; AFL-CIO president George Meany endorsed Richard Nixon's 1972 campaign for the US presidency, supporting 'a policy Canadians have nothing to do with, a war policy,' as a Trail smelterworker described it.[182] Social Credit cabinet minister Patricia Jordan, North Okanagan MLA, commended Meany's support for 'binding arbitration' and opposition to 'strikes of people making more than $7,500 a year.'[183] A section of BC's labour leadership, however, was not prepared to leave the Internationals. In 1971, the BCFL executive council condemned 'the disruptive tactics of the PPWC and other breakaway unions' and urged the Internationals to move 'quickly and decisively to provide full autonomy for their Canadian members.'[184] Four Internationals – Steel, Pulp & Sulphite, IBEW, and IAM – launched a 'Go for Unity Now!' campaign with the BCFL and CLC, hoping to win back 5,300 breakaway union members in BC.[185] Federal NDP leader David Lewis urged delegates at the 1972 Miami convention of the Amalgamated Meat Cutters to recognize 'a new Canadian nationalism' and support 'Canadian autonomy within the International.'[186]

An Old Leftist who engaged in a unique dialogue with the New Left, Jack Scott, located the breakaways in the context of capitalist crisis. In the final issue of his *BC Newsletter* he stated: 'The existing trade union movement, which is the only mass organization of the working people presently functioning, is incapable of dealing with the developing crisis, especially in view of the fact that it is controlled by the US bureaucrats who exert every effort to hold it in check.'[187] The breakaways, meanwhile, adopted militant tactics and a critique of capitalism to meet employers' attacks. Kevin Neish, who worked as a heavy-duty mechanic and CAIMAW shop-steward at the Newmount copper-gold-silver mine near Princeton in the 1970s, recalls a spirit of solidarity:

> CAIMAW was a great union. They supported other unions, they supported the Steelworkers – even though the head office of Steelworkers was raiding CAIMAW, because CAIMAW was an independent left-wing union – even when they were raiding us we would still support the [Steel] strikers from mines near us. We would send money and support to them, irregardless [*sic*] of the fact that they were raiding us.[188]

The growth of breakaway unions and a militant rank and file precipitated change in the policy and attitude of established labour unions, healing a decades-old wound in BC's working class. Delegates at the 1968 BCFL convention instructed officers to lobby the CLC for readmission of the UFAWU, a stance reaffirmed at two subsequent conventions.[189] However, opposition to red unions endured, with the Victoria Labour Council hotly debating constitutional amendments in 1969 against 'totalitarian agencies.'[190] Jack Phillips, representing Vancouver civic workers, declared at the 1970 BCFL convention: 'We've had enough of this McCarthyite garbage in the trade union movement. It's time these doddering old men heading the CLC were told that trade unionists want to solve the problems of today, not rehash the disputes of 20 years ago.'[191] Phillips proposed withholding per-capita dues, a tactic that had forced the CLC to admit his own CUPE local. In December 1972, the CLC's executive council relented and accepted the UFAWU's affiliation.[192] For nineteen years, fishermen and their allies had waged a determined fight to win readmission. Indicating a *détente* in BC's working class, their efforts bore fruit. On 7 February 1973, Elgin 'Scotty' Neish was seated as a delegate of the Victoria Labour Council, ending his twenty-two-year exile from the house of labour.[193] UFAWU delegates were seated at labour councils up and down the coast. A relic of labour's Cold War had been laid to rest.

In the preceding decades, the militant minority of BC workers had challenged the premises and practices of the industrial relations regime, in the face of an intransigent provincial bourgeoisie and hostile governments, courts, and allied agencies. Though weakened by red-baiting and the allure of an affluent society, this layer of working-class leaders and rank-and-file workers refused to follow the path of accommodation and compromise. Periodic struggles against repressive labour laws – Bills 33, 39, 42, 43, 87, 128 – served as lightning rods for latent working-class dissent. Key strikes – loggers in 1952, ironworkers and provincial government workers in 1959, oilworkers in 1965, electrical workers in 1966, fishers in 1967, telephone workers in 1969 – served as catalysts to wider industrial action and an oppositional working-class culture. Automation, unemployment, inflation, and workplace safety exposed basic antagonisms between worker and owner, as a new working class of women, youth, and public-sector and white-collar workers challenged existing patterns of power and authority. Finally, the discriminatory exercise of injunctions in labour disputes fuelled contempt for the rule of law and an openness to 'illegal' wildcat strikes. The inadequate responses of American-controlled International unions to these diverse oppositional currents revived the historic secessionist sentiment, giving rise to breakaway unions and lending an institutional form to the new militancy of the 1960s.

CHAPTER SIX

Political Change

We're out in the wild west here ... Their agenda was to stop us from coming into power at all costs. It cost them plenty but they paid. They bought and sold the governments, the corporations did ...

I wouldn't describe it as a 'New Left.' It was a maturing left. The baby was born. It had been through its diapers. We had a history with democratic socialists since the turn of the century. We nearly formed the government in '52. We should have had one in the '40s. But the Coalition ... went on from the forties, right through Social Credit. It broke down once, in '72.[1]

Dave Barrett, Premier of BC (1972–5)

The New Democratic Party (NDP), formed in 1961, represented an alliance between the Old Left, organized labour, and an emerging professional middle class, and explicitly invited 'liberally minded persons' to join its ranks.[2] The BC NDP was a paradoxical political animal – inheriting some of the best and worst characteristics of the CCF and organized labour. NDP politicians and rank-and-file members sustained oppositional currents in the corridors of power and BC's far-flung communities, at the same time that top-down practices endured. Janet Burns discovered 'a weak but significant relationship between trade union membership and New Democratic Party voting' but 'no statistically significant relationship between working-class self-identification' and party support.[3] Labour ties had both positive and negative features. They provided 'a bulwark against sudden' shifts but impeded the NDP's goal of 'broadening its base of support' because of the 'pronounced public aversion to the involvement of trade unions in the party.'[4] CCF-NDP veteran Dorothy Steeves confirms this view: 'in the public mind, the link up with the Trade Unions did us no good at all.'[5]

The rise of a new working class produced tension in the NDP, influencing the turbulent transitions from the Strachan to Berger to Barrett leaderships – and paving the road to victory in 1972. The militant minority of public-sector workers, youth, and professionals clashed with Old Left labour leaders. Women, who had played a prominent role in the CCF, at both the grassroots and legislative levels, continued to exert influence in the NDP as they moved toward a more explicity feminist politics. The Waffle challenge, which sought to restore socialism as the NDP's objective, was less acrimonious in BC, where sections of the establishment including Barrett signed the manifesto. The leadership of Dave Barrett, a social worker, signified changes in the structure and culture of BC's working class, from blue-collar industrial occupations to white-collar professions. Moreover, because he was Jewish, it also revealed increased acceptance of previously excluded groups. Fired from Oakalla Prison after he won the CCF nomination in 1960, Barrett defeated Social Credit labour minister Lyle Wicks in Dewdney, a rapidly suburbanizing riding on the eastern edge of Greater Vancouver. Barrett was part of the new working class that propelled his party to power:

> Most of the people up until the late 50s and early 60s had essentially working labour backgrounds. Skilled labour. An occasional teacher. The party began to change in the 60s as younger members came in. They came from a variety of professions and brought a focus that was different in some areas ... I came on the crest of the change.[6]

In 1972, as voters grew weary of 'Old Man' Bennett amid major industrial strife, and Social Credit support migrated to the Conservative Party, the NDP formed the first labour-backed government in BC history.

The New Party

The 1956 Winnipeg Declaration and TLC-CCL merger paved the way for a new political alignment on the Canadian left, a marriage between the CCF and CLC.[7] The impetus came from industrial Ontario, but the New Party movement extended throughout party and union ranks. The BCFL 1956 merger convention created a Political Education Committee to formulate legislative strategy with unions, cooperatives, farm groups, and parties including the CCF; a year later, BCFL delegates declared that 'the CCF warrants the support of the workers in British Columbia, as the best means to obtain their legislative aims.'[8] Several delegates opposed the motion, including boilermaker and LPPer Bill Stewart representing the Vancouver Labour Council, who said the CCL policy asking union members 'to support one political party ... has never worked.' N.W. Swanson of Vancouver Office Workers Local 378 opposed the motion because it would 'cause disruption in our organization ... the fastest growing union in Canada.' However, a majority of delegates, such as J. Moore of IWA Local 1-85, favoured the CCF, arguing that 'the Social Credit party of BC are debating a resolution to outlaw strikes by the labour movement in BC. That is the kind of political action you get from parties representing big business like MacMillan, Bloedel, Wenner-Gren and the CPR. They realize the importance of political action as the workers have yet to realize it.'[9]

The New Party took shape as BC's union density reached its historic peak – the apex of union strength in postwar North America, when 54 per cent of wage workers belonged to unions.[10] However, union strength did not translate into a surge in radical politics: 'With the industrialization of BC and the stabilization of the economy has come a certain conservatization of the workers,' the Trotskyist SEL observed.[11] Nonetheless, New Party talks proceeded, with the BC CCF executive appointing a committee to plan future cooperation. In May 1958, CCF convention delegates welcomed the CLC and BCFL's decision to formalize political involvement, and pledged 'co-operation and support in mobilizing the forces of farmer, labor, CCF and forward looking persons in British Columbia.'[12] A historic joint conference of the CCF and BCFL executives convened in May 1959. Commenting on limited wage gains at the negotiating table, and the use of injunctions against unions, BCFL secretary-treasurer Pat O'Neil told a group of UBC students that 'only through political action can the aims and objectives of the trade union movement be achieved.'[13] However, in summer 1959, a major strike wave threatened to derail New Party talks. Citing a protracted IWA strike, BC CCF secretary Harold Thayer feared that Bennett would call an election during the strike to 'save the province from economic chaos': 'Such an election would magnify our problems many times.'[14]

CCF members were far from unanimous on the New Party idea. Thayer conceded that 'there is a reaction setting in in this province regarding the merger ... because of the time it takes labor to organize to do a political job ... CCF members are becoming impatient. They want action and see none.' While the merger proposal had been 'welcomed generally,' some members 'were skeptical but went along.'[15] MLAs Cedric Cox and Leo Nimsick, who belonged to Mine-Mill and opposed Steel raiding, declared their contempt for the New Party idea. Dorothy Steeves was also 'against it,' describing the motivation as 'purely monetary ... The party thought the trade unions would pour money into our movement.'[16] George Home, CLC political education director and veteran of the anti-communist Red Wars, also disagreed with the move:

> I still think they should have built on the existing structure we had in the West and gradually built it up in the East. I'm an organizational person, and I figured that organization was the key. What I saw happening was that some people were attempting to hit the CCF over the head with a hammer and build a new organization closer to the Liberal party.[17]

Kootenay West MP Bert Herridge described himself as 'an orthodox CCFer.'[18] In 1960, the BC CCF executive went on record regretting that the National Committee for the New Party invited 'individuals to join New Party Clubs and have representation at a founding convention without any personal commitment' to the philosophy and program of the CCF and CLC.[19] One group not included in the New Party was the Farmers' Union, because 'such an endeavour would be useless in BC,' Thayer wrote. 'The Farmers' Union is in the hands of Socreds and non-political types. There is no hope of persuading the provincial organization to meet with the CCF and BC Federation of Labour.'[20] Despite these obstacles, there were signs of momentum. A new $100,000 headquarters opened on Vancouver's Broadway Street, and membership increased from 3,981 in 1958 to 5,058 by the end of 1959; Stephen Lewis, then a twenty-one-year-old undergraduate student from Ontario, worked as a BC CCF organizer in summer 1959. 'The morale of the movement is good,' Thayer noted, 'and it seems that only internal strife can keep the CCF from forming the next government.'[21]

Communists welcomed the New Party as an opportunity to end their protracted exile from the mainstream of Canadian working-class politics. Predictably, CCF and CLC leaders shunned these efforts. The BC CCF executive opposed a membership application from Orville Braaten, business agent of Pulp & Sulphite Local 433, on grounds of 'political instability' and past LPP association, but delegates at the 1959 convention overturned this recommendation and admitted Braaten into the CCF. When Braaten won the CCF nomination in North Vancouver in 1960, 'the right wing in their usual fashion got up as a body and left the hall.'[22] The BCFL's 1960 convention voted to limit participation in the BC Committee for the New Party to those prepared to 'work for election of a CCF government,' a move Communists described as 'a serious setback.' They fielded candidates in nineteen constituencies in the 1960 provincial election, citing failed efforts to be included as 'an integral part of the new alternative.'[23] Communist leader Tim Buck further alienated CCF leaders when he told a Victoria audience that sixty Communists belonged to New Party clubs. The night prior to the election, posters appeared on telephones poles around Vancouver linking the CCF with Communism.[24] On a brighter note, the irascible Tom Uphill of Fernie bowed out of the 1960 election – the first time since 1912 that his name did not appear on a ballot – to prevent a split in the working-class vote, the veteran MLA said.[25]

The 1960 election, the last contested under the CCF banner, produced the best outcome since 1952, despite determined opposition by major resource corporations and splits in labour's ranks. The Macmillan, Bloedel and Powell River company prohibited loggers from campaigning on company property, including bunkhouses. Three days before the writ was dropped, the forestry giant had been awarded 'one of the largest forest management licenses ever issued in BC,' M.J. Coldwell told a group of Powell River workers.[26] During the campaign, Mine-Mill circulated a letter to CCF candidates urging support for a Workmen's Compensation claim, prompting CCF campaign manager Grant MacNeil to warn 'all Candidates to refrain from public comment regarding current trade union jurisdictional disputes.'[27] Despite these obstacles, the CCF, running under the slogan *Put People First* and a pledge to nationalize the BC Electric Company, captured 16 seats, compared with 10 at dissolution, and improved its share of the vote from 28 per cent to 33 per cent; Social Credit support dropped to 39 per cent (from 46 per cent) and 32 seats (from 39). As Paddy Neale, Vancouver Labour Council secretary and a defeated CCF candidate in Vancouver-Burrard pointed out, fewer than 4,000 well-placed votes would have translated into a CCF majority.[28]

Dave Barrett's election in Dewdney – defeating Labour Minister Lyle Wicks, the sponsor of Bill 43, the employer-friendly Trade-Unions Act (1959) – was particularly gratifying for the CCF and labour. Barrett had been fired as a program officer at Oakalla prison for his political involvement. The *Vancouver Sun* highlighted the achievement of 'giant-killer David Barrett, the 29-year-old ex-civil servant who knocked the props out from under Wicks in Dewdney.' Wicks attributed his defeat to an influx of union members in the growing suburban areas of the formerly rural riding. The western end – containing Burquitlam, Coquitlam, and Port Moody – had nearly doubled in population in a few short years, and voted heavily for the CCF, while the eastern reaches remained loyal to Wicks and Social Credit. Wicks suggested, however, that Bill 43 was not a factor in his defeat, but conceded that the working-class voters in the suburbs 'did not appreciate the good that Bill 43 had done for the province.'[29]

The BC NDP

On 4 August 1961, delegates at the Ottawa Coliseum voted 784 to 743 to name their new organization the New Democratic Party, rather than the Social Democratic Party, emphasizing the party's newness rather than its socialism.[30] Tommy Douglas, CCF premier of Saskatchewan, was easily elected leader, defeating outgoing CCF leader Hazen Argue, MP for Assiniboia, who was supported by a majority of the CCF caucus but defected to the Liberal Party six months later.[31] Prominent members of the BC CCF, including Dewdney MLA Dave Barrett, were unable to attend the Ottawa convention, because of a special legislative session that nationalized the BC Electric Company: 'Bennett called the session to stop us from going back for the New Party convention,' Barrett suggests. 'We didn't attend. It didn't matter to me. It was just moving on with the party.'[32] At a Vancouver convention in October 1961, the BC NDP was born, acclaiming Strachan as leader and Tom Berger, a twenty-eight-year-old Vancouver lawyer, as president. Barrett told delegates: 'There is no place in the NDP for those of faint hearts or weak knees.'[33]

Prior to the Vancouver convention, Paddy Neale discussed the NDP's relationship with organized labour: 'It is as true for labor as it is for big business that we represent vested interests. But our special interests are the interests of the majority. It's as simple as this to us: we have the most people so we should have the most representation.'[34] However, ongoing ambivalence in the CCF rank and file was evident when federal secretary Carl Hamilton wrote to his provincial counterpart, Jessie Mendels, regarding the 'status of affiliated members at the constituency level ... Since the whole matter is a touchy one.'[35] Social Credit imposed a legislative roadblock between the NDP and BC unions: Bill 42, amendments to the Labour Relations Act that outlawed the automatic check-off of union dues for political purposes. Douglas described the legislation as 'restrictive, unfair and discriminatory.'[36] In December 1962, the NDP counted 195,500 affiliated members across Canada but only 29,000 in BC.[37]

Like the CCF, the NDP was not immune from internal strife. Partly, this reflected enduring Cold War crises on the left, which were manifested in the leadership's drive for moderation and battles in the early 1960s over NATO, NORAD, and Cuba.[38] Partly, this reflected institutional pressures in all parties, exacerbated by Cold War debates and the influence of the NDP's union affiliates. Partly, this inner-party conflict reflected deliberate efforts by the Trotskyist League for Socialist Action (LSA) and its youth wing the Young Socialists (YS), which pursued the policy of entryism in social democracy. On the eve of the Ottawa convention, the LSA pursued 'an anti-war program and a class struggle policy,' urging withdrawal from NATO and NORAD and a referendum on nuclear arms for Canada; the BC CCF responded by rejecting an application for membership from Ruth Houle, a Vancouver LSA member.[39] *Workers Vanguard* ran the headline: 'Keep McCarthyism out of New Democratic Party,' but the BC NDP leadership declared that any member distributing *Workers Vanguard* or *Press* was liable for expulsion.[40]

Railroader and leftist dissident Richard 'Lefty' Morgan had rejoined the CCF in 1960, following the demise of his short-lived Labour Party of Canada. Morgan was elected secretary of North Vancouver's Deep Cove CCF Club and attended the NDP's founding Ottawa convention as a delegate, along with Jerry Lebourdais, a communist militant in the Oilworkers' union. Commenting on the BC NDP convention in October 1961, Morgan said the party was 'in a very sick condition,' 'on its deathbed' from the standpoint of meaningful membership participation. 'On the other hand, if the party is to be one in which the individual member is regarded as the simple provider of willing hands at election times and a constant source of revenue at all times then there is perhaps some future for this machine of political forces.'[41]

In its formative years, the NDP fared better in federal politics than in BC provincial politics, where the free-enterprise vote gravitated behind Social Credit. In the June 1962 federal election, the party captured 10 seats (out of 21 across the country) with 31 per cent of the vote – surpassing the Liberals, Conservatives, and Social Credit. This result was marred, however, by Tommy Douglas's defeat in Regina, a casualty of the doctors' strike against Medicare.[42] Reflecting the strength of BC's parliamentary socialist tradition, Douglas was parachuted into Burnaby-Coquitlam and easily won a by-election with a majority of ballots cast.[43] However, Douglas warned a high-level Ottawa meeting of NDP and CLC leaders that the Liberals and New Democrats would be engaged 'in a head-on fight for the votes of non-political trade unionists and white collar workers in the urban areas of the country.'[44] Changes in Canada's class composition influenced NDP tactics in the unstable parliamentary climate of the 1960s. In the April 1963 federal election the NDP lost one BC seat, Tom Berger's in Vancouver-Burrard, and dropped to 17 seats in the House of Commons, but its share of the BC vote held at 30.3 per cent.[45]

In provincial politics, the NDP fell to 14 seats with 28 per cent of the vote in September 1963, a setback from the previous election when the CCF had cut into Social Credit support. The election appeared to confirm the fears of the New Party's detractors. NDP provincial secretary Ernie Hall identified 'a definite trend toward stability and away from the chance of a minority NDP government.'[46] *Vancouver Sun* columnist Jack Scott (not to be confused with the dissident communist of the same name), hardly an ally of the left, suggested that the 'only surprise … was that the NDP didn't lose more seats,' lamenting the party's willingness 'to compromise its basic philosophy to appear respectable.' Scott cited NDP support for NATO and disciplinary action against dissidents including MLA Cedric Cox and MP Bert Herridge, who was rapped 'across of the knuckles' for appearing at a May Day gathering. 'What no one seems to have said out loud is that, in fact, the NDP ran scared, that it went tippy-toe to avoid a frontal test of public opinion on what it really believes.'[47]

The conflict with Cox exposed divided opinions over Communist Cuba, as the United States sought to regain control over the rebel island ninety miles off the Florida coast. During the October 1962 Cuban Missile Crisis, Douglas had told the BCFL convention: 'The story of Castro is a people's revolution, that overthrew one of the bloodiest and corrupt, and most vicious dictatorships in the history of the Western Hemisphere … The policies that were followed on this Continent, pushed them into the arms of the Soviet Union.' Douglas expressed an idealism uncharacteristic of many politicians when he appealed to internationalism:

> My friends, the day is coming when honest working people, toiling people will have to reach their hands across the sea and across international boundaries and across the barriers of language, and join hands and say to the statesmen of the world, we want to live in peace, we want to build a

> world in which there will be security, a world in which social justice and economic security and human brotherhood will cover the earth as the waters now cover the sea.[48]

However, the BC NDP leadership clung to a stolid Cold War pragmatism. In January 1963, Cox, the Burnaby MLA who had filled the legislative seat and married the daughter of old Marxist Ernest Edward Winch, travelled to Cuba with the Fair Play for Cuba Committee (FPCC), which he chaired. Cox was the first Canadian politician to visit the island since the revolution, the FPCC claimed, and he had been invited by the Cuban ambassador, but Strachan requested that he cancel the trip.[49] Cox refused, and upon his return to Burnaby defiantly told a crowd of 500 people:

> The Americans are not at all concerned about the wealth of Cuba or the people of Cuba. What they are concerned about are the ideas that are implanted in the minds of the people of Cuba and these ideas have now spread out to all of Latin America. They can drop bombs on Cuba, they can kill every Cuban if they want, but they will not kill the ideas that are implanted in the minds of the Latin Americans now.[50]

These ideological tensions spawned a Socialist Caucus in the BC NDP. At the second provincial convention, in October 1962 (conventions were held annually until 1968), delegates refused membership to left-winger Rod Young, expelled eight New Democratic Youth (NDY) members, and suspended three others for distributing *Workers Vanguard* and belonging to the LSA.[51] Lefty Morgan objected to the convention proceedings, accusing Tom Berger of 'unfair and unjust conduct' in his handling of Young's appeal.[52] Cox and two other dissidents, Hugh Clifford and John Macey, subsequently announced the formation of the Socialist Caucus:

> Since the founding of the New Democratic Party and the widening of the perimeter of our Party to include the 'liberally minded', many old CCF'ers felt concern not only for the future of our socialist philosophy but also for the security of the socialist. The organized assault on the socialist youth and subsequent expulsions and the manner in which the recent Provincial election was conducted have justified our fear.

The caucus pledged to promote social ownership of natural resources and the means of production as 'the only practical economic basis upon which to build a new society,' aiming to win majority support for this policy.[53] Party leaders, however, dismissed the group as a 'Trotskyite front,' a 'bunch of screwballs' in the words of Tommy Douglas.[54]

In 1963, the BC NDY disciplined eleven more members for belonging to the LSA, an action sustained by the BC NDP executive, as thirty young Trotskyists were expelled across Canada, 'almost our entire NDY fraction.'[55] Provincial secretary Ernie Hall anticipated 'a great deal of trouble' at the 1963 provincial convention, and the next March the BC NDP executive declared LSA membership 'incompatible with membership in the NDP.' Vancouver Trotskyists Ruth and Reg Bullock were expelled, forcing YS members to avoid 'openly and formally' identifying with the League.[56] The expulsions curbed Socialist Caucus growth. The caucus was 'all but dead,' the Vancouver YS conceded, and 'with the exception of two or three clubs, the NDY in Vancouver is inactive.'[57] At the 1964 provincial convention, the Socialist Caucus 'was defeated on every issue, and was isolated by the end of the convention,' the federal secretary observed. Delegates approved changes to the party constitution making constituency associations (rather than clubs) the sole basis for representation of individual members.[58] After the convention, Socialist Caucus member John Macey, a lawyer, applied to the Registrar of Companies to create a society called the Canadian Commonwealth Federation – a move blocked by BC NDP leaders.[59]

Ideological strife was only one challenge confronting the young party, as the flurry of provincial and federal elections strained NDP finances. As party president Berger told the 1962 provincial convention, the Victory Fund Drive had not been a success, forcing the provincial office to adopt 'an austerity program' and 'tight money policy.' The $3 annual membership fee 'is not adequate,' Berger claimed.[60] Despite a $500 donation from the BC Hospital Workers in spring 1963, the party ended the year with a $24,350 cash deficit.[61] However, the NDP's federated structure and labour affiliation made it possible to collect and disburse funds across the country. Evading the Bill 42 restrictions on union donations, the Ontario-based United Auto Workers loaned $5,000 to the BC NDP for the 1963 election, disbursed through the federal party, which raised an additional $10,000 in donations. A similar device enabled BC locals of the United Packinghouse Workers to maintain NDP affiliation and contribute funds by way of sister locals in eastern Canada. IWA Local 1-80 of Duncan was advised to pay five cents per member per month for as many members as it could afford, and 'affiliate your entire membership using the check-off' if Bill 42 was declared *ultra vires* in the Supreme Court.[62] However, the impact of Bill 42 was apparent: at the end of 1965, only twelve BC union locals (out of 1,061) representing 2,374 workers (1 per cent of the organized working class) were affiliated in good standing; nine were United Packinghouse locals and all but one were located in the Lower Mainland.[63] 'Due to anti-Labour legislation affiliation is not good,' the party's Organization Committee concluded.[64]

In the 1960s, growing restlessness in workers' ranks spilled over into the BC NDP. Larry Sefton, a Steelworkers' director, objected to Kootenay West MP Bert Herridge's 'support for our enemies' in the Mine-Mill fight.[65] While MLAs Cedric Cox and Leo Nimsick were charter members of Mine-Mill, the leadership gravitated behind the raiders; former Steel staff representative Wally Ross was hired as provincial secretary in 1968.[66] Labour militancy and growing anti-war activism compelled the BC NDP 'to make the class basis of the party clear,' Socialist Caucus member Sheila Turgeon claimed after the 1965 federal election, when the NDP retained its nine BC seats with 32.9 per cent of the vote – a plurality among the four major parties.[67] Tommy Douglas declared himself in favour of a general strike in support of striking oil workers, a move applauded by the Socialist Caucus: 'By supporting the proposed general strike, the party dramatically jumped down from the colourless middle ground ... and unequivocally took sides.'[68] Staunch moderate Grace MacInnis, MP for Vancouver Kingsway, also supported the oil workers and later called for the nationalization of the Canadian steel industry, while MLAs Arthur Turner and Alex MacDonald demanded nationalization of the brewing monopolies, which had refused to negotiate with their workers. Pressure from the left impelled the party toward a more interventionist policy. Provincial leader Bob Strachan pledged to nationalize the BC Telephone Company.[69]

However, such stances did little to improve NDP fortunes, which plateaued in the mid-1960s a decade after Strachan took the helm. Prior to the 1966 election, provincial secretary Clive Lytle suggested the NDP appeal to voters as 'consumers rather than as producers,' fearing an emphasis on 'social problems affecting minorities' and 'welfare-statism' would be 'inviting electoral failure.'[70] This reflected the individualization of working-class culture, as the proliferation of televisions, automobiles, suburbs, and consumer durables strained traditional class loyalties. The NDP caucus grew from 14 to 16 seats, as its share of the vote expanded from 28 per cent to nearly 34 per cent, a result Lytle (who managed the campaign) described as 'quite satisfactory.'[71] But NDP gains provided little solace against W.A.C. Bennett's sixth consecutive victory, with a solid legislative majority. In the BCFL and other circles, pressure mounted for a change in leadership, spurring a recruitment campaign for Tom Berger, the BCFL's legal counsel and former MP, who captured one of two NDP seats in Vancouver-Burrard in 1966. Federal secretary Cliff Scotton congratulated Berger, expressing hope that the BC party 'will now start working to build the organization necessary to crack the Socred machine.'[72]

Berger had been elected party president in 1961, at age twenty-eight, after running unsuccessfully as a CCF provincial candidate in Vancouver Centre in 1960. He was among the 10 NDP MPs elected from BC in the 1962 federal election, capturing Vancouver-Burrard in a tight three-way race. His enthusiasm on the hustings and trail-blazing legal work earned him a reputation as a 'young man in a hurry.' As an MP, Berger introduced a number of private member's bills with proposals including a Civil Servants' Bill of Rights and Criminal Code amendments protecting the right of trade unions to participate in peaceful picketing.[73] However, the 1962 Parliament was short-lived, and in the March 1963 election Berger lost to a Liberal by over 2,000 votes. He ran again as a provincial candidate in Vancouver-Burrard in September 1963, but lost by 300 votes. Following this string of defeats, Berger returned to his legal career, establishing a practice in Vancouver. He successfully sued Bennett for slander in the case of former civil servant George Jones and drew headlines for work in labour law and aboriginal land claims.[74]

Bennett pejoratively described Berger as a 'city-slicker lawyer' rather than a member of the working class. Berger's base, however, rested squarely in organized labour. He worked as counsel for the BCFL and enjoyed the support of E.P. 'Pat' O'Neil, BCFL secretary-treasurer (1958–66) and Pulp & Sulphite's BC captain, and also political scientist Walter Young, a CCF-NDP loyalist who had served on the New Party committee.[75] In 1967, the campaign against Strachan broke into the open, triggering two years of bitter inner-party conflict. At a NDP provincial executive meeting on 13 April 1967, Berger announced his intention to seek the leadership. Union locals rushed to establish NDP affiliation so they could send delegates to the upcoming convention.[76] On 3 June, Strachan withstood the challenge, 277–178 votes, but Young described this result as 'a stay of execution.' Berger felt the vote would have gone differently if he had had another month to campaign.[77]

Influential NDP members were uneasy with Berger's ambition and particularly the conduct of some of his supporters. 'I was shocked that they were attacking a sitting leader,' Dave Barrett recalls, describing Strachan as 'tough as a rock, extremely bright,' with a 'good sense of humour underneath':

> I was totally on board with Strachan. I have nothing against Berger. To this moment, I'd trust my life with him, and I mean it. A wonderful guy. Extremely bright ... He was being pushed by a handful of people in the party, one or two MLAs. A hell of a good person to push. It's a question of the timing that really began to break up the group ... The mood for a lot of people was that it was too early. He had just got there.[78]

Across the country, NDP support surged to 26 per cent in a November 1966 Gallup poll, and a May 1967 Sudbury by-election win increased the federal caucus to 22 MPs.[79] However, Douglas's warning of stiff competition from Liberals for urban white-collar votes was confirmed. NDP fortunes stalled in the 1968 federal election, as the Trudeau Liberals surged to 16 BC seats with 42 per cent of the vote. The NDP's share of the BC vote held at 32.6 per cent but three BC MPs lost their seats – Douglas in the reconfigured Burnaby-Seymour riding, Bob Prittie in neighbouring Burnaby-Richmond, and Tom Barnett in Comox-Alberni by a scant 9 votes, a result declared void by the courts. Douglas fell to former BC Liberal leader Ray Perrault by 138 votes.[80] According to Eileen Dailly, the Burnaby North MLA who served as Douglas's official agent:

> It was a sad day, but I could see that Tommy was in great difficultly ... He wasn't in our riding much at all. Because the head office knew how popular he was, knew he was in demand all across the place. We had a heck of a time getting him just to stay where he had to win the seat. And I used to point this out to the federal office, and, 'Oh no, Tommy won't lose.' Tommy lost. It doesn't matter how popular you are. The people there want to see you. Ray Perrault was running around and having coffee parties every day and making speeches. Tommy was devastated. And you can't blame him.[81]

Douglas was easily parachuted into Nanaimo-Cowichan-The Islands, after old Marxist Colin Cameron passed away a month after the election, but party leaders were growing restless.[82] Stephen Lewis, MPP for

Scarborough West and son of York South MP David Lewis, flew to BC to urge Douglas to resign as leader.[83]

Bill 33 and the Boycott of Bennett's Mediation Commission

In 1968, Social Credit responded to a sharp upturn in strike activity – and a walkout by 1,100 ferryworkers – with yet another legislative device. Bill 33, the Mediation Commission Act, allowed for compulsory arbitration of any dispute considered threatening to 'the public interest or welfare' and transferred the power to end strikes from the Legislative Assembly to the Cabinet. Labour viewed the new legislation as a grave intrusion on the right to bargain freely and strike, 'the sharpest spike ever aimed at the heart of the provincial labour movement,' delegate Ed Haw told the Victoria Labour Council. The Communist Party accused the Bennett government of enacting 'the worst anti-labor legislation on this continent.'[84]

Labour reacted aggressively against Bill 33, particularly Section 18, which empowered the cabinet to declare a recommendation of the Commission binding in instances where an ill-defined 'public welfare' was at stake. Unions including the Vancouver Building Trades Council, Vancouver letter carriers, Amalgamated Transit Workers, ILWU, and several large IWA locals agreed to walk out if the legislation came into force. However, the BCFL leadership deflected demands for a general strike. A March 1968 conference, attended by union officials from across BC, was dismissed by the Trotskyist LSA as 'a conference of pork-choppers' called to 'head off "rash actions."'[85] While BCFL secretary Ray Haynes insisted that 'the door is not closed' on a general strike, the LSA noted a 'real deep cynicism among workers ... It is consequently the duty of militants who are leaders of strategic groups of workers, to recognize that the Fed leadership will not give leadership, and that it will come only if they are prepared to give leadership.'[86] Burnaby-Edmonds MLA Gord Dowding urged the NDP provincial council against making Bill 33 an issue in a May 1968 Vancouver South by-election, which was won by the NDP.[87]

When the Bennett government ignored labour's opposition and proclaimed Bill 33, the BCFL declared a boycott of the Mediation Commission hearings, a request 'overwhelmingly supported' by affiliated and unaffiliated unions.[88] Statements by the commission's chairman that 'There should be no collective bargaining for Civil Servants' only inflamed the public sector.[89] The BCGEA recruited John Fryer, a British-born labour economist and CLC research director, to transform their association into a union. In October 1969, BCGEA delegates voted 62–51 to rename their organization the BC Government Employees Union (BCGEU), a move rejected 51–47 a year earlier, and approved resolutions launching a 'Collective Bargaining Rights Now!' campaign, restructuring the organization along industrial lines, and increasing dues from $2 to $3 per month. 'We created an industrial union,' Fryer recalls.[90] BCGEU membership grew from 12,500 in 1969 to 16,000 in March 1972, four times the rate of growth of government services.[91] In September 1969, Bill 33's compulsory arbitration provisions were invoked for the first time, when the Mediation Commission imposed an agreement for police officers in Saanich and Oak Bay.[92]

As labour challenged the Mediation Commission Act, a group of economists debated solutions to BC's stormy industrial relations climate. J.T. Montague stated bluntly: 'The pressure of the strike remains the impetus to settlement,' a view echoed by Ronald Shearer: 'The threat of the strike is essential and as such it should not be outlawed.'[93] Stuart Jamieson pointed out that the federal Task Force on Industrial Relations 'strongly endorsed collective bargaining rather than legal regulation' and 'recommended reducing the scale and frequency of government intervention in, and restriction of, collective bargaining activities.'[94]

Bill 33 failed to curb growing industrial unrest. In 1969, meatcutters in the Canadian Food and Allied Workers' Union waged a three-month strike 'attempting to break the 40-hour week.' Despite a slick public-relations campaign by BC's major food retailers, the workers won the thirty-nine-hour week and other gains.[95] Also in 1969, telephone workers waged a successful six-week strike against the BC Telephone Company, while the Plumbers and Tunnel and Rock Workers engaged in lengthy and difficult strikes. The Oil, Chemical and Atomic Workers – at the centre of the 1965 general strike movement – walked out against the big oil companies on 21 May 1969, striking for five months in what the BCFL executive council described as 'one of the most bitter strikes waged in BC over the last few years.'[96] Militants in the Vancouver and District Labour Council (VDLC) attempted to reverse the BCFL's single-company boycott of Imperial Oil, which they described as 'ineffective.' The LSA urged 'united labour action. Shut down the refineries with mass picketing ... Would the government dare to arrest the whole labor leadership in Vancouver?' However, a VDLC decision for a mass rally and march to the Vancouver Court House to protest Bill 33 was rescinded.[97] Labour's fight against Bill 33 was undermined by the collaborationist stance of several union leaders, a rift exploited by the new Employers' Council of BC. Charles Stewart of the Amalgamated Transit Union served as 'labour' representative on the Mediation Commission earning $20,000 per year, while the Teamsters, led by Liberal Senator Ed Lawson, were similarly compromised. The BCFL executive council commented bitterly that despite 'sabotage by this political opportunist, the policy and strategy of this Federation with respect to Bill 33 have proven to be the only approach.'[98]

The Tom Berger Leadership and 1969 Defeat

Amid growing working-class anger at Social Credit, the NDP grappled with the question of leadership. In early 1969, Bob Strachan resigned as BC NDP leader. Dave Barrett, the Coquitlam MLA who had remained loyal to Strachan, declared his candidacy, as did Vancouver East MLA Bob Williams, SFU activist John Conway, and Tom Berger. At the April 1969 convention, Berger defeated Barrett by the narrow margin of 36 votes, 411–375.[99] Barrett leapt to the platform to make the vote unanimous, but animosity between the camps prevailed.

1969 was to be the year of NDP victory. Enthusiasm in the province was running high, a pre-election report noted, and many NDP supporters were 'convinced that victory is inevitable.'[100] Optimism surged with a string of NDP by-election victories, retaining Revelstoke-Slocan and Burnaby-Willington and capturing Vancouver South – 'a bellwether area with a high representation of young marrieds' – from Social Credit. The government lost two other by-elections to Liberals, in well-heeled North Vancouver-Capilano and Oak Bay. The tide was turning against Bennett, as Martin Robin observed:

> Bennett and his colleagues are anxious to revive British Columbia's traditional red bogey but its credibility is becoming harder to maintain. Public malaise, in a province prone to hysteria, has focused on the student movement and hippies, alongside which the NDP appears as an assemblage of pious clergy.[101]

Anticipation of an NDP breakthrough was not confined to the left. Provincial secretary Wally Ross suggested Bennett was 'scared stiff,' framing the campaign as a struggle between 'Christian free enterprise' and 'godless socialists,' promising 'take-home pay instead of strike pay,' and warning of 'the flight of frightened capital.'[102] The NDP targeted

14 Social Credit seats, 11 of which were needed to form government if all incumbent NDP MLAs retained their seats (the party predicted the Liberals would neither gain nor lose seats). To finance this effort, the NDP requested $4,000 per month from the labour movement of eastern Canada, beginning on 1 June and continuing until the election, to cover wages, transportation, and accommodation for four organizers in the targeted ridings. Steel, Packinghouse/Canadian Food and Allied Workers, CUPE, Canadian Brotherhood of Railway and Transport (CBRT), Pulp & Sulphite, and the CLC were approached. The IWA, whose 'contribution to the NDP of BC far outstrips that of any other single union,' was excluded from this appeal, said Ross.[103] CUPE pledged $3,000, with the proviso that 'information regarding this donation be handled carefully in BC' because many members 'were not particularly oriented towards the New Democratic Party.'[104] Funds were deposited in the BCFL's 'Fight Bill 33 Fund' and spent on organizers' wages, leaflets, and other campaign expenses. While this direct appeal to national union headquarters aggravated CLC secretary William Dodge, it successfully bypassed Bill 42 and generated crucial funds for the NDP's war chest.[105]

On 21 July 1969, Bennett called a summertime election, apparently 'to dilute the university vote to the greatest possible extent.'[106] He embarked on a frenzied 1,500-kilometre tour of the province, armed with a glossy election platform, *The Good Life*, paid for with $500,000 from the Social Credit war chest. Initially, federal NDP secretary Cliff Scotton expressed 'cautious optimism,' with thirty to forty NDP organizers from various provinces converging on BC, backed by the 'enthusiastic participation' of BC NDP members. However, 'poor canvassing conditions due to extensive vacation absences' undermined the party's grassroots campaigning style.[107] Midway through the campaign, momentum turned against the NDP. Bennett homed in on Berger's pledge to nationalize the BC Telephone Company, which had witnessed its first strike in fifty years. While Berger insisted, 'Our program so far as nationalization is concerned begins with the telephone company and ends with the telephone company,' the nationalization plank influenced undecided voters, who were susceptible to Bennett's anti-socialist appeals.[108] When the ballots were tallied on 27 August 1969, NDP members were confronted with a painful result: 12 NDP seats to 38 Social Credit and 5 Liberal; the party lost 4 seats, including Berger's in Vancouver-Burrard by 279 votes. While the party's share of the vote improved slightly to 34 per cent, and its vote total increased from 253,000 in 1966 to 332,000 in

1969, the verdict was clear. Less than a month after the election, Berger resigned as BC NDP leader, naming Dave Barrett 'de facto leader of the party.'[109]

The NDP faced a financial crisis: $63,000 debt for the provincial party and another $100,000 owed by local constituencies. Treasurer and defeated Vancouver South MLA Norm Levi recommended that all six organizers be laid off, and that the provincial office close until the financial picture improved. Provincial secretary Wally Ross tendered his resignation, but was later persuaded to remain until mid-1970. The *Democrat* suspended publication. 'I cannot stress too strongly the tremendous danger of the party marking time ... and falling back without some central co-ordinating office,' federal secretary Cliff Scotton warned.[110] MLA Dave Stupich of Nanaimo organized a BC Tomorrow Raffle to pay off the provincial and constituency debt.[111] The BCFL executive council, meanwhile, urged affiliates that 'this is the time to intensify our efforts on the political field.'[112] The BCFL Political Education Committee observed:

> it is unfortunate that Premier Bennett recognizing the fact that Social Democratic governments have only come to power through full trade union participation and support, has succeeded in persuading some trade unionists and NDP members to accept his view that unions should not participate in the NDP.[113]

The year 1969 closed with only 20,972 BC workers affiliated to the NDP through their unions, out of 292,000 unionized workers in province.[114] Despite mounting militancy and opposition to Social Credit labour laws, the NDP had failed to provide an effective vehicle for working-class agency. An aversion to socialism among a layer of workers, and a preference for extra-parliamentary change among others, undermined the NDP's appeal.

The Waffle

In the late 1960s a layer of New Left activists migrated into the NDP. At the 1965 federal convention in Toronto, dissidents had formed a federal Socialist Caucus, 'the first time socialists in the Party made an effort to coalesce a cross-country body of opposition to its reformist program and leadership.'[115] The group launched *Socialist Caucus Bulletin*, focused on labour issues and the Vietnam War. Kootenay West MP Bert Herridge led a march of 150 delegates to the US consulate, and the convention adopted a resolution opposing the war.[116] Caucus member Sheila Turgeon described the 1966 BC NDP convention as 'more democratic and relaxed' than previous meetings, marked by 'a reluctant swing to the left on Vietnam' but 'a further shift to the right programmatically on nationalization.' According to Turgeon, 'Between the stalwarts of the old CCF and the new socialists lay a broad gap of years. Dorothy Steeves typified the best tradition of the old CCF.'[117]

The NDP's appeal among young people was confirmed by the YS in 1966: 'for all its dedicated fulltime workers and unlimited publicity ... SUPA has never been able to muster a quarter the number of active members of the NDYC ... In spite of its leadership, the NDY because of its ties with the NDP has a far broader appeal than the New Left.'[118] SUPA chairman Jim Harding conceded that activists were moving into the NDY, confiding to a colleague that 'SUPA has failed ... to relate to radical potential.'[119] Another SUPA activist suggested the NDP's existence had made 'the emergence of a new left more difficult in Canada than in the case of the USA.'[120]

Young radicals and New Leftists occupied a precarious position in the NDP, which like the CCF imposed limits on dissent. 'The right wing is not prepared to tolerate indefinitely our presence and the growth of our influence,' the Vancouver YS noted in 1966.[121] In the spring of 1967, a fresh wave of expulsions purged the NDY of its 'socialist left wing,' imposing 'a puppet leadership on the Youth of do-nothing careerists.'[122] Nanaimo-Cowichan-The Islands MP Colin Cameron (threatened with expulsion for belonging to the Socialist Fellowship in 1950) signed a petition opposing 'the recent expulsions of young anti-Vietnam war activists'; Herridge (expelled for advocating cooperation with communists during the Second World War) donated money to the Committee to Defend the Expelled. The expulsions confirmed, according to the LSA/YS, 'the hostility and fear of the NDP leadership to a serious and viable youth movement.'[123] However, Trotskyists remained committeed to entryism, describing 'Labor's creation' of the NDP as 'the most significant political development' of the twentieth century:

> Conceived originally by the CCF and CLC leadership as a multi-class liberal-labor party, the NDP has taken root and grown as a class party, based in industrial urban centers, on the votes, organized muscle and financial strength of trade unions. The NDP presents a class alternative to the capitalist parties.[124]

In 1969, the most serious New Left challenge surfaced in the NDP – the Waffle. The BC Waffle, unlike its Ontario counterpart, never elicited the same scorn among provincial party leaders. The ideological distance between NDP leaders and dissidents – which John Bullen identifies as the major factor behind the group's demise in eastern Canada – was narrower in BC, reflecting the relative radicalism of the working-class movement.[125] Barrett and his group – which included MLAs Bob Williams, Jim Lorimer, Eileen Dailly, Alex MacDonald, and former MLA Norm Levi – signed the manifesto *For an Independent Socialist Canada* (appendix I), as did VDLC secretary-treasurer Paddy Neale, not necessarily because they shared its radical zeal, but in Barrett's words 'to encourage debate.'[126] 'It seemed harmless to me,' recalls Eileen Dailly, who was surprised by the uproar at the 1969 federal convention.[127] Levi, a social worker, was a former BC NDP president (1966–8) who had moved the party from annual to biannual conventions, but retained connections to a social-movement base.[128]

Formed in April 1969 and led by Queen's University instructor James Laxer (a SUPA activist and son of former communist organizer Robert Laxer) and University of Toronto economist Melville Watkins, author of an influential 1968 report on foreign ownership, the Waffle mounted the most significant challenge to the NDP leadership since the party's formation.[129] It combined a left-nationalist critique of foreign ownership with the more explicitly anti-capitalist politics associated with the New Left. From its inception, the Waffle was centred in Ontario, though it developed a presence in all provinces, particularly Saskatchewan and New Brunswick, where it briefly won control of the provincial party.[130] In BC, the NDY convention of October 1969 endorsed the Waffle Manifesto; Watkins met Vancouver supporters and delivered an address at UBC. However, of twenty-one federal NDP riding associations that endorsed the manifesto, only one – Tommy Douglas's old Burnaby-Seymour riding – was in BC.[131] At the Winnipeg convention in October 1969, delegates rejected the Waffle manifesto 499–268, favouring the leaderships' compromise 'Marshmallow' manifesto, *For a United and Independent Canada*.[132] During the debate VDLC secretary-treasurer Paddy Neale said he appeared 'on this side of the hall to show that the whole labour movement of Canada is not conservative ... Unless this party leads the way and says we have an alternative, and the alternative is public ownership of the means of distribution, the means of production, and of our natural resources, we are in trouble.'[133]

To the Waffle, however, the Winnipeg convention was only the 'first objective.'[134] Organizing efforts unfolded across the provinces in 1970: a Western Regional Waffle conference in Banff in April, a national Waffle conference in Toronto in August, and demonstrations against the continental energy resources deal. The Waffle hired a full-time organizer and published *Waffle News*, disparaging the moderate policy of the new Schreyer government in Manitoba and supporting striking Dunlop workers in Toronto.[135] In BC, Wafflers supported a tugboat workers' strike and protested an increase in BC Hydro rates. The BC Waffle released a report criticizing labour affiliation to the NDP, which it described as 'mere affiliation between bureaucracies ... leaving most of the members of both organizations out in the cold ... For affiliation to be useful, the abuses, manipulation and undemocratic structuring ... must be ended.'[136] At the 1970 BC NDP convention, which elected Dave Barrett as leader, the BC Waffle put forward a slate of officers – three of whom were elected – and presented a 'draft statement of principles' declaring that only the working class can 'uproot and transform the established power structure.'[137] A resolution was adopted eliminating fixed membership fees.[138] *Waffle News* estimated that 150–200 of 500 delegates supported Waffle candidates and resolutions.[139]

In 1971, Laxer declared his candidacy for the federal leadership vacated by Tommy Douglas, providing a lightning rod for opponents of the party establishment backing deputy leader David Lewis and International unions such as Steel. Laxer made public ownership of natural resources the centrepiece of his campaign, a position repudiated by Lewis, as was Laxer's call for accommodation of the separatist Parti Québécois.[140] 'Confrontation is the name of the political game these days in the NDP,' Victoria's *Daily Colonist* observed.[141] At the leadership convention in Ottawa in April 1971, Laxer mounted a surprisingly strong challenge, forcing the race to a fourth ballot where he lost to Lewis with 613–1,046 votes.[142] Frank Howard, MP for Skeena in northwestern BC, finished at the bottom of the first ballot, with 124 votes. Prior to voting, Douglas, who continued to serve as Nanaimo MP, warned against 'the extreme nationalizing tendencies of the party's left wing,' according to the *Vancouver Sun*.[143]

Opposition to the Waffle reflected earlier Cold War practices, imbued with a sense of urgency because of the rising breakaway union phenomenon. To International unionists at the helm of the CLC and NDP, the Waffle's left-nationalism was cause for concern. As early as 1962, Tommy Douglas had proposed a campaign focused on foreign ownership and control of Canada's economy, but Steel leaders Larry Sefton and Bill Mahoney were opposed because it would 'degenerate into an appeal to superficial nationalism and anti-Americanism.'[144] When the NDP's 1969 federal convention approved 'in principle' the idea of industrial democracy, a cause championed by Oshawa MP Ed Broadbent, CLC secretary William Dodge protested the lack of official labour input 'on this highly controversial subject.'[145] As the Waffle gained strength and began to encourage breakaway movements – like one at Stanley Steel Co. in Hamilton where 150 workers left the International in November 1971 – Steel drew a line in the sand. 'Support is no longer automatic,' Steel organizer Bob Mackenzie (later labour minister in Bob Rae's Ontario NDP government) informed David Lewis.[146] Mackenzie's Hamilton-Mountain NDP constituency association demanded 'exclusion from membership' for anyone belonging to 'any clearly identifiable ongoing political group.'[147]

Appeals were issued from across the country urging tolerance between the warring factions. 'In BC, we have "Wafflers", non-wafflers and anti-Wafflers,' the Langley constituency association declared, 'but so far we have managed to conciliate our differences towards that greater objective of winning seats whether the candidate is a waffler or not. There is no talk of disciplinary action and possible expulsion here.'[148] Vancouver's Point Grey adopted a similar stance, while Fort George requested more information from both camps.[149] The *Vancouver Sun*, however, considered the Waffle 'a threat' to the NDP's 'national credibility and its chances in a federal election,' and W.A.C. Bennett dared the provincial party to hold a leadership convention so moderates could replace Barrett, 'a member of the Waffle group.'[150] 'Bennett is making political hay out of the Ontario promoted split,' Langley campaign organizer Charlie Haddrell warned.[151] The stage was set for the Ontario NDP's June 1972 Orillia provincial council meeting, which culminated in an edict that the Waffle disband and the Waffle's decision at London to leave the NDP and form the Movement for an Independent Socialist Canada, which fielded candidates in the 1974 federal election.[152] 'It was a great movement, while it lasted,' communist Ben Swankey recalls. 'But they weren't strong enough to take over the NDP.'[153]

'It was definitely quite a tense time,' Eileen Dailly says. 'And yet they were quite a small group ... It's really sad, isn't it. Because to have any kind of split like that is not good for any major party, because the public's wondering what the heck's going on.'[154] But others saw the Waffle as a positive development for the NDP and the Canadian left. Dorothy

Steeves, an Old Leftist who belonged to the Waffle, felt it was important for the party to 'do something bold, and appeal to the imagination of people.'[155] The YS observed that 'student radicals who previously wrote off the NDP as a factor became involved in it through its Waffle caucus.' New Leftists gravitated to the NDP, the YS argued, because of its relevance as a labour party and the Waffle's anti-imperialist sentiment that resonated strongly among students.[156] According to Hilda Thomas, a UBC English instructor, feminist, and outspoken Waffler (and co-chair of the 1975 Rosemary Brown leadership campaign), 'an attempt was made to organize the remnants of the Waffle' at the Richmond home of MLA Harold Steves, but little came of it.[157] Leftist activities became concentrated in the party's Vancouver Area Council, and, a few years later, in the Left Caucus.[158] Outside the NDP, the Waffle's defeat was interpreted as confirmation that social democracy had 'sold out' to capitalism. Veteran communist Tom McEwen, *Pacific Tribune* editor, linked the Waffle to earlier left factions: 'Right-wing social democracy cannot "bed down" with bourgeois ideology and at the same time retain its pretentious claims of being "socialist." So its historic role, that of fomenting confusion and betrayal is preserved ... by getting rid of its dissidents.'[159]

Barrett and the Road to Power

Tom Berger's defeat in the 1969 election and subsequent resignation left the BC NDP leadership open. As runner-up in the leadership race, Barrett was the obvious successor. Moreover, his social-movement orientation made him amenable to the party's resurgent left wing. 'Barrett was a left-winger in his party,' Swankey recalls. 'A person you could work with. He had close connections with the rank and file, of the party and the people, and he still has.'[160] The NDP legislative caucus met after Berger resigned and elected the Coquitlam MLA as house leader.[161]

Animosity generated during the leadership fight, however, had not dissipated and a powerful labour group remained vehemently opposed to Barrett, a situation aggravated by the party's precarious financial situation. As Eileen Dailly recalls, there was 'a lot of tension' between Barrett and BCFL president Ray Haynes, whom LSA activist Allan Engler described as 'one of the most despised trade union leaders in BC ... the leader of the conservative craft union faction of the BC Fed.'[162] Party member Joyce Nash of Ladysmith asked: 'Why do men feel that their position can only be strong at the expense of others?'[163] Ironically,

Barrett moved into the NDP leadership at the moment union affiliation reached a record high.[164] 'It is not a labour party,' Barrett insists. 'It never has been a labour party. I would wish that everybody who worked or joined a union would vote for us. It's not that way. The perception has been deliberately created that the labour movement dominates.'[165]

In early 1970, as a leadership convention approached, the conflict between Barrett and the BCFL erupted. Barrett and the NDP caucus signed a declaration stating: 'As a group that hopes to govern this province for the benefit of all people, our view must reflect the broader public interest rather than the view of one single sector of society. Significant as the organized labor sector is, the public interest must prevail.'[166] A line had been drawn. Wally Ross, who had tendered his resignation as provincial secretary, observed that 'the issues in the BC section are clearly defined: 1) the accountability of elected members to the Convention; 2) the question of who runs the Party: the Caucus, or the Executive.'[167] Barrett embarked on a provincial tour in his Volvo, accompanied by SFU political scientist Martin Robin, to 'consolidate his position in the party' and lay the foundation for the next general election.[168] The two travelled to northern Prince George, then Prince Rupert, with stops along the way; collections at local meetings, attended by a half-dozen to several hundred members, covered the cost of accommodation, gas, and food. Robin parted with Barrett at Prince Rupert, and then Barrett travelled to the Okanagan. By the time of the leadership convention, held in Chilliwack in June 1970, Barrett had met, by his own account, with nearly every constituency association in the province outside the northeast. He was acclaimed leader of the BC NDP.[169]

The prize that had evaded Barrett a year earlier was now his. He began in earnest to prepare for the next election, still two and a half years away. 'I knew I had one shot and that was it,' Barrett recalls.[170] However, the rift with organized labour threw a curveball at the new leader, despite a convention resolution reaffirming 'strong ties' between the NDP and unions.[171] As the *Waffle News* reported in July 1970, 'the Barrett forces (which comprise the left and centre of the party) basically smashed the party's right wing at the convention.'[172] Haynes was defeated for the position of first vice-president by Paddy Neale, VDLC secretary and a Barrett ally.[173] A short time later, the BCFL called the mortgage on the BC NDP's Vancouver headquarters, leaving the party without office space. Barrett and his group – Williams, Lorimer, Levi, Dailly, MacDonald – responded by finding their own building, a vacant Swedish church near East Hastings and Victoria. Twenty-one debentures valued at $1,000 each were sold to party members, including Barrett, and the building was purchased for $21,000. Hartley Dent, an Anglican priest, was hired as provincial secretary.[174] Despite the tension, in November 1970 BCFL delegates rejected a motion to withdraw from the NDP, 'despite growing disaffection between some members of both organizations,' the *Globe and Mail* reported.[175]

The Fall of Social Credit

Social Credit tried in vain to legislate away mounting working-class unrest. In February 1970, the government introduced Bill 22, amending the Labour Relations Act to accredit employer organizations as bargaining agents. NDP MLA Ernie Hall complained that 'changes that are requested by the labour groups ... don't receive the same kind of speedy treatment.'[176] Bill 22 also altered the time-frame in which raiding was permitted, a move specifically designed to thwart a PPWC breakaway at Chemainus. In summer 1970, PPWC waged an eight-week strike against a multi-employer bargaining group, shutting down mills at Crofton, Harmac, Prince Rupert, Prince George, Castlegar, and Skookumchuk.[177] A strike by tugboat workers paralysed Lower Mainland sawmills and Vancouver's waterfront, prompting injunctions and a mass meeting of 400 trade unionists where labour leaders vowed to defy discriminatory court orders.[178] Indicating growing militancy in public-sector ranks, the Trotskyist *Labor Challenge* noted that 'The first signs of a new militancy have appeared in the BC Teachers' Federation.'[179]

In January 1971, at the opening of the legislature in Victoria, the BCFL organized a protest demonstration against Bennett's labour policies. Barrett reportedly told the crowd, 'This is your building,' and 200 protesters – described by an RCMP agent as mainly 'Hippies and VLF [Vancouver Liberation Front] types' – occupied the foyer and public gallery, disrupting the speech from the throne.[180] In the chamber the next day, James Charles Chabot, Social Credit MLA for Columbia River, took aim at labour's relationship to the NDP: 'They were flaunting the red flag out in the front, a red flag attached to banners such as these: "Jobs with the NDP Labour to Power."' Chabot claimed that Barrett's public tiff with Haynes and the BCFL leadership was a sham: 'When Ray Haynes tells him to jump, he asks, "how high?"' Voicing a familiar Socred theme, Chabot – who would replace Leslie Peterson as labour minister in April – issued a warning against labour militancy:

> The majority of time-loss due to strikes and lockouts that took place in Canada, took place in our Province. We have lost approximately three million man-days in 1970, almost half the national total, more time-loss than in the preceding decade in this Province. Economically this has had a very severe effect on our ability to render services to people ... Governments can no longer tolerate unions that would attempt to coerce their will upon the electorate, regardless of the consequences.

Describing the 'union shop' and 'closed shop' as forms of compulsion, Chabot said that BC labour took its position for granted: 'Some unions fail to appreciate this tremendous concession.' He advocated amendments to the Mediation Act to remove penalties against individual workers and increase penalties against unions.[181]

Such threats failed to stem the widening rank-and-file revolt. In March 1971, the BC Teachers' Federation (BCTF) staged a one-day strike, the first province-wide teachers' strike in BC or Canada; 500,000 students were affected as most of the union's 22,000 members walked out.[182] Later that month, the BCFL held a special convention where delegates declared that 'free collective bargaining, the existence of a strong trade union movement and vital democratic rights, such as the right to strike' were 'seriously threatened by British Columbia's power-intoxicated Social Credit government.' They instructed BCFL officers to mobilize 'the labour movement politically' and increase affiliations to the NDP.[183] However, ongoing tension was evident when the BCFL executive council declared: 'in spite of the reluctance of some in the Party to be associated with the trade union movement, the NDP still represents for trade unionists the only viable and meaningful alternative to the three old-line parties.'[184] In 1972, BC's working class reached a level of militancy unparalleled since the 1940s and surpassing all North American jurisdictions outside Quebec.[185]

Such was the context of the NDP's drive for power. Despite Barrett's distance from the captains of the BCFL, several important unions embraced political action in a bid to oust Social Credit, particularly the BCTF, which was livid over the Bill 3 amendments to the Public Schools Act that would have limited school spending and teacher salaries. An RCMP agent reported that 'the primary aim' of the BCTF's April 1972 annual meeting 'was to discuss ways of fighting against the British Columbia Government's controversial Bill 3.'[186] Union president Adam Robertson told delegates: 'We must leave the seeming security of our classrooms to enter the political arena.'[187] Delegates approved a strike vote and voted 495–84 for a special levy of one day's pay to build a $1.25-million political war chest, to 'finance citizens' committees in BC ridings' – a move opposed by Social Credit and the employer-friendly BC Supreme Court.[188] Mass rallies took place under the aegis of a 'Collective Bargaining Defence Committee,' bringing together teachers and other public-sector workers in what the RCMP called 'a common front.'[189] In May, CUPE BC described the Bennett government as 'a menace to working people' and pledged to join with BC teachers 'in their campaign ... to turn the Socreds out of office.'[190] As BCGEU secretary John Fryer recalls: 'The BCTF was absolutely critical' to Social Credit's defeat. 'W.A.C. Bennett considers in his grave that they were the ones that did him in. I know that for a fact.'[191]

The summer of 1972 was marked by militant job action – the high point of a year of industrial unrest that saw one-third of BC's unionized workers walk picket lines – 106,399 of 332,091 union members.[192] The BCGEU set up illegal pickets at twenty department of highways yards in May, and disrupted a Kamloops speech by Bennett and his highways minister, Phil Gaglardi.[193] In June, a lock-out of 30,000 construction workers prompted a back-to-work order under section 18 of the Mediation Commission Act, which the workers defied, and RCMP raids on the BC-Yukon Building Trades Council headquarters and a dozen union offices from Victoria to Prince Rupert to Cranbrook – on orders of Bennett's attorney general.[194] Also in June, 5,000 IWA workers wildcatted, shutting down three mills in the Alberni valley and logging operations at Inglewood and Squamish; within a week, all 28,000 coastal fallers had joined the strike. A settlement favourable to the fallers was reached after twenty-five days, but the *Vancouver Sun* reported that 'many rebel fallers followed through with a threat to stay off the job,' while Robert Bonner, Bennett's former attorney general and president of forestry giant MacMillan Bloedel, said the compensation package would hurt BC's export position.[195] In the Interior, 4,000 loggers wildcatted in anticipation of a legal strike, while the PPWC applied for certification at two IWA mills in Port Alberni.[196] In July, 2,800 Vancouver civic workers walked out, while a two-week strike of Cominco smelter workers in Trail, members of the United Steelworkers, spawned the breakaway Canadian Workers Union (CWU).[197]

The heightened militancy of BC workers in 1972 reflected pressures that had been building for decades, but also the inflationary squeeze on workers' wages that became acute in the 1970s.[198] W.A.C. Bennett called an election on 24 July, as his leadership came under fire by members of his own cabinet, including Gaglardi. As Dave Barrett recalls: 'Bennett was getting old. Phil Gaglardi was making noises that he wanted to be leader. That was a big issue in the campaign itself.'[199] The premier hoped for a repeat of his summer 1969 victory, with students and workers preoccupied with more leisurely pursuits.[200] However, after seven consecutive victories, the formula failed. Barrett employed an aggressive, populist strategy, designed to ridicule and discredit the decaying Social Credit regime. When Bennett accused Barrett of fomenting a demonstration in New Westminster, where a cabinet minister was injured, the NDP leader sued the premier. When Bennett warned of 'dangerous Marxists' in the NDP, Barrett jokingly asked, 'which one, Groucho, Harpo, or Zeppo? I just made it the theatre of the absurd that it was.'[201] The NDP platform, *A New Deal for People*, said that despite lofty promises, Social Credit delivered 'unemployment statistics, labour-management confrontations, battles with teachers and doctors, and welfare for too many of our citizens.' The NDP promised 'an end to the labour-management crisis' by repealing Bill 33 and discriminatory provisions in the Trade Unions Act and Labour Relations Act, restoring 'free collective bargaining' and the right of workers 'to a fair share of the fruits of their labour.'[202]

On 30 August 1972, a revived Conservative party under North Vancouver lawyer Derril Thomas Warren – 'a very bright young lawyer' – captured 13 per cent of the vote, attracting wayward Socred voters as the party's support dipped to 31 per cent. NDP support grew from 34 to 40 per cent and Dave Barrett formed a majority government with 33 of 58 legislative seats.[203] The free-enterprise monopoly on political power was broken. After twenty years, Bennett lost the premiership. After seventy years on the opposition benches, social democrats captured legislative power. A new chapter in BC working-class history began.

Conclusion

The NDP's 1972 victory reflected structural changes in British Columbia's working class and divisions within the provincial bourgeosie. As Daniel Koenig and others argued in a contemporary study, assessments that Social Credit 'defeated itself' provide only 'partial explanations.'[1] Throughout the 1950s and 1960s, Social Credit had enjoyed the support of a layer of workers, supplanting the crass partisanship of the old-line Liberal-Conservative Coalition with a populism that promised economic growth and social security short of CCF-NDP socialism. Rapid resource expansion and buoyant economic conditions provided the ingredients for success. However, beneath the veneer of W.A.C. Bennett's 'good life,' structural changes sowed the seeds for political change. Unemployment, automation, inflation, and restrictive labour laws generated discontent – among blue-collar resource-extraction workers and the emerging white-collar new working class in the cities. The NDP was well positioned to harness this discontent as the Fordist formula underpinning the postwar settlement unravelled. The party represented an alliance of the Old Left CCF tradition, blue-collar and white-collar workers, marginalized social groups, and upwardly mobile members of the urban middle class. The party's slate of candidates in 1972 reflected this diversity, including school teachers, a city planner, an accountant, a lawyer, an indigenous fisherman, and several social workers, two of them black and two of them (including Dave Barrett) Jewish. Social Credit faltered at a time when the BC NDP was riding a wave of electoral strength, coming to terms with its demons and sidestepping the Waffle controversy to present a favourable image to voters. The party's diverse electoral base was integral to victory in 1972. However, it also fuelled conflict after the NDP assumed the reins of government.

Since the Second World War, British Columbia's militant minority and the broader working class had engaged in a tug-of-war with employers over control of the province's resource wealth, the framework of industrial relations, and the limits of labour's social wage. While this conflict was mediated through collective bargaining and an expanding welfare state, tensions endured. The Cold War had blunted the edge of socialism, inducing crises in the Labor-Progressive Party and Co-operative Commonwealth Federation and propelling Social Credit to power. However, the militant minority nurtured an oppositional political culture throughout the 1950s in the labour, peace, and women's movements. Structural changes in BC's economy and working class laid the groundwork for political renewal as the historic affluence achieved during the 'long boom' of North American capitalism appeared vulnerable. Workers gravitated toward breakaway unions and a New Left that was industrially militant and politically radical – and more diverse and diffuse than earlier left formations.

In this postwar era, the militant and radical traditions of BC workers reached their logical end: a level of industrial conflict – 2.1 million striker-days in 1972 – that set the province apart from most North American jurisdictions and a class-polarized party system that more closely resembled European patterns of partisan alignment than North American 'brokerage' politics.[2] Labour's organizational muscle coming out of the successful war against fascism succeeded in unravelling the partisan coalitions that had governed BC since the inauguration of the party system in 1903; in the forty-nine years from 1903 to 1952, Conservative and Liberal governments alternated, or shared, power; in the forty-nine years from 1952 to 2001, new parties of the right and left – Social Credit and NDP – governed Canada's westernmost province.[3] Ironically, victory for the labour-backed NDP in 1972 occurred at the moment that labour's historic postwar gains began to unravel. The oil shocks of 1973, rampant inflation, and the competitiveness of German and Japanese manufacturing vis-à-vis North American industry eroded the economic strength underpinning collective bargaining and the welfare state's social wage; Fordist accommodation came under siege, foreshadowing the neo-liberal assault. BC's working class approached legislative power on the eve of a determined assault by an aggressive and global capitalist class.

Tug-of-War Rather than Compromise

Rather than a 'compromise,' industrial relations in postwar British Columbia more closely resembled a tug-of-war, a conflict between labour and capital over the terms of collective bargaining and the balance of power between workers and employers. From the moment that legislative jurisdiction over labour relations returned to the province in 1947, BC workers and employers applied pressure on governments to enact laws and regulations to their benefit. Even as partisan alignments shifted from the Liberal and Conservative parties to populist parties of the right and left, the basic conflict over the terms of industrial relations remained. Sections of the labour leadership made peace with expansionary postwar capitalism, but many unions remained defiant. The United Fishermen and Allied Workers' Union (UFAWU) refused to accept the prerogatives of private enterprise in the fishery; when the union was sidelined in the drive for industrial legality, the absence of union certification created an opening for militant leadership. The compliance of the judiciary in the jailing of UFAWU secretary Homer Stevens and president Steve Stavenes (and dozens of other labour leaders in this period) reflects the bias of the state and allied institutions in postwar industrial relations. The wide sympathy enjoyed by Stevens among fishers reflects the limited appeal of Cold War anti-communism among BC resource-sector workers, who accepted communist leadership as the most effective means of advancing their interests as workers.

The absence of 'compromise' in postwar industrial relations is further revealed by the predilection of wide sections of BC workers to engage in 'wildcat' strikes and other forms of job action proscribed by BC's postwar labour laws. The most articulated rejection of compromise took the form of 'breakaway' unions, where workers abandoned their parent International unions to forge independent and militant organizations such as the CIW, PPWC, CEWU, CASAW, and CAIMAW. That these breakaway unions emerged first in BC should not be viewed as accidental. The province had a deep tradition of independence, from both the labour leadership based in eastern Canada and International unions based in the United States. The province's resource-extraction economy was more conducive to industrial, rather than craft, unionism; the IWW had gained a strong following in BC in the first decades of the twentieth century; the One Big Union was initiated by BC socialists in 1919; the CIO took root among BC loggers, miners, and shipbuilders; communists advocating Canadian independence retained the loyalty of workers long after 'red' unions had been broken elsewhere – Mine-Mill and the UFAWU remained BC's second and third largest unions throughout the 1950s. Bolstered by the tradition of political independence dating back to the turn of the century, BC's militant minority was positioned to lead the effort for independent Canadian unions in the 1960s and 1970s.

In postwar British Columbia, collective bargaining and the social wage provided by an expanding welfare state insulated workers from the most glaring inequities of the private enterprise economy, giving rise to a level of union density and a degree of affluence that was without historical precedent. The expansion of public enterprise in the fields of transportation, energy, health and education drove economic growth in BC's hinterland, and contributed to economic diversification in established urban centres. Vancouver emerged as the service centre for western Canada, giving rise to a 'metropolis-hinterland' dynamic centred in the Lower Mainland, a 'city-state' in the words of New Leftist Jim Harding.[4] These structural changes in BC's economy combined with changes in the social fabric of the province. The increased participation of women in the paid labour force and the recognition of diverse ethnic groups altered the working-class experience and bolstered the militant minority's ranks. Technological innovation and automation also precipitated change within BC's working class, altering the work process, employment patterns, and the texture of working-class life. Technology fuelled the age of mass consumption, the proliferation of consumer durables and labour-saving devices. Technology also gave rise to the television age, hastening the individuation of working-class culture, and the proliferation of the automobile, which diluted collective bonds between workers and made possible suburbanization. The automobile, television, and suburbia signalled a departure from previously close-knit working-class communities, creating barriers to the collective agency of the working class – particularly in urban centres like Vancouver.

In the Old Left LPP and CCF, the militant minority engaged in a unique dialogue with emerging social groups – students, professionals, and upwardly mobile members of the middle class. In groups such as the BC Peace Council, Vancouver Committee for the Control of Radiation Hazards, Combined Universities Campaign for Nuclear Disarmament (CUCND), Voice of Women (VOW), and Student Union for Peace Action (SUPA), the Old Left and New Left mobilized around issues such as atomic testing, the rights of indigenous peoples and workers of colour, and the liberation struggles of colonial peoples from China to Cuba to Vietnam. Tied to the increased participation of women in the paid labour force, and ongoing male domination in labour unions and left parties, a layer of working-class women embraced women's liberation and the ideology of socialist feminism, demanding pay equity, public child care, and reproductive choice; these women worked to change the unions and parties, and some employed forms of direct action that conflicted with the narrow electoralism of the social-democratic NDP.

Disenchantment with the Communist Party's 'Stalinism,' graphically displayed by Soviet armed force in Hungary in 1956 and Czechoslovakia in 1968, and dissatisfaction with the CCF-NDP's limited parliamentary agenda, resuscitated leftist tendencies that had operated on the margins. Trotskyist and later Maoist formations grew on the wave of worker and student unrest – embracing a conception of revolutionary socialism that located these tendencies in the vanguard of a worker-student uprising against the colonialism, consumerism, and 'soullessness' of North American capitalism. The Trotskyists in Ross Dowson's Revolutionary Workers Party, League for Socialist Action, and Young Socialists challenged the CCF-NDP's moderate leadership, while Jack Scott's Maoist *Progressive Worker* offered a left-nationalist critique of organized labour. Another, more indigenously inspired, New Left formation – the Waffle – mounted the most formidable challenge to the NDP's dominant political strategy. Established working-class parties were influenced by this ferment; Barrett and many in his caucus signed the Waffle's manifesto *For an Independent Socialist Canada*.[5] Out of this constellation of social forces – more fragmented but also more dynamic than the waning institutional expressions of the Old Left – the NDP was elected to power in 1972.

The NDP's victory revealed the temporary dissolution of the free-enterprise coalition around Social Credit, rather than a huge increase in NDP support. Even so, it signified the beginning of a new era in working-class history and working-class politics, as BC workers were forced to grapple with the responsibilities of governing and the difficulties of implementing a socialist program in the confines of a globalizing, commodity-based capitalist economy. Wall Street's characterization of Barrett's BC as 'a Northern Chile' – and alleged CIA surveillance of Barrett and members of his cabinet – tells us something of the pressures confronting a socialist administration in Cold War North America.[6] Internally, the challenges facing BC labour and the NDP point to the persistent tug-of-war over labour relations – and reveal conflicts of ideology, policy, and organization reminiscent of Michels's 'Iron Law,' underscoring the difficulty of sustaining a culture of democracy in established institutions. While BC labour and the NDP went some distance in preserving mechanisms for grassroots control and collective agency, enduring 'top-down' methods left BC's working class vulnerable to the ascendant corporate assault. This was the contradiction of the NDP's 1972 'victory.'

In summation, the preceding study has documented the transition of British Columbia's working-class movement from one left formation to another – from Old Left parties at the inauguration of the Cold War in 1948 to the New Left politics of the 1970s – the social-movement activism and rank-and-file revolt that preceded the NDP's victory in 1972. Throughout this period, BC's militant minority and the broader working class engaged in a tug-of-war with employers over the shape the postwar industrial relations system would take, challenging labour laws to gain a larger share of BC's resource wealth and alter the balance of power in the provincial economy. While Cold War anti-communism weakened the appeal of more radical forms of working-class politics, an oppositional current was sustained in working-class parties (both large and small) and in the labour, peace, and women's movements. Structural and political changes in the 1960s buoyed older formations and contributed to the rise of a new working class and a New Left. Through Old and New Left formations, BC workers succeeded in transforming partisan alignments and elected the New Democratic Party to power in 1972. Persistent problems in their ranks – centring on the historic tension between democracy and organization – left working-class British Columbians vulnerable to the increasingly aggressive prescriptions of global capitalism in the 1970s and beyond.

Afterword

Addressing a crowd of NDP supporters in Coquitlam on the evening of his party's historic victory, premier-elect Dave Barrett declared: 'For 40 years, literally tens of thousands of people have worked in the CCF and NDP to bring this day about and I promise you this: I will not let their hopes or aspirations down. We will now move into a peoples' century in British Columbia.'[7] The self-described democratic socialist embraced an activist approach to governing: 'We were in a cabinet meeting, and somebody said, "Are we here for a long time, or a good time?" And my response was "a good time." I knew very well that even though we could push the vote up, based on what we did, we would not be fighting a divided right wing.'[8]

Beneath the euphoria of the NDP's working-class supporters and anxiety of the province's traditional elite, the August 1972 victory was bittersweet. For in the preceding quarter-century, the parliamentary socialist party *had* changed. The social pressures of Cold War conformity, and the corresponding narrowing of ideological belief, had transformed the substance of the CCF-NDP program from the wholesale embrace of a socialized economy to the advocacy of a more humane form of capitalism. Mirroring changes in social-democratic thinking from the British Isles and continental Europe to Australia and New Zealand, the New Democratic Party that was elected to government in 1972 posed a muted threat to private enterprise. To be sure, the government of Dave Barrett implemented policies that transcended those of the avowedly free enterprise Social Credit administrations that preceded and succeeded it. The Barrett NDP left a legacy of enlarged health, education, and social service sectors, limited nationalizations in the realm of coal, pulp-and-paper, natural gas distribution, and automobile insurance, and important legislative changes in the form of Community Resource Boards, the Human Rights Commission, a more equitable Labour Relations Board and Labour Code, strengthened regional governments, and the Agricultural Land Reserve. Unlike the elder and younger Bennett, Barrett incurred the wrath of mining interests for imposing steep increases in mineral royalties, and he had the courage to withstand the opposition of private insurance corporations in bringing automobile insurance under public ownership.[9]

However, other aspects of the Barrett NDP's record were more ambiguous. While the government extended bargaining rights to civil servants and transferred the power to grant injunctions during labour disputes from the courts to a reformed LRB, tension remained.[10] The government faced the legislature in February 1973 in the midst of a school janitors' strike in Victoria, amid calls for government intervention.[11] The premier's strained relations with the BCFL leadership, a symptom of inner-party fights in the 1960s, foreshadowed conflict between his government and unionized workers. During his tenure as premier, Barrett alienated sections of his working-class base by imposing legislative restrictions on the right of public-sector workers to strike, moves rigorously opposed by the militant minority.[12] Like Social Credit, labour militancy contributed to the NDP's downfall in 1975. The experience of the Barrett government tells us something of the limitations of a parliamentary strategy of social change – and the weaknesses of the New Left in pursuing its political agenda.

The election of the Barrett government marked the conclusion of a seventy-year project of attaining a socialist majority in the provincial house; it also marked the beginning of a new period in the working-class history of BC. The protest party, institutionally linked to organized labour, increasingly assumed the trappings of a *status quo* party, legislating striking workers back to work, imposing wage controls and other concessions on workers, and legitimizing hierarchical structures and practices within its own ranks. From 1972 onward, a heightened antagonism could be noted within the left, between an increasingly professionalized NDP bureaucracy and a militant minority aligned with the New Left, feminism, environmentalism, and sections of labour. While this antagonism was present in the CCF-NDP tradition from its inception, it became particularly pronounced following the election of NDP governments across the provinces.[13]

Larger structural changes were also on the horizon. BC labour approached political power at the moment that the ability of governments to restrain the power of capital began to unravel. As Gary Teeple has argued, the internationalization of capital, combined with the shift from Fordism to information technology and an international division of labour, eroded the bargaining power of workers in the industrialized countries.[14] The postwar settlement, which gave rise to the welfare state and an institutionalization of class conflict, became unhinged in the early 1970s. The oil shocks of 1973 aggravated inflationary pressures, while North American industry entered into a prolonged crisis in the face of the ascendant, competitive manufacturing sectors of Germany and Japan.[15] BC workers elected 'their' party to government at the moment that the basis for North American labour's historic postwar advance was undermined. Moreover, the assumptions that had formed the basis of postwar social democracy were being superseded by sweeping changes in the structure of international capitalism.[16]

As working-class agency was directed into diffuse, rather than institutional, channels, BC workers had less capacity to challenge the prerogatives of an increasingly aggressive global capitalist class – that, as always, sought to extract the maximum profit from the province's timber, mineral, and energy resources. This 'individualization' of the working-class experience reflected improvements in conditions in postwar BC, but diluted linkages between the militant minority and the broader working class, leaving workers vulnerable to the more hostile economic and political climate that emerged in the 1970s. Economic growth and the expansion of state services had elevated living standards and the economic security of workers, reducing the need for participation in unions and political parties. But the distance between many workers and 'their' institutions reflected a rupture that was not easily reversed. Bill White, president of the powerful Vancouver Shipyard Workers' Federation during the war, commented on declining union participation in the postwar era:

> Most fellas in a union today, they hardly know they're in it except for the nick in their paycheck, and half of them don't notice that ... Much as I hate to say it the closed shop has a lot to do with this. When you had to go out and sell your union to every member you worked harder to prove it was worth it and you kept more men in the field. Now the leadership can lay back in the head office and pay themselves big salaries because they know the dues are going to come rolling in anyway. I doubt there's a union in the country that had a shop stewards' movement like the one we had.[17]

BC's tradition of labour militancy and political radicalism had its foundations in the active participation of rank-and-file workers. By the 1970s, institutionalized collective bargaining and an institutionalized social-democratic party distanced workers from the locus of economic and political decision-making. Militant agency – their historic weapon against capitalist exploitation – had been paradoxically rendered essential and obsolete. The tug-of-war continued.

Appendices

Appendix A: Industrial unrest in BC, 1945–72

Year	# of strikes/lockouts	employers affected	workers involved	striker-days	workers affected as % of total union members
1945	18	18	6,810	65,595	6.19
1946	21	524	40,014	1,294,202	37.01
1947	25	65	6,386	153,168	5.35
1948	10	63	3,216	106,230	2.38
1949	11	44	3,007	31,692	2.10
1950	22	46	13,579	105,792	9.28
1951	26	120	3,326	74,722	2.11
1952	36	381	46,806	1,234,120	21.88
1953	36	113	8,207	260,335	3.67
1954	24	119	12,622	140,958	7.07
1955	24	63	3,695	44,000	1.80
1956	35	69	3,197	39,211	1.67
1957	35	98	8,914	225,869	4.13
1958	29	188	11,709	325,211	5.00
1959	34	233	33,443	1,423,268	15.25
1960	14	16	999	35,848	0.46
1961	17	28	1,638	34,659	0.74
1962	33	60	1,982	32,987	0.91
1963	23	27	824	24,056	0.37
1964	29	72	9,503	181,784	4.16
1965	40	88	6,755	104,430	2.84
1966	39	411	24,748	272,922	9.66
1967	54	101	11,371	327,167	4.15
1968	66	140	12,179	406,729	4.25
1969	85	–[a]	17,916	406,645	6.12
1970	81	–	46,649	1,684,463	15.04
1971	111	–	52,333	276,030	16.53
1972	101	–	106,399	2,120,848	32.04

Source: BC Department of Labour, *Annual Report* (1945–1972)

[a] Data on employers affected was not reported after 1969. See BC Department of Labour, *Annual Report* (1969–72).

Appendix B: Union Density in BC, 1945–72

Year	# labour organizations	# workers covered by collective agreements	# workers in the non-agricultural paid workforce[a]	Union density
1945	617	110,045	283,000	38.9
1946	636	108,125	322,000	33.6
1947	642	119,258	334,000	35.7
1948	715	135,320	338,000	40.0
1949	745	142,989	340,000	42.0
1950	761	146,259	335,000	43.6
1951	770	157,287	342,000	46.0
1952	772	170,036	362,000	47.0
1953	766	174,894	368,000	47.5
1954	795	178,533	370,000	48.2
1955	865	186,951	390,000	47.9
1956	869	191,952	421,000	45.6
1957	907	216,070	439,000	49.2
1958	952	233,972	434,000	53.9
1959	948	219,279	452,000	48.5
1960	923	215,437	448,000	48.1
1961	1,048	221,946	455,000	48.8
1962	1,043	216,685	477,000	45.4
1963	1,041	222,138	501,000	44.3
1964	1,057	226,690	529,000	42.9
1965	1,061	237,864	561,000	42.4
1966	1,064	256,241	597,000	42.9
1967	1,054	273,946	636,000	43.1
1968	1,092	287,502	663,000	43.4
1969	1,085	292,842	714,000	41.0
1970	1,010	310,222	722,000	43.0
1971	1,035	316,587	753,000	42.0
1972	1,079	332,091	794,000	41.8

Source: British Columbia Department of Labour, *Annual Report* (1945–72)

[a] In 1957, the Department of Labour began reporting data on union membership from 1 January of each year rather than 31 December of the previous year. My data reflect the latter terminology. Calculations of union density vary from year to year due to changing methodology on the total size of the labour force. In 1956, the Department replaced its own data with the Canadian Labour Force Estimates from the Dominion Bureau of Statistics, although even this data varied year over year. See BC Department of Labour, *Annual Report* (1948–72).

Appendix C: Party support in BC provincial elections, 1949–72

	1949	1952	1953	1956	1960	1963	1966	1969	1972
Lib %	61.35	23.46	23.59	21.77	20.90	19.98	20.24	19.03	16.40
(contested)	48	48	48	52	50	51	53	55	53
(won)	39	6	4	2	4	5	6	5	5
Con %	(Coalition)	16.84	5.60	3.11	6.72	11.27	0.18	0.11	12.67
(contested)		48	39	22	52	44	3	1	49
(won)		4	1	0	0	0	0	0	2
CCF/NDP %	35.1	30.78	30.85	28.32	32.73	27.80	33.62	33.92	39.59
(contested)	48	48	47	51	52	52	55	55	55
(won)	7	18	14	10	16	14	16	12	38
SC %	1.65	27.20	37.75	45.84	38.83	40.83	45.59	46.79	31.36
(contested)	16	47	48	52	52	52	55	55	55
(won)	0	19	28	39	32	33	33	38	10
LPP/CPC %	0.24	0.33	1.03	0.41	0.57	0.09	0.14	0.05	0.08
(contested)	2	5	25	14	19	4	6	4	5
(won)	0	0	0	0	0	0	0	0	0
Other %	1.66	1.39	1.18	0.55	0.25	0.03	0.23	0.10	0.10
(contested)	24	16	22	8	5	2	6	7	9
(won)	2	1	1	1	0	0	0	0	0

Source: British Columbia, *Statement of Votes*, 1949–72

Appendix D: CCF-NDP Federal Support in BC, 1935–72

Year	BC seats	BC share of vote (%)	Canada-wide seats	Canada-wide share of vote (%)
1935	3	32.7	7	9.31
1940	1	28.4	8	8.42
1945	4	29.4	28	15.55
1949	3	31.5	13	13.42
1953	7	26.6	23	11.28
1957	7	22.3	25	10.71
1958	4	24.5	8	9.51
1962	10	30.9	19	13.57
1963	9	30.3	17	13.24
1965	9	32.9	21	17.91
1968	7	32.6	22	16.96
1972	11	35.0	31	17.83
1974	2	23.0	16	15.44

Source: Canada, *Canadian Parliamentary Guide* (1935–74)

Appendix E: Structural Change in BC's Working Class, by Industry and Gender, 1941–71

	1941				1951				1961				1971			
	Men	Women	Total	%	Men	Women	Total	%	Men	Women	Total	%	Men	Women	Total	%
TOTAL	287,932	55,226	343,158	100.00	346,374	97,978	444,352	100.00	421,786	155,862	577,648	100.00	561,635	284,740	846,375	100.00
Forestry	18,134	162	18,296	5.33	24,403	508	24,911	5.61	20,429	639	21,068	3.65	22,885	1,665	24,550	2.90
Fishing	7,946	38	7,984	2.33	4,505	69	4,574	1.03	4,303	128	4,431	0.76	3,140	235	3,375	0.40
Mining	14,086	128	14,214	4.14	11,142	300	11,442	2.57	7,916	263	8,179	1.42	12,415	850	13,265	1.57
Oil & Gas	56	9	65	0.02	101	3	104	0.02	520	35	555	0.01	550	45	595	0.01
Agriculture	39,752	1,473	41,225	12.01	25,842	1,817	27,659	6.22	19,793	3,497	23,290	4.03	14,980	6,665	21,645	2.56
Manufacturing	61,976	5,262	67,238	19.59	91,150	11,559	102,709	23.11	98,618	14,401	113,019	19.57	115,845	20,460	136,305	16.10
Wood & Paper products	28,186	1,306	29,492	8.59	45,425	3,081	48,506	10.92	49,183	3,204	52,387	9.07	55,350	3,625	58,975	6.97
Pulp & Paper	3,116	117	3,233	0.94	7,087	813	7,900	1.78	10,292	1,253	11,545	2.00	15,385	1,570	16,955	2.00
Construction	19,446	115	19,561	5.70	30,148	573	30,721	6.91	35,343	955	36,298	6.28	54,910	3,065	57,975	6.85
Highways & Bridges	2,172	7	2,179	0.63	4,798	46	4,844	1.09	4,579	104	4,683	0.81	5,830	255	6,085	0.72
Electricity, Gas, and Water	1,716	99	1,815	0.53	4,247	532	4,779	1.08	5,339	948	6,287	1.10	7,610	1,260	8,870	1.05
Service	30,709	32,396	63,105	18.39	59,147	45,669	104,816	23.56	91,676	78,107	169,783	29.39	130,845	134,575	265,420	31.36
Direct Government	8,814	1,827	10,641	3.10	25,521	5,157	30,678	6.90	38,433	7,568	46,001	7.96	41,290	13,565	54,855	6.48
Education	2,795	4,095	6,890	2.01	5,035	6,118	11,153	2.51	11,091	12,953	24,044	4.16	23,895	27,120	51,015	6.03
Health	2,739	5,994	8,733	2.54	5,704	12,755	18,459	4.15	8,652	23,124	31,776	5.50	11,525	39,105	50,630	5.98
Transport & Communication	24,379	2,402	26,781	7.80	34,810	5,983	40,793	9.18	53,873	8,933	62,806	10.87	66,970	14,905	81,875	9.67
Retail Trade & Wholesale	30,749	10,408	41,157	11.99	47,327	23,258	70,585	15.88	65,499	33,779	99,278	17.19	86,970	53,335	140,305	16.58
Finance, Insurance & Real Estate	5,557	2,308	7,865	2.29	8,056	6,529	14,585	3.28	12,142	10,500	22,642	3.92	19,015	20,820	39,835	4.71
Hunting & Trapping	1,827	19	1,846	0.54	255	7	262	0.06	47	0	47	0.01	30	0	30	0.01
Not stated	2,446	321	2,767	0.81	5,342	1,174	6,516	1.47	12,147	4,620	16,767	2.90	36,640	28,170	64,810	7.66

Source: Statistics Canada, Census of Canada, 1941–71

Appendix F: Interim Manifesto, Labour Party of Canada, 1957

INTERIM MANIFESTO

Socialist Committee for the Organization of a Labour Party

(1) SOCIALISM

Socialism is a philosophy which gives rise to political action aimed at an international society in which the exploitation of one class by another shall be replaced by the government of all things in the interest of all men.

(2) NATIONALISM

The socialists hold that patriotism is a survival of past historical epochs, that civilized men owe allegiance to all humanity and are citizens of one world indivisible. The nation state which succeeded the feudal kingdoms must itself be succeeded by the parliament of the world. War is mass murder and must be renounced as an instrument of policy.

(3) HISTORY

Human beings distinguished themselves from animals by producing their own means of subsistence, altering their environment as well as being altered by it. It is the satisfaction of material human needs which is the prime force of history. The social and political superstructure of human society at any given epoch is designed to fulfill the needs of the division of labour at that period. The form of society, once determined, remains static while the methods of production evolve and create new divisions of labour. A time arrives when the methods of production have so far outmoded the political society that the latter becomes a check upon further human progress and a political change becomes inevitable. History is a record of productive evolution and political revolution. All past revolutions have been designed to remove one minority and replace it by another. The socialist revolution is designed to establish a majority and therefor differs from all preceding revolutions in that it can only be achieved by general consent, consciously and openly and without the intervention or creation of a new privileged class. Historically, socialism will realize the ideal of democracy for the first time in human experience. From each according to his ability and to each according to his need.

(4) ECONOMICS

The value of raw material and land is purely potential until human labour discovers and utilizes it. The difference between the value of commodities produced by labour and the wages paid to the labourer is profit. Profit, when transformed into capital, makes modern production possible. The socialists have no quarrel with profit, socially owned and directed to the benefit of human needs. The fight of the socialists is against the private ownership of capital directed to anti-social ends which constitutes exploitation of man by man. The socialists hold that the profit system is now in fundamental contradiction to the needs of mankind and has become a check on the further development of social evolution. This contradiction is the basic cause of imperialism, colonialism, modern war and periodical depression. It is the cause of the diversion of human inventive genius from the task of establishing an ever-rising standard of living for the world to a race to develop ever more frightful weapons of destruction.

(5) POLITICAL SOLUTION

The majority being necessary to the achievement of a world co-operative commonwealth, they being the producers as distinguished from the exploiters, the socialists propose to support them on all occasions in their struggles for better conditions under capitalism. The socialists will use the lessons of these conflicts to convince the majority of the need to abolish capitalism and replace it with the co-operative commonwealth. To these ends the socialists strive to organize a political party in Canada to be known as the LABOUR PARTY wherein men may be organized for education to arrive at emancipation. The socialists will conduct constant public educational meetings that the majority may become capable of performing their historic mission. The party will support all movements of colonial emancipation regardless of the short term disadvantages which may result to local or national interests or temporary alignment with dubious allies. It will unfurl its banner on all political levels open to it without compromise with any other party which may, by declaration or act, betray the principles here set forth. The LABOUR PARTY will oppose any other party which seeks to place the socialists of one country under the direction of the socialists of another country. The party will always hold out the hand of friendship to all other groups who may adopt these minimum principles.

Appendix F: (*Concluded*)

(6) IMMEDIATE PROGRAM

The struggle for the dignity of man against the police state, for better conditions under existing capitalism, against bureaucracy and dictatorship will not cause us to deviate from our final objective. Reform is not in the forefront and social ownership relegated to some distant future. The experience of two centuries has shown that gradualism in theory is perpetuity in practice. The following basic demands are a minimum for the period of transition :

- Abolition of unemployment through equal access to work and leisure for all.
- Progressive reduction of hours of labour and increase of the rewards of labour to keep pace with automation.
- A self-owned modern home for every family.
- Equal educational opportunity for every child limited only by ability.
- Equal medical and hospital care for all mentally or physically sick.
- Guaranteed political democracy through the abolition of unlimited campaign funds.
- An industrial and economic parliament subject to election to direct and develop the national wealth and productivity.
- Translation of smaller industries into co-operatives.
- Translation of local banks into credit unions.
- Religious freedom for all both to believe and not to believe.

Upon the broad principles embodied in these ten propositions and in accordance with the conceptions contained in the foregoing preamble, we pledge ourselves never to rest content until we have eradicated capitalism from the earth.

APPLICATION FOR MEMBERSHIP

I agree to the principles and propositions contained in the Manifesto and Immediate Program of the Committee for the organization of a LABOUR PARTY and apply to be enrolled as a member thereof.

NAME ....

STREET ....

TOWN OR CITY ....

ENDORSED BY ....

Dues one dollar per month, payable to Organizer, T. Gauthier, 3393 Worthington Drive, Vancouver, B.C., phone DExter 2967-M.

Source: 'Interim Manifesto – Socialist Committee for the Organization of a Labour Party,' n.d. [c. 1957], file 3, box 3, Rodney Young papers, University of British Columbia Special Collections

Appendix G: Peace Groups in British Columbia, 1950–72

British Columbia Peace Council (affiliate of Canadian Peace Congress)
Peace Will Win British Columbia
Victoria Peace Council
Trail Peace Council
Fraser Valley Peace Conference
Canadian Committee for the Control of Radiation Hazards, BC section
Voice of Women (VOW)
Canadian Campaign for Nuclear Disarmament, BC Branch
Canadian Campaign for Nuclear Disarmament, West End Group
Canadian Campaign for Nuclear Disarmament, Port Alberni Group
Canadian Campaign for Nuclear Disarmament, Prince George Group
Canadian Campaign for Nuclear Disarmament, Victoria Group
University of British Columbia Disarmament Club (CUCND)
Peace by Peaceful Means, BC
Peace by Peaceful Means, Victoria
Peace by Peaceful Means, Vancouver
Women's International League for Peace and Freedom, Vancouver
Student Union for Peace Action – University of British Columbia
New Left Committee – Simon Fraser University
Trade Union Fellowship for Peace
Canadian League for Peace and Democracy, Vancouver
Student Non-Violent Coordinating Committee, Vancouver
Canadian Youth for Nuclear Disarmament, BC
Peace Action League, Victoria
Vancouver Peace Action League
Vietnam Day Committee, Vancouver
Surrey Committee to End the War in Vietnam
North Shore Action for Peace Committee, Vancouver
Nuclear Disarmament Club, UBC
Student Association to End the War in Vietnam, BC
High School Students against the War in Vietnam, Vancouver
Vietnam Action Committee, Vancouver, BC
Committee to End Canadian Production for the US War, Vancouver
Artists Continuation Committee to End the War in Vietnam, Vancouver
Youth Committee to End the War in Vietnam
The League of Ex-Patriots, Vancouver
Drive to End All Nuclear Testing, Victoria
Canadian Coalition to Stop the Amchitka Nuclear Blast, BC
Student Mobilization Committees, BC
Coalition for Peace, Land and Bread, Vancouver

Source: Vols. 716–83, Previously Released Files series, RCMP Security Service, RG 146, CSIS records, LAC

Appendix H: 'Injunctions Won't Catch Fish nor Build Bridges'

It is almost amazing to see the attempts of the Structural Steel Association and Dominion Bridge to force the striking Ironworkers back on the job.

The closeness of the companies and the courts was never more clearly indicated than in this case, where not the slightest justification exists for the swiftly granted injunction which would force men back on the job in spite of being on a legal strike.

The operators and their spokesman, R.K. Gervin, have used the alleged danger of the new Second Narrows span in its present condition as the level for forcing the men back to work. But the men are not returning. 'A court order instructing men to return to work constitutes slavery,' is the way an official of the ironworkers has accurately put the issue.

There are half a million unemployed workers in Canada, the direct responsibility of employers and government. Why not an injunction ordering the employers and government to put them to work?

The question may sound silly but it's a sight more sensible than what the court is proposing to do in the case of the Ironworkers.

The answer given by the strikers is providing sensible leadership to the rest of the labour movement in the militant tradition that built unions in this province and won the conditions today's members enjoy.

Support announced Thursday by the Building Trades Council should be affirmed by all sections of organized labour. Struggles like the Battle of the Bridge can be won with trade union solidarity. Bill 43 can be made ineffective and wiped off the books in that manner.

There are big strikes in the offing, in the lumber and fishing industries in particular, both within the next few weeks.

United action by all labour can win these strikes despite the opposition of employers, government, and courts.

Injunctions can't catch fish, cut logs, nor in the case of the ironworkers' strike, can they build bridges.

Source: 'Injunctions Won't Catch Fish nor Build Bridges,' *Fisherman* (Vancouver), 26 June 1959

Appendix I: Waffle Manifesto

For an Independent Socialist Canada, 1969

1. Our aim as democratic socialists is to build an independent socialist Canada. Our aim as supporters of the New Democratic Party is to make it a truly socialist party.
2. The achievement of socialism awaits the building of a mass base of socialists, in factories and offices, on farms and campuses. The development of socialist consciousness, on which can be built a socialist base, must be the first priority of the New Democratic Party.
3. The New Democratic Party must be seen as the parliamentary wing of a movement dedicated to fundamental social change. It must be radicalized from within and it must be radicalized from without.
4. The most urgent issue for Canadians is the very survival of Canada. Anxiety is pervasive and the goal of greater economic independence receives widespread support. But economic independence without socialism is a sham, and neither are [*sic*] meaningful without true participatory democracy.
5. The major threat to Canadian survival today is American control of the Canadian economy. The major issue of our times is not national unity but national survival, and the fundamental threat is external, not internal.
6. American corporate capitalism is the dominant factor shaping Canadian society. In Canada, American economic control operates throughout the formidable medium of the multi-national corporation. The Canadian corporate elite has opted for a junior partnership with these American enterprises. Canada has been reduced to a resource base and consumer market within the American Empire.
7. The American Empire is the central reality for Canadians. It is an empire characterized by militarism abroad and racism at home. Canadian resources and diplomacy have been enlisted in the support of the empire. In the barbarous war in Vietnam, Canada has supported the United States through its membership on the International Control Commission and through sales of arms and strategic resources to the American military industrial complex.
8. The American empire is held together through worldwide military alliances and giant monopoly corporations. Canada's membership in the American alliance system and the ownership of the Canadian economy by American corporations precludes Canada's playing an independent role in the world. These bonds must be cut if corporate capitalism and the social priorities it creates are to be effectively challenged.

9. Canadian development is distorted by a corporate capitalist economy. Corporate investment creates and fosters superfluous individual consumption at the expense of social needs. Corporate decision-making concentrates investment in a few major urban areas, which become increasingly uninhabitable while the rest of the country sinks in underdevelopment.
10. The criterion that the most profitable pursuits are the most important ones causes the neglect of activities whose value cannot be measured bythe standards of profitability. It is not accidental that housing, education, medical care, and public transportation are inadequately provided for by the present social system.
11. The problem of regional disparities is rooted in the profit orientation of capitalism. The social costs of stagnant areas are irrelevant to the corporations. For Canada, the problem is compounded by the reduction of Canada to the position of an economic colony of the United States. The foreign capitalist has even less concern for balanced development of the country than the Canadian capitalist with roots in a particular region.
12. An independent movement based on substituting Canadian capitalists for American capitalists, or on public policy to make foreign corporations behave as if they were Canadian corporations, cannot be our final objective. There is not now an independent Canadian capitalism and any lingering pretensions on the part on Canadian businessmen to independence lack credibility. Without a strong national capitalist class behind them, Canadian governments, Liberal and Conservative, have functioned in the interests of international and particularly American capitalism, and have lacked the will to pursue even a modest strategy of economic independence.
13. Capitalism must be replaced by socialism, by national planning of investment and by the public ownership of the means of production in the interests of the Canadian people as a whole. Canadian nationalism is a relevant force on which to build to the extent that it is anti-imperialist. On the road to socialism, such aspirations for independence must be taken into account. For to pursue independence seriously is to make visible the necessity of socialism in Canada.
14. Those who desire socialism and independence for Canada have often been baffled and mystified by the problem of internal divisions within Canada. While the essential fact of the Canadian history in the past century is the reduction of Canada to a colony of the United States, with a consequent increase in regional inequalities, there is no denying the existence of two nations within Canada, each with its own language, culture,

and aspirations. This reality must be incorporated into the strategy of the New Democratic Party.

15. English Canada and Quebec can share common institutions to the extent that they share common purposes. So long as Canada is governed by those who believe that the national policy should be limited to the passive function of maintaining a peaceful and secure climate for foreign investment, there can be no meaningful unity between English and French Canadians. So long as the federal government refuses to protect the country from economic and cultural domination, English Canada is bound to appear to French Canadians simply as part of the United States. An English Canada concerned with its own national survival would create common aspirations that would help to tie the two nations together once more.
16. Nor can the present treatment of the constitutional issue in isolation from economic and social forces that transcend the two nations be anything but irrelevant. Politicians committed to the values and structure of a capitalist society drafted our present constitution a century ago. Constitutional change relevant to socialists must be based on the needs of the people rather than the corporations and must reflect the power of classes and groups excluded from effective decision-making by the present system.
17. A united Canada is of critical importance in pursuing a successful strategy against the reality of American imperialism. Quebec's history and aspirations must be allowed full expression and implementation in the conviction that new ties will emerge from the common perception of 'two nations, one struggle'. Socialists in English Canada must ally themselves with socialists in Quebec in this common cause.
18. Central to the creation of an independent socialist Canada is the strength and tradition of the Canadian working class and the trade union movement. The revitalization and extension of the labor movement would involve a fundamental democratization of our society.
19. Corporate capitalism is characterized by the predominant power of the corporate elite aided and abetted by the political elite. A central objective of Canadian socialists must be to further the democratization process in industry. The Canadian trade union movement throughout its history has waged a democratic battle against the so-called rights or prerogatives of ownership and management. It has achieved the important moral and legal victory of providing for working men an effective say in what their wages will be. At present management's 'right' to control technological change is being challenged. The New Democratic Party must provide leadership in the struggle to extend working men's influence into every area of industrial decision-making. Those who work must have effective

control in the determination of working conditions, and substantial power in determining the nature of the product, prices and so on. Democracy and socialism require nothing less.

20. Trade unionists and New Democrats have led in extending the welfare state in Canada. Much remains to be done: more and better housing, a really progressive tax structure, a guaranteed annual income. However, these are no longer enough. A socialist society must be one in which there is democratic control of all institutions, which have a major effect on men's lives and where there is equal opportunity for creative non-exploitative self-development. It is now time to go beyond the welfare state.
21. New Democrats must begin now to insist on the redistribution of power, and not simply welfare, in a socialist direction. The struggle for worker participation in industrial decision-making and against management 'rights' is such a move toward economic and social democracy.
22. By strengthening the Canadian labor movement, New Democrats will further the pursuit of Canadian independence. So long as the corporate elite dominates Canadian economic activity, and so long as workers' rights are confined within their present limits, corporate requirements for profit will continue to take precedence over human needs.
23. By bringing men together primarily as buyers and sellers of each other, by enshrining profitability and material gain in place of humanity and spiritual growth, capitalism has always been inherently alienating. Today, sheer size combined with modern technology further exaggerates man's sense of insignificance and impotence. A socialist transformation of society will return to man his sense of humanity, to replace his sense of being a commodity. But a socialist democracy implies man's control of his immediate environment as well, and in any strategy for building socialism, community democracy is as vital as the struggle for electoral success. To that end, socialists must strive for democracy at those levels that most directly affect us all - in our neighborhoods, our schools, and our places of work. Tenants' unions, consumers' and producers' cooperatives are examples of areas in which socialists must lead in efforts to involve people directly in the struggle to control their own destinies.
24. Socialism is a process and a program. The process is the raising of socialist consciousness, the building of a mass base of socialists, and a strategy to make visible the limits of liberal capitalism.
25. While the program must evolve out of the process, its leading features seem clear. Relevant instruments for bringing the Canadian economy under Canadian ownership and control and for altering the priorities established by corporate capitalism are to hand. They include extensive public

control over investment and nationalization of the commanding heights of the economy, such as the essential resources industries, finance and credit, and industries strategic to planning our economy. Within that program, workers' participation in all institutions promises to release creative energies, promote decentralization, and restore human and social priorities.

26. The struggle to build a democratic socialist Canada must proceed at all levels of Canadian society. The New Democratic Party is the organization suited to bringing these activities into a common focus. The New Democratic Party has grown out of a movement for democratic socialism that has deep roots in Canadian history. It is the core around which should be mobilized the social and political movement necessary for building an independent socialist Canada. The New Democratic Party must rise to that challenge or become irrelevant. Victory lies in joining the struggle.

(Waffle Resolution 133, debated at NDP Federal Convention, Winnipeg, October 1969. Defeated with 268 votes in favour and 499 against.)

BC Signatories to the Waffle Manifesto

Dave Barrett, MLA (Coquitlam)
Eileen Dailly, MLA (Burnaby North)
Gordon Dowding, MLA (Burnaby-Edmonds)
Jim Lorimer, MLA (Burnaby-Willingdon)
Alex MacDonald, MLA (Vancouver East)
Wally Ross, provincial secretary, BC NDP
Norm Levi, past president, BC NDP, former MLA (Vancouver South)
Paddy Neale, secretary-treasurer, Vancouver and District Labour Council
Terry Campbell, editor, NDY *Confrontations*
Prof. John Conway, Simon Fraser University
Prof. Gerry Sperling, Simon Fraser University
Dawn Carrell, BC NDY
Rob Hill, president, BC NDY
Guy Pockington, New Westminster, BC
Chris Thurrott, president, NDY
Dr Harry Winrob, Vancouver

Source: 'For an Independent Socialist Canada,' file 446-1, vol. 446, series IV-1, MG 28, Co-operative-Commonwealth Federation-New Democratic Party fonds, Library and Archives Canada

Notes

Introduction

1 'Library Stocks May Be Combed for Red-Tainted Literature,' *Daily Times*, 27 Jan. 1954.

2 David Montgomery, *The Fall of the House of Labor: The Workplace, the State, and American Labor Activism, 1865–1925* (New York: Cambridge University Press, 1985), 2; also Montgomery, *Workers' Control in America: Studies in the History of Work, Technology, and Labor Struggles* (New York: Cambridge University Press, 1979), 108; Montgomery, 'Immigrants, Industrial Unions, and Social Reconstruction in the United States, 1916–1923,' *Labour/Le Travail* 13 (Spring 1984), 110. For earlier usage of the term, notably Australia's Militant Minority Movement of the late 1920s and early 1930s, see Robin Gollan, *Revolutionaries and Reformists: Communism and the Australian Labour Movement, 1920–1955* (Canberra: Australian National University Press, 1975); also William Z. Foster, *Bankruptcy of the American Labor Movement* (Chicago: Trade Union Educational League, 1922), 23.

3 For the emerging literature on 'recreational democracy,' see Jenny Clayton, 'Making Recreational Space: Citizen Involvement in Outdoor Recreation and Park Establishment in British Columbia, 1900–2000,' PhD diss., University of Victoria, 2009; Alan MacEachern, *Natural Selections: National Parks in Atlantic Canada, 1935–1970* (Montreal and Kingston: McGill-Queen's University Press, 2001).

4 Gordon Hak, *Capital and Labour in the British Columbia Forest Industry, 1934–1974* (Vancouver: UBC Press, 2007), 5–6.

5 BC Department of Labour, *Annual Report* (1958), 70.

6 Paul Knox, 'Breakaway Unionism in Kitimat,' in Knox and Resnick, eds., *Essays in BC Political Economy* (Vancouver: New Star Books, 1974), 42–51;

Philip Resnick, 'The Breakaway Movement in Trail,' in Knox and Resnick, eds., *Essays in BC Political Economy*, 52–9; Jack Scott, 'British Columbia and the American Labour Movement,' in Knox and Resnick, eds., *Essays in BC Political Economy*, 33–41; Scott, *Canadian Workers, American Unions* (Vancouver: New Star, 1978); Bryan D. Palmer, *Canada's 1960s: The Ironies of Identity in a Rebellious Era* (Toronto: University of Toronto Press, 2009), 211–41.

7 BC Department of Labour, *Annual Report* (1972), 90.

8 Ian McKay, *Rebels, Reds, Radicals: Rethinking Canada's Left History* (Toronto: Between the Lines, 2005), 95, 133–44; also McKay, 'For a New Kind of History: A Reconnaissance of 100 Years of Canadian Socialism,' *Labour/Le Travail*, 46 (Fall 2000), 109; McKay, *Rebels, Reds, Radicals*, 144; also Patrick George Hill, 'A Failure of Unity: Communist Party-CCF Relations in British Columbia, 1935–1939,' MA thesis, University of Victoria, 1977; Raymond Frogner, '"Within Sound of the Drum": Currents of Anti-Militarism in the British Columbia Working Class in the 1930s,' MA thesis, University of Victoria, 1987; Irving Martin Abella, *Nationalism, Communism and Canadian Labour: The CIO, the Communist Party, and the Canadian Congress of Labour 1935–1956* (Toronto: University of Toronto Press, 1973) and Abella, 'Communism and Anti-Communism in the British Columbia Labour Movement: 1940–1948,' in David J. Bercuson, ed., *Western Perspectives* 1 (Toronto and Montreal: Holt, Rinehart, and Winston, 1974), 88–100.

9 Stuart Marshall Jamieson, *Times of Trouble: Labour Unrest and Industrial Conflict in Canada 1900–1966* (Ottawa: Task Force on Labour Relations, 1968).

10 Maurice Isserman, *If I Had a Hammer: The Death of the Old Left and the Birth of the New Left* (New York: Basic Books, 1987).

11 Palmer, *Canada's 1960s*, 5; Myrna Kostash, *Long Way from Home: The Story of the Sixties Generation in Canada* (Toronto: J. Lorimer, 1980); Cyril Levitt, *Children of Privilege: Student Revolt in the Sixties: A Study of Student Movements in Canada, the United States, and West Germany* (Toronto: University of Toronto Press, 1984); Norman Penner, *The Canadian Left: A Critical Analysis* (Scarborough: Prentice-Hall, 1977), 218–49; also James Harding, 'The New Left in British Columbia,' in Dimitrios I. Roussopoulos, ed., *The New Left in Canada* (Montreal: Black Rose, c. 1970), 17–40; Roussopoulos, ed., *Canada and Radical Social Change* (Montreal: Black Rose, 1973); Tim Reid and Julyan Reid, eds., *Student Power and the Canadian Campus* (Toronto: Peter Martin Associates, 1969).

12 The 'postwar compromise' is examined in Leo Panitch and Donald Swartz, *From Consent to Coercion: The Assault on Trade Union Freedoms*, third ed. (Aurora, ON.: Garamond, 2003), 9–21; Bryan D. Palmer, *Solidarity: The Rise and Fall of an Opposition in British Columbia* (Vancouver: New Star, 1987),

14–19; Palmer, 'The Rise and Fall of British Columbia's Solidarity,' in Palmer, ed., *The Character of Class Struggle: Essays in Canadian Working Class History, 1850–1985* (Toronto: McClelland and Stewart, 1986), 176–200; Don Wells, 'The Impact of the Postwar Compromise on Canadian Unionism: The Formation of an Auto Worker Local in the 1950s,' *Labour/Le Travail*, 36 (Fall 1995), 147–73.

13 Nelson Lichtenstein, *State of the Union: A Century of American Labor* (Princeton: Princeton University Press, 2002), 99; Palmer, *Canada's 1960s*, 212.

14 Palmer, *Canada's 1960s*, 212.

15 Hak, *Capital and Labour in the British Columbia Forest Industry*, 7–8.

16 Statistics Canada, *Census of Canada*, 1951, 1971. For data on wage inequality, see Paul Phillips and Erin Phillips, *Women and Work: Inequality in the Canadian Labour Market*, revised ed. (Toronto: Lorimer, 1993), 50–63; also Josie Bannerman, Kathy Chopik, and Ann Zurbrigg, 'Cheap at Half the Price: The History of the Fight for Equal Pay in BC,' in Barbara K. Latham and Roberta J. Pazdro, eds., *Not Just Pin Money: Selected Essays on the History of Women's Work in British Columbia* (Victoria: Camosun College, 1984), 296–313.

17 Gillian Creese, *Contracting Masculinity: Gender, Class, and Race in a White-Collar Union, 1944–1994* (Don Mills, ON: Oxford University Press, 1999), 207.

18 Creese, *Contracting Masculinity*, 47.

19 See Sylvia B. Bashevkin, *Toeing the Lines: Women and Party Politics in English Canada* (Toronto: University of Toronto Press, 1985); Joan Sangster, *Dreams of Equality: Women on the Canadian Left, 1920–1950* (Toronto: McClelland and Stewart, 1989); Linda Kealey, *Enlisting Women for the Cause: Women, Labour and the Left in Canada, 1890–1920* (Toronto: University of Toronto Press, 1998).

20 'Women in Politics,' *CCF News*, 26 Jan. 1949.

21 See Betty Griffin and Susan Lockhart, *Their Own History: Women's Contribution to the Labour Movement of British Columbia* (Vancouver: UFAWU/CAW Seniors Club, 2002); Dorothy Sue Cobble, *The Other Women's Movement: Workplace Justice and Social Rights in Modern America* (Princeton, NJ: Princeton University Press, 2005); Julie White, *Sisters in Solidarity: Women and Unions in Canada* (Toronto: Thompson Educational Publishing, 1993); Linda Briskin and Lynda Yanz, eds., *Union Sisters: Women in the Labour Movement* (Toronto: Women's Press, 1983); Latham and Pazdro, eds., *Not Just Pin Money*; Phillips and Phillips, *Women and Work*; Meg Luxton, 'Feminism as a Class Act: Working Class Feminism and the Women's Movement in Canada,' *Labour/Le Travail*, 48 (Fall 2001), 63–88.

22 The exclusionary immigration policies of the pre-war years and the wartime internment and expulsion of Japanese Canadians left an imprint on BC's demography: while 5 per cent of the provincial population in 1931 had been born in Asia, this proportion declined to 2.9 per cent in 1941 and 1.2 per cent in 1951. Between 1941 and 1951, the number of British Columbians of Japanese, Chinese, and 'other Asiatic' origin declined by 18,398. Statistics Canada, *Census of Canada*, 1931–51; *Transactions of the Ninth British Columbia Natural Resources Conference, February 22–25, 1956* (Victoria: BC Natural Resources Conference, 1956), 19–20; Werner Cohn, 'Persecution of Japanese Canadians and the Political Left in British Columbia, December 1941-March 1942,' *BC Studies*, 68 (Winter 1985–6), 3–22; Ken Adachi, *The Enemy That Never Was: A History of the Japanese Canadians* (Toronto: McClelland and Stewart, 1976). Racism within BC labour is examined in Gillian Creese, 'Class, Ethnicity and Conflict: The Case of Chinese and Japanese Immigrants, 1880–1923,' in *Workers, Capital, and the State in British Columbia* (Vancouver: UBC Press, 1988), 55–85; and Creese, 'Exclusion or Solidarity? Vancouver Workers Confront the "Oriental Problem,"' *BC Studies*, 80 (Winter 1988–9), 24–51; Patricia E. Roy, *A White Man's Province: British Columbia Politicians and Chinese and Japanese Immigrants, 1885–1914* (Vancouver: UBC Press, 1989) and Roy, *The Oriental Question: Consolidating a White Man's Province, 1914–41* (Vancouver: UBC Press, 2003); Peter Ward, *White Canada Forever: Popular Attitudes and Public Policy toward Orientals in British Columbia*, third ed. (Montreal and Kingston: McGill-Queen's University Press, 2002).
23 'Coalition Racism Scored by CCF,' *CCF News*, 29 Jan. 1948.
24 'A Contemptible Action,' *CCF News*, 29 Jan. 1948.
25 'Japanese,' *Pacific Tribune*, 30 Jan. 1948.
26 'CCF MLA Says Jap Canadians "Good Citizens,"' *Sun*, 22 Feb. 1950.
27 Harjit Daudharia, *Darshan* (Vancouver: Heritage House, 2004); Darshan Singh Sangha interview, 1985, F-77-item53 to F-77-item62, Hari Sharma Indo-Canadian Oral History Collection, Simon Fraser University Archives; Nall Singh, 'Racial Discrimination Even in Port Alberni,' *Fisherman*, 29 Oct. 1948; Nall Singh, 'Alberni Paper Waves "Red Bogey" but Silent on Race Discrimination,' *Pacific Tribune*, 29 Oct. 1948; Richard Rajala, 'Pulling Lumber: Indo-Canadians in the British Columbia Forest Industry, 1900–1998,' *BC Historical News*, 36 (Winter 2002/3), 1–13.
28 'Anti-Discrimination Group Formed,' *Fisherman*, 14 Nov. 1950; Dominique Clément, *Canada's Rights Revolution: Social Movements and Social Change, 1947–1982* (Vancouver: UBC Press, 2008).
29 Andrew Parnaby, *Citizen Docker: Making a New Deal on the Vancouver Waterfront, 1919–1939* (Toronto: University of Toronto Press, 2008), 98.

30 'Breach Made in Franchise Restrictions,' *CCF News*, 29 April 1948; 'Indians Granted BC Vote' and 'Two-Way Understanding,' *Native Voice* (Vancouver), March 1949; 'Indian MLA "Goes to Bat for White Man,"' *Sun*, 23 Feb. 1950.
31 'Indians Living on $9 a Month,' *Pacific Tribune*, 30 March 1956.
32 'Hospitality, Good Fellowship Reign at Brotherhood Meet,' *Fisherman*, 2 May 1950; 'Brotherhood Hears Stevens,' *Fisherman*, 18 April 1950.
33 Frank Calder address, *UFAWU Proceedings*, 24–9 March 1952, Vancouver, 315, Neish papers.
34 Calder address, *UFAWU Proceedings* (1952), 316; also *UFAWU Proceedings* (1947), 11–12, 27–8, 75–6. Relations between the NBBC and UFAWU are discussed in North, *A Ripple, a Wave: The Story of Union Organization in the BC Fishing Industry* (Vancouver: Fishermen Publishing Society, 1974), 10–11, 14–15, 57.
35 North, *A Ripple, a Wave*, 25.
36 See Leonard Peltier, *Prison Writings: My Life Is My Sun Dance* (New York: St Martin's Griffin, 1999); also Palmer, *Canada's 1960s*, 367–411.
37 Paul Tennant, *Aboriginal Peoples and Politics: The Indian Land Question in British Columbia, 1849–1989* (Vancouver: UBC Press, 1990); Union of British Columbia Indian Chiefs, *Stolen Lands, Broken Promises: Researching the Land Question in British Columbia*, second ed. (Vancouver: Union of British Columbia Indian Chiefs, 2005), 15–30; Jacqueline Patricia O'Donnell, 'The Native Brotherhood of British Columbia, 1931–1950: A New Phase in Native Political Organization,' MA thesis, University of British Columbia, 1985; Peter Parker, '"We Are Not Beggars": Political Genesis of the Native Brotherhood, 1931–1951,' MA thesis, Simon Fraser University, 1992.
38 As quoted in Steve Hewitt, *Spying 101: The RCMP's Secret Activities at Canadian Universities* (Toronto: University of Toronto Press, 2002), 157.
39 Tennant, *Aboriginal Peoples and Politics*, 133; Union of British Columbia Indian Chiefs, *Stolen Lands, Broken Promises*, 15–30.
40 Harding, 'The New Left in BC,' 37; Engler to Dick, 25 March 1968, file 57-10, Dowson fonds, LAC.
41 'A Personal Message,' n.d. [c. 1968], file 23-06, 'BC Provincial Series,' reel H1592, CPC fonds, LAC; 'Vancouver,' in 'YS/LJS Discussion Bulletin vol 4 no 2', June 1968, file 19-14 'B2-1968', vol. 14, Dowson fonds, LAC. Beynon provided statistics demonstrating the plight of indigenous people: the average age of death of indigenous men in Canada in 1963 was 33 compared with 60.5 for white men; the average family income for indigenous people was $1,600 per year in 1964, less than half the national average; only 9 per cent of indigenous homes had sewer or septic systems in 1962, and only

13 per cent had running water, compared with a national average of 92 per cent for sewage and water. Beynon demanded legislation banning all forms of discrimination; just settlement of aboriginal land claims; election of band councils with autonomy from 'interference' by Indian Agents and the Department of Indian Affairs; establishment of industries on or near reserves; a large-scale program of housing, water, and sanitation; an education program, developed in concert with indigenous people, 'to enable all Indians to acquire the level of education they may desire'; and 'a true history of the role of the Indian People in Canada.' Beynon received a scant 36 votes in the by-election, amounting to 0.35 per cent of the vote. Liberal candidate David Brousson was elected with 5,578 votes, followed by Social Credit candidate Peter Robinson, with 3,090 votes and Sidney Simons for the NDP, with 1,265 votes. See British Columbia, *Statement of Votes*, 1968.

42 'League for Socialist Action – Forums – British Columbia,' 17 May 1972, file 5, vol. 110, Previously Released Files series, RCMP Security Service, CSIS records, LAC.

43 See Serge Mallet, *La Nouvelle Classe Ouvrière* (Paris: Seuil, 1963), translation by Andreé and Bob Sheperd, *The New Working Class* (Nottingham: Spokesman Books, 1975); David Lockwood, 'The "New Working Class,"' *European Journal of Sociology*, 1:2 (1960), 248–59; Daniel Bell, *The Coming of Post-Industrial Society: A Venture in Social Forecasting* (New York: Basic Books, 1973); Duncan Gallie, *In Search of the New Working Class: Automation and Social Integration within the Capitalist Enterprise* (Cambridge: Cambridge University Press, 1978); James D. Wright, 'In Search of a New Working Class,' *Quantitative Sociology*, 1:1 (May 1978), 33–57; Harding, 'The New Left in BC,' 26–7.

44 Roberto Michels, *Political Parties: A Sociological Study of the Oligarchical Tendencies of Modern Democracy*, translated by Eden and Cedar Paul, with an introduction by Seymour Martin Lipset (1915; New York: Free Press, 1962), 365; Leo Zakuta, *A Protest Movement Becalmed: A Study of Change in the CCF* (Toronto: University of Toronto Press, 1964); Maurice Duverger, *Political Parties: Their Organization and Activity in the Modern State*, third ed., translated by Barbara and Robert North, with a foreword by D.W. Brogan (London: Methuen, 1964); Richard Hyman, *Industrial Relations: A Marxist Introduction* (London: Macmillan, 1975); Seymour Martin Lipset, *Agrarian Socialism: The Cooperative Commonwealth Federation in Saskatchewan. A Study in Political Sociology*, updated ed. (Garden City, NY: Anchor Books, 1968); K. Carroll and R.S. Ratner, 'Old Unions and New Social Movements,' *Labour/Le Travail*, 35 (1995), 195–221; Arend Lijphart, *Democracy in Plural Soci-*

eties: A Comparative Exploration (New Haven: Yale University Press, 1977); Leon D. Epstein, *Political Parties in Western Democracies* (New Brunswick, NJ: Transaction, 1980); Angelo Panebianco, *Political Parties: Organization and Power* (Cambridge and New York: Cambridge University Press, 1988); also Bruce Levine, David Montgomery, and Anson Rabinbach in *International Labor and Working-Class History*, 46 (Fall 1994); Elizabeth Faue, 'Paths of Unionization: Community, Bureaucracy, and Gender in the Minneapolis Labor Movement, 1935–1945,' in Ava Baron, ed., *Work Engendered: Toward a New Labor History* (Ithaca: Cornell University Press, 1991), 296–319; Mark Leier, *Red Flags and Red Tape: The Making of a Labour Bureaucracy* (Toronto: University of Toronto Press, 1995).

45 Leier, *Red Flags and Red Tape*.

46 See Walter D. Young, *Anatomy of a Party: The National CCF, 1932–1961* (Toronto: University of Toronto Press, 1969); Gad Horowitz, *Canadian Labour in Politics* (Toronto: University of Toronto Press, 1968); Dean E. McHenry, *The Third Force in Canada: The Cooperative Commonwealth Federation, 1932–1948* (Toronto, Berkeley and Los Angeles: University of Toronto Press and University of California Press, 1950); Ivan Avakumovic, *Socialism in Canada: A Study of the CCF-NDP in Federal and Provincial Politics* (Toronto: McClelland and Stewart, 1978); Desmond Morton, *The New Democrats, 1961–1986: The Politics of Change* (Toronto: Copp Clark Pittman, 1986); Norman Penner, *From Protest to Power: Social Democracy in Canada, 1900-Present* (Toronto: Lorimer, 1992); and Alan Whitehorn, ed., *Canadian Socialism: Essays on the CCF-NDP* (Toronto: Oxford, 1992). Important regional studies of the CCF-NDP include Lipset, *Agrarian Socialism*; Zakuta, *A Protest Movement Becalmed*; Nelson Wiseman, *Social Democracy in Manitoba: A History of the CCF-NDP* (Winnipeg: University of Manitoba Press, 1983); Gerald Caplan, *The Dilemma of Canadian Socialism: The CCF in Ontario* (Toronto: McClelland and Stewart, 1973); Dan Azoulay, *Keeping the Dream Alive: The Survival of the Ontario CCF/NDP, 1950–1963* (Montreal and Kingston: McGill-Queen's University Press, 1997); Ian McKay, 'The Maritime CCF: Reflections on a Tradition,' in McKay and Scott Milsom, eds., *Toward a New Maritimes: A Selection of Ten Years from New Maritimes* (Charlottetown: Ragweed Press, 1992), 67–83; Patrick J. Smith and Marshall W. Conley, '"Empty Harbours, Empty Dreams": The Democratic Socialist Tradition in Atlantic Canada,' in William J. Brennan, ed., *Building the Cooperative Commonwealth: Essays on the Democratic Socialist Tradition in Canada* (Regina: Canadian Plains Research Center, 1984), 227–52.

47 For the history of communism in BC, see Tom McEwen, *He Wrote for Us: The Story of Bill Bennett, Pioneer Socialist Journalist* (Vancouver: Tribune

Publishing Company, 1951); David Akers, 'Rebel or Revolutionary? Jack Kavanagh and the Early Years of the Communist Movement in Vancouver, 1920–1925,' *Labour/Le Travail*, 30 (Fall 1992), 9–44; Ben Swankey and Jean Evans Sheils, *'Work and Wages!': A Semi-Documentary Account of the Life and Times of Arthur H. (Slim) Evans 1890–1944: Carpenter, Miner, Labor Leader* (Vancouver: Trade Union Research Bureau, 1977); McEwen, *The Forge Glows Red: From Blacksmith to Revolutionary* (Toronto: Progress Books, 1974); Al King with Kate Braid, *Red Bait! Struggles of a Mine Mill Local* (Vancouver: Kingbird, 1998); Howard White, *A Hard Man to Beat: The Story of Bill White, Labour Leader, Historian, Shipyard Worker, Raconteur* (Vancouver: Pulp Press, 1983); Homer Stevens and Rolf Knight, *Homer Stevens: A Life in Fishing* (Madeira Park, BC: Harbour, 1992); John Stanton, *Never Say Die! The Life and Times of John Stanton, a Pioneer Labour Lawyer* (Ottawa: Steel Rail, 1987) and *My Past Is Now: Further Memoirs of a Labour Lawyer* (St John's: Canadian Committee on Labour History, 1994); Harry Rankin, *Rankin's Law: Recollections of a Radical* (Vancouver: November House, 1975).

48 See Reg Whitaker and Gary Marcuse, *Cold War Canada: The Making of a National Insecurity State, 1945–1957* (Toronto: University of Toronto Press, 1994); Mark Kristmanson, *Plateaus of Freedom: Nationality, Culture, and State Security in Canada, 1940–1960* (Don Mills, ON: Oxford University Press, 2003); Len Scher, *The Un-Canadians: True Stories of the Blacklist Era* (Toronto: Lester, 1992); Sean Griffin, ed., *Fighting Heritage: Highlights of the 1930s Struggle for Jobs and Militant Unionism in British Columbia* (Vancouver: Tribune Publishing Company, 1985); Maurice Rush, *We Have a Glowing Dream: Recollections of Working-Class and People's Struggles in BC from 1935 to 1996* (Vancouver: Centre for Socialist Education, 1996); Tim Buck, *30 Years, 1922–1952: The Story of the Communist Movement in Canada* (Toronto: Progress Books, 1952), Ivan Avakumovic, *The Communist Party in Canada: A History* (Toronto: McClelland and Stewart, 1975); Lita-Rose Betcherman, *The Little Band: The Clashes between the Communists and the Political and Legal Establishment in Canada, 1928–1932* (Ottawa: Deneau, 1982); Ian Angus, *Canadian Bolsheviks: The Early Years of the Communist Party of Canada* (Montreal: Vanguard, 1981); Norman Penner, *Canadian Communism: The Stalin Years and Beyond* (Toronto: Methuen, 1988); John Manley, '"Starve, Be Damned!": Communists and Canada's Urban Unemployed, 1929–1939,' *Canadian Historical Review*, 79 (Sept. 1998), 467–73; *Canada's Party of Socialism: History of the Communist Party of Canada, 1921–1976* (Toronto: Progress Books, 1982).

49 For the CCF-NDP tradition in BC, see Dorothy G. Steeves, *The Compassionate Rebel: Ernest Winch and the Growth of Socialism in Western Canada*

(Vancouver: J.J. Douglas, 1977); Daisy Webster, *Growth of the NDP in BC, 1900–1970: 81 Political Biographies* (Vancouver: New Democratic Party, 1970); Dave Barrett and William Miller, *Barrett: A Passionate Political Life* (Vancouver: Douglas and McIntyre, 1995); Carolyn Swayze, *Hard Choices: A Life of Tom Berger* (Vancouver/Toronto: Douglas and McIntyre, 1987); Irene Howard, *The Struggle for Social Justice in British Columbia: Helena Gutteridge, the Unknown Reformer* (Vancouver: UBC Press, 1992); S.P. Lewis, *Grace: The Life of Grace MacInnis* (Madeira Park, BC: Harbour, 1993); Ann Farrell, *Grace MacInnis: A Story of Love and Integrity* (Markham, ON: Fitzhenry and Whiteside, 1994); Richard Grey Stuart, 'The Early Political Career of Angus MacInnis,' MA thesis, University of British Columbia, 1970; Arthur Cathers, *Beloved Dissident Eve Smith, 1904–1988* (Blyth, ON: Drumadravy, 1997); Rosemary Brown, *Being Brown: A Very Public Life* (Toronto: Random House, 1989); Alex MacDonald, *'My Dear Legs ... ': Letters to a Young Social Democrat* (Vancouver: New Star, 1985).

50 See John Douglas Belshaw, *Colonization and Community: The Vancouver Island Coalfield and the Making of the British Columbian Working Class* (Montreal and Kingston: McGill-Queen's University Press, 2002); Lynn Bowen, *Boss Whistle: The Coal Miners of Vancouver Island Remember* (Lantzville: Oolichan, 1982); Mark Leier, *Where the Fraser River Flows: The Industrial Workers of the World in British Columbia* (Vancouver: New Star, 1990); Martin Robin, 'British Columbia: The Company Province,' in Robin, ed., *Canadian Provincial Politics: The Party Systems in the Ten Provinces*, second ed. (Scarborough: Prentice-Hall, 1978), 28–60; Carlos A. Schwantes, *Radical Heritage: Labor, Socialism, and Reform in Washington and British Columbia, 1885–1917* (Vancouver: Douglas and McIntyre, 1979); Philip Resnick, 'The Political Economy of BC – A Marxist Perspective,' in Paul Knox and Philip Resnick, eds., *Essays in BC Political Economy* (Vancouver: New Star, 1974), 3–12; Allen Seager, 'Socialists and Workers: The Western Canadian Coal Miners, 1900–21,' *Labour/Le Travail*, 16 (Fall 1985), 23–60; James Conley, 'Frontier Labourers, Crafts in Crisis and the Western Canadian Labour Revolt,' *Labour/Le Travail*, 23 (Spring 1989), 1–37; Robert A.J. McDonald, 'Lumber Society on the Industrial Frontier: Burrard Inlet, 1863–1886,' *Labour/Le Travail*, 33 (Spring 1994), 69–96. As Frederick Jackson Turner wrote in his famous 1893 essay, the frontier provided 'a new field of opportunity, a gate of escape from the bondage of the past ... scorn of older society, impatience of its restrains and its ideas, and indifference to its lessons.' Frederick Jackson Turner, 'The Significance of the Frontier in American History,' reprinted in George Rogers Taylor, ed., *The Turner Thesis Concerning the Role of the Frontier in American History*, revised ed. (Boston: D.C. Heath and Company, 1965), 19.

51 Paul A. Phillips, *No Power Greater: A Century of Labour in British Columbia* (Vancouver: BC Federation of Labour and the Boag Foundation, 1967), 164.
52 Ross Alfred Johnson, 'No Compromise – No Political Trading: The Marxian Socialist Tradition in British Columbia,' PhD diss., University of British Columbia, 1975; Ronald Grantham, 'Some Aspects of the Socialist Movement in British Columbia, 1898–1933' MA thesis, University of British Columbia, 1942; Martin Robin, *Radical Politics and Canadian Labour* (Kingston: Industrial Relations Centre, Queen's University, 1968); Gerald Friesen, 'Yours in Revolt: Regionalism, Socialism, and the Western Canadian Labour Movement,' *Labour/Le Travailleur*, 1 (1976), 141–57; A. Ross McCormack, *Reformers, Rebels, and Revolutionaries: The Western Canadian Radical Movement, 1899–1919* (Toronto and Buffalo: University of Toronto Press, 1977); Walter Young, 'Ideology, Personality and the Origin of the CCF in British Columbia,' *BC Studies*, 32 (Winter 1976–7), 139–62; Peter Campbell, *Canadian Marxists and the Search for a Third Way* (Montreal and Kingston, McGill-Queen's University Press, 1999); Peter Campbell, '"Making Socialists": Bill Pritchard, the Socialist Party of Canada, and the Third International,' *Labour/Le Travail*, 30 (Fall 1992), 42–65; Dorothy G. Steeves, *Builders and Rebels: A Short History of the CCF in British Columbia, 1932–1961* (Vancouver: BC Committee for the New Democratic Party, c. 1961) and Steeves, *The Compassionate Rebel*; Elaine Bernard, 'The Rod Young Affair in the British Columbia Co-operative Commonwealth Federation,' MA thesis, University of British Columbia, 1979; Gordon Stanley Wickerson, 'Conflict in the British Columbia Cooperative Commonwealth Federation and the "Connell Affair,"' MA thesis, University of British Columbia, 1970; Dorothy J. Roberts, 'Doctrine and Disunity in the British Columbia Section of the CCF, 1932–1956,' MA thesis, University of Victoria, 1972; and Christine J. Nichol, 'In Pursuit of the Voter: The British Columbia CCF, 1945–1950,' in Brennan, ed., *Building the Cooperative Commonwealth*, 123–40.
53 See Eric Tucker and Judy Fudge, *Labour before the Law: The Regulation of Workers' Collective Action in Canada, 1900–1948* (Don Mills: Oxford University Press, 2001); Ben Swankey, ed., *'Man along the Shore'! The Story of the Vancouver Waterfront As Told by Longshoremen Themselves 1860's-1975* (Vancouver: ILWU 500 Pensioners, 1978); Andrew Neufeld, *Union Store: The History of the Retail Clerks Union in British Columbia, 1899–1999* (Vancouver: United Food and Commercial Workers Union Local 1518, 1999); Gordon Hak, *Capital and Labour in the British Columbia Forest Industry, 1934–1974* (Vancouver: UBC Press, 2007); Jerry Lembcke and William M. Tattam, *One Union in Wood: A Political History of the International Woodworkers of America* (Madeira Park, BC: Harbour/International Publishers, 1984); Andrew

Neufeld and Andrew Parnaby, *The IWA in Canada: The Life and Times of an Industrial Union* (Vancouver: IWA/New Star Books, 2000); Grant MacNeil, *The IWA in British Columbia* (Vancouver: Western Canadian Regional Council No. 1 IWA, 1971); Elaine Bernard, *The Long Distance Feeling: A History of the Telecommunications Workers Union* (Vancouver: New Star, 1983); Gillian Creese, *Contracting Masculinity*; Jo Dunaway, *We're Your Neighbours: The Story of CUPE BC* (Vancouver: Canadian Union of Public Employees – BC Division, 2000); Patricia G. Webb, *The Heart of Health Care: The Story of the Hospital Employees' Union, the First 50 Years* (Vancouver: Hospital Employees' Union, 1994); Bruce McLean, *A Union amongst Government Employees: A History of the BC Government Employees' Union, 1919–1979* (Victoria: BCGEU, 1979); M.C. Warrior and Mark Leier, *Light at the End of the Tunnel: The First Forty Years: A History of the Tunnel and Rock Workers Union Local 168* (Vancouver: LIUNA, 1992); Bruce Lowther, *A Better Life: The First Century of the Victoria Labour Council* (Victoria: Victoria Labour Council, 1989); see also R.E. (Lefty) Morgan, *Workers' Control on the Railroad: A Practical Example 'Right under Your Nose,'* ed. G.R. Pool and D.J. Young (St John's: Canadian Committee on Labour History, 1994); Allen Seager and David Roth, 'British Columbia and the Mining West: A Ghost of a Chance,' in Craig Heron, ed., *The Workers' Revolt in Canada: 1917–1925* (Toronto: University of Toronto Press, 1998), 231–67; Gordon Hak, 'British Columbia Loggers and the Lumber Workers Industrial Union, 1919–1922,' *Labour/Le Travail*, 23 (Spring 1989), 67–90; Andrew Parnaby, 'What's Law Got to Do with It? The IWA and the Politics of State Power in British Columbia, 1935–1939,' *Labour/Le Travail*, 44 (Fall 1999), 9–46.

54 This more recent period is examined in Patricia Marchak, 'Class, Regional, and Institutional Sources of Social Conflict in BC,' *BC Studies*, 27 (Fall 1975), 30–49. For discussion of the political impact of earlier labour struggles, see Martin Robin, 'British Columbia: The Company Province,' in Robin, ed., *Canadian Provincial Politics: The Party Systems in the Ten Provinces*, second ed. (Scarborough: Prentice-Hall, 1978), 28–60; Robin, *The Rush for Spoils: The Company Province, 1871–1933* (Toronto: McClelland and Stewart, 1972); Robin, *Pillars of Profit: The Company Province, 1934–1972* (Toronto: McClelland and Stewart, 1973); Nelson Wiseman, *In Search of Canadian Political Culture* (Vancouver: UBC Press, 2007), 242–4 and 250–60; Philip Resnick, 'The Political Economy of BC – A Marxist Perspective,' in Paul Knox and Philip Resnick, eds., *Essays in BC Political Economy*, 3–12; Thomas Michael Sanford, 'The Politics of Protest: The Cooperative Commonwealth Federation and Social Credit League in British Columbia,' PhD diss., University of California, 1961; Phillips, *No Power Greater*; Schwantes,

Radical Heritage; Seager, 'Socialists and Workers'; Conley, 'Frontier Labourers'; Robert A.J. McDonald, 'Lumber Society on the Industrial Frontier.'

55 BC Department of Labour, *Annual Report* (1958), 70; Maurice Duverger, *Political Parties*.

56 As Douglas Kellner writes, 'From the time of its introduction in 1946, television promoted the ethos of anticommunism that defined cold war mentality.' Kellner, *Television and the Crisis of Democracy* (Boulder, San Francisco, and Oxford: Westview, 1990), 46. The impact of the mass media on framing the social-protest movements of the 1960s is explored in Todd Gitlin, *The Whole World Is Watching: Mass Media in the Making and Unmaking of the New Left* (Berkeley, Los Angeles, and London: University of California Press, 1980). See also 'TV to Be Used in Schools Here,' *Daily Times* (Victoria), 5 March 1959.

57 'Ban Bomb Broadcast Gag Keeps Stevens off Air,' *Fisherman* (Vancouver), 22 Aug. 1950.

58 Ibid.

59 'Union Denied Air Time; Will Protest,' *Vancouver Sun*, 15 April 1955.

60 See, for example, R.E. (Lefty) Morgan, *Workers' Control on the Railroad*.

61 Paul Thompson, *The Voice of the Past: Oral History*, second ed. (Oxford: Oxford University Press, 1988), 258. Historian Gordon Hak made a similar point, calling for a broadening of labour history's emphasis beyond 'the militant mining towns of the Kootenays and Vancouver Island and ... the small band of articulate socialist theorists in Vancouver.' Gordon Hak, 'The Socialist and Labourist Impulse in Small-Town British Columbia: Port Alberni and Prince George, 1911–33,' *Canadian Historical Review*, 70:4 (December 1989), 518.

62 Mark Leier, 'W[h]ither Labour History: Regionalism, Class and the Writing of BC History,' *BC Studies*, 111 (Fall 1996), 67.

63 *Transactions of the Ninth British Columbia Natural Resources Conference, February 22–25, 1956* (Victoria: BC Natural Resources Conference, 1956), 38–9.

64 Ibid., 40.

65 John Vanderkamp, 'Manpower Policies and the Adjustment of the Labour Force,' in R. Shearer, ed., *Exploiting Our Economic Potential: Public Policy and the British Columbia Economy* (Toronto: Holt, Rinehart and Winston, 1968), 129.

66 In 1951 only 40 per cent of BC residents had been born in the province. British Columbia, *Submission to the Royal Commission on Canada's Economic Prospects* (Victoria: Queen's Printer, 1955), 6.

67 Edwin R. Black, 'British Columbia: The Politics of Exploitation,' in Shearer, *Exploiting Our Economic Potential*, 27.

68 Tucker and Fudge, *Labour before the Law*; Peter McInnis, *Harnessing Labour Confrontation: Shaping the Postwar Settlement in Canada, 1943–1950* (Toronto: University of Toronto Press, 2002).

69 McInnis, *Harnessing Labour Confrontation*, 191.

70 As quoted in McInnis, *Harnessing Labour Confrontation*, 183.

71 See Bryan D. Palmer, 'Small Unions and Dissidents in the History of Canadian Trade Unionism,' in Mercedes Steedman et al., eds., *Hard Lessons: The Mine Mill Union in the Canadian Labour Movement* (Toronto: Dundurn, 1995), 39–49.

72 The relationship between postwar affluence and class politics is explored in George Lipsitz, *Rainbow at Midnight: Labor and Culture in the 1940s* (Chicago: University of Illinois Press, 1994); Daniel Bell, *The End of Ideology* (New York: Free Press, 1965); John Kenneth Galbraith, *The Affluent Society* (New York: Mentor, 1958); Ferdynand Zweig, *The Worker in an Affluent Society: Family Life and Industry* (New York: Free Press, 1962); John H. Goldthorpe et al., *The Affluent Worker: Political Attitudes* (London: Cambridge, 1968); Nick Tiratsoo, *Reconstruction, Affluence and Labour Politics: Coventry, 1945–1960* (London: Routledge, 1990); Lawrence Black, *Old Labour, New Britain? The Political Culture of the Left in Affluent Britain, 1951–64* (New York: Palgrave Macmillan, 2003); Magda Fahrni and Robert Rutherdale, eds., *Creating Postwar Canada: Community, Diversity, and Dissent, 1945–75* (Vancouver: UBC Press, 2008); David Lockwood, 'Sources of Variation in Working-Class Images in Society,' *Sociological Review*, 14 (1966), 249–67; David E. Butler and Donald Stokes, *Political Change in Britain: Forces Shaping Electoral Choice* (New York: St Martin's, 1969); Robert McKenzie and Allan Silver, *Angels in Marble: Working Class Conservatives in Urban England* (Chicago: University of Chicago Press, 1968); Martin Pugh, 'The Rise of Labour and the Political Culture of Conservatism, 1890–1945,' *History*, 87:288 (October 2002), 514–37; Michael Mann, 'Sources of Variation in Working-Class Movements in Twentieth-Century Europe,' *New Left Review*, 212 (July-August 1995), 14–54. For discussions of working-class consumerism, see Victoria de Grazia and Lizabeth Cohen, 'Class and Consumption,' *International Labor and Working-Class History*, 55 (1999), 1–5; Jackson Lears, 'A Matter of Taste: Corporate Cultural Hegemony in a Mass Consumption Society,' in Lary May, ed., *Recasting America: Culture and Politics in the Cold War* (Chicago: University of Chicago Press, 1989), 38–57; Lizabeth Cohen, 'The Class Experience of Mass Consumption: Workers as Consumers in Interwar America,' in Richard Wightman Fox and T.J. Jackson Lears, eds., *The Power of Culture: Critical Essay in American History* (Chicago: University of Chicago Press, 1993), 134–60; Clifford E.

Clark, Jr, 'Ranch-House Suburbia: Ideals and Realities,' in May, ed., *Recasting America*, 171–91; Lawrence B. Glickman, *A Living Wage: American Workers and the Making of Consumer Society* (Ithaca: Cornell University Press, 1997); Kathy M. Newman, 'From Sit-ins to "Shirt-ins": Why Consumer Politics Matter More Than Ever,' *American Quarterly*, 56:1 (March 2004), 213–21. The relationship between class and suburbia is explored in Richard Harris, 'The Suburban Worker in the History of Labor,' *International Labor and Working-Class History*, 64 (2003), 8–24; William Mann Dobriner, *Class in Suburbia* (Englewood Cliffs, NJ: Prentice-Hall, 1963); Bennett Berger, *Working Class Suburb: A Study of Auto Workers in Suburbia* (Berkeley: University of California Press, 1968).

73 Myrna Kostash, *Long Way from Home: The Story of the Sixties Generation in Canada* (Toronto: J. Lorimer, 1980); Harding, 'The New Left in British Columbia,' 17–40; Roussopoulos, ed., *Canada and Radical Social Change* (Montreal: Black Rose, 1973); Reid and Reid, eds., *Student Power and the Canadian Campus*; Douglas Owram, *Born at the Right Time: A History of the Baby-Boom Generation in Canada* (Toronto: University of Toronto Press, 1996); Cyril Levitt, *Children of Privilege: Student Revolt in the Sixties: A Study of Student Movements in Canada, the United States, and West Germany* (Toronto: University of Toronto Press, 1984); Norman Penner, *The Canadian Left: A Critical Analysis* (Scarborough: Prentice-Hall, 1977), 218–49.

74 See Leier, 'W[h]ither Labour History'; Jeremy Mouat, 'The Genesis of Western Exceptionalism: British Columbia's Hard Rock Miners, 1895–1903,' *Canadian Historical Review*, 71:3 (September 1990), 317–45; David Bright, 'The West Wants In: Regionalism, Class, and *Labour/Le Travail*, 1976–2002,' *Labour/Le Travail*, 50 (Fall 2002), 149–61; also Gregory S. Kealey, '1919: The Canadian Labour Revolt,' *Labour/Le Travail*, 13 (Spring 1984), 11–44. Leier, Kealey, and others responded to an earlier historiography that emphasized region over class. This 'western exceptionalist' framework can be found in David Bercuson, 'Western Labour Radicalism and the One Big Union: Myths and Realities,' in S.M. Trofimenkoff, ed., *The Twenties in Western Canada: Papers of the Western Canadian Studies Conference, March 1972* (Ottawa: National Museum of Man, 1972), 32–49 and 'Labour Radicalism and the Western Industrial Frontier, 1897–1919,' *Canadian Historical Review*, 57 (June 1977), 154–77; McCormack, *Reformers, Rebels, and Revolutionaries*; Bercuson, *Fools and Wise Men: The Rise and Fall of the One Big Union* (Toronto: McGraw-Hill Ryerson, 1978); see also Friesen, 'Yours in Revolt.'

75 Thompson, *The Voice of the Past*, 71, 20.

76 James Naylor, 'Working-Class History in English Canada in the 1980s: An Assessment,' *Acadiensis*, 19:1 (Fall 1989), 164.

77 Heron, 'Toward Synthesis in Canadian Working-Class History: Reflections on Bryan Palmer's Rethinking,' *Left History*, 1:1 (1993), 113–15.

1. The Political Economy of British Columbia

1 'Party Leaders Speak Out,' *Province* (Vancouver), 17 Sept. 1956.

2 For a study of BC's political economy from a radical viewpoint, see Philip Resnick, 'The Political Economy of BC – A Marxist Perspective,' in Paul Knox and Philip Resnick, eds., *Essays in BC Political Economy* (Vancouver: New Star, 1974), 3–12. Studies of BC's economic history are mainly of the boosterist variety, celebrating the efforts of individual industrialists while downplaying larger structural questions and labour relations. See, for example, G.W. Taylor, *Builders of British Columbia: An Industrial History* (Victoria: Morriss, 1982). In contrast, we find an earlier work of the same title, written by communist journalist William 'Ol' Bill' Bennett in the midst of the 1930s depression, William Bennett, *Builders of British Columbia* (Vancouver: Broadway Printers, 1937). The proceedings of the BC Natural Resources Conference (1948–64), which brought together representatives of industry, government, and academia, provide valuable data and analysis on the various industrial sectors.

3 Industrial Conciliation and Arbitration Act (1947), S.B.C. 1947 c. 44; BC Department of Labour, *Annual Report* (1947), 36–8. PC 1003, the Wartime Labour Relations Regulations of 17 February 1944, required employers to recognize, and negotiate with, employee committees chosen by workers. It outlined a procedure for union certification and banned company unions. Wartime Labour Relations Regulations, Order in Council P.C. 1003, 17 Feb. 1944, *Labour Gazette*, 44:2 (Feb. 1944), 136–43.

4 'Aim of Labor Bill 87 to Smash Trade Unions,' *Pacific Tribune* (Vancouver), 23 April 1948; BC Department of Labour, *Annual Report* (1947), 41–3. Responding to a wartime ban in 1943, the CPC rebranded itself the LPP, retaining the name until 1959. See *Canada's Party of Socialism: History of the Communist Party of Canada, 1921–1976* (Toronto: Progress Books, 1982).

5 'Labor Fights Fascist Curbs,' *Pacific Tribune*, 23 April 1948.

6 'The Daily Round!' *Pacific Tribune*, 15 Oct. 1948.

7 'Living Costs Up As Subsidy Is Removed,' *CCF News* (Vancouver), 12 Aug. 1948. The article notes that 'All foods in Canada are now released from price control, except sugar, sugar can syrups, can molasses, butter, and certain fresh canned fruits, vegetables and juices.' Also 'Oppose the Sales Tax,' *CCF News*, 11 March 1948; 'CCF Opposes New Sales Tax,' *CCF News*, 18 March 1948.

8 'The Daily Round!' *Pacific Tribune*, 30 April 1948.

9 'The Daily Round!' *Pacific Tribune*, 30 April 1948.

10 'BC Women Ask Steps to Hold Line on Prices,' *Fisherman*, 8 Aug. 1950; 'COL Up Again …Will It Ever Stop,' *Fisherman*, 8 Aug. 1950; also Dolly Smith Wilson, 'A New Look at the Affluent Worker: The Good Working Mother in Post-War Britain,' *Twentieth Century British History*, 17:2 (2006), 206–29.

11 'Interior Packers May Take Strike Action,' *CCF News*, 22 July 1948.

12 'Strike – The Vancouver Daily Province,' 13 July 1946, file 'Canadian Seamen's Union – Vancouver, BC,' vol. 2285, series A, RCMP Security Service, RG 146, Canadian Security Intelligence Service records [hereafter CSIS records], Library and Archives Canada [hereafter LAC]; 'Officers, Crews May Tie Up All Deep Sea Ports,' *Daily Tribune* (Toronto), 28 Oct. 1947; 'Mass Rally to Aid Seamen Urged upon Trades Council,' *Pacific Tribune*, 9 July 1948; Jim Green, *Against the Tide: The Story of the Canadian Seamen's Union* (Toronto: Progress Books, 1986), 167–9.

13 'Labor Board,' *CCF News*, 22 Jan. 1948.

14 'Govnt. Ties Labor,' *Pacific Tribune*, 16 April 1948; 'Aim of Labor Bill 87 to Smash Trade Unions,' *Pacific Tribune*, 16 April 1948; 'Labor Fights Fascist Curbs,' *Pacific Tribune*, 23 April 1948.

15 'CCF Battles against Anti-Labor Bill 87,' *Pacific Tribune*, 30 April 1948.

16 Ibid.; also 'Convention Urges New Labor Code,' *CCF News*, 3 June 1948.

17 'Labor Council Asks Resignation of CCL Nominee on Labor Board,' *Pacific Tribune*, 28 May 1948. Harry Strange, the CCL designate on the LRB, argued that the Bill 87 amendments were 'the best obtainable under the circumstances.' A majority of delegates to the Vancouver Labour Council (CCL), however, voted to demand his resignation. The TLC representative on the LRB, George Wilkinson, also supported the legislation.

18 'Repairs Aren't Enough, a New Act Is Needed,' *Fisherman*, 3 Dec. 1948. The UFAWU lobbied other TLC unions to adopt this position at a December 1948 conference of BC affiliates. The Victoria Trades and Labour Council originally called for the repeal of the Act, but at a subsequent meeting reversed this decision and instead called merely for 'amendments.' See 'Victoria Doings Take the Spotlight,' *Fisherman*, 20 Dec. 1948.

19 Minutes, 6 Oct. 1948, box 4, series IV, accession 80–59, Victoria Labour Council fonds, University of Victoria Archives and Special Collections (hereafter UVASC).

20 'Local Union Severely Critical of Labor Board Appointments,' *CCF News*, 15 Jan. 1948. Wilkinson claimed that 'The only two groups that are doing much yelling about it seem to be the CCF and LPP and every week seems

to bring further slander upon my head in the official "Comic" paper, the *Pacific Tribune*. Personally they make me sick. The recent hysteria among certain groups over the amendments to Bill 39 would be very amusing if it were not for the fact that many decent workers are gullible enough to believe the tripe these people peddle.' As quoted in Bruce Lowther, *A Better Life: The First Century of the Victoria Labour Council* (Victoria: Victoria Labour Council, 1989), 60.

21 'Labor Board,' *CCF News*, 22 Jan. 1948. The Coalition appointed J.P. Hogg, the government's legislative counsel, as temporary chairman.

22 'Certification Withdrawn from AFL Union in Dispute,' *Pacific Tribune*, 13 Feb. 1948. The certification battle at Dominion Rustproofing is described in Howard White, *A Hard Man to Beat: The Story of Bill White, Labour Leader, Historian, Shipyard Worker, Raconteur* (Vancouver: Pulp Press, 1983), 181–6.

23 'Labor Fights Fascist Curbs,' *Pacific Tribune*, 23 April 1948.

24 Ibid.

25 'Writ against IWA Shows How ICA Act Perils Unions,' *Pacific Tribune*, 21 May 1948; also 'ICA Act Used to Haul IWA Local into Court,' *Pacific Tribune*, 14 May 1948. The 'Smith' in Smith and Osberg Ltd was C.C. Smith, president of the Truck Loggers' Association of BC.

26 'Writ against IWA Shows How ICA Act Perils Unions,' *Pacific Tribune*, 21 May 1948.

27 The colonization and political development of BC is outlined in Margaret Ormsby, *British Columbia: A History* (Toronto: Macmillan, 1958); Patricia Roy and John Herd Thompson, *British Columbia: Land of Promises* (Toronto: Oxford University Press, 1995); Jean Barman, *The West beyond the West: A History of British Columbia*, revised ed. (Toronto: University of Toronto Press, 1996). Coal baron Robert Dunsmuir was granted 1,900,000 acres of prime coal and timber lands, and $750,000 cash to build seventy-eight miles of rail track between Victoria and the Island coalfields.

28 The decline of BC's manufacturing sector began much earlier, as outlined in John Sutton Lutz, 'Structural Changes in the Manufacturing Economy of British Columbia 1860–1915,' MA thesis, University of Victoria, 1988.

29 Robert A.J. McDonald, *Making Vancouver: Class, Status and Social Boundaries, 1863–1913* (Vancouver: UBC Press, 1996), 117–19.

30 For the origins of BC's party system, see Ross MacKenzie, 'A More Subtle Polity: The Provincial State and Party Politics in British Columbia, 1871–1903,' MA thesis, Simon Fraser University, 1992.

31 For a contemporary account of the Vancouver Island Miners' Strike (1912–14), see J. Kavanagh, *The Vancouver Island Strike* (Vancouver: BC Miners' Liberation League, c. 1913).

32 Ross Alfred Johnson, 'No Compromise – No Political Trading: The Marxian Socialist Tradition in British Columbia,' PhD diss., University of British Columbia, 1975; Benjamin Isitt, 'The Search for Solidarity: The Industrial and Political Roots of the Cooperative Commonwealth Federation in British Columbia, 1913–1928,' MA thesis, University of Victoria, 2003.

33 Theresa Ann Kerin, 'The Power of Indigenous Capital in a Company Province: An Analysis of the Ruling Class of British Columbia,' MA thesis, University of Victoria, 1977, iii; also John Addie, Allan Czepil, and Fred Rumsey, 'The Power Elite in BC,' in Knox and Resnick, *Essays in BC Political Economy*, 25–32.

34 See Martin Robin, *The Rush for Spoils: The Company Province, 1871–1933* (Toronto: McClelland and Stewart, 1972); Robin, *Pillars of Profit: The Company Province, 1934–1972* (Toronto: McClelland and Stewart, 1973); Thomas Michael Sanford, 'The Politics of Protest: The Cooperative Commonwealth Federation and Social Credit League in British Columbia,' PhD diss., University of California, 1961; also Andrew Yarmie, 'The State and Employers' Associations in British Columbia: 1900–1932,' *Labour/Le Travail*, 45 (Spring 2000), 53–101.

35 See, for example, Robin, *The Rush for Spoils*, 117–229; also 'Billion Dollar Steal,' *Pacific Tribune*, 7 May 1948.

36 'CCF Lambasts SC, Misses Giveaways,' *Pacific Tribune*, 10 Feb. 1956; '"Grass Roots" Base of Socreds Drying Up,' *Pacific Tribune*, 2 March 1956; 'Gargrave Urges Commission Probe Sturdy Charges,' *Pacific Tribune*, 27 Jan. 1956; 'Sommers Case Report Kept Secret,' *Province*, 20 Sept. 1956; 'Sommers-Sturdy Controversy,' Provincial Election Speakers Notes, Sept. 1956, file 450-2, CCF-NDP fonds, LAC; Betty O'Keefe and Ian Macdonald, *The Sommers Scandal: The Felling of Trees and Tree Lords* (Surrey, BC: Heritage House, 1999).

37 Bruce Hutchinson, *The Fraser* (Toronto: Clark, Irwin and Co., 1950), 189.

38 Provincial Elections Act Amendment Act, S.B.C. 1951 Ch. 25, assented to 18 April 1951. The new electoral system had been endorsed by the BC Conservative party at its 1947 convention, and by the BC Liberals in 1949. This suggests that both parties in the Coalition anticipated its eventual dissolution, and the need for an electoral mechanism to prevent a CCF victory. See Robin, *Pillars of Profit*, 92–3, 107, and 119–22. The operation of the Alternative Vote, commonly refererred to as the 'transferable ballot system' or 'preferential ballot system' at the time, is described in David J. Elkins, 'Politics Makes Strange Bedfellows: The BC Party System in the 1952 and 1953 Provincial Elections,' *BC Studies*, 30 (Summer 1976), 3–26; David J. Mitchell, *W.A.C. Bennett and the Rise of British Columbia* (Vancou-

ver/Toronto: Douglas and McIntyre, 1995), 126–7, 160–3. In brief, voters indicated their first, second, third, and fourth preferences on a ballot, with votes transferred from the lowest-ranking candidate until one candidate had achieved an outright majority; the procedure was more complicated in the multiple-member Vancouver and Victoria ridings. See also Barbara Horsfield, 'The Social Credit Movement in British Columbia,' BA essay, University of British Columbia, 1953, 88–9; also David M. Greer, 'Redistribution of Seats in the British Columbia Legislature, 1952–1978,' *BC Studies*, 38 (Summer 1978), 24–46.

39 Patrick L. McGeer, *Politics in Paradise* (Toronto: Peter Martin, 1972), 101.

40 Ronald B. Worley, *The Wonderful World of W.A.C. Bennett* (Toronto/Montreal: McClelland and Stewart, 1971), 59. Had the first-past-the-post, simple-majority system been in operation for the 1952 election, the CCF would have formed a minority government with 21 seats, compared with 14 Social Credit, 9 Liberal, 3 Conservatives, and 1 Labour, Tom Uphill. Under the new voting system, Social Credit formed a minority government with 19 seats to 18 for the CCF. See British Columbia, *Statement of Votes*, 1952.

41 Margaret Ormsby, 'T. Dufferin Pattullo and the Little New Deal,' *Canadian Historical Review*, 43:4 (December 1962), 277–97; J. Neil Sutherland, 'T.D. Pattullo as a Party Leader,' MA thesis, University of British Columbia, 1960; Robin, *Pillars of Profit*, 9–62.

42 Pattullo letter to *Vancouver Sun*, 4 Aug. 1942.

43 For the emergence of the Coalition and developments in the Liberal and Conservative parties, see George M. Abbott, 'Duff Pattullo and the Coalition Controversy of 1941,' *BC Studies*, 102 (Summer 1994), 30–53; George Malcolm Abbott, 'The Formation of the Liberal-Conservative Coalition in 1941,' MA thesis, University of Victoria, 1978; John Gordon Terpenning, 'Maitland and the British Columbia Conservative Party: The Struggle for Political Identity and Survival,' MA thesis, University of Victoria, 1988.

44 See British Columbia, *Statement of Votes*, 1945. While CCF support in BC grew from 33 per cent in 1941 to 37 per cent in the October 1945 provincial election, unity of free-enterprise forces, and disunity on the left, reduced CCF representation from 16 seats to 10. The presence of LPP candidates in several key ridings ensured the defeat of CCF candidates, among them left-winger Colin Cameron. For the experience of the Saskatchewan CCF, see Seymour Martin Lipset, *Agrarian Socialism: The Cooperative Commonwealth Federation in Saskatchewan. A Study in Political Sociology*, updated ed. (Garden City, NY: Anchor Books, 1968); an unsympathetic account is provided in Robert Tyre, *Douglas in Saskatchewan: The Story of a Socialist Experiment* (Vancouver: Mitchell, 1962).

45 Statement made in the legislative assembly, 15 March 1951, as quoted in Mitchell, *W.A.C. Bennett and the Rise of British Columbia*, 102; and Worley, *The Wonderful World of W.A.C. Bennett*, 41 and 55.
46 Forest Act Amendment Act, S.B.C. 1947 c. 38; *Industrial Development Act*, S.B.C. 1949 c. 31.
47 'Oust the Coalition: The Fight to Elect a CCF Government,' *Pacific Tribune*, 12 March 1948.
48 McGeer, *Politics in Paradise*, 99; 'CCF to Seek BC Hospital Probe,' *Sun*, 22 Feb. 1950; 'Gov't May Slash Hospital Extras,' *Sun*, 22 Feb. 1950; also A. Douglas Turnbull, 'Memoir: Early Years of Hospital Insurance in British Columbia,' *BC Studies*, 76 (Winter 1987–8), 58–81.
49 Statement in the legislature, 13 March 1951, as quoted in McGeer, *Politics in Paradise*, 100. The Hospital Insurance petition is cited in the address of IWA secretary-treasurer George Mitchell, *UFAWU Proceedings* (1952), Vancouver, 121, Neish papers.
50 McGeer, *Politics in Paradise*, 98–100; Robin, *Pillars of Profit*, 99; 'Coalition Hopelessly Muddled Hospital Insurance,' *CCF News*, 19 April 1950.
51 The results among the leading candidates were: Frank Mitchell (CCF), 2,837 (38.3 per cent); Alfred Wurtele (Independent, though aligned with Social Credit), 2,491 (33.7 per cent); Percival George (Coalition), 1,703 (23.0 per cent). See British Columbia, *Statement of Votes*, 1951.
52 Johnson fired Anscomb as finance minister and the Coalition was over. The 12 remaining Conservatives crossed the floor, replacing the 8-seat CCF as Official Opposition. With only 22 Liberals and 3 lingering Coalitionists on the government side – against 12 Conservatives, 7 CCFers, 2 independents (Bennett and Ralston), and the lone Uphill – Johnson's government remained in office on a razor-thin majority. McGeer, *Politics in Paradise*, 97–103; Horsfield, 'The Social Credit Movement in British Columbia,' 86. For the decline of the BC Conservative party, see Donald Keith Alper, 'From Rule to Ruin: The Conservative Party in British Columbia, 1928–1954,' PhD diss., University of British Columbia, 1975.
53 See Worley, *The Wonderful World of W.A.C. Bennett*; Mitchell, *W.A.C. Bennett and the Rise of British Columbia*. A more critical examination of Social Credit is provided in McGeer, *Politics in Paradise* and Paddy Sherman, *Bennett* (Toronto: McClelland and Stewart, 1966). Social Credit in Alberta is examined in C.B. Macpherson, *Democracy in Alberta: Social Credit and the Party System* (Toronto: University of Toronto Press, 1962); John A. Irving, *The Social Credit Movement in Alberta* (Toronto: University of Toronto Press, 1959), and Alvin Finkel, *The Social Credit Phenomenon in Alberta* (Toronto: University of Toronto Press, 1989). The political philosophy of Social Credit is articulated in C.H. Douglas, *Social Credit* (London: Eyre and Spottiswoode, 1933).

54 Following the death of Conservative leader Royal Lethington 'Pat' Maitland, Bennett challenged Coalition finance minister Herbert Anscomb for the party leadership in 1947, losing 319 votes to 188. In 1950, Bennett again challenged Anscomb, whom he criticized for retaining directorships in brewing and winery firms. However, Anscomb defeated Bennett by an even wider margin, 453 to 167, including half of the Kelowna delegation. McGeer, *Politics in Paradise*, 97 and 100; Worley, *The Wonderful World of W.A.C. Bennett*, 30–90; Robin, *Pillars of Profit*, 119–22.

55 For the origins of the BC Social Credit League, see Barbara Horsfield, 'The Social Credit Movement in British Columbia.' An early critique from the CCF perspective appeared in 'Social Credit Double-Talk,' *CCF News*, 25 March 1948.

56 Robin, *Pillars of Profit*, 123.

57 As Barbara Horsfield observed in her contemporary study of Social Credit, the party presented its platform to the public 'just at the time when a new, non-Socialistic force was needed to fill the vacuum left by the decline in popularity of the Liberals and Conservatives.' Major Douglas's central proposal of a dividend (or 'social credit') did not even appear in the party's 1952 platform or campaign literature. See Horsfield, 'The Social Credit Movement in British Columbia,' 75–8.

58 Frank Calder address, *UFAWU Proceedings*, 24–9 March 1952, Vancouver, 316, Neish papers.

59 Black, 'British Columbia: The Politics of Exploitation,' in Shearer, *Exploiting Our Economic Potential: Public Policy and the British Columbia Economy* (Toronto: Holt, Rinehart and Winston, 1968), 32.

60 Gordon Hak, 'Populism and the 1952 Social Credit Breakthrough in British Columbia,' *Canadian Historical Review*, 85:2 (June 2004), 277–96; also Kerin, 'The Power of Indigenous Capital in a Company Province,' 121.

61 D.V. Smiley, 'Canada's Poujadists: A New Look at Social Credit,' *Canadian Forum* 42 (1963), 123. A critique of such interpretations of Social Credit strength can be found in Mark Sproule-Jones, 'Social Credit and the British Columbia Electorate,' *BC Studies*, 11 (Fall 1971), 37–50.

62 Stephen G. Tomblin, 'W.A.C. Bennett and Province-Building in British Columbia,' *BC Studies*, 85 (Spring 1990), 45–61.

63 British Columbia, *A Brief Submitted to the Government of Canada by the Government of British Columbia on Federal-Provincial Co-operation in Economic Development* (Victoria: Queen's Printer, 1953), 3 and 19. This brief cited federal funding for similar capital projects in every region of Canada.

64 Worley, *The Wonderful World of W.A.C. Bennett*, 210–19. Bennett replaced the ailing Black Ball and Canadian Pacific Steamship services with one of the largest fleets in the world.

65 See J.H. Bradbury, 'Class Structures and Class Conflicts in "Instant" Resource Towns in British Columbia, 1965 to 1972,' *BC Studies*, 37 (Spring 1978), 3–18.
66 As Stuart Jamieson observed: 'British Columbia is the only province in Canada, and the only regional political unit on the North American continent, in which, between 1941 and 1956, the population of the main metropolitan areas grew *less* rapidly than the population over the province as a whole' (emphasis original). Jamieson, 'Regional Factors in Industrial Conflict: The Case of British Columbia,' *Canadian Journal of Economics and Political Science*, 28:3 (Aug. 1962), 410fn5; British Columbia, *Regional Industrial Index of British Columbia* (Victoria: Ministry of Trade and Industry, 1948) and British Columbia, *British Columbia Regional Index* (Victoria: Ministry of Economic Development, 1978).
67 See British Columbia, *Statement of Votes*, 1955 and 1956. Also 'Chinese Nominated in Jan. 9 By-Election,' *Province*, 21 Dec. 1955.
68 'CCF Lambasts SC, Misses Giveaways,' *Pacific Tribune*, 10 Feb. 1956; '"Grass Roots" Base of Socreds Drying Up,' *Pacific Tribune*, 2 March 1956; 'Gargrave Urges Commission Probe Sturdy Charges,' *Pacific Tribune*, 27 Jan. 1956.
69 Morgan to LPP constituency committees and provincial candidates, 22 Aug. 1956, file 23-02, 'BC provincial series,' reel H1592, CPC fonds, LAC.
70 '"Grass Roots" Base of Socreds Drying Up,' *Pacific Tribune*, 2 March 1956.
71 Gordon Hak, *Capital and Labour in the British Columbia Forest Industry, 1934–1974* (Vancouver: UBC Press, 2007); M. Patricia Marchak, *Green Gold: The Forestry Industry in British Columbia* (Vancouver: UBC Press, 1983); G.W. Taylor, *Timber: History of the Forest Industry in BC* (Vancouver: J.J. Douglas, 1975), 161–83. For an earlier period, see Joseph C. Lawrence, 'Markets and Capital: A History of the Lumber Industry of British Columbia 1778 to 1952,' MA thesis, University of British Columbia, 1957; Gordon Hak, *Turning Trees into Dollars: The British Columbia Coastal Lumber Industry, 1858–1913* (Toronto: University of Toronto Press, 2000).
72 Keith Reid and Don Weaver, 'Aspects of the Political Economy of the BC Forest Industry,' in Knox and Resnick, *Essays in BC Political Economy*, 18. H.R. MacMillan recorded $7-million in profits in 1947, yet paid only $140,000 in royalties to the BC government. Randolph Harding, CCF MLA (Kaslo-Slocan), raised the matter in the provincial legislature, proposing that the new 3 per cent provincial sales tax be scrapped and the revenue generated through increased corporate taxation of resource firms. 'This Week in the House,' *Pacific Tribune*, 9 April 1948.
73 British Columbia, *Transactions of the First Resources Conference* (Victoria:

Department of Lands and Forests, 1948), 89–90 (hereafter *BC Resources Conference*); Reid and Weaver, 'Aspects of the Political Economy of the BC Forest Industry,' 18.

74 Sue Baptie et al., *First Growth: The Story of British Columbia Forest Products Limited* (Vancouver: BC Forest Products, 1975).

75 Postwar consolidation in BC's forestry sector is described in Taylor, *Timber*, 161–83.

76 D.M. Carey, 'Forest Tenure in British Columbia,' in *BC Resources Conference* (1956), 271–6. Carey told the BC Natural Resource Conference that the proportion held by persons owning less than 20,000 acres declined from more than two-thirds to less than one-third of all Crown-granted land outside the E and N Lands on Vancouver Island.

77 Edwin R. Black, 'British Columbia: The Politics of Exploitation,' in Shearer, *Exploiting Our Economic Potential*, 35; also W.T. Stanbury and M.R. McLeod, 'The Concentration of Timber Holdings in the British Columbia Forest Industry, 1972,' *BC Studies* 17 (Spring 1973), 57–69.

78 Steeves to Cameron, 15 Jan. 1955, file 1-1, Colin Cameron collection (hereafter CCC), University of British Columbia Rare Books and Special Collections Division (hereafter UBCSC).

79 Nigel Morgan, *British Columbia Needs a New Forest Policy!* (Vancouver: Labor-Progressive Party, 1955), 4. The Big Five were MacMillan-Bloedel, Crown Zellerbach, Celanese Corporation of America, Powell River Company (soon to merge with MacMillan-Bloedel), and BC Forest Products.

80 Ibid., 17.

81 The 1947 Abbott Plan, which critics described as an extension of the European Marshall Plan, envisaged complete reciprocity with the US, the abolition of tariffs on trade. Mackenzie King approved talks with the US in January 1948, but soon repudiated the plan, fearing a backlash from voters. 'I could think of nothing that would destroy my name and reputation more than to be made the spearhead of a political fight which would be twisted into a final endeavour to bring about economic union with the US which would mean annexation, and separation from Britain,' King wrote in his diary in March 1948. While the plan 'might be sound economically, I believed it would be fatal politically.' Abbott shifted his tune, telling Toronto's Empire Club that 'we must reduce this dependence and begin the building of a more virile and independent economy of our own.' However, a year later, Lester Pearson, secretary of state for external affairs and Canada's former ambassador to the US, advised St Laurent: 'we must turn south.' See *Hansard, Debates of the House of Commons*, 16 Dec. 1947, 330; William Lyon Mackenzie King diary, 25 March 1948, <http://king.collectionscanada.ca>

(accessed 30 July 2007); Hector Mackenzie, 'The ABCs of Canada's International Economic Relations, 1945–1951,' in Greg Donaghy, ed., *Canada and the Early Cold War, 1943–1957* (Ottawa: Department of Foreign Affairs and International Trade, 1998), 225 and 230; 'Abbott Plan Reversal Sought by Convention,' *Fisherman*, 2 April 1948; *The Empire Club of Canada Speeches 1947–1948* (Toronto: Empire Club Foundation, 1948), 285–98; Tim Buck, *Canada: The Communist Viewpoint* (Toronto: Progress Books, 1948), 23–36.

82 'Pritchett Scores Bosses' Smear Campaign in Radio Broadcast,' *Pacific Tribune*, 20 Feb. 1948.

83 *BC Resources Conference* (1956), 214–16.

84 See Dianne Newell, *The Development of the Pacific Salmon-Canning Industry: A Grown Man's Game* (Montreal and Kingston: McGill-Queen's University Press, 1989); British Columbia, *Submission to the Royal Commission on Canada's Economic Prospects* (Victoria: Queen's Printer, 1955), 13.

85 In 1960, the British food conglomerate George Weston Ltd. acquired control of BC Packers. The web of ownership is illuminated by the following list of H.R. MacMillan's corporate affiliations in 1948: along with BC Packers and the H.R. MacMillan Export Co., MacMillan served as president of the Canadian Transport Co. Ltd., Canadian White Pine Co. Ltd., Alberni Pacific Lumber Co. Ltd., MacMillan Industries Ltd., Alberni Plywoods Ltd., Alpine Timber Co. Ltd., Northwest Bay Logging Co. Ltd., Shawnigan Lake Lumber Co. Ltd. He served as vice-president and director of London and Western Trusts Co. Ltd., and as a director of the Canadian Bank of Commerce, International Nickel Co. of Canada Ltd., Vancouver Creosoting Co. Ltd., Dominion Tar and Chemical Co. Ltd., Forest Investment Co. Ltd., Argus Corporation, and the Sino-Canadian Development Co. Ltd. He was a member of the Canadian Chamber of Commerce, among other groups. Information provided in Buck, *Canada*, 261.

86 British Columbia, *Submission to the Royal Commission on Canada's Economic Prospects* (Victoria: Queen's Printer, 1955), 13.

87 See 'Beginnings of BC's Co-ops,' *Fisherman*, 3 Oct. 1947; 'History of BC Fishery Unions Elaborated,' *Fisherman*, 7 Nov. 1947; 'Old-Time Fisherman Gives Some Early Union History,' *Fisherman*, 5 Dec. 1947; George North, edited by Hal Griffin, *A Ripple, a Wave: The Story of Union Organization in the BC Fishing Industry* (Vancouver: Fishermen Publishing Society, 1974); Percy Gladstone and Stuart Jamieson, 'Unionism in the Fishing Industry of British Columbia,' *Canadian Journal of Economics and Political Science*, 16:2 (May 1950), 1–11. The evolution of cooperatives in the coastal fishery and the steps culminating in the UFAWU's formation are detailed in *BC Resources Conference* (1956), 122–8; also *Proceedings and Resolutions of the*

Sixth Annual Convention United Fishermen's Federal Union of BC (hereafter *UFAWU Proceedings*), Vancouver, 20–4 March 1944, Kevin Neish papers (private collection).

88 'The Coalition Steals Our Forests for Uncle Sam,' *Pacific Tribune*, 18 June 1948.

89 A quarter-century later, following the NDP's victory, Columbia Cellulose (as the Celanese Company's BC assets were called) was purchased by the province and a new Crown Corporation formed, British Columbia Cellulose.

90 'The Coalition Steals Our Forests for Uncle Sam,' *Pacific Tribune*, 18 June 1948.

91 'Morgan Urges Action on New Forest Policy,' *Pacific Tribune*, 3 Feb. 1956.

92 Ibid.

93 Statistics Canada, *Census of Canada*, 1951; British Columbia, *Submission to the Royal Commission on Canada's Economic Prospects* (Victoria: Queen's Printer, 1955), 18.

94 *BC Resources Conference* (1956), 13, and British Columbia, *Documentary Submission to the Royal Commission on Canada's Economic Prospects* (Victoria: Queen's Printer, 1956), 13–15.

95 'The Coalition Steals Our Forests for Uncle Sam,' *Pacific Tribune*, 18 June 1948.

96 British Columbia, *Documentary Submission to the Royal Commission on Canada's Economic Prospects*, 51.

97 Morgan to LPP constituency committees and provincial candidates, 22 Aug. 1956, file 23-02 'BC election, 1956,' vol. 23, series IV-4 'BC provincial series,' reel H1592, MG 28, Communist Party of Canada fonds (hereafter CPC fonds), LAC.

98 'Masters in Our Own House,' *Pacific Tribune*, 2 March 1956; 'Giveaway of Resources Hit by Mine-Mill,' *Pacific Tribune*, 20 Jan. 1956; Ivan Avakumovic, *The Communist Party in Canada: A History* (Toronto: McClelland and Stewart, 1975), 182–6.

99 'Canadian Collieries' Propaganda Fails to Shake Stand of Island Coalminers,' *CCF News*, 5 Feb. 1958.

100 'Operators Provoked Coal Strike,' *Pacific Tribune*, 23 Jan. 1948; 'Coal Monopoly's Propaganda Drive Fails to Shake Island Miners' Stand,' *Pacific Tribune*, 13 Feb. 1956.

101 For the passage of the Coal and Petroleum Control Board Act (1937) and earlier skirmishes with the industry, see Robin, *Pillars of Profit*, 39–41.

102 'Oil on the Boil,' *CCF News*, 12 Feb. 1948.

103 'Oil Monopolies on Price-Gouge Strike,' *Pacific Tribune*, 6 Feb. 1948; 'Labor

Federation to Present Bill 39 Demands to Cabinet,' *Pacific Tribune*, 13 Feb. 1948.

104 *BC Resources Conference* (1956), 443 and 535.

105 'BC Power Commission Should Enter Gas Field,' *Pacific Tribune*, 3 Feb. 1956; 'CCF Lambasts SC, Misses Giveaways,' *Pacific Tribune*, 10 Feb. 1956; 'Did Socreds Make Deal?,' *Pacific Tribune*, 17 Feb. 1956.

106 'Public demand Can Will All-Canadian Pipeline,' *Pacific Tribune*, 16 March 1956.

107 See Stuart Jamieson, *Times of Trouble: Labour Unrest and Industrial Conflict in Canada, 1900–1966* (Ottawa: Task Force on Labour Relations, 1968), 419–22; Jamieson, *Industrial Relations in Canada* (Toronto: Macmillan, 1973), 67; Paul Phillips, *No Power Greater: A Century of Labour in British Columbia* (Vancouver: BC Federation of Labour and the Boag Foundation,1967), 155; Jack Scott, *A Communist Life: Jack Scott and the Canadian Workers' Movement, 1927–1985* (St John's: Canadian Committee on Labour History, 1988), 181–3.

108 For an early (and sympathetic) history of the BC Electric, see Cecil Maiden, *Lighted Journey: The Story of BC Electric* (Vancouver: British Columbia Electric Company, 1948). The company's streetcar operations are explored in Patricia E. Roy, 'The British Columbia Electric Railway Company, 1897–1928: A British Company in British Columbia,' PhD diss., University of British Columbia, 1970; and Roy, 'The Fine Arts of Lobbying and Persuading: The Case of the BC Electric Railway,' in David S. Macmillan, ed., *Canadian Business History: Selected Studies, 1497–1971* (Toronto: McClelland and Stewart, 1972), 239–54; also Taylor, *Builders of British Columbia*, 68–76, 178–83.

109 In 1945, its first year of operation, BCPC purchased the electric utilities in Nanaimo, Duncan, and Terrace, and also the West Canadian Hydro Electric Corporation; in 1946, BCPC acquired BC Electric generating plants at Port Alberni and Kamloops; in 1947, it expanded to Parksville-Qualicum, Royston, Cumberland, and opened the Elk Falls generating plant near Campbell River; in 1948, it acquired utilities at Lake Cowichan and Ladysmith, and in 1949, Courtenay, Comox, and Bowen Island. See BC Hydro Power Pioneers, *Gaslights to Gigawatts: A Human History of BC Hydro and Its Predecessors* (Vancouver: Hurricane Press, 1998); Worley, *The Wonderful World of W.A.C. Bennett* , 41.

110 In 1946, Cominco purchased all but one of the West Kootenay Power Company's generating plants, to supply its smelter at Trail. Alcan was granted power rights in the Industrial Development Act, S.B.C. 1949 c. 31.

BC Hydro Power Pioneers, *Gaslights to Gigawatts*; 'Aluminum Trust Set for Grab in BC,' *CCF News*, 6 April 1949.

111 'The Coalition Steals Our Forests for Uncle Sam,' *Pacific Tribune*, 18 June 1948.

112 'Public Power Urged by Nanaimo Mayor,' *Pacific Tribune*, 2 March 1956; British Columbia, *Submission to the Royal Commission on Canada's Economic Prospects* (Victoria: Queen's Printer, 1955), 17.

113 'Charge Bennett "Exporting Jobs,"' *Pacific Tribune*, 27 Jan. 1956; also 'Use the Columbia for Canada,' *Pacific Tribune*, 29 June 1956.

114 O'Keefe and Macdonald, *The Sommers Scandal*; Mel Rothenburger, *Friend o' Mine: The Story of Flyin' Phil Gaglardi* (Victoria: Orca, 1991); McGeer, *Politics in Paradise*, 186–214; '300 Protest Plan for Deas Tunnel,' *Sun*, 16 Feb. 1956; 'RCMP Probe Clears Gov't Cavalcade,' *Sun*, 28 June 1972; British Columbia, *Statement of Votes*, 1960.

115 As quoted in Black, 'British Columbia: The Politics of Exploitation,' in Shearer, ed., *Exploiting Our Economic Potential*, 27; British Columbia, *Statement of Votes*, 1960.

116 As quoted in Worley, *The Wonderful World of W.A.C. Bennett*, 234.

117 The United States provided an advance payment of $273-million (Canadian) upon ratification of the Treaty, to cover the construction costs for the dams. In addition, $64.4-million was provided in stages to mitigate flood damage downstream in Washington and Oregon. See *Industrial British Columbia* (Vancouver: Industrial British Columbia, c. 1966), 19; Neil A. Swanson, *Conflict over the Columbia: The Canadian Background on an Historic Treaty* (Montreal: McGill-Queen's University Press, 1979); Larratt Higgins, 'The Alienation of Canadian Resources: The Case of the Columbia River Treaty,' in Ian Lumsden, ed., *Close the 49th Parallel Etc.: The Americanization of Canada* (Toronto: University of Toronto Press, 1970), 223–40; James Laxer, *The Energy Poker Game: The Politics of the Continental Resources Deal* (Toronto/Chicago: New Press, 1970), 35–42.

118 Tension could be discerned, however, when three members of the Canadian Iron Workers union No. 1 Vancouver picketed the opening of the BC Legislature in January 1965, protesting a $150 initiation fee imposed by International unions for workers engaged on the Peace and Columbia projects. 'Ceremony Picketed,' *Sun*, 22 Jan 1965; BC Hydro Power Pioneers, *Gaslights to Gigawatts*; Worley, *The Wonderful World of W.A.C. Bennett*, 224–35.

119 Delegates at the 1962 BCFL convention unanimously endorsed a report opposing the export of Columbia River power to the United States. The

report was motivated by Orville Braaten, a paper worker and CCF-NDP dissident who was instrumental in the founding of the breakaway Pulp and Paper Workers of Canada (PPWC) the following year. See 'BC Labor Says Don't Export Power,' *Sun*, 27 Oct. 1961; 'Columbia for Canadians,' *Western Pulp and Paper Worker* (Vancouver), Sept. 1962.

120 *Canada's Party of Socialism*, 214; Maurice Rush interview, with author, 26 Feb. 2006, North Vancouver, BC.

121 'Hydro Defends Arrow Lakes Deals,' *Sun*, 13 April 1966; J.W. Wilson and Maureen Conn, 'On Uprooting and Rerooting: Reflections on the Columbia River Project,' *BC Studies*, 58 (Summer 1983), 40–54.

122 Tina Loo, 'Disturbing the Peace: Environmental Change and the Scales of Justice on a Northern River,' *Environmental History*, 12:4 (Oct. 2007), 895–919; Loo, 'People in the Way: Modernity, Environment, and Society on British Columbia's Arrow Lakes,' *BC Studies*, 142 and 143 (2004), 161–91; Susan Toller and Peter N. Nemetz, 'Assessing the Impact of Hydro Development: A Case Study of the Columbia River Basin in BC,' *BC Studies*, 114 (Summer 1997), 5–30.

123 'Hydro Defends Arrow Lakes Deals,' *Sun*, 13 April 1966.

124 *BC Resources Conference* (1956), 532.

125 British Columbia Hydro and Power Authority, *The Power of British Columbia* (Vancouver: Information Services Department, 1967).

126 W.A.C. Bennett as quoted in North, *A Ripple, a Wave*, 47–8.

127 'Stevens Backs Gillett on Salmon Protection,' *Pacific Tribune*, 6 Jan. 1956; also 'Plenty of Alternatives to Using Salmon Rivers' and 'Columbia Offer Must Be Snapped Up by BC,' *Fisherman*, 9 April 1957; 'The Fraser is a Salmon River,' Provincial Election Speakers Notes, September 1956, file 450-2, CCF-NDP fonds, LAC.

128 While Bennett pledged that the damming of the Fraser would not proceed 'until the fish problem can be solved,' the UFAWU official history claims a new energy study was conducted in 1972, and that the Fraser dam was only averted by the defeat of Social Credit at the polls. See North, *A Ripple, a Wave*, 48.

129 See 'Stop US Plans to Make BC a Military Target' [1960], file 23-08, 'BC provincial series,' reel H1592, CPC fonds, LAC.

130 See James Harding, 'The New Left in BC,' in Dimitrios I. Roussopolous, ed., *The New Left in Canada* (Montreal: Black Rose, c. 1970), 17–40. For a broad discussion of the New Left's economic views, from an American context, see Assar Lindbeck, *The Political Economy of the New Left: An Outsider's View*, second ed. (New York: Harper and Row, 1977). Contemporary Canadian studies of American economic domination include Ian

Lumsden, ed., for the University League for Social Reform, *Close the 49th Parallel Etc.: The Americanization of Canada* (Toronto: University of Toronto Press, 1970), James Laxer, *The Energy Poker Game*; Kari Levitt, *Silent Surrender: The Multinational Corporation in Canada* (Toronto: Macmillan, 1970); Dave Godfrey and Mel Watkins, eds., *Gordon to Watkins to You: A Documentary Battle for Control of Our Economy* (Toronto: New Press, 1970); Abraham Rotstein and Gary Lax, *Independence: The Canadian Challenge* (Toronto: Committee for an Independent Canada, 1972); Thomas L. Burton, *Natural Resource Policy in Canada: Issues and Perspectives* (Toronto: McClelland and Stewart, 1972); Richard C. Bocking, *Canada's Water: For Sale?* (Toronto: James Lewis and Samuel, 1972); Dimitrios I. Roussopoulos, ed., *Canada and Radical Social Change* (Montreal: Black Rose, 1973); Philip Sykes, *Sellout: The Giveaway of Canada's Energy Resources* (Edmonton: Hurtig, 1973); Laxer, *Canada's Energy Crisis* (Toronto: James Lewis and Samuel, 1974); also Laxer, *Canada's Economic Strategy* (Toronto: McClelland and Stewart, 1981); Richard Gwyn, *The 49th Paradox: Canada in North America* (Toronto: McClelland and Stewart, 1985); and Gordon Laxer, *Open for Business: The Roots of Foreign Ownership in Canada* (Toronto: Oxford University Press, 1989).

131 Harding, 'The New Left in BC,' 22.

132 Ibid., 24.

133 John Addie, Allan Czepil, and Fred Rumsey, 'The Power Elite in BC,' in Knox and Resnick, *Essays in BC Political Economy*, 30.

134 British Columbia, *Documentary Submission to the Royal Commission on Canada's Economic Prospects*, 50. The benefit of free trade for BC is explored by UBC economist Gordon R. Munroe, 'British Columbia's Stake in Free Trade,' in Shearer, *Exploiting Our Economic Potential*, 61–76.

135 Data generated from Statistics Canada, *Census of Canada*, 1941–71.

136 *Industrial British Columbia* (Vancouver: Industrial British Columbia, c. 1966), 36; Michael Dawson, 'Victoria Debates Its Post-Industrial Reality: Tourism, Deindustrialization, and Store-Hour Regulations, 1900–1958,' *Urban History Review*, 35:2 (March 2007), 14–24; Dawson, *Selling British Columbia: Tourism and Consumer Culture, 1890–1970* (Vancouver: UBC Press, 2004).

137 BC Department of Labour, *Annual Report* (1970), 86.

138 Statistics Canada, *Census of Canada*, 1941–71; BC Department of Labour, *Annual Report* (1971), 86. A total of 134,575 women worked in the service sector in 1971 compared to 130,845 men. Union density was 40.5 per cent, with 49,634 women belonging to unions compared with 57,798 men.

139 Nancy Christie, *Engendering the State: Family, Work and Welfare in Canada*

(Toronto: University of Toronto Press, 2000); also Ruth Roach Pierson, 'Gender and the Unemployment Insurance Debates in Canada, 1934–1940,' *Labour/Le Travail*, 25 (Spring 1990), 77–103. Canada's welfare state developed unevenly across the provinces, reflecting divided powers under the federal system and strong opposition to a social wage. In contrast, the Scandinavian states and other European jurisdictions approached 'cradle-to-grave' security, reflecting the ascendancy of social-democratic politics in the postwar decades.

140 Statistics Canada, *Census of Canada*, 1941–71.

141 British Columbia, *Submission to the Royal Commission on Canada's Economic Prospects*, 28–9.

142 'Night Sittings All This Week,' *Daily Times*, 3 March 1959.

143 McGeer, *Politics in Paradise*, 42.

144 As quoted in Dean H. Goard, 'People, Education, Labour and Natural Resources,' in *Inventory of the Natural Resources of British Columbia* (Victoria: BC Natural Resources Conference, 1964), 37.

145 G. Neil Perry, 'The Political Economy of Education,' in Shearer, *Exploiting Our Economic Potential*, 79–113.

146 John B. Macdonald, *Higher Education in British Columbia and a Plan for the Future* (Vancouver: University of British Columbia, 1962).

147 See Harding, 'The New Left in BC,' 26; 'College Receives Provincial Charter,' *Sun*, 12 April 1966; Maria J. Brown, 'Capilano College: A Study in the Development of a Regional or Community College,' *BC Studies*, 17 (Spring 1973), 43–56.

148 British Columbia, *Documentary Submission to the Royal Commission on Canada's Economic Prospects*, 55.

149 Statistics Canada, *Census of Canada*, 1961 and 1971.

150 See Harding, 'The New Left in BC,' 26 and 39; and Herbert Marcuse, *An Essay on Liberation* (Boston: Beacon Press, 1969); also Marcuse, 'On the New Left,' in Massimor Teodori, ed., *The New Left: A Documentary History* (Indianapolis: Bobbs-Merrill, 1969), 468–73. For Marcuse's views on the USSR, see *Soviet Marxism, A Critical Analysis* (London: Routledge and Kegan Paul, 1958).

151 'Unrest at Simon Fraser University,' n.d. [1968], file 93-A-00019 part 3, vol. 24, Previously Released Files Series, RCMP Security Service, CSIS records, LAC.

152 Harding, 'The New Left in BC,' 26–7.

153 Statistics Canada, *Census of Canada*, 1941–71. Education grew from 6,890 jobs in 1941 to 51,015 in 1971.

154 Addie, Czepil, and Rumsey, 'The Power Elite in BC,' in Knox and Resnick, *Essays in BC Political Economy*, 30; Edwin R. Black, 'British Columbia: The Politics of Exploitation,' in Knox and Resnick, *Essays in BC Political Economy*, 35. In the 1956 provincial election, the BC CCF highlighted the connections between big business and Social Credit's campaign war chest. See 'Social Credit Campaign Funds,' Provincial Election Speakers Notes, September 1956, file 450-2, CCF-NDP fonds, LAC.

2. Moscow on the Fraser

1 'Letter Hits US Entry Refusal,' *Fisherman*, 16 Jan. 1948; also 'We Don't Like Being Bullied,' *Fisherman*, 6 Feb. 1948.

2 Homer Stevens and Rolf Knight, *Homer Stevens: A Life in Fishing* (Madeira Park, BC: Harbour, 1992), 30, 184–90; Club Bulletin No. 8, 7 July 1969, file 23-38, 'BC provincial series,' reel H1592, CPC fonds, LAC; Maurice Rush, *We Have a Glowing Dream: Recollections of Working-Class and People's Struggles in BC from 1935 to 1996* (Vancouver: Centre for Socialist Education, 1996), 94; Ben Swankey interview, with author, 10 June 2005 and 14 Aug. 2005, Burnaby, BC.

3 See *Canada's Party of Socialism: History of the Communist Party of Canada, 1921–1976* (Toronto: Progress Books, 1982); Ivan Avakumovic, *The Communist Party in Canada: A History* (Toronto: McClelland and Stewart, 1975); Norman Penner, *Canadian Communism: The Stalin Years and Beyond* (Toronto: Methuen, 1988); Tim Buck, *30 Years, 1922–1952: The Story of the Communist Movement in Canada* (Toronto: Progress Books, 1952); Ian Angus, *Canadian Bolsheviks: The Early Years of the Communist Party of Canada* (Montreal: Vanguard, 1981); Lita-Rose Betcherman, *The Little Band: The Clashes between the Communists and the Political and Legal Establishment in Canada, 1928–1932* (Ottawa: Deneau, 1982); John Manley, '"Starve, Be Damned!": Communists and Canada's Urban Unemployed, 1929–1939,' *Canadian Historical Review*, 79 (Sept. 1998), 467–73 and 'Does the International Labour Movement Need Salvaging? Communism, Labourism, and the Canadian Trade Unions, 1921–1928,' *Labour/Le Travail*, 41 (Spring 1998), 147–80; Sean Griffin, *Fighting Heritage: Highlights of the 1930s Struggle for Jobs and Militant Unionism in British Columbia* (Vancouver: Tribune Publishing Company, 1985).

4 Irving Abella, *Nationalism, Communism and Canadian Labour: The CIO, the Communist Party, and the Canadian Congress of Labour, 1935–56* (Toronto: University of Toronto Press, 1973), 111.

5 For the organizational work of BC Communists, see Griffin, *Fighting Heritage*; Myrtle Bergren, *Tough Timber: The Loggers of BC – Their Story* (Toronto: Progress Books, 1966); Ben Swankey and Jean Evans Sheils, *'Work and Wages!': A Semi-Documentary Account of the Life and Times of Arthur H. (Slim) Evans 1890–1944: Carpenter, Miner, Labor Leader* (Vancouver: Trade Union Research Bureau, 1977); Al King with Kate Braid, *Red Bait! Struggles of a Mine Mill Local* (Vancouver: Kingbird, 1998); Gordon Hak, 'Red Wages: Communists and the 1934 Vancouver Island Loggers Strike,' *Pacific Northwest Quarterly*, 80:3 (July 1989), 82–3; Steve Brodie, *Bloody Sunday: Vancouver-1938: Recollections of the Post Office Sitdown of Single Unemployed*, ed. with an introduction by Sean Griffin, epilogue by Maurice Rush (Vancouver: Young Communist League, 1974); John Stanton, *Never Say Die! The Life and Times of John Stanton, a Pioneer Labour Lawyer* (Ottawa: Steel Rail, 1987) and *My Past Is Now: Further Memoirs of a Labour Lawyer* (St John's: Canadian Committee on Labour History, 1994). Fergus McKean opposed the wartime 'no-strike pledge' and the 'Liberal-Labor' slogan adopted by the National LPP leadership in 1945, the policy of supporting Liberals that cost the CCF seats in the federal and provincial elections that year. He also objected to the abandonment of the Communist Party in favour of the LPP, accusing Buck and his group of setting up 'a bourgeois parliamentary party.' At the August 1945 National Committee plenum, McKean delivered a two-hour speech accusing the LPP leadership of advocating 'Browderism,' the policy associated with US Communist leader Earl Browder that called for collaboration between the North American working class and bourgeoisie. McKean had earlier been suspended for allenging that the BC LPP leadership counted *agents provocateurs* among its ranks. At the August 1945 plenum, he widened this allegation of treachery to include Buck, and failed to adequately substantiate these charges before a specially appointed committee. In September 1945, McKean was expelled from the LPP. He then organized his own 'Communist Party of Canada,' but, according to the CPC's official history, 'wielded little influence and soon sank into oblivion.' See *Canada's Party of Socialism*, 148–9; Avakumovic, *The Communist Party in Canada*, 164–7; Penner, *Canadian Communism*, 199–200; Howard White, *A Hard Man to Beat: The Story of Bill White, Labour Leader, Historian, Shipyard Worker, Raconteur* (Vancouver: Pulp Press, 1983), 215; *Canadian Tribune* (Toronto), 17 Nov. 1945. McKean's internment during the war, the founding of the LPP, and related events are illuminated in 'F.A. McKean, n.d.,' file 95-A-00111 part 8, vol. 65, Previously Released Files series, RCMP Security Service, CSIS records, LAC; also Stanton, *My Past Is Now*, 50–9. A discussion of 'Browderism' is provided in Maurice Isserman, *If I Had a*

Hammer: The Death of the Old Left and the Birth of the New Left (New York: Basic Books, 1987), 5–6 and 11–14; Fergus McKean, *Communism Versus Opportunism: An Examination of the Revisionism of Marxism in the Communist Movement of Canada* (Vancouver: Organizing Committee, Communist Party of Canada, 1946).

6 Tim Buck, *Canada: The Communist Viewpoint* (Toronto: Progress Books, 1948), 252.

7 'Red Bogey in Nanaimo,' *Pacific Tribune*, 23 April 1948; see also Alvin Finkel, 'The Cold War, Alberta Labour, and the Social Credit Regime,' *Labour/Le Travail*, 21 (Spring 1988), 123–52.

8 'Here's the Complete Text of Nanaimo Libel Charges,' *Pacific Tribune*, 28 May 1948; 'Nanaimo,' *Pacific Tribune*, 28 May 1948; 'Anti-Fascist War Hero in Dock at Nanaimo on Libel Charges,' *Pacific Tribune*, 4 June 1948; 'Manson Says He'll Tolerate No Public Comment on Nanaimo Case,' *Pacific Tribune*, 18 June 1948.

9 Ross Alfred Johnson, 'No Compromise – No Political Trading: The Marxian Socialist Tradition in British Columbia,' PhD diss., UBC, 1975, 129.

10 'Anti-Fascist War Hero in Dock at Nanaimo on Libel Charges,' *Pacific Tribune*, 4 June 1948; 'Defend Nanaimo Labor,' *Pacific Tribune*, 28 May 1948. A more thorough discussion of the Vitkovich case is provided in Stanton, *My Past Is Now*, 67–88.

11 See Canada, *Royal Commission to Investigate Facts Relating to and the Circumstances Surrounding the Communication, by Public Officials and Other Persons in Positions of Trust of Secret and Confidential Information to Agents of a Foreign Power* (Ottawa: Queen's Printer, 1946); Dominique Clément, 'Spies, Lies and a Commission, 1946–8,' *Left History*, 7:2 (Fall 2000), 53–79; Mark Kristmanson, 'Pulp History: Repossessing the Gouzenko Myth,' in *Plateaus of Freedom: Nationality, Culture, and State Security in Canada, 1940–1960* (Don Mills, ON.: Oxford University Press, 2003), 137–80; Merrily Weisbord, *The Strangest Dream: Canadian Communists, the Spy Trials, and the Cold War* (Toronto: Lester and Orpen Dennys, 1983); John Sawatsky, *Gouzenko: The Untold Story* (Toronto: Macmillan, 1984); Reg Whitaker and Gary Marcuse, *Cold War Canada: The Making of a National Insecurity State, 1945–1957* (Toronto: University of Toronto Press, 1994).

12 The Right Honourable Louis St Laurent, the Maurice Cody Memorial Lecture, Jan. 1947, Convocation Hall, University of Toronto. As quoted in Buck, *Canada: The Communist Viewpoint*, 17.

13 As quoted in Buck, *Canada: The Communist Viewpoint*, 17.

14 The French and Italian Communist parties, which both participated in national-coalition governments following the defeat of Fascism, were

excluded from power from 1947 and 1948 onward, but maintained strong support among the electorate. See Perry Anderson, *Considerations on Western Marxism* (London: New Left Books, 1976), 35–42.

15 Whitaker and Marcuse, *Cold War Canada*, 362, 354.

16 Abella, *Nationalism, Communism and Canadian Labour*, 111–38; Abella, 'Communism and Anti-Communism in the British Columbia Labour Movement, 1940–1948,' in David Jay Bercuson, ed. *Western Perspectives 1: Papers of the Western Canadian Studies Conference, 1973* (Toronto and Montreal: Holt, Rinehart and Winston, 1974), 88–100; Whitaker and Marcuse, *Cold War Canada*, 287–90 and 351–3.

17 Harry A. Millis and Emily Clark Brown, *From the Wagner Act to Taft-Hartley: A Study of National Labor Policy and Labor Relations* (Chicago: University of Chicago Press, 1950); Steven E. Abraham, 'The Impact of the Taft-Hartley Act on the Balance of Power in Industrial Relations,' *American Business Law Journal*, 33:3 (Spring 1996), 341–63. Incongruities between Canadian and American labour legislation since the 1940s had contributed to divergent patterns of union density in the two countries. In 1948, 32 per cent of American workers belonged to unions, compared with 30 per cent in Canada. Union density in the United States peaked at 34 per cent in 1953. By 1972, only 26 per cent of American workers were organized into unions, while the Canadian total had increased to 34 per cent. In British Columbia, where the heavily unionized resource sectors dominated the economy, density peaked at 53.9 per cent in 1958. Data derived from the United States Bureau of Labor Statistics and BC Department of Labour, *Annual Report* (1948–72).

18 'Trail Paper Attempts to Split Smeltermen,' *Pacific Tribune*, 24 Sept. 1948; 'US Border Bans Hit Union Rights,' *Pacific Tribune*, 17 Sept. 1948; Jack Scott, *A Communist Life: Jack Scott and the Canadian Workers Movement, 1927–1985* (St John's: Canadian Committee on Labour History, 1988), 92. For the banning of Pritchett and the IWA, see 'IWA Officials Win Right to Enter United States,' *Pacific Tribune*, 20 Feb. 1948. For a personal account of dealings with border officials, see 'IWA Delegate Reveals "Iron Curtain" Location,' *Pacific Tribune*, 1 Oct. 1948. During the war, Pritchett, international president of the powerful IWA and a communist, had been barred from the United States. See Jerry Lembcke and William M. Tattam, *One Union in Wood: A Political History of the International Woodworkers of America* (Madeira Park, BC: Harbour, 1984), 75–9; Scott, *A Communist Life*, 118–19.

19 'IUMMS Executive Term Millard Statements "Malicious Nonsense,"' *Pacific Tribune*, 27 Feb. 1948.

20 'Miners Score Interference with Union,' *Pacific Tribune*, 12 March 1948; also 'Labor Council Moves to Reserve Top CCL Policy,' *Pacific Tribune*, 27 March 1948.

21 'Labor Lobby,' *Pacific Tribune*, 9 April 1948; 'CMA Wants Hitlerite Clauses in Revised Act,' *Pacific Tribune*, 16 April 1948; also 'Taft-Hartley Formula Sought by Employers,' *Pacific Tribune*, 16 Jan. 1948; 'Come Out from behind the Red Curtain!,' *Fisherman*, 12 March 1948; 'Out with the Reds, Back the "Open Shop,"' *Fisherman*, 29 Oct. 1948; 'PEI "Hitler" Labor Law under Blistering Attack,' *Fisherman*, 9 April 1948.

22 'Murphy Raps Mining Association for Refusal to State Proposals,' *Pacific Tribune*, 23 Jan. 1948.

23 See Benjamin Isitt, 'Elusive Unity: The Canadian Labor Party in British Columbia, 1924–1928,' *BC Studies*, 163 (Fall 2009), 33–64; Benjamin Isitt, 'The Search for Solidarity: The Industrial and Political Roots of the Cooperative Commonwealth Federation in British Columbia, 1913–1928,' MA thesis, University of Victoria, 2003, 142–79; Manley, 'Does the International Labour Movement Need Salvaging?'; Manley, 'Canadian Communists, Revolutionary Unionism, and the "Third Period": The Workers' Unity League, 1929–1935,' *Journal of the Canadian Historical Association*, 5 (1994), 167–91; Martin Robin, *Radical Politics and Canadian Labour* (Kingston: Industrial Relations Centre, Queen's University, 1968), 252–67.

24 Patrick George Hill, 'A Failure of Unity: Communist Party-CCF Relations in British Columbia, 1935–1939,' MA thesis, University of Victoria, 1977; Raymond Frogner, '"Within Sound of the Drum": Currents of Anti-Militarism in the British Columbia Working Class in the 1930s,' MA thesis, University of Victoria, 1987.

25 In 1943, the CCF provincial convention voted to form a special committee to investigate the issue, and provincial secretary Frank McKenzie held a meeting with BC communist Tom McEwen. In response to the convention decision, Coldwell threatened to either disband the BC section or resign as leader. See A. MacInnis to McKenzie, 14 June 1943; McKenzie to A. MacInnis, 24 June 1943, file 72-16, Angus MacInnis Collection (hereafter AMC), UBCSC; Walter D. Young, *Anatomy of a Party: The National CCF, 1932–61* (Toronto: University of Toronto Press, 1969), 277–80; Penner, *Canadian Communism*, 200–1; S.P. Lewis, *Grace: The Life of Grace MacInnis* (Madeira Park, BC: Harbour, 1993), 173 and 183. In 1948, following the death of the sitting Coalition MLA in Rossland-Trail, the BC CCF leadership readmitted Herridge, likely in the hopes of recapturing the working-class provincial riding that had been lost in 1945 as a result of the CCF and 'People's

CCF' split. See 'Unity Aided by Herridge,' *Pacific Tribune*, 13 Aug. 1948; also Abella, 'Communism and Anti-Communism in the British Columbia Labour Movement: 1940–1948,' 88–100.

26 Beginning in 1941, when CCFer Charlie Millard succeeded in winning control of the powerful Steelworkers' organization in Ontario, CCF and CCL officials set their sights on BC labour. As Angus MacInnis wrote to provincial president and MLA Arthur Turner, 'if we play our cards right we can make our support of the trade union movement quite solid.' At the time, communists controlled the VLC, IWA, Mine-Mill, Dock and Shipyard Workers, and the Boilermakers' and Iron Shipbuilders' unions. The latter experienced an explosion in growth, from 200 members in 1939 to 13,000 two years later, as wartime demand gave rise to a massive expansion in shipbuilding. In December 1942, a communist slate won executive elections for the Boilermakers. The CCL cancelled the election, placed the union under trusteeship, and seized the union's funds. MacInnis recommended that members of the National Executive and other prominent CCFers 'be careful not to say anything about the dispute existing now between the National Council of the Canadian Congress of Labour and the Boilermakers' Union in Vancouver.' When the CCL action was challenged in the courts, and subsequently overturned, the CCL and its CCF allies learned an important lesson: 'To defeat the Communists would require more than an *ad hoc*, confused programme. It would require a well-organized, coordinated plan of attack.' Abella, 'Communism and Anti-Communism in the British Columbia Labour Movement,' 88–100; Gad Horowitz, *Canadian Labour in Politics* (Toronto: University of Toronto Press, 1968); Young, *Anatomy of a Party*, 254–84; 'Victoria Local Resents SGWS Officers' Tactics,' *CCF News*, 13 Sept. 1945.

27 The motion carried on a vote of 53–44. See 'Council Votes CCF Support,' *Pacific Tribune*, 13 Feb. 1948; 'Labor Council Endorses CCF,' *CCF News*, 12 Feb. 1948; 'Upset in Vancouver Labor Council Reflects Unbalanced Representation,' *Pacific Tribune*, 30 Jan. 1948; 'G. Home Heads Labor Council,' *CCF News*, 29 Jan. 1948.

28 'Unity at Polls Vital – Buck' and 'Convention Plans for Election of CCF Govn't,' *Pacific Tribune*, 19 March 1948. See also British Columbia, *Statement of Votes*, 1945; *Canadian Parliamentary Guide*, 1945.

29 'Trade Council Scores UBC Hoodlum Group' and 'Planned Provocation,' *Pacific Tribune*, 19 March 1948.

30 'Police Action Scored,' *Pacific Tribune*, 6 Feb. 1948; 'Port Alberni Council Rejects Censure of LPP for Price Parade, Protests Embargo Lift,' *Pacific Tribune*, 20 Aug. 1948; 'Protest Meeting Speakers Heckled,' *Sun*, 15 Sept. 1948.

31 'O'Brien Acquittal Seen as BCFL Vindication,' *Pacific Tribune*, 27 Feb. 1948.
32 For developments in the CSU in BC, see file 'Canadian Seamen's Union – Vancouver, BC,' vol. 2285, series A, RCMP Security Service, CSIS records, LAC; 'Support Seamen, It's Your Fight Too,' *Fisherman*, 16 July 1948; 'Rally July 23 to Back Seamen,' *Pacific Tribune*, 16 July 1948; 'Shipowners Get Set to Extend War on CSU,' *Pacific Tribune*, 10 Sept. 1948; 'Labor's Rights Threatened by Vicious Board Ruling,' *Fisherman*, 19 Dec. 1950; Jim Green, *Against the Tide: The Story of the Canadian Seamen's Union* (Vancouver: Progress Books, 1986), 170–2; John Stanton, *The Life and Death of a Union: The Canadian Seamen's Union, 1936–1949* (Toronto: Steel Rail, 1979); Jack Scott, *Canadian Workers, American Unions* (Vancouver: New Star, 1978), 172–207. In May 1949, the Victoria Trades and Labour Council went on record 'as recognizing the Seafarers International Union as the only Union for seamen.' Minutes, 18 May 1949, box 4, series IV, accession 80–59, Victoria Labour Council fonds, UVASC. The Red Wars in the Vancouver shipyards are recounted in White, *A Hard Man to Beat*, 172–86.
33 'Local AFL Council Attacks Communists,' *CCF News*, 27 May 1948; 'TLC Resolution Echoes Chamber of Commerce Line,' *Pacific Tribune*, 21 May 1948; 'Who Profits by Red-Baiting?,' *Pacific Tribune*, 4 June 1948.
34 'Who Profits by Red-Baiting?,' *Pacific Tribune*, 4 June 1948.
35 White, *A Hard Man to Beat*, 161.
36 'Big Struggle This Year Seen by IWA Leader,' *Fisherman*, 2 April 1948; 'Red Baiters Lose in IWA Vote,' *Pacific Tribune*, 19 March 1948; 'IWA Leaders Win Election,' *Fisherman*, 19 March 1948.
37 Rush, *We Have a Glowing Dream*, 106; 'VLC Critical of Lobby "Walkout" Disruption,' *Pacific Tribune*, 16 April 1948.
38 King with Braid, *Red Bait!*, 76–84; 'Mine-Mill Union at Trail Wins Backing,' *Fisherman*, 4 April 1950; 'Battle with Murphy Costs Half-Million,' *Sun*, 22 Sept. 1951; 'CCL Executive Suspends Murphy from Conventions for Two Years,' *CCF News*, 2 Sept. 1948; Abella, *Nationalism, Communism, and Canadian Labour*, 101–2, 124.
39 Jack Webster, *Webster – An Autobiography of a Veteran BC Journalist* (Vancouver: Douglas and McIntyre, 1990), 35 and 37.
40 'Union Wreckers,' *Pacific Tribune*, 27 Aug. 1948; also Rush, *We Have a Glowing Dream*, 105–7; 'Murphy Will Appeal to CCL Convention,' *Pacific Tribune*, 27 Aug. 1948; 'CCL Delegates Gagged, Mine-Mill Suspension Upheld by Slim Margin,' *Pacific Tribune*, 10 Sept. 1948; 'Carlin Puts Case to CCL Unions, Wants Mine-Mill Reinstated,' *Pacific Tribune*, 10 Sept. 1948; Abella, *Nationalism, Communism, and Canadian Labour*, 124–7.
41 Mahoney to Tallman, 9 Sept. 1948, United Steelworkers of America papers

(private papers at USWA District office, Toronto), as quoted in Abella, *Nationalism, Communism and Canadian Labour*, 126–7; also 'BC Federation Plans European Peace Tour,' *Pacific Tribune*, 10 Sept. 1948; 'Mahoney Clique Stages Stayaway from BCFL,' *Pacific Tribune*, 17 Sept. 1948; 'John Clark to Address BC Federation Meet,' *Pacific Tribune*, 3 Sept. 1948; George Home interview, as quoted in Olenka Melnyk, *No Bankers in Heaven: Remembering the CCF* (Toronto and Montreal: McGraw-Hill Ryerson, 1989), 63–4.

42 'As We See It,' *Pacific Tribune*, 10 Sept. 1948.

43 'O'Brien Quits Chair of BC Federation,' *Pacific Tribune*, 12 Nov. 1948.

44 'Steel Raids Mine-Mill Vancouver,' *Pacific Tribune*, 3 Sept. 1948; 'Raiding Tactics Denied by Union,' *Sun*, 15 Sept. 1948; 'Steel Organizer Claims Congress Backs Raid on Mine-Mill Union,' *Pacific Tribune*, 17 Sept. 1948.

45 'Right to Choose Union, Leaders Basic,' *Fisherman*, 22 Oct. 1948.

46 'TLC Backs Bengough on Hall Suspension,' *Pacific Tribune*, 24 Sept. 1948; 'Defeat Scheme to Split Congress,' *Pacific Tribune*, 1 Oct. 1948; 'TLC Convention Backs Executive,' *CCF News*, 14 Oct. 1948; 'Hall Splitters Routed,' *Pacific Tribune*, 15 Oct. 1948; 'TLC Unions in BC Rebuff New Hall Group,' *Pacific Tribune*, 10 Dec. 1948; Whitaker and Marcuse, *Cold War Canada*, 325–8; *Trades and Labor Congress Convention Proceedings*, Oct. 1948, Victoria, BC, 77–8; Stevens and Knight, *Homer Stevens*, 92; also 'Alex Gordon Named TLC Vice-President' and 'Election of Alex Gordon Tribute to UFAWU,' *Fisherman*, 3 Oct. 1947.

47 'Fadling's Line Hasn't Paid Off,' *Pacific Tribune*, 16 July 1948. The conflict in the IWA and the formation of the WIUC is examined in Lembcke and Tattam, *One Union in Wood*, 103–34; Abella, *Nationalism, Communism and Canadian Labour*, 111–38; and Stanton, *Never Say Die!*, 197–208.

48 'Reporter Fingerman on IWA,' *Pacific Tribune*, 20 Aug. 1948. At the beginning of 1948, the contours of the dispute were clear. *CCF News* attacked Pritchett and other IWA leaders for sparring with the International over CIO support for Taft-Hartley and the Marshall Plan. Pritchett, meanwhile, accused the BC lumber bosses of dragging in 'the cheap tactic of the red bogey.' See 'Pritchett's Labor Unity Double-Talk,' *CCF News*, 8 Jan. 1948; 'Pritchett Scores Bosses' Smear Campaign in Radio Broadcast,' *Pacific Tribune*, 20 Feb. 1948.

49 'Fadling's Line Hasn't Paid Off,' *Pacific Tribune*, 16 July 1948; also Lembcke and Tattam, *One Union in Wood*, 125.

50 As quoted in 'Employers' Labor Letter Exposes Plot to Destroy IWA Leadership,' *Pacific Tribune*, 13 Aug. 1948.

51 'Employers' Labor Letter Exposes Plot to Destroy IWA Leadership,' *Pacific Tribune*, 13 Aug. 1948.

52 'Communist Leadership,' *CCF News*, 23 Sept. 1948; 'Murphy Blasts "CCF News" Smear on IWA Conciliation Board Award,' *Pacific Tribune*, 1 Oct. 1948.

53 'CCL Asked to Suspend Mahoney on IWA Charges,' *Pacific Tribune*, 3 Sept. 1948; 'IWA President Criticizes Tactics Used by BC District Officers,' *CCF News*, 30 Sept. 1948; also 'IWA Scores Again,' *Pacific Tribune*, 24 Sept. 1948; 'IWA Members Open War on "White Bloc,"' *Pacific Tribune*, 17 Sept. 1948; 'US Border Bans Hit Union Rights,' *Pacific Tribune*, 17 Sept. 1948; also 'Washington IWA Asks Entry Bars Be Lifted to BC Delegates,' *Pacific Tribune*, 10 Sept. 1948; 'IWA Delegate Reveals Iron Curtain,' 1 Oct. 1948.

54 'LPP Leadership Splits with IWA,' *CCF News*, 7 Oct. 1948; also 'Why the WIUC Was Born,' *Fisherman*, 5 Nov. 1948; Lembcke and Tattam, *One Union in Wood*, 125; Scott, *A Communist Life*, 118. According to Jack Scott, the BC District was informed of the planned trusteeship by Karly Larsen, a communist union leader in Washington State.

55 Betty Griffin interview, 11 Aug. 2005, North Vancouver, BC. Labour lawyer John Stanton claims that Murphy and Morgan outvoted Pritchett, who favoured a membership referendum on disaffiliation from the IWA. This view is confirmed by Rush, who wrote that Murphy was 'one of the strongest advocates of the breakaway tactic. This was one of his big mistakes, but as I mentioned before, he was not alone.' Stanton, *Never Say Die!*, 201–2; Rush, *We Have a Glowing Dream*, 166; Scott, *A Communist Life*, 118–21.

56 Griffin interview, 11 Aug. 2005.

57 'LPP Leadership Splits with IWA,' *CCF News*, 7 Oct. 1948; 'IWA International President Charges Communist Leaders with Disruption,' *CCF News*, 7 Oct. 1948.

58 'WIUC Asks Certification of 3 Locals As Drive Debunks Fadling Claims,' *Pacific Tribune*, 15 Oct. 1948; 'Loggers Reject IWA, Solid with New Union,' *Fisherman*, 22 Oct. 1948; 'WIUC Installs Charters in Nine New Unions,' *Pacific Tribune*, 22 Oct. 1948; 'WIUC Takes Job Action, Wins Two Encounters,' *Fisherman*, 12 Nov. 1948; 'WIUC Strike Action Enforces Contract,' *Pacific Tribune*, 12 Nov. 1948; 'IWA Loses Only 3000 to Rebel Union,' *Sun*, 28 Dec. 1948; 'Defends Union's Strike Fund; Dalskog Jailed As WIU Urged Unity in Wage Drive,' *Canadian Tribune* (Toronto), 18 April 1949; 'BC Union Official Defies Court Order; Put under Arrest,' *Montreal Gazette*, 8 April 1949; 'Here are the facts' [IWA leaflet], c. 1948, file 'Woodworkers Industrial Union of Canada – Vancouver, BC,' vol. 2285, series A, RCMP Security Service, CSIS records, LAC; see also *The Union Woodworker* (Vancouver), 1948–50, in vol. 3526, Registry Files, RCMP Security Records, RG18-F-3,

LAC; Lembcke and Tattam, *One Union in Wood*, 129–34; Scott, *A Communist Life*, 121. In the summer of 1951, the IWA announced that it was sending more organizers into the Cranbrook area to unseat the WIUC. 'Communist Attempts to Organize on West Coast Ships Unsuccessful,' *Daily Colonist* (Victoria), 25 July 1951; 'The WIUC, Past, Present, and Future,' *The Woodpecker* (Cranbrook), 16 Nov. 1955, file 'Woodworkers Industrial Union of Canada – Cranbrook, BC,' vol. 2285, series A, RCMP Security Service, CSIS records, LAC.

59 Lembcke and Tattam, *One Union in Wood*, 131 and 133.

60 Stephen Gray, 'Woodworkers and Legitimacy: The IWA in Canada, 1937–1957,' PhD diss., Simon Fraser University, 1989, 431.

61 Erni Knott, *Development of the Coastal Wood Industry in BC* (Sooke, BC, 1996), 14–15. Unpublished manuscript in possession of author.

62 Grace Tickson interview, with author, 20 July 2005, Nanaimo, BC.

63 Griffin interview, 11 Aug. 2005.

64 Ibid. Another Communist, Jack Scott, suggested that 'The IWA was the beginning of the downfall of the CP' in BC. Scott, *A Communist Life*, 118.

65 White, *A Hard Man to Beat*, 172–86, 192, 197.

66 'The Red Threat to Our Pacific Gateway,' *Financial Post* (Toronto), 12 Dec. 1953.

67 'Labour Review April 1962,' file 'Trade unions: Comm. Penetration Canada,' vol. 2213, series A, RCMP Security Service, CSIS records, LAC. The RCMP wrote that the Vancouver, Port Alberni, and Prince Rupert ILWU locals 'are Communist controlled at the local level in addition to the executive level.'

68 '"Reds Build Springboard" – Alsbury Says Communists Major Threat in BC,' *Sun*, 13 Feb. 1956.

69 Report on 'Trade Union Research Bureau,' 20 Oct. 1965, file 'Oil, Chemical and Atomic Workers International Union, 9–601 Vancouver, BC,' vol. 2157, series A, RCMP Security Service, CSIS records, LAC; 'Memorandum to Inspector Parent Re: Communist Penetration of trade unions,' 7 May 1963; 'Labour Review April 1962,' file 'Trade unions: Comm. Penetration Canada,' vol. 2213, series A, RCMP Security Service, CSIS records, LAC.

70 Report on 'Trade Union Research Bureau,' 20 Oct. 1965, file 'Oil, Chemical and Atomic Workers International Union, 9–601 Vancouver, BC,' vol. 2157, series A, RCMP Security Service, CSIS records, LAC. In 1962, the RCMP Security Service noted that the BCGEA's Essondale branch, representing workers at the provincial mental institution, was 'Communist Infiltrated.' 'Labour Review April 1962,' file 'Trade unions: Comm. Penetration Canada,' vol. 2213, series A, RCMP Security Service, CSIS records, LAC;

Swankey interview, 10 June 2005; John Fryer interview, with author, 11 April 2006, Victoria, BC.

71 'Communist Wins Election,' *Sun*, 10 Nov. 1972.

72 Stevens and Knight, *Homer Stevens*, 101.

73 '15 Red-Backed Candidates Running for Seats in BC,' *Province*, 6 Dec. 1961.

74 'Homer Stevens Delegate to World Youth Festival,' *Fisherman*, 23 May 1947; 'Canadian Youth Termed Shock Brigade, Honored, *Fisherman*, 3 Oct. 1947; 'Banquet Oct. 17 to Greet Youth Festival Delegates,' 10 Oct. 1947; Stevens and Knight, *Homer Stevens*, 79–83 and 184–90; Grace Stevens interview, with author, 9 Aug. 2005, Nanaimo, BC. Stevens left the party following the Soviet invasion of Czechoslovakia in 1968, but returned three years later.

75 Resolution No. 104 'Red-Baiting,' *UFAWU Proceedings*, 17–21 March 1947, Vancouver, Neish papers; see also '47 Resolution to Stem Union-Busting Drive,' *Fisherman*, 9 April 1948; 'Fishermen Reap the Returns of Unity,' *Pacific Tribune*, 30 July 1948.

76 Speech by Elgin Neish, 11 Oct. 1952, *The Peace Conference of the Asian and Pacific Regions Bulletin, October 2–12, 1952, Peking*, English ed. (Peking: Secretariat of the Peace Conference of the Asian and Pacific Regions, 1952), 146, Neish papers; 'China Does Want Our Goods,' *Fisherman*, 4 Nov. 1952; 'Conference Seeks 75,000 Names for Peace,' *Fisherman*, 6 June 1950; 'Alex Gordon Nominated to World Peace Congress,' *Fisherman*, 17 Oct. 1950; 'World Peace Congress Outlines Job to Be Done,' *Fisherman*, 12 Sept. 1950; 'World Peace Congress to Forge New Charter,' *Fisherman*, 15 Nov. 1950; 'Britain Ends Long Tradition of Freedom, Bars Leading Peace Congress Delegates,' *Fisherman*, 21 Nov. 1950; 'Europe's People Want Peace, Rebuild Devastated Areas,' *Fisherman*, 12 Dec. 1950; 'Declaration to People Issued by Peace Congress' and 'Peace Program for United Nations,' *Fisherman*, 19 Dec. 1950; 'End War by Negotiation UFAWU Executive Urges' and 'End War in Korea,' *Fisherman*, 5 Dec. 1950.

77 Social Credit and CCF MLAs endorsed the idea, but action wasn't taken until 1975 when the Barrett NDP amended the Workmen's Compensation Act. 'By Sea, Land They Came to Victoria Demanding Justice' and 'Lobby Presses Legislature for Full Compensation,' *Fisherman*, 18 March 1952; George North, *A Ripple, a Wave: The Story of Union Organization in the BC Fishing Industry* (Vancouver: Fishermen Publishing Society, 1974), 42; 'All BC fishermen covered by compensation January 1,' *Fisherman*, 28 Nov. 1975.

78 'Auxiliary Wants Coast Guard,' *Pacific Tribune*, 23 March 1956. Delegates at the UFAWU auxiliaries' sixth annual convention in 1956 adopted a resolu-

tion reiterating this stance. Prior to the coast guard's inception in 1962, the Marine Service performed many coastal defence functions, as did the navy in the early twentieth century. Located in the Department of Marine and Fisheries after Confederaton, the Marine Service moved into the Department of Transport in the 1930s and became the Canadian Coast Guard in 1962, with operations extending from the Atlantic, Arctic, and Pacific coasts to the St Lawrence Seaway and the Great Lakes.

79 Griffin interview, 11 Aug. 2005; Kevin Neish interview, with author, 11 May 2006, Victoria, BC.

80 Minutes, 19 April 1950, box 5, series IV, accession 80–59, Victoria Labour Council fonds, UVASC; also Minutes, 1 March 1950; Bruce Lowther, *A Better Life: The First Century of the Victoria Labour Council* (Victoria: Victoria Labour Council, 1989), 17; 'TLC Delegates Remove Showler as Council Head' and 'Showler's Swan Song,' *Fisherman*, 14 Feb. 1950; 'TLC Condemns Ban of "Red" Nominee,' *Sun*, 22 Feb. 1950; 'Bengough Ruling Backed by Trades Council Meet,' *Fisherman*, 14 March 1950. Showler was defeated in elections for the VLTC presidency at the same meeting, after serving eight years in that position. In October 1947, Showler had been defeated for the TLC vice-presidency by UFAWU business agent Alex Gordon. 'Alex Gordon Named TLC Vice-President,' *Fisherman*, 3 Oct. 1947.

81 'TLC Veers Sharply Right,' *Fisherman*, 19 Sept. 1950. The statement was made by the chairman of the TLC's constitution committee.

82 North, *A Ripple, a Wave*, 34; 'Victoria Local Says Ban "Cannot Go Unchallenged"'; 'Gervin Threatens to Disband Meet to Force Ban on UFAWU Delegates'; 'Telegram from UFAWU'; and 'Peace, Communism and Madness,' *Fisherman*, 21 Nov. 1950; 'UFAWU Hits Bar on Delegates,' *Fisherman*, 5 Dec. 1950; Minutes, 6 Dec. 1950; also 19 July 1950, box 5, series IV, accession 80–59, Victoria Labour Council fonds, UVASC; 'Victoria Local Rebukes TLC over Ban on Neish' and 'UFAWU Locals Will Stick to Democracy,' *Fisherman*, 12 Dec. 1950; Lowther, *A Better Life*, 18.

83 Neish's expulsion followed a year of hearings and legal exchanges. The original charge had been levelled in February 1954, by fellow Legionnaire Frank Partridge, a known anti-communist, outlining Neish's association with the Peace Council and LPP, his trip to China in 1952, and his criticism of the Canadian military's conduct in Korea. Neish contracted Vancouver lawyer Harry Rankin as he prepared his defence. In January 1955, the charges against Neish were sustained and he was expelled from the Legion's Britannia Branch No. 7. See Partridge to Secretary, 23 Feb. 1954 ('Charge against Elgin Neish'); Chairman (Trial Committee) to Neish, 5 March 1954; Anderson to Parker, 9 March 1954; Parker to Neish, 19 March

1954; Rankin to Neish, 29 March 1954, Ray Gardner to Neish, 20 Jan. 1955. File 'Expulsion from Legion,' Neish papers; 'Fight Looms over Legion Suspension,' *Sun*, 20 Jan. 1955.

84 As quoted in North, *A Ripple, a Wave*, 35.

85 Stevens and Knight, *Homer Stevens*, 96–8; North, *A Ripple, a Wave*, 40–1.

86 'Combines Probe Termed Illegal,' *Pacific Tribune*, 18 May 1956; 'UFAWU Says Probe Gov't Attack on Union,' *Pacific Tribune*, 1 June 1956; 'BC Labor Hits Combines Probe,' *Pacific Tribune*, 8 June 1956; 'Combines Probe Arouses Storm' and 'Westminster CCF Protests Probe,' *Pacific Tribune*, 15 June 1956; 'Irwin Raps "Stupidity" of Combines Probe,' *Pacific Tribune*, 22 June 1956; 'Protest Rises against Probe,' *Tribune*, 29 June 1956. Initiated under pressure of the Gillnetters Association and major fishing firms, the investigation centred on whether or not the UFAWU represented an unlawful 'conspiracy,' and whether or not fishers were actually workers. The companies had always argued that because they owned their own boats, fishers were 'co-adventurers' rather than workers, a view confirmed in the precedent-setting 1946 case between the Zwicker Company and the Canadian Fishermen's Union in Nova Scotia. The UFAWU argued, however, that boats were simply tools in the fishing trade, 'whether the traditional rowboat of yesteryear or today's costly power vessel with its modern electronic equipment.' The investigators found in favour of the company, concluding the fishers had engaged in a conspiracy in restraint of trade; no further action was taken, however, when the UFAWU pointed out that the true combine in BC was the monopoly controlled by George Weston Ltd and the Canadian Fishing Company. North, *A Ripple, a Wave*, 40–1; Stevens and Knight, *Homer Stevens*, 101; A.W.R. Carrothers, *The Labour Injunction in British Columbia: A Study of the Operation of the Injunction in Labour-Management Disputes in British Columbia, 1946–1955 with Particular Reference to the Law of Picketing* (Toronto and Montreal: CCH Canadian Ltd., 1956), 145–7.

87 This allegation appears in Al King's biography, which states: '[Harvey] Murphy always charged that Mine Mill was sold to the Steelworkers for $50,000 – that that's what it cost for the CCL to sanction the raid on Mine Mill. The CCL never denied it.' King, *Red Bait!*, 76, also 77–84; 'Mine-Mill Union at Trail Wins Backing,' *Fisherman*, 4 April 1950; 'Battle with Murphy Costs Half-Million,' *Sun*, 22 Sept. 1951; Francis 'Buddy' DeVito, 'We're Still Here,' in Mercedes Steedman et al., eds., *Hard Lessons: The Mine Mill Union in the Canadian Labour Movement* (Toronto: Dundurn, 1995), 162. Between the wars, Trail was dominated by a company union, but communist organizer Arthur 'Slim' Evans made inroads in the late 1930s. In 1944, Mine-Mill achieved certification as a result of PC 1003, which required employers to

recognize unions and outlawed company unions. The first collective agreement was negotiated in 1944. See King, *Red Bait!*, 34–51; Mike Solski and John Smaller, *Mine Mill: The History of the International Union of Mine, Mill and Smelter Workers in Canada since 1895* (Ottawa: Steel Rail, 1984), 33–53.

88 Harvey Murphy address, *UFAWU Proceedings*, 24–9 March 1952, Vancouver, 11, Neish papers; also Scott, *A Communist Life*, 96–7. The executive defection was announced in a full-page ad, 'We're Staying with CIO-CCL,' *Trail-Times*, 9 Feb 1950; 'Ousted Mine Union Men Assail CIO-CCL,' *Sun*, 20 Feb. 1950.

89 As quoted in Solski and Smaller, *Mine Mill*, 50; see also King, *Red Bait!*, 70–9.

90 'Steel Raid Stymied, Defeat for Disruption,' *Fisherman*, 16 May 1950; Burton to Dowson, 8 March 1950, file 9-2 'Trail, BC 1949–1950,' vol. 2, Canadian Trotskyist Movement fonds (hereafter CTM fonds), series IV 11, MG 28, LAC; 'Raiding Methods Hit,' *Fisherman*, 10 Oct. 1950; 'Labor Backs Mine Mill,' *Fisherman*, 18 April 1950; 'Union Raiding Vicious, Deserves Condemnation' and 'Anti-Raiding Conference Friday,' *Fisherman*, 11 April 1950.

91 'Labor Board Queried,' *Sun*, 1 Aug. 1950.

92 Dowson to Burton, 28 May 1950, file 9-2, vol. 2, CTM fonds, LAC.

93 Murphy address, *UFAWU Proceedings* (1952), 11, Neish papers; Rosslund (Burton) to Dowson, 5 Aug. 1950; *Mine-Mill Bulletin* (Trail), 1 Sept. 1950, file 9-2, vol 2, CTM fonds, LAC.

94 'Union Expulsion First at CCL National Meet,' *Fisherman*, 17 Oct. 1950; Solski and Smaller, *Mine Mill*, 33–40; Steedman et al., eds., *Hard Lessons*. The same convention voted to expel the entire Canadian section of the Electrical, Radio and Machine Workers' Union.

95 Rush, *We Have a Glowing Dream*, 165; 'How a Red Union Bosses Atom Workers at Trail, BC,' *Maclean's Magazine* (Toronto), 67:7 (1 April 1951), 7–9 and 57–8. See also 'BC in Running for Heavy Water,' *Sun*, 12 April 1966; C.D. Andrews, 'Cominco and the Manhattan Project,' *BC Studies*, 11 (Fall 1971), 51–62.

96 'The Red Threat to Our Pacific Gateway,' *Financial Post* (Toronto), 12 Dec. 1953.

97 King, *Red Bait!*, 111; Solski and Smaller, *Mine Mill*, 42.

98 Murphy address, *UFAWU Proceedings* (1952), 8–9, Neish papers; 'Battle with Murphy Costs Half-Million,' *Sun*, 22 Sept. 1951.

99 Jack Phillips interview, with Dave Werlin and Don Bouzek, 8–9 March 2003, Alberta Labour History Institute.

100 'Fight for Democracy Say Barred Unionists,' *Fisherman*, 3 Oct. 1950.
101 Ibid.
102 'Civic Workers Stick Up for Right to Elect Officers, Run Own Affairs,' *Fisherman*, 14 Nov. 1950; 'Union Executive, Three Locals Vote Disapproval of TLC Policy,' *Fisherman*, 7 Nov. 1950; 'UFAWU Attacks Actions of Berg,' *Fisherman*, 15 Nov. 1950; 'Sets Up Dual Union, Wants 28's Records,' *Fisherman*, 5 Dec. 1950.
103 'Parks Board Employee Reports Members Are Sticking to Union,' *Fisherman*, 21 Nov. 1950; 'Sets Up Dual Union, Wants 28's Records,' *Fisherman*, 5 Dec. 1950; 'TLC Bars Local 28 Delegates, Unionists Becoming "Fed Up,"' *Fisherman*, 12 Dec. 1950; Jack Phillips interview, 8–9 March 2003.
104 'IWA Chiefs Seek Power to Bar Reds,' *Sun*, 20 Jan. 1955.
105 'George Lakusta Addresses the Jury,' n.d. [c. 1960], file 23-03, 'BC provincial series,' reel H1592, CPC fonds, LAC.
106 'UAW Local Calls for Parley of Whole Union on Edict,' *Canadian Tribune*, 12 March 1951; file 'Canadian Seamen's Union – Vancouver, BC,' vol. 2285, series A, RCMP Security Service, CSIS records, LAC; 'Communist Attempts to Organize on West Coast Ships Unsuccessful,' *Colonist*, 25 July 1951; Green, *Against the Tide*, 293.
107 'Union Wreckers Linked to RCMP,' *Pacific Tribune*, 20 Jan. 1956.
108 Ibid.; 'McCuish Gets 15-Year Gag,' *Pacific Tribune*, 17 Feb. 1956.
109 'RCMP Charged with Intimidatory Visits,' *Pacific Tribune*, 20 Jan. 1956.
110 'Big Business Backs Kuzych,' *Pacific Tribune*, 20 Jan. 1956.
111 Ibid.; also Ian MacDonald, 'Class Conflict and Political Factionalism: A History of Local 213 of the International Brotherhood of Electrical Workers, 1901–1961,' MA thesis, Simon Fraser University, 1986.
112 'Expelled Unionist Gets Interim Injunction,' *Pacific Tribune*, 1 June 1956.
113 'Kuzych Case Decision Threat to Unions,' *Fisherman*, 20 June 1950; 'Shipyard Union's Legality Attacked,' *Sun*, 22 Feb. 1950; White, *A Hard Man to Beat*, 132–46. Jack Scott offers a different interpretation of the Kuzych case in Scott, *A Communist Life*, 114–17.
114 'Big Business Backs Kuzych,' *Pacific Tribune*, 20 Jan. 1956.
115 'Union Wreckers Linked to RCMP,' *Pacific Tribune*, 20 Jan. 1956.
116 'McCarthyist Motion Would Limit Affiliation to New Congress,' *Pacific Tribune*, 10 Feb. 1956.
117 '"Reds Build Springboard" – Alsbury Says Communists Major Threat in BC,' *Sun*, 13 Feb. 1956; also 'Third of BC Unionists Bow to Reds,' *Province*, 11 Feb. 1956; 'BC Red Unionists "Toe Moscow Line,"' *Sun*, 14 Feb. 1956; 'Reds Found in All Ranks of Society,' *Sun*, 15 Feb. 1956; 'Communists Die Hard, Says Alsbury,' *Sun*, 16 Feb. 1956.

118 'Labor Unity Real Alsbury Target,' *Pacific Tribune*, 24 Feb. 1956; 'Labor Council Refuses to Censure Alsbury,' *Sun*, 15 Feb. 1956.
119 Ibid.
120 'Alsbury's Articles Held "Comfort to Employers,"' *Pacific Tribune*, 9 March 1956.
121 'Why Labor Must Have Annual Conventions,' *Pacific Tribune*, 10 Feb. 1956.
122 'McCarthyite Section Stirs Protest at CLC Parley,' *Pacific Tribune*, 27 April 1956; also 'United Labor Million Strong,' *Pacific Tribune*, 27 April 1956.
123 Whitaker and Marcuse, *Cold War Canada*, 364–83; *Canada's Party of Socialism*, 218.
124 'Open Letter to Mr. Philpott,' *Fisherman*, 1 Aug. 1950; also 'People of Canada Join Fight for World Peace,' *Fisherman*, 18 July 1950; Tim Buck to 'Comrades,' 16 Aug. 1950, file 2, box 26; 'LPP Demands Peace in Korea,' 26 Jan. 1951, file 1, box 4, MSS 179, Robert S. Kenny Collection, University of Toronto Fisher Rare Book Library (hereafter Fisher Library); 'Endicott to Speak in City,' *Pacific Tribune*, 6 Feb. 1948; also 'Chiang Kai-Shek Kills Unionist,' *Fisherman*, 22 Oct. 1948; 'Workers Strike, Chiang Totters,' *Fisherman*, 19 Nov. 1948; 'Canada Scuttles UN for War Alliance' and '"Marshall Plan" Markets,' *Pacific Tribune*, 12 Nov. 1948.
125 'Viet Nam Fights for Freedom,' *Pacific Tribune*, 27 Feb. 1948; also 'Britain Snubs Russia, Backs Indo-China's Anti-Red Gov't,' *Sun*, 7 Feb. 1950; Harry Rankin, *Rankin's Law: Recollections of a Radical* (Vancouver: November House, 1975), 76.
126 'Report of the BC Council to the YCL Convention,' n.d. [c. 1962], file 53-04 'Correspondence Re: British Columbia 1961–1962', vol. 53, series IV-4, MG 28, CPC fonds, LAC.
127 'Lauds UFAWU Peace Stand,' *Fisherman*, 15 Aug. 1950; also 'British Trade Unionists Describe Visit to Russia,' *Fisherman*, 12 Sept. 1950.
128 In March 1950, representatives from fifty-two countries assembled in Stockholm for the World Peace Committee meetings and issued the appeal. In May, 1,700 delegates endorsed the Stockholm Appeal at the Canadian Peace Conference, Toronto. 'Conference Seeks 75,000 Names for Peace,' *Fisherman*, 6 June 1950; 'Introduction to the Report of the Canadian Peace Congress,' 6 May 1950, file 'WIUC–Vancouver, BC,' vol. 2285, series A, RCMP Security Service, CSIS records, LAC. According to a report in the *Fisherman*, 471,119 signatures were collected by 11 November 1950, though no BC breakdown is provided. Maurice Rush, however, writes in his memoirs that 200,000 signatures were collected across Canada by the end of 1950, and nearly 300,000 by the end of 1951. See 'Nearly 500,000 Canucks Endorse Peace Appeal,' *Fisherman*, 5 Dec. 1950; Rush, *We Have*

a Glowing Dream, 98 fn12. Also *Peace* (Trail), 23 Aug. 1950, Rossland-Trail Peace Committee Bulletin No. 2, file 9-2, vol. 2, CTM fonds, LAC; 'Conference Seeks 75,000 Names for Peace,' *Fisherman*, 6 June 1950; 'People of Canada Join Fight for World Peace,' *Fisherman*, 18 July 1950; 'Peace Signers Total 224 Millions,' *Fisherman*, 8 Aug. 1950; 'Hiroshima was atom-bombed five years ago … No Hiroshimas for Canada – Sign the Petition' (Advertisement for the Canadian Peace Congress), *Fisherman*, 15 Aug. 1950; 'Complete All Petitions, Must Be In by October 2,' *Fisherman*, 19 Sept. 1950; 'Peace Petition Drive Extended Full Month,' *Fisherman*, 3 Oct. 1950.

129 Burton to Dowson, 3 April 1950, file 9-2, vol. 2, CTM fonds, LAC.

130 'Don't Be a Blind Signer,' *Sun*, 28 July 1950; 'Idealists, Idiots and Traitors,' *Province*, 28 July 1950; 'Why Don't Dailies Want A-Bomb Ban?' *Fisherman*, 1 Aug. 1950; 'People of Canada Join Fight for World Peace,' *Fisherman*, 18 July 1950; 'Subversive Activities in the Woodworkers Industrial Union of Canada,' 27 Nov. 1950, file 'WIUC–Cranbrook, BC,' vol. 2285, series A, RCMP Security Service, CSIS records, LAC. In September 1951, the *Sun* claimed: 'The A-Bomb is the greatest single factor which may prevent outbreak of war in the near future … Russia has a big enough land force to march to the English Channel "any time they want to," but would not, because our knowledge of atomic warfare is much greater.' 'A-Bomb Seen War Stopper,' *Sun*, 22 Sept. 1951.

131 'Peace Drive Continues Despite Arrests,' *Fisherman*, 15 Aug. 1950. Charges of 'obstructing a police officer' against Phillips and the others were dismissed by a Vancouver magistrate. 'Peace Petitioner Wins Case against "Obstruction" Charge,' *Fisherman*, 17 Oct. 1950. Similar police action against 'Ban-the-Bomb' campaigning occurred in Toronto. See 'Toronto Cops Beat Vet for Peace Petitioning' and 'Brutal Police Beating Described by Petitioner,' *Fisherman*, 5 Sept. 1950.

132 'Open Letter to Mr. Philpott,' *Fisherman*, 1 Aug. 1950. Philpott ran as an Independent, capturing 6,583 votes to Rush's 637. Liberal candidate William Mott won the election with 8,727 votes, while CCF candidate Ronald William Irvine finished third with 5,769 votes and the Progressive Conservative, Leslie Christmas, finished fourth with 3,068 votes. See *Canadian Parliamentary Guide*, 1949.

133 'Blessed Are the Peacemakers,' *Fisherman*, 23 May 1950; also Rankin, *Rankin's Law*, 75. Responding to the Dean of Canterbury's public association with BC peace activists, Victoria resident Frank H. Partridge wrote a letter of protest to British Prime Minister Clement Atlee in July 1951. 'Victoria Man Tells Atlee Views on Dean,' *Colonist*, 24 July 1951.

134 See Rankin, *Rankin's Law*, 76.

135 Mark Kristmanson, 'I Came to Sing: Paul Robeson on the Border,' *Plateaus of Freedom*, 181, 211, 226. Kristmanson argues that 'the security forces know better that the nation is constituted far less stably than it appears to be. Short of actual war, it maintains itself restlessly by fear, distrust, rumours, and selective memories, and by sensing, surveillance, subterfuge, sabotage, and secrecy.' See Paul Robeson, *The Peace Arch Concerts* (Folk Era Records, 1998); Laurel Sefton MacDowell, 'Paul Robeson in Canada: A Border Story,' *Labour/Le Travail*, 51 (Spring 2003), 177–221; Murphy address, *UFAWU Proceedings* (1952), Vancouver, 13, Neish papers; *Canada's Party of Socialism*, 183; King, *Red Bait!*, 114–18. Robeson's passport had been revoked in 1950 after he refused to sign an anti-communist declaration. While US citizens did not require passports to enter Canada, US border officials prevented Robeson from entering Canada to perform at the 1952 Mine-Mill concert in Vancouver.

136 'Robeson Bar Stirs Up Storm,' *Pacific Tribune*, 20 April 1956; 'Robeson Gets Ovation on Return to Toronto after Five-Year Ban,' *Pacific Tribune*, 17 Feb. 1956. Also 'My Fight for a Passport,' *Pacific Tribune*, 13 July 1956.

137 *Canada's Party of Socialism*, 219–20; Rankin, *Rankin's Law*, 76; also Cheddi Jagan, *Forbidden Freedom: The Story of British Guiana* (London: Lawrence and Wishart, 1954) and *The West on Trial: The Fight for Guyana's Freedom* (London: Michael Joseph, 1966). Antonios 'Tony' Ambatielos, secretary of the Greek Maritime Workers' Federation, visited Vancouver in April 1969, after he was imprisoned for eighteen years and stripped of his citizenship by the Junta. See Club Bulletin No. 4, 19 March 1969, file 23-38, 'BC provincial series,' reel H1592, CPC fonds, LAC.

138 'Buck Addresses Soviet Communist Congress,' *Pacific Tribune*, 24 Feb. 1956.

139 Scott, *A Communist Life*, 131.

140 King, *Red Bait!*, 120–2; Tickson interview, 20 July 2005; Griffin interview, 11 Aug. 2005; Swankey interview, 14 Aug. 2005.

141 'Covert Measures-Check Mate-"D" Operation,' 21 March 1956, vol. 130, accession 1992–93/251, access request AH-1998–00059, Records of the McDonald Commission, RG 33/128, LAC, as quoted in Steve Hewitt, *Spying 101: The RCMP's Secret Activities at Canadian Universities, 1917–1999* (Toronto: University of Toronto Press, 2002), 31; vols. 1993–2285, series A, RCMP Security Service, CSIS records, LAC; *Civil Liberties Digest* (Vancouver Branch, League for Democratic Rights), 1955–6, vol. 3521; *Magyar Hirado* (BC Hungarian Newsreel), 1957–8, vol. 3523, Registry Files, RCMP Security Records, RG 18 F-3, LAC.

142 *Canada's Party of Socialism*, 190–1. During the 1953 federal election, the CCF declared in its program that 'to outlaw communism and to engage in "McCarthyism" and witch-hunting is to weaken the very freedoms we are trying to protect.' See 'CCF Federal Program,' 11 March 1953, file 'Elections 1953 – Slogans (1952–1953),' vol. 131, CCF-NDP fonds, LAC.

143 'Confusing Civil Liberty with Treason Legislation,' *Sun*, 26 Jan. 1954.

144 In 1954, the Victoria Trades and Labour Council (TLC) received correspondence from Jack Phillips, secretary of the League for Democratic Rights, urging 'a Bill of Rights for Canada' that would guarantee 'the right to freedom from discrimination; the right to freedom of speech; assembly, association and religion; the right to citizenship, personal liberty, fair trial and equality before the law; the right to petition and to government by the people.' Minutes, 3 Feb. 1954, box 5, series IV, accession 80–59, Victoria Labour Council fonds, UVASC; *Canada's Party of Socialism*, 191.

145 'RCMP Intimidation Aired in Legislature,' *Pacific Tribune*, 4 Mar 1955.

146 Griffin interview, 11 Aug. 2005. Rankin does not mention threats against his wife, but recalls the presence of the 'Red surveillance squad' at rallies during the Rosenberg-Sobell trials. Rankin, *Rankin's Law*, 104.

147 Griffin interview, 11 Aug. 2005; Tom McEwen, *He Wrote for Us: The Story of Bill Bennett, Pioneer Socialist Journalist* (Vancouver: Tribune Publishing Company, 1951), 152–3.

148 Tickson interview, 20 July 2005.

149 'Marshall Issues Statement,' *Daily Times*, 27 Jan. 1954; 'Book-Burning Plan Blamed on Murdoch,' *Daily Times*, 26 Jan. 1954; 'Library Association Asks Marshall Hearing,' *Daily Times*, 28 Jan. 1954. See also various materials in *The Marshall case, Victoria, BC, 1954: news clippings, correspondence and some related documents connected with the intellectual freedom conflict between the Victoria Public Library Board and librarian John Marshall* (1998), compiled and annotated by Phillip Teece, O25.213 MAR, Local History Collection, Greater Victoria Public Library.

150 Transcript of 'Broadcast by Elgin Neish – Feb 5, 1954 – 6:55 a.m. – CKDA,' file 'Book Burning 1950s,' Neish papers. At the time, Neish was a candidate for city alderman. He challenged the Junior Chamber of Commerce to disclose on 'whose authority they set themselves up as an un-American activities committee.' The organization responded, declaring that 'Elgin Neish by his own many statements and actions has clearly shown where his sympathies and beliefs lie.' Neish interpreted this as confirmation of the Jaycees' 'persecution of citizens who are so bold as to disagree with them.' See 'Jaycees' Activities Challenged,' *Colonist*, 29 Jan. 1954;

'Jaycees Attack Neish, Critic of Red Expose,' *Daily Times*, 30 Jan. 1954; 'Statement by Elgin Neish,' 1 Feb. 1954, file 'Book Burning 1950s,' Neish papers. See also 'Librarian Tenders Her Resignation,' *Colonist*, 4 Feb. 1954; 'Three Board Members Go "Or I Go,"' Says Librarian,' *Daily Times*, 4 Feb. 1954; 'What's It All About,' *Colonist*, 5 Feb. 1954.

151 'Library Stocks May Be Combed for Red-Tainted Literature,' *Daily Times*, 27 Jan. 1956; also 'Book-Burning Plan Blamed on Murdoch,' *Daily Times*, 26 Jan. 1954; 'Victoria Mayor Hit Over "Book Burning,"' *Sun*, 28 Jan. 1954; 'Reeves' Right to Vote Sought on City-Ruled Library Board' and 'Junior Chamber Opposes "Book-Burning" Proposal,' *Daily Times*, 28 Jan. 1954; '"Misrepresented," Mayor Claims'; 'Mayor's Library Nominee Ousted after Bitter Battle'; 'Murdoch Seeks Help of RCMP'; 'Legislature May Hear Book-Burning Dispute'; 'Mrs. Lougheed Claims Press Uses Communistic Methods,' *Colonist*, 29 Jan. 1954; 'BC Group Opposes Book-Burning,' *Colonist*, 29 Jan. 1954; various letters on the topic 'Censorship,' *Colonist*, 29 Jan. 1954; 'Marshall Case before Board on Wednesday,' *Daily Times*, 3 Feb. 1954; 'Citizens Cry Halt to "Book Burnings,"' *Daily Times*, 27 Jan. 1954; 'CCF Group Protests Marshall's Dismissal,' *Daily Times*, 28 Jan. 1954. The Victoria Trades and Labour Council (TLC) went on record calling 'for the resignation of the Mayor and Alderman Murdoch because of the very bad publicity created through his attitude and reported remarks on book-burning.' Minutes, 3 Feb. 1954, box 5, series IV, accession 80–59, Victoria Labour Council fonds, UVASC. W.A.C. Bennett, meanwhile, steered clear of the controversy, saying: 'I am 100 per cent opposed to what people call McCarthyism and witch-hunting.' 'Bennett Keeps Clear of Battle of Books,' *Daily Times*, 30 Jan. 1954.

152 'Library Stocks May Be Combed for Red-Tainted Literature,' *Daily Times*, 27 Jan. 1954. John Marshall was belatedly vindicated, in 1998, when the Greater Victoria Library Board issued a formal apology to the then-seventy-three-year-old retired professor of library science. Marshall and his wife, Betsy English, flew from Toronto for a ceremony where the apology was publicly provided by the Board's chairperson. The BC Library Association renamed its Intellectual Freedom Award the John Marshall Award. See 'Library Puts Cold War to Rest,' *Victoria News*, 23 Oct. 1998; 'The 1954 Marshall Case,' *Check It Out* magazine (Victoria), (Winter 1999), 6–9. In possession of author.

153 Legal Professions Act Amendment Act, S.B.C. 1948, c. 36, s. 17.

154 'Law Society Lifts Ban Placed on Student Vet,' *Pacific Tribune*, 6 Aug. 1948; also W. Wesley Pue, 'Banned from Lawyering: William John Gordon Mar-

tin, Communist,' *BC Studies*, 162 (Summer 2009), 111–36; Rankin, *Rankin's Law*, 68–9; Whitaker and Marcuse, *Cold War Canada*, 228–90.

155 Rankin, *Rankin's Law*, 72; also 61–72, 207–19.

156 *Canada's Party of Socialism*, 214; Maurice Rush interview, with author, 26 Feb. 2006, North Vancouver, BC.

157 Neish interview, 11 May 2006. Communist-influenced cultural activities were described despairingly by Tom Alsbury in 'Reds Found in All Ranks of Society,' *Sun*, 15 Feb. 1956; also 'The Red Threat to Our Pacific Gateway,' *Financial Post*, 12 Dec. 1953. The formation of ethnic federations in the CPC – among Ukrainians, Jews, and Finns – is described in William Rodney, *Soldiers of the International: A History of the Communist Party of Canada, 1919–1929* (Toronto: University of Toronto Press, 1968); Penner, *Canadian Communism*, 268–84. For youth organizations, see 'Report of the BC Council to the YCL Convention,' n.d. [c. 1962], file 53-04 'Correspondence Re: British Columbia 1961–1962', vol. 53, series IV-4.

158 Boyd to Neish, 4 May 1961; 'Exclusion Proceedings Under Section 235(c) of the Immigration and Nationality Act, re NEISH, Elgin,' file 'Letter barring Scotty from USA,' Neish papers. The provisions of the Immigration and Nationality Act (McCarran-Walter Act, 1952) barring entry into the United States on ideological grounds were not repealed until 1990.

159 Neish interview, 11 May 2006.

160 Tickson interview, 9 Aug. 2005.

161 'Put the People's Interests First!,' LPP Victoria Constituency Leaflet, Nov. 1953, file 23-01, 'BC provincial series,' reel H1592, CPC fonds, LAC. In the by-election, held on 24 Nov. 1953 to provide a seat for Social Credit Finance Minister Einar Gunderson, Blakey received a meagre 161 votes, or 0.8 per cent of total, compared to 8,456 votes (41.3 per cent) for the Liberal candidate, who narrowly defeat Gunderson (40.9 per cent). CCF candidate Alfred Matthews received 2,495 votes (12.1 per cent) See British Columbia, *Statement of Votes*, 1953.

162 Tickson interview, 9 Aug. 2005; 'Unity at Polls Vital – Buck' and 'Convention Plans for Election of CCF Govn't,' *Pacific Tribune*, 19 March 1948.

163 'This Congress Will Go Down in History,' *Pacific Tribune*, 23 March 1956; also 'LPP Resolution on CPSU 20th Congress,' *Pacific Tribune*, 25 May 1956; 'CPSU Replies to Criticism,' *Pacific Tribune*, 13 July 1956. Originally, the *Tribune* reported only on Russia's glowing achievements under the Five-Year Plan. See 'USSR Planning Great Advances,' *Pacific Tribune*, 24 Feb. 1956.

164 Scott, *A Communist Life*, 131. According to Jack Scott, the Canadian del-

egation consisted of Morgan, Buck, Leslie Morris, and William Kashtan. Gregory Kealey adds Stanley Ryerson. See Gregory S. Kealey, 'Stanley Bréhaut Ryerson: Canadian Revolutionary Intellectual,' *Studies in Political Economy*, 8 (Summer 1982), 14–24.

165 'Khrushchev Talk on Stalin Bares Details of Rule Based on Terror; Charges Plot for Kremlin Purges,' *New York Times*, 5 June 1956.

166 Prior to the Hungarian crisis, dissent in the Soviet bloc was revealed when riots broke out among workers in Poznan, Poland. 'Riots Won't Bar Wider Democracy,' *Pacific Tribune*, 6 July 1956; 'Public Probe of Polish Riots,' *Pacific Tribune*, 13 July 1956.

167 'CPSU 20th Congress,' *Pacific Tribune*, 20 July 1956.

168 'UJPO Asks Full Facts of Anti-Jewish Crimes,' *Pacific Tribune*, 18 May 1956; Gerald Tulchinsky, 'Family Quarrel: Joe Salsberg, the "Jewish" Question, and Canadian Communism,' *Labour/Le Travail*, 56 (Fall 2005), 149–73; Scott, *A Communist Life*, 132–3.

169 *Canada's Party of Socialism*, 193.

170 At a National Committee meeting in May 1956, the 'revisionists' were in the minority, but succeeded in restoring Joe Salsberg to the National Executive Committee (NEC), reversing a 1953 decision that had removed Salsberg because of alleged Zionist sympathies. Salsberg's return gave the 'revisionists' a majority on the NEC and control over the *Canadian Tribune*. On 18 June 1956, the *Tribune* printed the entire text of Khrushchev's speech, which the orthodox 'Leninist' group alleged had been doctored by the CIA. At the end of June, the 'revisionist'-dominated NEC issued a statement criticizing the Soviet Communist Party for failing to provide a Marxist explanation of Stalinism. In August, the NEC called a special plenum of the National Committee to discuss growing disunity in the party, and opened the party press to discussion on the issue. A commission was struck to investigate the 1947 expulsion of three leading Quebec members, which the Quebec LPP executive considered a 'Canadian counterpart' to the anti-democratic practices exposed by Khrushchev. The expulsions had stemmed from the 'incorrect practice' of applying 'administrative measures' to solve 'ideological differences,' the commission concluded. Dissent in the Quebec LPP mushroomed into a wholesale rejection of the Leninist principle of 'democratic centralism,' the cornerstone of decision-making and leadership in the various Communist parties. Guy Caron called for 'a decisive break with the ideological subservience to the CPSU,' rejected the principle of proletarian dictatorship, and proposed the LPP's transformation into an educational association akin to former American Communist leader Earl Browder's Communist Political

Association. On 15 October, Caron and five other Quebec LPP executive members left the party. On 28 October, the special plenum of the LPP National Committee convened in Toronto. Buck, Kashtan, Salsberg, Leslie Morris, William Kardash, and Stanley Ryerson had returned from Moscow, where they discussed Khrushchev's revelations with CPSU leaders, including Khrushchev. However, the 'revisionist' NEC was divided on its interpretation of the Moscow delegation's report, and prior to the Toronto plenum demanded Buck's resignation as party secretary and replacement by a three-member secretariat pending the next convention. 'LPP Explain Re-election of Salsberg on Executive Body,' *Pacific Tribune*, 13 July 1956; Buck to National Committee members, 6 July 1956, file 2, box 26, MSS 179, Kenny Collection, Fisher Library; Tulchinsky, 'Family Quarrel,' 156–9; *Canada's Party of Socialism*, 193–207; Avakumovic, *The Communist Party in Canada*, 224–34; Penner, *Canadian Communism*, 241–8; Kealey, 'Stanley Brehaut Ryerson: Canadian Revolutionary Intellectual,' 14–24; Isserman, *If I Had a Hammer*, 5–6 and 11–14; Scott, *A Communist Life*, 131.

171 Scott, *A Communist Life*, 131.

172 Tickson interview, 9 Aug. 2005.

173 Swankey interview, 10 June 2005. At the 1958 BC convention, the first he attended since moving from Alberta, Swankey was elected to serve on the BC provincial committee. Across Canada, dissent erupted. Toronto organizer Norman Penner, son of Winnipeg alderman Jacob Penner, called for closer cooperation with the CCF and advocated the LPP's democratization, including referenda on major issues and 'democratic debates': 'We have become highly institutionalized, we have made organization our chief concern instead of ideology, and have built ourselves into a tight, closely knit party along Stalin's lines.' Ontario LPP leader Stewart Smith, once a firm Buck ally, called for 'a new socialist alignment' not tied to Marxism-Leninism. Toronto communist Robert Laxer rejected the dictatorship of the proletariat and advocated the parliamentary path to socialism, suggesting the LPP had failed 'to see that the qualitative change to socialism will be the result of quantitative changes.' 'Norman Penner's Amendment,' n.d. [c. 1956], file 6, box 4, Kenny Collection, Fisher Library; *Canada's Party of Socialism*, 198–9; Penner, *Canadian Communism*, 245; Avakumovic, *The Communist Party in Canada*, 231.

174 Penner, *Canadian Communism*, 244. The thirteen-day plenum, which opened on 28 October 1956, was marked by sharp divisions, with Buck defending democratic centralism and accusing those who advocated cooperation with the CCF of 'revisionism,' since the CCF was not a Marxist party. Midway through the plenum, Soviet military intervention

in Hungary intensified the conflict. To some LPP members, it was proof that '"Stalinism" had not died with Stalin.' The Hungarian issue was so divisive that plenum delegates abstained from taking a position, instead referring the question to the incoming NEC. Tulchinsky, 'Family Quarrel,' 160.

175 Avakumovich, *The Communist Party in Canada*, 229–30; *Canada's Party of Socialism*, 200–3; Penner, *Canadian Communism*, 244–5.

176 Scott, *A Communist Life*, 131; Avakumovic, *The Communist Party in Canada*, 231–2. An article by McEwen attacking Salsberg appeared in *National Affairs Monthly* (Toronto), April 1957, 4–5. For the burning of the contentious *Tribune* supplement, see Penner, *Canadian Communism*, 242–4.

177 *Canada's Party of Socialism*, 204–5; 'Resolution Introduced by JB Salsberg – Toronto,' n.d. [c. 1957], file 6, box 4, Kenny Collection, Fisher Library. Salsberg called on the upcoming LPP convention to pledge 'itself to support the Socialist gains in Hungary' and allow Imre Nagy and comrades Rakosi and Geroe 'the full opportunity to defend themselves and to explain their policies and actions not only to the Hungarian people but also the working class of the world.'

178 Penner, *Canadian Communism*, 247; *Canada's Party of Socialism*, 205–6; 'Keynote Speech of Tim Buck,' April 1956, file 7, box 4, Kenny Collection, Fisher Library; also 'Proposed Rules and Order for 6th National LPP Convention,' 1 April 1957; 'Memorandum prepared by NEC for delegates to convention,' n.d. [c. 1957]; 'Resolution from the National Jewish Committee, LPP (Resident Board),' n.d. [c. 1957], file 7, box 4; 'Resolution Introduced by JB Salsberg – Toronto,' n.d. [c. 1957]; 'Draft Programmatic Statement,' n.d. [c. 1957]; 'Decision on the LPP Program,' 19–22 April 1957, file 6, box 4, Kenny Collection, Fisher Library. Voting on the draft policy resolution reflected the uneven strength of the 'Leninist' and 'revisionist' camps: 122 delegates voted in favour with only 20 delegates opposed. In balloting for the 51-member National Committee, Smith and Salsberg received the fewest votes of the 83 delegates nominated. 'The revisionists were reduced to a tiny minority on the incoming NC,' the official history records.

179 'General Resolutions,' 4 April 1957; 'Proposed amendments to the party constitution,. 4 April 1957; 'Resolution on Draft Policy Resolution and Amendments' and 'Resolutions to Draft Policy Resolution,' n.d. [c. 1957], file 7, box 4, Kenny Collection, Fisher Library.

180 'Mad-Dog Faction Leaves Trail of Wreckage,' *Advocate* (Toronto), April 1957, in file 57-11, Dowson fonds, LAC.

181 'Stalinism Canadian Type,' n.d. [c. 1958], 8; 'Notes on LPP Convention,' n.d. [1957], file 57-11, Dowson fonds, LAC.

182 'RCMP Activities Violate Civil Rights,' *Pacific Tribune*, 20 July 1956; File 'Covert Measures – Check Mate – "D" Operation,' 21 March 1956, box 130, accession 1992–93/251, access request AH-1998–00059, Records of the McDonald Commission, RG 33/128, LAC; as quoted in Hewitt, *Spying 101*, 31. This tactic was rare, Hewitt suggests: 'Instead, monitoring and gathering intelligence on the activities of targeted organizations and individuals became the usual activity of Canada's national police. The procedures that were utilized included opening mail, tapping telephone lines, and planting listening devices.'

183 Scott, *A Communist Life*, 137–9.

184 Swankey interview, 10 June 2005; *Canada's Party of Socialism*, 210; Buck to LPP members, June 1959, file 2, box 26, Kenny Collection, Fisher Library.

185 Griffin interview, 11 Aug. 2005.

186 Morgan to Tom Morris (YCL national secretary), 29 Jan. 1962; Morris to Morgan, 5 Feb. 1962; Glyn to Tom [Morris], n.d. [c. 1962]; Tom [Morris] to Glyn, 5 Feb. 1962; 'Provincial Council Meeting,' 9 Jan. 1962; 'BC Council Meeting,' 23 Jan. 1962; 'Advance Report,' n.d. [c. 1962]; 'Provincial Council Meeting,' 13 Feb. 1962, file 53-04, vol. 53, CPC fonds, LAC. On 13 February 1962, the BC Provincial Council of the YCL approved a resolution stating: 'That we send a letter to Nat. office saying that we recognize our mistake on the Dec. issue distribution as a breach of democratic centralism; and that we schedule an educational on democratic centralism in Prov. Council.'

187 Scott, *A Communist Life*, 149, 152. Scott reiterates this point: 'China was not central ... Our position was us versus the Party leadership on the question of a programme for Canada.'

188 Statement of BC Provincial Executive Regarding Dissolution of 'Special Club,' 8 July 1964, file 'China-Soviet Split/CP Expulsions,' Neish papers; Scott, *A Communist Life*, 142–4

189 Scott, *A Communist Life*, 140–8; Scott, *Canadian Workers, American Unions*, 206–7. According to Scott, the party leadership supported the Norris Commission's recommendation to place the SIU under a government-appointed trusteeship, a stance mirrored by the CLC. Scott and other dissidents, however, agreed 'the corruption has to end, but it's got to be done by the trade union movement, not by the government, and particularly not by a government that was responsible for the goddamn situation in the first place' [by bringing Hal Banks into Canada].

190 Scott, *A Communist Life*, 149–52; Ronald C. Keith, *The Diplomacy of Zhou Enlai* (Houndsmills: Macmillan, 1989), 112–13; 'Chinese and Soviet Letters on Current Differences in the World Communist Movement,' 'Open Letter of the Central Committee of the Communist Party of the Soviet Union,' and 'The Struggle for Peace Is the Supreme Duty,' *Pacific Tribune Special Supplement*, 26 June 1963; *Canada's Party of Socialism*, 223–8. For the earlier Tito-Stalin split, see 'Tito's Tactics,' *Pacific Tribune*, 23 July 1948; 'A Socialist View of World Affairs,' *CCF News*, 1 July 1948. In January 1969, the Sino-Soviet conflict assumed military proportions when Soviet and Chinese forces clashed on Damansky Island in the Ussuri River, the boundary between the two socialist states. See 'China: Cultural Revolution or Counter-Revolutionary Coup,' *Pacific Tribune Special Supplement*, 21 March 1969.

191 Scott, *A Communist Life*, 149–54.

192 See Text of Sino-India Border Dispute Speech, file 'China-Soviet Split/CP Expulsions,' Neish papers; Scott, *A Communist Life*, 155.

193 Scott, *A Communist Life*, 155.

194 Statement of BC Provincial Executive CPC Re Expulsion of Jack Scott, 11 Aug. 1964, file 'China-Soviet Split/CP Expulsions,' Neish papers; also Statement of BC Provincial Executive Regarding Dissolution of 'Special Club,' 8 July 1964; Scott, *A Communist Life*, 157.

195 J.A. Scott to National Committee, 7 June 1964, file 'China-Soviet Split/CP Expulsions,' Neish papers (also file 138-6 'CPC Misc 1964–1967,' vol. 138, CTM fonds, LAC); Statement of BC Provincial Executive Regarding Dissolution of 'Special Club,' 8 July 1964, file 'China-Soviet Split/CP Expulsions,' Neish papers.

196 Statement of BC Provincial Executive CPC Re Expulsion of Jack Scott, 11 Aug. 1964, file 'China-Soviet Split/CP Expulsions,' Neish papers.

197 Neish interview, 11 May 2006; Minutes of Provincial Committee meeting, 23 May 1964, file 24-25 'British Columbia Provincial Committee Meetings, Minutes,' vol. 24, reel H1593, CPC fonds, LAC.

198 *Canada's Party of Socialism*, 227.

199 Rush, *We Have a Glowing Dream*, 93–4.

200 'Party Organization and Style of Work,' n.d., file 23-23, 'BC provincial series,' reel H1592, CPC fonds, LAC.

201 See Helen Garry to Vancouver City Committee, 23 Nov. 1967; Caron to Morgan, 14 Dec. 1967, file 23-37, 'BC provincial series,' reel H1592, CPC fonds, LAC.; also *Canada's Party of Socialism*, 148–9, McKean, *Communism Versus Opportunism*.

202 'LSA Internal Bulletin,' 6 May 1968, 10, file 57-10, Dowson fonds, LAC;

Helen Garry to Vancouver City Committee, 23 Nov. 1967; Caron to Morgan, 14 Dec. 1967, file 23-37, 'BC provincial series,' reel H1592, CPC fonds, LAC.

203 'Report from Regional Committee of the Delta-New Westminster Region of the Communist Party of Canada,' 22 Jan. 1967, file 23-30, 'BC provincial series,' reel H1592, CPC fonds, LAC.

204 Swankey interview, 14 Aug. 2005.

205 Stevens and Knight, *Homer Stevens*, 187–8. A Soviet interpretation of the Czechoslovakian crisis is provided in V.V. Zagladin, ed., *The World Communist Movement: Outline of Strategy and Tactics* (Moscow: Progress Publishers, 1973), 472.

206 Club Bulletin No. 8, 7 July 1969, file 23-38, 'BC provincial series,' reel H1592, CPC fonds, LAC; 'Resolution,' 15 Dec. 1968, file 24-61 'Special Convention. Agenda, Resolutions. 14–15 Dec 1968,' and file 24-62 'Special Convention, Agenda, Nominating Form, 15–16 Mar. 1969,' reel H1593, CPC fonds, LAC; Rush, *We Have a Glowing Dream*, 94; Avakumovic, *The Communist Party in Canada*, 269; *Pacific Tribune*, 3 Jan. 1969.

207 Swankey interview, 10 June 2005 and 14 Aug. 2005.

208 Stevens and Knight, *Homer Stevens*, 184–90; Grace Stevens interview, with author, 9 Aug. 2005, Nanaimo, BC; Minutes of BC Provincial Committee meeting, 17 Dec. 1970, file 24-25 'British Columbia Provincial Committee Meetings, Minutes,' vol. 24, reel H1593, CPC fonds, LAC.

209 Avakumovic, *The Communist Party in Canada*, 269; Scott, *A Communist Life*, 218–19. According to Avakumovic, Boylan was expelled for his criticism of the Czechoslovakian invasion and for removing 'without authorization ... a substantial sum of money and the mailing plates of the magazine.'

210 Swankey interview, 14 Aug. 2005.

211 Rush, *We Have a Glowing Dream*, 94; *Canada's Party of Socialism*, 237.

212 White, *A Hard Man to Beat*, 209.

213 'Communist Party of Canada, Vancouver City Convention, Nov 23–24,' RCMP report, 10 Dec. 1963, file 'Canadian Iron Workers,' vol. 2257, series A, RCMP Security Service, CSIS records, LAC.

214 White, *A Hard Man to Beat*, 215.

215 Buck, *Canada: The Communist Viewpoint*, 243.

216 Roberto Michels, *Political Parties: A Sociological Study of the Oligarchical Tendencies of Modern Democracy* (1915; New York: Free Press, 1962), 365.

217 Jack Phillips interview, 8–9 March 2003. In 1991–2, a fratricidal war further depleted the ranks of BC's Communist Party, as the Soviet beacon faded into the dustbin of history. Two groups vied for control, an upstart revisionist group arrayed against the party's old guard, which included

Rush and Betty and Hal Griffin. While the revisionist challenge was contained, the split resulted in the *Pacific Tribune*'s demise, after forty-five years of continuous publication. Griffin retains detailed records of the split at her North Vancouver home. She remains committed to the political tradition to which she devoted her life: 'There will always be a need for a Communist Party. Sooner or later, it's going to be there, whether it's called that or not ... Capitalism is a pretty miserable way to run six billion people.' Griffin interview, 11 Aug. 2005; Betty Griffin papers, private collection.

3. Socialism Postponed

1 President's Report, 'Report of Officers to the 1947 Provincial Convention CCF British Columbia – Yukon Section,' file 1-5, Colin Cameron collection (hereafter CCC), UBCSC.

2 Steeves was a Dutch immigrant and lawyer by training, who had belonged to the Socialist Party of Holland in her youth and joined the CCF through the Vancouver branch of the League for Social Reconstruction (LSR). Report of first vice-president (D.G. Steeves), 'Report of Officers to the 1947 Provincial Convention CCF British Columbia – Yukon Section,' file 1-5, CCC, UBCSC.

3 Peter Campbell, '"Making Socialists": Bill Pritchard, the Socialist Party of Canada, and the Third International,' *Labour/Le Travail*, 30 (Fall 1992), 42–65; Dorothy Gretchen Steeves, *The Compassionate Rebel: Ernest Winch and the Growth of Socialism in Western Canada* (Vancouver: Boag Foundation, 1977); Christine J. Nichol, 'In Pursuit of the Voter: The British Columbia CCF, 1945–1950,' in William J. Brennan, ed., *Building the Cooperative Commonwealth: Essays on the Democratic Socialist Tradition in Canada* (Regina: Canadian Plains Research Center, 1984), 123–40.

4 The typology 'left' and 'right,' applied to the BC CCF in Elaine Bernard's thesis on the Rod Young affair, is sustained for the sake of clarity. See Elaine Bernard, 'The Rod Young Affair in the British Columbia Co-operative Commonwealth Federation,' MA thesis, University of British Columbia, 1979.

5 Martin Robin, *Pillars of Profit: The Company Province, 1934–1972* (Toronto: McClelland and Stewart, 1973), 104.

6 The *CCF News* closely followed the legislative achievements of kindred parties, in the areas of labour legislation, human rights and social ownership. See, for example, 'Lessons from the Saskatchewan Election,' *CCF News*, 1 July 1948; 'Sask CCF Officials Report Improved Financial Position,'

CCF News, 29 July 1948; 'Labor Government Makes Progress Dealing with Housing Problem,' *CCF News*, 22 July 1948; 'New Zealand to Build State Paper Pulp Mill,' *CCF News*, 22 Jan. 1948; 'No Extremes of Wealth and Poverty in New Zealand,' *CCF News*, 10 June 1948; 'Social Security Benefits Boost N.Z. Workers Wages,' *CCF News*, 1 July 1948, 'New Zealand Health Services,' *CCF News*, 22 July 1948; 'Crown Corporations in Saskatchewan 1955,' Provincial Election Speakers Notes, Sept. 1956, file 450-2, CCF-NDP fonds, LAC; Jean Larmour, 'The Douglas Government's Changing Emphasis on Public, Private, and Co-operative Development in Saskatchewan, 1944–1961,' in Brennan, ed., *Building the Cooperative Commonwealth*, 161–80; also 'Cost of Nationalization,' *Sun*, 31 May 1948; Seymour Martin Lipset, *Agrarian Socialism: The Cooperative Commonwealth Federation in Saskatchewan. A Study in Political Sociology*, updated ed. (Garden City, NY: Anchor Books, 1968); Ralph Miliband, *Parliamentary Socialism: A Study in the Politics of Labour* (London: Merlin, 1973); Leo Panitch, *Social Democracy and Industrial Militancy: The Labour Party, the Trade Unions, and Incomes Policy, 1945–1974* (Cambridge: Cambridge University Press, 1976). Correspondence between the National CCF and kindred parties in South Africa, Australia, Italy, Finland, Jamaica, Britain, and the USA can be found in files 436–1 to 436–14, CCF-NDP fonds, LAC.

7 Reg Whitaker and Gary Marcuse, *Cold War Canada: The Making of a National Insecurity State, 1945–1957* (Toronto: University of Toronto Press, 1994), 272.

8 See Bernard, 'The Rod Young Affair in the British Columbia Co-operative Commonwealth Federation.' Young won a June 1948 Vancouver Centre by-election. The war veteran and UBC law student had been twice suspended as a member of the Co-operative Commonwealth Young Movement (CCYM) in the 1930s, for his association with Trotskyism. At the 1934 national convention in Winnipeg, Young had challenged Tommy Douglas for the CCYM leadership. In 1937, when he was serving on the BC provincial executive, he was suspended for nine months, for belonging to 'a leftist faction' and being 'a disruptive element.' At the time, Young belonged a group called the Young Socialist League. In the House of Commons, Young remained at the centre of controversy. A statement to the effect that Canadians had been sending 'a bunch of crooks to Parliament' embarrassed party leaders, as did his opposition to the North Atlantic Treaty Organization (NATO), though Hansard indicates he voted in favour of the security pact. National secretary David Lewis wrote to Grace MacInnis, expressing concern over 'pro-Soviet' and pacifist opposition to NATO within the CCF. In a letter to Barry Richards, a Manitoba MLA who was suspended and later expelled for LPP ties, Young wrote: 'I am in principle

opposed to a military pact as an instrument for maintaining peace … I believe a Socialist party should be able to produce a Socialist policy to fit the need internationally.' He called for the creation of a 'third force' by social-democratic governments at the UN, independent of American or Soviet influence, to prevent atomic war. However, as Angus MacInnis wrote in 1953, when Young was again vying for the CCF nomination in Vancouver Centre, 'Rodney voted for the North Atlantic Treaty. The vote on it was 185 with none against.' See A. MacInnis to MacDonald, 19 March 1953, file 73-5 'Correspondence 1953'; 'Record of Rod Young as a Member of Parliament,' file 4-9; 'Rod Young's Position on the North Atlantic Treaty,' file 73-3 'Correspondence 1950,' AMC, UBCSC; D. Lewis to G. MacInnis, 22 Feb. 1949, file 4-7; Young to Richards, 24 March 1949, file 4-9, GMC, UBCSC; Hansard, *Debates of the House of Commons*, 29 April 1949, 2791–7; S.P. Lewis, *Grace: The Life of Grace MacInnis* (Madeira Park, BC: Harbour, 1993, 199.

9 See British Columbia, *Statement of Votes*, 1956.

10 David Lewis, *The Good Fight: Political Memoirs, 1909–1958* (Toronto: Macmillan, 1981), 411.

11 Al King with Kate Braid, *Red Bait! Struggles of a Mine Mill Local* (Vancouver: Kingbird, 1998), 35 and 49.

12 'Uphill Has Represented Fernie in Legislature for 36 Years,' *Pacific Tribune*, 10 Feb. 1956; Tom Langford and Chris Frazer, 'The Cold War and Working-Class Politics in the Coal Mining Communities of the Crowsnest Pass, 1945–1958,' *Labour/Le Travail*, 49 (Spring 2002), 43–81; Robert McDonald, '"Just a Working Man": Tom Uphill,' in Wayne Norton and Tom Langford, eds., *A World Apart: The Crowsnest Communities of Alberta and British Columbia* (Kamloops: Plateau, 2000), 99–112. Born near Bristol, England in 1874, Uphill began work in the mines at age fourteen and migrated to Canada in 1906. He served as president of the Fernie Miners' Union and was elected alderman and mayor of Fernie during the First World War. In 1916, Uphill was narrowly defeated as a Conservative candidate in the provincial election, capturing 826 votes (42.4 per cent) to 903 (46.4 per cent) for the Liberal victor and 218 votes (11.2 per cent) for third-place Socialist candidate John McDonald. In 1920, Uphill ran as a Federated Labour Party candidate and was elected, serving continuously as a Labour MLA until his retirement in 1960, at age eighty-six. Uphill remained Fernie's mayor until 1945, when he was narrowly defeated, but served again from 1950 until 1955, when he resigned due to deteriorating health. As an independent 'Labour' MLA, Uphill astutely evaded the political minefield of CCF-CPC relations, although Langford and Frazer argue that he worked closely with the CPC-LPP. Uphill had visited the USSR in the 1930s, and attended

the 1952 World Peace Congress in Vienna. He supported the LPP-initiated 'Labour Representation Committee' which fielded candidates in the 1952 provincial election, and waffled between Social Credit leader W.A.C. Bennett and CCF leader Harold Winch as Lieutenant Governor Clarence Wallace decided who would head a minority government. Uphill ultimately sided with the CCF, but Bennett became premier. From that point forward, the CCF abstained from fielding a candidate in Fernie. In 1960, Uphill was succeeded by a Liberal, with the CCF finishing third, behind Social Credit, while the LPP did not contest the seat. See British Columbia, *Statement of Votes*, 1916–60; 'Mayor Uphill to Peace Congress,' *Fernie Free Press*, 11 Dec. 1952.

13 Ronald Grantham, 'Some Aspects of the Socialist Movement in British Columbia, 1898–1933,' MA thesis, University of British Columbia, 1942; Ross Alfred Johnson, 'No Compromise – No Political Trading: The Marxian Socialist Tradition in British Columbia,' PhD diss., University of British Columbia, 1975; Gerald Friesen, 'Yours in Revolt: Regionalism, Socialism, and the Western Canadian Labour Movement,' *Labour/Le Travailleur*, 1 (1976), 141–57; A. Ross McCormack, *Reformers, Rebels, and Revolutionaries: The Western Canadian Radical Movement, 1899–1919* (Toronto and Buffalo: University of Toronto Press, 1977); Peter Campbell, *Canadian Marxists and the Search for a Third Way* (Montreal and Kingston: McGill-Queen's University Press, 1999); Ian McKay, *Rebels, Reds, Radicals: Rethinking Canada's Left History* (Toronto: Between the Lines, 2005), 150–4.

14 H. Winch to D. Lewis, 13 Oct. 1948, file 73-1 'Correspondence 1948,' AMC, UBCSC; 'Off to Far North,' *CCF News*, 9 Sept. 1948; also 'Dawson City Supplement,' *CCF News*, 18 Nov. 1948. In October 1961, shortly after the NDP was formed, federal secretary Carl Hamilton wrote to BC provincial secretary Jessie Mendels officially requesting that the BC NDP 'give what attention it can to the question of organization in the Yukon.' The mayor of Dawson City had reportedly expressed interest in the New Party. See Hamilton to Mendels, 5 Oct. 1961; Mendels to Hamilton, 16 Oct. 1961; Hamilton to Regier, 1 Dec. 1961; Grier to Mendels, 15 Aug. 1962, file 450-12, CCF-NDP fonds, LAC.

15 See Anne Burger, 'The Communist Party of Canada during the Great Depression: Organizing and Class Consciousness,' MA thesis, Simon Fraser University, 2004.

16 Ernest Edward Winch was an old socialist from the First World War era, president of the Vancouver Trades and Labor Council during the Ginger Goodwin general strike of 1918 and head of the Lumber Workers' Industrial unit of the One Big Union. He was secretary of the Socialist Party of

Canada when it became the founding section of the BC CCF in 1932, and along with son Harold was elected to the BC legislature in 1933. In 1936, conflict erupted with CCF House Leader Rev. Robert Connell, a Victoria botanist, who condemned the pro-communist leanings of the elder Winch. The CCF membership refused, in a convention vote, to follow Connell's lead and he defected from the CCF to found the short-lived BC Constructive Party. Connell was joined by MP J.S. Taylor and old socialists Vic Midgley (his executive secretary) and Bill Pritchard (editor of the *Commonwealth* newspaper), rivals of Winch since the OBU days. In the subsequent election, the BC Constructive Party contested 14 seats, none of which it won, and garnered 2 per cent of the popular vote, before disappearing from the political scene. See Gordon Stanley Wickerson, 'Conflict in the British Columbia Cooperative Commonwealth Federation and the "Connell Affair,"' MA thesis, University of British Columbia, 1973; Steeves, *The Compassionate Rebel*, 107–21.

17 The conflict between Stephen and the party is discussed in Patrick George Hill, 'A Failure of Unity: Communist Party-CCF Relations in British Columbia, 1935–1939,' MA thesis, University of Victoria, 1977. In the 1937 general election, Stephen shunned the provincial leadership and ran as the CCF candidate in Alberni-Nanaimo, capturing 3,129 votes to 3,616 for the Liberal victor. British Columbia, *Statement of Votes*, 1937.

18 Walter D. Young, 'Ideology, Personality and the Origin of the CCF in British Columbia,' *BC Studies*, 32 (Winter 1976–7), 139.

19 Bernard, 'The Rod Young Affair,' 85.

20 Arthur Cathers, *Beloved Dissident Eve Smith, 1904–1988* (Blyth, ON: Drumadravy Books, 1997), 147.

21 Muriel to G. MacInnis, 19 April 1946, file 4-4, Grace MacInnis Collection (hereafter GMC), UBCSC. Muriel explained this point to MacInnis: 'Since I joined the Movement four years ago I have worked very actively from the first month, tried to keep up with current CCF literature & thought, also with current events and then tried to study Socialism and make up for not having been born in a Socialist background. When I heard all the phrases used at the Convention, I wondered if I would ever catch up. Yet I can't help thinking that I am a good Socialist & CCFer. We cannot raise a whole race of Socialists in time to do something now. We must convert & use people that are in the world now.'

22 ''Bye Comrade, 'Lo Friend, May Be New CCF Greeting,' *Daily Times*, 11 April 1953. In the 1950s, as the moderate faction triumphed over the left wing, the party considered changing the greeting from 'comrade' to 'friend.'

23 James Naylor, 'Pacifism or Anti-Imperialism: The CCF Response to the Outbreak of World War II,' *Journal of the Canadian Historical Association*, 6 (1997), 234.

24 A. MacInnis to D. Lewis, 17 Jan. 1941, file 72-14, AMC, UBCSC. In another letter, MacInnis articulated a socialist argument in support of the war effort: 'The purpose of the Lend-Lease Bill is not to solve any of the problems of capitalism. Its purpose is to enable Great Britain to win the war ... Socialism may, of course, be the solution to all our difficulties but there is no such thing as a clear jump from capitalism to socialism and if Hitler wins, the opportunity which we have had of attempting to build a new society to our heart's desire, will disappear.' A. MacInnis to A. Webster, 20 March 1941, file 72-14, AMC, UBCSC.

25 Jamieson to G. MacInnis, 28 July 1940, file 4-4, GMC, UBCSC. Jamieson referred to a meeting with a Mr Calvert, of Princeton University, who was writing a BA thesis on the CCF.

26 Leo Zakuta, *A Protest Movement Becalmed: A Study of Change in the CCF* (Toronto: University of Toronto Press, 1964), 141–52.

27 James Naylor argues that the approach of the CCF left wing derived from a socialist, rather than a pacifist, critique of war and imperialism. This working-class internationalism had its origins in the SPC, and remained the dominant perspective in the BC CCF during the 1940s and into the 1950s. J.S. Woodsworth's famous stand in the House of Commons in September 1939 received wide support among the BC leadership and rank and file, who condemned the National Council's support for the war. The Saanich, Renfrew, and Penticton CCF Clubs issued a circular attempting to have the Council's position overturned, while the provincial executive narrowly approved the position on a 5–4 vote. In a letter to her father, Grace MacInnis indicated that Colin Cameron (provincial organizer), Bert Gargrave (*Federationist* editor), and Barry Mather supported his position. Naylor, 'Pacifism or Anti-Imperialism,' especially footnotes 107–11; 'Maitland Dislikes CCF's War Stand,' *Daily Times*, 3 Nov. 1939; 'CCF Chiefs Repudiate Attack on War Loan,' *Sun*, 28 Feb. 1941; Dorothy Steeves interview, with Marlene Karnouk, 4 April 1973, T0182:0001, BC Archives; Walter D. Young, *Anatomy of a Party: The National CCF, 1932–61* (Toronto: University of Toronto Press, 1969), 192.

28 'Colima Picketing,' *CCF News*, 1 Jan. 1948.

29 'Victoria News,' *CCF News*, 8 Jan. 1948.

30 'Convention Footnotes,' *CCF News*, 3 June 1948; 'CCF Urged to Plan Program for BC,' *Sun*, 28 May 1948; 'CCF Research for Election Victory,' *Sun*, 29 May 1948; 'Nationalized Brew Is CCF Proposal,' *Sun*, 31 May 1948; also

'North Atlantic Pact,' *CCF News*, 2 Feb. 1949. This stance was reiterated in 1949, when delegates to the BC CCF convention refused to endorse the North Atlantic Pact. See A. Burton (a.k.a. Steve Rosslund), 'Whether the CCF?,' c. Sept. 1950, file 9-2, vol. 2, CTM fonds, LAC.

31 Rod Young won an 8 June 1948 by-election, with 9,518 votes to 7,348 votes for the Liberal and 4,965 votes for the Progressive Conservative. The LPP did not contest the by-election. During the campaign, Young attracted controversy when he shared a May Day platform in Nanaimo with Harold Pritchett, the communist leader of the IWA. National CCF leader M.J. Coldwell wired Colin Cameron, then provincial secretary, accusing Young of violating a National Council policy prohibiting cooperation with communists, and threatening to cancel a Vancouver speaking tour. Cameron condemned the 'dictatorial and preemptory tone' of Coldwell's telegram. Cameron to A. MacInnis, 13 May 1948; A. MacInnis to Cameron, 13 May 1948; A. MacInnis to Cameron, 14 May 1948; Cameron to M.J. Coldwell, 15 May 1948; file 73-1 'Correspondence, 1948,' AMC, UBCSC; *Canadian Parliamentary Guide*, 1948.

32 'The CCF Convention,' *Pacific Tribune*, 10 Sept. 1948.

33 'CCF Divides in Debate on ERP' and 'CCF Meets in Convention,' *Pacific Tribune*, 27 Aug. 1948; 'Strengthening the CCF,' *Pacific Tribune*, 16 July 1948. After an hour of debate, convention chair Stanley Knowles shut off discussion and the convention voted overwhelmingly in favour of the Marshall Plan, with only two votes opposed.

34 'Provincial Council Decides Full-Time Organizer Needed,' *CCF News*, 5 Aug. 1948; 'Unity Aided by Herridge,' *Pacific Tribune*, 13 Aug. 1948; 'Morgan Hails Unity Talks,' *Pacific Tribune*, 21 May 1948; Herbert Wilfred Herridge interview, with Peter Stursberg, n.d. [c. spring 1967], 38–41, file 46-9, vol. 46, series D78, MG 31, LAC. According to her biographer, Grace MacInnis viewed Herridge as 'a hypocrite, a big landlord who dabbled in communism. Angus, among others, believed Herridge was really working for the LPP, boring into the CCF from within.' When Herridge was elected to the House of Commons in 1945 as an Independent CCF (or 'People's CCF') candidate in Kootenay West, and subsequently admitted into the CCF caucus, Angus 'never acknowledged Herridge's presence in the House of Commons, even to say good morning, even though they were both part of the CCF caucus from 1945 until Angus retired in 1957.' S.P. Lewis, *Grace*, 173 and 183.

35 'A Socialist View of World Affairs,' *CCF News*, 1 July 1948.

36 A. MacInnis to D. Lewis, 18 Oct. 1948, file 73-1, AMC, UBCSC.

37 D. Lewis to A. MacInnis, 25 Oct. 1948, file 73-1, AMC, UBCSC. He added:

'I still have very great respect for her intellectual capacity, and I have a strong feeling that it is her isolation from the studies and research and discussion which go on at this end, which is responsible for a great deal of the gap between us.'

38 Anti-communism in the CCF is explored in Whitaker and Marcuse, *Cold War Canada*, 268–84; Young, *Anatomy of a Party*, 282–4. For attempts at unity in the 1930s, see Hill, 'A Failure of Unity.'

39 A. MacInnis to Coldwell, 27 Oct. 1950, file 73-3, AMC, UBCSC.

40 'CCF and Unity,' *Pacific Tribune*, 9 April 1948; also 'Right and Wrong,' *CCF News*, 10 June 1948.

41 'The Difference between Communism and Socialism,' *CCF News*, 5 Feb. 1948.

42 'Coalition Wages Dirty Campaign in Saanich,' *CCF News*, 26 Feb. 1948; also 'LPP Withdraws Candidate, Gives Support to Cameron,' *Pacific Tribune*, 23 Jan. 1948; 'CCF "Analysis" of Saanich Vote Indicates Reason Coalition Won,' *Pacific Tribune*, 5 March 1948. Cameron received 4,405 votes to 5,942 for his Coalition opponent Arthur Ash. See British Columbia, *Statement of Votes*, 1948.

43 '"The Spectre of Communism": 1848 to 1948,' *CCF News*, 26 Feb. 1948.

44 'Writers Digest,' *CCF News*, 4 March 1948.

45 'The Red Witch-Hunts,' *CCF News*, 12 Aug. 1948.

46 'M'Innis Opposes Bill to Outlaw Comm'st Party,' *CCF News*, 29 April 1948.

47 A. MacInnis to D. Lewis, 27 Oct. 1948, 73-1, AMC, UBCSC.

48 Alsbury to G. MacInnis, 20 June 1949, file 4-5 'Correspondence 1946–1951,' GMC, UBCSC.

49 'TLC Delegates Remove Showler as Council Head,' *Fisherman*, 14 Feb. 1950.

50 'Bengough Ruling Backed by Trades Council Meet,' *Fisherman*, 14 March 1950.

51 In Rossland-Trail, the death of the sitting Coalition member culminated in a narrow CCF victory in October 1948. CCFer James Quinn took 4,847 votes (51 per cent) to 4,622 (48.8 per cent) for Coalition candidate Alexander Turnbull, increasing the CCF opposition to 11 seats. In all other by-elections, CCF candidates were defeated. In North Okanagan (December 1945), Point Grey (June 1946), and Cariboo (February 1948), the CCF lost to Coalitionists, though the social composition of each riding did not favour the party. Colin Cameron's attempted return to the legislature in Saanich in February 1948 improved the CCF margin over the previous election, with 4,405 votes (39 per cent) to 5,902 (53 per cent) for Coalition candidate Arthur Ash, but fell short. In a November 1948 South Okana-

gan by-election triggered by W.A.C. Bennett's run for federal office, Bruce Woodsworth (Grace MacInnis's brother and son of J.S.), took 4,335 votes (46 per cent) – an impressive improvement from the party's 35 per cent in 1945 – but lost to the Coalition's Robert Brown-Clayton, who garnered 5,088 votes (54 per cent). See British Columbia, *Statement of Votes*, 1945–9.

52 The CCF candidate in Yale, Kelowna mayor and hardware merchant Owen Jones, defeated Bennett by nearly 5,000 votes, claiming the seat for the CCF the first time. The second by-election was won by Rod Young in Vancouver Centre. *Canadian Parliamentary Guide*, 1948 and 1949.

53 In 1945, 175,960 voters cast ballots for the CCF. In 1949, this increased to 245,284. The Coalition was returned with 61 per cent of the vote. The only incumbents who retained their seats were Ernest and Harold Winch, and Arthur Turner, in the working-class strongholds of Burnaby and Vancouver East. They were joined by four new members. In remote Atlin, CCFer Frank Calder became the first Aboriginal legislator in Canada. Reversing the outcome of the 1945 contest, he edged out his Coalition opponent by six votes. The remaining seats were in mining regions along BC's southern boundary. In Grand Forks-Greenwood, Rupert Haggen won by 49 votes. In Kaslo-Slocan, Randolph Harding won with 53 per cent of the vote. In the southeast, Leo Nimsick claimed the new Cranbrook seat for the CCF. British Columbia, *Statement of Votes*, 1949.

54 While the Social Credit League had appeared periodically since its triumph in neighbouring Alberta in 1935, it remained a marginal force until the late 1940s. As fissures began to emerge in Coalition ranks, Social Credit gained strength. In Delta and Dewdney, the combined CCF-Social Credit vote in 1949 surpassed support for the Coalition candidates. In Chilliwack, a farming community in the Fraser Valley with a strong evangelical Christian bent, Social Credit nearly matched the CCF with over 2,400 votes. This outcome foreshadowed the explosion of Social Credit support in 1952. See Barbara Horsfield, 'The Social Credit Movement in British Columbia,' BA essay, University of British Columbia, 1953; 'Social Credit Double-Talk,' *CCF News*, 25 March 1948.

55 T.C. Douglas to Grace MacInnis, 26 Sept. 1949, file 4-5, GMC, UBCSC.

56 In Vancouver East, Angus MacInnis won his fifth straight election, while in Kootenay West, Bert Herridge, once again in the CCF fold, retained his seat. In the interior riding of Yale, CCFer Owen Jones was re-elected, albeit by a narrower margin. Rod Young was less fortunate, as he lost Vancouver Centre to the Liberals. In Cariboo, Bill Irvine lost his seat in a straight two-way race against a Liberal. The same dynamic cost the CCF its Skeena seat. A third incumbent, James Matthew, was challenged by a single Con-

servative in Kootenay East, and was narrowly defeated. Grace MacInnis, contesting her first federal election, finished second to a Liberal in Vancouver South. In the new riding of Burnaby-Richmond, Dorothy Steeves came within 300 votes of defeating the Liberal, while LPPer Tom McEwen took 1,558 votes. Besieged by Coalitionists from the right and LPPers from the left, CCFers had difficulty capturing a plurality of the vote. *Canadian Parliamentary Guide*, 1950.

57 Ingle to A. MacInnis, 30 June 1949, file 73-2, AMC, UBCSC. Ingle outlined the factors he believed contributed to the loss: '(a) The North Atlantic Pact business; (b) the Nova Scotia and British Columbia set backs [provincial elections]; (c) the disruptive work of the communists in Trade Unions that should have been overwhelmingly on our side; (d) prosperity.' The 'North Atlantic Pact business' referred to the refusal of the 1949 BC CCF convention, held in Vancouver, to endorse National CCF caucus support for the North Atlantic Pact. See A. Burton (a.k.a. Steve Rosslund), 'Whether the CCF?,' n.d. (c. Sept. 1950), file 9-2, vol. 2, CTM fonds, LAC; 'North Atlantic Pact,' *CCF News*, 2 Feb. 1949.

58 Forsey to G. MacInnis, 20 July 1949; a third perspective on the 1949 election defeat is provided in D. Lewis to A. MacInnis, 4 July 1949, file 73-2, AMC, UBCSC.

59 A. MacInnis to D. Lewis, 6 July 1949, file 73-2, AMC, UBCSC.

60 A. MacInnis to McKenzie, 18 April 1950, file 73-3, AMC, UBCSC.

61 For collaboration between the National CCF leadership and BC's moderate faction, see D. Lewis to A. MacInnis, 10 July 1949 (telegram); A. MacInnis to D. Lewis, 17 July 1949, file 73-2, AMC, UBCSC. This correspondence relates to a *CCF News* article by Cameron, critical of the CCF leadership, which resulted in 'a mild vote of censure' by the provincial executive. MacInnis confided to Lewis that he was unsure of how to respond to Cameron's charges, 'not because Colin's slanderous and irresponsible statements are hard to answer, but because one had to keep in mind what effect an appropriate reply would have on the movement.' Grant MacNeil and other 'responsible CCF people' were 'particularly fearful' of Angus's 'outspokenness.'

62 G. MacInnis to D. Lewis, 13 July 1950, file 4-5, GMC, UBCSC.

63 Neither was present at the meeting, which Grace's brother Bruce Woodsworth described as 'a real knock-em-down and pick-em-up pitched battle of personalities, ideologies, lies, distortions, innuendoes.' B. Woodsworth to G. and A. MacInnis, 10 April 1950, file 4-5, GMC, UBCSC. Woodsworth, warned in advance by his sister and brother-in-law, set his sights on the left: 'after the first hour of numbing shock at hearing all the horrible things

you two had been secretly engaged in a strong rightist sabotage thrust at the CCF's vitals, I cast discretion into the winds, and pitched right into: 1. Rod. Y.; 2. D. Steeves; 3. Cameron – in that order.'

64 G. Webster to G. MacInnis, 1 March 1950, file 4-5, GMC, UBCSC. At the provincial council meeting, Gladys Webster paid little attention to the predictable statements of leftists such as George Weaver, Bill Mandale, and Eve Smith, more concerned about Steeves and Cameron 'because they are out of character in becoming armchair philosophers.' She could not believe they 'sincerely support the narrow, doctrinaire view of socialism.' Rather, she felt they had taken a stand – 'a sort of refuge' – and would go to any length to justify that stand. Steeves discussed the class struggle, and conflict between 'trade unions and owners,' while Cameron, in supporting the theory of the 'state withering away,' was 'living a hundred years in advance of the times.'

65 B. Woodsworth to G. and A. MacInnis, 10 April 1950, file 4-5, GMC, UBCSC.

66 Defeated CCF MLA Bert Gargrave was instrumental in the Steel raid. Prior to the convention, Trotskyist Aubrey Burton of Trail observed: 'The rank and file CCF are disgusted and angered by the role assumed by these leaders and there is little doubt that things may pop up at the coming BC CCF convention.' See Burton to Dowson, 8 March 1950, file 9-2, vol. 2, CTM fonds, LAC; also King, *Red Bait!*, 74.

67 Woodsworth cited a trip by Gladys Webster and Don Capon to Kelowna and Vernon, to coordinate the activities of the CCYM. For details of a February 1950 meeting in the Burrard constituency, where the right was dominant, see B. Woodsworth to G. and A. MacInnis, 10 April 1950; G. Webster to G. MacInnis, 1 March 1950, file 4-5, GMC, UBCSC.

68 In elections for convention chairperson, Tom Alsbury defeated Cameron by a margin of nearly two to one: 'it proved to be an accurate portent (at least partially) of future voting strength.' In presidential elections, MacNeil defeated Cameron 76–32 votes; Jamieson defeated Cameron for first vice-president 66–46; however, in voting for second vice-president, Rod Young defeated Jim Bury on a narrow 56–55 vote. For other executive positions, only one 'pseudo-revolutionary,' Dave Stupich, was elected. However, one of two National Council seats went to Steeves on the left, who defeated Grace MacInnis, Jamieson, Mackenzie, and others. In a ballot for the second seat, Young nearly defeated Arthur Turner. B. Woodsworth to G. and A. MacInnis, 10 April 1950, file 4-5, GMC, UBCSC. Woodsworth suggested this resolution carried 'when there probably wasn't quorum.' (It was 11:30 pm on a Saturday night, with roughly 60 delegates in attendance.) An ex-

planation of Rod Young's election is provided in Burton to Dowson, 4 May 1950, file 9-2, vol. 2, CTM fonds, LAC.

69 A. MacInnis to B. Woodsworth, 21 April 1950, file 4-5, GMC, UBCSC.

70 G. MacInnis to D. Lewis, 13 July 1950, file 4-5, GMC, UBCSC. In delegate selection meetings in the constituencies, Vancouver East 'chose a man with a fellow-travelling record and a loud voice'; Rod Young was selected in Vancouver Centre and leftist Bill Mandale won in Vancouver South. The right was successful in electing Arnold Webster in Burrard and Tom Alsbury in Burnaby-Richmond. In Comox, Colin Cameron persevered by two votes over former MLA Joe Corsbie, who 'may have weird spots but I think they lie in other directions.' MacInnis concluded that, 'taking it over the province, the other crowd will probably have the majority numerically – although we shall have the better debating strength.'

71 G. MacInnis to D. Lewis, 13 July 1950, file 4-5, GMC, UBCSC.

72 Steeves to Cameron, 11 July 1950, file 1-1, CCC, UBCSC; 'The Birth of a Socialist,' *CCF News*, 26 July 1950.

73 Burton to Dowson, 4 May 1950; Dowson to Rosslund (Burton), 28 May 1950, file 9-2, vol. 2, CTM fonds, LAC. On the eve of the national convention, Sooke CCF Club secretary B.P. Johnson formally protested CCF support for American military action in Korea. 'Protest on Korea,' *CCF News*, 19 July 1950.

74 'No Compromise on Korean Aggression' and 'CCYM Delegates Support Western Action,' *CCF News*, 26 July 1950; 'CCF Supports UN on Korea,' *Province*, 28 July 1950; Young, *Anatomy of a Party*, 233.

75 'CCF Counter Attacks "Stockholm Appeal,"' *Province*, 29 July 1950; 'Delegates Spurn Peace Petition,' *CCF News*, 2 Aug. 1950; Young, *Anatomy of a Party*, 281–2; Steeves, *The Compassionate Rebel*, 206; 'A Word to the Wives – I Wouldn't Ban the Bomb,' *CCF News*, 12 April 1950. In December 1951, the National Executive directed the BC executive to take action against Winch, Nimsick, and Turner. The provincial section refused, claiming the MLAs had forgotten about the 1950 resolution when they signed the petition.

76 'National Council Instructed to Modernize Regina Manifesto,' *CCF News*, 2 Aug. 1950; Young, *Anatomy of a Party*, 126–30, 170–4; Alan Whitehorn, *Canadian Socialism: Essays on the CCF-NDP* (Toronto: Oxford University Press, 1992): 3–50; S.P. Lewis, *Grace*, 210–11.

77 Rosslund (Burton) to Dowson, 5 Aug. 1950, file 9-2, vol. 2, CTM fonds, LAC.

78 'Booklet Banned by Convention,' *Sun*, 29 July 1950; 'Tract Banned Because It Conflicts with New CCF Executive Policy,' *Sun*, 4 Aug. 1950. Smith, an avowed leftist, had set up a literature table outside the convention hall in

the Hotel Vancouver. Several materials, including the contentious pamphlet, had been published by the Socialist Labour Party of Great Britain. According to Smith's account, a man named Eggleston from Trail, who was not a delegate, violently threw the offending pamphlet on the floor, referring to it as 'god-damned Trotskyist stuff.' David Lewis and Tommy Douglas, who were nearby, joined Eggleston in demanding the pamphlet be removed. When Smith and her brother-in-law John Smith refused, Lewis charged to a microphone, attacking 'this woman' for 'criticizing our sister party in Great Britain.' Despite the pleas of speakers including BC leader Harold Winch, a majority of delegates voted with Lewis to remove the pamphlet. Smith then seized the microphone from Thérèse Casgrain, who was chairing the session, attempting to explain her position; shouting ensued between the rival factions, leading Douglas to appeal for unity. In the aftermath, the BC executive voted to condemn Smith for her action and dismiss her as chair of the Political Education Committee. Smith viewed the incident as 'a natural corollary of the greatly modified form of "socialism" that is being handed down to us by our leaders.' For Smith's notes on the incident, see Cathers, *Beloved Dissident Eve Smith*, 118–20; also Rosslund (Burton) to Dowson, 1 Aug. 1950; Dowson to Burton, 21 July 1950, file 9-2, vol. 2, CTM fonds, LAC.

79 Ingle to G. MacInnis, 23 Aug. 1950, file 4-5, GMC, UBCSC. This gesture provided little solace to Grace, who was bitter over the refusal of Lewis and others to support Angus for National Chairman, a position vacated by Frank Scott. S.P. Lewis, *Grace*, 206–7; Ann Farrell, *Grace MacInnis: A Story of Love and Integrity* (Markham, ON: Fitzhenry and Whiteside, 1994), 184–7.

80 'Minutes of Left Wing Conference,' 25 Aug. 1950, file 4-9, GMC, UBCSC; Cathers, *Beloved Dissident Eve Smith*, 120. The moderates seized on this development. As Steeves informed Cameron: 'Somebody sent Jessie [Mendels] – anonymously – the minutes of the rebel meeting and the fat was sizzling. Some of them evidently think this a godsent opportunity to expel Rod, for moving the resolution to disaffiliate. A resolution was moved and carried to set up a trial committee on Rod, only Dave Stupich, Thomas and myself voting against. Grace MacInnis was there and fairly chattering with vindictive rage.' Steeves to Cameron, 23 Sept. 1950, file 1-1, CCC, UBCSC; Coldwell to A. MacInnis, 7 Nov. 1950, file 73-3, AMC, UBCSC.

81 Cathers, *Beloved Dissident Eve Smith*, 131; R.E. 'Lefty' Morgan, *Workers' Control on the Railroad: A Practical Example 'Right under Your Nose'* (St John's: Canadian Committee on Labour History, 1994).

82 'Summary of Minutes of Socialist Fellowship,' n.d., file 73-21 'Miscellaneous,' AMC, UBCSC; 'Minutes of Meeting of Socialist Caucus,' 1 Oct. 1950;

Gretchen to Colin, 23 Sept. 1950, file 1-1, CCC, UBCSC; 'Joint Meeting Provincial Executive Members and CCYM Executive and CCYM Club Representatives,' 28 Jan. 1951, file 4-10, GMC, UBCSC; Cathers, *Beloved Dissident Eve Smith*, 145–52.

83 'Minutes of Meeting of Socialist Caucus,' 1 Oct. 1950, file 1-1, CCC, UBCSC; *Material for Thought* (Vancouver), July 1950, file 4-10, GMC, UBCSC.

84 Cameron to E. Smith, 23 Jan. 1951, as quoted in Cathers, *Beloved Dissident Eve Smith*, 125–6.

85 'Report of Trial Board Appointed to Hear the Complaint of Colin Cameron,' 23 Sept. 1950, file 4-10, GMC, UBCSC.

86 Cameron to E. Smith, 23 Jan. 1951, as quoted in Cathers, *Beloved Dissident Eve Smith*, 125–6.

87 Cameron called for an end to 'silly resolutions,' yet enclosed a donation of $5 for the Fellowship, stressing it was 'not dues.' Cameron to E. Smith, n.d., as quoted in Cathers, *Beloved Dissident Eve Smith*, 126; also 'Report of the Provincial Secretary on the Socialist Fellowship,' n.d. [Jan. 1951], file 73-21, AMC; Steeves to Cameron, 23 Sept. 1950, file 1-1, CCC, UBCSC.

88 G. Webster to G. MacInnis, 11 Feb. 1951, file 4-10, GMC, UBCSC.

89 G. Webster to G. MacInnis, 5 April 1951, file 4-10, GMC, UBCSC.

90 MacNeil to G. MacInnis, 6 March 1951, file 4-10, GMC, UBCSC. According to Frank McKenzie, the debate had to be focused on loyalty, rather than foreign policy, for the moderates to succeed. In constituencies across the province, jostling ensued between supporters of the two camps. In April, Burrard voted to forward the resolution against 'an organization within an organization' to the convention, and approved a slate of moderate delegates. Victoria, Oak Bay, and other clubs, however, went to the Fellowship. McKenzie to G. MacInnis, 19 Feb. 1951; G. Webster to G. MacInnis, 5 April 1951; Jamieson to G. MacInnis, 17 April 1951; Jamieson to G. MacInnis, 26 April 1951, file 4-10, GMC, UBCSC.

91 Resolution of Provincial Executive, n.d., and Resolution of National Council, 17 March 1951, file 73-4, 'Correspondence 1951,' AMC; MacNeil to Ingle, 6 March 1951; MacNeil to G. MacInnis, 6 March 1951; G. Webster to G. MacInnis, 5 April 1951; Jamieson to G. MacInnis, 17 April 1951, file 4-10, GMC, UBCSC; S.P. Lewis, *Grace*, 213–14; Cathers, *Beloved Dissident Eve Smith*, 127–9.

92 S.P. Lewis, *Grace*, 213–14.

93 Jamieson to G. MacInnis, 17 April 1951, file 4-10, GMC, UBCSC. However, moderates including Frank McKenzie, a lawyer, and Alex MacDonald questioned '"Under what article of the Constitution," or upon "what specific evidence could you expel them?"' This prompted Jamieson to ask

MacInnis: 'If you know how, please let us know. I feel definitely it has to be done. If we can't do it, then the National will have to.'

94 Jamieson to G. MacInnis, 26 April 1951; also 'Report of Trial Board Appointed to Hear the Complaint of Colin Cameron,' 23 Sept. 1950, file 4-10, GMC, UBCSC; S.P. Lewis, *Grace*, 212–14.

95 Jamieson to G. MacInnis, 17 April 1951, file 4-10, GMC, UBCSC.

96 Burton to Dowson, 18 April 1950, file 9-2, vol. 2, CTM fonds, LAC. Following the 1950 Vancouver convention, Burton observed that 'Coldwell has finished his party in this area now, there is no disputing this but whether it's [*sic*] effect will be of a permanent nature is of course as I said a matter for conjecture, a lot will undoubtedly depend on how much Herridge's personal influence can counter the disillusionment with the CCF in the minds of the workers here.' Rosslund (Burton) to Dowson, 5 Aug. 1950, file 9-2, vol. 2, CTM fonds, LAC.

97 MacNeil to G. MacInnis, 6 March 1951, file 4-10 'Personal Subject Files – Trial of Tom Alsbury for "Character Assassination of Colin Cameron," 1950–1957,' GMC, UBCSC.

98 MacNeil to G. MacInnis, 6 March 1951, file 4-10, GMC, UBCSC. In December 1951, the Fellowship had adopted a resolution calling 'upon the working class of this country to muster under its banner.' 'Report of the Provincial Secretary on the Socialist Fellowship,' n.d. [Jan. 1951], file 73-21, AMC, UBCSC.

99 MacNeil to G. MacInnis, 6 March 1951, file 4-10, GMC, UBCSC.

100 Jamieson to G. MacInnis, 18 Feb. 1951, file 4-10, GMC, UBCSC.

101 Smith – who battled tuberculosis throughout her adult life – resigned from the CCF and retired to an acreage on South Pender Island. According to her biographer: 'She could not in the end continue to support a party that abandoned political education, paid mere lip service to internal democracy, allowed its leaders to ignore party policies, and increasingly tended to be controlled by self-perpetuating cliques.' According to Cathers, leftists differed on the ideological crisis in the CCF. Eve and John Smith felt there had been a betrayal of socialism, while Doug Cameron felt a majority in the party had never been committed to socialist principles. Cathers, *Beloved Dissident Eve Smith*, 94 and 150.

102 LaFrance to E. Smith, 12 May 1951, as quoted in Cathers, *Beloved Dissident Eve Smith*, 128.

103 McKenzie to G. MacInnis, 15 May 1951, file 4-10, GMC, UBCSC. According to Smith, the Fellowship's 'swan song' was a Nanaimo conference where Mainland delegates went too far in their ridicule of Coldwell,

alienating supporters on Vancouver Island. Cathers, *Beloved Dissident Eve Smith*, 129; also S.P. Lewis, *Grace*, 214.

104 G. MacInnis to MacNeil, 23 May 1951, file 4-10, GMC, UBCSC. Grace expressed her appreciation for MacNeil's work: 'had it not been for your courage in grasping that particular nettle of the Fellowship and obtaining the help you needed at the time of the National Council meeting, British Columbia might now be lost as far as the CCF is concerned.' She felt the 'well-known habit of awarding consolation prizes when we think we have won a victory' had to be discarded, to prevent Steeves and her group from using 'the CCF News as a means – the most powerful means – of building themselves up again and fostering the fog of confusion which led to trouble before ... I think it is *the* moment to make a change in British Columbia.'

105 Cathers, *Beloved Dissident Eve Smith*, 127.

106 Jamieson to G. MacInnis, 24 Nov. 1951, file 4-5, GMC, UBCSC. According to Jamieson, the left intended to raise the issue of the *CCF News* at the next Provincial Council meeting: 'I am hoping we can improve the paper and take the wind out of their sails.' In January 1951, McKenzie and Webster had lodged a formal complaint against Steeves's foreign-policy writings in a letter to the provincial executive. However, the committee appointed to consider the charges found there had been no 'studied misrepresentation of CCF policy by CCF News.' In March, MacNeil wrote to national secretary Lorne Ingle regarding Steeves's control of the paper: 'In her capacity as Chairman of the CCF News Committee she has slanted editorial material, despite frequent protests, toward the views held by the Fellowship.' After the right strengthened their control at the May convention, Steeves was placed on the defensive. By November, MacNeil had supplanted her as chair of the committee, but as a conciliatory gesture allowed her to remain on the committee. Jamieson lamented this concession to the left: 'The "Thaw" in the cold war in BC is having its effect early I am afraid.' Jamieson to G. MacInnis, 24 Nov. 1951, file 4-5; MacNeil to Ingle, 6 March 1951; G. MacInnis to MacNeil, 23 May 1951; 'Report of the Administration Committee on the Complaint filed by F. McKenzie and A. Webster against the CCF News Committee,' 15 Feb. 1951, file 4-10, GMC; McKenzie and Webster to Mendels, 23 Jan. 1951, file 73-21, AMC, UBCSC.

107 See David J. Elkins, 'Politics Makes Strange Bedfellows: The BC Party System in the 1952 and 1953 Provincial Elections,' *BC Studies*, 30 (Summer 1976), 3–26.

108 Patrick L. McGeer, *Politics in Paradise* (Toronto: Peter Martin, 1972), 101.

109 British Columbia, *Statement of Votes*, 1951.
110 H. Winch to G. MacInnis, 25 Feb. 1952, file 4-6, GMC, UBCSC. Winch discussed the implications the new voting system. While the government had not yet announced whether the general election would be conducted in accordance with the new rules, Winch believed that statements by Johnson and Wismer pointed in this direction, as did a directive to the chief electoral officer to draft an explanation. According to Winch, the electoral system adopted in BC 'is one unknown in the democratic world.' He was particularly critical of how the transferable ballot would be applied in multiple-member ridings, which included his own. Winch raised these concerns in his response to the Throne Speech, and warned the attorney general that the election results, due to irregularities in the amended Act, could be subject to a Court challenge; however, there is no evidence that Winch or the CCF mounted a legal challenge to the 1952 results. Bill 108, the Elections Act Amendment Act, is mentioned briefly in Jamieson to G. MacInnis, 17 April 1951, file 4-10, GMC, UBCSC.
111 'Political Action, Unity, Major Needs,' *Sun*, 22 Sept. 1951.
112 Steeves to Cameron, 4 June 1951, file 1-1, CCC, UBCSC.
113 Debate on Resolution L-11 Labor Representation, *UFAWU Proceedings* (1952), 330–1, Neish papers.
114 David J. Mitchell, *W.A.C. Bennett and the Rise of British Columbia* (Vancouver/Toronto: Douglas and McIntyre, 1995), 172. According to Mitchell, Uphill 'had written to Bennett several times during the election campaign and its aftermath; apparently, he hoped to become minister of mines if Social Credit did squeeze its way into power.' As Elkins argued, Social Credit benefited the most from the preferential-voting system. The Liberals and Conservatives were most negatively impacted, reduced to 6 and 4 seats, respectively, from 23 and 12 at dissolution. Elkins, 'Politics Makes Strange Bedfellows,' 3–26; Gordon Hak, 'Populism and the 1952 Social Credit Breakthrough in British Columbia,' *Canadian Historical Review*, 85:2 (June 2004), 277–96.
115 See Wickerson, 'Conflict in the British Columbia Cooperative Commonwealth Federation and the "Connell Affair."'
116 McKenzie to Val, 6 April 1953, file 4-6 'Correspondence, 1952–1956,' GMC, UBCSC.
117 A. Webster to A. and G. MacInnis, 28 Feb. 1953, file 73-6 'Correspondence 1953,' AMC, UBCSC.
118 MacNeil to G. MacInnis, 9 March 1953, file 4-6, GMC, UBCSC.
119 McKenzie to Val, 6 April 1953, file 4-6, GMC, UBCSC.
120 'Winch Quits as CCF Head,' *Colonist*, 29 March 1953; 'Convention to Pick

Leader April 13–15,' *Colonist*, 28 March 1953; 'Winch Definite on Resignation,' *Province*, 30 March 1953; 'Winch Action Clouds BC Picture,' *Daily Times*, 30 March 1953; 'Mr Winch and the CCF,' *Daily Times*, 30 March 1953; Mitchell, *W.A.C. Bennett*, 196–200.

121 'CCF Executive Endorses Webster,' *Province*, 10 April 1953; 'Nobody Wants to Win CCF Leadership,' *Province*, 10 April 1953; 'Winch Definitely Out as CCF Chief,' *Sun*, 10 April 1953; 'Winch Retirement Final; Webster May Lead CCF,' *Daily Times*, 10 April 1953; 'Webster Elected New CCF Leader,' *Colonist*, 11 April 1953; 'CCF Party Unanimously Sweeps Webster to Leadership,' *News Herald*, 11 April 1953; 'Arnold Webster Named CCF Provincial Leader,' *Sun*, 11 April 1953; 'CCF Rallies behind Vancouver's Webster,' *Daily Times*, 11 April 1953; also Arnold Alexander Webster fonds, UBCSC. At the convention, delegates considered changing the traditional greeting in the BC CCF from 'comrade' to 'friend.' As mentioned at the beginning of the chapter, 'comrade' had been used since 1932, reflecting traditions in the pre-CCF Socialist Party. 'Bye Comrade, 'Lo Friend, May Be New CCF Greeting,' *Daily Times*, 11 April 1953.

122 British Columbia, *Statement of Votes*, 1953.

123 Young defeated Vancouver lawyer Alex MacDonald for the CCF nomination. Two weeks before the nominating convention, MacDonald confided to Angus MacInnis that 'the outlook is not good.' MacDonald recommended against having the provincial executive 'refuse consent' to Young, suggesting that 'while the National might, if it had the power, it would not be wise to use the Provincial to start up a big Convention rabbit now. It is better to take a chance, and do our best.' MacInnis responded that 'there are very good reasons why Rodney's name should not be approved by the executive,' but that a motion to that effect by Grant MacNeil had elicited little support; moreover, 'there is no provision for such action as they would expect in our National Constitution.' However, against MacDonald's advice, the provincial executive refused consent to Young's candidacy, a decision overturned at the convention. In the general election, Young finished third, with 4,516 votes, behind a Social Credit candidate (4,946 votes) and a Liberal (8,259 votes). See MacDonald to A. MacInnis, 13 March 1953; A. MacInnis to MacDonald, 19 March 1953, file 73-6, AMC, UBCSC; 'Internal CCF Row Looms over Young,' *Sun*, 7 April 1953; 'Report Rouses Dispute,' *Colonist*, 11 April 1953; 'Report Sparks Argument during CCF Convention,' *News Herald*, 11 April 1953; 'Report of Provincial Executive Committee to 1955 Provincial Convention,' file 4-6, GMC, UBCSC; Canada, *Canadian Parliamentary Guide*, 1953.

124 McKenzie to G. MacInnis, 6 April 1952, file 4-6, GMC, UBCSC.

125 'CCFer Knows 50 Ex-Reds in Party,' *Sun*, 12 June 1954. Young made his remarks during debate on a Sooke CCF Club resolution that described the drive against Communism as 'witchhunting and Red-baiting' and 'merely a screen for the attack of big business on all working class organization bringing the threat of fascism.' Also 'CCF Movement "Set Back Ten Years" by "Proud-to-Be-Called-Red Remark,"' *Province*, 12 June 1954; '"Proud If Called Red," Says CCF Rod Young,' *Province*, 12 June 1954; 'Proud to Be Called a Red, Says CCF Member,' *Daily Times*, 12 June 1954.

126 'Emergency Resolution,' 1954 BC CCF Convention, file 4-9, GMC, UBCSC; '"Proud to Be Called a Red," Says CCFer; Ouster Beaten,' *Colonist*, 13 June 1954; 'Young Remains in CCF, but Remarks Repudiated,' *News Herald*, 14 June 1954; 'Young Escapes CCF Expulsion,' *Sun*, 14 June 1954; 'The CCF Keeps Its Rebel,' *Sun*, 15 June 1954; 'Rod Young Resigns from CCF after Suspension Ordered,' *Daily Times*, 12 July 1954; 'CCF Suspends Young, He Quits,' *Province*, 12 July 1954; 'Young Skips "Trial," Quits CCF Party,' *Sun*, 12 July 1954; 'Young Resigns from CCF Party,' 13 July 1954; 'Eventual Reinstatement for Young, Say Island CCFers,' *Colonist*, 14 July 1954; 'Party "Trial" of Rod Young Postponed,' *Sun*, 24 July 1954; '"Most-Talked of CCFer" Won't Attend Convention,' *Sun*, 15 April 1955; Bernard, 'The Rod Young Affair'; Young, *Anatomy of a Party*, 282–3. As Dorothy Steeves wrote after the convention, the controversy arose over 'one of the foolish Sooke resolutions, condemning "red-baiting, witch-hunting", etc ... Rod gained no policy point by these idiotic statements ... I feel that whatever happens, Rod has ditched himself in the CCF now and he may not be a member much longer.' Citing Tom Alsbury's growing isolation among CCF trade-union members, Steeves wrote: 'Well, we shall be well rid of both of them.' Steeves to Cameron, 13 June 1954, file 1-1, CCC, UBCSC.

127 Bernard, 'The Rod Young Affair,' 79.

128 D. Lewis, *The Good Fight*, 429.

129 'Biggest CCF Convention in 15 Years Opens,' *Province*, 15 April 1955; 'Two Leftists Elected to CCF Executive,' *Sun*, 18 April 1955; 'CCF Strife Blamed on Executive,' *Sun*, 15 April 1955; 'CCF Slump Blamed on Party Plot,' *Sun*, 15 April 1955; 'CCF Plans Drive against Trotskyist Plotters Here,' *Sun*, 11 April 1955; 'Just One Trotskyist Got Cameron's Help,' *Daily Times*, 13 April 1955; '"Trotskyites" Cost CCF '52 Election,' *Sun*, 14 April 1955. '"Trotskyism" Charge, Labor Policy Split CCF Delegates,' *Sun*, 16 April 1955; 'Trotsky Communists Aim for Class War, Revolution,' *Sun*, 16 April 1955. The *Sun* reported that the North Vancouver trials, which occurred in January, would become entangled with the *Box 16* controversy. In execu-

tive elections, Steeves defeated Jessie Mendels for first vice-president on a 79–75 vote, while Winch defeated Home for second vice-president 83–70. However, for president, Frank McKenzie easily defeated David Stupich 94–57. During the convention, British Labour Party leader Clement Atlee addressed a crowd of 3,500 at a CCF-sponsored rally in Vancouver's Exhibition Gardens. 'Attlee Pins World's Hope on Democratic Socialism,' *Sun*, 18 April 1955.

130 'CCF Strife Blamed on Executive,' *Sun*, 15 April 1955. Stupich, an outgoing member of the provincial executive, and past president Joseph Corsbie refused to sign the executive report 'Program for Action' and presented their own 'minority report' to the convention. 'The Program for Action and the Campaign for a CCF government,' n.d. [1955], file 9, box 3; 'A Call for Action to the CCF,' n.d. [1955], file 2, box 3, Rodney Young papers, UBCSC.

131 'Trotsky Communists Aim for Class War, Revolution,' *Sun*, 16 April 1955; '"Trotskyism" Charge, Labor Policy Split CCF Delegates,' *Sun*, 16 April 1955.

132 'Report of the Provincial Executive Committee to the 1955 Provincial Convention,' file 4-6, GMC, UBCSC.

133 'Our Movement Is in Peril,' n.d. [1955], file 4-6, GMC, UBCSC.

134 Ibid.; also 'The Program for Action and the Campaign for a CCF Government,' n.d. [1955], file 9, box 3, Rodney Young papers, UBCSC.

135 Young, *Anatomy of a Party*, 3–11, 287–308.

136 Zakuta, *A Protest Movement Becalmed*, 4–5, 141–2.

137 In October 1950, MacInnis had urgently wired Coldwell, who was in New York with a Canadian delegation for Korea talks: 'Crossing thirty-eighth parallel by South Koreans unwise and very disturbing STOP war danger tremendously and needlessly increased STOP suggest you strongly urge Canadian delegation oppose crossing border by any armed forces and United Nations instruct all troops return south of border STOP Indias stand appears correct STOP.' In a letter sent the same day, MacInnis wrote: 'It is also of first importance that all bombing by U.N., U.S., or any other forces should stop at once. Bombing industrial works or the homes of the people is not a good way to teach democracy.' Coldwell responded that 'if the United Nations will, as I think they will, decide to unify the country by sending a force across the 38th Parallel, we will have to support the action. I had hoped this would not be necessary.' A. MacInnis to Coldwell, 1 Oct. 1950; Coldwell to A. MacInnis, 6 Oct. 1950, file 73-3, AMC, UBCSC. At the National Convention that summer, Angus had been sidelined by Lewis and other national leaders in his bid to succeed Frank

Scott as national chairman. According to S.P. Lewis, 'It was the most bitter disappointment of Angus's political life, and the beginning of his decline … For the first time since the CCF's founding in 1932, he was not on the national council.' S.P. Lewis, *Grace*, 206–7.

138 A. MacInnis to Coldwell, 27 Oct. 1950, file 73-3, AMC, UBCSC.

139 'Webster Quits as Leader of Provincial CCF Party,' *Sun*, 9 March 1956; 'Webster Quits as CCF Leader,' *Province*, 9 March 1956; 'Webster Quits as CCF Leader,' *Daily Times*, 9 March 1956.

140 Webster to A. MacInnis, n.d. [Sept. 1953], file 73-6, AMC, UBCSC.

141 Steeves to Cameron, 5 Sept. 1955, file 1-1, CCC, UBCSC.

142 While the CCF proposed 'horizontal division of ownership,' the IWA felt that the 'industry is built vertically and won't work any other way…. The IWA likes FML's [Forest Management Licences], with reforms, that is.' According to Steeves, Dave Stupich of Nanaimo was the only executive member who voted against withdrawing the forestry brief. Steeves to Cameron, 15 Jan. 1955, file 1-1, CCC, UBCSC.

143 Steeves to Cameron, 15 Jan. 1955, file 1-1, CCC, UBCSC.

144 'CCF Lambasts SC, Misses Giveaways,' *Pacific Tribune*, 10 Feb. 1956.

145 '"Militant Socialist" Chosen by CCF as Provincial Chief,' *Sun*, 7 April 1956. Strachan defeated fellow MLAs Arthur Turner and Leo Nimsick, who entered the race at the last moment. According to Steeves: 'The caucus would have been unanimous on [Randolph] Harding, but were otherwise split. Ernie [Winch] told me that the ten who were present voted 5 for Bob, 3 for Macdonald and 2 for Turner … In the convention Macdonald declined to run and the left had decided in despair to vote for Turner, when Nimsick came up as a dark horse nomination and so they switched to him, he got 35 votes, Turner only 19 and I was surprised to see him get that much.' Also 'Strachan to Seek CCF Leadership,' *Colonist*, 18 March 1956; 'Strachan Seeking CCF Leadership,' *Province*, 19 March 1956; 'CCF Officials Favour Strachan for Leader As Webster Quits,' *Colonist*, 10 March 1956; 'Party Battle in CCF Ranks Looms over Rightist Move,' *Herald*, 29 March 1956; 'BC CCF Elects New House Leader, No Discussion of Party Policy,' *Workers Vanguard* (Toronto), May 1956, file 24-6, Dowson fonds, LAC.

146 'Political Pot Boils,' *Sun*, 9 April 1956.

147 'BC CCF Convention Faces Big Tasks,' *Workers Vanguard*, March 1956, file 24-6, Dowson fonds, LAC.

148 'Adhere to Manifesto,' *CCF News*, 6 April 1949.

149 'Time for Revolt, Says CCF Leader,' *Calgary Herald*, 10 Nov. 1943; 'CCF Would Enforce Socialism Aid of Police, Military,' *Ottawa Journal*, 10 Nov.

1943; 'Misinterpret Winch Coldwell Comments,' *Toronto Daily Star*, 11 Nov. 1943.

150 A committee consisting of Lewis, Coldwell, and Scott had proposed a draft electoral program modifying the CCF's socialization plank to allow room for private enterprise under a CCF government. The national leadership was motivated, Lewis claimed, by 'the need to allay unjustified fears and suspicions, in the hope of increasing support for the party.' D. Lewis, *The Good Fight*, 257; 'Lewis Denies "Win Election" Statement,' *Sun*, 9 Dec. 1944; 'Cash Worries CCF Topic,' *Montreal Star*, 30 Nov. 1944.

151 'CCF Parley Orders Appendix for Basic Regina Manifesto,' *Sun*, 29 July 1950; 'National Council Instructed to Modernize Regina Manifesto,' *CCF News*, 2 Aug. 1950; Young, *Anatomy of a Party*, 170–1. The CCF national caucus had endorsed an 'innocuous' resolution on 22 July 1950 empowering the National Council to begin drafting a new statement of principles, according to Young.

152 'The CCF Convention,' *Canadian Forum*, Sept. 1950, 124. The Frankfurt Declaration was adopted at the first congress of the Socialist International in July 1951 and stated that 'socialist planning … is compatible with the existence of private ownership in important fields.'

153 'CCF Parley Orders Appendix for Basic Regina Manifesto,' *Sun*, 29 July 1950.

154 Ibid.

155 'Comrades of the CCF,' 5 Aug. 1950; Burton to Dowson, 18 April 1950, file 9-2, vol. 2, CTM fonds, LAC. Prior to the 1950 CCF Convention, Burton reported that the CCF left and MLAs including Leo Nimsick and Randolph Harding believed 'the CCF can yet be rescued and returned to the principles of the Regina Manifesto.'

156 After the 1950 convention, a committee had been appointed to draft the statement in consultation with party units, consisting of David Lewis, Frank Scott, Andrew Brewin, Tommy Douglas, Lorne Ingle, Hazen Argue, Grace MacInnis, Joe Noseworthy, Francois Laroche, and Clarie Gillis. However, the thirty-page draft contained six areas of disagreement, and a revised version prepared by Ingle and Grace MacInnis failed to ease concerns in the National Council and provincial sections. In March 1952 the council postponed consideration of the matter until the 1954 convention. However, prior to that convention the National Council again rejected a revised draft. The BC section's concerns were discussed at the National Executive meeting of 29 Feb. 1952. See Young, *Anatomy of a Party*, 126–8 and 172–3.

157 'Notes on National Council Meeting,' 13–15 Jan. 1956, file 7-9 'National

Council Meeting, Rough Notes, 1956,' vol. 7, CCF-NDP fonds, LAC; 'Federation Envisioned by Douglas,' *Pacific Tribune*, 29 June 1956; also Young, *Anatomy of a Party*, 128.

158 'Notes on National Council Meeting,' 13–15 Jan. 1956, file 7-9, CCF-NDP fonds, LAC.

159 'CCF Endorses New Platform,' *Winnipeg Free Press*, 4 Aug. 1956; also '"Old Guard" Loses Battle of Socialism,' *Winnipeg Free Press*, 2 Aug. 1956; 'Last Stand by CCF Diehards,' *Winnipeg Free Press*, 3 Aug. 1956; 'CCF Hopes for New Life from Manifesto's Death,' *Winnipeg Free Press*, 4 Aug. 1956.

160 'Timely Reminder,' *Sun*, 6 Aug. 1956. According to the *Sun*, 'Since nationalization disappointed the hopes of many British socialists and disillusioned the workers who expected so much from it, the emphasis has shifted to ways of promoting and preserving individual rights in any form of society ... In Canada there's no reasonable chance that the CCF, at least for a long time, can hope to supplant the Liberal party. But it could move into the Liberal party and give it the necessary spur to be what its name implies and what its present leadership has forgotten.' Also Frank H. Underhill, 'The Winnipeg Declaration of the CCF,' in *In Search of Canadian Liberalism* (Toronto: Macmillan, 1960), 243–7.

161 The fourteen Ontario members had been expelled in April 1955, and appealed the decision to the Winnipeg convention. Mitchell and SEL president George Stanton arranged a dissident meeting at the Winnipeg Labour Temple, coinciding with the convention, but influential CCFers in the Winnipeg Trades and Labour Council succeeded in having the booking cancelled. Their appeal was rejected by convention delegates. 'CCF "Closed Door" on the Truth-Trotskyists,' *Winnipeg Free Press*, 3 Aug. 1956; 'Fourteen Reds Ousted by Ontario CCF Party,' *Sun*, 9 April 1955.

162 'Running in the Federal Election and Our Orientation,' n.d. [c. 1957], file 57-11, Dowson fonds, LAC.

163 'Farm-Labor Clash in CCF,' *Winnipeg Free Press*, 4 Aug. 1956.

164 Morgan to LPP constituency committees and provincial candidates, 22 Aug. 1956, file 23-02 BC elections 1960, 'BC provincial series,' reel H1592, CPC fonds, LAC.

165 '"Bulk of Labor" Voted CCF, Says Home,' *Sun*, 20 Sept. 1956; British Columbia, *Statement of Votes*, 1956.

166 '"Public Is Only Interested in Half-a-Mile of Black Top,"' *Sun*, 20 Sept. 1956.

167 '"Money Beat Us," Says Bitter CCF,' *Sun*, 20 Sept. 1956.

168 'Premier Douglas Not Surprised by BC Vote,' *Sun*, 20 Sept. 1956.

169 Morgan to LPP constituency committees and provincial candidates, 22 Aug. 1956, file 23-02, 'BC provincial series,' reel H1592, CPC fonds, LAC.
170 E.E. Winch to Ingle, 13 Dec. 1956, as quoted in Steeves, *The Compassionate Rebel*, 210.
171 Steeves, *The Compassionate Rebel*, 111
172 'Confidential – For National Committee Members Only,' Socialist Educational League, 3 Jan. 1957, file 19-2 'Discussion Documents and Reports, n.d. 1955–1959,' CTM fonds, LAC; 'Running in the Federal Election and Our Orientation,' n.d. [c. 1957], file 57-11, Dowson fonds, LAC; 'Pre-Election Report – Socialist Committee for the Organization of a Labour Party in Canada,' 19 Nov. 1957, file 3, box 3, Rodney Young papers, UBCSC; also 'Provisional Constitution'; Pool and Young, 'Introduction,' in Morgan, *Workers' Control on the Railroad*, 23–4.
173 BC Federation of Labour (CLC), *Report of Proceedings of Second Convention* (hereafter *BCFL Proceedings*) (1957), 74. In 1954, Dorothy Steeves confided to Colin Cameron that Tom Alsbury was falling out of favour within the Vancouver Trades and Labour Council: 'the CCFers are withdrawing their votes from him and the only thing which keeps him in office (with a greatly reduced vote) is the Liberal vote.' A year later, Steeves reported that the 'AFL BC Congress threw out the rightists ... I am told that Tom is now as discredited as Gervin – that he is trying to get the NPA nomination for Mayor and that no CCF trade unionists will vote for him.' Steeves to Cameron, 13 June 1954; Steeves to Cameron, 9 Oct. 1955, file 1-1, box 1, CCC, UBCSC.
174 In 1966, Alsbury ran against NDPers Tom Berger and Ray Parkinson in the two-member riding. He received 7,584 votes to 9,849 votes for Berger and 9,498 for Parkinson. A year later, he returned to Vancouver City Council under the NPA banner, capturing the tenth and final council seat with 35,448 votes. BC NDP president Norm Levi, a future MLA and cabinet minister, finished thirteenth with 27,471 votes. See British Columbia, *Statement of Votes*, 1966; 'Here's Final Result of Civic Vote Race,' file 23-23 Vancouver municipal elections 1966, 'BC provincial series,' reel H1592, CPC fonds, LAC.

4. Other Lefts

1 'Outline of Manifesto,' 2 Jan. 1967, file 9, box 16a, CUCND-SUPA archives, McMaster Archives and Research Collections (hereafter MARC).
2 Maurice Isserman, *If I Had a Hammer: The Death of the Old Left and the Birth of the New Left* (New York: Basic, 1987).

3 Ibid., 36–75.

4 This description is provided in Dowson to Burton, 25 April 1950, file 9-2, vol. 2, CTM fonds, LAC; for the significance of the Vancouver branch, see Dowson to Vancouver Executive, 5 May 1948, file 10-2 'Vancouver Branch 1947,' vol. 2, CTM fonds, LAC.

5 Bryan D. Palmer, 'Maurice Spector, James P. Cannon, and the Origins of Canadian Trotskyism,' *Labour/Le Travail*, 56 (Fall 2005), 91–148; Ian McKay, 'Revolution Deferred: Maurice Spector's Political Odyssey, 1928–1941,' Paper presented to the Canadian Historical Association Annual Meeting, Halifax, May 2003; Ian Angus, *Canadian Bolsheviks: The Early Years of the Communist Party of Canada* (Montreal: Vanguard, 1981); Elaine Bernard, 'A History of BC Trotskyism as seen through *Labour Challenge* and *Workers Vanguard*, 1945–1961,' <http://www.socialisthistory.ca/Docs/History/Bernard-BC_Trot.htm#8> (accessed 10 Nov. 2006); Heather McLeod, 'Not Another God-Dam Housewife: Ruth Bullock, the "Woman Question" and Canadian Trotskyism,' MA thesis, Simon Fraser University, 1993; also Gary O'Brien, 'Maurice Spector and the Origin of Canadian Trotskyism,' MA thesis, Carleton University, 1974; Ross Dowson, 'Maurice Spector, 1898–1968,' *Workers Vanguard*, 26 Aug. 1968.

6 'Trotskyites Seek Trouble,' *Labor Statesman* (Vancouver), 27 Jan. 1928.

7 In 1941, the three dissidents were charged with violating the War Measures Act (1914) and Defense of Canada Regulations (1940) for possessing copies of *Island Clarion*, *Internationalism*, *Conscription Is a Matron's Betrayal*, and *Democracy, Civil Liberties, Economic Conditions*, which were considered 'prejudicial to the safety of the state or the efficient prosecution of the war'; the accused were sentenced to nine months imprisonment. See 'History of Policing in Oak Bay,' *Oak Bay News*, 7 Feb. 2001; Bernard, 'A History of BC Trotskyism.'

8 In 1950, Ross Dowson referred to 'the stinking record of Harvey Murphy during the war, his battling for the no-strike pledge, his support of the Liberals in the 1945 election.' Dowson to Burton, 25 April 1950, file 9-2, vol. 2, CTM fonds, LAC.

9 The LPP summoned White before a special tribunal that consisted of provincial leader Nigel Morgan, *Tribune* editor Tom McEwen, and Gary Culhane, a political rival who was gunning for White's job as union president. While he was acquitted, its accusatory tone contributed to White's decision to leave the LPP in 1949. McQuillan belonged to the DeLeonite Socialist Labor Party (SLP), a non-Trotskyist group, and had run as an SLP candidate in Vancouver Centre in the 1945 federal election, taking 319 votes. His SLP colleague Paul Debragh took 140 votes in Vancouver-

Burrard. Howard White, *A Hard Man to Beat: The Story of Bill White, Labour Leader, Historian, Shipyard Worker, Raconteur* (Vancouver: Pulp Press, 1983), 174–5; Canada, *Canadian Parliamentary Guide*, 1945.

10 'New Trotskyite Sheet,' *Pacific Tribune*, 20 Feb. 1948.

11 'IWA Routs Stalinists, Way Open to New Gains,' *Labor Challenge* (Vancouver), Nov. 1948; Jerry Lembcke and William M. Tattam, *One Union in Wood: A Political History of the International Woodworkers of America* (Madeira Park, BC: Harbour/International Publishers, 1984), 205 fn83; also Ruth and Reg Bullock fonds, UBCSC.

12 Bernard, 'A History of Trotskyism in BC.'

13 Dowson to Rosslund (Burton), 25 Sept. 1950, file 9-2, vol. 2, CTM fonds, LAC; also Ross Dowson, 'Our Orientation to the NDP – as a strategy and its tactical application' (1970), Socialist History Project <http://www.socialisthistory.ca/Docs/CCF-NDP/Orientation-Dowson-1970.htm> (accessed 10 Nov. 2006); Ross Dowson, 'Trotskyism and the NDP,' *Labor Challenge* (Toronto), file 31-16, vol. 31, Dowson fonds, LAC; *Revolutionary Trotskyist Bulletin No. 3: Trotskyism and the CCF/NDP: Documents from 1938 to 1973* (Toronto 1978), cited in Palmer, 'Maurice Spector, James P. Cannon, and the Origins of Canadian Trotskyism,' 139, fn75.

14 Dorothy G. Steeves, *The Compassionate Rebel: Ernest Winch and the Growth of Socialism in Western Canada* (Vancouver: J.J. Douglas, 1977), 114–15.

15 Dowson to Burton, 8 Jan. 1949, file 9-2, vol. 2, CTM fonds, LAC.

16 'Former CCF Members Form *Labor Challenge* Group,' *Labor Challenge*, mid-Sept. 1946, as quoted in Bernard, 'A History of BC Trotskyism.'

17 'Three BC LPP Members Break; Support RWP,' *Labor Challenge*, Dec. 1946, as cited in Bernard, 'A History of BC Trotskyism'; 'CCF Delegate from BC Issues Call for Revolutionary Program,' *Labor Challenge*, mid-Aug. 1946; 'Former CCF Members Form *Labor Challenge* Group,' *Labor Challenge*, mid-Sept. 1946; and 'National Convention Launches the Revolutionary Workers Party,' *Labor Challenge*, mid-Oct. 1946, as cited in Bernard, 'A History of BC Trotskyism'; Lembcke and Tattam, *One Union in Wood*, 205 fn83.

18 Dowson to Burton, 8 Jan. 1949, file 9-2, vol. 2, CTM fonds, LAC. William Green was president of the American Federation of Labor (AFL) (1924–52), advocating labour-management cooperation and taking a hard line during the CIO split in the 1930s. Percy Bengough, a machinist by trade, was secretary of the Vancouver Trades and Labor Council (1921–42) and president of the Trades and Labor Congress of Canada (TLC) (1943–54). Aaron R. Mosher was president of the Congress of Canadian Labour (CCL), a former leader of the Canadian Brotherhood of Railway Employees and an avowed anti-communist.

19 Dowson to Burton, 8 Jan. 1949, file 9-2, vol. 2, CTM fonds, LAC. The RWP's orientation was outlined in a May 1950 'seven-point program' for Burton's political work in the year ahead: '(1) Clarification and organization of the BC Left CCF; (2) Formation of the Trail CCF Left into a club; (3) Defeat of the Right-Steelworkers raid; (4) Increased circulation of the L.C. as an educational and propaganda organ; (5) Exposure of the right-wing CCF through educational efforts; (6) Exposure of the Stalinists [*sic*] role in the Labor Movement; (7) Recruitment of membership.' Burton to Dowson, 4 May 1950, file 9-2, vol. 2, CTM fonds, LAC.

20 Kane (Dowson) to Burton, 29 Sept 1949, file 9-2, vol. 2, CTM fonds, LAC. Dowson often wrote under the pseudonym Paul Kane.

21 Burton to Dowson, 8 March 1950, file 9-2, vol. 2, CTM fonds, LAC. Charlie Millard was Canadian director of the United Steelworkers of America (USWA). Mosher and Millard were influential in curbing communist influence in Canadian unions.

22 Burton to Dowson, 18 April 1950; Dowson to Burton 25 April 1950, file 9-2, vol. 2, CTM fonds, LAC. According to Dowson, the Penticton convention proved 'there is a very broad leftist tendency in BC which the left despite all its weaknesses managed to tap.' After the convention, Dowson received a 'red hot letter' from CCF leftist Eve Smith alleging that the *Labor Challenge* coverage of the convention had threatened to sink the left at Penticton and urged the RWP to 'try to develop a little political sense.' Dowson to Burton, 25 April 1950, file 9-2, vol. 2, CTM fonds, LAC.

23 Burton to Dowson, April 1950, file 9-2, vol. 2, CTM fonds, LAC; Burton to Dowson, n.d. [c. May 1950]; 'To All CCF Leftists in Trail,' n.d. [c. May 1950]; Dowson to Burton 25 April 1950, file 9-2, vol. 2, CTM fonds, LAC.

24 Burton worked for the municipality of Tadanac, a sister community to Trail. Dowson to Burton, 28 May 1950; Rosslund (Burton) to Dowson, 2 Nov. 1950, file 9-2, vol. 2, CTM fonds, LAC.

25 Dowson to Burton, 28 May 1950, file 9-2, vol. 2, CTM fonds, LAC; 'Unity through Democratic Discipline,' *CCF News*, 26 April 1950. Dowson wrote that 'Comrade Bullock in his last letter suggested that you should take on a pseudonym for party correspondence etc. I think it would be advisable since you are working in the CCF. Take your choice if the above is suitable alright.'

26 Burton to Dowson, 1 Aug. 1950; Dowson to Rosslund (Burton), 21 July 1950, file 9-2, vol. 2, CTM fonds, LAC. Dowson noted that 'CCFers are tremendously influenced by the BLP and developments within it.'

27 Rosslund (Burton) to Dowson, 1 Aug. 1950, file 9-2, vol. 2, CTM fonds, LAC.

28 Burton to Young, 7 Aug. 1950, file 9-2, vol. 2, CTM fonds, LAC.
29 Rosslund (Burton) to Dowson, 1 Aug. 1950; 'Comrades of the CCF,' 5 Aug. 1950, file 9-2, vol. 2, CTM fonds, LAC.
30 Dowson to Rosslund (Burton), 21 Aug. 1950; Rosslund (Burton) to Dowson, 5 Aug. 1950, file 9-2, vol. 2, CTM fonds, LAC.
31 Dowson to Burton 25 April 1950, file 9-2, vol. 2, CTM fonds, LAC.
32 Burton to Dowson, 4 May 1950; Burton to Dowson, n.d. (c. May 1950), file 9-2, CTM fonds, LAC. Earlier evidence of internal strife can be found in Vancouver branch to Members at Large, n.d. (c. April 1947); Dowson to Vancouver Executive, 11 March 1947; Dowson to Vancouver Executive, 16 April 1947; Dowson to Vancouver Executive, 5 May 1948, file 10-2, vol. 2, CTM fonds, LAC.
33 In August 1950, Young described Burton as 'a Trotskyist provocateur, which I suppose in a way I was.' Rosslund (Burton) to Dowson, 5 Aug. 1950, file 9-2, vol. 2, CTM fonds, LAC; also 'Trotskyists and the CCF,' *Labour Challenge*, mid-April 1951, as quoted in Bernard, 'A History of Trotskyism in BC'; S.P. Lewis, *Grace: The Life of Grace MacInnis* (Madeira Park, BC: Harbour, 1993), 213–14.
34 Dowson to Burton 25 April 1950, file 9-2, vol. 2, CTM fonds, LAC.
35 Dowson to Rosslund (Burton), 28 May 1950, file 9-2, vol. 2, CTM fonds, LAC.
36 Dowson to Rosslund (Burton), 2 Aug. 1950, file 9-2, vol. 2, CTM fonds, LAC. Emphasis added.
37 Dowson to Rosslund (Burton), 25 Sept. 1950, file 9-2, vol. 2, CTM fonds, LAC.
38 Rosslund (Burton) to Dowson, 2 Nov. 1950, file 9-2, vol. 2, CTM fonds, LAC.
39 Ibid.; Rosslund (Burton) to 'Reg, Ruth and all Vancouver Comrades,' 8 Oct. 1950, file 9-2, vol. 2, CTM fonds, LAC.
40 Dowson to Rosslund (Burton), 23 Oct. 1950; A. Burton (a.k.a. Steve Rosslund), 'Whether the CCF?,' n.d. [c. Sept. 1950], file 9-2, vol. 2, CTM fonds, LAC.
41 Dowson to Rosslund (Burton), 27 Nov. 1950, file 9-2, vol. 2, CTM fonds, LAC.
42 Dowson to Murray and Barry, 27 Sept. 1951; Dowson to Gang (Barry and Murray), 9 Aug. 1951; Dowson to Barry and Murray, 19 Oct 1951, file 49-10 'E2-1951-From,' vol. 49, Dowson fonds, LAC. Barry suggested, however, that 'Burton has our CCF orientation … Maybe someday you will learn the elements of how to work with comrades. You don't come in from the outside like a visiting school inspector and grill and pound your com-

rades, you try to establish a friendly working relationship with them, and try to get across as much as possible in the brief period of your stay … If I wanted to try and wield the big stick I'd join the army.' Barry to Dowson, 28 Oct. 1951, file 49-9 'E2-1951-to,' vol. 49, Dowson fonds, LAC. There is no evidence of contact between Burton and the RWP (or later Trotskyist formations) after 1952. In the early 1960s, he was hired as business agent of Civic Workers Local 343, and attended CUPE's founding convention as one of two Local 343 delegates. See Jo Dunaway, *We're Your Neighbours: The Story of CUPE BC* (Vancouver: Canadian Union of Public Employees – BC Division, 2000), 10.

43 Fitzgerald (M. Dowson) to Rosslund (Burton), 17 March 1952, file 9-2, vol. 2, CTM fonds, LAC. Murray Dowson wrote under the pseudonym T. Fitzgerald.

44 Bernard, 'A History of Trotskyism in BC.'

45 Barry to Dowson, 5 July 1952, file 49-11 'E2-1951-to,' vol. 49, Dowson fonds, LAC; also Hugh to Ross, 18 June 1954; Hugh to Ross and Murray, 21 Sept. 1954; Bill to Ross, 24 Oct. 1954, file 11-2 'Vancouver Branch 1954,' vol. 2, CTM fonds, LAC. It does not appear that MacPhee was formally associated with the RWP, though in 1960 he visited Dowson in Toronto and expressed displeasure with the conduct of Jerry and Ruth Houle. *Workers Vanguard* reported on a Cuba motion MacPhee made at the 1960 BCFL convention. 'BC Labor to Find Truth about Cuba,' *Workers Vanguard*, mid-Oct. 1960; Dowson to J. and R. Houle, 31 July 1960, file 57-8, Dowson fonds, LAC; Angus MacPhee fonds, UBCSC.

46 In the early 1950s, the Fourth International faced the most acute internal crisis since Trotsky's death in 1940. A group of dissidents issued a 'Militant Open Letter,' attacking the leadership of Michel Pablo and Ernest Mandel as 'revisionist' and triggering an organizational break in the Trotksyist left. See correspondence on 'Militant Open Letter' and 'Pabloists,' file 11-2 'Vancouver Branch 1954'; also file 15-2 'Cannon, James P Correspondence 1954–1961,' vol. 2, CTM fonds, LAC.

47 'CCF Plans Drive against Trotskyist Plotters Here,' *Sun*, 11 April 1955; 'Just One Trotskyist Got Cameron's Help,' *Daily Times*, 13 April 1955; '"Trotskyites" Cost CCF '52 Election,' *Sun*, 14 April 1955; '"Trotskyism" Charge, Labor Policy Split CCF Delegates,' *Sun*, 16 April 1955; 'Trotsky Communists Aim for Class War, Revolution,' *Sun*, 16 April 1955; 'Fourteen Reds Ousted by Ontario CCF Party,' *Sun*, 9 April 1955; Kane to Friends, 24 Oct. 1954; Dowson to Reg Bullock, 3 Dec. 1954, file 11-2 'Vancouver Branch 1954,' vol. 2, CTM fonds, LAC.

48 'Socialist Education League Organized,' *Workers Vanguard*, Dec. 1955, as

quoted in Bernard, 'A History of BC Trotskyism'; 'Running in the Federal Election and Our Orientation,' n.d. [c. 1957], file 57-11, Dowson fonds, LAC.

49 Ibid.; 'Confidential – For National Committee Members Only,' Socialist Educational League, 3 Jan. 1957, file 19-2 'Discussion Documents and Reports, n.d. 1955–1959,' CTM fonds, LAC.

50 Dowson later questioned SIC's ongoing validity, describing it as 'a hangover from this regroupment era,' set up with the practical purpose of providing 'a place where *we* could meet, keep our files, work out from' (emphasis original). He questioned whether SIC was 'continuing in old ways' and detracting from 'really getting into the new labor party.' Dowson to J. and R. Houle, 31 July 1960, file 57-8, Dowson fonds, LAC; 'The Need for the LSA & What It Wants,' *Workers Vanguard*, mid-June 1961; 'Vancouver Socialist Forum Discusses Military Budget,' *Workers Vanguard*, mid-Feb. 1959, as quoted in Bernard, 'A History of BC Trotskyism'; Ross Dowson, 'Our Orientation to the NDP – as a strategy and its tactical application' (1970), *Socialist History Project* <http://www.socialisthistory.ca/Docs/CCF-NDP/Orientation-Dowson-1970.htm> (accessed 10 Nov. 2006).

51 J. Houle to Dowson, 28 Dec. 1960, file 57-8, Dowson fonds, LAC. The SWP is discussed in 'A Reply to Comrade Frazer,' n.d. [c. 1967], *YS/LJS Discussion Bulletin*, March 1967, file 19-13, Dowson fonds, LAC. For information on Bruce and SIC's activities in Vancouver, see 'The Need for the LSA & What It Wants,' *Workers Vanguard*, mid-June 1961; Bernard, 'A History of BC Trotskyism'; 'Socialist Forum,' 10 Feb. [1961], panel with Malcolm Bruce, file 57-8, Dowson fonds, LAC; 'Malcolm Bruce, 1880–1967,' *Workers Vanguard*, mid-May 1967.

52 Dowson to [Vancouver] Comrades, 29 Dec. 1960; 'NC Meeting Minutes,' 25 Sept. 1960, file 57-8, Dowson fonds, LAC. The National Committee brainstormed a number of names for the new organization: Socialist Labor League, League for Socialist Action, Socialist Action League, Socialist Educational League, Socialist Workers Alliance (League), League for Socialist Policy, Socialist Unity League, and Workers Socialist League.

53 Dowson to [Vancouver] Comrades, 25 Feb. 1961, file 57-8, Dowson fonds, LAC.

54 Branch 2 member Fred McNeil (a Vancouver Labour Council delegate from ILWU Local 507) withdrew his nomination for the Vancouver Centre CCF candidacy, despite 'a resolution endorsing him' by the council of CCF clubs in the riding, branch member Jerry Houle informed Dowson. The Branch 2 executive, consisting of McNeil and Ruth and Reg Bullock, decided that McNeil should withdraw, under pressure from the BC CCF

executive. In the Stanley Park Club nominating meeting, Tom Berger took 40 votes to 40 for William Dennison and 24 for SIC member Harold Rittberg. Berger and Dennison went on to win the nomination for the two-member riding, but lost the election by a wide margin to Social Credit candidates. See R. and J. Houle to Dowson, 27 June 1960; R. and J. Houle to Dowson, 10 July 1960; J. Houle to Dowson, 28 July 1960; J. Houle to Dowson, 2 Aug. 1960; J. Houle to Dowson, 8 Aug. 1969, file 57-8, Dowson fonds, LAC; British Columbia, *Statement of Votes*, 1960. For debate on the New Party structure and the question of formal affiliation versus deep entryism, see Ruth Bullock to Dowson, 16 Sept. 1960, file 57-8, Dowson fonds, LAC. Vancouver's Fair Play for Cuba Committee is discussed in Dowson to [Vancouver] Comrades, 29 Dec. 1960; Dowson to [Vancouver] Comrades, 25 Feb. 1961; J. Houle to Dowson, 21 Nov. 1960; 'Hello Ross & the comrades of the PC,' 23 Nov. 1960; J. Houle to Dowson, 28 Dec. 1960, file 57-8, Dowson fonds, LAC. Dowson cited a 5 November 1960 picket demonstration called by the City Executive in the name of the Fair Play for Cuba Committee, which Dowson felt was 'somewhat premature … when in reality no committee existed outside ourselves.' See 'Hands Off Cuba,' Nov. 1960, file 57-8, Dowson fonds, LAC.

55 'Minutes of Political Committee,' 1 Jan. 1961, file 57-8, Dowson fonds, LAC; J. Houle to Dowson, 28 July 1960; R. and J. Houle to Dowson, 10 July 1960; J. Houle to Dowson, 16 Sept. 1960; Dowson to J. Houle, 30 Sept. 1960, file 57-8, Dowson fonds, LAC. Branch 1 objected to changes Bruce had made to articles for the newspaper. As Ruth and Jerry Houle wrote to Dowson: 'How can branch 1 be responsible to an editor who is opposed to them "politically."'

56 Dowson to R. and J. Houle, 1 March 1961; R. Houle to Dowson, 7 March 1961; also J. Houle to Dowson, 21 June 1960; R. and J. Houle to Dowson, 27 June 1960; R. and J. Houle to Dowson, 10 July 1960; Dowson to J. and R. Houle, 31 July 1960; J. Houle to Dowson, 21 Nov. 1960; Shelley Rogers to Branch 2 Comrades, 23 Dec. 1960; Dowson to J. and R. Houle, 3 Jan. 1961, file 57-8, Dowson fonds, LAC. Jerry Houle wrote to Dowson in November 1960 about fellow Branch 2 members 'Ruth, Reg, Fred and Malcolm' who, 'being in the majority in the convention looked upon this as a stick with which to beat branch one.' Houle described Ruth Bullock as 'a real case. I have never met a person who can be so vicious, petty and personal.' In late December 1960, Bullock assisted a move by Shelley Rogers to have Houle recalled as Branch 2 delegate to SIC's City Executive Committee.

57 'Found League for Socialist Action,' *Workers Vanguard*, mid-June 1961, file 57-8, Dowson fonds, LAC.

58 'Pre-Election Annual report,' n.d. [c. Nov. 1957]; 'Provisional Constitution,' n.d., file 3, box 3, Rodney Young papers, UBCSC; Pool and Young, 'Introduction: R.E. (Lefty) Morgan, His Life and Work,' in R.E. 'Lefty' Morgan, *Workers' Control on the Railroad: A Practical Example 'Right under Your Nose'* (St John's: Canadian Committee on Labour History, 1994), 23–4; D. Randall, 'Ex-CCF MP Attempts to Organize New Socialist Party on West Coast,' *Workers Vanguard*, 2:3 (Feb. 1957), 4.
59 'Pre-Election Annual report,' n.d. [c. Nov. 1957], file 3, box 3, Rodney Young papers, UBCSC.
60 'Provisional Constitution,' n.d., file 3, box 3, Rodney Young papers, UBCSC.
61 'Interim Manifesto – Socialist Committee for the Organization of a Labour Party,' n.d. [c. 1957], file 3, box 3, Rodney Young papers, UBCSC.
62 Steeves to Cameron, 25 March 1957; Steeves to Cameron, 18 Feb. 1957, file 1-1, Cameron fonds, UBCSC.
63 Jack Scott, *A Communist Life: Jack Scott and the Canadian Workers Movement, 1927–1985* (St John's: Canadian Committee on Labour History, 1988), 140.
64 J. Houle to Dowson, 21 June 1960, file 57-8, Dowson fonds, LAC.
65 Ibid.
66 J. Houle to Dowson, 28 July 1960, file 57-8, Dowson fonds, LAC. According to Jack Scott, 'the Trotskyists, as usual, were three or four or five different factions and often fighting one another.' Scott, *A Communist Life*, 148.
67 Dowson to J. and R. Houle, 3 Jan. 1961, file 57-8, Dowson fonds, LAC.
68 Bruce to City Committee Executive, 14 Dec. 1960, file 57-8, Dowson fonds, LAC.
69 'Socialist Forum,' 10 Feb. [1961], panel with Malcolm Bruce, file 57-8, Dowson fonds, LAC.
70 Scott, *A Communist Life*, 140–9. According to Scott: 'A lot of Trotskyists were going to Cuba with delegations and so on in the early days.' The Columbia River for Canada Committee formed during the protracted negotiations over the Columbia River Treaty. The committee argued that the river's vast hydro-electric potential should serve domestic, rather than US, interests.
71 Scott, *A Communist Life*, 140–9.
72 Pool and Young, 'Introduction: R.E. (Lefty) Morgan, His Life and Work,' 25–31.
73 Scott, *A Communist Life*, 158–9. According to Scott, Endicott gravitated toward a spontaneous view of revolution, 'the theory that the Cuban Revolution was a mass movement with no party involved.' He proposed building up a similar movement in Canada and attending to a party at a

later stage. Scott criticized Endicott's position in a letter mailed to contacts across the country, further aggravating the dispute.

74 'Editorial,' *Progressive Worker* (Vancouver), Oct. 1964.

75 Scott, *A Communist Life*, 158–9.

76 Ibid., 159–60, 172; 'Ex-Union Leader Loses Appeal,' *Sun*, 28 Dec. 1965.

77 Lebourdais captured a meagre 274 votes (1.3 per cent) while Winch was easily returned with a resounding 11,854 votes (57 per cent), nearly triple the total for his nearest Liberal opponent. Canada, *Canadian Parliamentary Guide*, 1965.

78 Scott, *A Communist Life*, 159–60, 185–203.

79 *Progressive Worker*, Oct. 1964 to *BC Newsletter* (Vancouver), June/July 1970. Scott refers to individual CPC members being pressured into subscribing to five copies of the *Pacific Tribune*, then incinerating them, unopened. The *Tribune*, like other Communist papers, was also financed by bulk subscriptions from the USSR. Scott, *A Communist Life*, 161–2.

80 As quoted in 'Tom McEwen,' *Pacific Tribune*, 16 Oct. 1964.

81 'LSA Internal Bulletin,' 6 May 1968, 8, file 57-10; also 'Political Resolution as adopted by the founding convention of the Young Socialists,' July 1965, in *Youth Discussion Bulletin*, April 1966, file 19-12, box 12, Dowson fonds, LAC.

82 Scott, *A Communist Life*, 172–4.

83 'Progressive Workers Movement: A Reassessment of Our Role and Some Cutbacks in Activity,' *BC Newsletter* (Vancouver), June/July 1970; Scott, *A Communist Life*, 174.

84 Scott, *A Communist Life*, 162.

85 Ibid., 249; 'Malcolm Bruce, 1880–1967,' *Workers Vanguard*, mid-May 1967.

86 According to Jack Scott: 'The CP even worked with their bitter enemies the Trotskyists. They didn't get along too well but they met anyhow.' Scott, *A Communist Life*, 167. See also 'Revised Draft Constitution' YS, and 'Our Campus Work,' *Youth Discussion Bulletin* (Vancouver), May 1965, file 19-11, box 19, Dowson fonds, LAC.

87 Khrushchev told the twentieth congress of the CPSU: 'After all, around Trotsky were people whose origin cannot by any means be traced to bourgeois society. Part of them belonged to the party intelligentsia and a certain part were recruited from among the workers.' Khrushchev suggested that those communists who 'broke with Trotskyism and returned to Leninist positions' were not deserving of the harsh treatment meted out under Stalin. Khrushchev speech, Twentieth Congress of the CPSU, Moscow, 25 Feb. 1956.

88 Ivan Avakumovic, *The Communist Party in Canada: A History* (Toronto: McClelland and Stewart, 1975), 261–2.

89 'A New Wind From the East Side,' file 23-23, 'BC provincial series,' reel H1592, CPC fonds, LAC; 'BC NDP Youth Hit by YCL: Stalinist youth condemn NDY platform calling for a socialist Canada as Trotskyite,' *Workers Vanguard*, Dec. 1961, file 24-6, vol. 24, Dowson fonds, LAC. The Communists declared that the issue 'was not a socialist program, but a democratic program that could move us forward towards Socialism.'

90 'Political Resolution as adopted by the founding convention of the Young Socialists,' July 1965, in *Youth Discussion Bulletin*, April 1966, file 19-12, box 19; 'For an Open Organization,' Dec. 1966, in *Young Socialists Discussion Bulletin*, Feb. 1967, file 19-13, box 19, Dowson fonds, LAC.

91 'Draft Press Resolution,' YS National Executive Committee, 16 March 1967, *YS/LJS Discussion Bulletin*, March 1967; also J. Frazer, 'Notes on YSF,' n.d. [c. 1967]; 'Our University Work,' YS National Executive Committee, n.d. [c. 1967]; J. Frazer, 'A Contribution to the Discussion of the Political Resolution,' n.d. [1967]; 'Amendments to Political Resolution,' n.d. [c. 1967]; 'A Reply to Comrade Frazer,' n.d. [c. 1967], *Young Socialists Discussion Bulletin*, Feb. 1967, file 19-13, box 19, Dowson fonds, LAC.

92 'Bill 33 and Ferryworkers,' *Workers Vanguard*, 4 March 1968; 'Bill 33 and Ferryworkers,' (draft), in *Vancouver Branch Discussion Bulletin*, 3 April 1968; Engler to Fidler, 8 March 1968; Engler to Dowson, 18 March 1968; Fidler to Engler, 20 March 1968; Engler to Fidler, 22 March 1968; Fidler to Engler, 23 March 1968; Dowson to Vancouver Branch, 25 March 1968, Dowson to West Coast Correspondent, 27 March 1968, file 57-10, vol. 57, Dowson fonds, LAC; see also Fidler to Engler, 15 Nov. 1967. The Vancouver branch voted 30–5 against distributing issue no. 144 of the *Vanguard*, which contained a heavily edited article by Allen Engler, west coast editor of the paper (writing under the pseudonym L. Kavanagh), on 'Bill 33 and Ferryworkers.' Engler and his Vancouver comrades objected to the removal of comments criticizing the NDP's reluctance to campaign against Bill 33 in a Vancouver South by-election, and also a shift in emphasis that gave 'the wrong impression of Ray Haynes' intentions' by downplaying efforts by the BCFL leadership to avert a general strike against the legislation. As Engler informed Dowson, 'since we are involved in the struggles here, we are convinced we are more competent to make assessments' than the editor '3,000 miles away.' Following a conciliatory letter from Dick Fidler, *Vanguard* editor, Engler insisted that the Vancouver branch did not disagree with 'the line of the movement' but 'with you and Ross thinking that

you are the movement.' He called for internal discussion on the application of democratic centralism in the LSA, the nature of the revolutionary paper, and the national question in English Canada. Dowson responded that 'a general strike represents a climax at a certain stage of the struggle,' suggesting the Vancouver comrades, who were 'outside the ranks of the trade union movement,' were unrealistic in their assessment of the situation. Dowson advised the more modest strategy of urging a BCFL lobby to Victoria the day Bill 33 came up for final reading.

93 'Introduction to Pre-Convention Discussion' in 'YS/LJS Discussion Bulletin vol. 4 no 1,' June 1968, file 19-14, vol. 19, Dowson fonds, LAC; also 'Draft Political Resolution,' submitted by YS National Executive Committee, 29 April 1967; 'Vancouver,' in 'YS/LJS Discussion Bulletin vol 4 no 2', June 1968; Dave C., Judy P. and Heidi F., 'Anti-War,' n.d. [c. 1968]; Ian A. and David P., 'Animal, Vegetable, or Mineral,' 24 June 1968, file 19-14, vol. 19, Dowson fonds, LAC.

94 'Vancouver,' in 'YS/LJS Discussion Bulletin vol 4 no 2', June 1968, file 19-14, vol. 19, Dowson fonds, LAC; also 'Draft Political Resolution' and 'Proposed Constitutional Amendments,' YS/LJS Central Executive Council, Oct. 1969, file 19-16, vol. 19, Dowson fonds, LAC.

95 Dowson, 'On the Tendency Formation Statement,' 20 Nov. 1968, file 57-9, Dowson fonds, LAC

96 Scott, *A Communist Life*, 166–7; Canadian Party of Labour fonds, UBCSC.

97 Scott, *A Communist Life*, 162 and 166.

98 Ibid., 166–7, 216, 224; also 'Amendments to Political Resolution,' n.d. [c. 1967]; 'A Reply to Comrade Frazer,' n.d. [c. 1967], *YS/LJS Discussion Bulletin*, file 19-13, box 19, Dowson fonds, LAC.

99 'Report to the BC Provincial Convention of the Young Communist League on Education Work, 31 March-1 April 1962,' file 53-04 'Correspondence Re: British Columbia 1961–1962,' vol. 53, series IV-4 'Young Communist League,' CPC fonds, LAC.

100 See Club Bulletin No. 8, 7 July 1969, file 23-38, 'BC provincial series,' reel H1592, CPC fonds, LAC; 'Report of the BC Council to the YCL Convention,' n.d. [c. 1962], file 53-04 'Correspondence Re: British Columbia 1961–1962', vol. 53, 'Young Communist League' series, CPC fonds, LAC.

101 'Hail the Ushering in of the Second Year of the Great 1970s!' *The Worker/Mass Line/People's Canada Daily News* joint supplement, 30 Dec. 1970, file 138-8 'CPC (ML) – Leaflets, clippings n.d., 1970–1972,' vol. 138, CTM fonds, LAC; Scott, *A Communist Life*, 215–23; White, *A Hard Man to Beat*, 214–15; Avakumovic, *The Communist Party in Canada*, 260–1.

102 Hansard, *Debates of the House of Commons*, 16 Oct. 1970, 197.

103 The group Direct Action! gained notoriety in the early 1980s for a string of bombings that targeted the Cheekye-Dunsmuir power substation under construction near Parksville on Vancouver Island, the 'Red Hot Video' chain of pornography shops, and the Litton Industries plant near Toronto, where ten workers were injured. One member of the Squamish Five, Brent Taylor, had been active in Victoria's anti-war movement as a high school student in the early 1970s. See Neish interview, 11 May 2006; Ann Hansen, *Direct Action: Memoirs of an Urban Guerilla* (Toronto: Between the Lines, 2001). For clashes between the CPCML and rival groups, see Betty Griffin interview, 11 Aug. 2005, North Vancouver, BC; Geoffrey Reaume, 'Portraits of People with Mental Disorders in English Canadian History,' *Canadian Bulletin of Medical History*, 17:1/2 (2000), 93–125.

104 'Crusade against Progress,' *Pacific Tribune*, 27 Feb. 1948.

105 'City Chinese Rap Arms Shipment,' *Pacific Tribune*, 9 Jan. 1948; also 'Munitions Will Be Loaded for China Despite Demonstration,' *Sun*, 18 Dec. 1947; Jim Green, *Against the Tide: The Story of the Canadian Seamen's Union* (Toronto: Progress Books, 1986), 170–2; 'Labor Council,' *CCF News*, January 1948.

106 'Colima Picketing,' *CCF News*, 1 Jan. 1948; 'Munitions Will Be Loaded for China Despite Demonstration,' *Sun*, 18 Dec. 1947; '"Arms Ship" Argument Ended Here,' *Sun*, 22 Dec. 1947. Loosmore authored an MA thesis on the early history of BC socialism. See T.R. Loosmore, 'The British Columbia Labour Movement and Political Action, 1878–1906,' MA thesis, University of British Columbia, 1954.

107 'Chinese Will Remember,' *Fisherman*, 19 Nov. 1948; 'Workers Strike, Chiang Totters,' *Fisherman*, 19 Nov. 1948; Green, *Against the Tide*, 171.

108 '"Hands Off China" – Arms Ship Picketed,' *Pacific Tribune*, 19 Nov. 1948. The *Islandside* had been the target of labour pickets in late 1947 and early 1948 while loading munitions at Halifax. Green, *Against the Tide*, 171–2.

109 'Labor Council Aids Women in Peace Float for PNE,' *Pacific Tribune*, 16 July 1948.

110 'CCF Women Protest School Recruiting,' *CCF News*, 18 March 1948; Irene Howard, *The Struggle for Social Justice in British Columbia: Helena Gutteridge, the Unknown Reformer* (Vancouver: UBC Press, 1992), 244–57. Howard claims that Cold War debates over China, Czechoslovakia, and NATO created splits in the WILPF Vancouver branch.

111 'Protest on Korea,' *CCF News*, 19 July 1950.

112 Burton to Dowson, 4 May 1950, file 9-2, vol. 2, CTM fonds, LAC.

113 'Hands Off Indo-China, CCF Urges,' *Sun*, 14 June 1954.

114 'Conscription Rejected by Boys' Parliament,' *Pacific Tribune*, 6 Jan. 1956.

115 Ray Gardner to Neish, 20 Jan. 1955, file 'Expulsion from Legion,' Neish papers.

116 'Peace Mission to Press Resolution at Victoria,' *Pacific Tribune*, 6 Jan. 1956; 'House Adopts Peace Motion,' *Pacific Tribune*, 9 March 1956. The Legislature passed the resolution on 29 February 1956.

117 'City Council Deaf to LPP Plea for Support on Ban on H-Bomb,' *Pacific Tribune*, 23 March 1956; 'Labor Backs Peace Motion,' *Pacific Tribune*, 17 Feb. 1956.

118 'Radiation Has Doomed Many, Scientist Warns' and 'CCW Appeals for Halting of Atomic Tests,' *Pacific Tribune*, 23 March 1956. The *Tribune* cited evidence from British biochemist J.B.S. Haldane, based on observation of the effects of radiation on laboratory animals. Haldane presented his finding at a meeting of Science for Peace, and provided reports to atomic officials in Britain, India, and Japan. See also 'H-Tests Pose Cancer Threat,' *Pacific Tribune*, 20 July 1956; 'Ottawa Not Alarmed over Atomic Fallout,' *Sun*, 15 April 1955.

119 'Why We Support Cedric Cox' [1957], file 23-08, 'BC provincial series,' reel H1592, CPC fonds, LAC.

120 *Canada's Party of Socialism: History of the Communist Party of Canada, 1921–1976* (Toronto: Progress Books, 1982), 215.

121 Carter and Daoust, 'From Home to House: Women in the BC Legislature,' in Barbara K. Latham and Roberta J. Pazdro, eds., *Not Just Pin Money: Selected Essays on the History of Women's Work in British Columbia* (Victoria: Camosun College, 1984), 393 and 400; Arthur Cathers, *Beloved Dissident Eve Smith, 1904–1988* (Blyth, ON: Drumadavy, 1997), 165–72.

122 'Welcome to Vancouver – Dr. Linus Pauling,' n.d. [c. 1960], file 57-8, vol. 57, Dowson fonds, LAC. From 1952 to 1954, Pauling's passport was revoked by the US State Department and restored to allow him to receive the Nobel Prize in Sweden. In 1963, Pauling was awarded a second Nobel Prize for his radiation hazards work, which contributed to the Partial Test Ban Treaty signed between the United States and Soviet Union that year.

123 'Radiation Hazards Meeting, UBC Auditorium, Friday, Oct. 7/60'; 'The Arms Race or Human Race: No Nuclear Arms for Canada,' 9 Feb. 1961, file 57-8, vol. 57, Dowson fonds, LAC.

124 'Radiation Hazards Meeting, UBC Auditorium, Friday, Oct. 7/60,' 9 Feb. 1961, file 57-8, vol. 57, Dowson fonds, LAC; 'Stop US Plans to Make BC a Military Target' [1960], file 23-08, 'BC provincial series,' reel H1592, CPC fonds, LAC.

125 Kay Macpherson, *When in Doubt, Do Both: The Times of My Life* (Toronto: University of Toronto Press, 1994), 89–100.

126 T.C. Douglas address, 24 Oct. 1962, *BCFL Proceedings* (1962), 83; also 'CCF Convention Demands Canada Break from NATO Military Pact,' *Workers Vanguard*, Sept. 1960; 'Fails to Adopt Anti-War Policy after Stormy Two Day Debate: CCF-CLC Brass Employ Every Trick to Curb and Defeat Anti-Nato Forces,' *Workers Vanguard*, Aug. 1961, file 24-6, vol. 24, Dowson fonds, LAC.

127 *BCFL Proceedings* (1962), 24.

128 'Bomb Tests Condemned by City Labor Council,' *Pacific Tribune*, 4 March 1962.

129 Cathers, *Beloved Dissident Eve Smith*, 165–8.

130 Tony Hyde, 'Student Union for Peace Action: An Analysis,' Sept. 1967, file 10, box 16a, CUCND-SUPA archives, MARC.

131 'No Connection,' *Ubyssey*, 3 Oct. 1961.

132 'UBC Anti-Bombers,' *Ubyssey*, 3 Oct. 1961. Students from several universities picketed Parliament for seventy-three hours on Thanksgiving Weekend – one hour for every thousand people killed at Hiroshima – and subsisted on water alone to highlight the radiation dangers to the food supply.

133 Herbison to Pape, 6 May 1963; Boothroyd to Herbison, 30 Sept. 1963; Dalton to Boothroyd, 1 Dec. 1963; Boothroyd to John, 10 Dec. 1963, Boothroyd to John, 31 Dec. 1963, file 'University of British Columbia 1962–1964,' box 4, CUCND-SUPA archives, MARC.

134 'Hands Off Cuba,' Nov. 1960; Dowson to [Vancouver] Comrades, 29 Dec. 1960; Dowson to Comrades, 25 Feb. 1961; R. Houle to Dowson, 7 March 1961, file 57-8, Dowson fonds, LAC. Dowson felt the picket was 'somewhat premature.'

135 Dowson to [Vancouver] Comrades, 25 Feb. 1961, 57–8, vol. 57, Dowson fonds, LAC.

136 'BC Labor to Find Truth about Cuba,' *Workers Vanguard*, mid-Oct. 1960; *BCFL Proceedings* (1960), 142; also *BCFL Proceedings* (1962), 37, 50.

137 Pool and Young, 'Introduction,' in Morgan, *Workers' Control on the Railroad*, 24–6.

138 'Keep Heads Cool, Douglas Tells NDP,' *Sun*, 27 Oct. 1962.

139 'We're Being Watched,' *Ubyssey*, 18 Jan. 1963; also 'Communist Party of Canada – Students' Club – U.B.C.,' 22 Oct. 1962, file 96-A-00045, pt 5, vol. 2872, Previously Released Files series, RCMP Security Service, CSIS records, LAC; Steve Hewitt, '"Information Believed True": RCMP Security Intelligence Activities on Canadian University Campuses, 1911–1971,' *Canadian Historical Review*, 81:2 (June 2000), 200–4.

140 Hansard, *Debates of the House of Commons*, 21 Jan. 1963, 2920.

141 'Redcoats Still Hunt Campus Reds,' *Ubyssey*, 31 Jan. 1964; Peter Bower, 'I Spy with My Little Red Eye,' *Martlet* (Victoria), 10 March 1964; Hewitt, '"Information Believed True,"' 208.
142 See Ben Swankey, *Keep Canada Out! Why Canada Should Not Join the OAS* (Vancouver: Canadian Cuban Friendship Committee, 1965), BC Archives.
143 *Canada's Party of Socialism*, 215–17, 227.
144 Minutes, 15 Sept. 1965, box 4, series IV, accession 76–11, Victoria Labour Council fonds, UVASC.
145 'Comox Project,' Summer 1965, file 'Kootenay Project 1965,' box 18, CUCND-SUPA archives, MARC; Harrison et al. to Friend, 15 May 1965, file 95-A-00064, vol. 36, Previously Released Files series, RCMP Security Service, CSIS records, LAC.
146 'Marcher Evades Border Barrier,' *Daily Times*, 20 May 1965; 'Line-Jumper Jailed Here,' *Colonist*, 22 May 1965; 'NDP Chief Will Probe Border Ban,' *Daily Times*, 22 May 1965; 'Fourteen-Day Peace March – Victoria to Comox, BC,' RCMP report, 21 May 1965, file 95-A-00064, vol. 36, Previously Released Files series, RCMP Security Service, CSIS records, LAC.
147 Neish interview, 11 May 2006.
148 'YS/JSL Draft Political Resolution,' [1968], p .1, file 19-14, vol 19, Dowson fonds, LAC.
149 'Elect a Democratic Majority,' [1963], file 23-05, 'BC provincial series,' reel H1592, CPC fonds, LAC. The ICC consisted of Canada, Poland, and India, representing the non-communist, communist, and non-aligned countries.
150 Hilda Thomas interview, with author, 28 Feb. 2004, Toronto, Ontario; Vancouver Vietnam Action Committee fonds, UBCSC.
151 'Children's Crusade Dies on the Street,' *Province*, 23 Aug. 1965; 'Activists Reunite over Star Wars,' *Sun*, 16 Aug. 1985.
152 'Report from Regional Committee of the Delta-New Westminster Region of the Communist Party of Canada,' 22 Jan. 1967, file 23-30, 'BC provincial series,' reel H1592, CPC fonds, LAC.
153 Read to 'Supa People,' 29 March 1966, file 'University of British Columbia 1966,' box 4, CUCND-SUPA, MARC; 'Babes-in-Arms Join City Peace Parade,' *Province*, 28 March 1966; 'Protesting War' and 'Viet Protesters Halted by Police,' *Sun*, 28 March 1966; also 'Protesters Here Burn US Flag,' *Sun*, 11 April 1966; 'Viet Nam Draft Splits Australia,' *Sun*, 12 April 1966.
154 'VOW Efforts Supported,' *Fisherman*, 1 April 1966; 'Protests and Demonstrations re: US Action in Vietnam – Canada,' 30 March 1966, file 2, vol. 110, Previously Released Files Series, RCMP Security Service, CSIS records, LAC.

155 Hansard, *Debates of the House of Commons*, 2 April 1965, 13108.

156 Hansard, *Debates of the House of Commons*, 13 Feb. 1967, 12988–12990; also 'Douglas Backs Viet Aid Group' and 'Douglas Defends Support of Group Sending Reds Aid,' *Sun*, 13 April 1966. Douglas faced criticism for publicly supporting the Canadian Aid for Viet Nam Civilians Committee.

157 Engler to Dowson, 12 Feb. 1968, file 57-10, Dowson fonds, LAC.

158 'Concert to Support the Vietnamese National Liberation Front,' *Ubyssey*, 15 March 1968. Clarke, formerly president of the Vancouver Marine Workers and Boilermakers, had been bitten by a police dog during the 1962 Allied Engineering strike and was one of four labour leaders jailed for a defying an injunction during the 1966 Lenkurt Electric strike. In the 1960s, Clarke worked closely with Trotskyist groups such as the LSA; LSA member Joe Irving performed at the 1968 NFL benefit concert. On 6 July 1969, Clarke died of a heart attack and was eulogized in the LSA's *Workers Vanguard*. See 'Tom Clarke,' *Workers Vanguard*, 14 July 1969, file 446-30, CCF-NDP fonds, LAC; 'Concert to Support the Vietnamese National Liberation Front,' *Ubyssey*, 15 March 1968; Scott, *A Communist Life*, 183; 'Allied Engineering Strike 1962,' file 3-3, box 3, Marine Workers and Boilermakers Industrial Union Local No. 1 fonds, UBCSC; 'Allied Engineering Strike Vancouver BC 1962,' file 41a-w, vol. BC 1429, 'Photo Inventory,' BCFL fonds, UBCSC.

159 'Political Report,' *Youth Discussion Bulletin* (Vancouver), April 1966, file 19-12; 'Our Campus Work,' *Youth Discussion Bulletin* (Vancouver), May 1965, file 19-11; 'Draft Anti-War Resolution,' YS/LJS Central Executive Council, n.d. [c. Oct. 1969], file 19-16, vol. 19, Dowson fonds, LAC.

160 Neish interview, 11 May 2006. The 3 Nov. 1971 walk-out was organized under the banner the Student Amchitka Antiwar Committee (SAAC), and initiated by the Victoria YS branch. High-school students, particularly women, played a major role in organizing the protest. NDP leader Dave Barrett addressed the crowd, blaming the Amchitka tests on 'mad scientists and politicians.' For details of the event and plans leading up to it, see 'Victoria YS/LJS Report,' n.d. [1971], 'Cross-Country Fall Anti-War Reports for YS/LJS Plenum,' Dec. 1971, file 20-1, vol. 21, Dowson fonds, LAC.

161 'Report on the Kootenay Project,' 1 Sept. 1965, file 'Kootenay Project 1965,' box 18, CUCND-SUPA archives, MARC; 'What is the War Resisters League?' [pamphlet], n.d. [c. 1965], file 95-A-00064, vol. 36, Previously Released Files series, RCMP Security Service, CSIS records, LAC. SUPA field secretary Peter Boothroyd observed that 'The noose of conscription is drawing tighter and tighter around the necks of all males of military

age in the United States. For the first time in that country there is the beginnings of an active resistance to this conscription, on a very wide scale. Not only complete pacifists but many other young men who disagree strongly with American military policy and/or the right of the State to force people into war are trying to organize resistance of many different kinds to conscription. One idea that some people have begun looking into is the dramatizing of the deep disenchantment with United States militarism on the part of many students and others by bringing them into Canada ... To bring a draftee would be illegal, and would likely mean jail for both the Canadian host and the draftee. But it's possible some Doukhobors seeing a similarity between this situation and their own in past years, may want to take that risk and support some serious opponents to the draft – not to hide him but to aggressively support him.'

162 'Dissenting Teachers to Be Fired,' *Ubyssey*, 23 Oct. 1970; 'Repressive Law Looms under Cover of WMA,' *Labor Challenge*, 9 Nov. 1970; Dominique Clement, 'Rights in the Age of Protest: A History of the Human Rights and Civil Liberties Movement in Canada, 1962–1982,' Ph.D. diss., Memorial University of Newfoundland, 2005, 204–5; 'The Santo Domingo of Pierre Elliot Trudeau,' *Last Post* (Montreal), Special Report, Oct. 1970, file 446-18, CCF-NDP fonds, LAC.

163 'Viet Nam Protest to Be Allowed,' *Ubyssey*, 30 Oct. 1970; also 'Quebec Enemy Is Structural,' *Ubyssey*, 23 Oct. 1970; 'End Repressive Laws,' *Labor Challenge*, 9 Nov. 1970; 'The Challenge of the New Youth Radicalization,' YS/LJS Central Executive Council, 1970, file 19-17, vol. 17, Dowson fonds, LAC. For a discussion of the response of Vancouver's New Left to the imposition of the War Measures Act, including the activities of the Free Canada, Free Quebec Committee, see Scott, *A Communist Life*, 223–6.

164 'Quebec Liberation Support March Set,' *Ubyssey*, 14 Oct. 1971.

165 For a brief history of the SCM, see 'Students Learn and Share at Four-Month SCM Camps,' *Sun*, 27 Oct. 1962.

166 'Police Watch Mayor's Effigy Burn,' *Daily Times*, 30 Jan. 1954; 'Book "Purge" Protested by College Group,' 28 Jan. 1954; 'Junior Chamber Opposes "Book-Burning" Proposal,' *Daily Times*, 28 Jan. 1954. The SCM chapter wrote to the Library Board, opposing 'the suppression of books, periodicals and pamphlets pertaining to religious, social or political ideas or beliefs.' On 29 January 1954, an attempted march through the city centre was blocked by Victoria's chief of police, so the students relocated to the college campus where they burned the mayor's effigy.

167 J.M. Rockingham to Army Headquarters, 23 May 1963, 'University of Victoria Contingent COTC,' file 2001-09/VI, vol. 212, accession 83–84/215,

RG 24, Department of National Defence fonds, LAC; also Paul Axelrod and John G. Reid, eds., *Youth, University and Canadian Society: Essays in the Social History of Higher Education* (Kingston, ON: McGill-Queen's University Press, 1989).

168 As quoted in Julyan Reid, 'Some Canadian Issues,' in Tim Reid and Julyan Reid, eds., *Student Power and the Canadian Campus* (Toronto: Peter Martin Associates, 1969), 7.

169 'Night Sittings All Week,' *Daily Times*, 3 March 1959.

170 John Conway and Jim Harding, 'A Structure for Radical Action,' n.d. [c. Dec. 1964], file 'Supa founding conf,' box 17, CUCND-SUPA materials, MARC. While CUCND had been weakened by a tense debate over nonviolent direct action, 'a small group of people, perhaps fifty, had discovered politics through the organization, and a core of them wished to act politically within it,' Tony Hyde observed. SUPA retained 'the peace issue as the organization's main concern' but developed 'an SDS-style organization whose prime activity would be dispossessed organizing.' At SUPA's founding conference, Saskatchewan activist Jim Harding was elected chairman. Tony Hyde, 'Student Union for Peace Action: An Analysis,' Sept. 1967, file 10, box 16a, CUCND-SUPA archives, MARC.

171 '"Radical" in as 1st Veep on Recount,' *Ubyssey*, 16 Feb. 1966.

172 'League for Socialist Action – Vancouver, BC,' 29 Aug. 1967, file 2, vol. 110, Previously Released Files series, RCMP Security Service, CSIS records, LAC; 'Vancouver,' in 'YS/LJS Discussion Bulletin vol 4 no 2,' June 1968; also 'Canadian Universities and Our Student Work,' n.d. [c. 1968]; Joe Fraser, 'Introduction to Pre-Convention Discussion,' 21 May 1968; 'Draft Political Resolution,' submitted by YS National Executive Committee, 29 April 1967, file 19-14, vol. 19, Dowson fonds, LAC. The YS described SFU's SDU as a group run by a 'small clique' with 'no elected leadership.'

173 Don Roebuck, 'The Question of Priorities: Viet Nam or Student Syndicalism,' 4 Feb. 1968, file 7, box 16a, CUCND-SUPA archives, MARC.

174 'Vancouver,' in 'YS/LJS Discussion Bulletin vol 4 no 2,' June 1968, file 19-14, Dowson fonds, LAC.

175 'Draft Political Resolution,' submitted by YS National Executive Committee, 29 April 1967, file 19-14; 'LSA Internal Bulletin,' 6 May 1968, 8, file 57-10; also 'Political Resolution as adopted by the founding convention of the Young Socialists,' July 1965, in *Youth Discussion Bulletin*, April 1966, file 19-12; 'Canadian Universities and Our Student Work,' n.d. [c. 1968]; Joe Frazer, 'Introduction to Pre-Convention Discussion,' 21 May 1968; 'Draft Political Resolution,' submitted by YS National Executive Commit-

tee, 29 April 1967, file 19-14; Gary P. and Walter B., 'The Canadian Student Movement,' *YS/LJS Discussion Bulletin*, June 1969, file 19-15, box 19, Dowson fonds, LAC.

176 Peggy Morton and Myrna Wood, '1848 and All That or Whatever Happened to the Working Class?,' *NLC Bulletin*, Nov. 1967, 9–15, file 8, box 16a, CUCND-SUPA archives, MARC. The November 1967 *NLC Bulletin* was dedicated to Che Guevara, who had been killed a month earlier in Bolivia.

177 'Summary of Discussions,' 24–5 Jan. 1968, file 7; also 'Minutes, New Left Committee,' 29–30 Sept. 1967; Shepherd to NLC Members, 3 Oct. 1967, file 11; 'Statement of Resignation,' *NLC Bulletin*, Nov. 1967, 2–3, file 8, box 16a, CUCND-SUPA archives, MARC. SUPA's 1967 general membership conference in Goderich, Ontario, where the New Left Committee was formed, included thirty-six activists from Ontario and Quebec but not a single delegate for the western provinces or Atlantic Canada. Predictably, the NLC's twelve-member executive consisted solely of activists from Toronto, Kingston, Ottawa, and Montreal. 'Elected New Left Committee,' n.d. [c. 1967], file 7; 'List of Participants at SUPA General Membership Conference,' 5–10 Sept. 1967, file 11, box 16a, CUCND-SUPA archives, MARC.

178 'CUS Vote Plagues Two More Schools,' *Ubyssey*, 25 Oct. 1968; 'CUS Dealt Knockout, Lethbridge Opts Out,' *Ubyssey*, 29 Oct. 1968; see also 'SFU Postpones CUS Decision,' *Ubyssey*, 24 Oct. 1968.

179 'We Are Not Guilty!,' file 57-11; 'Report from Simon Fraser University,' Dec. 1968, file 19-14, Dowson fonds, LAC; 'Unrest at Simon Fraser University,' n.d. [1968], file 93-A-00019 part 3, vol. 24, Previously Released Files series, RCMP Security Service, CSIS records, LAC; file 150-1 'SFU Dept. Issues 1969,' vol. 150, CTM fonds, LAC. The occupation was coordinated by members of Students for a Democratic University (SDU) from SFU, UBC, Vancouver Community College, and Selkirk College and lasted from 20 to 23 November, ending when SFU president Ken Strand called in the RCMP to forcibly remove the students. Following the occupation, SFU students voted 2,400–1,200 against a general strike to protest the arrests, with approximately 65 per cent of the student body voting. Also Dionysios Rossi, 'Mountaintop Mayhem: Simon Fraser University, 1965–1971,' MA thesis, Simon Fraser University, 2003; Reid and Reid, eds., *Student Power and the Canadian Campus*, 155–6; Doug Owram, *Born at the Right Time: A History of the Baby-Boom Generation in Canada* (Toronto: University of Toronto Press, 1996), 242–7.

180 'Committee Takes Over SFU Department,' *Globe and Mail*, 19 July 1969.

In September 1969, the PSA Department went on strike, but the response from faculty and students in other departments was mixed. See 'PSA Department Votes to Strike,' *Sun*, 23 Sept. 1969; 'PSA – What's Happening?' 11 Sept. 1969; 'SFU Comix,' n.d. [1969]; Strand to All Members of the University, file 150-2 'SFU Dept. Issues 1969,' vol. 150, CTM fonds, LAC.

181 'Uniondom,' *Ubyssey*, 14 Oct. 1971.

182 Sue Clause and Abie Weisffseld, 'Student Strike,' in 'YS/LJS Discussion Bulletin vol 4 no 2,' June 1968; file 19-14, Dowson fonds, LAC.

183 See Jeanette Taylor, *River City: A History of Campbell River and the Discovery Islands* (Madeira Park, BC: Harbour, 1999), 190–7; 'Fight Brewing at Senior High,' *Campbell River Courier*, 6 Oct. 1971; 'Knowplace: An Answer to Boredom,' *Province*, 4 Oct. 1969; 'A Research Proposal Concerning the Feasibility of Setting up a Free University in the Greater Victoria (British Columbia) Area,' 28 Feb. 1967, file 'Victoria 1963–1964,' box 4, CUCND-SUPA archives, MARC.

184 In Paris, students at the Sorbonne created a political crisis that culminated in a national general strike, factory occupations, and General De Gaulle's brief retreat to Baden-Baden, Germany. In Chicago, students and other young people converged on the Democratic Party Convention, where they were met with a brutal police response. In Montreal, West Indian students occupied the computing centre at Sir George Williams (now Concordia) University, as a protest against racial discrimination, and during an altercation with police destroyed $2-million of equipment. 'Sir George Williams Loses Its Innocence,' *Canadian Forum* (Toronto), April 1969, 2–4; 'The Apocalyptic Fires,' *Canadian Dimension* (Feb. 1969); 'Freedom for Sir George Williams Students,' May 1971, file 20-1, vol. 20, Dowson fonds, LAC; Patrick Seale and Maureen McConville, *Red Flag/Black Flag: French Revolution 1968* (New York: Ballantine, 1968); Jules Witcover, *The Year the Dream Died: Revisiting 1968 in America* (New York: Warner, 1997).

185 T.C. Douglas address at McMaster University, Hamilton, 30 May 1969, as quoted in Dale Lovick, ed., *Till Power Is Brought to Pooling: Tommy Douglas Speaks* (Lantzville, BC: Oolichan, 1979), 211–13.

186 'Address to student body Selkirk College, Castlegar Nov. 8 '67,' file 1-2 'Manuscripts: Articles, Speeches, and Broadcasts (including transcripts),' Box 1, CCC, UBCSC.

187 James Harding, 'The New Left in British Columbia,' in Dimitrios I. Roussopoulos, ed., *The New Left in Canada* (Montreal: Black Rose, c. 1970), 30.

188 Harry Rankin, *Rankin's Law: Recollections of a Radical* (Vancouver: November House, 1975), 115–16.

189 'The Victoria Project,' *NLC Bulletin*, Oct. 1967; 'Addenda: Analysis of Kingston and the KCP,' *NLC Bulletin*, Nov. 1967, file 8, box 16a, CUCND-SUPA archives, MARC; Paul Phillips interview, with author, 13 April 2006, Victoria, BC; 'Hippie Image of CYC Outdated Says Clarke,' *Ubyssey*, 15 March 1968; Saul Alinsky, *Rules for Radicals: A Pragmatic Primer for Realistic Radicals* (New York: Random House, 1971); Abbie Hoffman, *Steal This Book* (New York: Pirate Editions, 1971). Tony Hyde wrote that 'a debate over the involvement of SUPA people in the CYC' contributed to the split at Goderich, Ontario. A section of SUPA joined the CYC and became influential within the organization. See Tony Hyde, 'Student Union for Peace Action: An Analysis,' Sept. 1967, file 10, box 16a, CUCND-SUPA archives, MARC.

190 'Prof Club Invaded,' 'Raucous Ruckus Rouses Faculty Club,' and 'Cast Off Bonds Rubin Tells 2000,' *Ubyssey*, 25 Oct. 1968; also 'Hip Yippie Rubin Raps for Youth,' *Ubyssey*, 24 Oct. 1968.

191 Harding, 'The New Left in BC,' 35–6; Dominique Clément, *Canada's Rights Revolution: Social Movements and Social Change, 1947–1982* (Vancouver: UBC Press, 2008); Clément, 'Rights in the Age of Protest,' 205–12; Michael Boudreau, 'The Struggle for a Different World ... in the Angry Seventies: The Youth International Party and the 1971 Gastown Riot,' paper presented at Centre for Canadian Studies Mobilizations and Engagement Conference, Sackville, NB, 2007; 'Campbell Okays Police Riot Sticks,' *Sun*, 8 June 1972; 'City Police Get More Riot Gear,' *Sun*, 20 June 1972; British Columbia, Report of Dohn Commission of Enquiry into Gastown Riot (1971).

192 Michael Walzer, 'The New Left,' reprinted in Reid and Reid, eds., *Student Power and the Canadian Campus*, 16–17; also Owram, *Born at the Right Time*.

193 'Why Weed Out Natives in BC Fishing Industry?' *Fisherman*, 19 Dec. 1950; George North, *A Ripple, a Wave: The Story of Union Organization in the BC Fishing Industry* (Vancouver: Fishermen Publishing Society, 1974), 45; also Keith Reid and Don Weaver, 'Aspects of the Political Economy of the BC Forest Industry,' in Paul Knox and Philip Resnick, eds., *Essays in BC Political Economy* (Vancouver: New Star, 1974), 18.

194 Steeves, *The Compassionate Rebel*, 147–55.

195 'BCA Program' [1960] and 'Pollution Must Be Stopped Now!', file 23-09, 'BC provincial series,' reel H1592, CPC fonds, LAC.

196 'For Leadership and Planning,' file 23-12, 'BC provincial series,' reel H1592, CPC fonds, LAC.

197 Neish interview, 11 May 2006. The role of the Trotskyist YS (and also the CPC, NDP, YND, Maoists, Yippies, university students, and high-school

students) in the Amchitka campaign, which included school walk-outs on 6 October and 3 November 1971, is discussed in 'Vancouver,' n.d. [1971], 'Cross-Country Fall Anti-War Reports for YS/LJS Plenum,' Dec. 1971, file 20-1, vol. 20, Dowson fonds, LAC.

198 Eryk Martin, 'When Red Meets Green: Perceptions of Environmental Change in the BC Communist Left, 1937–1978,' MA thesis, University of Victoria, 2008; Barrett interview, 24 April 2006.

199 'Healthy Waffle Base at BC Provincial Convention,' *Waffle News*, July 1970, file 446-18, CCF-NDP fonds, LAC.

200 Minutes, 17 Feb. 1971, Victoria Labour Council papers (not yet remitted to UVASC), as quoted in Bruce Lowther, *A Better Life: The First Century of the Victoria Labour Council* (Victoria: Victoria Labour Council, 1989), 44–5. See 'Coastal Oil Slick Threatens Birds' and 'Park Pickets,' *Sun*, 27 April 1971.

201 North, *A Ripple, a Wave*, 29; 'Secondary Sewage beyond Richmond's Means,' *Sun*, 23 Sept. 1969.

202 Robert Hunter, *The Greenpeace to Amchitka: An Environmental Odyssey* (Vancouver: Arsenal Pulp Press, 2004); Frank Zelco and Kristine Kern, 'Greenpeace and the Development of International Environmental Activism in the 1970s,' in Ursula Lehmkulh and Hermann Wellenreuther, eds., *Historians and Nature: Comparative Approaches to Environmental History* (Oxford, NY: Berg, 2007), 296–318; John-Henry Harter, 'Environmental Justice for Whom? Class, New Social Movements, and the Environment: A Case Study of Greenpeace Canada, 1971–2000,' *Labour/Le Travail*, 54 (Fall 2004), 83–119.

203 Various documents, file 23-29, 'BC provincial series,' reel H1592, CPC fonds, LAC. The California grape boycott began in 1967, mobilizing wine drinkers across North American to support the United Farm Workers' organizing drive, led by César Chavéz.

204 Demonstrating the impact of New Left ideas on Old Left stalwarts, Ross Dowson, a father of Canadian Trotskyism, became a dissident in the League for Socialist Action in 1972: 'It is the norm in a Bolshevik organization for its press to expound the line that was last officially established … The August issue [of Labor Challenge], designed for mass distribution during the BC elections, studiously evades recognizing … the anti-US imperialist sentiment … going so far as to excerpt almost all mention of the weight of US capital investment in BC.' The election that elevated the BC NDP to power had a cathartic effect in the Trotskyist Left. Dismayed over a policy that 'dissociated our movement from Canadian nationalism,' which he viewed as a bridge to a broader anti-capitalist politics, Dowson initiated a United Tendency within the LSA in March 1973,

aligned with the minority tendency in the Fourth International. Ross Dowson, 'Memorandum II on Labor Challenge,' 29 Oct. 1972; 'Memorandum on the August Issue of Labor Challenge,' 14 Aug. 1972, file 26-12, vol. 26, Dowson fonds, LAC; also J. Henderson and D. Fidler, 'In Reply to Comrade Dowson's Memorandum,' n.d. [1972]; G. Addison, 'In Reply to Comrade Dowson's Memorandum II on Labor Challenge,' 20 Nov. 1972; 'Declaration of the United Tendency,' 16 March 1973; G. Addison, 'In Reply to Comrade Dowson's Memorandum II on Labor Challenge,' 20 Nov. 1972, file 26-12, vol. 26, Dowson fonds, LAC.

5. New Militancy

1 'A New Wind from the East Side,' CPC City Committee report, [c. 1966], file 23-23, 'BC provincial series,' reel H1592, CPC fonds, LAC.
2 Jane Jenson and Rianne Mahon, 'Representing Solidarity: Class, Gender and the Crisis in Social Democratic Sweden,' *New Left Review*, I/201 (Sept.-Oct. 1993), 88; Richard Fantasia, 'The Wildcat Strike and Industrial Relations,' *Industrial Relations Journal*, 14:2 (June 1983), 74–86; Samuel R. Friedman, *Teamster Rank and File: Power, Bureaucracy, and Rebellion at Work and in a Union* (New York: Columbia University Press, 1982); Frank Kashner, 'A Rank and File Revolt at GE,' *Radical America*, 12:6 (Nov./Dec. 1978), 43–60.
3 See the *Woodpecker* (Cranbrook), 21 Nov. 1956; also various records in file 'Woodworkers Industrial Union of Canada – Cranbrook, BC,' vol. 2285, series A, RCMP Security Service, CSIS records, LAC; 'Union's Stormy History Over,' *Province*, 1 March 1957; 'Lumber Unions Sign No-Raiding Agreement,' *Pacific Tribune*, 16 Nov. 1956.
4 Thomas R. Berger, 'Report and Recommendations on the Use of Injunctions in Labour Disputes,' 30 Oct. 1966, in Berger, *Injunctions in British Columbia* (Vancouver: British Columbia Federation of Labour, c. 1966), 10 and 17; A.W.R Carrothers, *The Labour Injunction in British Columbia: A Study of the Operation of the Injunction in Labour-Management Disputes in British Columbia, 1946–1955 with Particular Reference to the Law of Picketing* (Toronto: CCH Canadian Ltd., 1956), 194.
5 'Labor Demands Repeal of Federal Slave Law,' *Fisherman*, 5 Sept. 1950. The parallel Vancouver Trades and Labor Council (TLC) and Vancouver Labour Council (CCL), like similar bodies in Victoria, reflected the North America-wide split between AFL and CIO unions between the late 1930s and mid-1950s.

6 See Leo Panitch and Donald Swartz, *From Consent to Coercion: The Assault on Trade Union Freedoms*, third ed. (Aurora, ON: Garamond, 2003) 247–52.
7 'Labor Demands Repeal of Federal Slave Law,' *Fisherman*, 5 Sept. 1950.
8 'Watch Your Dollar, It's Getting Smaller,' *Fisherman*, 15 Aug. 1950; 'It's Up to Labor,' *Fisherman*, 5 Sept. 1950; 'Inflation on the March Aided by New Budget,' *Fisherman*, 3 Oct. 1950.
9 'When Is Inflation?,' *CCF News*, 12 Aug. 1948; 'Strikes and Price Control,' *CCF News*, 16 Aug. 1950.
10 'Price Controls Given Go-By in New Supplementary Budget,' *Fisherman*, 12 Sept. 1950.
11 'O'Neil Proclaims Politics a Must,' *Ubyssey*, 30 Oct. 1959.
12 See *Fed Up Newsletter* (Vancouver), 1973–5; Bill Coughlan et al., *The Food Co-op Handbook: How to Bypass Supermarkets to Control the Quality and Price of Your Food* (Boston: Houghton Mifflin, 1975).
13 Harvey Murphy address, *UFAWU Proceedings*, 24–9 March 1952, Vancouver, 10, Neish papers.
14 See Mark Leier, *Red Flags and Red Tape: The Making of a Labour Bureaucracy* (Toronto: University of Toronto Press, 1995).
15 Murphy address, *UFAWU Proceedings* (1952), 10–11.
16 Stuart Jamieson, 'Regional Factors in Industrial Conflict: The Case of British Columbia,' *Canadian Journal of Economics and Political Science*, 28:3 (Aug. 1962), 408–9, 415; BC Department of Labour, *Annual Report* (1952), 120; 'The Red Threat to Our Pacific Gateway,' *Financial Post*, 12 Dec. 1953; 'Close to 10,000 Idled in BC Labor Eruptions,' *Financial Post*, 12 Dec. 1953. The 1952 IWA strike was only the most prolonged of thirteen major strikes that rocked the sector in the 1950s, accounting for 66 per cent of all striker-days in BC.
17 'Poje to Stay in Jail until Next Thursday,' *Sun*, 19 Sept. 1952; Grant MacNeil, *The IWA in British Columbia* (Vancouver: Western Canadian Regional Council No. 1 IWA, 1971), 45; Carrothers, *Labour Injunction in BC*, 11–23.
18 Jamieson, 'Regional Factors in Industrial Conflict,' 410.
19 George Mitchell address, *UFAWU Proceedings* (1952), 121–2, Neish papers.
20 Jamieson, 'Regional Factors in Industrial Conflict,' 416. For earlier efforts to amend the ICA Act, see 'Provincial Cabinet Gets TLC's Brief,' *Sun*, 1 Feb. 1950; 'Labor Group Urges Union Shop Clause,' *Sun*, 22 Feb. 1950.
21 'CCF Convention Demands Shelving of New Labor Act,' *Sun*, 14 June 1954; 'Delegates Pledge Labor Act Repeal,' *Province*, 12 June 1954; 'CCF Parley Adopts Labor Policy,' *Province*, 12 June 1954.

22 'CCF Labor Platform Rejected,' *Sun*, 16 April 1955; also 'BCFL Statement of Policy on 1956 election,' 26 Aug. 1956, file 450-2, CCF-NDP fonds, LAC.
23 *BCFL Proceedings* (1956), 87. Resolution from Vancouver and District Labour Council.
24 Jamieson, 'Regional Factors in Industrial Conflict,' 409; Jamieson, *Times of Trouble: Labour Unrest and Industrial Conflict in Canada, 1900–1966* (Ottawa: Task Force on Labour Relations, 1968), 374.
25 'Strike Action Closes District Sawmills,' *Nelson Daily News*, 10 Oct. 1953.
26 Jamieson, 'Regional Factors in Industrial Conflict,' 412. Jamieson also argues that while multi-employer sectoral bargaining reduces the number of 'interest' strikes, 'when they do occur they tend to be larger and more prolonged.'
27 Jamieson, 'Regional Factors in Industrial Conflict,' 413–14.
28 John Stanton, *Never Say Die!: The Life and Times of John Stanton, a Pioneer Labour Lawyer* (Ottawa: Steel Rail, 1987) 212; 'Gervin Becomes Open Spokesman for Big Business,' *Pacific Tribune*, 16 March 1956. Gervin had headed a 1950 TLC delegation to the BC legislature. See 'Provincial Cabinet Gets TLC's Brief,' *Sun*, 1 Feb. 1950.
29 'Gervin Becomes Open Spokesman for Big Business,' *Pacific Tribune*, 16 March 1956.
30 'Dictatorship,' *CCF News*, 12 Aug. 1948.
31 J. Bury speech, *BCFL Proceedings*, 15–18 Nov. 1956, Vancouver, 84.
32 'China Does Want Our Goods,' *Fisherman*, 4 Nov. 1952.
33 'Anti-Discrimination Group Formed,' *Fisherman*, 14 Nov. 1950.
34 Knute Buttedahl address, *UFAWU Proceedings* (1952), 220, Neish papers.
35 Buttedahl address, *UFAWU Proceedings* (1952), 220; also 'Six Provinces Have Fair Practices Acts,' *Pacific Tribune*, 8 June 1956. Biographical information on Buttedahl, secretary of the Vancouver Labour Council (CCL), is provided in Ross Lambertson, 'The Black, Brown, White, and Red Blues: The Beating of Clarence Clemons,' *Canadian Historical Review*, 85:4 (Dec. 2004), 762.
36 'Bill 33 "Good Step" but Still Falls Short,' *Pacific Tribune*, 30 March 1956; Fair Employment Practices Act, S.B.C. 1956, c. 16.
37 [Chinese Language Leaflet, 1963], file 23-02, 'BC provincial series,' reel H1592, CPC fonds, LAC. Leaflets were also mailed to subscribers of the Russian-language press and to Russian miners in BC. See [Russian Language Leaflet, 1963], file 23-02, 'BC provincial series,' reel H1592, CPC fonds, LAC. Also 'Labor Newsvendor Dies,' *Pacific Tribune*, 25 June 1948; 'Labor Press Loses Devoted Salesman,' *Fisherman*, 2 July 1948; Women's School for Citizenship report, 22 March 1949, file 'Woodworkers Industrial

Union of Canada – Vancouver, BC,' vol. 2285, series A, RCMP Security Service, CSIS records, LAC; 'Alfred Quan,' *Fisherman*, 9 May 1950; 'BC Japanese Canadian Meet Endorses Fisheries Program,' *Fisherman*, 7 Feb. 1950; 'Japanese Canadians Join UFAWU Readily,' *Fisherman*, 2 May 1950; Rolf Knight and Maya Koisumi, *A Man of Our Times: The Life-History of a Japanese-Canadian Fisherman* (Vancouver: New Star, 1976), 105–28; Harjit Daudharia, *Darshan* (Vancouver: Heritage House, 2004); Darshan Singh Sangha interview, 1985, F-77-item53 to F-77-item62, Hari Sharma Indo-Canadian Oral History Collection, Simon Fraser University Archives.

38 The mechanics of merger in British Columbia's capital is illuminated in 'Minutes of Merger Committee Meeting,' 17 May 1956 and 24 May 1956; 'Draft Constitution and By-laws for the Merger Council,' n.d. [1956], box 5, series IV, accession 80–59, Victoria Labour Council fonds, UVASC.

39 I.M. Abella, 'Lament for a Union Movement,' in Ian Lumsden, ed., *Close the 49th Parallel Etc.: The Americanization of Canada* (Toronto: University of Toronto Press, 1970), 90.

40 'BC Trade Unionists Fight US Dictation,' *Pacific Tribune*, 29 June 1956.

41 'Mine-Mill Parley Backs Union Split,' *Sun*, 20 Jan. 1955; 'Murphy Spikes Province Story on Kitimat Raid,' *Pacific Tribune*, 20 Jan. 1956; 'Workers at Yale Lead on Strike,' *Pacific Tribune*, 30 March 1956. As mentioned in chapter 1, the American Taft-Hartley Act (1947) was the legislative embodiment of postwar anti-communism, substantially amending the National Labor Relations Act (Wagner Act) of 1935 and requiring union officers from the local to international levels to take anti-communist oaths. Taft-Hartley also prohibited the 'closed shop' and secondary boycotts, and strengthened the powers of the National Labor Relations Board to prevent strikes. See Harry A. Millis and Emily Clark Brown, *From the Wagner Act to Taft-Hartley: A Study of National Labor Policy and Labor Relations* (Chicago: University of Chicago Press, 1950); Irving Richter, *Labor's Struggles, 1945–1950: A Participant's View* (Cambridge: Cambridge University Press, 1994).

42 Al King with Kate Braid, *Red Bait!: Struggles of a Mine Mill Local* (Vancouver: Kingbird, 1998), 127; Mercedes Steedman, 'Introduction' to Steedman et al., eds., *Hard Lessons: The Mine Mill Union in the Canadian Labour Movement* (Toronto: Dundurn, 1995), 8.

43 'Retain Independence,' *Woodpecker* (Cranbrook), 7 Nov. 1955, in file 'Woodworkers Industrial Union of Canada – Cranbrook, BC,' vol. 2285, series A, RCMP Security Service, CSIS records, LAC.

44 *The Amplifier: Voice of the Rank and File Movement for Democratic Action* (Portland), March 1961-Jan. 1964, Angus MacPhee Collection, UBCSC; Betty Griffin and Susan Lockhart, *Their Own History: Women's Contribu-*

tion to the Labour Movement in British Columbia (Vancouver: UFAWU/ CAW Seniors Club, 2002), 179; boxes 1–5, MacPhee Collection, UBCSC; 'Where Is Western Canada,' *Western Pulp and Paper Worker* (Vancouver), 1956, as quoted in 'The Early History of Pulp, Paper and Woodworkers of Canada,' Pulp, Paper and Woodworkers of Canada website, n.d. <http:// www.ppwc.bc.ca/ppwchist01.pdf> (accessed 8 March 2005), 3–20. Pulp & Sulphite was led in BC by Pat O'Neil, BCFL secretary treasurer from 1958 to 1966. As the union's history records: 'Branch plant mentality ruled the day.' At the May 1956 International convention in Milwaukee, the Western Council argued that new pulp mills in Hinton, Alberta and northern Saskatchewan should be included in its jurisdiction. A majority of delegates, however, disagreed. The merger talks with the IWA, which ultimately failed, were driven by the American leaderships, excluding Local 433 members and the Western Council; while Pulp & Sulphite counted only 5,500 BC members compared with the IWA's 34,000, internationally Pulp & Sulphite was the larger union, representing 160,000 workers compared with the 95,000 in the IWA. See 'Pulp-Sulphite IWA Confer,' *Pacific Tribune*, 1 June 1956.

45 'Tunnel Workers Back Officers in Fight,' *Pacific Tribune*, 25 May 1956.

46 'Injunction Won by Hod Carriers,' *Pacific Tribune*, 13 July 1956. Also 'Tunnel, Rock Workers Fight for BC scale,' *Pacific Tribune*, 18 May 1956; 'Tunnel Workers Win Pact for BC Rates,' *Pacific Tribune*, 1 June 1956; 'City Unions Resent US Interference,' *Pacific Tribune*, 8 June 1956; M.C. Warrior and Mark Leier, *Light at the End of the Tunnel: The First Forty Years: A History of the Tunnel and Rock Workers Union Local 168* (Vancouver: LIUNA, 1992). Local 168 pledged loyalty to the CLC, but VTLC president Lloyd Whalen said: 'We can't interfere, but no one regrets that more than I do.'

47 'Tunnel Local Wins Victory' and 'Tunnel Workers,' *Pacific Tribune*, 20 July 1956. Tunnel and Rock Workers at Quesnel in central BC also struck for the BC wage scale. See 'Injunction Appealed,' *Pacific Tribune*, 27 July 1956.

48 'The Mergers,' *Woodpecker* (Cranbrook), 21 Nov. 1955, in file 'Woodworkers Industrial Union of Canada – Cranbrook, BC,' vol. 2285, series A, RCMP Security Service, CSIS records, LAC; 'Issues Confronting Unity Congress Are Far Wider Than Call Would Imply,' *Pacific Tribune*, 3 Feb. 1956; 'Why Labor Must Have Annual Conventions,' *Pacific Tribune*, 10 Feb. 1956; 'Delegates Dispute Ruling on Convention,' *Pacific Tribune*, 16 March 1956; 'Merger Constitution Needs Close Scrutiny,' *Pacific Tribune*, 23 March 1956.

49 *BCFL Proceedings*, (1956), 91.

50 Ibid., 92.

51 Ibid., 101 and 90. The Marine Workers and Boilermakers' resolution called

on the CLC 'to open its doors to all Trade Unions in Canada now outside the Canadian Labour Congress.'

52 See *BCFL Proceedings* (1957–72).

53 Grant MacNeil, *The IWA in British Columbia* (Vancouver: Western Canadian Regional Council No. 1 IWA, 1971), 50.

54 *BCFL Proceedings* (1957), 67.

55 BC Department of Labour, *Annual Report* (1958), 116. This report records union density at 55.18 per cent of the paid labour force, which was calculated using an earlier formula. The lower amount has been cited in the text to allow for accurate comparison for the duration of the period under study. See appendix B.

56 'CCF Council Statement on BC Shipping Strike,' file 7-11 'National Council, Executive and Table Officers Minutes 1957–1958,' vol. 7, CCF-NDP fonds, LAC; Panitch and Swartz, *From Consent to Coercion*, appendix II, 247.

57 Stanton, *Never Say Die!*, 123–4; International Association of Bridge, Structural and Ornamental Iron Workers Local 712 fonds, UBCSC.

58 'Injunctions Won't Catch Fish nor Build Bridges,' *Fisherman*, 26 June 1959; file 1073 'George North,' box 7, John Stanton Fonds, UBCSC; Stanton, *Never Say Die!*, 123–31.

59 James Harding, 'The New Left in British Columbia,' in Dimitrios I. Roussopolous, ed., *The New Left in Canada* (Montreal: Black Rose, c. 1970), 28; BC Department of Labour, *Annual Report* (1959), 45; 'Labor Peace Claimed due to Socred Legislation,' *Ubyssey*, 28 Sept. 1961. Bill 43 replaced an old law on the BC statutes, the Trade-Unions Act (1902), which had relieved 'unions and their members from liability in damages and to an injunction in respect of certain types of union activity.' However, as Carrothers observed: 'the statute, perhaps because of its tortuous phraseology and consequent ambiguity, has been ignored or explained away more often than it has been applied.' According to Berger, Carrothers's criticisms of the use of injunctions in labour disputes 'carry more weight today than in the past,' because of the provisions of the old Trade-Unions Act. Berger, 'Report and Recommendations on the Use of Injunctions in Labour Disputes,' in Berger, *Injunctions in British Columbia*, 10; Carrothers, *The Labour Injunction in British Columbia*, xxiii–xxiv, 38; Charles Lipton, *The Trade Union Movement in Canada, 1827–1959*, second ed. (Montreal: Canadian Social Publications, 1968), 315. Lipton described Bill 43 as 'anti-labour legislation which facilitated injunctions against picketing.'

60 Harry Rankin, *Rankin's Law: Recollections of a Radical* (Vancouver: November House, 1975), 137.

61 'New Democratic Party Policy Statement' and 'Report and Recommenda-

tions on the Use of Injunctions in Labour Disputes,' in Berger, *Injunctions in British Columbia*, 7, 13–14; Jamieson, *Times of Trouble*, 386.

62 BC Department of Labour, *Annual Report* (1959), 45; also Constitution Act Amendment Act, S.B.C. 1959 c. 17.

63 Lipton, *The Trade Union Movement in Canada*, 315.

64 Ibid., 315.

65 'Lumber Bosses Must Disgorge,' n.d. [c. 1959], file 12, box 49, MSS 179, Kenny Collection, Fisher Library.

66 MacNeil, *The IWA in British Columbia*, 51; Lipton, *The Trade Union Movement in Canada*, 315–16.

67 'Walkoff First for Workers,' *Fisherman*, 31 July 1959; George North, *A Ripple, a Wave: The Story of Union Organization in the BC Fishing Industry* (Vancouver: Fishermen Publishing Society, 1974), 25; Lipton, *The Trade Union Movement in Canada*, 316; 'Fishermen Endorse New Wage Contract,' *Pacific Tribune*, 27 July 1956; BC, Department of Labour, *Annual Report* (1959), 66.

68 Bruce McLean, *A Union amongst Government Employees: A History of the BC Government Employees' Union, 1919–1979* (Vancouver: BCGEU, 1979), 74–7.

69 The Vancouver postal workers' proposal for a one-day strike in December 1959, part of a federal public-sector dispute involving 150,000 workers, is described in Lipton, *The Trade Union Movement in Canada*, 317.

70 Patricia G. Webb, *The Heart of Health Care: The Story of the Hospital Employees' Union, the First 50 Years* (Vancouver: Hospital Employees' Union, 1994), 19–26, 33–7. Certification of Hospital Employees' Local 371 as the official bargaining agent at Victoria's Royal Jubilee Hospital was discussed at the Victoria Trades and Labour Council (TLC-AFL) in 1949. Minutes, 7 Dec. 1950, box 5, series IV, accession 80–59, Victoria Labour Council fonds, UVASC.

71 Public Schools Act Amendment Act, S.B.C. 1947 c. 79 s. 101; F. Henry Johnson, *A History of Public Education in British Columbia* (Vancouver: University of British Columbia Publications Centre, 1964), 248–50. The BCTF first entertained the idea of affiliation in 1938, striking a committee that was sharply divided and subsequently shelved the matter. Ibid., 248, 240–1; *BCTF Handbook, 1967–1968* (Vancouver: BCTF, 1967), 7, in 'file AH-2000.00123 part 2,' vol. 110, Previously Released Files series, RCMP Security Service, CSIS records, LAC. In 1942, the Rural Teachers' Association voted to merge with the BCTF.

72 'Affiliation to Labor Has Brought Many Benefits to Teachers,' *Pacific Tribune*, 23 March 1956.

73 UBC education professor Maxwell A. Cameron was appointed as a one-person commission in November 1944, conducting an inquiry into

education administration in BC. Cameron's report, tabled in the legislature in February 1946, underpinned the Public Schools Act Amendment Act (1946), which reorganized the province's schools into seventy-four school districts. 'N. Shore Teachers Win Salary Gains,' *Sun*, 14 Feb. 1950; '$42,000 More for Surrey Teachers,' *Sun*, 20 Feb. 1950.

74 Johnson, *History of Public Education in BC*, 249.

75 'Affiliation to Labor Has Brought Many Benefits to BC Teachers,' *Pacific Tribune*, 23 March 1956.

76 *BC Teacher*, 35:8 (May-June 1956), 392B as quoted in Johnson, *History of Public Education in BC*, 249.

77 *BCFL Proceedings* (1956), 95.

78 'Political Rights,' *CCF News*, 22 July 1948.

79 McLean, *A Union amongst Government Employees*, 3–4 and 47–9. The union formed as the British Columbia Provincial Government Employees' Association, before dropping 'Provincial' in 1949. In 1969, 'union' replaced 'association,' giving rise to the BCGEU.

80 McLean, *A Union amongst Government Employees*, 50 and 66–8.

81 British Columbia, *Report of a Board of Reference into the British Columbia Civil Service Act* (Victoria: Queen's Printer, 1959), 39–50.

82 Minutes, 29 Jan. 1958, box 1, series IV, accession 76–11, Victoria Labour Council fonds, UVASC.

83 'Injunction Halts Picketing Civil Service Back to Work,' *Daily Times*, 13 March 1959; 'Civil Servants Standing Firm; Government Remains Silent,' *Daily Times*, 12 March 1959; 'CS Chief Gives Ultimatum,' *Daily Times*, 11 March 1959; McLean, *A Union amongst Government Employees*, 73–7; Lipton, *The Trade Union Movement in Canada*, 316.

84 Constitution Act Amendment Act, S.B.C. 1959 c. 17 s. 2. The Constitution Act, passed in 1871 when BC entered Confederation, sets out the powers of the executive and legislative branches of government.

85 McLean, *A Union amongst Government Employees*, 82–3; Bruce Lowther, *A Better Life: The First Century of the Victoria Labour Council* (Victoria: Victoria Labour Council, 1989), 40.

86 Fryer interview, 11 April 2006; McLean, *A Union amongst Government Employees*, 83.

87 Stuart Jamieson, *Industrial Relations in Canada* (Toronto: Macmillan, 1973), 131.

88 Swankey interview, 10 June 2005.

89 'Communist controlled locals of unions not controlled by communists at the top executive level,' 1 May 1963; 'Memorandum Re: Communist penetration of trade unions,' 14 May 1963, file 'Trade unions: Comm. Pen-

etration Canada,' vol. 2213, series A, RCMP Security Service, CSIS records, LAC.

90 Jo Dunaway, *We're Your Neighbours: The Story of CUPE BC* (Vancouver: Canadian Union of Public Employees – BC Division, 2000), 2–3.

91 The 1964 strike lasted two and a half weeks, while the 1966 strike lasted six weeks. Both disputes were referred to the province's Industrial Inquiry Commission, and settled on terms recommended in the commission's report. 'City Outside Staff Serves Strike Notice,' *Sun*, 13 April 1966; BC Department of Labour, *Annual Report* (1964), 65 and *Annual Report* (1966), 85.

92 Phillips sheds light on the reasoning behind CUPE's decision to admit the communist-led civic workers local: '[CUPE National president] Stan Little and these people, they wanted to build the biggest national union in the country. They wanted certain changes in the directions that the labour movement would follow. They looked at [Outside Civic Workers president] Don Guise and myself and some others as people who will live only so long. "We can handle them, we can live with them. We'll take them in. It'll help us in our bigger battle."' Jack Phillips interview, 8–9 March 2003; Paul A. Phillips, *No Power Greater: A Century of Labour in British Columbia* (Vancouver: BC Federation of Labour and the Boag Foundation, 1967), 157; Dunaway, *We're Your Neighbours*, 16; 'Outside Staff Walks Out,' *Sun*, 7 May 1966.

93 Jack Phillips interview, 8–9 March 2003.

94 'Strike Halts BC Mail Service,' *Sun*, 23 July 1965.

95 'Mail Strike Backlash Feared' and 'Postal Workers Reject Strike 4–1,' *Sun*, 23 Aug. 1965; Joe Davidson and John Deverell, *Joe Davidson* (Toronto: Lorimer, 1978); 73–8; Jean-Claude Parrot, *My Union, My Life: Jean-Claude Parrot and the Canadian Union of Postal Workers* (Halifax: Fernwood, 2005).

96 The Trotskyist LSA observed in 1967 that CUPW 'offers good prospects for militant leadership.' 'League for Socialist Action-Vancouver, BC,' 29 Aug. 1967, file AH-2000.00123 part 3, vol. 110, Previously Released Files series, RCMP Security Service, CSIS records, LAC.

97 'Election Research Circular No. 2,' 18 July 1960, file 23-03, 'BC provincial series,' reel H1592, CPC fonds, LAC; 'Jobless Total Up 52,000 in Month,' *Sun*, 18 Feb. 1950; 'Cries of "Liar" at Jobless Aid Parley,' *Sun*, 22 Feb. 1950; 'CCL Launching Jobless Union,' *Sun*, 23 Feb. 1950.

98 BC's maximum workweek had remained at forty-four hours since 1946. 'Election Research Circular No. 2,' 18 July 1960, file 23-03, 'BC provincial series,' reel H1592, CPC fonds, LAC.

99 McGarvie to Ruth [Houle], 23 Dec. 1960, file 57-8, Dowson fonds, LAC.

100 'British Columbia Federation of the Unemployed,' c. 1960, LAC, RG 146, A2006–00621, STACK-04, p69. The federation included representatives of the Vancouver and Victoria Building Trades Councils and the labour councils of Vancouver, Victoria, Nelson-Trail, Prince George, Prince Rupert, Nanaimo, Kitimat-Terrace, Kelowna, Kamloops, and Dawson Creek.
101 'Victoria Jobless Plan Demonstration,' *Pacific Tribune*, 6 Jan. 1961.
102 Jamieson, *Times of Trouble*, 415.
103 'General Resolutions,' 1957 LPP convention, file 7, box 4, Kenny Collection, Fisher Library.
104 'Elect a Democratic Majority,' file 23-05, 'BC provincial series,' reel H1592, CPC fonds, LAC; *Canada's Party of Socialism: History of the Communist Party of Canada, 1921–1976* (Toronto: Progress Books, 1982), 243–4.
105 Jamieson, *Times of Trouble*, 398. Jamieson defines 'large' strikes as those involving at least 5,000 workers or resulting in 100,000 striker-days. Ibid., 374.
106 'Labor Vows to Battle Prosecution,' *Sun*, 26 Oct. 1962; *BCFL Proceedings* (1962), 61–2, 87–9.
107 Jack Scott, *A Communist Life: Jack Scott and the Canadian Workers' Movement, 1927–1985* (St John's: Canadian Committee on Labour History, 1988), 183; 'Allied Engineering Strike 1962,' file 3-3, box 3, Marine Workers and Boilermakers Industrial Union Local No. 1 fonds, UBCSC; 'Allied Engineering Strike Vancouver BC 1962,' file 41a-w, vol. BC 1429, 'Photo Inventory,' BCFL fonds, UBCSC. Following the Allied Engineering strike, Vancouver aldermanic candidate Harry Rankin pledged to outlaw the use of police dogs during labour disputes. 'Labor Won't Back Rankin,' *Sun*, 21 Nov. 1962; Rankin, *Rankin's Law*, 149–50.
108 Vince Ready, 'Forward,' in King, *Red Bait!*, ix, 132.
109 'City Ironworkers Win Injunction,' *Sun*, 17 Nov. 1964; '35 Electricians Fired with Approval of Union,' *Sun*, 13 March 1965; 'Walkout Slows Pulp Mill Job,' *Sun*, 15 March 1965; 'Early History of PPWC,' 25–6.
110 'Pickets Stop $12 Million Plant Job,' *Sun*, 28 July 1965. The wildcat was triggered by a dispute between Canadian Betchel, the company building the plant, and IBEW over interpretation of a contract clause regarding a room and board allowance of $7.20 per day.
111 'BC Election Platform of the Communist Party' [1960], file 23-03, 'BC provincial series,' reel H1592, CPC fonds, LAC.
112 'A Message for All Trade Unionists,' [1960], file 23-03, 'BC provincial series,' reel H1592, CPC fonds, LAC.
113 BC Department of Labour, *Annual Report* (1961), 29; 'Labor Peace Claimed

due to Socred Legislation,' *Ubyssey*, 28 Sept. 1961; 'Social Credit Campaign Funds,' Provincial Election Speakers Notes, Sept. 1956, file 450-2, CCF-NDP fonds, LAC; Paul Phillips, *No Power Greater*, 156–7.

114 'Minority Union Strike Ban Sought by Manufacturers,' *Sun*, 26 Oct. 1962.

115 Ibid., 119.

116 J.T. Montague, 'Effective Industrial Relations Policies in a Developing Economy,' in R. Shearer, ed., *Exploiting Our Economic Potential: Public Policy and the British Columbia Economy* (Toronto: Holt, Rinehart and Winston, 1968), 122.

117 The strike and related sympathetic action is described in Jamieson, *Times of Trouble*, 419–22; Jamieson, *Industrial Relations in Canada*, 67; Phillips, *No Power Greater*, 155; Scott, *A Communist Life*, 181–3. See also file 'Oil, Chemical and Atomic Workers International Union, 9–601 Vancouver, BC,' vol. 2157, series A, RCMP Security Service, RG 146, CSIS fonds, LAC; 'Gov't Vote for Oil Workers,' *Sun*, 24 Aug. 1965.

118 Scott, *A Communist Life*, 181–3; 'The Shellburn Story,' *Progressive Worker*, 31 Oct. 1965; 'Ex-Union Leader Loses Appeal,' *Sun*, 28 Dec. 1965; 'Oil Strike Spreads with Ioco Walkout,' *Sun*, 6 Nov. 1965. Lebourdais lost his job as a result of the sit-down strike, the only one of nine dismissed workers not reinstated. 'It was not a PW [Progressive Worker] strike in the sense that the PW made a decision that it should happen,' Scott claims, but 'it was a PW strike in that a leading member and certainly a number of strong supporters of PW were the ones who instigated it ... Lebourdais had led the thing but didn't know where it was going. I told him you don't do things like that.' Conditions were starkly different from the famous Detroit sit-down strikes of the 1930s that had established the CIO, Scott insisted, urging against the tactic. At Imperial Oil's Ioco refinery, strikers attributed their walkout to the suspension of thirty-five workers and Imperial Oil's refusal to recognize the union and bargain in good faith. Jamieson, *Times of Trouble*, 419.

119 'Won't Permit Full Oil Shutdown,' *Sun*, 8 Nov. 1965.

120 Jamieson, *Times of Trouble*, 420.

121 'Labor Girds for Showdown over Oil Strike Extension,' *Sun*, 10 Nov. 1965.

122 'Oil Strike Could Tie Up Industry,' *Sun*, 12 Nov. 1965; 'Avoid Oil Tieup, Peterson Warns,' *Sun*, 15 Nov. 1965; 'Big Unions Favour Walkout,' *Sun*, 17 Nov. 1965; Engler to Dick, 25 March 1968, file 57-10, Dowson fonds, LAC; Jamieson, *Times of Trouble*, 421.

123 'Liar Charge Made,' *Sun*, 18 Nov. 1965; 'General Strike Plan Idiotic, Attorney-General Declares,' *Sun*, 17 Nov. 1965.

124 Ibid.; 'Avoid Oil Tieup, Peterson Warns,' *Sun*, 15 Nov. 1965; 'Oil Tie-Up Put Off for 9 More Days' and 'Merger Union Style,' *Sun*, 16 Nov 1965.

125 'Tough Strike Line Urged by Business,' *Sun*, 22 Nov 1965; 'Truce Plan Drawn to Avert Oil Crisis,' *Sun*, 24 Nov 1965; Jamieson, *Times of Trouble*, 421; Jamieson, *Industrial Relations in Canada*, 67.

126 'BC Strike Off,' *Globe and Mail*, 25 Nov. 1965; 'BC General Strike Averted,' *Sun*, 24 Nov. 1965; 'Price Increases Next Step, BC Oil Companies Warn,' *Sun*, 25 Nov. 1965.

127 'Communist Party Will Nominate Ten Candidates in BC Election,' press release, 6 April 1966, file 23-05, 'BC provincial series,' reel H1592, CPC fonds, LAC.

128 Jamieson, *Times of Trouble*, 429–35.

129 Ibid., 441–6.

130 'International Association of Bridge, Structural and Ornamental Ironworkers – Local 97, Vancouver,' RCMP report, 1 June 1960, file 'Canadian Iron Workers,' vol. 2257; 'Labour Review April 1962,' file 'Trade unions: Comm. Penetration Canada,' vol. 2213, series A, RCMP Security Service, CSIS records, LAC; 'BC Ironworkers Local No. 1 Answers False Unity Cry,' *Workers Vanguard*, 31 Dec. 1963.

131 They formed Seamen's Section (Local 400) of the Canadian Brotherhood of Railway, Transport and General Workers (CBRT), called 'Vocal 400' for its social-movement unionism and support for sailors from underdeveloped countries seeking to unionize ships sailing under flags of convenience. 'WCSU Meet to Vote on Merger with SIU,' *Pacific Tribune*, 29 June 1956; Jim Green, *Against the Tide: The Story of the Canadian Seamen's Union* (Toronto: Progress Books, 1986), 293–4.

132 Dowson to J. and R. Houle, 31 July 1960, file 57-8, Dowson fonds, LAC.

133 'Appeal for Unity of Iron Workers in British Columbia,' 28 Oct. 1963; 'Canadian Iron Workers Union – Local #1 – Communist Activities Within,' RCMP report, 20 Dec. 1963, file 'Canadian Iron Workers,' vol. 2257, series A, RCMP Security Service, CSIS records, LAC.

134 'Canadian Iron Workers, Local No. 1, Vancouver,' RCMP report, 22 Oct. 1963, file 'Canadian Iron Workers,' vol. 2257, series A, RCMP Security Service, CSIS records, LAC; 'Union Plea Kills "Corporate Device,"' *Sun*, 24 Feb. 1964; 'City Ironworkers Win Injunction,' *Sun*, 17 Nov. 1964; 'Ironworkers Vow Continued Picket,' *Sun*, 10 March 1964; 'Ceremony Picketed,' *Sun*, 22 Jan. 1965.

135 Castlegar workers objected to a 'pre-contract' agreement between the company, Celgar, and the United Pulp and Paperworkers Union (UPPU). They joined the Western Pulp & Paper Council and requested that Pulp

& Sulphite organize the mill, a move resisted by the AFL-CIO. While 70 per cent of the Castlegar workers signed a petition requesting decertification of UPPU, Pulp & Sulphite conceded jurisdiction, prompting the formation of PPWC Local 1 in June 1962. Meanwhile, at the 1962 CLC convention, Braaten defended Mine-Mill and condemned Steel raiding, prompting an attack from the podium by William Mahoney, a CLC vice-president and Steel director. In September 1962, Braaten and MacPhee, Prince Rupert Local 408 president, were prevented from attending Pulp & Sulphite's International convention in Detroit. US border officials allegedly had a list of BC delegates singling out the two dissident pulp and paper workers, who were questioned on Cuba and Communism. Al Smith of Woodfibre, BC, described the Detroit convention proceedings as 'a machine in action...determined to maintain the status quo in spite of the wishes of the rank and file.' 'Early History of PPWC,' 5–24; 'New Mill to Boost Kootenays Industry,' *Sun*, 16 Feb. 1956; Angus MacPhee papers, UBCSC. MacPhee, who had earlier been aligned with the Trotskyist Revolutionary Workers Party (RWP), was active in the Prince Rupert Pulp & Sulphite Local, and served as PPWC first vice-president (1964–7); secretary-treasurer (1968–9); Local 4 (Prince Rupert) business agent and National Board representative; and president (1977–82).

136 Within a month of PPWC's founding convention in Vancouver in January 1963, Crofton workers voted 94.6 per cent and Woodfibre workers voted 92 per cent in favour of PPWC, forming Locals 2 and 3. Later that spring, they were joined by Prince Rupert workers who decertified from Pulp & Sulphite Local 408; Angus MacPhee, then president of the Western Pulp & Paper Council, resigned to lead PPWC Local 4. All three locals won certification from the LRB in June 1963. This marked, according the union's official history, 'the end of an era ... the last comparatively easy certification achieved by PPWC.' Vancouver Local 5 was strenuously resisted by the International and remnants of Pulp & Sulphite Local 433, which clung tenuously to the sixteen Lower Mainland certifications; workers at the Crown Zellerbach Richmond plant voted against the new union, while other smaller workplaces voted to join Local 5, which was certified by the end of 1963. At the new Northwood Mill in Prince George, Pulp & Sulphite signed up seven construction workers and went on to represent the entire workforce. 'Early History of PPWC,' 17–26; Angus MacPhee papers, UBCSC.

137 'Early History of PPWC,' 28–37, 45–56; Griffin and Lockhart, *Their Own History*, 179. An estimated 820 of 870 Harmac workers belonged to PPWC Local 8 and paid monthly dues, but the LRB declared that $40,000 was the

property of Pulp & Sulphite Local 695. The International asked management to fire PPWC members on grounds that they refused to pay dues to Local 695 and were ineligible for employment. The LRB wavered, fearing wildcat action, and on 1 July 1967 granted automatic certification to PPWC Local 8. In 1968, Prince George workers voted overwhelmingly to join PPWC, after management fired five PPWC leaders who conducted a vigorous five-month picket outside the plant gates. Also in 1968, PPWC Local 15 won certification at the Skookumchuk pulp mill near Cranbrook. However, many other PPWC drives in the late 1960s and early 1970s – at Houston (Local 17) and Mackenzie (Local 18) in northern BC, and Chemainus on Vancouver Island – failed in the face of employer-International collusion, 'pre-contract' certification, and the LRB's discriminatory rulings.

138 This incident led to the appointment of retired BC judge R.A. Sargent to head a public inquiry, and the jailing of PPWC president Orville Braaten for refusing to testify on previous radical activities. 'Early History of PPWC,' 38–43; 'Labour Review April 1962,' file 'Trade unions: Comm. Penetration Canada,' vol. 2213, series A, RCMP Security Service, CSIS records, LAC.

139 Griffin and Lockhart, *Their Own History*, 179; 'Early History of PPWC,' 30–1.

140 'Early History of PPWC,' 35 and 42.

141 Scott, *A Communist Life*, 177–80.

142 Berger, *Injunctions in British Columbia*, 16; Rankin, *Rankin's Law*, 150.

143 'Lenkurt Electric Company of Canada – North Burnaby, British Columbia,' 1966/04, file 183, Strikes and Lockouts Files, vol. 3117, Microfilm reel T-3419, Department of Labour Records, RG27, LAC; 'Lenkurt Electric Co. of Canada Ltd. Strike (Legal) 1966,' file 5-16, box 5, BCFL records, UBCSC; also 'Lenkurt Electric Co. of Canada Ltd. – Miscellaneous correspondence,' file 8-10, box 8 and 'Lenkurt Electric (Canada) Ltd. – Strike by the International Brotherhood of Electrical Workers,' file 30-9, box 30.

144 The CCU was the central body of the breakaway union movement in Canada, founded at a 1969 Sudbury convention, which Succamore attended. Veteran organizers Madeleine Parent and Kent Rowley were also influential, along with CAIMAW and PPWC. While the CCU never attracted more than a small percentage of Canadian union members, it influenced moves toward autonomy and independence in various Internationals. Affiliated membership peaked at about 40,000 members in the 1980s, but in the 1990s a number of affiliates left the CCU, including CAIMAW, CASAW, the Canadian Textile and Chemical Union, and

the remnants of Mine-Mill, which all joined the Canadian Auto Workers (CAW). In 2000, the CCU closed its national office in Nanaimo but decided to continue operating as a central body, despite a decline to around 7,000 members. See Confederation of Canadian Unions fonds, LAC.

145 CAIMAW had formed in Winnipeg in 1964 as a breakaway from the International Molders' Union. At the special 1971 convention that elected Succamore, CAIMAW took a turn to the left, away from business unionism toward a clearly defined program of independent Canadian unionism based on rank-and-file control. Despite its formidable challenge to the Internationals, employer and state opposition and successful autonomy and independence struggles in larger unions impeded CAIMAW's growth. In 1991, CAIMAW's 6,500 members voted 82 per cent in favour of merging with CAW, which had severed ties with parent UAW in 1985. Patricia Atherton, 'CAIMAW: Portrait of a Union,' MA thesis, University of British Columbia, 1981; CAIMAW fonds, UBCSC.

146 Scott, *A Communist Life*, 179. For the development of breakaway unionism, see various issues of *Progressive Worker* and *BC Newsletter* (Vancouver), Oct. 1964-June/July 1970.

147 Elaine Bernard, *The Long Distance Feeling: A History of the Telecommunications Workers Union* (Vancouver: New Star, 1983), 130.

148 'Injunctions in Labour Disputes,' Box 64, BCFL records, UBCSC; Tom Berger, *Injunctions in British Columbia*.

149 'Report from Regional Committee of the Delta-New Westminster Region of the Communist Party of Canada,' 22 Jan. 1967, file 23-30, 'BC provincial series,' reel H1592, CPC fonds, LAC.

150 North, *A Ripple, a Wave*, 30–42; Stanton, *Never Say Die!*, 133–48; Rankin, *Rankin's Law*, 122–36; file 3041 'UFAWU Contempt, first appeal,' box 10; files 3055, 3075, 3076, 3138, box 11, John Stanton fonds, UBCSC. The genesis of the strike was a jurisdictional dispute between the UFAWU and the much smaller Deep Sea Fisherman's Union (DSFU), which was exploited by the Prince Rupert Vessel Owners' Association. In March 1967, the UFAWU called a strike of all Prince Rupert trawlers and shoreworkers to protect its jurisdiction.

151 Stanton, *Never Say Die!*, 137; 'Dohm Picked to Head Stock Exchange,' *Sun*, 23 Dec. 1971; 'Dohm Forced to Quit as Exchange Head,' *Sun*, 9 Nov. 1972.

152 Stanton, *Never Say Die!*, 141–7.

153 'Minutes of the Trawl Membership Meeting,' 19 June 1967, Neish papers.

154 Homer Stevens and Rolf Knight, *Homer Stevens: A Life in Fishing* (Madeira Park, BC: Harbour, 1992), 170.

155 Ibid., 171–2; Stanton, *Never Say Die!*, 141.

156 'WA Women Answer "Marching Mothers,"' *Fisherman*, 9 June 1967.

157 Canada, *Canadian Parliamentary Guide*, 1974.

158 Stevens and Knight, *Homer Stevens*, 171.

159 Engler to Dick, 18 Nov. 1967, file 57-9, Dowson fonds, LAC. By the mid-1970s, Thompson was elected IWA president for BC District 1 and also VDLC president. See Hansard, *Official Report of the Debates of the Legislative Assembly*, 25 Feb. 1974, 484; 7 April 1975, 1064; 'Most Farms Big Business – IWA Chief,' *Colonist*, 23 Jan. 1975; MacNeil, *The IWA in British Columbia*, 56–7. In October 1967, 4,000 loggers in the southern Interior and 1,000 loggers in the northern Interior went on strike demanding parity with coastal IWA members, the latter remaining out for seven and a half months.

160 Engler to Dick, 18 Nov. 1967, file 57-9, Dowson fonds, LAC.

161 Harding, 'The New Left in BC,' 30 and 21.

162 'League for Socialist Action-Vancouver, BC,' 29 Aug. 1967, file AH-2000.00123 part 3, vol. 110, Previously Released Files series, RCMP Security Service, CSIS records, LAC.

163 'LSA Internal Bulletin,' 6 May 1968, 8, file 57-10, Dowson fonds, LAC.

164 Bernard, *The Long Distance Feeling*, 128–44.

165 Gillian Creese, *Contracting Masculinity: Gender, Class, and Race in a White-Collar Union, 1944–1994* (Toronto: Oxford University Press, 1999), 47–50; see also Julia Smith, 'Organizing the Unorganized: The Service, Office, and Retail Workers' Union of Canada (SORWUC), 1972–1986,' MA thesis, Simon Fraser University, 2009. In 1972, 1,200 BC Hydro workers in Local 378 wildcatted for two days as a protest against a time-management study recommending 25 per cent staff reductions and reprisals against seventeen workers for a 'work-to-rule' campaign. Management was forced to back down.

166 'Trade Unions – British Columbia,' 17 Dec. 1969, file 'Canadian Iron Workers,' vol. 2257, series A, RCMP Security Service, CSIS records, LAC.

167 King, *Red Bait!*, 132–40.

168 Ibid., 140–9; Mike Solski and John Smaller, *Mine Mill: The History of the International Union of Mine, Mill and Smelter Workers in Canada since 1895* (Ottawa: Steel Rail, 1984), xi; Steedman et al., eds., *Hard Lessons*.

169 King, *Red Bait!*, 151–2. Mine-Mill explored a merger with Steel, the Quebec-based Confederation of National Trade Unions, and International Building Labourers, which included the BC Rock and Tunnel Workers.

170 John Stanton, *My Past Is Now: Further Memoirs of a Labour Lawyer* (St John's: Canadian Committee on Labour History, 1994), 115–17.

171 King, *Red Bait!*, 144.

172 Allen Seager, 'Memorial: To a Departed Friend of the Working Man,' *Bulletin of the Committee on Canadian Labour History*, 4 (Autumn 1977), 12–13.

173 Jack Scott, 'British Columbia and the American Labour Movement,' in Paul Knox and Philip Resnick, eds., *Essays in BC Political Economy* (Vancouver: New Star, 1974), 33; Scott, *A Communist Life*, 252–3; Howard White, *A Hard Man to Beat: The Story of Bill White, Labour Leader, Historian, Shipyard Worker, Raconteur* (Vancouver: Pulp Press, 1983), 218.

174 Ibid., 135, 218.

175 'Union Hall Outlines,' *Trail Times*, 13 Dec. 1972. The context of Murphy's letter was a speech by Kent Rowley, of the breakaway CCU, lambasting the 1967 merger. A clipping of this letter is included in file 11, box, 49, Kenny Collection, Fisher Library; 'Red Rose Dies at 73,' *Province*, 3 May 1977.

176 King, *Red Bait!*, 152.

177 Paul Knox, 'Breakaway Unionism in Kitimat,' in Knox and Resnick, eds., *Essays in BC Political Economy*, 42–51; also J.H. Bradbury, 'Class Structures and Class Conflicts in "Instant" Resource Towns in British Columbia, 1965 to 1972,' *BC Studies*, 37 (Spring 1978), 3–18.

178 'Dissatisfaction Leads to Break,' *Ubyssey*, 2 Feb. 1973; Paul Knox, 'Breakaway Unionism in Kitimat,' in Knox and Resnick, eds., *Essays in BC Political Economy*, 43; 'Early History of PPWC,' 58–62. CASAW withstood a concerted attempt by Steel to regain certification, remaining fiercely independent and rejecting a merger with CAIMAW in 1978. CASAW won certification at the Giant gold mine in Yellowknife, NWT in 1978 and Alcan's Extrusion Plant in Richmond, BC in 1991 (raided from Steel at the request of the plant's 120 workers). However, a long strike against concessions at the Giant mine, which ran from May 1992 to November 1993 and culminated in the death of nine miners in an explosion, and an unsuccessful 1992 strike at Alcan's Richmond plant that ended in its closure, dealt CASAW a fatal blow. In 1994, CASAW members voted 76 per cent to merge with CAW. Klaus A. Mueller, Sr, 'CASAW History: The Early Days,' *CAW Local 2301 website*, n.d. < http://www.caw2301.ca / history.htm> <http://www.caw2301.ca/early.htm> (accessed 20 Nov. 2006); CASAW correspondence (1976–81), files 13 and 14 'CCU affiliates,' series 4, CAIMAW fonds, UBCSC.

179 Knox, 'Breakaway Unionism in Kitimat,' 47–8.

180 This data appeared in the Corporations and Labour Unions Returns Act (CALURA) report, which required corporations and unions to reveal their returns annually. In 1973, CLC president Donald McDonald described the reports as 'misleading, inaccurate and incomplete,' demanding they

be revised or eliminated. 'Government report grossly inaccurate – CLC president,' 7 Nov. 1973, file 436-27, CCF-NDP fonds, LAC; Canadian Textile and Chemical Union (CCU), 'The Scandal of the American Steal of Canadian Money,' n.d. [c. 1970], file 436-24, CCF-NDP fonds, LAC; 'Early History of PPWC,' 47.

181 Knox, 'Breakaway Unionism in Kitimat,' 45.

182 As quoted in Resnick, 'The Breakaway Movement in Trail,' in Knox and Resnick, eds., *Essays in BC Political Economy*, 57.

183 Hansard, *Official Report of the Debates of the Legislative Assembly*, 15 Feb. 1972, 502.

184 'Report of the BCFL Executive Council,' *BCFL Proceedings* (1971), 10–11.

185 'Breakaway Union Members Urged to Return to the Fold,' *Sun*, 9 Dec. 1971.

186 As quoted in Ross Dowson, 'Memorandum II on Labor Challenge,' 29 Oct. 1972, file 26-12, Dowson fonds, LAC. The 'Limits of "Autonomy"' are discussed in Jack Scott, *Canadian Workers, American Unions* (Vancouver: New Star, 1978), 208–14.

187 'Editorial Statement: BC's Labour Situation Is Due to National Problems That Labour Movement Leaders Will Neither Recognize Nor Effectively Combat,' *BC Newsletter* (Vancouver), June/July 1970.

188 Neish interview, 11 May 2006.

189 'Supplement to the Report of the Officers' Report Committee,' *BCFL Proceedings* (1969); 'Report of the BCFL Executive Council,' *BCFL Proceedings* (1970), 12–13; North, *A Ripple, a Wave*, 37–8.

190 Minutes, 4 June 1969, Victoria Labour Council papers (not yet remitted to UVASC), as quoted in Lowther, *A Better Life*, 45.

191 'Act Now on Jobs, Demands Labor,' *Pacific Tribune*, 24 Nov. 1970.

192 At the November 1972 BCFL convention, delegates – many of them sporting stickers reading '72-UFAWU' – had lambasted CLC president William Dodge, urging the UFAWU's readmission. The union's protracted struggle following its 1953 'suspension' is described in North, *A Ripple, a Wave*, 34–9; also *BCFL Proceedings* (1956–72); 'Delegates Hit CLC Bosses,' *Sun*, 9 Nov. 1972.

193 Minutes, 7 Feb. 1973, Victoria Labour Council papers (not yet remitted to UVASC), as quoted in Lowther, *A Better Life*, 46.

6. Political Change

1 Barrett interview, 24 April 2006.

2 As quoted in Stanley Knowles, *The New Party* (Toronto: McClelland and Stewart, 1961), 127.

3 Janet Mary Christine Burns, 'Trade Union Membership, Working Class Self-Identification, and Support for the New Democratic Party,' MA thesis, University of Victoria, 1981, iii, 41–3; also Vincent Keddie, 'Class Identification and Party Preference among Manual Workers: The Influence of Community, Union Membership and Kinship,' *Canadian Review of Sociology and Anthropology*, 17:1 (1980), 24–36; John C. Leggett, 'The Persistence of Working-Class Consciousness in Vancouver,' in John Allan Fry, ed, *Economy, Class and Social Reality: Issues in Contemporary Canadian Society* (Toronto: Butterworths, 1979), 230–43.
4 Wallace Gagne and Peter Regenstreif, 'Some Aspects of New Democratic Party Urban Support in 1965,' *Canadian Journal of Economics and Political Science*, 33:4 (1967), 260.
5 Dorothy Steeves interview, with Marlene Karnouk, 4 April 1973, T0182:0001, BC Archives.
6 Barrett interview, 24 April 2006.
7 Knowles, *The New Party*; David Lewis, *The Good Fight: Political Memoirs, 1909–1958* (Toronto: Macmillan, 1981) , 481–507.
8 *BCFL Proceedings*, 24–7 Oct. 1957, Vancouver, 60; 'BCFL Statement of Policy on 1956 election,' 26 Aug. 1956, file 450-2, CCF-NDP fonds, LAC; Paul A. Phillips, *No Power Greater A Century of Labour in British Columbia* (Vancouver: BC Federation of Labour and Boag Foundation, 1967), 153. In February 1954, the CCF's Lower Island Industrial Club invited the Victoria Trades & Labor Council (TLC) to send two delegates to a Trade Union Conference, which took place in the Victoria CCF Hall on 21 February 1954. Minutes, 3 Feb. 1954, box 5, series IV, accession 80–59, Victoria Labour Council fonds, UVASC.
9 *BCFL Proceedings* (1957), 60 and 63.
10 BC Department of Labour, *Annual Report* (1958), 116. Union density peaked in the United States at 35 per cent of all workers in 1954. For state totals, see Barry T. Hirsch, David A. Macpherson, and Wayne G. Vroman, 'Estimates of Union Density by State,' *Monthly Labor Review*, 124:7 (July 2001), 51–5.
11 'Confidential – For National Committee Members Only,' Socialist Educational League, 3 Jan. 1957, file 19-2 'Discussion Documents and Reports, n.d. 1955–1959,' CTM fonds, LAC.
12 As quoted in Lewis, *The Good Fight*, 497, 493. The CCF committee consisted of Strachan, Angus MacInnis, and Alex MacDonald, newly elected Vancouver Centre MP.
13 'O'Neil Proclaims Politics a Must,' *Ubyssey*, 30 Oct. 1959; 'Minutes of Joint Conference,' 29 May 1959, file 450-3, CCF-NDP fonds, LAC.

14 Thayer to Hamilton, 23 June 1959, file 450-1, vol. 450, CCF-NDP fonds, LAC.
15 Ibid.
16 Dorothy Steeves interview, 4 April 1973; 'Review of Constituencies,' n.d. [c. 1960], file 450-3, CCF-NDP fonds, LAC.
17 George Home interview, as quoted in Olenka Melnyk, *No Bankers in Heaven: Remembering the CCF* (Toronto and Montreal: McGraw-Hill Ryerson, 1989), 64.
18 Herbert Wilfred Herridge interview, with Peter Stursberg, n.d. [c. spring 1967], 40, file 46-9, vol. 46, series D78, MG 31, LAC.
19 Thayer to Hamilton, 8 April 1960, file 450-4, CCF-NDP fonds, LAC. The BC CCF executive also expressed displeasure over the format and content of the *New Party Newsletter*, declaring unanimously that the publication 'in its present form does not seem to serve a useful purpose in this province.'
20 Thayer to Hamilton, 2 June 1959, file 450-4, CCF-NDP fonds, LAC.
21 Thayer to Hamilton, 8 Jan. 1959; 'Opening of our New Provincial CCF Building, 517 East Broadway,' 3 April 1959; Thayer to Hamilton, 8 Jan. 1960, file 450-4, CCF-NDP fonds, LAC. For details of Stephen Lewis's organizing work, see Thayer to Hamilton, 8 Jan. 1960; Hamilton to Thayer, 3 Feb. 1959; Thayer to Hamilton, 5 Feb. 1963; Hamilton to Thayer, 13 Feb. 1959; Hamilton to Thayer, 3 March 1959; Hamilton to Thayer, 22 April [1959]; Hamilton to Thayer, 1 July 1959, file 450-4, CCF-NDP fonds, LAC.
22 R. and J. Houle to Dowson, 27 June 1960, file 57-8, Dowson fonds, LAC. Braaten and fellow CCFer Hugh Clifford, whom the Trotskyist Socialist Information Centre had supported, were soundly defeated in the election in the two-member riding, receiving roughly half the votes of the Liberal and Social Credit candidates. British Columbia, *Statement of Votes*, 1960.
23 'Only All-In United Action For People's Needs Can Create An Effective Electoral Alternative' [c. 1960], file 23-03, 'BC provincial series,' reel H1592, CPC fonds, LAC.
24 '"Reds Busy in New Party" Buck Taunt Riles Strachan,' *Colonist*, 1 Sept. 1960; 'Red Infiltration Remarks Misinterpreted, Says Buck,' *Colonist*, 7 Sept. 1960; 'Talk of Hiring BC Reds to Hurt CCF Isn't New,' *Sun*, 3 Sept. 1960; 'An Old Story,' *Sun*, 6 Sept. 1960; 'Defeat of Wicks Worth Whole Fight, Says [*sic*] CCFers,' *Sun*, 13 Sept. 1960; 'Some observations on the British Columbia Provincial Election, Sept. 12. 1960,' n.d. [1960], file 450-11, CCF-NDP fonds, LAC.
25 'Uphill Sure Liberal Would Win,' *Sun*, 13 Sept. 1960; 'Review of Constituencies,' n.d. [c. 1960], file 450-3, CCF-NDP fonds, LAC.

26 CCF Campaign Headquarters, Press Release, 26 Aug. 1960, file 450-11, CCF-NDP fonds, LAC.

27 MacNeil to CCF candidates, 20 Aug. 1960; MacNeil to CCF candidates, 24 Aug. 1960, file 450-11, CCF-NDP fonds, LAC.

28 'CCF 4,000 Votes Short,' *Sun*, 13 Sept. 1960; 'CCF Policy for BC,' n.d. [1959], file 450-8; MacNeil to CCF candidates, 4 Aug. 1960; 'Some observations on the British Columbia Provincial Election, Sept. 12. 1960,' n.d. [1960], file 450-11, CCF-NDP fonds, LAC; '5500 Cheer Tommy Douglas in Largest-Ever Rally,' *Sun*, 3 Sept. 1960; British Columbia, *Statement of Votes*, 1960. The margin of victory in Comox, Lillooet, Nanaimo, Omenica, Prince Rupert, Salmon Arm, Vancouver-Burrard, Skeena, and Yale totalled 3,852 votes.

29 'Defeat of Wicks Worth Whole Fight, Says [*sic*] CCFers,' *Sun*, 13 Sept. 1960; Barrett interview, 24 April 2006.

30 Desmond Morton, *New Democrats, 1961–1986: The Politics of Change* (Toronto: Copp Clark Pittman, 1986), 27, also 23; Nelson Wiseman and Benjamin Isitt, 'Social Democracy in Twentieth-Century Canada: An Interpretive Framework,' *Canadian Journal of Political Science*, 40:3 (September 2007), 572. Morton described the vote on the party's name as 'the only major grassroots uprising of the convention,' an initiative spearheaded by 'a handful of Ontario CCFers' who 'pushed, lobbied and manipulated their way past procedural roadblocks and won acceptance of their favourite.' In total, '2084 delegates, alternates, guests and officials' attended the founding convention.

31 Jessie Mendels to Hamilton telegram, 19 Feb. 1962, file 450-12, CCF-NDP fonds, LAC. Argue had been elected CCF MP in 1945, at age twenty-four, and became House Leader after Coldwell lost his seat in the 1958 Diefenbaker sweep. Argue was elected National Leader at the CCF's final convention in August 1960, a move opposed by Lewis and other party heavyweights who sought to leave the position vacant in anticipation of Douglas leading the new party. Argue was roundly defeated for the NDP leadership, losing to Douglas in a 380–1,391 vote. In the 1962 election, he ran as a Liberal and was narrowly returned. In the subsequent elections, in 1963 and 1965, Argue was defeated, but returned to public office when Pearson appointed him to the Senate in 1966. From 1980 to 1984, Argue served as minister of state responsible for the Canadian Wheat Board, after the Trudeau Liberals failed to elect a single MP west of Winnipeg. See Morton, *New Democrats*, 26; *Canadian Parliamentary Guide* (1945–65).

32 Barrett interview, 24 April 2006.

33 As quoted in Carolyn Swayze, *Hard Choices: A Life of Tom Berger* (Vancouver/Toronto: Douglas and McIntyre, 1987), 92; see also 'New Democrats

Pick Leader and Manifesto of Old CCF,' *Sun*, 30 Oct. 1961; 'BC News Party Backs Strachan, Right of Appeal,' *Globe and Mail*, 30 Oct. 1961.

34 'Labor Should Be Political – Neale,' *Ubyssey*, 3 Oct. 1961.

35 Hamilton to J. Mendels, 5 Oct. 1961; also Mendels to Hamilton, 17 July 1961; Mendels to Hamilton, 7 Dec. 1961; Hamilton to Mendels, 19 Dec. 1961; Mendels to Grier, 23 June 1962; Mendels to Grier, 19 July 1962; Grier to Mendels, 10 Aug. 1962; Grier to Mendels, 13 Aug. 1962, file 450-12, CCF-NDP fonds, LAC. Mendels's inquiries to federal office were triggered by requests from the communist-dominated Marine Workers and Boilermakers and UFAWU for affiliation. The question arose over whether a Communist (or Liberal, Conservative, or Social Credit party member) would be eligible to represent an NDP-affiliated union at a provincial or federal convention. Grier responded that the NDP's credential form would likely include a statement stating that the delegate did not belong to another party, similar to language on membership forms. This would 'solve the problem without drawing undue attention to it.' In 1967, BCFL secretary-treasurer Ray Haynes, a staunch craft unionist, asked the federal secretary to notify him if 'the Boilermakers Union applies for affiliation. I think we've got to take a long hard look at this one.' In 1970, a procedure was ingrained in Article 6.1 of the federal NDP constitution, requiring affiliated delegates to sign an undertaking agreeing to abide by the party's constitution and principles, and attesting that they are 'not a member or supporters of any other party.' Scotton to Gabelman, 8 Jan. 1970, file 450-19; see also Haynes to Scotton, 24 Nov. 1967; Scotton to Haynes, 1 Dec. 1967, file 436-21, CCF-NDP fonds, LAC.

36 T.C. Douglas address, 24 Oct. 1962, *BCFL Proceedings* (1962), 78; Labour Relations Act Amendment Act (1961), S.B.C. 1961 c. 31 s. 5; BC Department of Labour, *Annual Report* (1961), 29; Phillips, *No Power Greater*, 156–7. Bill 42 became law on 27 March 1961.

37 Minutes of meeting between CLC Executive Council and representatives of the NDP, 12 Dec. 1962, Chateau Laurier Hotel, Ottawa, file 436-17, CCF-NDP fonds, LAC.

38 The Ottawa convention had voted to remain in NATO. 'Fails to Adopt Anti-War Policy after Stormy Two Day Debate,' *Workers Vanguard*, Aug. 1961, file 24-6, Dowson fonds, LAC.

39 Kent to Vancouver Comrades, 20 Feb. 1961; 'Minutes of the PC Meeting,' 14 Feb. 1961; Thayer to Houle, 22 Feb. 1961, file 57-8, vol. 57, Dowson fonds, LAC. The entryist strategy, predicated on recruiting revolutionaries from the mass organizations of the working class, was described succinctly in a 1950 letter from Ross Dowson, secretary of the Revolutionary Workers

Party (RWP), to Aubrey Burton of Trail, BC: 'The French turn as it is called in our movement is a tactical maneuver designed to overcome the general isolation that the revolutionary vanguard finds itself in today.' Dowson to Rosslund (Burton), 25 Sept. 1950, file 9-2, vol. 2, CTM fonds, LAC.

40 'Keep McCarthyism Out of New Democratic Party,' *Workers Vanguard*, mid-Sept. 1961; 'Protest This Proscription on the Vanguard & Press!,' *Workers Vanguard*, mid-Dec. 1961; 'Ban on Vanguard a Prophesy of a Witch Hunt in BC NDP?' *Workers Vanguard*, mid-Jan. 1962, file 24-6, Dowson fonds, LAC; also Ross Dowson, 'Trotskyism and the NDP,' *Labor Challenge*, n.d., file 31-16, Dowson fonds, LAC.

41 Pool and Young, 'Introduction,' in R.E. 'Lefty' Morgan, *Workers' Control on the Railroad: A Practical Example 'Right under Your Nose'* (St John's: Canadian Committee on Labour History, 1994), 27–8; Jack Scott, *A Communist Life: Jack Scott and the Canadian Workers' Movement* (St John's: Canadian Committee on Labour History, 1988), 144.

42 'Result of Federal Election – Power of New Democrats,' Strachan Press Release, 20 June 1962; Grier to Mendels, 21 June 1962, file 450-12, CCF-NDP fonds, LAC; *Canadian Parliamentary Guide*, 1962. Douglas received 12,736 votes to 22,164 for Conservative Ken More. See *Canadian Parliamentary Guide*, 1962; also Robin F. Badgley and Samuel Wolfe, *Doctors' Strike: Medical Care and Conflict in Saskatchewan* (Toronto: Macmillan, 1967). Prior to the election, BC secretary Jessie Mendels and federal secretary Carl Hamilton had discussed the difficulties involved in scheduling Douglas, who was sought after by party units across the country. Mendels suggested that for BC to make a good showing in the election, 'the seats we hope to win will have to receive attention over and above the pressures that tend to get priority on the other side of the Rocky Mountain barrier.' Hamilton to Mendels, n.d. [1962]; Mendels to Hamilton, 26 Feb. 1962, file 450-12, CCF-NDP fonds, LAC.

43 Mendels to Douglas, 12 July 1964, file 450-12, CCF-NDP fonds, LAC; also Grier to Mendels, 4 July 1962, file 450-12, CCF-NDP fonds, LAC; *Canadian Parliamentary Guide*, 1962. Burnaby-Coquitlam was vacated by Erhart Regier, the sitting NDP member. Douglas's legacy in Saskatchewan, criticized in Robert Tyre's *Douglas in Saskatchewan: The Story of a Socialist Experiment* (Vancouver: Mitchell, 1962), which was widely distributed in BC, dogged the NDP. Mendels to Grier, 2 Nov. 1962; Grier to Mendels, 13 Nov. 1962, file 450-14, CCF-NDP fonds, LAC; Tyre, *Douglas in Saskatchewan*.

44 Minutes of meeting between CLC Executive Council and representatives of the NDP, 12 Dec. 1962, Chateau Laurier Hotel, Ottawa, file 436-17, CCF-NDP fonds, LAC.

45 *Canadian Parliamentary Guide*, 1963. New Democrat Max Saltsman won a November 1964 Waterloo South by-election, increasing the NDP federal caucus to 18 seats. *Canadian Parliamentary Guide*, 1964.

46 Hall to Grier, 16 Oct. 1963, file 450-13; 'Observations on the 1963 British Columbia Provincial Election,' n.d. [1963], file 450-15, CCF-NDP fonds, LAC; British Columbia, *Statement of Votes*, 1963.

47 'Jack Scott,' *Sun*, n.d. [Oct. 1963], clipping in file 24-6, Dowson fonds, LAC.

48 T.C. Douglas address, 24 Oct. 1962, *BCFL Proceedings* (1962), 84–6.

49 'Guest of Castro for Cuba Trip, BC New Democrat Criticized,' *Globe and Mail*, 8 Jan. 1963.

50 Cedric Cox speech, Jan. 1963, in Fair Play for Cuba Committee, *Four Canadians Who Saw Cuba* (March 1963), Socialist History Project <http://www.socialisthistory.ca/Docs/1961-/Cuba/FourCanadians.htm> (accessed 4 November 2006).

51 'Protest Witch-Hunt in West Coast NDP,' *Workers Vanguard*, mid-Dec. 1962, file 24-6, Dowson fonds, LAC; 'Our Work in the NDY,' n.d. [c. 1962], file 19-9, Dowson fonds, LAC; Grier to Mendels telegram, 20 Nov. 1962, file 450-14, CCF-NDP fonds, LAC. Federal secretary Terry Grier wired Mendels, stating: 'I personally concur your position this matter re youth jurisdiction. Federal constitution leaves discipline to province and federal youth constitution states discipline is responsibility of provincial youth sections subject to special arrangements made jointly in province.'

52 Young's application for membership had been rejected by the BC executive earlier in 1962. When he appealed this decision to the convention, Tom Berger (a lawyer) ruled that Young present his case before he had heard the executive's case against him. Morgan took issue with this procedure, alleging that Berger had 'ruled in his own favour,' a procedure 'tantamount to forcing a lawyer to defend a client who is not yet charged.' See '62 Convention Report,' Lefty Morgan Papers, as quoted in Pool and Young, 'Introduction,' in Morgan, *Workers' Control on the Railroad*, 28.

53 'What is the Socialist Caucus?' n.d. [c. 1963], file 24-6, Dowson fonds, LAC. The Socialist Caucus distributed a brief questioning 'The Myth of Swedish Socialism,' n.d., file 24-6, Dowson fonds, LAC. John Macey was a lawyer and former president of the BC Young Liberals, who contested the Lillooet riding for the CCF in 1960. 'Review of Constituencies,' n.d. [c. 1960], file 450-3, CCF-NDP fonds, LAC.

54 'Canada's Screwball Left: The Trotskyites,' *New Democrat* (Toronto), Aug. 1965, file 24-10, Dowson fonds, LAC. An exposé in the *New Democrat*, the party's official organ in eastern Canada, suggested there were 500 Trotskyists in Canada 'divided into a number of factions' and led by Ross Dow-

son, 'secretary of the Canadian Trotskyite movement.' The Ontario NDP had earlier denied membership to Dowson's younger brother Hugh. Jim Bury (Ontario NDP provincial secretary) to George Burt (UAW Canadian director), 1 Oct. 1963, file 436-18, CCF-NDP fonds, LAC.

55 'International Report of the Young Socialists of Canada,' Dec. 1966, in *Young Socialists Discussion Bulletin*, Feb. 1967, file 19-13, Dowson fonds, LAC.

56 Hall to Grier, 28 Oct. 1963; 'Call to Convention,' 19 Aug. 1963, file 450-14; 'Important statement,' 28 May 1964, file 450-13, CCF-NDP fonds, LAC; Brock to Bannon, 20 Aug. 1964, file 19-10, Dowson fonds, LAC; Ruth Bullock to 'Comrades' (Fed. Exec. Committee, NDP), 6 July 1965; Grier to Bullock, 21 July 1965, file 450-14, CCF-NDP fonds, LAC.

57 Brock to Bannon, 20 Aug. 1964; Brock to Bannon, 11 Sept. 1964, file 19-10, Dowson fonds, LAC.

58 'British Columbia,' n.d. [1964], file 450-14, CCF-NDP fonds.

59 Wood to J. MacKenzie, 10 July 1964; F. McKenzie to Registrar of Companies, 10 July 1964; Hall to Grier, 14 July 1964; Grier to Hall, 21 July 1964; Grier to provincial secretaries, 21 July 1964, file 450-14, CCF-NDP fonds. John H. Wood, administrative officer of the BC NDP legislative caucus in Victoria, wrote a confidential letter to party president Jack MacKenzie, stating: 'The Registrar feels they would be trading on the history of the CCF and is looking for an excuse to turn down the application; for example, a written protest from the New Democratic Party.'

60 'NDP in Financial Hole, Parley Told,' *Sun*, 26 Oct. 1962; also Mendels to Grier, 27 June 1961 [*sic* for 1962]; Grier to Mendels, 9 Nov. 1962, file 450-13, CCF-NDP fonds, LAC.

61 Grier to MacDonald, 18 June 1963, file 436-17; 'Report of Organization Committee,' n.d. [1964], file 450-5, CCF-NDP fonds, LAC. See also 'BC – 1964 Contributions – MPs and MLAs,' n.d. [1965], file 450-13, CCF-NDP fonds, LAC. Tommy Douglas and former provincial leader Arnold Webster topped the contribution list at $600 each, while several MPs and MLAs including Frank Howard, Tony Gargrave, Lois Haggen, Frank Calder, Leo Nimsick, and Dave Barrett made no donation. A note appended to the list identifies Kootenay West MP Bert Herridge's $50 donation as the 'first in history!' while leftist dissident Colin Cameron, Nanaimo-Cowichan-The Islands MP, 'say's [*sic*] he won't contribute.' In May 1964, BC secretary Ernie Hall confided to federal secretary Terry Grier that 'the past two months have been hell' from the financial standpoint. Hall to Grier, 1 June 1964, file 450-13, CCF-NDP fonds, LAC.

62 Grier to Linder, 10 July 1963; also Grier to Hall, 9 Sept. 1963; Grier to Hall,

22 Oct. 1963; Grier to Hall, 5 Nov. 1963; Grier to Hall, 27 Jan. 1963, file 450-13, Grier to Burt, 6 Feb. 1964, file 436-18, CCF-NDP fonds, LAC. For the response of BCFL and NDP leaders to circumvent Bill 42, see 'Interview with Mr. Pat O'Neil, BCFL,' 17 Jan. 1966; Scotton to Ross, 4 Feb. 1970, file 450-16, Dodge to Greer, 'Re: Meeting Nov. 21, 1964,' file 436-19, CCF-NDP fonds, LAC. In November 1964, a joint meeting of NDP and CLC leaders agreed 'it was not feasible to handle British Columbia affiliations via the CLC office.' CLC political education director George Home agreed to discuss the matter with the BCFL to 'work out an acceptable solution.' For a list of past and present affiliates, including their history of affiliation and financial contribution to the NDP, see Grier to Hall, 28 July 1964, file 450-16, CCF-NDP fonds, LAC.

63 'Confidential – Affiliated Locals – British Columbia as at December 31, 1965,' n.d. [1966]; 'Confidential – Affiliated Locals Part II – British Columbia locals in arrears on dues payments as at December 31, 1965,' n.d. [1966], file 436-18; Grier to Hall, 22 Feb. 1966, file 450-14, CCF-NDP fonds, LAC; BC Department of Labour, *Annual Report* (1965). The other affiliated locals were BC Interior Fruit and Vegetable Workers Union Local 1572 (a directly chartered affiliate of the CLC), representing 100 workers with headquarters in Penticton, Steelworkers Local 6721, representing 175 Vancouver workers, and Retail Wholesale Local 580 representing 600 Vancouver workers. Another sixteen union locals were in arrears, having paid per-capita in 1965 to send delegates to provincial and federal conventions; these included eight IWA locals representing 14,900 workers and several locals of Steel, Retail Wholesale, Amalgamated Clothing Workers, Surrey Firefighters, Vancouver Plumbers, and North Burnaby oil workers with a combined membership of about 2,600. Sixteen other locals had tenuous claims to affiliation, with all but three having had no communication with federal office in the preceding three years. At the end of 1965, there were 237,864 organized workers in BC. A year later, affiliation to the NDP had improved marginally to fourteen locals in good standing representing 4,215 workers (out of a total of twenty-seven affiliates representing 19,157 workers). However by 1968, only 13,000 BC unionists were affiliated to the NDP, out of 290,000 union members. Engler to Dick, 8 March 1968, file 57-10, Dowson fonds, LAC; 'Confidential – British Columbia – Locals affiliated as at December 31, 1966,' n.d. [1967]; 'Confidential – Affiliated Locals 3 months or more in appears as at December 31, 1966,' 31 March 1967, file 436-20, CCF-NDP fonds, LAC.

64 'Report of Organization Committee,' n.d. [1964], file 450-5, CCF-NDP fonds, LAC.

65 Sefton to Grier, 15 Feb. 1965; Fenwick to Grier, 7 April 1965, file 436-18, CCF-NDP fonds, LAC; 'What's with the NDP?' *Miners' Voice* (Toronto), 8 April 1965. Herridge had addressed the 1964 Mine-Mill convention, 'taking a whack at the Steelworkers Union.'

66 Daisy Webster, *Growth of the NDP in BC 1900–1970: 81 Political Biographies* (Vancouver: New Democratic Party, 1970), 97. For Ross's relationship to Steel, see Ross to Hamilton, 14 Feb. 1962, file 436-18, CCF-NDP fonds, LAC. He served as CLC director of organization before working as BC provincial secretary. Ross to Home, 4 Jan. 1967, file 436-21, CCF-NDP fonds, LAC.

67 'BC Report,' *Socialist Caucus Bulletin*, Nov. 1965, file 24-10, Dowson fonds, LAC; *Canadian Parliamentary Guide*, 1965. Behind the scenes, tension percolated between NDP elected officials and rank-and-file party members. The Prince Rupert NDP Club disavowed any responsibility for the Skeena federal riding's election debt, citing MP Frank Howard's 'apparent reluctance to work with and assist the Prince Rupert Club.' Crampton to Howard, 27 Dec. 1965; Grier to Howard, 13 Jan. 1966; Howard to Grier, 19 Jan. 1966, file 450-14, CCF-NDP fonds, LAC.

68 'Tommy Douglas and the BC General Strike,' *Socialist Caucus Bulletin*, Nov. 1965, file 24-10, Dowson fonds, LAC.

69 'Bill 33 and the Ferryworker,' *Vancouver Branch Discussion Bulletin*, 3 April 1968; Engler to Dick, 8 March 1968; 'Our Press,' n.d. [c. 1968], file 57-10, Dowson fonds, LAC. Also 'Strike Dries Up Five Breweries,' *Sun*, 23 Aug. 1965.

70 C. Lytle, 'Submission to Strategy and Issues Committee,' n.d. [1966]; also 'Claim Better Living in BC!', n.d. [1966]; 'Report of BC Provincial Campaign Committee,' 25 June 1966, file 450-17, CCF-NDP fonds, LAC. Lytle suggested the NDP focus on quality of life issues such as ending water and air pollution and protecting green spaces, appealing to 'British Columbians as consumers rather than as producers ... In our present relatively affluent society ... most of our people are concerned primarily with the problems they face as consumers and as individuals seeking enjoyment and satisfaction out of life ... If we concentrate a campaign on social problems affecting minorities or on welfare-statism, we will, I submit, be inviting electoral failure.'

71 Lytle to Bury, 14 Sept. 1966, file 450-17, CCF-NDP fonds, LAC; British Columbia, *Statement of Votes*, 1966.

72 Scotton to Berger, 13 Sept. 1966, file 450-17, CCF-NDP fonds, LAC. Berger was elected with 9,849 votes to 7,584 for the closest Social Credit candidate, former CCFer and Vancouver mayor Tom Alsbury; fellow New

Democrat Ray Parkinson took 9,498 votes. See British Columbia, *Statement of Votes*, 1966.

73 Swayze, *Hard Choices*, 93–4. In the 1960 provincial election, Berger received 6,530 votes, while the Social Credit winners in the two-member riding received 8,516 and 8,227 votes. In the 1962 federal election, Berger won the seat with 9,173 votes, to 9,079 votes for his Liberal competitor and 8,651 for the Conservative. British Columbia, *Statement of Votes*, 1960; *Canadian Parliamentary Guide*, 1962.

74 'Lawyer Attacks Bennett Remarks,' *Sun*, 13 April 1966; Swayze, *Hard Choices*, 97–100. In the 1963 federal election, Berger received 9,998 votes to 12,048 for Ron Basford. In the 1963 provincial election, Berger received 10,345 votes to 10,612 for his nearest Social Credit opponent in the two-member riding. See *Canadian Parliamentary Guide*, 1963; British Columbia, *Statement of Votes*, 1963.

75 Swayze, *Hard Choices*, 103. A year earlier, O'Neil had been ambivalent about labour support for the NDP, informing provincial secretary Ernie Hall that even if Bill 42 was not in effect 'unions and union members would still support candidates according to their own likes or dislikes. There would be no blanket change.' 'Interview with Mr. Pat O'Neil, BCFL,' 17 Jan. 1966; Scotton to Ross, 4 Feb. 1970, file 450-16, CCF-NDP fonds, LAC.

76 Lytle to Scotton, 27 April 1967, file 450-14, CCF-NDP fonds, LAC. BC NDP secretary Clive Lytle informed federal secretary Cliff Scotton that 'I understand a fair amount [of affiliations are] coming in from the BC Federation of Labour during the next few weeks.'

77 Swayze, *Hard Choices*, 102; 'Strachan Scores Decisive Victory,' *Sun*, 5 June 1967; Lytle to Scotton, 23 Jan. 1967; Lytle to Scotton, 27 April 1967, file 450-14, CCF-NDP fonds, LAC.

78 Barrett interview, 24 April 2006.

79 'The Political Situation and the Gallup Poll,' n.d. [c. Nov. 1968], file 436-20, CCF-NDP fonds, LAC; *Canadian Parliamentary Guide*, 1967. The BC NDP released organizer Michael Lewis, son of David, to work on the Sudbury campaign, a common practice where personnel were exchanged between provincial sections. Scotton to Lytle, 19 April 1967; Lytle to Scotton, 27 April 1967, file 450-14; Lytle to Bury, 14 Sept. 1966, file 450-17, CCF-NDP fonds, LAC.

80 *Canadian Parliamentary Guide*, 1968; Ross to Scotton, 10 March 1969; Scotton to Ross, 13 March 1969, file 450-19, CCF-NDP fonds, LAC. Douglas received 17,753 votes to 17,891 for Perrault, while the Conservative and Social Credit candidates were far behind, with 3,206 and 702 votes. In

Comox-Alberni, Tom Barnett was elected in a subsequent by-election in April 1969, with 12,612 votes to 12,357 for Liberal Richard Durante. In the 1968 general election, Durante had squeaked by Barnett, 11,939 votes to 11,930.

81 Dailly interview, 2 Aug. 2005. Prior to the election, Norm Levi had raised the implications of boundary changes. See Ross to Douglas, 29 March 1968, file 450-19, CCF-NDP fonds, LAC.

82 Douglas was returned to the House of Commons in a February 1969 by-election, which he won with 19,730 votes (57 per cent) to 12,897 for Liberal candidate Eric Winch and 1,966 votes for Conservative Magdalenus Verbrugge. Scotton requested funds from several national union headquarters for the by-election campaign, pointing out that 'the Trudeau government is turning out to be a very "conservative" operation ... Big business feels that the Prime Minister is their kind of man.' Unions including the UAW and CUPE responded with donations. Scotton to Dennis McDermott (Canadian Director, UAW), 19 Dec. 1968, file 436-22; Ross to Scotton, 2 Oct. 1968, file 450-19; Scotton to Hartman, 27 March 1969; Hartman to Scotton, 25 March 1969, file 436-23, CCF-NDP fonds, LAC; *Canadian Parliamentary Guide*, 1969.

83 Walter Stewart, *The Life and Political Times of Tommy Douglas* (Toronto: McArthur and Company, 2003), 269; Thomas H. McLeod and Ian McLeod, *Tommy Douglas: The Road to Jerusalem* (Edmonton: Hurtig, 1987), 168, 171–2; Doris French Shackleton, *Tommy Douglas* (Toronto: McClelland and Stewart, 1975), 286.

84 'Draft Platform – Why Bennett Must Go?' [1969], file 23-06, 'BC provincial series,' reel H1592, CPC fonds, LAC; Bruce Lowther, *A Better Life: The First Century of the Victoria Labour Council* (Victoria: Victoria Labour Council, 1989), 44; Mediation Commission Act, S.B.C. 1968 c. 26 s 18; BC Department of Labour, *Annual Report* (1968), 11; J.T. Montague, 'Effective Industrial Relations Policies in a Developing Economy,' in R. Shearer, ed., *Exploiting Our Economic Potential* (Toronto: Holt, Rinehart and Winston, 1968) 124; 'Bill 33 and the Ferryworkers,' *Workers Vanguard*, 3 March 1968, file 57-10, Dowson fonds, LAC.

85 Engler to Dick, 8 March 1968; Engler to Dick, 25 March 1968, file 57-10, Dowson fonds, LAC.

86 Dick to Engler, 23 March 1968; Engler to Dick, 25 March 1968, file 57-10, Dowson fonds, LAC.

87 'Bill 33 and the Ferryworker,' *Vancouver Branch Discussion Bulletin*, 3 April 1968; Engler to Dick, 8 March 1968, file 57-10, Dowson fonds, LAC. Party president Norm Levi won the seat with 10,289 votes, to 8,309 for Social

Credit candidate George Wainborn and 7,356 for Liberal Edward 'Sandy' Robinson. British Columbia, *Statement of Votes*, 1968.

88 Stuart Jamieson, *Industrial Relations in Canada* (Toronto: Macmillan, 1973), 129; also 'Report of the BCFL Executive Council,' *BCFL Proceedings* (1969), 6–7.

89 As quoted in Hansard, *Official Report of the Debates of the Legislative Assembly*, 22 Jan. 1971, 11.

90 Fryer interview, 11 April 2006; Bruce McLean, *A Union amongst Government Employees: A History of the BC Government Employees' Union, 1919–1979* (Victoria: BCGEU, 1979), 92–3. Fryer was hired in the midst of a tense factional fight in the BCGEA. In his words, the lines of demarcation were between 'conservatives' based in Victoria and the Okanagan and 'real trade unionists.' The latter group courted him, and finessed the hiring through the divided provincial executive.

91 McLean, *A Union amongst Government Employees*, 103.

92 See Minutes, 17 Sept. 1969, Victoria Labour Council papers (not yet remitted to UVASC), as quoted in Lowther, *A Better Life*, 45.

93 J.T. Montague, 'Effective Industrial Relations Policies in a Developing Economy,' in Shearer, *Exploiting Our Economic Potential*, 123, and Shearer, 'Public Policy and the British Columbia Economy: Conclusions of the Series,' in Shearer, *Exploiting Our Economic Potential*, 150.

94 Jamieson, *Industrial Relations in Canada*, 130.

95 'Report of the BCFL Executive Council,' *BCFL Proceedings* (1969), 3.

96 'Report of the BCFL Executive Council,' *BCFL Proceedings* (1969), 4; also BC Department of Labour, *Annual Report* (1969), 53.

97 'Break the Chains on the Labour Movement!' n.d. [July 1969], file 57-9, Dowson fonds, LAC; 'Need Militant Strategy to Win BC Oil Strike,' *Workers Vanguard*, 14 July 1969, file 446-30, CCF-NDP fonds, LAC.

98 'Report of the BCFL Executive Council,' *BCFL Proceedings* (1970), 3–5; 'Report of the BCFL Executive Council,' *BCFL Proceedings* (1969), 1; James Harding, 'The New Left in British Columbia,' in Dimitrios I. Roussopoulos, ed., *The New Left in Canada* (Montreal: Black Rose, c. 1970), 30.

99 'Berger Vows No Compromise If NDP Forms Government,' 'Berger Win Tension-Packed,' and '"City Slicker Lawyer" to Be Called Leader,' *Sun*, 14 April 1969; Swayze, *Hard Choices*, 103; Webster, *Growth of the NDP*, 82. W.A.C. Bennett responded to Berger's win by repeating his description of the new leader as a 'city-slicker lawyer.' Fourth-place finisher John Conway, an SFU student who pledged to take the party back to its socialist roots, told delegates that 'we have seen machine pitted against machine, bloc against bloc and personality against personality.' In December 1968,

BCFL secretary Ray Haynes wired federal NDP secretary Cliff Scotton: 'Urgently require up to date list of BC locals affiliated to New Democratic Party with paid up affiliation.' Scotton responded that provincial secretary Wally Ross had the 'most recent BC affiliation lists.' In March 1969, Scotton had informed the BC NDP that fourteen union locals were in good standing and eligible to send delegates to the convention: eight Steel locals, five IWA locals, and the lone BC Interior Fruit and Vegetable Workers 1572, a directly chartered CLC affiliate. However, in the intervening period prior to the convention, nine additional locals – representing 7,113 workers – were granted credentials, though no affiliation fees were remitted to federal office. Scotton wrote to the BC party after the convention: 'These locals had, among them, 25 delegates at the convention and in order for no questions to be raised as to their entitlement, we should be in receipt of their affiliation fees according to the established requirements.' Scotton to Ross, 13 March 1969, file 450-19, CCF-NDP fonds, LAC; Haynes to Scotton, 10 Dec. 1968; Scotton to Haynes, 11 Dec. 1968, file 436-22, CCF-NDP fonds, LAC.

100 Ross to Provincial Officers, 20 May 1969, file 450-21, CCF-NDP fonds, LAC.

101 Martin Robin, 'Victoria Letter,' *Canadian Forum* (Toronto), April 1969, 9–11; British Columbia, *Statement of Votes*, 1968–9.

102 Ross to Provincial Officers, 20 May 1969, file 450-21, CCF-NDP fonds, LAC.

103 Ibid.; Ross to Scotton, 2 Oct. 1968; Scotton to Ross, 10 Oct. 1968, Hartman to Ross, 30 July 1969, file 450-19, CCF-NDP fonds, LAC.

104 Hartman to Ross, 30 July 1969, file 450-19, CCF-NDP fonds, LAC.

105 Ross to Dodge, 27 June 1969, file 450-20; Ross to Hartman, 5 Aug. 1969, file 450-19, CCF-NDP fonds, LAC.

106 Ross to Scotton, 16 July 1969, file 450-19, CCF-NDP fonds, LAC.

107 Scotton to Federal Officers, 31 July 1969, file 450-20, CCF-NDP fonds, LAC; Swayze, *Hard Choices*, 105.

108 Swayze, *Hard Choices*, 105–6; Elaine Bernard, *The Long Distance Feeling: A History of the Telecommunications Workers' Union* (Vancouver: New Star, 1983), 128–44.

109 'Berger Resigns as Leader of NDP, Nods to Barrett,' *Sun*, 22 Sept. 1963; also 'Help Sought As Barrett Tackles Job,' *Sun*, 23 Sept. 1969; British Columbia, *Statement of Votes*, 1969. Several explanations were offered for the NDP's defeat. See Enid Page (Vancouver Centre canvass organizer), 'Thoughts on the Election Campaign,' 2 Sept. 1969; Thayer to Scotton, 3 Sept. 1959, file 450-21, CCF-NDP fonds, LAC.

110 Scotton to Nash, 14 Nov. 1969, file 450-19, CCF-NDP fonds, LAC. Also 'Norm Levi Memo to Table Officers, Financial crisis in the NDP of BC,' 20 Oct. 1969, file 450-20; Haynes to All Affiliates, 13 March 1970; Nash to Cliff, 7 Nov. 1969; Scotton to Ross, 12 Nov. 1969; Scotton to Nash; Ross to Scotton, 30 June 1970; 'Province-Wide Fund Raising Drive,' 17 Feb. 1970, file 450-19, CCF-NDP fonds, LAC. In June 1970, Ross resigned for a final time, serving as provincial secretary until 15 Sept. 1970.

111 'Province-Wide Fundraising Drive,' 17 Feb. 1970; Haynes to All Affiliates, 13 March 1970; Carter to 'All Provincial Constituency Association Executives,' 17 April 1970; 'Haynes to CLC Delegates,' 15 May 1970; 'BC Tomorrow Committee,' 19 May 1970; 'To all BC Tomorrow Prize Winners and Solicitors,' 19 June 1970; Carter to Scotton, 30 Sept. 1970, file 450-19, CCF-NDP fonds, LAC.

112 'Report of the BCFL Executive Council,' *BCFL Proceedings* (1969), 8.

113 'Report of BCFL Political Education Committee,' *BCFL Proceedings* (1969), 1.

114 'Report on Affiliation to the NDP and Comparison with Affiliation to the CLC,' n.d. [1970], file 436-25, CCF-NDP fonds, LAC. Half of these union members belonged to CLC affiliated unions. BC NDP membership peaked at 17,000 at the end of 1969. It had hovered around 9,000 since the party's formation in 1961, but the 1969 leadership race created a surge in new members. The next year, when Barrett ran uncontested for the leadership, NDP membership declined to 11,248. See Thayer to Hamilton, 8 Jan. 1960, file 450-4; Report of Organization Committee, n.d. [1964], file 450-5; J.H. to Scotton, 15 March 1968, file 450-20; Ross to Provincial Officers, 20 May 1969, file 450-21; Scotton to Dodge, 16 Feb. 1971, file 436-25, vol. 436, CCF-NDP fonds, LAC.

115 'British Columbia Report,' *Socialist Caucus Bulletin*, Jan. 1966, file 24-10, Dowson fonds.

116 'NDP stages march to US consulate,' n.d. [Aug. 1965], file 24-10, Dowson fonds; 'Seven Years of Struggle to End the War,' *Labor Challenge*, 9 Aug. 1971; 'Federal NDP Convention Resolutions 1965,' file 68-5, box 5, BC NDP fonds, UBCSC.

117 'British Columbia NDP Convention,' *Socialist Caucus Bulletin*, May 1966, file 24-10, Dowson fonds, LAC; 'BC Section Federal Socialist Caucus,' [Resolutions to 1966 BC NDP convention], 7 Feb. 1966, file 43-1 '1969 BC Provincial Convention – Socialist Caucus Intervention (file 1 of 2),' vol. 43, CTM fonds, LAC.

118 'Political Report,' *Youth Discussion Bulletin* (Vancouver), April 1966, file 19-12, Dowson fonds, LAC.

119 Jim [Harding] to Mike [Rowan], 10 April 1966, file 9, box 16a, CUCND-SUPA archives, MARC.
120 Stan Grey speech, 'Fall Training Institute,' SUPA Federal Council Meeting, n.d. [c. 1966], file 8, box 16a, CUCND-SUPA archives, MARC.
121 'Political Report,' *Youth Discussion Bulletin* (Vancouver), April 1966, file 19-12, Dowson fonds, LAC.
122 'Some Developments in the NDP,' Vancouver, 27 May 1968, file 57-10; 'Introduction to Pre-Convention Discussion,' 21 May 1968; 'Draft Political Resolution,' submitted by YS National Executive Committee, 29 April 1967, file 19-14; Committee to Defend the Expelled, *Stop the Expulsions in the NDP!* (Toronto: Committee to Defend the Expelled, n.d. [c. 1967]), in file 24-11, Dowson fonds, LAC. The expulsions centred in the Ontario NDY, where a dozen members were expelled for belonging to or supporting the LSA, but included two Quebec NDY members, including future *Workers Vanguard* editor Dick Fidler, and Lyle Severin in BC.
123 'Some Developments in the NDP,' Vancouver, 27 May 1968, file 57-10, Dowson fonds, LAC; Committee to Defend the Expelled, *Stop the Expulsions in the NDP!*, 6–7, in file 24-11, Dowson fonds, LAC. By May 1968, YS activist Joe Fraser concluded that 'the NDY is non-existent practically.'
124 'LSA Internal Bulletin,' 6 May 1968, p. 8, file 57-10, Dowson fonds, LAC.
125 John Bullen, 'The Ontario Waffle and the Struggle for an Independent Socialist Canada,' *Canadian Historical Review*, 64:2 (June 1983), 188–215. For a concise history of the Waffle and a list of signatories to the manifesto, see 'Confidential: Chronological survey of documents dealing with the Waffle group within the NDP and also public comments based on their activity,' n.d. [1972], file 446-25, CCF-NDP fonds, LAC.
126 Barrett interview, 24 April 2006; 'For an Independent Socialist Canada,' file 446-1, CCF-NDP fonds, LAC.
127 Dailly interview, 2 Aug. 2005.
128 President's Report, April 1968, file 450-9; Wally to Harney, 28 Feb. 1968, file 450-19, CCF-NDP fonds, LAC; Norman Levi interview, with author, 19 April 2006, Victoria, BC. In 1966, the Socialist Caucus nominee for BC NDP president, John Macey, had called for 'a democratic party with annual conventions and no political expulsions.' 'British Columbia NDP Convention,' *Socialist Caucus Bulletin*, May 1966, file 24-10, Dowson fonds, LAC.
129 For the origins of the Waffle, see 'Minutes of meeting held in Kingston,' 26 July 1969; Thayer to Endicott, 3 Sept. 1969, file 446-4; 'Why is the Waffle Called the Waffle,' n.d. [1969], file 446-7, CCF-NDP fonds; Mike [Rowan] to Jim [Harding], 26 April 1966; 'Outline of Manifesto,' 2 Jan.

1967, file 9, box 16a, CUCND-SUPA archives, MARC; James Laxer, *Red Diaper Baby: A Boyhood in the Age of McCarthyism* (Vancouver/Toronto: Douglas and McIntyre, 2004).

130 See Patrick Webber, '"For a Socialist New Brunswick": The New Brunswick Waffle, 1967–1972,' MA thesis, University of New Brunswick, 2008; 'You Remember New Brunswick,' *Waffle News*, July 1970, file 446-18; 'Extracts from "For a Socialist New Brunswick" – Resolution as endorsed at NDP New Brunswick Convention 1971,' 25 Sept. 1971, file 446-25, CCF-NDP fonds, LAC; 'Walkouts Break Up NB NDP Convention,' *Labor Challenge* (Toronto), 11 Oct. 1971; 'Report on the Maritime suspensions,' 30 Oct. 1971, file 26-14, Dowson fonds, LAC.

131 'Manifesto Comes of Age,' 'Recent Strides,' and 'The Watkins Tour,' *Waffle Weekly*, 20 Oct. [1969], file 32-3, Dowson fonds, LAC.

132 'Debate on the Resolutions: "For a United and Independent Canada" (C-17) and "For an Independent Socialist Canada" (R-133),' 30 Oct. 1969, pp. 18–19, file 446-7, CCF-NDP fonds, LAC; 'NDP delegates reject Watkins manifesto by margin of nearly 2 to 1,' *Globe and Mail*, 31 Oct. 1969; 'The Watkins Manifesto: "For an Independent Socialist Canada,"' *New Democrat* (Toronto), Sept.-Oct. 1969, in file 446-9, CCF-NDP fonds, LAC; 'The Marshmallow,' *Waffle Weekly*, 20 Oct. [1969], file 32-3, Dowson fonds, LAC.

133 'Debate on the Resolutions: "For a United and Independent Canada" (C-17) and "For an Independent Socialist Canada" (R-133),' 30 Oct. 1969, pp. 18–19, file 446-7, CCF-NDP fonds, LAC.

134 'Solidarity Forever,' *Waffle Weekly*, 20 Oct. [1969], file 32-3, Dowson fonds, LAC.

135 'Western Regional NDP Waffle Conference,' 25–6 April 1970; 'National Waffle Conference,' 1–3 Aug. 1970; 'Agenda – National Waffle Conference,' n.d. [Aug. 1970], file 446-12; 'Stop the Continental Energy Resource Deal – Demonstration at [Toronto] City Hall, Saturday, September 12,' n.d. [Sept. 1970]; 'Yankees, Oil and Gas, Canada and the NDY,' n.d. [Sept. 1970], file 446-5; 'Money Matters,' file 446-6; 'We've got an NDP government; but the Dept. of Industry & Commerce is still the Same old Way!' n.d. [c. 1969], file 446-7; 'Dunlop Workers Fight for Their Jobs,' *Waffle News*, n.d. [c. 1970], file 446-18, CCF-NDP fonds, LAC.

136 'Labour Affiliation to the NDP,' BC Waffle discussion paper, n.d. [c. 1969], file 446-8; 'Recent Activities of the BC Waffle,' *Waffle News*, May 1970, file 446-18, CCF-NDP fonds, LAC.

137 'BC Waffle Slate,' n.d. [1970], 'BC Waffle Draft Statement of Principles,' n.d. [1970]; 'BC, BC, BC, BC, BC, BC, BC,' *Waffle News*, Feb. 1970; 'More

from 20th Century BC,' *Waffle News*, May 1970; 'Healthy Waffle Base at BC Provincial Convention,' *Waffle News*, July 1970, file 446-18, CCF-NDP fonds, LAC. The Waffle contested every position except party leader. Its nominee for first vice-president, VDLC secretary-treasurer Paddy Neale, who had been endorsed by Barrett's group, was elected. Wafflers Dawn Carrell and Harold Winrob were elected as members-at-large.

138 The resolution declared that 'the annual membership fee in the NDP of BC shall be determined by the member, rather than by the party … There shall be neither maximum nor minimum membership fee, but rather, that each shall decide how much a socialist society is worth to him or her.' On 4 October 1970, the BC provincial council voted to withhold 50 per cent of the federal membership fee quota to defray costs to the 1971 federal convention. This action spurred moves toward a federal travel pool. 'Substitute Resolution Prepared by the Officers,' 7 June 1970; Scotton to Dent, 9 Dec. 1970, file 450-20, CF-NDP fonds, LAC.

139 'Healthy Waffle Base at BC Provincial Convention,' *Waffle News*, July 1970, file 446-18, CCF-NDP fonds, LAC.

140 'Lewis New Release,' 28 Jan. 1971; 'Public Ownership of Canadian Resource Industries,' Waffle resolution prepared for NDP Federal Council, 15–17 Jan. 1971; 'Public Ownership and the NDP,' n.d. [1971], file 446-19, CCF-NDP fonds, LAC. Ed Broadbent, the Oshawa NDP MP who also vied for the leadership, suggested: 'A faction within a party can be best handled not by the creation of a counter-faction but by serious and determined efforts to generate imaginative policies that transcend minority interests.' Broadbent News Release, 2 Feb. 1971, file 446-22, CCF-NDP fond, LAC.

141 'The Technique of Confrontation,' *Colonist*, 21 Feb. 1971; also 'Max Saltsman and the Wafflers,' *Colonist*, 19 Feb. 1971.

142 'NDP Requires 4 Ballots to Elect Lewis as Leader' and 'Lewis Asserts His Command: No Pandering to the Waffle,' *Globe and Mail*, 26 April 1971; 'How Labor Outmanoeuvred the Waffle,' and 'Complete Public Ownership of Oil, Mines Is Rejected 3–1 by New Democratic Convention,' *Globe and Mail*, 24 April 1971; *Waffle Bulletin*, issue no. 1, 21 April 1971, file 446-20; 'For an Independent Socialist Canada: Resolutions prepared by the Waffle Movement in the NDP,' April 1971, file 446-7, CCF-NDP fonds, LAC. The Waffle candidate for federal president, Carol Gudmundson of Saskatoon, was also defeated. See 'Carol Gudmundson, President,' n.d. [1971], file 446-9; 'Left slate for Party Executive,' 23 April 1972, file 446-20, CCF-NDP fonds, LAC

143 '"Adapt or Get Out," Lewis tells Waffle,' *Sun*, 26 April 1971; 'Mr. Doug-

las's Swan Song,' 23 April 1971. Also 'Two Dangers Facing Canada, Douglas Tells NDP Meeting,' 21 April 1971; 'New Democrats Have Gone Full Circle,' 'NDP Bids Tommy Farewell,' and 'Waffle Defeated in NDP Vote Test,' *Sun*, 23 April 1971; 'Waffle Rejected on Eve of Voting' and 'NDP Hedges on Quebec,' *Sun*, 24 April 1971; 'David Lewis's Problem' and 'Old Leader, Old Democratic Party,' *Sun*, 26 April 1971.

144 Minutes of meeting between CLC Executive Council and representatives of the NDP, 12 Dec. 1962, Chateau Laurier Hotel, Ottawa, file 436-17, CCF-NDP fonds, LAC. Douglas's suggestion was supported by at least one International labour leader, George Burt, Canadian director of the United Auto Workers.

145 Dodge to Scotton, 13 Jan. 1970; Blakeney (A.E.B.) Scotton to Dodge, 15 Jan. 1970, file 436-24; Ed Broadbent, 'Challenging the Rights of Management,' *New Democrat* (Toronto), Sept.–Oct. 1969, in file 446-9; Dennis McDermott (UAW International vice-president and Canadian director) to D. Lewis, 25 Jan. 1972; D. Lewis to Brisbois (UAW Local 199 president), file 436-26, CCF-NDP fonds, LAC.

146 Mackenzie to D. Lewis, 7 June 1972, file 446-4, CCF-NDP fonds, LAC; see also 'Hamilton Workers Dump US Union!' n.d. [c. 1970], file 446-5; 'Dunlop Workers Fight for Their Jobs,' *Waffle News*, n.d. [1970], file 446-18; 'Labor and the NDP,' n.d. [Aug. 1970], file 446-12; 'The Issues at Texpack,' *Waffle Labor News*, n.d. [c. Sept. 1971], file 41-12 'Waffle – Misc. 1972/1973,' vol. 41, CTM fonds, LAC; 'A socialist program for Canadian trade unions, Issued by the NDP-Waffle Labour Committee,' n.d. [1972], file 446-28; Ontario Waffle Labour Committee, 'For a Fully Independent and Militant Union Movement in Canada,' n.d. [1974], file 32-7, Dowson fonds, LAC. Also Ed Finn, 'Canadianizing Unions,' *New Democrat* (Toronto), Sept.-Oct. 1969, in file 446-9; 'A Programme for Reform,' n.d. [c. 1969], file 446-8; and various correspondence in file 436-24, CCF-NDP fonds, LAC.

147 'Hamilton Mountain Resolution,' n.d. [1972], file 446-23 'Ontario Waffle Debate'; Laxer et al. to Brother or Sister, 5 March 1972, file 446-6; Ontario Waffle to Ontario Executive, n.d. [1972], file 446-23, CCF-NDP fonds, LAC.

148 Carpenter to Gordon Brigden (Ontario NDP secretary), 8 June 1972; also Brigden to Carpenter, 13 June 1972, file 446-4; Haddrell to Brigden, 14 May 1972; Brigden to Haddrell, 19 May 1972, file 446-27, CCF-NDP fonds, LAC. When Alberta NDP MLA and provincial leader Grant Notley signed a petition against the expulsions, he received a strong rebuke from Brigden: 'All other provincial leaders and executives have been very careful to remain neutral.' Another letter of complaint was received from

Moose Jaw MP John L. Skoberg. Brigden to Notley, 22 June 1972; Skoberg to Brigden, 8 June 1972; Scotton to Skoberg, 9 June 1972, file 446-4, CCF-NDP fonds, LAC.

149 Howard to Scotton, 4 June 1972; Scotton to Howard, 9 June 1972; Holtby to Scotton, 13 July 1972, file 446-27, CCF-NDP fonds, LAC.

150 'Choking on a Waffle,' *Sun*, 25 May 1972, 'Bennett, Barrett Tangle,' *Province*, 15 June 1972.

151 Haddrell to Brigden, 15 June 1972, file 446-4, CCF-NDP fonds, LAC.

152 Ontario NDY to Executive, 27 April 1972, file 446-23; Kelly Crichton (Ontario Waffle Steering Committee) to Waffler, 19 June 1972; Watkins to Provincial Council delegates, 19 June 1972; Pitman and Harney to Fellow New Democrats, 21 June 1972; 'Associate Membership Resolution,' n.d. [1972]; Quarter to Delegate, 24 June 1972; Scotton to Federal Council, 26 June 1972; 'Resolution Re: The Waffle Group,' 24 June 1972, file 446-4, CCF-NDP fonds, LAC. The Orillia council, 'the largest delegate council meeting ever held by the party in Ontario,' voted 217–88 for a resolution stating that 'the present structure and behaviour of the Waffle cannot continue' and that 'public activities must be undertaken only by constituency associations, the Provincial Executive or Council, or other duly-constituted bodies within the party.' While this action was supported by diverse party units including the *Kootenay West Sentinel*, an NDP organ in BC's southern interior, it inflamed the left. Following the Orillia council, four leading Wafflers resigned as NDP federal candidates: Laxer (York East), Watkins (Parkdale), George Gilks (Hamilton West), and Ellie Prepas (Trinity). At a fractious August 1972 Waffle conference outside London, Ont., a majority decided to leave the NDP and form MISC. A minority, including members of the Trotskyist LSA, opposed this move because it 'would reduce us to a sterile sect isolated from the existing mass audience for socialism.' See 'Waffle Withdraws from Ontario NDP, Militants Remain to Try to Out Lewis,' *Globe and Mail*, 21 Aug 1972; 'Orillia – The End of the Beginning,' *Waffle News*, July-Aug. 1972; *Waffle Election Special*, n.d. [1972], file 41-12 'Waffle-Misc. 1972/1973,' vol. 41, CTM fonds, LAC; 'Democratic Dissent,' *Kootenay West Sentinel* (Kinnaird, BC), n.d. [1972], vol. 446–23; Gilks et al. to Waffler, 19 July 1972; Minutes of proceedings of London Waffle Conference, 19–20 Aug. 1972; Bass et al., 'Toward a Movement for an Independent Socialist Canada,' Aug. 1970; Flexer et al., 'Resolution drafted for consideration at Waffle Conference,' 19–20 Aug. 1970; Flexer et al., 'A Fighting Strategy for the Waffle,' n.d. [Aug. 1972]; 'Proposed Agenda and Rules of Procedure, Waffle Conference,' 19–20 Aug. 1972; 'Resolution' [formation of MISC with list of supporting

delegates], 19 Aug. 1972; Sweet to Fellow NDP members, 24 Aug. 1972, file 446-4; 'Meeting of the organizing committee of the Movement for an Independent Socialist Canada,' n.d. [c. Sept. 1972]; 'The Ontario Waffle Movement for an Independent Socialist Canada, Protem Committee,' n.d. [1970], CCF-NDP fonds, LAC. For criticism of MISC from a left perspective, see Canadian Party of Labour, 'Class War, not Nationalist Research: Stop "Railroad" By Laxer & Watkins,' n.d. [1972]; 'A Call for a Left Caucus,' n.d. [1972], file 446-29, CCF-NDP fonds, LAC; 'From Watkins to Laxer to Lewis: NDP Puts Squeeze on Socialism,' n.d. [1972], file 41-12 'Waffle-Misc. 1972/1973,' vol. 41, CTM fonds, LAC.

153 Swankey interview, 10 June 2005.

154 Dailly interview, 2 Aug. 2005.

155 Steeves interview, 4 April 1973.

156 'YS/LJS Executive Council Plenum Reports,' Dec. 1971, file 20-1 'B2-1971,' Dowson fonds, LAC.

157 Hilda Thomas interview, with author, 28 Feb. 2004, Toronto, Ontario.

158 See 'League for Socialist Action (LSA) – Vancouver, BC,' 4 May 1972, file 5, vol. 110, Previously Released Files series, RCMP Security Service, CSIS records, LAC; file 41-12 'Waffle – Misc. 1972/1973,' vol. 41, CTM fonds, LAC.

159 Tom McEwen, *The Forge Glows Red: From Blacksmith to Revolutionary* (Toronto: Progress Books, 1974), 234.

160 Swankey interview, 10 June 2005.

161 Barrett interview, 24 April 2006; 'Press Conference,' 26 Sept. 1969, file 450-19, CCF-NDP fonds, LAC.

162 Dailly interview, 2 Aug. 2005; Engler to Dick, 25 March 1968, file 57-10, Dowson fonds.

163 Nash to Scotton, 7 Nov. 1969, file 450-19, CCF-NDP fonds, LAC.

164 Federal secretary Cliff Scott credited the 'highest ever affiliated membership in BC' to the efforts of provincial secretary Wally Ross, who insisted that affiliates be paid up in order to send delegates to the convention. Bill 42 was ignored. 'The real or imagined or rationalized barriers to affiliation, for fear of the law, do not seem to have materialized.' Scotton to Ross, 4 Feb. 1970, file 450-16, CCF-NDP fonds, LAC.

165 Barrett interview, 24 April 2006.

166 'Statement by the Provincial Caucus of the New Democratic Party,' March 1970, file 450-19, CCF-NDP fonds, LAC.

167 Ross to Scotton, 30 June 1970, file 450-19, CCF-NDP fonds, LAC.

168 This account is gleaned from a participant who provided information on the condition of anonymity.

169 'Barrett Elected Leader by Acclamation,' *Sun*, 6 June 1970; Barrett interview, 24 April 2006.
170 Barrett interview, 24 April 2006.
171 'NDP Reaffirms Union Tie,' *Sun*, 8 June 1970.
172 'Healthy Waffle Base at BC Provincial Convention,' *Waffle News*, July 1970, file 446-18, CCF-NDP fonds, LAC.
173 'NDP Reaffirms Union Tie,' *Sun*, 8 June 1970.
174 This account is gleaned from a participant who provided information on the condition of anonymity. See also Hansard, *Official Report of the Debates of the Legislative Assembly*, 27 Jan. 1971, 96. Dent was hired in August 1970. In late 1971, he was replaced by twenty-seven-year-old Hans Brown, a former Waffler, federal secretary of the New Democratic Youth, and executive assistant to Tommy Douglas. Brown worked on the Jim Laxer leadership campaign. See Scotton to Barrett, 1 Oct. 1971; Brown to Barrett, 10 Nov. 1971; Scotton to Stupich, 23 Nov. 1971; Stupich to Scotton, 1 Dec 1971, file 450-19, CCF-NDP fonds, LAC; Webster, *Growth of the NDP in BC*, 97.
175 'BC Labor to Continue NDP Link,' *Globe and Mail*, 4 Nov. 1970; 'Act Now on Jobs, Demands Labor,' *Pacific Tribune*, 24 Nov. 1970.
176 Hansard, *Official Report of the Debates of the Legislative Assembly*, 16 March 1970, 650.
177 'Early History of PPWC,' 54–7. In the wake of the strike, Social Credit invoked Section 18 of the Mediation Commission Act to end a strike of 55 electricians, members of IBEW Local 230, at MacMillan Bloedel's Port Alberni pulp mill, claiming 5,000 millworkers and loggers would be idled. 'Gov't Invokes Compulsion, Ending Six-Hour Strike,' *Sun*, 26 Sept. 1970.
178 'Recent Activities of the BC Waffle,' *Waffle News*, May 1970, file 446-18, CCF-NDP fonds, LAC; 'Union Picket Boat Hampers Barge Tows,' *Sun*, 23 April 1971.
179 'BC Teachers' Militancy,' *Labor Challenge*, 4 May 1970, file AH-2000.00123 part 3, vol. 110, Previously Released Files series, RCMP Security Service, CSIS records, LAC.
180 RCMP Security Service report, 'Protests and Demonstrations – British Columbia,' 25 Jan. 1971, file 'Victoria Labour Council,' vol. 2134, series A, RCMP Security Service, RG 146, CSIS fonds, LAC; 'Unruly Demonstrators Invade Legislature Opening,' *Daily Times*, 11 Jan. 1971; 'Wild Mob Mauls Session Start,' *Colonist*, 22 Jan. 1971; 'Unionist Roasts "Fiasco,"' *Colonist*, 4 Feb. 1971; '"On to Victoria" Jobs Rally Pushed by Labor,' *Pacific Tribune*, 22 Jan. 1971.
181 Hansard, *Official Report of the Debates of the Legislative Assembly*, 22 Jan. 1971, 8–10.

182 Two weeks before the strike, Social Credit tabled Bill 47, legislation ending compulsory union membership in the BCTF and barring teachers from standing for election to school boards. The immediate cause of the strike, however, was a dispute over the pensions of retired teachers. See 'Teachers Closed Shop under Axe,' *Province*, 2 March 1971; 'Teachers Strike Friday on Pension Issue,' *Sun*, 18 March 1971; 'Teachers' Strike Empties Classrooms across BC,' *Sun*, 19 March 1971.
183 'Report of the BCFL Executive Council,' *BCFL Proceedings* (1971), 7.
184 Ibid., 8.
185 BC Department of Labour, *Annual Report* (1972), 90.
186 'BC Teachers Federation – British Columbia,' 26 April 1972, file 5, vol. 110, Previously Released Files series, RCMP Security Service, CSIS records, LAC. The agent noted that delegates were 'much more radically inclined than in the past,' which was attributed to a generational shift: delegates 'averaged 30 years of age and there were very few … delegates in their 50's and 60's.'
187 'The President Reports to the 1972 Annual General Meeting,' file 5, vol. 110, Previously Released Files series, RCMP Security Service, CSIS records, LAC.
188 'BC Teachers Federation – British Columbia,' 26 April 1972; 'League for Socialist Action (LSA) – Vancouver, BC,' 4 May 1972; 'League for Socialist Action – Forums – British Columbia,' 17 May 1972, file 5, vol. 110, Previously Released Files series, RCMP Security Service, CSIS records, LAC; 'Court Bars Teachers from Collecting Funds for Ousting Bennett,' *Globe and Mail*, 1 July 1972; 'Teachers' Militant Stance Could Spark Resignations,' *Sun*, 7 April 1972; 'Oust Socreds Urge Teachers,' *Pacific Tribune*, 7 April 1972; 'Permanent Political Action Hinted by BC Teachers,' *Sun*, 17 May 1972, 'Report Cites Teacher Body,' *Sun*, 13 June 1972; 'Teachers' Federation Awaits Legal Opinion,' *Sun*, 15 June 1972; 'Teachers Challenge Levy,' *Sun*, 21 June 1972; 'Teachers' Decisions Indicated Invalid,' *Sun*, 25 June 1972; 'BC Teachers' Fund Not Set Up to Defeat Socred Gov't, Official Tells Judge,' *Sun*, 28 June 1972. Supreme Court Justice W.R. McIntyre issued an interim injunction restraining the BCTF from spending the funds; $900,000 of the anticipated $1.25-million levy had already been raised. The court's ruling followed an application from two BCTF members, Byron Baker of Victoria and Esther Hall of New Westminster, who belonged to the Social Credit League and claimed the levy was invalid since it had been approved by convention delegates rather than a membership referendum. The case rested on whether the BCTF's constitution conflicted with the BC Societies Act.

189 'Guidelines April Key Sector – Education,' 28 April 1972; 'League for Socialist Action (LSA) – Vancouver, BC,' 4 May 1972; 'League for Socialist Action – Forums – British Columbia,' 17 May 1972, file 5, vol. 110, Previously Released Files series, RCMP Security Service, CSIS records, LAC; '6 Groups Join Teacher Salary Restriction Fight,' *Sun*, 2 March 1972; 'Teachers Urged to Consider Strike,' *Sun*, 10 March 1972. A rally at the Pacific National Exhibition auditorium attracted 500 people and speakers including Conservative leader Derril Warren, Liberal MLA Barrie Clark, NDP leader Dave Barrett, BCFL secretary-treasurer Ray Haynes, and UFAWU president Homer Stevens.

190 'CUPE Resolutions Call for Defeat of Socreds,' *Province*, 2 June 1972.

191 Fryer interview, 11 April 2006.

192 BC Department of Labour, *Annual Report* (1972), 90. A total of 106,399 workers accounted for 2,120,848 striker-days, representing 32.1 per cent of BC's 332,091 union members.

193 McLean, *A Union amongst Government Employees*, 113.

194 Security Service (Vancouver) to OTT3, 20 June 1972, file 'IBEW Local 230, Victoria, BC,' vol. 2245, series A, RCMP Security Service, CSIS records, LAC; 'Back-to-Work Deadline Brings Labor Confusion,' *Sun*, 14 June 1972; 'Socred Intimidation Charged by Labour,' *Sun*, 21 June 1972. The raids were conducted in Vancouver, Nanaimo, Kitimat, New Westminster, Vernon, Kelowna, Victoria, Penticton, Cranbrook, Prince Rupert, Duncan, Prince George, Powell River, Nelson, and Kamloops.

195 'Many Fallers Still Out – Coast Woodworkers Back on Job,' *Sun*, 17 July 1972; also 'Wildcat IWA Strike Shuts 3 BC Mills,' 'Unions Must Abide by Rule of Law,' *Sun*, 15 June 1972; 'IWA, Forest Negotiators Getting Down to "Crunch,"' *Sun*, 20 June 1972; 'Walkout Roll Put at 12,000 As Forest Talks Stall,' *Sun*, 21 June 1972; '28,000 Woodworkers Strike, Shut Down Forest Industry,' *Sun*, 21 June 1972.

196 Ibid.; 'Southern Interior IWA Backs Strike,' *Province*, 13 June 1972; 'Early History of PPWC,' 64–5. The applications by PPWC Local 23, Somass Division, and Local 24, Alberni Division, were defeated, with majorities at both worksites voting to remain with the IWA.

197 Jo Dunaway, *We're Your Neighbours: The Story of CUPE BC* (Vancouver: Canadian Union of Public Employees – BC Division, 2000), 35; Resnick, 'The Breakaway Movement in Trail,' in Paul Knox and Philip Resnick, *Essays in BC Political Economy* (Vancouver: New Star, 1974), 52–9. In January 1973, CWU applied for certification at Cominco, but the LRB denied the application in March on the grounds that CWU officers had not been properly elected at the union's founding convention. The NDP govern-

ment sustained this decision and Steel retained certification. One CWU worker observed that the labour representatives on the LRB all came from International unions. While it ultimately failed, the CWU certification drive at Trail shed light on the contagious spread of breakaway unionism in BC. 'Celgar out here has broken away from the big union,' a CWU supporter told Resnick. 'They're getting those little things fixed, one by one. And they're not having anywhere near the trouble. This is the way I think we can run this.'

198 Working conditions pertaining to hours worked, union coverage, vacations, and other benefits are illuminated in BC Department of Labour, *Working Conditions in British Columbia Industry 1972* (Victoria: Research Branch BC Dept. of Labour, 1973).

199 Barrett interview, 24 April 2006.

200 'Teachers, Province About to Collide,' *Globe and Mail*, 8 April 1972; 'It's Bennett against Teachers in BC Election,' *Ottawa Citizen*, 12 April 1972.

201 Barrett interview, 24 April 2006.

202 'NDP – A New Deal for People' [1972 platform], *The Democrat* (Vancouver), 12:3, Sept. 1972, file 41-16, vol. 41, CTM fonds, LAC.

203 British Columbia, *Statement of Votes*, 1972.

Conclusion

1 Daniel Koenig et al., 'The Year That British Columbia Went NDP: NDP Voter Support Pre- and Post-1972,' *BC Studies*, 24 (Winter 1974–5), 66.

2 The pattern of labour militancy was approximated only in Quebec and Newfoundland, which, like BC, had high levels of union density in the resource-extraction sectors. Statistics Canada, *Labour Force Historical Review* (2004).

3 See Donald E. Blake et al., 'Sources of Change in the BC Party System,' *BC Studies*, 50 (Summer 1981), 3–28.

4 James Harding, 'The New Left in British Columbia,' in Dimitrios I. Roussopolous, ed., *The New Left in Canada* (Montreal: Black Rose, c. 1970), 22.

5 Outside BC, Oshawa MP Ed Broadbent was an early Waffle supporter, though he later distanced himself from the group. See Judy Steed, *Ed Broadbent: The Pursuit of Power* (Markham, ON: Viking, 1988), 140–64, 172–3.

6 'A Northern Chile?,' *Barron's* (Boston), 2 April 1973; Hansard, *Official Report of the Debates of the Legislative Assembly*, 12 April 1973, 2610; 14 March 1974, 1171. CIA surveillance of Barrett, Alex MacDonald, and Frank Calder – and the leaking of documents to Social Credit – was alleged by

Edmonton publisher Mel Hurtig in 1975, citing an unnamed source. Dave Barrett and William Miller, *Barrett: A Passionate Political Life* (Vancouver: Douglas and McIntyre, 1995), 106–7, 110; Mel Hurtig interview, with author via telephone, 19 June 2008, Vancouver to Victoria.

7 Dave Barrett victory speech, Coquitlam, 30 Aug. 1972, CBC Radio Archives <http://archives.cbc.ca/IDC-1–73–1637–11304/politics_economy/british_columbia_elections/clip3> (accessed 16 April 2007).

8 Barrett interview, 24 April 2006.

9 The activist orientation of the Barrett NDP is illuminated in 'Action in British Columbia,' *Cooperative Press Associates* (Ottawa), 29 Sept. 1972, file 436-26, vol. 436, CCF-NDP fonds, LAC; also Lorne J. Kavic and Gary Brian Nixon, *The 1200 Days: A Shattered Dream: Dave Barrett and the NDP in BC 1972–75* (Coquitlam, BC: Kaen, 1978), 145–64; Barrett interview, 24 April 2006; Dailly interview, 2 Aug. 2005; Levi interview, 19 April 2006.

10 Labour Code, SBC 1973 (2d Sess.), c. 122; Public Service Labour Relations Act, SBC 1973 c. 144; Hansard, *Official Report of the Debates of the Legislative Assembly*, 25 Oct. 1973, 951–74; 'BC Labor Minister's Workload,' *Cooperative Press Associates* (Ottawa), 29 Sept. 1972, file 436-26, CCF-NDP fonds; Bruce McLean, *A Union amongst Government Employees: A History of the BC Government Employees' Union, 1919–1979* (Victoria: BCGEU, 1979), 122–6; 'Labor Law Change 1½–2 Years Away,' *Sun*, 10 Nov. 1972. 'The BC Mediation Commission will officially die Nov. 20,' the *Sun* reported.

11 See Hansard, *Official Report of the Debates of the Legislative Assembly*, 6 Feb. 1973.

12 Kavic and Nixon, *The 1200 Days*, 145–64; also 'Teachers Fight Cutbacks,' *Labour Challenge* (Toronto), 4 March 1974, file 5, vol. 110, Previously Released Files series, RCMP Security Service, CSIS records, LAC.

13 Leo Zakuta, *A Protest Movement Becalmed: A Study of Change in the CCF* (Toronto: University of Toronto Press, 1964); also Norman Penner, *From Protest to Power: Social Democracy in Canada, 1900-Present* (Toronto: Lorimer, 1992). The experience of the Barrett NDP government is examined in Kavic and Nixon, *The 1200 Days*, and Barrett and Miller, *Barrett*. James McAllister discusses the strengths and limitations of Manitoba's first NDP government in *The Government of Edward Schreyer: Democratic Socialism in Manitoba* (Kingston and Montreal: McGill-Queen's University Press, 1984). The Ontario experience is explored in George Ehring and Wayne Roberts, *Giving Away a Miracle: Lost Dreams, Broken Promises, and the Ontario NDP* (Oakville, ON: Mosaic Press, 1993); Thomas Walkom, *Rae Days: The Rise and Follies of the NDP* (Toronto: Key Porter, 1994); and Bob Rae, *From Protest to Power: Personal Reflections on a Life in Politics* (Toronto: Viking, 1996).

14 Gary Teeple, *Globalization and the Decline of Social Reform: Into the Twenty-First Century*, second ed. (Aurora, ON: Garamond Press, 2000).
15 See James Laxer, *Canada's Energy Crisis* (Toronto: James Lewis and Samuel, 1974); John F. Helliwell et al., eds., *Oil and Gas in Canada: The Effects of Domestic Policies and World Events* (Ottawa: Canadian Tax Foundation, 1989).
16 See Francis Fox Piven, 'The Decline of Labor Parties: An Overview,' in Piven, ed., *Labor Parties in Postindustrial Society* (Cambridge: Polity Press, 1991), 1–19.
17 Howard White, *A Hard Man to Beat: The Story of Bill White, Labour Leader, Historian, Shipyard Worker, Raconteur* (Vancouver: Pulp Press, 1983), 210.

Bibliography

Interviews

Dave Barrett, 24 April 2006, Esquimalt, with author.
Eileen Dailly, 2 August 2005, Victoria, with author.
Bill Doherty, 29 January 2007, Victoria, with author.
John Fryer, 11 April 2006, Oak Bay, with author.
Betty Griffin, 11 August 2005 and 26 February 2006, North Vancouver, with author.
Herbert Wilfred Herridge, n.d. (c. spring 1967), with Peter Stursberg, n.d. [c. spring 1967], LAC.
Mel Hurtig, 18 June 2008, from Vancouver via telephone, with author.
Norm Levi, 19 April 2006, Victoria, with author.
Kevin Neish, 11 May 2006, Victoria, with author.
Jack Phillips, 8–9 March 2003, Edmonton, with Dave Werlin and Don Bouzek, Alberta Labour History Institute collection.
Paul Phillips, 13 April 2006, Victoria, with author.
Maurice Rush, 26 February 2006, North Vancouver, with author.
Dorothy Gretchen Steeves, 4 April 1973, Vancouver, with Marlene Karnouk, BC Archives.
Ben Swankey, 10 June 2005 and 14 August 2005, Burnaby, with author.
Hilda Thomas, 28 February 2004, Toronto, with author.
Grace Tickson, 20 July 2005 and 9 August 2005, Nanaimo, with author.

Archival Collections

Library and Archives Canada, Ottawa

Communist Party of Canada fonds
Co-operative Commonwealth Federation and New Democratic Party fonds

Canadian Labour Congress fonds
Canadian Security Intelligence Service records
Canadian Trotskyist Movement fonds
Department of Labour records
Department of National Defence records
H.W. Herridge fonds
Ross Dowson fonds
Royal Canadian Mounted Police records
Tim Buck fonds
William Lyon Mackenzie King diaries

British Columbia Archives, Victoria

Dorothy Gretchen Steeves Oral History Records
Robert M. Strachan Collection
W.A.C. Bennett Collection

University of British Columbia Special Collections, Vancouver

Angus MacInnis Memorial Collection
Angus MacPhee fonds
Arnold Alexander Webster fonds
British Columbia Federation of Labour fonds
British Columbia New Democratic Party fonds
Canadian Association of Industrial, Mechanical and Allied Workers fonds
Canadian Party of Labour fonds
Colin Cameron fonds
Doukhobor fonds
Grace MacInnis fonds
International Association of Bridge, Structural and Ornamental Iron Workers Local 712 fonds
International Union of Mine, Mill and Smelterworkers (Canada) fonds
John Stanton fonds
Marine Workers and Boilermakers Industrial Union Local No. 1 fonds
New Democratic Party fonds
Rodney Young fonds
Ruth and Reg Bullock fonds
Vancouver Vietnam Action Committee fonds

University of Victoria Archives and Special Collections

Boilermakers fonds
Byron Johnson fonds
Cordova Bay CCF Club fonds
NDP Saanich and the Islands Constituency Association fonds
Victoria Labour Council fonds

Simon Fraser University Archives

Hari Sharma Indo-Canadian Oral History Collection
Marge Hollibaugh Women's Movement Collection

University of Toronto Thomas Fisher Rare Book Library

Robert S. Kenny Collection
J.S. Woodsworth Memorial Collection

McMaster University Archives and Research Collections, Hamilton

Combined University Campaign for Nuclear Disarmament-Student Union for Peace Action fonds

Greater Victoria Public Library Local History Room

Marshall Case papers

Private Collections

Betty Griffin papers
Kevin Neish papers
Grace Stevens papers
Grace Tickson papers

Newspapers and Magazines (selected issues)

Advocate (Toronto), April 1957
Amplifier (Portland), 1961–4
Barron's (Boston), 1973
Calgary Herald, 1945

Canadian Dimension (Winnipeg), 1969–72
Canadian Forum (Toronto), 1948–72
Canadian Tribune (Toronto), 1956–7
CCF News (Vancouver), 1948–60
Civil Liberties Digest (Vancouver), 1955–6
Daily Colonist (Victoria), 1948–72
Daily Province and *Province* (Vancouver) 1948–72
Daily Times (Victoria), 1948–72
Daily Tribune (Toronto), 1947
Fed Up Newsletter (Vancouver), 1973–5
Fernie Free Press, 1952
Financial Post (Toronto), 1953
Fisherman (Vancouver), 1948–72
Forward (Toronto), 1974
Globe and Mail (Toronto), 1948–72
Labor Challenge (Toronto), 1946–60
Labor Statesman (Vancouver), 1948–60
Maclean's Magazine (Toronto), 1951
Material for Thought (Vancouver), 1950
Magyar Hirado (Vancouver), 1957–8
Miners' Voice (Sudbury), 1965
Montreal Star, 1944
National Affairs Monthly (Toronto), April 1957
Native Voice (Vancouver), 1949–53
New Democrat (Toronto), 1961–72
New Left Committee Bulletin (Toronto), 1967–8
New Party Newsletter (Toronto), 1960
New York Times, 1956
Ottawa Citizen, 1948–72
Ottawa Journal, 1943
Pacific Tribune (Vancouver), 1948–72
Peace (Trail), 1950
Pedestal (Vancouver), 1970
Press (Vancouver), 1956–61
Progressive Worker and *BC Newsletter* (Vancouver), 1964–70
Province: See *Daily Province*
'756' Review: Official Organ of Aircraft Lodge 756 I.A.M. (Vancouver), July 1943
Scan (Vancouver), 1968
Socialist Caucus Bulletin, 1964–6
Trail Times, 1948–72

Ubyssey (Vancouver), 1959–72
Union Woodworker (Vancouver), 1948–50
Vancouver Sun and *Sun* (Vancouver), 1948–72
Waffle Weekly (Toronto), 1970
Waffle News (Toronto), 1971
Western Pulp and Paper Worker (Vancouver), 1956–62
Winnipeg Free Press, 1948–72
Woodpecker (Cranbrook), 1950–7
Workers Vanguard (Toronto), 1961–72
Young Socialist Forum (Toronto), 1961–72

Government Documents

British Columbia

A Brief Submitted to the Government of Canada by the Government of British Columbia on Federal-Provincial Co-operation in Economic Development. 1953.
Department of Labour. *Annual Reports*. 1946–72.
Documentary Submission to the Royal Commission on Canada's Economic Prospects. 1956.
Industrial British Columbia. Vancouver: Industrial British Columbia, c. 1966.
Ministry of Trade and Industry. *Regional Industrial Index of British Columbia*. 1948–72.
Report of a Board of Reference into the British Columbia Civil Service Act. 1959.
Report of Royal Commission on Education (Chant Commission). 1960.
Report of Royal Commission on the Forest Resources of British Columbia (First Sloan Commission), 1945.
Royal Commission on the Forest Resources of British Columbia (Second Sloan Commission). 1956.
Statement of Votes. 1948–72.
Submission to the Royal Commission on Canada's Economic Prospects. 1955.
Transactions of the Natural Resources Conference. 1948–72.

Canada

Census of Canada. 1941–71.
Commission on the Case Involving Victor George Spencer, 1966. British Columbia Archives. GR 1983.
Hansard. *Debates, House of Commons, Dominion of Canada*. 1948–72.
Report of Royal Commission on Canada's Economic Prospects. 1956.

Royal Commission to Investigate Facts Relating to and the Circumstances Surrounding the Communication, by Public Officials and Other Persons in Positions of Trust of Secret and Confidential Information to Agents of a Foreign Power. 1946.

Legislation

British Columbia. Electric Power Act. S.B.C. 1945 c. 22.
British Columbia. Public Schools Act Amendment Act. S.B.C. 1946 c. 64.
British Columbia. Forest Act Amendment Act. S.B.C. 1947 c. 38.
British Columbia. Provincial Elections Act Amendment Act. S.B.C. 1947 c. 28.
British Columbia. Industrial Conciliation and Arbitration Act. S.B.C. 1947 c. 44.
British Columbia. Public Schools Act Amendment Act. S.B.C. 1947 c. 79.
British Columbia. Civil Service Act Amendment Act. S.B.C. 1948 c. 5.
British Columbia. Hospital Insurance Act. S.B.C. 1948 c. 28.
British Columbia. Industrial Conciliation and Arbitration Act Amendment Act. S.B.C. 1948 c. 31.
British Columbia, Legal Professions Act Amendment Act. S.B.C. 1948 c. 36.
British Columbia. Provincial Elections Act Amendment Act. S.B.C. 1949 c. 19.
British Columbia. Industrial Development Act. S.B.C. 1949 c. 31.
British Columbia. Provincial Elections Act Amendment Act. S.B.C. 1951 c. 25.
British Columbia. Provincial Elections Act Amendment Act. S.B.C. 1953 c. 5.
British Columbia. Equal Pay Act. S.B.C. 1953 c. 6.
British Columbia. Labour Relations Act. S.B.C. 1954 c. 17.
British Columbia. Fair Employment Practices Act, S.B.C. 1956 c. 16.
British Columbia. Forest Act. S.B.C. 1956 c. 20.
British Columbia. Constitution Act Amendment Act. S.B.C. 1959 c. 17.
British Columbia. Trade-Unions Act. S.B.C. 1959 c. 90.
British Columbia. Labour Relations Act Amendment Act. S.B.C. 1961 c. 31.
British Columbia. Mediation Commission Act. S.B.C. 1968 c. 26.
British Columbia. Labour Relations Act Amendment Act. S.B.C. 1970 c. 16.
British Columbia. Labour Code. S.B.C. 1973 c. 122.
British Columbia. Public Service Labour Relations Act. S.B.C. 1973 c. 144.
Canada. Wartime Labour Relations Regulations (Privy Council Order 1003). 1944.
Canada. Dominion Elections Act Amendment Act. 1948.
Canada. Maintenance of Railway Operations Act. 1950.
Canada. BC Coast Steamship Service Act. 1958.
Canada. Medical Care Act. 1968.

Pamphlets and Contemporary Publications

Berger, Thomas R. *Injunctions in British Columbia*. Vancouver: British Columbia Federation of Labour, c. 1966.

British Columbia Federation of Labour (CLC). *Convention Proceedings*, 1956–72.

– *A Handbook on the Great Conspiracy*. Vancouver. 1965. BC Archives.

British Columbia Hydro and Power Authority. *The Power of British Columbia*. Vancouver: Information Services Department, 1967.

British Columbia Natural Resources Conference. *Proceedings*, 1948–72.

– *Inventory of the Natural Resources of British Columbia*. Victoria: BC Natural Resources Conference, 1964.

Buck, Tim. *30 Years, 1922–1952: The Story of the Communist Movement in Canada*. Toronto: Progress Books, 1952.

– *Canada: The Communist Viewpoint*. Toronto: Progress Books, 1948.

Committee to Defend the Expelled. *Stop the Expulsions in the NDP!* Toronto: Committee to Defend the Expelled, n.d. (c. 1967).

Davidoff, Fred Nicolas. *Autobiography of Fred Nicolas Davidoff, Books I–VI, BC Penitentiary, Box 'M'*. New Westminster: Unpublished manuscript, 1966.

Dowson, Ross. *The Power & Dilemma of the Trade Unions*. Toronto: League for Socialist Action, 1968. In File 'Trade Unions: Trotskyist Activities Within,' vol. 2002, series A, RCMP Security Service, RG 146, CSIS records, LAC. (Orig. pub. in *Workers Vanguard*, Spring/Summer 1967).

Empire Club. *The Empire Club of Canada Speeches 1947–1948*. Toronto: Empire Club Foundation, 1948.

Fair Play for Cuba Committee. *Four Canadians Who Saw Cuba*. March 1963.

Foster, William Z. *Bankruptcy of the American Labor Movement*. Chicago: Trade Union Educational League, 1922.

Hoffman, Abbie. *Steal This Book*. New York: Pirate Editions, 1971.

Holt, Simma. *Terror in the Name of God: The Story of the Sons of Freedom Doukhobors*. Toronto: McClelland and Stewart, 1964.

Industrial British Columbia. Vancouver: Industrial British Columbia, c. 1966. [no author]

Jagan, Cheddi. *Forbidden Freedom: The Story of British Guiana*. London: Lawrence and Wishart, 1954.

– *The West on Trial: The Fight for Guyana's Freedom*. London: Michael Joseph, 1966.

Kavanagh, J. *The Vancouver Island Strike*. Vancouver: BC Miners' Liberation League, c. 1913.

Knowles, Stanley. *The New Party*. Toronto: McClelland and Stewart, 1961.

Macdonald, John B. *Higher Education in British Columbia and a Plan for the Future*. Vancouver: University of British Columbia, 1962.

MacInnes, Tom. *Oriental Occupation of British Columbia*. Vancouver: Vancouver Sun Publishing Company, 1927.

MacNeil, Grant. *The IWA in British Columbia*. Vancouver: Western Canadian Regional Council No. 1 IWA, 1971.

McKean, Fergus. *Communism Versus Opportunism: An Examination of the Revisionism of Marxism in the Communist Movement of Canada*. Vancouver: Organizing Committee, Communist Party of Canada, 1946.

Morgan, Nigel. *British Columbia Needs a New Forest Policy!* Vancouver: Labor Progressive Party, 1955.

Progressive Workers Movement. *(Draft) Statement of Principles*. Vancouver (c. 1965). Queen's University Special Collections.

Rotstein, Abraham, and Gary Lax. *Independence: The Canadian Challenge*. Toronto: Committee for an Independent Canada, 1972.

Steeves, Dorothy G. *Builders and Rebels: A Short History of the CCF in British Columbia, 1932–1961*. Vancouver: BC Committee for the New Democratic Party, c. 1961.

Swankey, Ben. *Keep Canada Out! Why Canada Should Not Join the OAS*. Vancouver: Canadian Cuban Friendship Committee, 1965. BC Archives.

Tyre, Robert. *Douglas in Saskatchewan: The Story of a Socialist Experiment*. Vancouver: Mitchell, 1962.

Union of British Columbia Indian Chiefs. *Submission on Native Title*. 6 October 1971.

United Fishermen and Allied Workers Union. *Convention Proceedings*. 1944–52.

War Resisters League. *What Is the War Resisters League?* New York (c. 1965). LAC.

Books

Abella, Irving Martin. *Nationalism, Communism and Canadian Labour: The CIO, the Communist Party, and the Canadian Congress of Labour, 1935–56*. Toronto: University of Toronto Press, 1973.

Adachi, Ken. *The Enemy That Never Was: A History of the Japanese Canadians*. Toronto: McClelland and Stewart, 1976.

Alinsky, Saul. *Rules for Radicals: A Pragmatic Primer for Realistic Radicals*. New York: Random House, 1971.

Anderson, Perry. *Considerations on Western Marxism*. London: New Left Books, 1976.

Angus, Ian. *Canadian Bolsheviks: The Early Years of the Communist Party of Canada*. Montreal: Vanguard, 1981.

Avakumovic, Ivan. *The Communist Party in Canada: A History*. Toronto: McClelland and Stewart, 1975.

– *Socialism in Canada: A Study of the CCF-NDP in Federal and Provincial Politics*. Toronto: McClelland and Stewart, 1978.

Axelrod, Paul, and John G. Reid, eds. *Youth, University and Canadian Society: Essays in the Social History of Higher Education*. Montreal and Kingston: McGill-Queen's University Press, 1989.

Azoulay, Dan. *Keeping the Dream Alive: The Survival of the Ontario CCF/NDP, 1950–1963*. Montreal and Kingston: McGill-Queen's University Press, 1997.

Badgley, Robin F., and Samuel Wolfe. *Doctors' Strike: Medical Care and Conflict in Saskatchewan*. Toronto: Macmillan, 1967.

Baptie, Sue, et al. *First Growth: The Story of British Columbia Forest Products Limited*. Vancouver: BC Forest Products, 1975.

Barman, Jean. *The West beyond the West: A History of British Columbia*. Revised ed. Toronto: University of Toronto Press, 1996.

Barrett, Dave, and William Miller. *Barrett: A Passionate Political Life*. Vancouver: Douglas and McIntyre, 1995.

Bashevkin, Sylvia B. *Toeing the Lines: Women and Party Politics in English Canada*. Toronto: University of Toronto Press, 1985.

BC Hydro Power Pioneers. *Gaslights to Gigawatts: A Human History of BC Hydro and Its Predecessors*. Vancouver: Hurricane Press, 1998.

Bell, Daniel. *The Coming of Post-Industrial Society: A Venture in Social Forecasting*. New York: Basic Books, 1973.

– *The End of Ideology*. New York: Free Press, 1965.

Belshaw, John Douglas. *Colonization and Community: The Vancouver Island Coalfield and the Making of the British Columbian Working Class*. Montreal and Kingston: McGill-Queen's University Press, 2002.

Bennett, William. *Builders of British Columbia*. Vancouver: Broadway Printers, 1937.

Bercuson, David J. *Fools and Wise Men: The Rise and Fall of the One Big Union*. Toronto: McGraw-Hill Ryerson, 1978.

Berger, Bennett. *Working Class Suburb: A Study of Auto Workers in Suburbia*. Berkeley: University of California Press, 1968.

Bergren, Myrtle. *Tough Timber: The Loggers of BC – Their Story*. Toronto: Progress Books, 1966.

Bernard, Elaine. *The Long Distance Feeling: A History of the Telecommunications Workers Union*. Vancouver: New Star, 1983.

Betcherman, Lita-Rose. *The Little Band: The Clashes between the Communists and the Political and Legal Establishment in Canada, 1928–1932*. Ottawa: Deneau, 1982.

Black, Lawrence. *Old Labour, New Britain? The Political Culture of the Left in Affluent Britain, 1951–64*. New York: Palgrave Macmillan, 2003.

Bocking, Richard C. *Canada's Water: For Sale?* Toronto: James Lewis and Samuel, 1972.

Bowen, Lynn. *Boss Whistle: The Coal Miners of Vancouver Island Remember*. Lantzville: Oolichan, 1982.

Briskin, Linda, and Lynda Yanz, eds. *Union Sisters: Women in the Labour Movement*. Toronto: Women's Press, 1983.

Brodie, Steve. *Bloody Sunday: Vancouver-1938: Recollections of the Post Office Sitdown of Single Unemployed*. Edited with an introduction by Sean Griffin. Epilogue by Maurice Rush. Vancouver: Young Communist League, 1974.

Brown, Rosemary. *Being Brown: A Very Public Life*. Toronto: Random House, 1989.

Burton, Thomas L. *Natural Resource Policy in Canada: Issues and Perspectives*. Toronto: McClelland and Stewart, 1972.

Butler, David E., and Donald Stokes. *Political Change in Britain: Forces Shaping Electoral Choice*. New York: St Martin's, 1969.

Campbell, Peter. *Canadian Marxists and the Search for a Third Way*. Montreal and Kingston, McGill-Queen's University Press, 1999.

Canadian Parliamentary Guide. 1935–72.

Canada's Party of Socialism: History of the Communist Party of Canada, 1921–1976. Toronto: Progress Books, 1982. [no author]

Caplan, Gerald. *The Dilemma of Canadian Socialism: The CCF in Ontario*. Toronto: McClelland and Stewart, 1973.

Carrothers, A.W.R. *The Labour Injunction in British Columbia: A Study of the Operation of the Injunction in Labour-Management Disputes in British Columbia, 1946–1955 with Particular Reference to the Law of Picketing*. Toronto and Montreal: CCH Canadian, 1956.

Cathers, Arthur. *Beloved Dissident Eve Smith, 1904–1988*. Blyth, ON: Drumadravy, 1997.

Christie, Nancy. *Engendering the State: Family, Work and Welfare in Canada*. Toronto: University of Toronto Press, 2000.

Clément, Dominique. *Canada's Rights Revolution: Social Movements and Social Change, 1947–1982*. Vancouver: UBC Press, 2008.

Cobble, Dorothy Sue. *The Other Women's Movement: Workplace Justice and Social Rights in Modern America*. Princeton, NJ: Princeton University Press, 2005.

Coughlan, Bill, et al. *The Food Co-op Handbook: How to Bypass Supermarkets to Control the Quality and Price of Your Food*. Boston: Houghton Mifflin, 1975.
Crean, Susan. *Grace Hartman: A Woman for Her Time*. Vancouver: New Star, 1995.
Creese, Gillian. *Contracting Masculinity: Gender, Class, and Race in a White-Collar Union, 1944–1994*. Toronto: Oxford University Press, 1999.
Creese, Gillian, and Veronica Strong-Boag, eds. *British Columbia Reconsidered: Essays on Women*. Vancouver: Press Gang, 1992.
Daudharia, Harjit. *Darshan*. Vancouver: Heritage House, 2004.
Davidson, Joe, and John Deverell. *Joe Davidson*. Toronto: Lorimer, 1978.
Dawson, Michael. *Selling British Columbia: Tourism and Consumer Culture, 1890–1970*. Vancouver: UBC Press, 2004.
Diamond, Sara. *Women's Labour History in British Columbia, 1930–48*. Vancouver: Press Gang, 1980.
Dobriner, William Mann. *Class in Suburbia*. Englewood Cliffs, NJ: Prentice-Hall, 1963.
Douglas, C.H. *Social Credit*. London: Eyre and Spottiswoode, 1933.
Dunaway, Jo. *We're Your Neighbours: The Story of CUPE BC*. Vancouver: Canadian Union of Public Employees – BC Division, 2000.
Duverger, Maurice. *Political Parties: Their Organization and Activity in the Modern State*. Third ed. Translated by Barbara and Robert North. London: Methuen, 1964.
Ehring, George, and Wayne Roberts. *Giving Away a Miracle: Lost Dreams, Broken Promises, and the Ontario NDP*. Oakville, ON: Mosaic Press, 1993.
Epstein, Leon D. *Political Parties in Western Democracies*. New Brunswick, NJ: Transaction, 1980.
Fahrni, Magda, and Robert Rutherdale, eds. *Creating Postwar Canada: Community, Diversity, and Dissent, 1945–75*. Vancouver: UBC Press, 2008.
Farrell, Ann. *Grace MacInnis: A Story of Love and Integrity*. Markham, ON: Fitzhenry and Whiteside, 1994.
Finkel, Alvin. *The Social Credit Phenomenon in Alberta*. Toronto: University of Toronto Press, 1989.
Friedman, Samuel R. *Teamster Rank and File: Power, Bureaucracy, and Rebellion at Work and in a Union*. New York: Columbia University Press, 1982.
Fudge, Judy, and Eric Tucker. *Labour before the Law: The Regulation of Workers' Collective Action in Canada, 1900–1948*. Toronto: Oxford University Press, 2001.
Galbraith, John Kenneth. *The Affluent Society*. New York: Mentor, 1958.
Gallie, Duncan. *In Search of the New Working Class: Automation and Social Integration within the Capitalist Enterprise*. Cambridge: Cambridge University Press, 1978.

Gitlin, Todd. *The Whole World Is Watching: The Mass Media in the Making and Unmaking of the New Left*. Berkeley, Los Angeles, and London: University of California Press, 1980.

Glickman, Lawrence B. *A Living Wage: American Workers and the Making of Consumer Society*. Ithaca: Cornell University Press, 1997.

Godfrey, Dave, and Mel Watkins, eds. *Gordon to Watkins to You: A Documentary Battle for Control of Our Economy*. Toronto: New Press, 1970.

Goldthorpe, John H., et al. *The Affluent Worker: Political Attitudes*. London: Cambridge University Press, 1968.

Gollan, Robin. *Revolutionaries and Reformists: Communism and the Australian Labour Movement, 1920–1955*. Canberra: Australian National University Press, 1975.

Green, Jim. *Against the Tide: The Story of the Canadian Seamen's Union*. Toronto: Progress Books, 1986.

Green, Valerie. *No Ordinary People: Victoria's Mayors since 1862*. Victoria: Beach Holme Publishers, 1992.

Griffin, Betty, and Susan Lockhart. *Their Own History: Women's Contribution to the Labour Movement in British Columbia*. Vancouver: UFAWU/CAW Seniors Club, 2002.

Griffin, Sean, ed. *Fighting Heritage: Highlights of the 1930s Struggle for Jobs and Militant Unionism in British Columbia*. Vancouver: Tribune Publishing Company, 1985.

Gwyn, *Richard. The 49th Paradox: Canada in North America*. Toronto: McClelland and Stewart, 1985.

Hak, Gordon. *Capital and Labour in the British Columbia Forest Industry, 1934–1974*. Vancouver: UBC Press, 2007.

– *Turning Trees into Dollars: The British Columbia Coastal Lumber Industry, 1858–1913*. Toronto: University of Toronto Press, 2000.

Hansen, Ann. *Direct Action: Memoirs of an Urban Guerilla*. Toronto: Between the Lines, 2001.

Harris, Cole. *The Resettlement of British Columbia: Essays on Colonialism and Geographical Change*. Vancouver: UBC Press, 1997.

Hawthorn, Harry B., ed. *The Doukhobors of British Columbia*. Vancouver: University of British Columbia and J.M. Dent and Sons, 1955.

Helliwell, John F., et al., eds. *Oil and Gas in Canada: The Effects of Domestic Policies and World Events*. Ottawa: Canadian Tax Foundation, 1989.

Heron, Craig. *Booze: A Distilled History*. Toronto: Between the Lines, 2003.

Heron, Craig, ed. *The Workers' Revolt in Canada: 1917–1925*. Toronto: University of Toronto Press, 1998.

Hewitt, Steve. *Spying 101: The RCMP's Secret Activities at Canadian Universities, 1917–1999*. Toronto: University of Toronto Press, 2002.

Horowitz, Gad. *Canadian Labour in Politics*. Toronto: University of Toronto Press, 1968.

Howard, Irene. *The Struggle for Social Justice in British Columbia: Helena Gutteridge, the Unknown Reformer*. Vancouver: UBC Press, 1992.

Hunter, Robert. *The Greenpeace to Amchitka: An Environmental Odyssey*. Vancouver: Arsenal Pulp Press, 2004.

Hutchinson, Bruce. *The Fraser*. Toronto: Clark, Irwin and Co., 1950.

Hyman, Richard. *Industrial Relations: A Marxist Introduction*. London: Macmillan, 1975.

Iacovetta, Franca, and Mariana Valverde, eds. *Gender Conflicts: New Essays in Women's History*. Toronto: University of Toronto Press, 1992.

Irving, John A. *The Social Credit Movement in Alberta*. Toronto: University of Toronto Press, 1959.

Isserman, Maurice. *If I Had a Hammer: The Death of the Old Left and the Birth of the New Left*. New York: Basic Books, 1987.

Jamieson, Stuart Marshall. *Industrial Relations in Canada*. Toronto: Macmillan, 1973.

– *Times of Trouble: Labour Unrest and Industrial Conflict in Canada, 1900–1966*. Ottawa: Task Force on Labour Relations, 1968.

Janzen, William. *Limits on Liberty: The Experience of Mennonite, Hutterite and Doukhobor Communities in Canada*. Toronto: University of Toronto Press, 1990.

Johnson, F. Henry. *A History of Public Education in British Columbia*. Vancouver: University of British Columbia Publications Centre, 1964.

Kavic, Lorne J., and Garry Brian Nixon. *The 1200 Days: A Shattered Dream: Dave Barrett and the NDP in BC 1972–75*. Coquitlam: Kaen, 1978.

Kealey, Gregory S., and Bryan D. Palmer. *Dreaming of What Might Be: The Knights of Labor in Ontario, 1880–1900*. Toronto: New Hogtown Press, 1987.

Kealey, Gregory S., and Peter Warrian, eds. *Essays in Canadian Working Class History*. Toronto: McClelland and Stewart, 1976.

Kealey, Linda. *Enlisting Women for the Cause: Women, Labour and the Left in Canada, 1890–1920*. Toronto: University of Toronto Press, 1998.

Kealey, Linda, and Joan Sangster, eds. *Beyond the Vote: Canadian Women and Politics*. Toronto: University of Toronto Press, 1989.

Keith, Ronald C. *The Diplomacy of Zhou Enlai*. Houndsmills: Macmillan, 1989.

Kellner, Douglas. *Television and the Crisis of Democracy*. Boulder, San Francisco, and Oxford: Westview, 1990.

Kilian, Crawford. *Go Do Some Great Thing: The Black Pioneers of British Columbia*. Vancouver: Douglas and McIntyre, 1978.

King, Al, with Kate Braid. *Red Bait! Struggles of a Mine Mill Local*. Vancouver: Kingbird, 1998.

Knight, Rolf. *Indians at Work: An Informal History of Native Indian Labour in British Columbia, 1858–1930*. Vancouver: New Star Books, 1996.

Knight, Rolf, and Maya Koisumi. *A Man of Our Times: The Life-History of a Japanese-Canadian Fisherman*. Vancouver: New Star, 1976.

Knott, Erni. 'Development of the Coastal Wood Industry in BC.' Sooke, BC: Unpublished manuscript, 1996.

Knox, Paul, and Philip Resnick, eds. *Essays in BC Political Economy*. Vancouver: New Star, 1974.

Kostash, Myrna. *Long Way from Home: The Story of the Sixties Generation in Canada*. Toronto: J. Lorimer, 1980.

Kristmanson, Mark. *Plateaus of Freedom: Nationality, Culture, and State Security in Canada, 1940–1960*. Don Mills, ON: Oxford University Press, 2003.

Latham, Barbara K., and Roberta J. Pazdro, eds. *Not Just Pin Money: Selected Essays on the History of Women's Work in British Columbia*. Victoria: Camosun College, 1984.

Laxer, Gordon. *Open for Business: The Roots of Foreign Ownership in Canada*. Toronto: Oxford University Press, 1989.

Laxer, James. *Canada's Economic Strategy*. Toronto: McClelland and Stewart, 1981.

– *Canada's Energy Crisis*. Toronto: James Lewis and Samuel, 1974.

– *The Energy Poker Game: The Politics of the Continental Resources Deal*. Toronto and Chicago: New Press, 1970.

– *Red Diaper Baby: A Boyhood in the Age of McCarthyism*. Vancouver and Toronto: Douglas and McIntyre, 2004.

Leier, Mark. *Where the Fraser River Flows: The Industrial Workers of the World in British Columbia*. Vancouver: New Star Books, 1990.

– *Red Flags and Red Tape: The Making of a Labour Bureaucracy*. Toronto: University of Toronto Press, 1995.

Lembcke, Jerry, and William M. Tattam. *One Union in Wood: A Political History of the International Woodworkers of America*. Madeira Park, BC: Harbour/International Publishers, 1984.

Levitt, Cyril. *Children of Privilege: Student Revolt in the Sixties: A Study of Student Movements in Canada, the United States, and West Germany*. Toronto: University of Toronto Press, 1984.

Levitt, Kari. *Silent Surrender: The Multinational Corporation in Canada*. Toronto: Macmillan, 1970.

Lewis, David. *The Good Fight: Political Memoirs, 1909–1958*. Toronto: Macmillan, 1981.

Lewis, S.P. *Grace: The Life of Grace MacInnis*. Madeira Park, BC: Harbour, 1993.
Lichtenstein, Nelson. *State of the Union: A Century of American Labor*. Princeton: Princeton University Press, 2002.
Lijphart, Arend. *Democracy in Plural Societies: A Comparative Exploration*. New Haven: Yale University Press, 1977.
Lindbeck, Assar. *The Political Economy of the New Left: An Outsider's View*. Second ed. New York: Harper and Row, 1977.
Lipset, Seymour Martin. *Agrarian Socialism: The Cooperative Commonwealth Federation in Saskatchewan. A Study in Political Sociology*. Updated ed. Garden City, NY: Anchor Books, 1968.
Lipsitz, George. *Rainbow at Midnight: Labor and Culture in the 1940s*. Chicago: University of Illinois Press, 1994.
Lipton, Charles. *The Trade Union Movement in Canada, 1827–1959*. Second ed. Montreal: Canadian Social Publications, 1968.
Logan, Harold. *The History of Trade-Union Organization in Canada*. Chicago: University of Chicago Press, 1928.
– *Trade Unions in Canada: Their Development and Functioning*. Toronto: Macmillan, 1948.
Lovick, Dale, ed. *Till Power Is Brought to Pooling: Tommy Douglas Speaks*. Lantzville, BC: Oolichan, 1979.
Lowther, Bruce. *A Better Life: The First Century of the Victoria Labour Council*. Victoria: Victoria Labour Council, 1989.
Lumsden, Ian. *Close the 49th Parallel Etc.: The Americanization of Canada*. Toronto: University of Toronto Press, 1970.
MacEachern, Alan. *Natural Selections: National Parks in Atlantic Canada, 1935–1970*. Montreal and Kingston: McGill-Queen's University Press, 2001.
MacDonald, Alex. *'My Dear Legs … ': Letters to a Young Social Democrat*. Vancouver: New Star, 1985.
Macmillan, David S., ed. *Canadian Business History: Selected Studies, 1497–1971*. Toronto: McClelland and Stewart, 1972.
Macpherson, C.B. *Democracy in Alberta: Social Credit and the Party System*. Toronto: University of Toronto Press, 1962.
Macpherson, Kay. *When in Doubt, Do Both: The Times of My Life*. Toronto: University of Toronto Press, 1994.
McAllister, James. *The Government of Edward Schreyer: Democratic Socialism in Manitoba*. Kingston and Montreal: McGill-Queen's University Press, 1984.
McCormack, A. Ross. *Reformers, Rebels, and Revolutionaries: The Western Canadian Radical Movement, 1899–1919*. Toronto and Buffalo: University of Toronto Press, 1977.

McDonald, Robert A.J. *Making Vancouver: Class, Status and Social Boundaries, 1863–1913*. Vancouver: UBC Press, 1996.

McEwen, Tom. *The Forge Glows Red: From Blacksmith to Revolutionary*. Toronto: Progress Books, 1974.

– *He Wrote for Us: The Story of Bill Bennett, Pioneer Socialist Journalist*. Vancouver: Tribune Publishing Company, 1951.

McGeer, Patrick L. *Politics in Paradise*. Toronto: Peter Martin, 1972.

McHenry, Dean E. *The Third Force in Canada: The Cooperative Commonwealth Federation, 1932–1948*. Toronto, Berkeley, and Los Angeles: University of Toronto Press and University of California Press, 1950.

McInnis, Peter. *Harnessing Labour Confrontation: Shaping the Postwar Settlement in Canada, 1943–1950*. Toronto: University of Toronto Press, 2002.

McKay, Ian. *Rebels, Reds, Radicals: Rethinking Canada's Left History*. Toronto: Between the Lines, 2005.

McKenzie, Robert, and Allan Silver. *Angels in Marble: Working Class Conservatives in Urban England*. Chicago: University of Chicago Press, 1968.

McLean, Bruce. *A Union amongst Government Employees: A History of the BC Government Employees' Union, 1919–1979*. Victoria: BCGEU, 1979.

McLeod, Thomas H., and Ian McLeod. *Tommy Douglas: The Road to Jerusalem*. Edmonton: Hurtig, 1987.

McNaught, Kenneth. *A Prophet in Politics: A Biography of J.S. Woodsworth*. Toronto: University of Toronto Press, 1959.

Maiden, Cecil. *Lighted Journey: The Story of BC Electric*. Vancouver: British Columbia Electric Company, 1948.

Mallet, Serge. *La Nouvelle Classe Ouvrière*. Paris: Seuil, 1963. Translation by Andréeand Bob Shepherd.*The New Working Class*. Nottingham: Spokesman Books, 1975.

Marchak, M. Patricia. *Green Gold: The Forestry Industry in British Columbia*. Vancouver: UBC Press, 1983.

Marcuse, Herbert. *An Essay on Liberation*. Boston: Beacon Press, 1969.

– *Soviet Marxism, A Critical Analysis*. London: Routledge and Kegan Paul, 1958.

Marks, Lynne. *Revivals and Roller Rinks: Religion, Leisure, and Identity in Late Nineteenth Century Small-Town Ontario*. Toronto: University of Toronto Press, 1996.

May, Lary, ed. *Recasting America: Culture and Politics in the Cold War*. Chicago: University of Chicago Press, 1989.

Melnyk, Olenka. *No Bankers in Heaven: Remembering the CCF*. Toronto and Montreal: McGraw-Hill Ryerson, 1989.

Michels, Roberto. *Political Parties: A Sociological Study of the Oligarchical*

Tendencies of Modern Democracy. Translated by Eden and Cedar Paul, with an introduction by Seymour Martin Lipset. 1915; New York: Free Press, 1962.

Miliband, Ralph. *Parliamentary Socialism: A Study in the Politics of Labour*. London: Merlin, 1973.

Millis, Harry A., and Emily Clark Brown. *From the Wagner Act to Taft-Hartley: A Study of National Labor Policy and Labor Relations*. Chicago: University of Chicago Press, 1950.

Mitchell, David J. *W.A.C. Bennett and the Rise of British Columbia*. Vancouver/Toronto: Douglas and McIntyre, 1995.

Montgomery, David. *The Fall of the House of Labor: The Workplace, the State, and American Labor Activism, 1865–1925*. New York: Cambridge University Press, 1985.

– *Workers' Control in America: Studies in the History of Work, Technology, and Labor Struggles*. New York: Cambridge University Press, 1979.

Morgan, R.E. 'Lefty'. *Workers' Control on the Railroad: A Practical Example 'Right under Your Nose'*. Ed. G.R. Pool and D.J. Young. St John's: Canadian Committee on Labour History, 1994.

Morton, Desmond. *The New Democrats, 1961–1986: The Politics of Change*. Toronto: Copp Clark Pittman, 1986.

Municipal Historical Society. *Your Worship, Members of Council: Highlights from Municipal Reform Movements in the Lower Mainland*. Vancouver: Municipal Historical Society, 1980.

Myers, Gustavus. *The History of Canadian Wealth*. 1914; New York: Argosy Antiquarian, 1968.

Neufeld, Andrew. *Union Store: The History of the Retail Clerks' Union in British Columbia, 1899–1999*. Vancouver: United Food and Commercial Workers Union Local 1518, 1999.

Neufeld, Andrew, and Andrew Parnaby. *The IWA in Canada: The Life and Times of an Industrial Union*. Vancouver: IWA Canada/New Star Books, 2000.

Newell, Dianne. *The Development of the Pacific Salmon-Canning Industry: A Grown Man's Game*. Montreal and Kingston: McGill-Queen's University Press, 1989.

Newton, Janice. *The Feminist Challenge to the Canadian Left, 1900–1918*. Montreal and Kingston: McGill-Queen's University Press, 1995.

North, George. *A Ripple, A Wave: The Story of Union Organization in the BC Fishing Industry*. Ed. Hal Griffin. Vancouver: Fishermen Publishing Society, 1974.

O'Keefe, Betty, and Ian Macdonald. *The Sommers Scandal: The Felling of Trees and Tree Lords*. Surrey, BC: Heritage House, 1999.

Ormsby, Margaret. *British Columbia: A History*. Toronto: Macmillan, 1958.
Owram, Douglas. *Born at the Right Time: A History of the Baby-Boom Generation in Canada*. Toronto: University of Toronto Press, 1996.
Palmer, Bryan D. *Canada's 1960s: The Ironies of Identity in a Rebellious Era*. Toronto: University of Toronto Press, 2009.
– *Solidarity: The Rise and Fall of an Opposition in British Columbia*. Vancouver: New Star, 1987.
– *Working-Class Experience: Rethinking the History of Canadian Labour, 1800–1991*. Second ed. Toronto: McClelland and Stewart, 1992.
Panebianco, Angelo. *Political Parties: Organization and Power*. Cambridge and New York: Cambridge University Press, 1988.
Panitch, Leo. *Social Democracy and Industrial Militancy: The Labour Party, the Trade Unions, and Incomes Policy, 1945–1974*. Cambridge: Cambridge University Press, 1976.
Panitch, Leo, and Donald Swartz. *From Consent to Coercion: The Assault on Trade Union Freedoms*. Third ed. Aurora, ON: Garamond, 2003.
Parnaby, Andrew. *Citizen Docker: Making a New Deal on the Vancouver Waterfront, 1919–1939*. Toronto: University of Toronto Press, 2008.
Parrot, Jean-Claude. *My Union, My Life: Jean-Claude Parrot and the Canadian Union of Postal Workers*. Halifax: Fernwood, 2005.
Peltier, Leonard. *Prison Writings: My Life Is My Sun Dance*. New York: St Martin's Griffin, 1999.
Penner, Norman. *Canadian Communism: The Stalin Years and Beyond*. Toronto: Methuen, 1988.
– *The Canadian Left: A Critical Analysis*. Scarborough: Prentice-Hall, 1977.
– *From Protest to Power: Social Democracy in Canada, 1900-Present*. Toronto: Lorimer, 1992.
Pentland, H. Clare. *Labour and Capital in Canada 1650–1860*. Ed. Paul Phillips. Toronto: Lorimer, 1981.
Phillips, Paul A. *No Power Greater: A Century of Labour in British Columbia*. Vancouver: BC Federation of Labour and Boag Foundation, 1967.
Phillips, Paul A., and Erin Phillips. *Women and Work: Inequality in the Canadian Labour Market*. Revised ed. Toronto: Lorimer, 1993.
Piven, Francis Fox, ed. *Labor Parties in Postindustrial Society*. Cambridge: Polity Press, 1991.
Rae, Bob. *From Protest to Power: Personal Reflections on a Life in Politics*. Toronto: Viking, 1996.
Rankin, Harry. *Rankin's Law: Recollections of a Radical*. Vancouver: November House, 1975.
Rebick, Judy. *Ten Thousand Roses: The Making of a Feminist Revolution*. Toronto: Penguin, 2005.

Reid, Tim, and Julyan Reid, eds. *Student Power and the Canadian Campus*. Toronto: Peter Martin Associates, 1969.

Richter, Irving. *Labor's Struggles, 1945–1950: A Participant's View*. Cambridge: Cambridge University Press, 1994.

Robin, Martin. *Radical Politics and Canadian Labour*. Kingston: Industrial Relations Centre, Queen's University: 1968.

– *The Rush for Spoils: The Company Province, 1871–1933*. Toronto: McClelland and Stewart, 1972.

– *Pillars of Profit: The Company Province, 1934–1972*. Toronto: McClelland and Stewart, 1973.

– *Shades of Right: Nativist and Fascist Politics in Canada, 1920–1940*. Toronto: University of Toronto Press, 1992.

Rodney, William. *Soldiers of the International: A History of the Communist Party of Canada, 1919–1929*. Toronto: University of Toronto Press, 1968.

Rothenburger, Mel. *Friend o' Mine: The Story of Flyin' Phil Gaglardi*. Victoria: Orca, 1991.

Roussopolous, Dimitrios I., ed. *The New Left in Canada*. Montreal: Black Rose, 1970.

– ed. *Canada and Radical Social Change*. Montreal: Black Rose, 1973.

Roy, Patricia E. *A White Man's Province: British Columbia Politicians and Chinese and Japanese Immigrants, 1885–1914*. Vancouver: University of British Columbia Press, 1989.

– *The Oriental Question: Consolidating a White Man's Province, 1914–41*. Vancouver: UBC Press, 2003.

Roy, Patricia E., and John Herd Thompson. *British Columbia: Land of Promises*. Toronto: Oxford University Press, 1995.

Rush, Maurice. *We Have a Glowing Dream: Recollections of Working-Class and People's Struggles in BC from 1935 to 1995*. Vancouver: Centre for Socialist Education, 1996.

Ryerson, Stanley B. *1837: The Birth of Canadian Democracy*. Toronto: Francis White, 1937.

Sangster, Joan. *Dreams of Equality: Women on the Canadian Left, 1920–1950*. Toronto: McClelland and Stewart, 1989.

Sangster, Joan, ed. *Beyond the Vote: Canadian Women and Politics*. Toronto: University of Toronto Press, 1989.

Sartori, Giovanni. *Parties and Party Systems: A Framework for Analysis*. Cambridge and New York: Cambridge University Press, 1976.

Sawatsky, John. *Gouzenko: The Untold Story*. Toronto: Macmillan, 1984.

Scher, Len. *The Un-Canadians: True Stories of the Blacklist Era*. Toronto: Lester, 1992.

Schwantes, Carlos A. *Radical Heritage: Labor, Socialism, and Reform in Washing-*

ton and British Columbia, 1885–1917. Vancouver: Douglas and McIntyre, 1979.

Scott, Jack. *A Communist Life: Jack Scott and the Canadian Workers Movement, 1927–1985*. Ed. and intro. Bryan D. Palmer. St John's: Canadian Committee on Labour History, 1988.

– *Canadian Workers, American Unions*. Vancouver: New Star, 1978.

Scotton, Clifford A. *Canadian Labour and Politics*. Ottawa: Political Education Department of the Canadian Labour Congress, 1966.

Seale, Patrick, and Maureen McConville. *Red Flag/Black Flag: French Revolution 1968*. New York: Ballantine, 1968.

Shackleton, Doris French. *Tommy Douglas*. Toronto: McClelland and Stewart, 1975.

Shearer, R., ed. *Exploiting Our Economic Potential: Public Policy and the British Columbia Economy*. Toronto: Holt, Rinehart and Winston, 1968.

Sherman, Paddy. *Bennett*. Toronto: McClelland and Stewart, 1966.

Smith, Peter L. *Multitude of the Wise: UVic Remembered*. Victoria: Alumni Association of the University of Victoria, 1993.

Solski, Mike, and John Smaller. *Mine Mill: The History of the International Union of Mine, Mill and Smelter Workers in Canada since 1895*. Ottawa: Steel Rail, 1984.

Stainsby, Jill, Honoree Newcombe, Jacqui Parker-Snedker, and Paul Reniers. *AUCE and TSSU: Memoirs of a Feminist Union, 1972–1993*. Vancouver: Teaching Support Staff Union Publishing, 1993.

Stanton, John. *The Life and Death of a Union: The Canadian Seamen's Union, 1936–1949*. Toronto: Steel Rail, 1979.

– *My Past Is Now: Further Memoirs of a Labour Lawyer*. St John's: Canadian Committee on Labour History, 1994.

– *Never Say Die!: The Life and Times of John Stanton, a Pioneer Labour Lawyer*. Ottawa: Steel Rail, 1987.

Steed, Judy. *Ed Broadbent: The Pursuit of Power*. Markham, ON: Viking, 1988.

Steedman, Mercedes, et al., eds. *Hard Lessons: The Mine Mill Union in the Canadian Labour Movement*. Toronto: Dundurn, 1995.

Steeves, Dorothy G. *The Compassionate Rebel: Ernest Winch and the Growth of Socialism in Western Canada*. Vancouver: J.J. Douglas, 1977.

Stevens, Homer, and Rolf Knight. *Homer Stevens: A Life in Fishing*. Madeira Park, BC: Harbour, 1992.

Stewart, Walter. *The Life and Political Times of Tommy Douglas*. Toronto: McArthur and Company, 2003.

Sufrin, Eileen Tallman. *The Eaton Drive: The Campaign to Organize Canada's Largest Department Store, 1948–1952*. Toronto: Fitzhenry and Whiteside, 1982.

Swankey, Ben, ed. *'Man along the Shore'! The Story of the Vancouver Waterfront As Told by Longshoremen Themselves 1860's-1975*. Vancouver: ILWU 500 Pensioners, 1978.

Swankey, Ben, and Jean Evans Sheils. *'Work and Wages!': A Semi-Documentary Account of the Life and Times of Arthur H. (Slim) Evans 1890–1944: Carpenter, Miner, Labor Leader*. Vancouver: Trade Union Research Bureau, 1977.

Swanson, Neil A. *Conflict over the Columbia: The Canadian Background on an Historic Treaty*. Montreal and Kingston: McGill-Queen's University Press, 1979.

Swayze, Carolyn. *Hard Choices: A Life of Tom Berger*. Vancouver/Toronto: Douglas and McIntyre, 1987.

Sykes, Philip. *Sellout: The Giveaway of Canada's Energy Resources*. Edmonton: Hurtig,1973.

Tarasoff, Koozma J. *A Pictorial History of the Doukhobors*. Saskatoon: Modern Press, 1969.

Tarasoff, Koozma J., ed. *Spirit-Wrestlers' Voices: Honouring Doukhobors on the Centenary of Their Migration to Canada in 1899*. New York, Ottawa, Toronto: Legas, 1999.

Tarasoff, Koozma J., and Robert B. Klymasz, eds. *Spirit Wrestlers: Centennial Papers in Honour of Canada's Doukhobor Heritage*. Ottawa: Canadian Museum of Civilization, 1995.

Taylor, G.W. *Builders of British Columbia: An Industrial History*. Victoria: Morriss, 1982.

– *Timber: History of the Forest Industry in BC*. Vancouver: J.J. Douglas, 1975.

Taylor, Jeanette. *River City: A History of Campbell River and the Discovery Islands*. Madeira Park, BC: Harbour, 1999.

Teeple, Gary. *Globalization and the Decline of Social Reform: Into the Twenty-First Century*. Second ed. Aurora, ON: Garamond Press, 2000.

Tennant, Paul. *Aboriginal Peoples and Politics: The Indian Land Question in British Columbia, 1849–1989*. Vancouver: UBC Press, 1990.

Thompson, Paul. *The Voice of the Past: Oral History*. Second ed. Oxford: Oxford University Press, 1988.

Thomson, Ann. *Winning Choice on Abortion: How British Columbia and Canadian Feminists Won the Battles of the 1970s and 1980s*. Vancouver: Trafford, 2005.

Tiratsoo, Nick. *Reconstruction, Affluence and Labour Politics: Coventry, 1945–1960*. London: Routledge, 1990.

Tucker, Judy, and Eric Fudge. *Labour before the Law: The Regulation of Workers' Collective Action in Canada, 1900–1948*. Don Mills: Oxford University Press, 2001.

Turner, Arthur J. *Somewhere – A Perfect Place*. Vancouver: Boag Foundation, 1981.

Underhill, Frank H. *In Search of Canadian Liberalism*. Toronto: Macmillan, 1960.

Union of British Columbia Indian Chiefs. *Stolen Lands, Broken Promises: Researching the Land Question in British Columbia*. Second ed. Vancouver: Union of British Columbia Indian Chiefs, 2005.

Vogel, Donna. *Challenging Politics: COPE, Electoral Politics and Social Movements*. Halifax: Fernwood, 2003.

Walkom, Thomas. *Rae Days: The Rise and Follies of the NDP*. Toronto: Key Porter, 1994.

Ward, Peter. *White Canada Forever: Popular Attitudes and Public Policy toward Orientals in British Columbia*. 3rd ed. Montreal and Kingston: McGill-Queen's University Press, 2002.

Ware, Alan. *Political Parties and Party Systems*. Oxford and New York: Oxford University Press, 1995.

Warrior. M.C., and Mark Leier. *Light at the End of the Tunnel: The First Forty Years: A History of the Tunnel and Rock Workers Union Local 168*. Vancouver: LIUNA, 1992.

Webb, Beatrice. *My Apprenticeship*. London: Longmans, Green, and Co., 1926.

Webb, Patricia G. *The Heart of Health Care: The Story of the Hospital Employees' Union, the First 50 Years*. Vancouver: Hospital Employees' Union, 1994.

Webster, Daisy. *Growth of the NDP in BC, 1900–1970: 81 Political Biographies*. Vancouver: New Democratic Party, 1970.

Webster, Jack. *Webster – An Autobiography of a Veteran BC Journalist*. Vancouver: Douglas and McIntyre, 1990.

Weisbord, Merrily. *The Strangest Dream: Canadian Communists, the Spy Trials, and the Cold War*. Toronto: Lester and Orpen Dennys, 1983.

Whitaker, Reg. *Double Standard: The Secret History of Canadian Immigration*. Toronto: Lester & Orpen Dennys, 1987.

Whitaker, Reg, and Gary Marcuse. *Cold War Canada: The Making of a National Insecurity State, 1945–1957*. Toronto: University of Toronto Press, 1994.

White, Howard. *A Hard Man to Beat: The Story of Bill White, Labour Leader, Historian, Shipyard Worker, Raconteur*. Vancouver: Pulp Press, 1983.

White, Julie. *Sisters in Solidarity: Women and Unions in Canada*. Toronto: Thompson Educational Publishing, 1993.

Whitehorn, Alan. *Canadian Socialism: Essays on the CCF-NDP*. Toronto: Oxford University Press, 1992.

Wiseman, Nelson. *In Search of Canadian Political Culture*. Vancouver: UBC Press, 2007.

– *Social Democracy in Manitoba: A History of the CCF-NDP*. Winnipeg: University of Manitoba Press, 1983.

Witcover, Jules. *The Year the Dream Died: Revisiting 1968 in America*. New York: Warner, 1997.

Woodcock, George, and Ivan Avakumovic. *The Doukhobors*. Toronto: McClelland and Stewart, 1976.

Worley, Ronald B. *The Wonderful World of W.A.C. Bennett*. Toronto/Montreal: McClelland and Stewart, 1971.

Young, Walter D. *Anatomy of a Party: The National CCF, 1932–61*. Toronto: University of Toronto Press, 1969.

Zagladin, V.V., ed. *The World Communist Movement: Outline of Strategy and Tactics*. Moscow: Progress Publishers, 1973.

Zakuta, Leo. *A Protest Movement Becalmed: A Study of Change in the CCF*. Toronto: University of Toronto Press, 1964.

Zweig, Ferdynand. *The Worker in an Affluent Society: Family Life and Industry*. New York: Free Press, 1962.

Articles

Abbott, George M. 'Duff Pattullo and the Coalition Controversy of 1941.' *BC Studies*, 102 (Summer 1994), 30–53.

Abella, Irving. 'Communism and Anti-Communism in the British Columbia Labour Movement, 1940–1948.' In David Jay Bercuson, ed. *Western Perspectives 1: Papers of the Western Canadian Studies Conference, 1973*. Toronto and Montreal: Holt, Rinehart and Winston, 1974: 88–100.

– 'Lament for a Union Movement.' In Ian Lumsden, ed. *Close the 49th Parallel Etc.: The Americanization of Canada*. Toronto: University of Toronto Press, 1970: 75–91.

Abraham, Steven E. 'The Impact of the Taft-Hartley Act on the Balance of Power in Industrial Relations.' *American Business Law Journal*, 33:3 (Spring 1996), 341–63.

Akers, David. 'Rebel or Revolutionary? Jack Kavanagh and the Early Years of the Communist Movement in Vancouver, 1920–1925.' *Labour/Le Travail*, 30 (Fall 1992), 9–44.

Andrews, C.D. 'Cominco and the Manhattan Project.' *BC Studies*, 11 (Fall 1971), 51–62.

Azoulay, Dan. '"Winning Women for Socialism": The CCF and Women, 1947–1961.' *Labour/Le Travail*, 36 (Fall 1995), 59–90.

Belisle, Donica. 'Exploring Postwar Consumption: The Campaign to Unionize Eaton's in Toronto, 1948–1952.' *Canadian Historical Review*, 86:4 (December 2005), 641–72.

Bercuson, David J. 'Labour Radicalism and the Western Industrial Frontier, 1897–1919.' *Canadian Historical Review*, 57 (June 1977), 154–77.

– 'Western Labour Radicalism and the One Big Union: Myths and Realities.' In S.M. Trofimenkoff, ed. *The Twenties in Western Canada: Papers of the Western Canadian Studies Conference, March 1972*. Ottawa: National Museum of Man, 1972: 32–49.

Blake, Donald E., et al. 'Sources of Change in the BC Party System.' *BC Studies*, 50 (Summer 1981), 3–28.

Bradbury, J.H. 'Class Structures and Class Conflicts in "Instant" Resource Towns in British Columbia, 1965 to 1972.' *BC Studies*, 37 (Spring 1978), 3–18.

Bright, David. 'The West Wants In: Regionalism, Class, and *Labour/Le Travail*, 1976–2002.' *Labour/Le Travail*, 50 (Fall 2002), 149–61.

Brown, Maria J. 'Capilano College: A Study in the Development of a Regional or Community College.' *BC Studies*, 17 (Spring 1973), 43–56.

Bullen, John. 'The Ontario Waffle and the Struggle for an Independent Socialist Canada.' *Canadian Historical Review*, 64:2 (June 1983), 188–215.

Campbell, Peter. '"Making Socialists": Bill Pritchard, the Socialist Party of Canada, and the Third International.' *Labour/Le Travail*, 30 (Fall 1992), 42–65.

Carroll, William K., and Rennie Warburton. 'Feminism, Class Consciousness and Household Work Linkages among Registered Nurses in Victoria.' *Labour/Le Travail*, 24 (Fall 1989), 131–45.

Carroll, William K., and R.S. Ratner. 'Old Unions and New Social Movements.' *Labour/Le Travail*, 35 (Spring 1995), 195–221.

Clément, Dominique. 'Spies, Lies and a Commission, 1946–8.' *Left History*, 7:2 (Fall 2000), 53–79.

Cohen, Lizabeth. 'The Class Experience of Mass Consumption: Workers as Consumers in Interwar America.' In Richard Wightman Fox and T.J. Jackson Lears, eds. *The Power of Culture: Critical Essay in American History.* Chicago: University of Chicago Press, 1993: 134–60.

Cohn, Werner. 'Persecution of Japanese Canadians and the Political Left in British Columbia, December 1941-March 1942.' *BC Studies*, 68 (Winter 1985–6), 3–22.

Conley, James. 'Frontier Labourers, Crafts in Crisis and the Western Canadian Labour Revolt.' *Labour/Le Travail*, 23 (Spring 1989), 1–37.

Cox, Robert W., and Stuart M. Jamieson. 'Canadian Labor in Continental Perspective.' *International Organization*, 28:4 (Autumn 1974), 803–26.

Creese, Gillian. 'Class, Ethnicity and Conflict: The Case of Chinese and Japanese Immigrants, 1880–1923.' In Rennie Warburton, ed. *Workers, Capital, and the State in British Columbia.* Vancouver: UBC Press, 1988: 55–85.

– 'Exclusion or Solidarity?: Vancouver Workers Confront the "Oriental Problem."' *BC Studies*, 80 (Winter 1988/9), 24–51.

Dawson, Michael. 'Leisure, Consumption, and the Public Sphere: Postwar Debates over Shopping Regulations in Vancouver and Victoria during the Cold War.' In Magda Fahrni and Robert Rutherdale, eds. *Creating Postwar Canada: Community, Diversity, and Dissent, 1945–1975.* Vancouver: University of British Columbia Press, 2007: 193–216.

– 'Victoria Debates Its Post-Industrial Reality: Tourism, Deindustrialization, and Store-Hour Regulations, 1900–1958.' *Urban History Review*, 35:2 (March 2007), 14–24.

DeLottinville, Peter. 'Joe Beef of Montreal: Working Class Culture and the Tavern, 1869–1889.' *Labour/Le Travail*, 8/9 (Fall 1981/Spring 1982), 9–40.

De Grazia, Victoria, and Lizabeth Cohen. 'Class and Consumption.' *International Labor and Working-Class History*, 55 (1999), 1–5.

Elkins, David J. 'Politics Makes Strange Bedfellows: The BC Party System in the 1952 and 1953 Provincial Elections.' *BC Studies*, 30 (Summer 1976), 3–26.

Fantasia, Richard. 'The Wildcat Strike and Industrial Relations.' *Industrial Relations Journal*, 14:2 (June 1983), 74–86.

Faue, Elizabeth. 'Paths of Unionization: Community, Bureaucracy, and Gender in the Minneapolis Labor Movement, 1935–1945.' In Ava Baron, ed. *Work Engendered: Toward a New Labor History*. Ithaca: Cornell University Press, 1991: 296–319.

Finkel, Alvin. 'Canadian Immigration Policy and the Cold War, 1945–1980.' *Journal of Canadian Studies*, 21:3 (Fall 1986), 53–69.

– 'The Cold War, Alberta Labour, and the Social Credit Regime.' *Labour/Le Travail*, 21 (Spring 1988), 123–52.

Fox, Bonnie J. 'The Feminist Challenge: A Reconsideration of Social Inequality and Economic Development.' In Robert J. Brym and Fox, eds. *From Culture to Power: The Sociology of English Canada*. Toronto: Oxford University Press, 1989: 120–67.

Friesen, Gerald. 'Yours in Revolt: Regionalism, Socialism, and the Western Canadian Labour Movement.' *Labour/Le Travailleur*, 1 (1976), 141–57.

Gagne, Wallace, and Peter Regenstreif. 'Some Aspects of New Democratic Party Urban Support in 1965.' *Canadian Journal of Economics and Political Science*, 33:4 (1967), 247–60.

Gladstone, Percy, and Stuart Jamieson. 'Unionism in the Fishing Industry of British Columbia.' *Canadian Journal of Economics and Political Science*, 16:2 (May 1950), 1–11.

Greer, David M. 'Redistribution of Seats in the British Columbia Legislature, 1952–1978.' *BC Studies*, 38 (Summer 1978), 24–46.

Hak, Gordon. 'British Columbia Loggers and the Lumber Workers Industrial Union, 1919–1922.' *Labour/Le Travail*, 23 (Spring 1989), 67–90.

– 'Populism and the 1952 Social Credit Breakthrough in British Columbia.' *Canadian Historical Review*, 85:2 (June 2004), 277–96.

– 'Red Wages: Communists and the 1934 Vancouver Island Loggers Strike.' *Pacific Northwest Quarterly*, 80 (1989), 82–90.

– 'The Socialist and Labourist Impulse in Small-Town British Columbia: Port Alberni and Prince George, 1911–33.' *Canadian Historical Review*, 70:4 (December 1989), 519–42.

Harding, James. 'The New Left in British Columbia.' In Dimitrios I. Roussopolous, ed. *The New Left in Canada*. Montreal: Black Rose, c. 1970: 17–40.

Harris, Richard. 'The Suburban Worker in the History of Labor.' *International Labor and Working-Class History*, 64 (2003), 8–24.

Harter, John-Henry. 'Environmental Justice for Whom? Class, New Social Movements, and the Environment: A Case Study of Greenpeace Canada, 1971–2000.' *Labour/Le Travail*, 54 (Fall 2004), 83–119.

Heron, Craig. 'Toward Synthesis in Canadian Working-Class History: Reflections on Bryan Palmer's Rethinking.' *Left History*, 1:1 (1993), 109–21.

Hewitt, Steve. '"Information Believed True": RCMP Security Intelligence Activities on Canadian University Campuses, 1911–1971.' *Canadian Historical Review*, 81:2 (June 2000), 191–228.

Higgins, Larratt. 'The Alienation of Canadian Resources: The Case of the Columbia River Treaty.' In Ian Lumsden, ed. *Close the 49th Parallel Etc.: The Americanization of Canada*. Toronto: University of Toronto Press, 1970.

Hirsch, Barry T., David A. Macpherson, and Wayne G. Vroman. 'Estimates of Union Density by State.' *Monthly Labor Review*, 124:7 (July 2001), 51–5.

Isitt, Benjamin. 'Elusive Unity: The Canadian Labor Party in British Columbia, 1924–1928.' *BC Studies*, 163 (Fall 2009), 33–64.

Jamieson, Stuart. 'Regional Factors in Industrial Conflict: The Case of British Columbia,' *Canadian Journal of Economics and Political Science*, 28:3 (August 1962) 405–16.

Jenson, Jane, and Rianne Mahon. 'Representing Solidarity: Class, Gender and the Crisis in Social Democratic Sweden.' *New Left Review*, I/201 (September-October 1993) 76–100.

Kashner, Frank. 'A Rank and File Revolt at GE.' *Radical America*, 12:6 (November/December 1978), 43–60.

Kealey, Gregory S. '1919: The Canadian Labour Revolt.' *Labour/Le Travail*, 13 (Spring 1984), 11–44.

– 'H.C. Pentland and the Writing of Canadian Working-Class History.' *Canadian Journal of Political and Social Theory*, 3 (1979), 79–94.

– 'Stanley Bréhaut Ryerson: Canadian Revolutionary Intellectual.' *Studies in Political Economy*, 8 (Summer 1982), 14–24.

– 'Stanley Bréhaut Ryerson: Marxist Historian.' *Studies in Political Economy*, 9 (Fall 1982), 103–71.

Keddie, Vincent. 'Class Identification and Party Preference among Manual Workers: The Influence of Community, Union Membership and Kinship.' *Canadian Review of Sociology and Anthropology*, 17:1 (1980), 24–36.

Knox, Paul. 'Breakaway Unionism in Kitimat.' In Paul Knox and Philip Resnick, eds. *Essays in BC Political Economy*. Vancouver: New Star Books, 1974: 42–51.

Koenig, Daniel, et al. 'The Year That British Columbia Went NDP: NDP Voter Support Pre- and Post-1972.' *BC Studies*, 24 (Winter 1974–5), 65–86.

Kristianson, G.L. 'The Non-Partisan Approach to BC Politics: The Search for a Unity Party, 1972–1975.' *BC Studies*, 33 (Spring 1977), 13–29.

Lambertson, Ross. 'The Black, Brown, White, and Red Blues: The Beating of Clarence Clemons.' *Canadian Historical Review*, 85:4 (December 2004), 755–76.

Langford, Tom, and Chris Frazer. 'The Cold War and Working-Class Politics in the Coal Mining Communities of the Crowsnest Pass, 1945–1958.' *Labour/Le Travail*, 49 (Spring 2002), 43–81.

Larmour, Jean. 'The Douglas Government's Changing Emphasis on Public, Private, and Co-operative Development in Saskatchewan, 1944–1961.' In William J. Brennan, ed. *Building the Cooperative Commonwealth: Essays on the Democratic Socialist Tradition in Canada*. Regina: Canadian Plains Research Center, 1984: 161–180.

Leggett, John C. 'The Persistence of Working-Class Consciousness in Vancouver.' In John Allan Fry, ed. *Economy, Class and Social Reality: Issues in Contemporary Canadian Society*. Toronto: Butterworths, 1979: 230–43.

Leier, Mark. 'W[h]ither Labour History: Regionalism, Class and the Writing of BC History.' *BC Studies*, 111 (Fall 1996), 61–75.

– 'Responses to Professors Palmer, Strong-Boag, and McDonald.' *BC Studies*, 111 (Fall 1996), 93–8.

Levine, Bruce. 'The History of Politics and the Politics of History.' *International Labor and Working-Class History*, 46 (Autumn 1994), 58–62.

Lockwood, David. 'Sources of Variation in Working-Class Images in Society.' *Sociological Review*, 14 (1966), 249–67.

– 'The "New Working Class."' *European Journal of Sociology*, 1:2 (1960), 248–59.

Loo, Tina. 'Disturbing the Peace: Environmental Change and the Scales of Justice on a Northern River.' *Environmental History*, 12:4 (October 2007), 895–919.

– 'People in the Way: Modernity, Environment, and Society on British Columbia's Arrow Lakes.' *BC Studies*, 142 and 143 (2004), 161–91.

Luxton, Meg. 'Feminism as a Class Act: Working Class Feminism and the Women's Movement in Canada.' *Labour/Le Travail*, 48 (Fall 2001), 63–88.

– 'From Ladies' Auxiliaries to Wives' Committees.' In Linda Briskin and Lynda Yanz, eds. *Union Sisters: Women in the Labour Movement*. Toronto: Women's Press, 1983: 333–47.

MacDowell, Laurel Sefton. 'Paul Robeson in Canada: A Border Story.' *Labour/Le Travail*, 51 (Spring 2003), 177–221.

Mackenzie, Hector. 'The ABCs of Canada's International Economic Relations, 1945–1951.' In Greg Donaghy, ed. *Canada and the Early Cold War, 1943–1957*. Ottawa: Department of Foreign Affairs and International Trade, 1998: 215–50.

McDonald, Robert A.J. '"Just a Working Man": Tom Uphill.' In Wayne Norton and Tom Langford, eds. *A World Apart: The Crowsnest Communities of Alberta and British Columbia*. Kamloops: Plateau, 2000: 99–112.

– 'Lumber Society on the Industrial Frontier: Burrard Inlet, 1863–1886.' *Labour/Le Travail*, 33 (Spring 1994), 69–96.

– 'The West Is a Messy Place.' *BC Studies*, 111 (Fall 1996), 88–92.

McKay, Ian. 'For a New Kind of History: A Reconnaissance of 100 Years of Canadian Socialism.' *Labour/Le Travail*, 46 (Fall 2000), 69–125.

– 'The Maritime CCF: Reflections on a Tradition.' In Ian McKay and Scott Milsom, eds. *Toward a New Maritimes: A Selection of Ten Years from New Maritimes*. Charlottetown,: Ragweed Press, 1992: 67–83

– 'Revolution Deferred: Maurice Spector's Political Odyssey, 1928–1941.' Paper presented to the Canadian Historical Association Annual Meeting, Halifax, May 2003.

– 'Three Faces of Canadian Labour History.' *History Workshop*, 24 (1987), 172–9.

Manley, John. 'Canadian Communists, Revolutionary Unionism, and the "Third Period": The Workers' Unity League, 1929–1935.' *Journal of the Canadian Historical Association*, 5 (1994), 167–91.

– 'Does the International Labour Movement Need Salvaging? Communism, Labourism, and the Canadian Trade Unions, 1921–1928.' *Labour/Le Travail*, 41 (Spring 1998), 147–80.

– '"Starve, Be Damned!": Communists and Canada's Urban Unemployed, 1929–1939.' *Canadian Historical Review*, 79 (September 1998), 467–73

Mann, Michael. 'Sources of Variation in Working-Class Movements in Twentieth-Century Europe.' *New Left Review*, 212 (July-August 1995), 14–54.

Marcuse, Herbert. 'On the New Left.' In Massimor Teodori, ed. *The New Left: A Documentary History*. Indianapolis: Bobbs-Merrill, 1969: 468–73.

Marchak, Patricia. 'Class, Regional, and Institutional Sources of Social Conflict in BC.' *BC Studies*, 27 (Fall 1975), 30–49.

Marks, Lynne. 'Heroes and Hallelujahs: Labour History, Bryan Palmer and the Social History of Religion in English Canada.' *Histoire Sociale/Social History*, 67 (2001), 169–86.

Miller, Fern. 'Vancouver Civic Political Parties: Developing a Model of Party-System Change and Stabilization.' *BC Studies*, 25 (Spring 1975), 3–31.

Montgomery, David. 'Immigrants, Industrial Unions, and Social Reconstruction in the United States, 1916–1923.' *Labour/Le Travail*, 13 (Spring 1984), 101–13.

Mouat, Jeremy. 'The Genesis of Western Exceptionalism: British Columbia's Hard Rock Miners, 1895–1903.' *Canadian Historical Review*, 71:3 (September 1990), 317–45.

– 'Vic Midgley Writes Home: A Letter from New Zealand, 1939.' *Labour/Le Travail*, 30 (Fall 1992), 205–12.

Naylor, James. 'Pacifism or Anti-Imperialism: The CCF Response to the Outbreak of World War II.' *Journal of the Canadian Historical Association*, 6 (1997), 213–37.

– 'Working-Class History in English Canada in the 1980s: An Assessment.' *Acadiensis*, 19:1 (Fall 1989), 156–69.

Newman, Kathy M. 'From Sit-ins to "Shirt-ins": Why Consumer Politics Matter More Than Ever.' *American Quarterly*, 56:1 (March 2004), 213–21.

Nichol, Christine J. 'In Pursuit of the Voter: The British Columbia CCF, 1945–1950.' In William J. Brennan, ed. *Building the Cooperative Commonwealth: Essays on the Democratic Socialist Tradition in Canada*. Regina: Canadian Plains Research Center, 1984: 123–40.

Ormsby, Margaret. 'T. Dufferin Pattullo and the Little New Deal.' *Canadian Historical Review*, 43:4 (December 1962), 277–97.

Page, Donald M. 'The Development of a Western Canadian Peace Movement.' In S.M. Trofimenkoff, ed. *The Twenties in Western Canada: Papers of the Western Canadian Studies Conference, March 1972*. Ottawa: National Museum of Man, 1972: 75–106.

Palmer, Bryan D. 'Class and the Writing of History: Beyond BC.' *BC Studies*, 111 (Fall 1996), 76–84.

– 'Maurice Spector, James P. Cannon, and the Origins of Canadian Trotskyism.' *Labour/Le Travail*, 56 (Fall 2005), 91–148.

– 'Old Positions/New Necessities: History, Class, and Marxist Metanarrative.' In Ellen Meiksins Wood and John Bellamy Foster, eds. *In Defense of History: Marxism and the Postmodern Agenda*. New York: Monthly Review Press, 1997: 65–73.

– 'The Rise and Fall of British Columbia's Solidarity.' In Palmer, ed. *The Character of Class Struggle: Essays in Canadian Working Class History, 1850–1985*. Toronto: McClelland and Stewart, 1986: 176–200.

Parnaby, Andrew. 'What's Law Got to Do with It? The IWA and the Politics of State Power in British Columbia, 1935–1939.' *Labour/Le Travail*, 44 (Fall 1999), 9–46.

Pentland, H. Clare. 'The Lachine Strike of 1843.' *Canadian Historical Review*, 29 (September 1948), 255–77.

Pierson, Ruth Roach. 'Gender and the Unemployment Insurance Debates in Canada, 1934–1940.' *Labour/Le Travail*, 25 (Spring 1990), 77–103.

Piven, Francis Fox. 'The Decline of Labor Parties: An Overview.' In Piven, ed. *Labor Parties in Postindustrial Society*. Cambridge: Polity Press, 1991: 1–19.

Pue, W. Wesley. 'Banned from Lawyering: William John Gordon Martin, Communist.' *BC Studies*, 162 (Summer 2009), 111–36.

Pugh, Martin. 'The Rise of Labour and the Political Culture of Conservatism, 1890–1945.' *History*, 87:288 (October 2002), 514–37.

Rajala, Richard A. 'Pulling Lumber: Indo-Canadians in the British Columbia Forest Industry, 1900–1998.' *BC Historical News*, 36:1 (Winter 2002/3), 1–13.

Reaume, Geoffrey. 'Portraits of People with Mental Disorders in English Canadian History.' *Canadian Bulletin of Medical History*, 17:1/2 (2000), 93–125.

Robin, Martin. 'British Columbia: The Company Province.' In Robin, ed. *Canadian Provincial Politics: The Party Systems in the Ten Provinces*. Second ed. Scarborough: Prentice-Hall, 1978: 28–60.

Robin, Martin. 'The Social Basis of Party Politics in British Columbia.' *Queen's Quarterly*, 72 (Winter 1965–6), 679–90.

Roy, Patricia E. 'The Oriental "Menace" in British Columbia.' In S.M. Trofimenkoff, ed. *The Twenties in Western Canada: Papers of the Western Canadian Studies Conference, March 1972*. Ottawa: National Museum of Man, 1972: 243–58.

Sangster, Joan. 'Feminism and the Making of Canadian Working-Class History: Exploring the Past, Present and Future.' *Labour/Le Travail*, 46 (Fall 2000), 127–66.

– '"Women and the New Era": The Role of Women in the Early CCF, 1933–1940.' In William J. Brennan, ed. *Building the Cooperative Commonwealth: Essays on the Democratic Socialist Tradition in Canada*. Regina: Canadian Plains Research Center, 1984: 69–98.

Sarra, Janis. 'Trade Union Women and the NDP.' In Linda Briskin and Lynda

Yanz, eds. *Union Sisters: Women in the Labour Movement*. Toronto: Women's Educational Press, 1983: 348–59.

Seager, Allen. 'Memorial: To a Departed Friend of the Working Man.' *Bulletin of the Committee on Canadian Labour History*, 4 (Autumn 1977), 9–13.

– 'Socialists and Workers: The Western Canadian Coal Miners, 1900–21.' *Labour/Le Travail*, 16 (Fall 1985), 23–60.

– 'Workers, Class, and Industrial Conflict in New Westminster, 1900–1930.' In Rennie Warburton and David Coburn, eds. *Workers, Capital and the State in British Columbia: Selected Papers*. Vancouver: University of British Columbia Press, 1988: 117–40.

Seager, Allen, and David Roth. 'British Columbia and the Mining West: A Ghost of a Chance.' In Craig Heron, ed. *The Workers' Revolt in Canada: 1917–1925*. Toronto: University of Toronto Press, 1998: 231–67.

Sethna, Christabelle, and Steve Hewitt. 'Clandestine Operations: The Vancouver Women's Caucus, the Abortion Caravan, and the RCMP.' *Canadian Historical Review*, 90:3 (September 2009), 463–96.

Smith, Andrea B. 'The CCF, NPA and Civic Change: Provincial Forces behind Vancouver Politics, 1930–1949.' *BC Studies*, 53 (Spring 1982), 45–65.

Smith, Patrick J., and Marshall W. Conley. '"Empty Harbours, Empty Dreams": The Democratic Socialist Tradition in Atlantic Canada.' In William J. Brennan, ed. *Building the Cooperative Commonwealth: Essays on the Democratic Socialist Tradition in Canada*. Regina: Canadian Plains Research Center, 1984: 227–52.

Sproule-Jones, Mark. 'Social Credit and the British Columbia Electorate.' *BC Studies*, 11 (Fall 1971), 37–50.

Stanbury, W.T., and M.R. McLeod. 'The Concentration of Timber Holdings in the British Columbia Forest Industry, 1972.' *BC Studies*, 17 (Spring 1973), 57–69.

Strong-Boag, Veronica. 'Moving beyond Tired "Truths": Or, Let's Not Fight the Old Battles.' *BC Studies*, 111 (Fall 1996), 84–92.

Taylor, Georgina M. '"The Women … Shall Help Lead the Way": Saskatchewan CCF-NDP Women Candidates in Provincial and Federal Elections, 1934–1965.' In William J. Brennan, ed. *Building the Cooperative Commonwealth: Essays on the Democratic Socialist Tradition in Canada*. Regina: Canadian Plains Research Center, 1984: 141–60.

Tennant, Paul. 'The NDP Government of British Columbia: Unaided Politicians in an Unaided Cabinet.' *Canadian Public Policy*, 3:4 (Autumn 1977), 489–503.

Toller, Susan, and Peter N. Nemetz. 'Assessing the Impact of Hydro Development: A Case Study of the Columbia River Basin in BC.' *BC Studies*, 114 (Summer 1997), 5–30.

Tomblin, Stephen G. 'W.A.C. Bennett and Province-Building in British Columbia.' *BC Studies*, 85 (Spring 1990), 45–61.

Tulchinsky, Gerald. 'Family Quarrel: Joe Salsberg, the "Jewish" Question, and Canadian Communism.' *Labour/Le Travail*, 56 (Fall 2005), 149–73.

Turnbull, A. Douglas. 'Memoir: Early Years of Hospital Insurance in British Columbia.' *BC Studies*, 76 (Winter 1987–8), 58–81.

Turner, Frederick Jackson. 'The Significance of the Frontier in American History.' Paper originally delivered to the American Historical Association, Chicago, 1893; reprinted in George Rogers Taylor, ed. *The Turner Thesis Concerning the Role of the Frontier in American History*. Revised ed. Boston: D.C. Heath and Company, 1965.

Walsh, Susan. 'The Peacock and Guinea Hen: Political Profiles of Dorothy Gretchen Steeves and Grace MacInnis.' In Gillian Creese and Veronica Strong-Boag, eds. *British Columbia Reconsidered: Essays on Women*. Vancouver: Press Gang, 1992: 73–89.

Wells, Don. 'The Impact of the Postwar Compromise on Canadian Unionism: The Formation of an Auto Worker Local in the 1950s.' *Labour/Le Travail*, 36 (Fall 1995), 147–73.

Wilson, Dolly Smith. 'A New Look at the Affluent Worker: The Good Working Mother in Post-War Britain.' *Twentieth Century British History*, 17:2 (2006), 206–29.

Wilson, J.W., and Maureen Conn. 'On Uprooting and Rerooting: Reflections on the Columbia River Project.' *BC Studies*, 58 (Summer 1983), 40–54.

Wiseman, Nelson, and Benjamin Isitt. 'Social Democracy in Twentieth-Century Canada: An Interpretive Framework.' *Canadian Journal of Political Science*, 40:3 (September 2007), 567–89.

Wright, James D. 'In Search of a New Working Class.' *Quantitative Sociology*, 1:1 (May 1978), 33–57.

Yarmie, Andrew. 'The State and Employers' Associations in British Columbia: 1900–1932.' *Labour/Le Travail*, 45 (Spring 2000), 53–101.

Yerbury, J.C. 'The "Sons of Freedom" Doukhobors and the Canadian State.' *Canadian Ethnic Studies*, 16:2 (1984), 47–70.

Young, Walter D. 'Ideology, Personality and the Origin of the CCF in British Columbia.' *BC Studies*, 32 (Winter 1976–7), 139–62.

Zaborsky, Deborah. 'Feminist Politics: The Feminist Party of Canada.' *Women's Studies International Forum*, 10:6 (1987), 613–21.

Zelco, Frank, and Kristine Kern. 'Greenpeace and the Development of International Environmental Activism in the 1970s.' In Ursula Lehmkulh and Hermann Wellenreuther, eds. *Historians and Nature: Comparative Approaches to Environmental History*. Oxford, NY: Berg, 2007: 296–318.

Theses and Dissertations

Abbott, George Malcolm. 'The Formation of the Liberal-Conservative Coalition in 1941.' MA thesis, University of Victoria, 1978.

Alper, Donald Keith. 'From Rule to Ruin: The Conservative Party in British Columbia, 1928–1954.' PhD diss., University of British Columbia, 1975.

Atherton, Patricia. 'CAIMAW: Portrait of a Union.' MA thesis, University of British Columbia, 1981.

Bernard, Elaine. 'The Rod Young Affair in the British Columbia Co-operative Commonwealth Federation.' MA thesis, University of British Columbia, 1979.

Burger, Anne. 'The Communist Party of Canada during the Great Depression: Organizing and Class Consciousness.' MA thesis, Simon Fraser University, 2004.

Burns, Janet Mary Christine. 'Trade Union Membership, Working Class Self-Identification, and Support for the New Democratic Party.' MA thesis, University of Victoria, 1981.

Clark, Terry. 'Mass Media and the New Democrats: Making Sense of the Election Campaign.' MA thesis, University of Victoria, 1993.

Clayton, Jenny. 'Making Recreational Space: Citizen Involvement in Outdoor Recreation and Park Establishment in British Columbia, 1900–2000.' PhD diss., University of Victoria, 2009.

Clément, Dominique. 'Rights in the Age of Protest: A History of the Human Rights and Civil Liberties Movement in Canada, 1962–1982.' PhD diss., Memorial University of Newfoundland, 2005.

Fisher, Edward George. 'The Effects of Changes in Labour Legislation on Strike Activity in British Columbia, 1945–1975.' PhD diss., University of British Columbia, 1979.

Frogner, Raymond. '"Within Sound of the Drum": Currents of Anti-Militarism in the British Columbia Working Class in the 1930s.' MA thesis, University of Victoria, 1987.

Grantham, Ronald. 'Some Aspects of the Socialist Movement in British Columbia, 1898–1933.' MA thesis, University of British Columbia, 1942.

Gray, Stephen. 'Woodworkers and Legitimacy: The IWA in Canada, 1937–1957.' PhD diss., Simon Fraser University, 1989.

Hak, Gordon Hugh. 'On the Fringes: Capital and Labour in the Forest Economies of the Port Alberni and Prince George Districts, British Columbia, 1910–1939.' PhD diss., Simon Fraser University, 1986.

Hill, Patrick George. 'A Failure of Unity: Communist Party-CCF Relations in British Columbia, 1935–1939.' MA thesis, University of Victoria, 1977.

Horsfield, Barbara. 'The Social Credit Movement in British Columbia.' BA essay, University of British Columbia, 1953.

Isitt, Benjamin. 'The Search for Solidarity: The Industrial and Political Roots of the Cooperative Commonwealth Federation in British Columbia, 1913–1928.' MA thesis, University of Victoria, 2003.

– 'Tug-of-War: The Working Class and Political Change in British Columbia, 1948–1972.' PhD diss., University of New Brunswick, 2008.

Johnson, Ross Alfred. 'No Compromise – No Political Trading: The Marxian Socialist Tradition in British Columbia.' PhD diss., University of British Columbia, 1975.

Kerin, Theresa Ann. 'The Power of Indigenous Capital in a Company Province: An Analysis of the Ruling Class of British Columbia.' MA thesis, University of Victoria, 1977.

Knox, Paul Graham. 'The Passage of Bill 39: Reform and Repression in British Columbia's Labour Policy.' MA thesis, University of British Columbia, 1974.

Lawrence, Joseph C. 'Markets and Capital: A History of the Lumber Industry of British Columbia 1778 to 1952.' MA thesis, University of British Columbia, 1957.

Loosmore, T.R. 'The British Columbia Labour Movement and Political Action, 1878–1906.' MA thesis, University of British Columbia, 1954.

Lowe, Lana C. 'A Strategic Analysis of the Union of British Columbia Indian Chiefs.' MA report, University of Victoria, 2004.

Lutz, John Sutton. 'Structural Changes in the Manufacturing Economy of British Columbia 1860–1915.' MA thesis, University of Victoria, 1988.

– 'Work, Wages and Welfare in Aboriginal-Non-Aboriginal Relations, British Columbia, 1849–1970.' PhD diss., University of Ottawa, 1994.

MacDonald, Ian. 'Class Conflict and Political Factionalism: A History of Local 213 of the International Brotherhood of Electrical Workers, 1901–1961.' MA thesis, Simon Fraser University, 1986.

MacKenzie, Bruce Alan. 'Party and Press Portrayals of the British Columbia CCF-NDP: 1937–1979.' MA thesis, University of Victoria, 1981.

MacKenzie, Ross. 'A More Subtle Polity: The Provincial State and Party Politics in British Columbia, 1871–1903.' MA thesis, Simon Fraser University, 1992.

McLeod, Heather. 'Not Another God-Dam Housewife: Ruth Bullock, the

"Woman Question" and Canadian Trotskyism.' MA thesis, Simon Fraser University, 1993.
Martin, Eryk. 'When Red Meets Green: Perceptions of Environmental Change in the BC Communist Left, 1937–1978.' MA thesis, University of Victoria, 2008.
Mathes, Raymond Walter. 'The Mediative Role of the Labour Relations Board of British Columbia in Disputes Involving Illegal Work Stoppages.' MSc thesis, University of British Columbia, 1982.
May, Edwin Peter. 'The Nishga Land Claim, 1873–1973.' MA thesis, Simon Fraser University, 1980.
McCallum, Todd. '"A Modern Weapon for Modern Man": Marxist Masculinity and the Social Practices of the One Big Union, 1919–1924.' MA thesis, Simon Fraser University, 1995.
O'Brien, Gary. 'Maurice Spector and the Origins of Canadian Trotskyism.' MA thesis, Carleton University, 1974.
O'Donnell, Jacqueline Patricia. 'The Native Brotherhood of British Columbia, 1931–1950: A New Phase in Native Political Organization.' MA thesis, University of British Columbia, 1985.
Parker, Peter. '"We Are Not Beggars": Political Genesis of the Native Brotherhood, 1931–1951.' MA thesis, Simon Fraser University, 1992.
Paulson, Marilee Reimer. 'Ideological Practice in Labour News Reporting.' MA thesis, University of British Columbia, 1975.
Roberts, Dorothy J. 'Doctrine and Disunity in the British Columbia Section of the CCF, 1932–56.' MA thesis, University of Victoria, 1972.
Rossi, Dionysios. 'Mountaintop Mayhem: Simon Fraser University, 1965–1971.' MA thesis, Simon Fraser University, 2003.
Roy, Patricia E. 'The British Columbia Electric Railway Company, 1897–1928: A British Company in British Columbia.' PhD diss., University of British Columbia, 1970.
Ruff, Norman John Robert. 'Labour Unions and the Canadian Political Process.' MA thesis, McMaster University, 1964.
Sanford, Thomas Michael. 'The Politics of Protest: The Cooperative Commonwealth Federation and Social Credit League in British Columbia.' PhD diss., University of California, 1961.
Scott, Gerry. 'Beyond Equality: British Columbia New Democrats and Native Peoples, 1961–1979.' MA thesis, Simon Fraser University, 1991.
Simpson, Bernard. 'The Political Career of Harold Winch in British Columbia's Legislative History, 1933–1953.' BA essay, University of British Columbia, 1964.
Smith, Julia. 'Organizing the Unorganized: The Service, Office, and Retail

Workers' Union of Canada (SORWUC), 1972–1986.' MA thesis, Simon Fraser University, 2009.
Stuart, Richard Grey. 'The Early Political Career of Angus MacInnis.' MA thesis, University of British Columbia, 1970.
Sutherland, J. Neil. 'T.D. Pattullo as a Party Leader.' MA thesis, University of British Columbia, 1960.
Terpenning, John Gordon. 'Maitland and the British Columbia Conservative Party: The Struggle for Political Identity and Survival.' MA thesis, University of Victoria, 1988.
Thorn, Brian. '"The Hand That Rocks the Cradle Rocks the World": Women in Vancouver's Communist Movement, 1935–1945.' MA thesis, Simon Fraser University, 2001.
Walsh, Susan. 'Equality, Emancipation and a More Just World: Leading Women in the British Columbia Cooperative Commonwealth Federation.' MA thesis, Simon Fraser University, 1984.
Wasserlein, Frances. '"An Arrow Aimed at the Heart": The Vancouver Women's Caucus and the Abortion Campaign 1969–1971.' MA thesis, Simon Fraser University, 1990.
Webber, Patrick. '"For a Socialist New Brunswick": The New Brunswick Waffle, 1967–1972.' MA thesis, University of New Brunswick, 2008.
Wickerson, Gordon Stanley. 'Conflict in the British Columbia Cooperative Commonwealth Federation and the "Connell Affair."' MA thesis, University of British Columbia, 1973.

Online Sources (World Wide Web)

Barrett, Dave. Victory speech. Coquitlam. 30 August 1972. CBC Archives <http://archives.cbc.ca/IDC-1-73-1637-11304/politics_economy/british_columbia_elections/clip3> (accessed 16 April 2007).
Fair Play for Cuba Committee. *Four Canadians Who Saw Cuba*. March 1963. Socialist History Project <http://www.socialisthistory.ca/Docs/1961-/Cuba/FourCanadians.htm> (accessed 4 November 2006).
Bernard, Elaine. 'A History of BC Trotskyism As Seen through Labour Challenge and Workers<apos?> Vanguard, 1945–1961.' Unpublished paper, available at <http://www.socialisthistory.ca/Docs/History/Bernard-BC_Trot.htm#8> (accessed 10 November 2006).
Daniel, K.S, P.B. McCarter, and D.E. Hay. 'The Construction of a Database of Pacific Herring Catches Recorded in British Columbia from 1888 to 1950.' Canadian Technical Report of Fisheries and Aquatic Sciences 2368, (2001) <http://www.pac.dfo-mpo.gc.ca/sci/ herring/herspawn/hcatch01.htm> (accessed 15 February 2005).

Dowson, Ross. 'Our Orientation to the NDP – as a Strategy and Its Tactical Application.' (1970) Socialist History Project <http://www.socialisthistory.ca/Docs/CCF-NDP/Orientation-Dowson-1970.htm> (accessed 10 November 2006).
'The Early History of Pulp, Paper and Woodworkers of Canada.' Pulp, Paper and Woodworkers of Canada website, n.d. <http://www.ppwc.bc.ca/ppwchist01.pdf> (accessed 8 March 2005). [no author]
Mueller, Klaus A. Sr. 'CASAW History: The Early Days.' CAW Local 2301 website, n.d.<http://www.caw2301.ca/early.htm> (accessed 20 November 2006); also 'History of CAW 2301.' n.d. <http://www.caw2301.ca/history.htm> (accessed 20 November 2006)

Illustration Credits

The Fisherman (Vancouver): Flotilla of fishing boats at the BC legislature, 1952 ('By Sea, Land They Came To Victoria Demanding Justice,' 18 March 1952); Korean boy and an American GI, 1950 (3 October 1950).

Library and Archives Canada: Social Credit election poster, 1956 (File 23-02 'Elections-Provincial 1956', vol. 23, series IV-4, Communist Party of Canada fonds, MG 28); Communist Party leaflet opposing the Columbia River Treaty (File 26-11 'Columbia River Project, Press Releases, Leaflets, Clippings, n.d. 1960–1964,' vol. 26, reel H1594, CPC fonds); Cuba meeting (File 26-14 'Cuba, leaflets, n.d.,' vol. 26, reel H1594, CPC fonds); Communist Party of Canada Women's Committee peace leaflet (File 26-17 'Disarmanent – Peace Movement, n.d. 1960, 1963,' vol. 26, reel H1594, CPC fonds); Radiation Hazards poster ('The Arms Race or Human Race: No Nuclear Arms for Canada,' 9 Feb. 1961, file 57-8, vol 57, R10995, Dowson fonds); Communist provincial election leaflet (File 23-04 'Elections – Provincial 1963,' vol. 23, reel H1592, CPC fonds); Communist poster opposing Bill 33 (File 26-06 'Bill 33 – Mediation Commission, Press Releases, Leaflets, Clippings, n.d. 1968–1970,' vol. 26, reel H1594, CPC fonds).

Bruce McLean, *A Union amongst Government Employees: A History of the BC Government Employees' Union, 1919–1979* (Vancouver: BCGEU, 1979): BC Government Employees' Association (BCGEA) picketers, page 75; BC Government Employees' Union (BCGEU) banner, page 94.

Kevin Neish papers (private collection), Victoria, BC: Elgin 'Scotty' Neish, Fidel Castro, and Gladys Neish.

Pacific Tribune (Vancouver): Bea Zucco's sit-down strike ('Women's sitdown dramatizes plight of silicosis victims,' 9 March 1956): Labour's response to Bill 87 ('Unions Won't Stand for Destruction by Law,' 30 April 1948).

Jack Reid: Strike Vote at Rivers Inlet, March 1959 (Photograph by Jack Reid, published in George North, *A Ripple, A Wave: The Story of Union Organization in the BC Fishing Industry* [Vancouver: Fishermen Publishing Society, 1974], 28–29).

Grace Stevens papers (private collection), Nanaimo, BC: Delegates at the annual convention of the Women's Auxiliary of the UFAWU.

Grace Tickson papers (private collection), Nanaimo, BC: Trade with China march; Grace Tickson election poster.

University of British Columbia Library, Rare Books and Special Collections: Camp Woodsworth (BC NDP collection, box 47, envelope 47-6a-1); UFAWU activists celebrate George North's release (Fisherman Publishing Society Collection, BC 1532/2/2); UFAWU march at the BC legislature (Fisherman Publishing Society Collection, BC 1532/20/18); The British Columbia New Democratic Party legislative caucus, 1967 (Dave Barrett Collection, BC 1964/24).

***Vancouver Province*:** Vancouver peace march ('Babes-in-arms join city peace parade,' 28 March 1966).

***Vancouver Sun*:** RCMP officers and strikers clash at a British American Oil Co. refinery (19 October 1965).

***Victoria Times Colonist*:** Black Panthers ('Panthers Stride UVic,' *Victoria Daily Colonist*, 20 August 1968).

Index